The World

PROGRAM AUTHORS

Dr. Candy Dawson Boyd
Professor, School of Education
Director of Reading Programs
St. Mary's College
Moraga, California

Dr. Geneva Gay
Professor of Education
University of Washington
Seattle, Washington

Rita Geiger
Director of Social Studies and
Foreign Languages
Norman Public Schools
Norman, Oklahoma

Dr. James B. Kracht
Associate Dean for Undergraduate
Programs and Teacher Education
College of Education
Texas A&M University
College Station, Texas

Dr. Valerie Ooka Pang
Professor of Teacher Education
San Diego State University
San Diego, California

Dr. C. Frederick Risinger
Director, Professional Development
and Social Studies Education
Indiana University
Bloomington, Indiana

Sara Miranda Sanchez
Elementary and Early Childhood
Curriculum Coordinator
Albuquerque Public Schools
Albuquerque, New Mexico

CONTRIBUTING AUTHORS

Dr. Carol Berkin
Professor of History
Baruch College and the Graduate
Center
The City University of New York
New York, New York

Lee A. Chase
Staff Development Specialist
Chesterfield County Public Schools
Chesterfield County, Virginia

Dr. Jim Cummins
Professor of Curriculum
Ontario Institute for Studies in
Education
University of Toronto
Toronto, Canada

Dr. Allen D. Glenn
Professor and Dean Emeritus
Curriculum and Instruction
College of Education
University of Washington
Seattle, Washington

Dr. Carole L. Hahn
Professor, Educational Studies
Emory University
Atlanta, Georgia

Dr. M. Gail Hickey
Professor of Education
Indiana University-Purdue
University
Fort Wayne, Indiana

Dr. Bonnie Meszaros
Associate Director
Center for Economic Education and
Entrepreneurship
University of Delaware
Newark, Delaware

Editorial Offices: Glenview, Illinois • Parsippany, New Jersey • New York, New York
Sales Office: Parsippany, New Jersey • Duluth, Georgia • Glenview, Illinois •
   Coppell, Texas • Ontario, California

www.sfsocialstudies.com

Content Consultants

Catherine Deans-Barrett
World History Specialist
Northbrook, Illinois

Dr. Michael Frassetto
Studies in Religions
Independent Scholar
Chicago, Illinois

Dr. Gerald Greenfield
Hispanic-Latino Studies
History Department
University of Wisconsin, Parkside
Kenosha, Wisconsin

Dr. Frederick Hoxie
Native American Studies
University of Illinois
Champaign, Illinois

Dr. Cheryl Johnson-Odim
Dean of Liberal Arts and Sciences and
    Professor of History
African American
    History Specialist
Columbia College
Chicago, Illinois

Dr. Michael Khodarkovsky
Eastern European Studies
University of Chicago
Chicago, Illinois

Robert Moffet
U.S. History Specialist
Northbrook, Illinois

Dr. Ralph Nichols
East Asian History
University of Chicago
Chicago, Illinois

Classroom Reviewers

Diana Vicknair Ard
Woodlake Elementary School
St. Tammany Parish
Mandeville, Louisiana

Dr. Charlotte R. Bennett
St. John School
Newburgh, Indiana

Sharon Berenson
Freehold Learning Center
Freehold, New Jersey

Betsy Blandford
Pocahontas Elementary School
Powhatan, Virginia

Gloria Cantatore
Public School #5
West New York, New Jersey

LuAnn Curran
Westgate Elementary School
St. Petersburg, Florida

Louis De Angelo
Office of Catholic Education
Archdiocese of Philadelphia
Philadelphia, Pennsylvania

Dr. Trish Dolasinski
Paradise Valley School District
Arrowhead Elementary School
Glendale, Arizona

Dr. John R. Doyle
Director of Social Studies Curriculum
Miami-Dade County Schools
Miami, Florida

Dr. Roceal Duke
District of Columbia Public Schools
Washington, D.C.

Peggy Flanagan
Roosevelt Elementary School
Community Consolidated School
    District #64
Park Ridge, Illinois

Mary Flynn
Arrowhead Elementary School
Glendale, Arizona

Sue Gendron
Spring Branch ISD
Houston, Texas

Su Hickenbottom
Totem Falls Elementary School
Snohomish School District
Snohomish, Washington

Sally Hunter
Highland Park Elementary School
Austin ISD
Austin, Texas

Allan Jones
North Branch Public Schools
North Branch, Minnesota

Brandy Bowers Kerbow
Bettye Haun Elementary School
Plano ISD
Plano, Texas

Sandra López
PSJA Service Center
San Juan, Texas

Martha Sutton Maple
Shreve Island School
Shreveport, Louisiana

Lyn Metzger
Carpenter Elementary School
Community Consolidated School
    District #64
Park Ridge, Illinois

Marsha Munsey
Riverbend Elementary School
West Monroe, Louisiana

Christine Nixon
Warrington Elementary School
Escambia County School District
Pensacola, Florida

Liz Salinas
Supervisor
Edgewood ISD
San Antonio, Texas

Beverly Scaling
Desert Hills Elementary School
Las Cruces, New Mexico

Madeleine Schmitt
St. Louis Public Schools
St. Louis, Missouri

Barbara Schwartz
Central Square Intermediate School
Central Square, New York

Ronald Snapp
North Lawrence Community Schools
Bedford, Indiana

Lesley Ann Stahl
West Side Catholic Consolidated
    School
Evansville, Indiana

Carolyn Moss Woodall
Loudoun County of Virginia Public
    Schools
Leesburg, Virginia

Suzanne Zaremba
J. B. Fisher Model School
Richmond Public Schools
Richmond, Virginia

ISBN: 0-328-01766-3

Contents

Social Studies Handbook

Let the Discovery Begin	H2
Building Citizenship Skills	H4
Building Geography Skills: Five Themes of Geography	H6
Building Geography Skills: Map and Globe Skills Review	H8
Building Research Skills	H16

Unit 1 — Early Civilizations and Cultures

Begin with a Primary Source	2
Meet the People	4
Reading Social Studies Sequence	6

Chapter 1 • Digging Up the Past

Lesson 1 • Early Gatherers and Hunters	**10**
Dorling Kindersley The Ice Age	12
Here and There Prehistoric Cave Art	13
Citizen Heroes Stone Age Healers	17
Lesson 2 • Early Farmers	**18**
Then and Now New Crop Development	20
Chart and Graph Skills Use Parallel Time Lines	24
Lesson 3 • Developing Cultures	**26**
Chapter 1 Review	30

Chapter 2 • Early Civilizations

Lesson 1 • The Fertile Crescent	**34**
Map Adventure You're a Mesopotamian Trader	38
Lesson 2 • Mesopotamia	**40**
BIOGRAPHY Gilgamesh	44
BIOGRAPHY Sargon	47
Lesson 3 • Babylonia and Assyria	**48**
BIOGRAPHY Hammurabi	51
Lesson 4 • Hebrews, Phoenicians, and Lydians	**54**
Thinking Skills Make Inferences	60
Chapter 2 Review	62

End with Literature The Epic of Gilgamesh	64
Unit 1 Review	66
Discovery Channel School Unit Project	68

"With patience and a spirit of adventure, nothing is too far away."

—Said by Father Alberto de Agostini about the Cave of the Hands, 1941

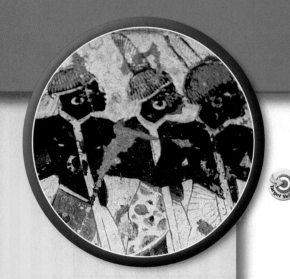

Unit 2 Early Civilizations in Africa and Asia

Begin with a Primary Source   70
Meet the People   72
Reading Social Studies   Summarize   74

Chapter 3 • Ancient Egypt and Nubia

Lesson 1 • The Lifeline of the Nile   **78**
   Map and Globe Skills   Compare Maps at Different Scales   82
Lesson 2 • Life in Egypt   **84**
   Dorling Kindersley   Egyptian Writing   86
   Citizen Heroes   Tomb Builders   88
   BIOGRAPHY   Hatshepsut   91
Lesson 3 • Nubia and Egypt   **92**
   Map Adventure   You're a Guide for Piankhi   94
Chapter 3 Review   96

Chapter 4 • Ancient China

Lesson 1 • The Geography of China   **100**
   Chart and Graph Skills   Interpret Climographs   104
Lesson 2 • China's Past   **106**
   BIOGRAPHY   Qin Shi Huangdi   113
Lesson 3 • Legacy of Thought   **114**
Chapter 4 Review   118

Chapter 5 • Ancient India and Persia

Lesson 1 • Geography of South Asia   **122**
   Then and Now   Harappa and Sahiwal, Pakistan:
    Land of Cotton   126
Lesson 2 • India and Persia   **128**
   Here and There   Class Systems   131
   BIOGRAPHY   Chandragupta Maurya   135
Lesson 3 • Hinduism   **136**
Lesson 4 • Buddhism   **140**
   Literature and Social Studies   The Jataka Tales   141
   Research and Writing Skills   Gather and Report Information   144
Chapter 5 Review   146

End with a Song   A Boat on the Lake   148
Unit 2 Review   150
Discovery Channel School   Unit Project   152

"I will lead the army on water and on land, to bring marvels from God's-Land."

—Probably said by Queen Hatshepsut of Egypt

Unit 3 Early Civilizations in the Americas

Begin with a Primary Source	154
Meet the People	156
Reading Social Studies *Compare and Contrast*	158

Chapter 6 • Mesoamerican Civilizations

Lesson 1 • Geography of Mesoamerica	**162**
Map and Globe Skills *Use Map Projections*	166
Lesson 2 • The Olmec and the Maya	**168**
Literature and Social Studies *Popol Vuh*	171
Lesson 3 • The Aztecs	**174**
Here and There *The Age of European Exploration*	178
BIOGRAPHY *Moctezuma II*	181
Chapter 6 Review	182

Chapter 7 • The Early Peoples of South America

Lesson 1 • Geography of South America	**186**
Lesson 2 • The Chavín and the Mochica	**190**
Map and Globe Skills *Use Latitude and Longitude*	194
Lesson 3 • The Inca	**196**
Map Adventure *You're an Inca Runner*	200
Citizen Heroes *Caring for Culture*	202
BIOGRAPHY *Pachacuti*	203
Chapter 7 Review	204

Chapter 8 • Early North American Peoples

Lesson 1 • Geography of North America	**208**
Lesson 2 • The Southwestern Peoples	**212**
Thinking Skills *Detect Bias*	216
Lesson 3 • The Mound Builders	**218**
Lesson 4 • Early Canadians	**222**
Then and Now *The Inuit*	223
BIOGRAPHY *Deganawidah*	225
Smithsonian *Inuit Artifacts*	226
Issues and Viewpoints *The Future of Rain Forests*	228
Chapter 8 Review	230
End With Literature *An Inuit Story*	232
Unit 3 Review	234
Discovery Channel School *Unit Project*	236

"With such wonderful sights to gaze on we did not know what to say, or if this was real that we saw before our eyes."

—account given by Spaniard Bernal Diaz on seeing Tenochtitlan, c. 1560.

Unit 4 Mediterranean Empires

Begin with a Primary Source 238
Meet the People 240
Reading Social Studies Main Idea and Details 242

Chapter 9 • Ancient Greece

Lesson 1 • The Geography of Greece **246**
  Here and There The Nok of Africa 250
Lesson 2 • The Greek City-States **252**
  Literature and Social Studies The Aeneid 253
  Fact File Greek Gods and Goddesses 254
  BIOGRAPHY Pericles 257
  Map and Globe Skills Compare City Maps
    at Different Scales 258
Lesson 3 • The Golden Age of Athens **260**
  Map Adventure You're Leading the Spartans 261
  Fact File The Greek Philosophers 262
  BIOGRAPHY Socrates 265
Lesson 4 • Alexander the Great **266**
  DK Dorling Kindersley Greek Columns 270
Chapter 9 Review 272

Chapter 10 • Ancient Rome

Lesson 1 • Rome's Beginnings **276**
  Research and Writing Skills Use Primary and
    Secondary Sources 280
Lesson 2 • The Roman Republic **282**
Lesson 3 • The Roman Empire **288**
  Citizen Heroes Warrior and Philosopher 293
Lesson 4 • The Rise of Christianity **294**
Lesson 5 • Rise and Fall **298**
  Then and Now Same City Different Name 301
  BIOGRAPHY Eudocia 305
Chapter 10 Review 306

End with Literature The Persian Wars 308
Unit 4 Review 310
Discovery Channel School Unit Project 312

"Let them enjoy indeed the title of citizens."

—Emperor Claudius, as
recorded by Tacitus, A.D. 48

Unit 5 The Medieval World

Begin with a Primary Source   314
Meet the People   316
Reading Social Studies *Sequence*   318

Chapter 11 • Byzantine Empire and Ancient Arabia

Lesson 1 • Geography of the Byzantine Empire   **322**
Lesson 2 • The Greatness of the Byzantine Empire   **326**
    BIOGRAPHY *Justinian and Theodora*   329
Lesson 3 • Development of Islam   **330**
Lesson 4 • The Islamic World   **334**
    Map Adventure *You're a Navigator*   337
    Citizen Heroes *Respecting Other Cultures*   339
    Chart and Graph Skills *Interpret Line Graphs*   340
Chapter 11 Review   342

Chapter 12 • Asian Empires

Lesson 1 • Empires of Asia   **346**
Lesson 2 • Chinese Dynasties   **350**
    Fact File *Dynasty Achievements and Advancements*   351
    Dorling Kindersley *Paper, Printing, and Books*   354
Lesson 3 • The Khmer   **356**
    Then and Now *The Khmer*   358
Lesson 4 • Japan in Isolation   **360**
    Research and Writing Skills *Gather and Report Information*   364
Chapter 12 Review   366

> *"I have not told half of what I saw."*
>
> —Said by Marco Polo on his deathbed about his travels across Asia, 1324

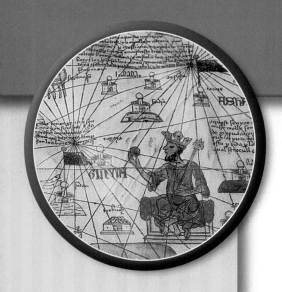

Chapter 13 • African Empires

Lesson 1 • Geography of Africa   **370**

Lesson 2 • West African Kingdoms   **374**
    Literature and Social Studies   A Wise Ruler   376
    BIOGRAPHY Sundiata   379

Lesson 3 • East, Central, and Southern Africa   **380**
    Research and Writing Skills   Use the Internet   386

Chapter 13 Review   388

Chapter 14 • Medieval Europe

Lesson 1 • Geography of Europe   **392**

Lesson 2 • Rulers and Invaders   **396**
    BIOGRAPHY Charlemagne   399

Lesson 3 • Life in the Middle Ages   **400**
    Here and There   The Beothuk   404

Lesson 4 • Crusades, Trade, and the Plague   **406**
    Map and Globe Skills   Use a Time Zone Map   412

Chapter 14 Review   414

End with a Legend   The Round Table   416
Unit 5 Review   418
Discovery Channel School   Unit Project   420

Unit 6 Discovery, Expansion, and Revolutions

Begin with a Primary Source	422
Meet the People	424
Reading Social Studies Summarize	426

Chapter 15 • New Beginnings

Lesson 1 • The Renaissance	**430**
Here and There An Asian Renaissance	433
Lesson 2 • Trade Routes and Conquests	**438**
Map Adventure You're an Explorer	440
BIOGRAPHY Elizabeth I	443
Lesson 3 • European Colonization	**444**
Research and Writing Skills Interpret Political Cartoons	450
Chapter 15 Review	452

Chapter 16 • Ideas and Movements

Lesson 1 • Revolutions in the Americas	**456**
Literature and Social Studies Latin American Liberator	461
BIOGRAPHY Simón Bolívar	463
Smithsonian American Revolution	464
Lesson 2 • The French Revolution	**466**
Citizen Heroes A Pioneer for Women's Rights	471
Research and Writing Skills Compare Primary Sources	472
Lesson 3 • The Industrial Revolution	**474**
Lesson 4 • The Second Industrial Revolution	**478**
Chapter 16 Review	482

Chapter 17 • Imperialism, Nationalism, and Unification

Lesson 1 • Expanding Empires	**486**
Chart and Graph Skills Interpret Circle Graphs	490
Lesson 2 • Imperialism in East Asia	**492**
BIOGRAPHY Meiji	497
Lesson 3 • New Nations	**498**
Then and Now German Reunification	500
Chapter 17 Review	504

End with a Song Así es mi tierra	506
Unit 6 Review	508
Discovery Channel School Unit Project	510

"Get gold, humanely if possible, but at all hazards— get gold."

—King Ferdinand of Spain, 1511

Unit 7 A World in Opposition

Begin with a Primary Source 512
Meet the People 514
Reading Social Studies *Cause and Effect* 516

Chapter 18 • The World at War

Lesson 1 • Headed Toward War **520**
Chart and Graph Skills *Compare Parallel Time Lines* 524
Lesson 2 • The Great War **526**
BIOGRAPHY Vera Brittain 533
Lesson 3 • After the War **534**
Fact File *Casualties and Debt of the Great War* 536
Chapter 18 Review 538

Chapter 19 • From Peace to War

Lesson 1 • Good to Bad Times **542**
Then and Now *Prices of Goods in the United States* 544
Lesson 2 • World War II **548**
BIOGRAPHY Winston Churchill 555
Smithsonian *A World at War* 556
Lesson 3 • The Aftermath **558**
Chart and Graph Skills *Interpret Bar Graphs* 562
Chapter 19 Review 564

Chapter 20 • The Cold War

Lesson 1 • The Soviets Advance **568**
Fact File *The Nuclear Arms Race* 571
Citizen Heroes *Reaching the Roof of the World* 573
Thinking Skills *Solve Complex Problems* 574
Lesson 2 • Communism in China **576**
Map Adventure *You're an American Journalist* 577
BIOGRAPHY Mao Zedong 581
Lesson 3 • The Cold War Heats Up **582**
Literature and Social Studies *The Clay Marble* 584
Here and There *War in Algeria* 585
Issues and Viewpoints *The Public Speaks Out* 588
Chapter 20 Review 590

End with a Song *Over There* 592
Unit 7 Review 594
Discovery Channel School *Unit Project* 596

"Never in the field of human conflict has so much been owed by so many to so few."

—said by Winston Churchill during the Battle of Britain, August 20, 1940

Unit 8　New Nations and a New Century

Begin with a Primary Source　　598
Meet the People　　600
Reading Social Studies　Draw Conclusions　　602

Chapter 21 • New Nations

Lesson 1 • Independence　　**606**
　Here and There　New States in the Middle East　　611
　BIOGRAPHY Julius Nyerere　　613
Lesson 2 • The Middle East　　**614**
　BIOGRAPHY Menachem Begin and Anwar el-Sadat　　619
Lesson 3 • Eastern Europe　　**620**
　Thinking Skills　Determine Accuracy of Information　　624
Chapter 21 Review　　626

Chapter 22 • Cooperation, Conflict, and Challenges

Lesson 1 • Economic Cooperation　　**630**
　Chart and Graph Skills　Interpret Cartograms　　634
Lesson 2 • Conflicts of Identity　　**636**
　Literature and Social Studies　What the World Needs　　638
　BIOGRAPHY Aung San Suu Kyi　　642
　Citizen Heroes　The Struggle for Peace　　643
Lesson 3 • Political Conflicts and Challenges　　**644**
　Fact File　The World Unites　　648
Chapter 22 Review　　650

Chapter 23 • Living in the 21st Century

Lesson 1 • Population Growth and Change　　**654**
　Map and Globe Skills　Compare Distribution Maps　　658
Lesson 2 • Earth's Environment　　**660**
　Map Adventure　You're Visiting an Amazon Village　　662
Lesson 3 • Energy　　**664**
Lesson 4 • Technology　　**668**
　Then and Now　Computers　　669
　DK Dorling Kindersley　Telecommunication　　670
Chapter 23 Review　　672

End with a Poem　The Garden We Planted Together　　674
Unit 8 Review　　676
Discovery Channel School　Unit Project　　678

"We must learn to think globally. . . . No single region or nation can isolate itself from the rest of the world."

—Gro Harlem Brundtland in *Our Common Future*, a 1987 United Nations report

Reference Guide

Atlas	R1
Geography Terms	R20
Countries of the World	R22
World History Time Line	R29
Gazetteer	R41
Biographical Dictionary	R50
Glossary	R58
Index	R69

★ BIOGRAPHY ★

Gilgamesh	44
Sargon	47
Hammurabi	51
Hatshepsut	91
Qin Shi Huangdi	113
Chandragupta Maurya	135
Moctezuma II	181
Pachacuti	203
Deganawidah	225
Pericles	257
Socrates	265
Eudocia	305
Justinian and Theodora	329
Sundiata	379
Charlemagne	399
Elizabeth I	443
Simón Bolívar	463
Meiji	497
Vera Brittain	533
Winston Churchill	555
Mao Zedong	581
Julius Nyerere	613
Menachem Begin and Anwar el-Sadat	619
Aung San Suu Kyi	642

Maps

Beringia and Possible
  Migration Paths   15
Domesticated Animals and Crops   21
The Fertile Crescent   35
Empire of Hammurabi   49
Judah, 925 B.C.   57
Phoenician Trade Routes   58
Ancient Egypt   79
Nubia and Egypt   93
China: Physical   101
Shang Dynasty and Zhou Dynasty   109
Great Wall of China   110
South Asia: Physical   124
Aryan Migration Map   130
Persian Empire, 500 B.C.   132
Spread of Hinduism   138
The Spread of Buddhism After
  500 B.C.   142
Central America and
  Mexico: Physical   163
Olmec and Mayan Empires   170
Aztec Empire   175
South America: Physical   187
Inca Empire   198
Climate Zones of the
  United States and Canada   210
Hohokam and Anasazi Cultures   214
Mississippian, Adena, and
  Hopewell Cultures   220
Greece: Physical   247
Peloponnesian War, 431–404 B.C.   263
Alexander's Conquests   267
Italian Peninsula   277
Roman Expansion, 133 B.C.   286
Roman Empire, about A.D. 14   290
Spread of Christianity   296
Division of the Roman Empire   300
Invaders of the Roman Empire   303
The Byzantine Empire: Physical   323
The Byzantine Empire   327
Spread of Islam   332
Asia: Physical   347
Mogul Empire   348
Mongol Empire   352
Khmer Kingdom   357
Japan, 1603   362
Africa: Physical   371
Spread of Bantu Speakers   373
Empires of Ghana, Mali,
  and Songhai   377
African Trade Routes   383
Europe: Physical   393
Charlemagne's Empire   397
The First Crusade   407
The Silk Road   409
The Spread of the Plague   410
Italian City-States, c. 1500   431
Spread of Protestantism   436
European Voyages of Exploration   441
European Colonization of the
  Americas by 1620   446
Slavery and the Triangular Trade   448
The 13 Colonies   457
Mexico, Central America,
  and South America   460
The French Empire, 1805–1812   469
Impact of the Suez Canal on
  European-Indian Trade   488
China: Territory Gained by European
  Imperialists and Japan   494
Italy and Germany, 1850   499
Italy and Germany, 1871   501
Canada, New Zealand,
  and Australia   502
Europe in 1914   522
The Battles of Verdun and
  the Somme   529
The Soviet Union in 1922   531
Europe in 1914/Europe in 1919   535
Japanese Aggression in China   546
Hitler's Aggression to 1939   549
World War II in Europe
  and Asia   552–553
The Iron Curtain   569
Cuban Missile Crisis   574
Korea, 1953   583
The Tet Offensive, 1968   586
African Independence in
  the Twentieth Century   608
Independence in South
  and Southeast Asia   610
Old City of Jerusalem   616–617
Israel and the Occupied Territories
  Since 1947   617
A New Eastern Europe   622
Trading Blocs   632
The Balkans   637
Rwanda and Burundi   638
Northern Ireland   639
International Terrorist Attacks,
  1978–2001   645

Skills

Reading Social Studies Skills
Sequence   6
Summarize   74
Compare and Contrast   158
Main Ideas and Details   242
Sequence   318
Summarize   426
Cause and Effect   516
Draw Conclusions   602

Map and Globe Skills
Compare Maps at Different Scales   82
Use Map Projections   166
Use Latitude and Longitude   194
Compare City Maps at
  Different Scales   258
Use a Time Zone Map   412
Compare Distribution Maps   658

Thinking Skills
Make Inferences   60
Detect Bias   216
Solve Complex Problems   574
Determine Accuracy of Information   624

Research and Writing Skills
Gather and Report Information   144
Use Primary and
  Secondary Sources   280
Gather and Report Information   364
Use the Internet   386
Interpret Political Cartoons   450
Compare Primary Sources   472

Chart and Graph Skills
Use Parallel Time Lines   24
Interpret Climographs   104
Interpret Line Graphs   340
Interpret Circle Graphs   490
Compare Parallel Time Lines   524
Interpret Bar Graphs   562
Interpret Cartograms   634

Fact File

Greek Gods and Goddesses   254
The Greek Philosophers   262
Dynasty Achievements
  and Advancements   351
Casualties and Debt of
  the Great War   536
The Nuclear Arms Race   571
The World Unites   648

Citizen Heroes

Stone Age Healers   17
Tomb Builders   88
Caring for Culture   202
Warrior and Philosopher   293
Respecting Other Cultures   339
A Pioneer for Women's Rights   471
Reaching the Roof of the World   573
The Struggle for Peace   643

Issues and Viewpoints

The Future of Rain Forests	228
The Public Speaks Out	588

Then and Now

New Crop Development	20
Harappa and Sahiwal, Pakistan: Land of Cotton	126
The Inuit	223
Same City Different Name	301
The Khmer	358
German Reunification	500
Prices of Goods in the United States	544
Computers	669

Here and There

Prehistoric Cave Art	13
Class Systems	131
The Age of European Exploration	178
The Nok of Africa	250
The Beothuk	404
The Asian Renaissance	433
War in Algeria	585
New States in the Middle East	611

Literature and Social Studies

The Jataka Tales	141
Popol Vuh	171
The Aeneid	253
A Wise Ruler	376
Latin American Liberator	461
The Clay Marble	584
What the World Needs	638

Map Adventure

You're a Mesopotamian Trader	38
You're a Guide for Piankhi	94
You're an Inca Runner	200
You're Leading the Spartans	261
You're a Navigator	337
You're an Explorer	440
You're an American Journalist	577
You're Visiting an Amazon Village	662

Graphic Organizers

Sequence	6
Sequence	16
Sequence	23
Main Idea and Details	29
Sequence	30
Cause and Effect	39
Main Ideas and Details	46
Sequence	53
Main Idea and Details	59
Sequence	62
Summarize	74
Summarize	81
Summarize	90
Summarize	95
Summarize	96
Summarize	103
Summarize	112
Summarize	117
Summarize	118
Summarize	127
Summarize	134
Summarize	139
Summarize	143
Summarize	146
Compare and Contrast	158
Compare and Contrast	165
Compare and Contrast	173
Main Idea and Details	180
Compare and Contrast	182
Compare and Contrast	189
Main Idea and Details	193
Main Idea and Details	201
Compare and Contrast	204
Compare and Contrast	211
Compare and Contrast	215
Compare and Contrast	221
Compare and Contrast	224
Compare and Contrast	230
Main Idea and Details	242
Main Idea and Details	251
Compare and Contrast	256
Main Idea and Details	264
Cause and Effect	271
Main Idea and Details	272
Main Idea and Details	279
Main Idea and Details	287
Draw Conclusions	292
Main Idea and Details	297
Cause and Effect	304
Main Idea and Details	306
Sequence	318
Sequence	325
Sequence	328
Main Idea and Details	333
Cause and Effect	338
Sequence	342
Sequence	349
Main Idea and Details	355
Cause and Effect	359
Cause and Effect	363
Sequence	366
Summarize	373
Summarize	378
Summarize	385
Sequence	388
Cause and Effect	395
Sequence	398
Main Idea and Details	405
Cause and Effect	411
Sequence	414
Summarize	426
Summarize	437
Summarize	442
Summarize	449
Summarize	452
Compare and Contrast	462
Summarize	470
Compare and Contrast	477
Main Idea and Details	481
Summarize	482
Summarize	489
Cause and Effect	496
Sequence	503
Summarize	504
Cause and Effect	516
Cause and Effect	523
Cause and Effect	532
Cause and Effect	537
Cause and Effect	538
Cause and Effect	547
Cause and Effect	554
Cause and Effect	561
Cause and Effect	564
Cause and Effect	572
Cause and Effect	580
Cause and Effect	587
Cause and Effect	590
Draw Conclusions	602
Draw Conclusions	612
Draw Conclusions	618
Draw Conclusions	623
Draw Conclusions	626
Cause and Effect	633
Draw Conclusions	641
Draw Conclusions	649
Draw Conclusions	650
Draw Conclusions	657
Cause and Effect	663
Draw Conclusions	667
Draw Conclusions	671
Draw Conclusions	672

Charts, Graphs, Tables & Diagrams

Diagram: Crowns of Upper and Lower Egypt 85
Climograph: Beijing 104
Climograph: Hong Kong 104
Climograph: Urumchi 105
Chart: The Roman Alphabet 292
Line Graph: Population of Major Cities, A.D. 100–622 340
Line Graph: Population of Major Cities, A.D. 800–1100 341
Line Graph: World Urban Population, 1950–2000 343
Diagram: How a Steam Engine Works 475
Bar Graph: Population of Great Britain, 1750–1850 476
African Colonies and Protectorates (Area), 1914 490
Bar Graph: Military Casualties for World War II 562
Bar Graph: National Income of War Powers, 1937 562
Bar Graph: Percentage of National Income Spent on Defense, 1937 563
Table: Population and Growth Rate of Russia, 1960–2000 624
Circle Graph: Gross Domestic Product 631
Cartogram: World Population, 2001 634
Cartogram: GDP of Countries, 2001 635
Chart: Terrorist Attacks Against Americans 647
Cartogram: Population of South America 651
Bar Graph: Urban Population Growth 655
Bar Graph: World Population Growth, 2001 656
Diagram: The Greenhouse Effect 661
Circle Graph: Sources of Energy as Percent of Total 665
Circle Graph: Carbon Dioxide Production 665

Time Lines

Early Civilizations and Cultures 2
Early Gatherers and Hunters 10
Early Farmers 18
Developing Cultures 26
Chapter 1 Review 30

The Fertile Crescent 34
Mesopotamia 40
Babylonia and Assyria 48
Hebrews, Phoenicians, and Lydians 54
Chapter 2 Review 62
Early Civilizations in Africa and Asia 70
The Lifeline of the Nile 78
Life in Egypt 84
Nubia and Egypt 92
Chapter 3 Review 96
China's Past 106
Great Wall of China 110
Legacy of Thought 114
Chapter 4 Review 118
India and Persia 128
Chapter 5 Review 146
Early Civilizations in the Americas 154
The Olmec and the Maya 168
The Aztecs 174
Chapter 6 Review 182
The Chavín and the Mochica 190
The Inca 196
Chapter 7 Review 204
The Southwestern Peoples 212
The Mound Builders 218
Early Canadians 222
Chapter 8 Review 230
Mediterranean Empires 238
The Geography of Greece 246
The Greek City-States 252
The Golden Age of Athens 260
Alexander the Great 266
Chapter 9 Review 272
Rome's Beginnings 276
The Roman Republic 282
The Roman Empire 288
The Rise of Christianity 294
Rise and Fall 298
Chapter 10 Review 306
The Medieval World 314
The Greatness of the Byzantine Empire 326
Development of Islam 330
The Islamic World 334
Chapter 11 Review 342
Empire of Asia 346
Chinese Dynasties 350
The Khmer 356
Japan in Isolation 360
Chapter 12 Review 366
The Geography of Africa 370
West African Kingdoms 374
East, Central, and Southern Africa 380
Chapter 13 Review 388
Rulers and Invaders 396
Life in the Middle Ages 400

Crusades, Trade, and the Plague 406
Chapter 14 Review 414
Discovery, Expansion, and Revolutions 422
The Renaissance 430
Inventions 434
Trade Routes and Conquests 438
European Colonization 444
Chapter 15 Review 452
Revolutions in the Americas 456
The French Revolution 466
The Industrial Revolution 474
The Second Industrial Revolution 478
Inventions 478–479
Chapter 16 Review 482
Expanding Empires 486
Imperialism in East Asia 492
New Nations 498
A World in Opposition 512
Chapter 17 Review 504
Headed Toward War 520
The Great War 526
After the War 534
Chapter 18 Review 538
Good to Bad Times 542
World War II 548
The Aftermath 558
Chapter 19 Review 564
The Soviets Advance 568
Communism in China 576
The Cold War Heats Up 582
Chapter 20 Review 590
New Nations and a New Century 598
Independence 606
The Middle East 614
Eastern Europe 620
Chapter 21 Review 626
Economic Cooperation 630
Conflicts of Identity 636
Political Conflicts and Challenges 644
Chapter 22 Review 650
Population Growth and Change 654
Earth's Environment 660
Energy 664
When Fossil Fuels May Run Out? 665
Technology 668
Chapter 23 Review 672

Let the Discovery Begin

Lumbering over the landscape, woolly mammoths search for food. Fast-forward some 20,000 years: Reindeer herders in Siberia find prehistoric mammoth bones buried in ice. The excitement about this fantastic discovery soon gave way to challenges when scientists tried to remove the mammal carefully from the frozen earth. Scientists hope to clone the animal's cells to bring this species back from extinction. Read on for more discoveries and challenges in the world's history. Your next discovery awaits.

Building Citizenship Skills

There are six ways to show good citizenship: caring, respect, responsibility, fairness, honesty, and courage. In your textbook, you will learn about people who used these ways to help their community, state, and country.

Caring
Think about what someone else needs without having to be asked.

Respect
Treat others as you would want to be treated, and accept differences among people.

Responsibility
Do what you think is expected of you and think before you act.

Fairness
Take turns and follow instructions and rules. Listen to other people.

Honesty
Tell the truth and follow through with what you say you will do.

Courage
Do what is right even when the task is challenging.

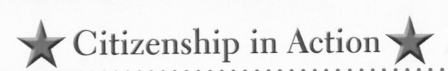

★ Citizenship in Action ★

Good citizens make careful decisions. They solve problems in a logical way. How will these sixth-graders handle each situation as good citizens?

Decision Making

These students need to choose a theme for the school book fair. Before making a decision, they should follow these steps:

1. **Tell what decision you need to make.**

2. **Gather information.**

3. **List your choices.**

4. **Tell what might happen with each choice.**

5. **Act according to your decision.**

Problem Solving

These students think their school needs a clean-up day. They should follow these steps to attack the problem:

1. **Name the problem.**

2. **Find out more about the problem.**

3. **List ways to solve the problem.**

4. **Talk about the best way to solve the problem.**

5. **Solve the problem.**

6. **Then, figure out how well the problem was solved.**

Building Geography Skills

Five Themes of Geography

Geography is the study of the relationship between physical features, climate, and people. This study can be divided into five themes that help you understand why Earth has such a wide variety of places. The themes below reveal something different about one of these places, the Acropolis of Athens in Greece.

Location

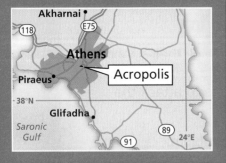

Where can something be found?
The Acropolis is located at about 38°N, 24°E.

Place

How is this area different from others?
The Acropolis is about a 10-acre flat-topped rocky hill around which Athens was built.

Human/Environment Interaction

How have people changed this place?
On top of the Acropolis, the ancient Greeks built magnificent temples and palaces.

Region

What is special about the region in which the Acropolis is located? Athens is on a plain in central Greece, bordered on the west, north, and east by mountains.

Movement

How has movement changed this place? Conquering armies passed through Athens, leaving the buildings on the Acropolis in ruins that stand today.

What Are Hemispheres?

Places on Earth can be located in general or specific terms. The most general way is by hemisphere. A hemisphere is any one of four overlapping halves of Earth.

Northern Hemisphere

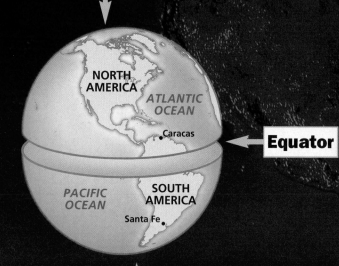

Equator

Southern Hemisphere

A place can be in either the **Northern** or **Southern Hemisphere**. That means it is in one of the halves above or below the imaginary east–west line known as the Equator. On the continent of South America, in what hemisphere is Santa Fe, Argentina? Caracas, Venezuela?

A place can also be in either the **Western** or **Eastern Hemisphere**. That means it is in one of the halves on either side of the imaginary north-south line known as the Prime Meridian. On the continent of Africa, is Cairo, Egypt, in the Eastern or Western Hemisphere? Of course, any place east or west will also be somewhere north or south—and vice versa. In what other hemisphere is Santa Fe? Cairo?

Eastern Hemisphere

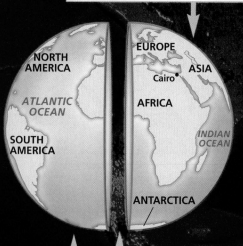

Western Hemisphere

Prime Meridian

Use Latitude and Longitude

The most exact way to locate places on Earth is by using imaginary lines of latitude and longitude. These lines are numbered by degrees [°].

Lines of **latitude** run east and west around Earth. They are also called **parallels** because the lines are always parallel, or the same distance apart. The equator is the longest latitude line, halfway between the poles, and is 0° latitude. All other latitude lines are up to 90°, either north or south of the equator.

Lines of **longitude,** or **meridians,** run north and south around Earth. However, unlike those of latitude, lines of longitude are all the same size and are not parallel. The **prime meridian** is 0° longitude, and all other longitude lines are up to 180°, either east or west of it. The 180° line is directly behind the prime meridian.

When used together, latitude and longitude form a pattern of crossed lines called a **global grid**. This allows any location on Earth to have an exact or nearly exact location, sometimes called a geographic address. (On globes these lines are usually shown at intervals of 10 degrees or more.) Look at the globes below and find New Orleans. Its geographic address is stated as 30°N, 90°W. Caracas and Beijing are not located at a point where lines cross. You would estimate their addresses to be about 10°N, 66°W and about 40°N, 116°E. What would you estimate is the geographic address of Santa Fe?

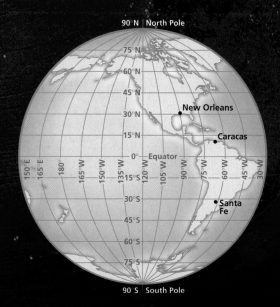

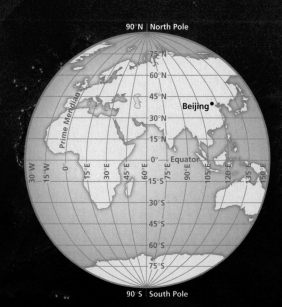

Section 1: Basic Maps

Understand Map Projections

A map projection is a way of showing the round Earth on a flat surface, such as on a page of a book. There are several kinds of projections. However, it is impossible to transfer exactly the image of a round Earth to a flat surface. All projections have one or more errors, or distortions, in showing size, shape, distance, or direction.

Three of these projections are Mercator, equal-area, and Robinson. On a Mercator projection, places away from the equator appear larger and farther apart than they usually are. This is because longitude lines are shown parallel, which they are not.

An equal-area projection corrects some of this distortion by curving all longitude lines, except for the prime meridian, toward the poles. This makes the relative sizes of continents much more accurate.

Since 1988 the Robinson projection, a type of equal-area projection, has become widely used. It minimizes overall distortion by more accurately showing both shape and size.

In reality the island of Greenland is about one-eighth the size of Africa. Which projections do you think show Greenland the most and least accurately? Why do you think that Africa and Australia are the least distorted continents on the three projections?

Mercator Projection

Equal-Area Projection

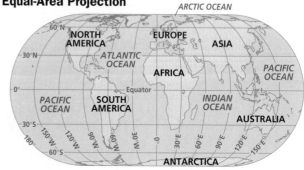

Robinson Projection

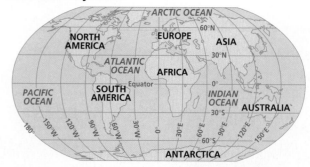

Use Map Features to Help Read Maps

A **political map** shows cities, states, and countries. A **physical map** adds landforms and water. What kind of map is on this page?

A **compass rose** is a pointer for cardinal directions: north, south, east, and west. On the compass roses in this textbook, north is marked with an "N." A compass rose also shows **intermediate directions,** which are pointers halfway between those for cardinal directions. They show northeast, southeast, southwest, and northwest. What country is northeast of Pakistan? northwest of Afghanistan?

A **key,** or legend, is the box in which a map's symbols—marks, drawings, or colors—are explained. What does the reddish-brown color tell you? In what height range is Karachi, Pakistan? What does the star in a circle stand for?

A **scale** helps you estimate real distances on Earth. It marks off very small distances to stand for miles and kilometers. About how many miles apart are Kabul and Kandahar?

Some maps have a **locator,** a small globe or flat map. It shows you where the subject of the main map can be found in a larger area of Earth. Are Afghanistan and Pakistan part of Asia or Africa?

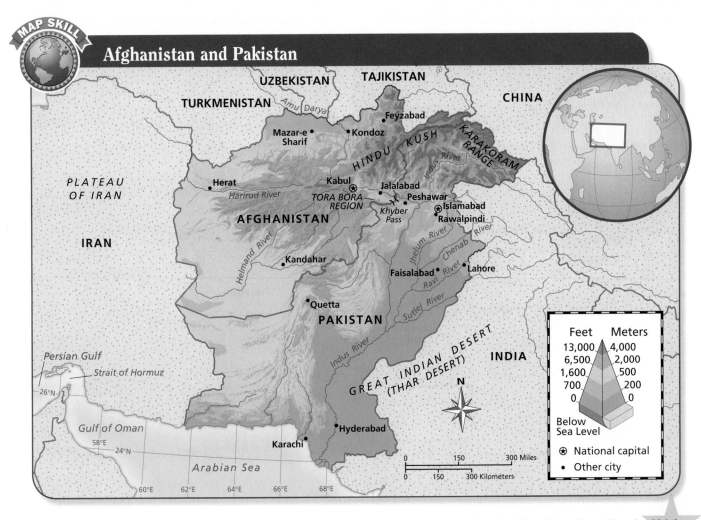

MAP SKILL

Afghanistan and Pakistan

UZBEKISTAN

TAJIKISTAN

TURKMENISTAN

CHINA

Amu Darya

Feyzabad

Mazar-e Sharif

Kondoz

HINDU KUSH

KARAKORAM RANGE

Indus River

PLATEAU OF IRAN

Herat

Harirud River

Kabul

Jalalabad

TORA BORA REGION

Peshawar

Khyber Pass

Islamabad

Rawalpindi

AFGHANISTAN

IRAN

Helmand River

Kandahar

Jhelum River

Chenab River

Faisalabad

Ravi River

Lahore

Sutlej River

Quetta

PAKISTAN

Indus River

GREAT INDIAN DESERT (THAR DESERT)

INDIA

Persian Gulf

Strait of Hormuz

26°N

Gulf of Oman

58°E

24°N

Karachi

Hyderabad

Arabian Sea

60°E   62°E   64°E   66°E   68°E

N

Feet	Meters
13,000	4,000
6,500	2,000
1,600	500
700	200
0	0

Below Sea Level

⊛ National capital
• Other city

0   150   300 Miles

0   150   300 Kilometers

Compare Maps of Different Scales

As you know, a map's scale allows you to estimate real distances on Earth. Oftentimes scales are set up so that one inch on a map stands for a certain number of actual miles or kilometers.

However, maps can have different scales. For example, one-inch on a scale may stand for 500 miles on one map but only 100 miles on another. On a **small-scale map,** where an area of Earth is larger, a one-inch measurement represents a

larger distance. The map below at the left shows countries at the southern tip of Africa. One inch on the scale stands for 500 actual miles. About how far is it in miles from Lusaka, the capital of Zambia, to Maseru, the capital of Lesotho?

The map below at the right shows Lesotho and is a **large-scale map.** Its scale represents a shorter distance on Earth. About how far is it in miles from Maseru to the city of Thaba-Tseka to the east? Imagine how difficult it would have been to make such an accurate measurement between the two cities on a small-scale map.

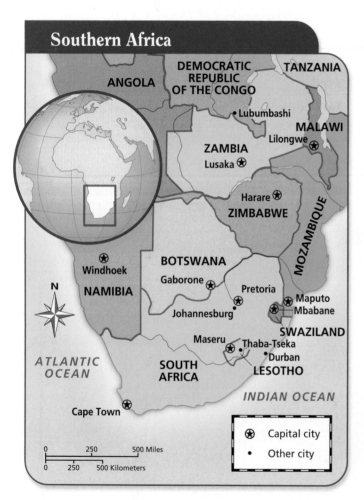

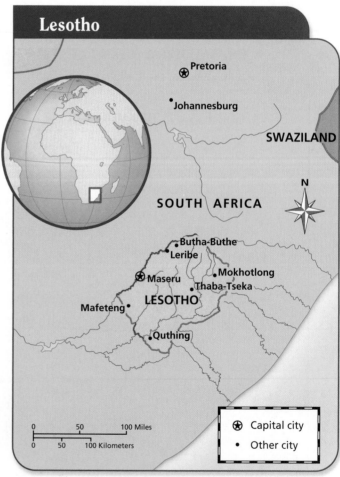

Section 2: Special-Purpose Maps

Interpret a Distribution Map

A **distribution map** shows the pattern of something spread out over an area. Such a map can show this pattern for a city, a region, countries, a continent, and even the whole world at a time.

The subjects of distribution maps can be the locations of languages, religions, rainfall, oil, natural vegetation, or safe drinking water. For example, this population map of China shows, on average, where the people of China live. Similar to an elevation key, the key in a distribution map may have boxes of color and just a few other symbols. Do more people live in eastern China or western China? Name the city with more than 10 million inhabitants. What is the population range of the city of Hong Kong? Where would you guess that the mountainous and desert regions of China are located? What hints at this fact?

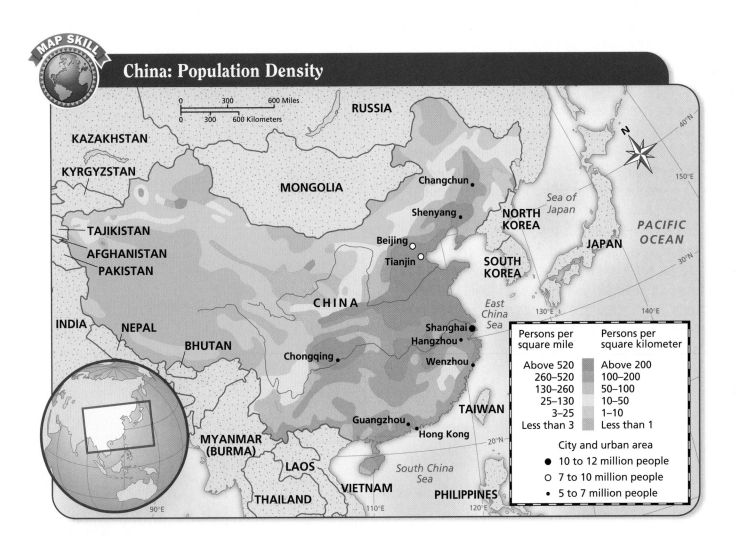

MAP SKILL

China: Population Density

Persons per square mile	Persons per square kilometer
Above 520	Above 200
260–520	100–200
130–260	50–100
25–130	10–50
3–25	1–10
Less than 3	Less than 1

City and urban area
- 10 to 12 million people
○ 7 to 10 million people
• 5 to 7 million people

Read a Road Map

A road map shows automobile routes between towns and cities for a region, county, state, or whole country. Major and minor roads or paved and unpaved roads are usually shown through the use of thick and thin lines or by use of color. Maps for countries found in atlas collections usually do not show road numbers such as those found on road maps for the United States.

The different sizes of cities that are connected by roads are also indicated. If a map has no key, then usually the bigger the dot means the bigger the city. However, sometimes a map key will show a population range for cities. For example, a certain sized dot may stand for cities with a size between 1 and 2 million.

The map of Chile in South America helps tell the story of this country's unusual physical geography. Chile is 2,650 miles long from north to south but only 265 miles wide east to west at its widest point. The country's southernmost region, from Puerto Montt to Porvenir, is almost entirely filled with glaciers, lakes, thick forests, and rugged, rocky land not suitable for farming. Do you think many people live there? How does the road map tell you this? What does the road map indicate about traveling by automobile between the far southern cities of Punta Arenas and Porvenir?

Chile: Major and Minor Roads

National capital
Other city
Major road
Minor road

Read a Time Zone Map

A time zone is a one-hour measurement of time. One day on Earth has 24 hours, and so there are 24 different time zones. All places within a time zone have the same time.

However, to avoid breaking some island groupings and large population areas into different time zones, all zones are irregular from north to south. Also, in some zones, people have shifted to half-hour markings. This creates non-standard time zones.

The figures across the top of the world time-zone map below show that it is noon at the Prime Meridian, known as Greenwich Mean Time. You can then tell what time it is anywhere in the world. (Twelve hours to the west, at the International Date Line, it is midnight and a new day is arriving.) The figures across the bottom tell you how many hours ahead or behind any place in the world is from Greenwich Mean Time.

When it is 6 A.M. in Mexico City, what time is it in Moscow, Russia? How many hours apart are clocks in Buenos Aires, Argentina, and Dublin, Ireland? The middle of Australia has non-standard time. If it had standard time, how many hours ahead of Greenwich Mean Time would the region be?

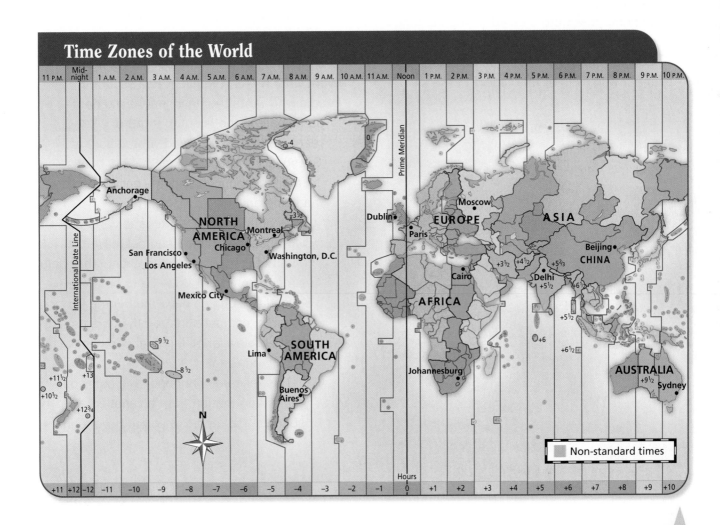

Time Zones of the World

Building Research Skills
Gathering and Reporting Information

When you need to find information for a report or project, there are three main resources you can use:

Technology Resources

Print Resources

Community Resources

Whichever resource you decide to use, be aware that the information you need can be found in two main types of sources.

Primary sources are firsthand historical documents that were created during the time period of an event in history. They were written by people who witnessed or participated in the event or who lived at that time.

Primary sources include journals, diaries, letters, speeches, autobiographies, photographs, interviews or eyewitness accounts, menus, programs, inventory lists, bills, receipts, and wills. Primary sources are valuable tools for creating an accurate research report.

Secondary sources are descriptions of an event written after the event has occurred. People who wrote the descriptions did not participate in the event, but rather researched the event and wrote about it. Secondary sources include history books, textbooks, nonfiction books, encyclopedias, and biographies.

Use both types of sources to carry out your research. Primary sources have the benefit of immediacy to the event. They help us focus on what it was like to be there. Secondary sources have the benefit of research, comparisons to other events and points-of-view, and historical perspective in judging an event.

This research handbook will help you gather information from a variety of sources and report what you have found.

Technology Resources

Use the Internet

The Internet is a system of linked computers that can store information to be accessed by people around the world. The World Wide Web (WWW), which is part of the Internet, has many resources. Through the World Wide Web, you can access on-line encyclopedias, dictionaries, almanacs, and Web sites for many different organizations, universities, companies, individuals, projects, and museums.

Information on the World Wide Web can be updated. Because anyone can create a Web site, it is important to evaluate information and determine what is accurate and what is not. It is also important to know from where the information comes. If it is posted by a reliable company or organization, the information is most likely correct. With any information you use, you should find three reliable sources that give similar information.

Remember to take notes so that you have a record of what you found and where you found it. For Web sites, list the complete Web address. On the computer, you can mark sites you want to look at again by clicking BOOKMARKS at the top of your screen and choosing ADD BOOKMARK. This will allow you to quickly return to that site at another time.

Search Engines

Before you turn on your computer, think about what you need to research. If you want to research the history of your town, for example, write down some key words that you can use to search the World Wide Web. The name of your town or city would be a good search term. The names of well-known people from your town's past would also be good search terms. You might want to use the names of landmarks or geographical sites in your town.

If you have not used the Internet before, you might want to ask a librarian, teacher, or parent for help.

Searching by Subject— To begin your search, click on SEARCH or NET SEARCH at the top of your screen. Then type one of your subject or key words into the search field. Finally, click SEARCH, FIND, or GO.

A list of possible sites will be displayed. Click on the one that you think best fits your search topic. Many Web sites have connections to other Web sites with additional information, or links. These links are usually in a different color. If you click on the colored words, you are taken to a new Web site.

If you cannot find what you need, try a different search engine. Not all search engines search Web sites in the same way.

Archaeology
www.abcd.org

World Wide Web sites have Uniform Resource Locators, or URLs. A URL is like an address. If you already know the address of a site that might have the information you need, type it in the LOCATION/GO TO box. This is an example of a URL: *www.webaddress.org.*

These addresses are found in many places. You may have seen Web addresses on television or in magazines. Some magazines, newspapers, or television shows have their own URLs that you can also search.

Print Resources

There are many reference tools that you can use to find information. A reference tool is a source that provides information.

We have already discussed Web sites, encyclopedias, dictionaries, and other resources that you can find online. Books such as atlases, almanacs, dictionaries, and encyclopedias are also reference tools. Most libraries have shelves of reference materials that cannot be checked out but can be used for research while you are at the library.

Encyclopedia An encyclopedia is a collection of articles, listed alphabetically, on various topics. When you need basic information quickly, an encyclopedia is a good choice. Electronic encyclopedias, available on the Internet or CD-ROM, have sound and video clips, in addition to written words.

Dictionary A dictionary is an alphabetical collection of words that includes the meanings of each word. It is the best source for checking the correct spelling of a word. Each entry in the dictionary usually includes the preferred pronunciation of a word and its part of speech. Some dictionaries also include information about the origin of a word, or the language from

which the word comes. Many dictionaries also include abbreviations, names, and explanations of well-known people and places.

Atlas An atlas is a collection of maps. If you want to find out about a geographical location, you would look in an atlas. Some atlases contain only one particular kind of map. Others have a variety of maps showing political boundaries, elevation, crops, population, natural resources, languages spoken, or historical developments. Teachers and librarians can help you find the type of atlas that would best help in your search for information.

Almanac An almanac is a book or computer media that lists many facts about a variety of topics. Almanacs are usually organized in sections by topic. Much of the information is given in charts, tables, and lists. Almanacs are usually updated every year, so they have the latest statistics on populations, economics, sports records, political events, weather, and other topics.

Nonfiction Books A nonfiction book is a factual book about a specific topic that was researched and written by someone who is knowledgeable on that topic. Nonfiction books can be a valuable reference tool.

In a library, all nonfiction books are numbered and placed in order on the shelves. Books on the same subject are grouped together. Whether your library has an online computer catalog or a card catalog, you can search for a book by title, subject, author, or key word.

Once you find information on a book that you want, look for the call number of the book. The call number is usually located on the bottom spine of the book binding. That number will guide you to the area of the library where you will find the book. A librarian can also help you find the book.

930	ANCIENT AMERICAS
ENC	Green, Jen; Macdonald, Fiona; Steele, Philip; and Stotter, Michael.
	The Encyclopedia of the Ancient Americas: The Everyday Life of America's Native Peoples, [by] Jen Green, Fiona Macdonald, Philip Steele, and Michael Stotter; London: Southwater, 2001.
	256 p. ill.
	1. ANCIENT AMERICAS I. Title

Subject

930	THE ENCYCLOPEDIA OF THE ANCIENT
ENC	AMERICAS
	The Encyclopedia of the Ancient Americas: The Everyday Life of America's Native Peoples, [by] Jen Green, Fiona Macdonald, Philip Steele, and Michael Stotter; London: Southwater, 2001.
	256 p. ill.
	1. ANCIENT AMERICAS I. Title

Title

930	Green, Jen; Macdonald, Fiona; Steele,
ENC	Philip; and Stotter, Michael.
	The Encyclopedia of the Ancient Americas: The Everyday Life of America's Native Peoples; London: Southwater, 2001. 256 p. ill.
	1. ANCIENT AMERICAS I. Title

Author

Periodicals A periodical, such as a newspaper or a magazine, is published on a regular basis—daily, weekly, or monthly. For this reason, the information in a periodical is usually more current than that found in a book. Most libraries have a special periodical section. Many magazines and newspapers also have their own Web sites where you can read all or part of the publication online.

Libraries have guides that list magazine articles by subject. The *Children's Magazine Guide* and the *Readers' Guide to Periodical Literature* are the most commonly used guides.

Periodical guides list information by title, subject, and author. Each entry lists the title of the article or story, the author, the name and date of the magazine, and the page number on which the article appears. If your library has the magazine, you can borrow it and read the article. If your library does not have it, then your library can usually borrow it or have the article copied from another library.

Community Resources

In addition to the Internet and reference tools, the people and resources in your community are good sources of information. If you are studying the Vietnam War, for instance, you can visit history museums or contact a local historical society. Perhaps you know someone who lived at the time of the Vietnam War. You might want to interview that person for more information.

Interviews

An interview is a good way to find out what people in your community know. This means asking them questions about the topic you are studying. Follow these steps:

Plan Ahead

- List the people you want to interview.
- Call or write to ask permission. Let the person know who you are, the name of your school and project, and why you need the information.
- Agree on a time and a place for the interview.
- Gather background information about the topic that you want to discuss.
- Write down questions that you want to ask at the interview.

Ask, Listen, Record

- Ask questions clearly.
- Listen carefully to gather information and to think of additional questions.
- Be polite. Do not interrupt or argue.
- Write notes so that you will remember what was said. Write down the person's actual words as much as possible. If possible, use a tape recorder to help you remember.

Wrap-up

- Thank the person when you are finished with the interview.
- Send a thank you note.

Use a Survey

Another way to find information in your community is to conduct a survey. A survey is a list of questions that you ask people and a record of their answers. This gives you an idea about what the people in your community know, think, or feel about a subject. You can use either yes-and-no questions or short-answer questions. To record the information you gather, you will want to make a tally sheet with a column for each question.

The following steps will help you plan a survey:

- Write down a list of questions.
- Decide where and when you want to conduct the survey and how many people you want to ask.
- Use a tally sheet when conducting the survey so that you can record people's answers.
- After you have completed the survey, look through the responses and write down what you found out.

Write for Information

Another way to obtain information from people or organizations in your community is to send an email or write a letter asking for information. Use the following steps to write for information:

- Plan what you want to say before you write it down or type it up.
- Be neat and careful about spelling, grammar, and punctuation.
- Explain who you are and why you are writing.
- Thank the person.
- You may want to include a self-addressed, stamped envelope so that the person or organization will be able to reply more easily.

Vietnam War

Where were you during the Vietnam War?	How old were you during the war?	How did the war affect Americans?	What memories do you have?
I signed up for the Marines and served in Cambodia.	I was 18 when I signed up.	There was a lot of protesting against the war. It made everyone think about why the U.S. was involved in a war so far away.	There are some I don't want to talk about. But I remember my buddies and good times playing cards and wishing we'd get home soon.
Oklahoma City, Oklahoma	I was 10 when it ended.	I don't remember too much about it. I do remember my grandmother being worried that her two sons would be drafted.	I remember the news on TV almost every evening had something about the war.

Writing a Research Report

Prewrite

- Choose a topic for your report. Your teacher may tell you what kind of report to research and write and how long it should be.
- Generate questions about your topic to help narrow it and focus your report.
- Use a variety of sources to find information and answer your questions.
- Evaluate your sources to determine which will be the most helpful.
- Take notes from your sources.
- Review your notes and write down the main ideas related to the topic that you want to present in your report. Two or three main ideas should be enough for most reports.
- Organize your notes into an outline, listing each main idea and the details that support it.

Write a First Draft

- Using your outline and your notes, quickly write down what you have learned. You can correct mistakes when you revise your draft. It is important to get your ideas on paper.
- Write in paragraph form. Each paragraph should be about a new idea.
- When you quote something directly from your sources, write down from which source the quotation came.
- When you are finished, your report should be organized with a strong introduction, a solid summary of information, a conclusion, and the list of sources you used.

Revise

- Read over your rough draft. Does it make sense? Does it answer the questions you asked? Does it clearly explain facts and ideas? Do your ideas flow from one to the next in an organized way? Do you need more information about any main idea? Will the report hold a reader's interest?
- Change any sentences or paragraphs that do not make sense. Add anything that will make your ideas clear.
- Check your quotations to make sure they are accurate and that you have noted from which source the quotation came.

Edit

- Proofread your report. Correct any errors in spelling, capitalization, punctuation, or usage.

Publish

- Add illustrations, maps, time lines, or other graphics that will add to the report.
- Create a table of contents.
- Write or type a final copy of your report as neatly as possible.

Early Civilizations and Cultures

*How does studying ancient cultures
affect our lives today?*

UNIT 1

Begin with a Primary Source

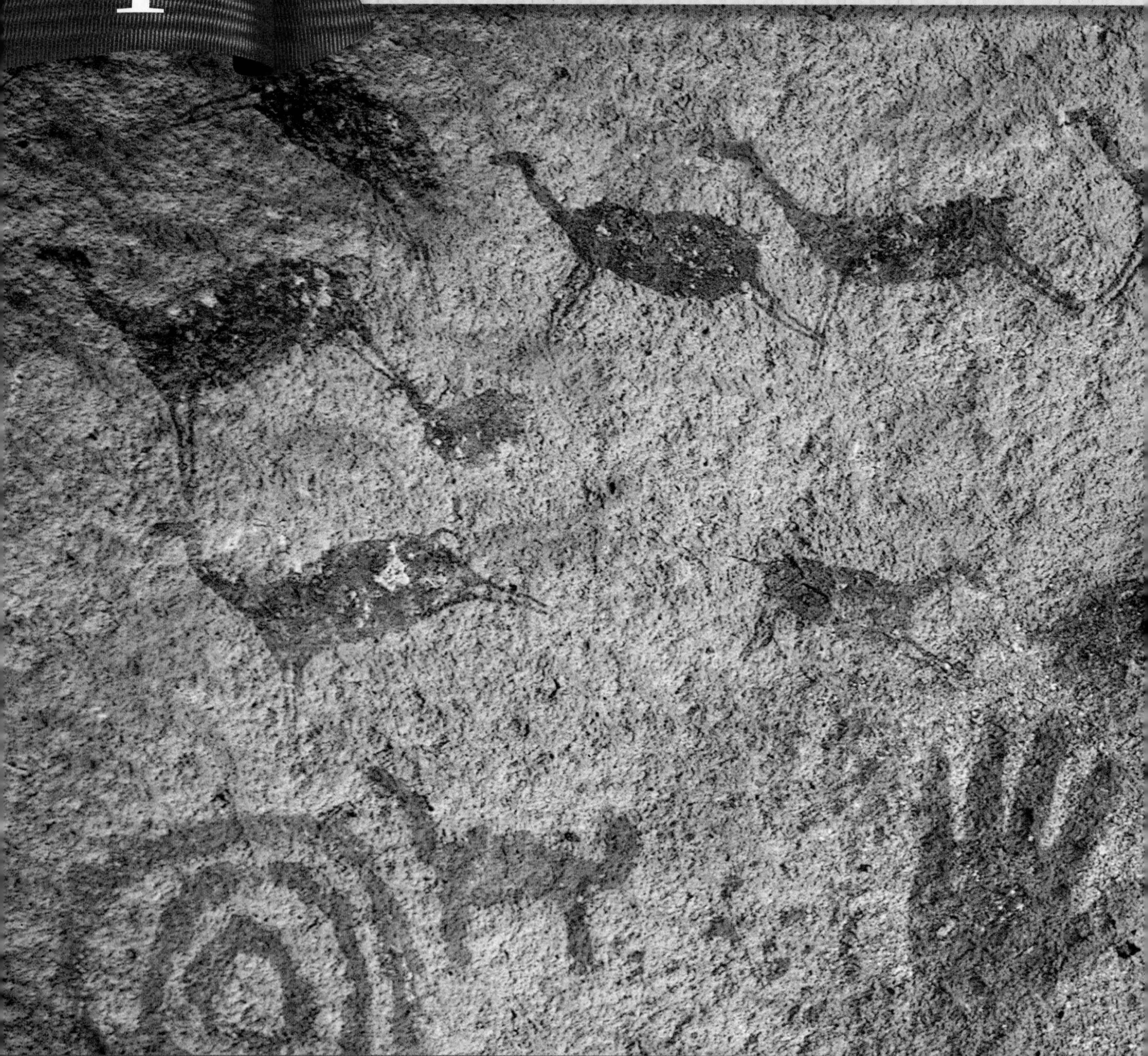

30,000 years ago

20,000 years ago

about 17,000 years ago
Cave paintings
in Lascaux

> **"With patience and a spirit of adventure, nothing is too far away."**
>
> —Said by Father Alberto de Agostini about the Cave of the Hands, 1941

Cave art message left by prehistoric people living in South America

10,000 years ago   **present**

about 11,000 years ago
Clovis culture in the Americas

about 10,000 years ago
End of Ice Age
Beginning of farming

about 9,000 years ago
Earliest date Cave of
the Hands could have
been painted.

about 5,200 years ago   Invention of writing

about 5,500 years ago
One of the first civilizations
rises in the Fertile Crescent.

Meet the People

Gilgamesh

c. 2700 B.C.
Birthplace: Unknown
King of Uruk
· Hero of legendary tales

Sargon

reigned c. 2334 B.C.–2279 B.C.
Birthplace: Unknown
Mesopotamian ruler
· Founded the Kingdom of Akkad
· Built the world's first great empire
· Ruled some 65 cities

Abraham

c. 1800 B.C.
Birthplace: Ur
Hebrew leader
· According to the Bible, God promised Canaan to Abraham's people.
· According to the Torah, Abraham agreed that he and his family would worship only one God.
· Considered to be the first Jew

Hammurabi

c. 1810 B.C.–1750 B.C.
Birthplace: Babylon
Mesopotamian ruler
· Established the Babylonian Empire
· Declared Babylon the capital of his empire
· Proclaimed a set of written laws to govern his empire

| 3000 B.C. | 2800 | 2600 | 2400 | 2200 | 2000 B.C. |

Gilgamesh
c. 2700 B.C.

Sargon
reigned c. 2334 B.C.–2279 B.C.

Moses

c. 1200 B.C.
Birthplace: Egypt
Hebrew leader
- Led the Hebrews out of slavery in Egypt
- According to the Torah, received the Ten Commandments from God

Deborah

c. 1224 B.C.–1184 B.C.
Birthplace: ancient Israel
Judge
- Encouraged a military leader to lead the tribes of Israel in an attack on the Canaanites
- Believed that a woman would triumph in the battle against the Canaanites

David

c. 1030 B.C.–962 B.C.
Birthplace: Bethlehem in ancient Judah
Hebrew ruler
- United the Hebrew tribes
- Second king of ancient Israel

Solomon

c. 1000 B.C.–925 B.C.
Birthplace: Jerusalem in ancient Israel
King of ancient Israel
- Built the First Temple at Jerusalem
- Considered the greatest king of Israel

1800   1600   1400   1200   1000 B.C.   800

Abraham
c. 1810 B.C.

Hammurabi
c. 1800 B.C.–1750 B.C.

Deborah
c. 1224 B.C.–1184 B.C.

Moses
c. 1200 B.C.

David
c. 1030 B.C.–962 B.C.

Solomon
c. 1000 B.C.–925 B.C.

Reading Social Studies

Early Civilizations and Cultures

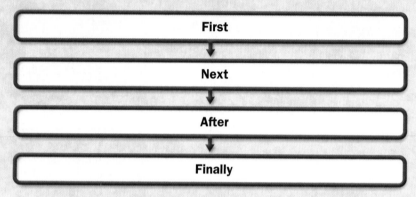

Sequence

Sequence refers to the order of events.

First
Next
After
Finally

- Sometimes writers use clue words such as *first*, *next*, *after*, and *finally* to signal sequence.

- Keeping track of dates on a time line will help you keep events in their correct sequence.

Read the following paragraph. The clue words that tell the **sequence** of events have been highlighted.

One of the **first** things archaeologists do is to choose a place, or a site, where they think ancient people once lived. **Next,** they use string and stakes to mark the area with a grid of squares. Once the grid is complete, they start digging. When they uncover objects, they map the location of the artifacts. **After** they dig up an item, they mark it. **Finally** they wrap the item carefully to study it at a **later** time.

Finding Ancient Americans

In 1932 archaeologists working in New Mexico found clues about humans who had lived in the region thousands of years ago. Based on the age of arrowheads and other tools they found, researchers made some conclusions. They said that ancient people lived near Clovis, New Mexico, more than 11,000 years ago.

Initially, the researchers developed an explanation to tell how they thought people came to Clovis. The first people to reach the Americas were hunters of large animals. They may have crossed a land bridge that linked Siberia in Asia to the Americas. Researchers said that this happened during the last Ice Age—about 11,500 years ago. Later, the ice sheets melted, and the ocean level rose, covering the land bridge.

During the last 20 years or so, some researchers have begun to question that explanation. Discoveries in Virginia, South Carolina, and other places have shown that people may have arrived in the Americas much earlier. These people may have come at several different times and from many different places.

In the summer of 2000, researcher Albert Goodyear examined a pale yellow rock at the Topper site in South Carolina. The rock had sharp, angled edges and was much older than the finds near Clovis. Goodyear said, "Nature can't make this; a human being has to do it very carefully." Finds like these are calling the old explanation of who the first Americans were into question. More research will need to be completed before we have a definite answer for "Who were the first Americans?"

Use the reading strategy of sequence to answer these questions.

1 When do some researchers believe the first people reached the Americas?

2 Did Goodyear's discovery in South Carolina come before or after the finds in Clovis?

Digging Up the Past

Lesson 1

12,500 years ago
Beringia
Early people survive as hunters and gatherers.

1

Lesson 2

about 4,000–4,500 years ago
Skara Brae
People begin to form communities.

2

Lesson 3

about 32,000–5,000 years ago
Chauvet
Cave paintings show how prehistoric cultures lived.

3

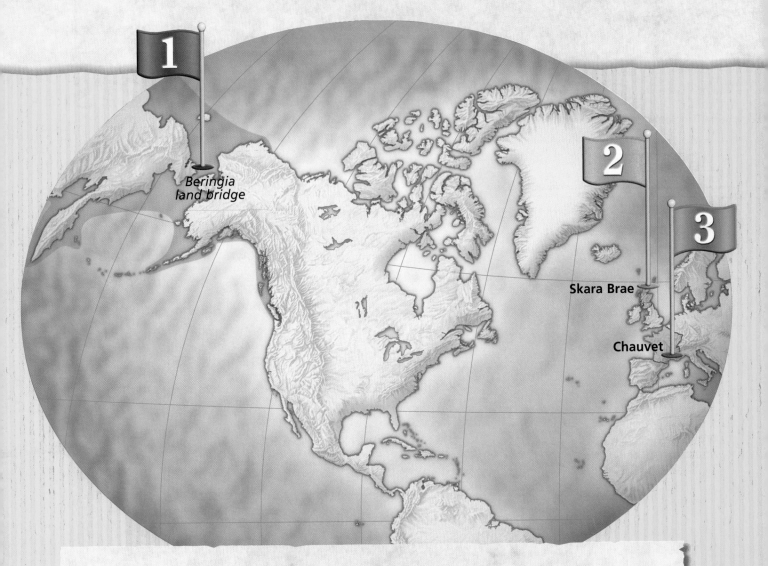

1 Beringia land bridge

2 Skara Brae

3 Chauvet

Why We Remember

Why do people live where they do? Why do people have many different ways of life? One way to learn about who we are is to study how people lived and worked in the past. Studying about the past helps us learn about the first people who were living on Earth, how they lived, and what problems they faced. Learning about the past can help us begin to understand why we have certain customs. Why are some regions of Earth crowded, while others are not? The information we gain from studying peoples who lived long ago helps fill in the picture of how we live today. Learning about ancient peoples from long ago helps us learn about ourselves.

Beringia
land bridge

near
Clovis

PREVIEW

Focus on the Main Idea
We use archaeology to learn about early peoples.

PLACES
Clovis
Tassili
Beringia
Monte Verde
Topper site

VOCABULARY
prehistory
archaeology
archaeologist
artifact
migrate
glacier

TERMS
Ice Age

4 million years ago **present**

3.5 millon years ago
Early humans in
East Africa

1.6 million years ago
Ice Age begins.

about 11,000 years ago
Clovis culture in North America

Early Gatherers and Hunters

You Are There

Dig, sift, sift. Dig, sift, sift. Beads of sweat roll down your face. The salt stings your eyes, but you try to focus. Your hands grip the wooden shovel handle. Earlier you trekked through the dense oak forest, where multicolored patches of sunlight decorated the forest floor. Now, as you kneel on the floor of a 6-foot-deep gray sand pit, the 95°F South Carolina heat burns your neck. You sift through sand that flowed out of the Savannah River thousands of years ago. Your eyes search the sand, looking for little razor blade-type things with sharp, slanted edges. Suddenly, you notice a sparkle in the sand. Could it be an arrowhead or a stone tool once used for cutting animal hide? This is the day you dreamed about. You are an archaeologist, and you have just made a great discovery!

▶ These tools help archaeologists dig up the past.

Sequence As you read, keep events in their correct time order.

Studying Prehistory

You just read about digging for tools from a period long ago, which is called prehistory. **Prehistory** is that long period of time before people developed systems of writing and written language. Prehistoric people did not leave books, newspapers, or letters to help us understand how they lived. However, even without written information, we can learn about prehistoric people and their way of life.

Archaeology (ahr kee AHL uh jee) is the study of past cultures through the things that remain such as buildings, tools, or pottery. The main task of an **archaeologist** is the careful uncovering of evidence, or clues, from the past. Archaeologists are most interested in finding and analyzing ancient **artifacts,** objects made by people long ago.

Artifacts can include tools, weapons, jewelry, and pottery. Artifacts of prehistoric people include sharpened stones for cleaning flesh from animal hides, bone needles for sewing hides together for clothing, and cords and knots used to tie together hides for shelter. A location with many hard rock flint chips might have been the workplace of a toolmaker. Archaeologists also are interested in the ashes of ancient campfires, the bones of animals left after a meal, or even nut shells. These items become prized puzzle pieces that help complete a picture of the past. Then archaeologists can draw conclusions about the daily lives of ancient peoples.

Artifacts tell us that ancient people hunted both small and large animals for food. Hides of larger animals were used for clothing and shelter. Ancient people also ate berries, fruits, nuts, wild grains, and roots that they gathered from nearby forests and meadows. They needed to move around in order to find a constant source of animals and fruit. For this reason early peoples are described as hunters and food gatherers.

REVIEW How can objects we find today tell us about people who lived before written history?
🔄 Sequence

▶ **Archaeologists, along with other scientists, literally "dig into" the past to learn how early peoples lived.**

Early Peoples

One way to learn about early peoples is to study the artifacts they left behind. Scientists have developed several ways to estimate the age of an artifact.

By comparing and analyzing the ages of thousands of artifacts, researchers believe that early peoples lived in parts of East Africa nearly 3.5 million years ago. Working together, archaeologists and historians believe that humans moved, or **migrated,** from East Africa to Europe and Asia thousands of years ago. As they studied these migrations they began to ask, "Who were the first Americans? Where did they come from? How did they get here?"

How archaeologists answer these questions can tell us a lot about how scholars piece together the puzzle of prehistory.

REVIEW Do archaeologists believe that humans moved first from East Africa or Europe?
⟳ **Sequence**

Early Americans

About 70 years ago, archaeologists found a variety of human-made objects near **Clovis,** New Mexico. The arrowheads, hammerstones, bone tools, and scrapers were estimated to be about 11,000 years old.

Eleven thousand years ago, Earth was still in an **Ice Age.** During this time—from about 1.6 million years ago until about 10,000 years ago—huge ice sheets, called **glaciers,** covered great stretches of land. Occasionally the glaciers grew and spread toward the equator. As glaciers spread over more of the earth, temperatures fell. However, when the glaciers retreated, temperatures rose. Vast expanses of land then became available for plant growth and animal grazing.

REVIEW When did archaeologists find evidence of Clovis people in America?
⟳ **Sequence**

 DORLING KINDERSLEY EYEWITNESS BOOK

The Ice Age

Archaeologists have found evidence of human life during the Ice Age. In 1926 they discovered a 10,000-year-old leaf-shaped stone point in Folsom, New Mexico. Archaeologists later found a 11,000-year-old stone point near Clovis, New Mexico, as well as spear points in the Great Lakes area and New England. They have identified common materials, shapes, and sizes in these artifacts. Why do you think early Ice Age hunters started using spear points made of copper?

Slated spear point

Copper spear point

Chipped-stone spear point

Larger Clovis point

Folsom point

Small Clovis point

Improved Technology
After the Ice Age ended, hunters became more skilled in tool making. They looked for better materials like slate and copper to make their weapons.

12

Prehistoric Cave Art

At about the same time that prehistoric people were making tools in the Americas, prehistoric people were painting on cave walls in Africa. Many of the paintings show animals grazing or people hunting. This painting discovered in **Tassili** in North Africa shows women and children with cattle. Archaeologists believe that it was painted between about 5500 B.C. and 3500 B.C.

ATLANTIC OCEAN

EUROPE

Mediterranean Sea

ALGERIA

AFRICA

■ Tassili region
— Present-day boundaries

▶ Scenes of cattle grazing, hunting, and family life were painted by different prehistoric peoples living in North Africa.

A Migration Path

The discovery of human-made objects near Clovis challenged archaeologists to explain how early people made their way to what is now New Mexico. Study of the Ice Age shape and boundaries of Asia and the Americas revealed that during parts of the Ice Age, the seas were lower than they are today. When the seas were lower a vast area of land, Beringia —now called the Bering Strait—stretched from Asia to North America. During times of the lowest seas, Beringia stretched for about 1,000 miles from north to south and formed what is sometimes called a "land bridge." Animals from either side of the "bridge" were able to migrate between Asia and the Americas. Of course, people also could cross the bridge to follow the animals they hunted for food.

Once archaeologists established that animals and people could have been able to walk from Asia to North America, they offered the following explanation. Bands, or small groups, of hunters left Asia more than 11,500 years ago. They may have moved across Beringia to present-day Alaska. From there the hunters traveled south,

moving through an ice-free passage between two immense glaciers. In less than 1,000 years, they may have reached what is now the American Southwest. They migrated eastward toward the center of North America and, within another 1,000 years, they had made their way to the tip of South America. Look for parts of this theory, or educated guess, in this legend of the Great Basin Paiute people:

> *"Ice had formed ahead of them. It reached all the way to the sky. The people could not cross it . . . . A Raven flew up and struck the ice and cracked it. Coyote said, 'The people can't get across the ice.' Another Raven flew up again and cracked the ice again. Coyote said, 'Try again.' Raven flew up again and broke the ice. The people ran across."*

REVIEW How long ago did the landmass of Beringia exist? ⟳ Sequence

▶ **The Paiute people may have crossed the Bering Strait more than 11,500 years ago.**

Beringia and Possible Migration Paths

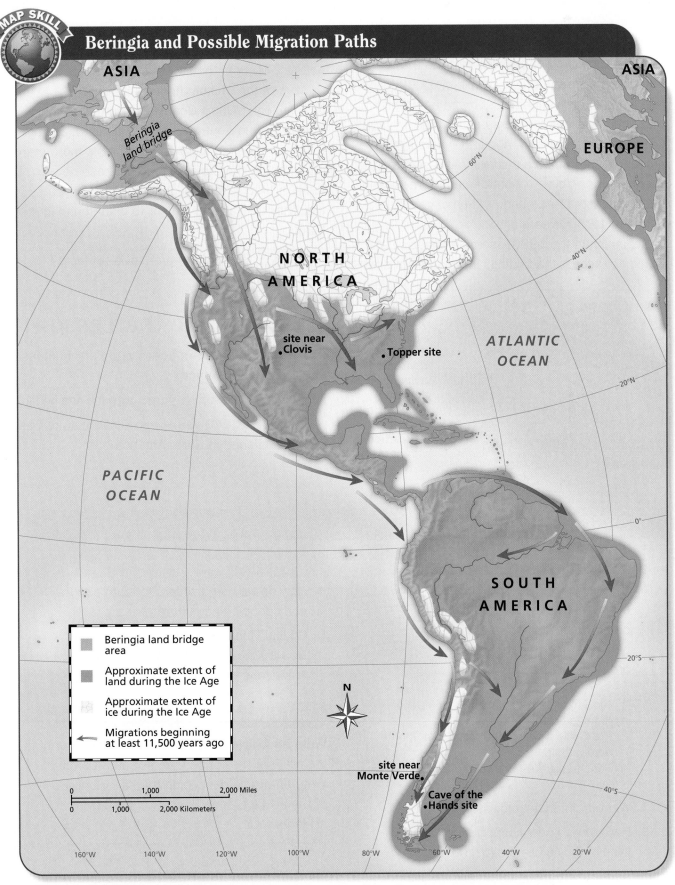

ASIA

ASIA

EUROPE

Beringia land bridge

NORTH AMERICA

60°N

40°N

site near Clovis

• Topper site

ATLANTIC OCEAN

20°N

PACIFIC OCEAN

0°

SOUTH AMERICA

20°S

Legend:

Beringia land bridge area

Approximate extent of land during the Ice Age

Approximate extent of ice during the Ice Age

Migrations beginning at least 11,500 years ago

N

site near Monte Verde •

Cave of the • Hands site

40°S

0   1,000   2,000 Miles

0   1,000   2,000 Kilometers

160°W   140°W   120°W   100°W   80°W   60°W   40°W   20°W

▶ You can trace what may have been migration routes of the first Americans by following the red arrows on the map.

MAP SKILL Understand Hemispheres *What hemisphere is shown on this map?*

15

Different Paths

For years, scholars believed that the first Americans were the Clovis people of 11,000 years ago. If an archaeologist found an artifact that seemed older, scholars doubted the artifact was real, not the theory. About 20 years ago, archaeologists made a discovery at a site near Monte Verde, Chile, in South America. They found artifacts from a band of hunter-gatherers, dating to 12,500 years ago.

Beginning in the 1990s, some archaeologists would not accept the findings in the Chilean site.

▶ Some of the artifacts at Monte Verde included pieces of wooden poles and stakes tied with cords.

Why? Because that would mean that the first Americans entered North America 1,000 years before scientists thought they did!

Word of the Chilean findings spread. Archaeologist Albert Goodyear returned to the Topper site in South Carolina and dug deeper. His team then found small stone tools more than a foot below the Clovis artifacts. These newly found artifacts were as much as 18,000 years old. They also looked similar to ones found in Europe.

REVIEW How old are pre-Clovis artifacts?
⟳ Sequence

Summarize the Lesson

- **about 3.5 million years ago** Early humans lived in East Africa.

- **about 1.6 million years ago** Ice Age began.

- **about 11,000 years ago** Clovis culture was established in North America.

LESSON 1 REVIEW

Check Facts and Main Ideas

1. ⟳ **Sequence** The following events are not in chronological order. On a separate piece of paper, list them in the correct order.

   - Clovis points are found in New Mexico.
   - Ice Age begins.
   - Pre-Clovis artifacts are found near Monte Verde, Chile.
   - People migrate from Asia to North America.

2. What is an archaeologist?

3. How do we know about the people who lived in Clovis years ago?

4. How do we use artifacts to learn about early people and cultures?

5. **Critical Thinking: *Evaluate Information*** Do we know for certain who the first Americans were? Explain your answer.

Link to ⌒⌒ Writing

Write an Article Suppose you are a member of the team at the Topper site in South Carolina. Write an article describing the importance of the artifacts found beneath the Clovis artifacts.

BUILDING CITIZENSHIP

Caring

Respect

⭐ Responsibility

Fairness

Honesty

Courage

Stone Age Healers

The hunters and gatherers who lived during the Stone Age risked injury every day. They were exposed to many diseases, ranging from the common cold to joint problems. How did early humans deal with sickness and injuries?

Early on, prehistoric humans made medicines from herbs. They also figured out the basics of the human body by studying the bodies of animals. Over time, they learned a lot about illnesses and injuries. Healers are responsible for passing this knowledge to the next generation of healers.

By about 7000 B.C. or even earlier, Stone Age healers could pull infected teeth, set broken bones, cut off limbs, and even perform brain surgery! The healers would perform brain surgery on someone who had headaches or head wounds. To treat the person, a Stone Age surgeon cut a round hole in the patient's skull. Early humans believed that disease was the work of angry gods. The opening in the patient's skull could have been a way for the evil spirit to escape.

The instruments of Stone Age surgeons were not much different from prehistoric hunting tools. The flint knives they used were sharper than steel scalpels used by surgeons today. No one knows if the operations really cured the patients. But archaeological findings show that some patients did survive the surgery. This indicates that the surgeons were remarkably skilled.

▶ **These surgical tools were used by the ancient Egyptians. They are made of bronze, while Stone Age surgeons used tools made of stone.**

Responsibility in Action

Link to Current Events Healers have the responsibility to help their patients. Research the story of a person who helps heal people. How is he or she responsible?

Skara Brae

SCOTLAND

10,000 years ago — present

about 10,000 years ago
First animals are domesticated.
Old Stone Age ends.
New Stone Age begins.

about 4,500 years ago
People living in Skara Brae

about 5,000 years ago
New Stone Age ends.

PREVIEW

Focus on the Main Idea
Communities began to develop during the Stone Age.

PLACES
Skara Brae

VOCABULARY
technology
domesticate
harvest
excavation site
agriculture
surplus
nomad
social division
climate
carbon dating

TERMS
Stone Age
Old Stone Age
New Stone Age

Early Farmers

You Are There
The air is close. The stone ceiling seems so low that you feel as though you should crawl. The ceiling, together with the stone walls, forms a covered walkway linking eight Stone Age dwellings. You move from house to house, noting that one is much like another. Each has a large square room with a central fireplace. The beds on either side have mattresses made of straw and blankets of sheepskin or deerskin. A dresser with shelves stands along the wall opposite the doorway. All the furniture—cupboards, dressers, even beds—is made of stone!

Sand dunes buried this village of Skara Brae in northern Scotland more than 4,500 years ago. Only uncovered in the 1800s, it offers many clues about Stone Age life to archaeologists.

Sequence While you read, keep events in their correct time order.

▶ The ruins at Skara Brae are located in the Orkney Islands, north of Scotland.

The Stone Age

When archaeologists uncover artifacts like those at **Skara Brae**, they try to group together artifacts and events in prehistoric times. For example, they study the physical conditions of Earth to determine the dates of the Ice Age. Archaeologists also group artifacts from a period of time called the Stone Age. During the **Stone Age**, humans relied primarily on stone tools. In certain regions, humans also made weapons and tools out of wood, bone, or antlers.

The Stone Age covers a vast amount of time. Archaeologists divide this time into two contrasting periods. The greater length of time, the **Old Stone Age**, lasted from about 3.5 million years ago to about 10,000 years ago. Although this is a lot of time, little progress was made. **Technology**, or the way in which humans produce the items they use, improved at a slow rate. Today, think about how fast technology has changed in your lifetime.

During the Old Stone Age, humans relied on pebble or stone tools, as well as hand axes. Rough, pitted surfaces and uneven cutting edges characterize tools made during the Old Stone Age. As the Stone Age progressed, humans began to use wood, horn, antler, and bone tools. These materials could be worked only with the aid of harder rock tools. Bone proved to be a particularly useful material for barbed fishhooks, needles, and small leatherworking instruments.

The **New Stone Age** began roughly 10,000 years ago and lasted until about 5,000 years ago. During the New Stone Age, humans made great improvements in technology in a shorter time span. The beginning of the New Stone Age was marked by new techniques in stoneworking. Polished rock tools then came into widespread use.

When the last of the glaciers retreated at the end of the Ice Age, humans began to experiment with growing wild plants as food crops. At the same time, humans began to **domesticate**, or tame, wild animals. The New Stone Age ended when humans discovered metals and metalworking.

REVIEW How do archaeologists group together the artifacts they find? **Summarize**

▶ **During the Stone Age, people mostly used stone tools and weapons. By about 7000 B.C., humans had fire-making techniques.**

Early Farming

As archaeologists examine a site, they are careful to look for any signs of plant life. From their studies we know that grains—wheat, rice, barley, and so on—were among the first plants to be domesticated, or cultivated for human use.

Plant remains may also tell us how plants were domesticated. For example, wild einkorn (INE corn), a type of wheat, breaks easily and releases seeds into the wind. This helps the wild plant spread seeds easily. However, it is more difficult to **harvest,** or gather, wild plants because the seeds scatter too much. As a result, people selected plants to grow that would not lose their seeds when harvested.

Plant remains and tools of domesticating crops can be found at an **excavation site,** where

▶ Threshing removes seeds from the stalk of a plant. In general, the seed is the part of the plant you can eat.

archaeologists dig up artifacts. These artifacts tell us about ancient grain processing techniques. Plants were grown for food and for practical use. For instance, jute (JOOT), a wild plant, was domesticated because its stalks had strong fibers. These fibers were then used to make rope and fishing nets.

REVIEW Why do archaeologists study plant remains? **Main Idea and Details**

Then and Now: New Crop Development

Domestication of plants did not stop after the Stone Age ended. For example, about two hundred years ago, farmers domesticated the sugar beet, a sugar-yielding plant. Less than one hundred years ago, farmers domesticated the mint plant for use in teas, flavorings, and beauty products.

Today, dozens of plants are being considered for domestication. In the United States, domesticating native plum trees may provide Kansas farmers an additional cash crop. Some crops that have been domesticated for years are being studied for new uses.

▶ International studies show that a crop of high-oil content, such as sunflowers, might someday provide a source of human-made fuel.

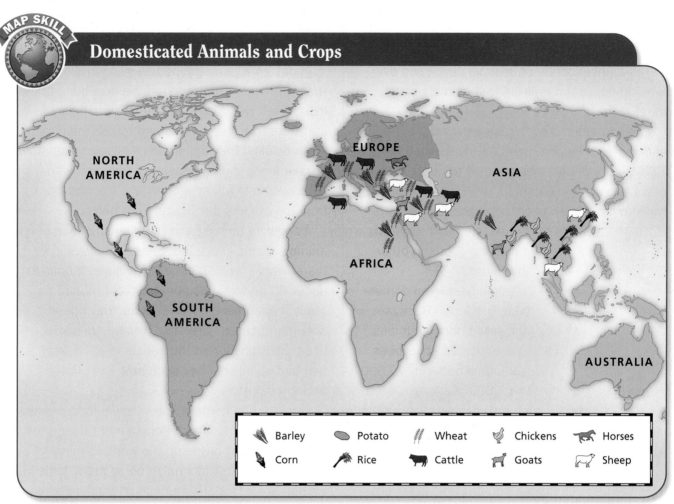

NORTH AMERICA

EUROPE

ASIA

AFRICA

SOUTH AMERICA

AUSTRALIA

Icon	Name	Icon	Name	Icon	Name	Icon	Name	Icon	Name
🌾	Barley	🥔	Potato	🌾	Wheat	🐓	Chickens	🐎	Horses
🌽	Corn	🌾	Rice	🐄	Cattle	🐐	Goats	🐑	Sheep

▶ Often the same animal or plant was domesticated about the same time in several different locations.

MAP SKILL Use a Distribution Map *Where were most of the first animals and plants domesticated?*

Domestic Animals

About 10,000 years ago, humans began to recognize that animals could be useful to them. They began to domesticate dogs, goats, cattle, and sheep. Domesticated animals differ from wild animals in several ways. Their survival depends on humans; and they develop traits that are not found in the wild.

Sheep and goats were among the first animals to be domesticated. Later, people realized that animals could also be kept to produce milk and wool. These by-products could then be sold. Cattle provided meat for food and skin for clothing and shelter.

▶ Chickens were domesticated at least 4,000 years ago.

Animals also were used to plow fields. In this way cattle made a great contribution to the development of **agriculture,** or the raising of plants and animals for human use. One family could now raise more crops than they needed and sell the **surplus,** or the extra supply.

REVIEW How did the domestication of some animals affect agriculture? *Cause and Effect*

21

More Useful Creatures

The domestication of animals developed over time. People soon realized that animals could meet many of their needs.

Early domesticated horses provided meat and skin. Later, they were used for transportation for **nomads,** or people who traveled from place to place. Donkeys and camels provided additional ways to move both people and goods. These animals helped people travel great distances carrying goods to other communities.

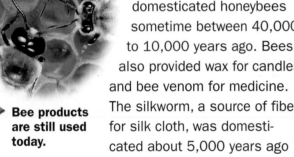

People have even domesticated insects! Because they liked honey, humans domesticated honeybees sometime between 40,000 to 10,000 years ago. Bees also provided wax for candles and bee venom for medicine. The silkworm, a source of fiber for silk cloth, was domesticated about 5,000 years ago in China.

▶ **Bee products are still used today.**

REVIEW How did early humans decide what animals to domesticate? *Draw Conclusions*

Village Life

About 2400 B.C., the people living in Skara Brae, the place you visited at the beginning of the lesson, left the village. Archaeologists believe that a terrible storm came and forced them to leave quickly. They did not even have enough time to take along their belongings! Archaeologists have pieced together what village life was like from the objects the villagers left behind.

Along with farming and the domestication of animals came village life. Skara Brae was in many ways a typical Stone Age village. It housed about 50 people. People used tools made from stone, beach pebbles, and bone. They raised sheep and cattle. They also farmed. Villagers used their location at the seashore to harvest fish and shellfish. They decorated their flat-bottomed pottery.

Farmers and herders, the village's food producers, raised surplus food. Because of the surplus, the village could divide up the work, forming **social divisions.** A toolmaker could make tools in exchange for food. Farmers could exchange surplus crops for meat or sheepskins. This change of lifestyle, from hunting and gathering to farming, led people to a new stage of development.

REVIEW What led to the development of social divisions? *Main Idea and Details*

▶ **Some grass-covered stones are all that remain of the New Stone Age village of Skara Brae.**

The Iceman

Archaeologists have made other discoveries that tell us about people living during the New Stone Age. Some tell us about how people lived in different **climates,** or the average weather conditions of places over a long span of time.

In 1991 two German tourists hiking in the snowcapped Alps in Europe found the body of a man. With him were found a stone knife and a small ax with a copper blade. His clothing was made mostly of deerskin to protect him from the cold climate. The food he carried included mushrooms, animal bones, and berries.

By looking at the Iceman's ax and knife, archaeologists could estimate that the man lived during or after the New Stone Age. How did they know this? The clue was in the ax with the copper blade. Archaeologists

▶ **This ash-handled flint dagger was probably used by the Iceman to cut leather or game.**

have learned from other excavations that copper was widely used during the New Stone Age.

To determine the age of the Iceman even more accurately, scientists used another method called **carbon dating.** All living things contain the element carbon. Scientists can date things based on what happened to the carbon over time. When scientists used carbon dating, they determined that the Iceman lived about 5,300 years ago.

REVIEW How do comparing artifacts and using carbon dating help us learn about how early people lived? **Draw Conclusions**

Summarize the Lesson

- **about 3.5 million years ago** Old Stone Age began.

- **about 10,000 years ago** First animals were domesticated and New Stone Age began.

- **about 5,000 years ago** New Stone Age ended.

- **about 4,500 years ago** People lived in Skara Brae.

LESSON 2   REVIEW

Check Facts and Main Ideas

1. **Sequence** The following events are not in the correct order. On a separate piece of paper, list them in correct chronological order.

   - Domesticated crops
   - Social divisions within a community
   - Production of surplus food
   - Domesticated animals
   - Technology improves.

2. What characteristics defined the Stone Age?

3. What is domestication?

4. How did farming crops and raising animals change how people lived?

5. **Critical Thinking:** *Make Inferences* How can we know what animals Stone Age people domesticated?

Link to ⬤⬤ **Writing**

Write a List Suppose you are an archaeologist exploring a village such as Skara Brae. Make a list of what artifacts you would look for to support the theory that the villagers raised sheep.

Use Parallel Time Lines

What? Time lines help you understand when something happened. Time lines help you put events in sequence, the correct chronological order. They are a way to help you visualize the order in which events occurred.

The time line below shows that the last Ice Age began about 2 million years ago and lasted until about 10,000 years ago.

2 million years ago	100,000	80,000	60,000	40,000	20,000	10,000

Last Ice Age

The break in the time line means that a part of the time line has been left out. In this case the years between 2 million years ago and 100,000 years ago have been left out of the time line.

Why? Calendars, dates, and time lines help us keep track of time. We can use them to find out whether an event happened very long ago or not too long ago. The time period between events may be represented in different ways on a time line. This is because throughout the world people use different calendars.

▶ **Mammoths ranged widely across Europe, Asia, and North America. They died out about 10,000 years ago.**

The calendar used in most parts of the world is based on the birth of Jesus Christ. This kind of calendar lists the events that happened before Christ was born as B.C., or "before Christ." It lists other events as A.D. The letters A.D. stand for the Latin words *anno Domini*, which mean "in the year of our Lord."

Some time lines are labeled B.C.E., which stands for "before the Common Era." These time lines also use C.E. for "in the Common Era." Other time lines, particularly time lines that record events in prehistory, are labeled Y.A. for years ago. The terms B.C.E. and B.C., as well as A.D. and C.E., refer to the same years.

Some events took place at a general, rather than a specific, time. We use the Latin term *circa*, or *c.*, which means "about," for approximate, or almost exact, dates. The last Ice Age ended c. 10,000 years ago.

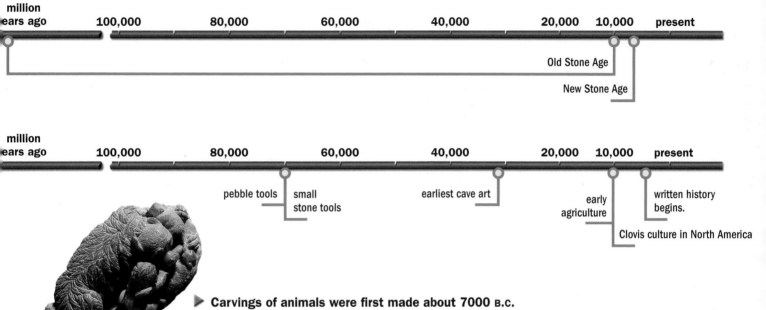

| million years ago | 100,000 | 80,000 | 60,000 | 40,000 | 20,000 | 10,000 | present |

Old Stone Age

New Stone Age

| million years ago | 100,000 | 80,000 | 60,000 | 40,000 | 20,000 | 10,000 | present |

pebble tools | small stone tools

earliest cave art

early agriculture

written history begins.

Clovis culture in North America

▶ **Carvings of animals were first made about 7000 B.C.**

How? Parallel time lines are useful for showing how events are related in time. The following steps will help you read time lines.

- Identify the length of time represented by the entire time line.
- Determine the length of time between each section and tick mark of the time line.
- Notice how events are marked in the time line. A [O] generally indicates a single point in time. The green lines show that an event lasted for a long period of time.
- Each labeled year has a blue tick mark. The white tick marks help show smaller time periods between the blue tick marks.

The two time lines represent time from 3 million years ago to the present. Use the time line to find out when the Old Stone Age ended. Follow the Old Stone Age line to the right. You can see that it ends at 10,000. This means the Old Stone Age lasted until about 10,000 years ago.

Study the other time line. Notice at the right of the time line that the beginning of written history occurred about 5,000 years ago.

Look at the top and bottom time lines. Compare the years of the Old Stone Age with the beginning of written history. You can see that written history began after the Old Stone Age ended.

Think and Apply

1 When did the earliest cave art appear?

2 What major event occurs near the end of the Old Stone Age?

3 What part of the Stone Age took place during the last Ice Age?

20,000 years ago   5,000 years ago   present

20,000 years ago
Hunter-gatherer
cultures exist.

5,000 years ago
Farming techniques
improve.

5,000 years ago
Complex cultures develop.

Chauvet

PREVIEW

Focus on the Main Idea
We use archaeology to learn
about how early cultures
developed.

PLACES
Cave of the Hands
Lascaux
Altamira
Chauvet

VOCABULARY
culture
anthropology
landform
geography
diverse

TERMS
Late Stone Age

Developing Cultures

You Are There
It is just after breakfast. You prepare for the highlight of your trip to Patagonia, a land in South America. You take a deep breath and step into the cave. After you've walked about 75 feet, your guide casts the lantern light onto a cave wall. An amazing scene appears. Hundreds of hand-prints, animal figures, and symbols cover the wall. You shudder. The paintings are amazing! You see paintings of ten hunters approaching dozens of llamas. Then you notice outlines of feet and of human figures, as well as patterns of geometric shapes. Among the paintings are handprints in black, brown, violet, yellow, and red. They seem to be waving at you from thousands of years ago.

▶ **This prehistoric cave lamp could have led ancient hunters into a safe place to rest.**

Main Idea and Details As you read, keep track of the main idea in each section.

Contacting Cultures

In the study of people, like those who painted the **Cave of the Hands** as many as 9,000 years ago, **culture** includes the technology, customs, beliefs, and art of those people. Sometimes, culture can be described as the way in which individuals and groups react to their environment. **Anthropology** is the study of how people have developed and live in cultural groups. Archaeology is a branch of anthropology.

Physical features of Earth such as plants and landforms encouraged the development of cultures. A **landform** is a surface feature such as a valley, plain, hill, or mountain. The study of the relationship between physical features, climate, and people is called **geography.**

During the **Late Stone Age,** or the end of the New Stone Age, there were several **diverse,** or different, peoples living in the Americas. Each diverse group had its developing culture. These cultures represented the different populations that migrated to the Americas from other regions.

Each of these cultures relied on the resources available to them. For example, a culture living in the desert relied on plant stems or fibers to make twine, nets, baskets, sandals, and animal traps. A culture living near mountains used rocks to make tools and weapons.

Small bands of people came together to form villages only after they had learned to grow crops. Corn, beans, and squash became the most important crops. They also are known as the "Three Sisters."

Ancient stone and simple pebble tools and sharp-pointed spears found in East Africa indicate Stone Age hunting and fishing cultures. In Central Africa, large, well-fired pots were decorated with designs to make them resemble baskets. Harpoons provide evidence for a fishing culture.

During the Ice Age, when sea levels were lower, a group of people from the Southeast Asia region migrated to islands in the Pacific. Their simple hunter-gatherer culture seems to have developed some ocean-going skills. In fact, some scientists believe that this culture had contact with the Americas. As evidence researchers point to the sweet potato, an American plant that also was grown in the Pacific.

▶ **The sweet potato was first cultivated in South America.**

REVIEW What is culture? **Main Idea and Details**

▶ **In the mid-20th century, adventurer Thor Heyerdahl and a small crew sailed on a primitive boat from the coast of South America to islands in the Pacific Ocean. He hoped to show that it might have been possible for these two cultures to have made contact in prehistoric times.**

Cultures Develop

In Europe the variety of landforms, climates, and soil produced many different cultures. Once farming was established, gradual settlement followed. Cultures increased their use of available resources. Throughout Europe, the major crops were grains, beans, peas, and lentils. Citrus trees grew well in warmer climates. Apples were grown in more temperate, or mild, climates.

The picture we have of the many Stone Age European cultures rests primarily on the technology and other artifacts these cultures left behind. However, in the last 200 years, archaeologists have found information-rich artifacts left behind by prehistoric cultures. These artifacts paint a picture of early peoples and their daily life.

REVIEW In Europe, what developed after farming was established? ⊙ Sequence

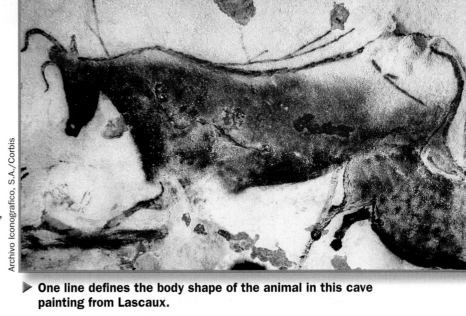

▶ One line defines the body shape of the animal in this cave painting from Lascaux.

Archivo Iconografico, S.A./Corbis

▶ Early peoples used milling stones to grind corn kernels.

▶ Corn, beans, and squash were first grown in the Americas between 6500 B.C. and 3500 B.C.

Prehistoric Art

At most prehistoric sites, archaeologists piece together the puzzle of a culture by using only the culture's tools and discards, or throwaways. A wealth of information can be found in pictures drawn by prehistoric people themselves. Archaeologists have discovered rocks engraved with human figures, horses, birds, and wild cattle at sites in Spain, Portugal, Australia, and South Africa. Some of these works of art are about 20,000 years old.

Prehistoric cave paintings can be found mostly in northern Spain and southern France. At **Lascaux** (las KOE) in southern France, cave art from about 17,000 years ago is protected deep in the ground from the damp climate. The paintings, drawings, and engravings on cave walls and ceilings provide a valuable view of the prehistoric world. The paintings reveal that the artists lived with, and hunted, horses, bison, mammoth, deer, and occasionally panthers and rhinoceroses. Colors range from red, brown, black and white, to yellow—all ground from nearby rock and stone. Paints were made by mixing the ground rock with saliva or animal fat. Then the paints were applied with fingers or simple brushes. Similar cave paintings appear on the ceiling of a cave at **Altamira,** Spain.

Even the caves themselves offer important information. Randall White, a researcher studying cave paintings from about 32,000 years ago at Chauvet in southern France commented:

> *"On the floor . . . everything is basically in place—torch fragments, stone tools, fire pits, and bones. We have well-preserved evidence of all the activities that were going on in and around these paintings. And that's critical."*

From the cave paintings, it seems that the caves served as places for spiritual and hunting rites. Over time, different humans visited the caves and added to the paintings several times for thousands of years. For all the information the cave paintings provide, questions remain. Why did artists paint a limited number of animals? Why are many paintings, drawings, and engravings in hard to reach places within caves? Why were some caves decorated but apparently not lived in? Archaeologists are still searching for answers.

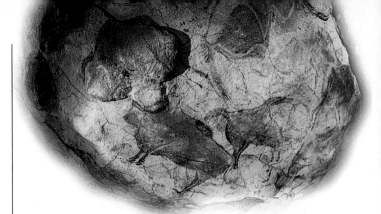

▶ **This cave art ceiling painting at Altamira, Spain, shows bison similar to those painted at Lascaux.**

REVIEW What do similar examples of cave art in many different countries tell us about the people living in prehistoric times? **Draw Conclusions**

Summarize the Lesson

- **20,000 years ago** Hunter-gatherer cultures existed.
- **5,000 years ago** Farming techniques started to improve.
- **5,000 years ago** Complex cultures developed.

LESSON 3   REVIEW

Check Facts and Main Ideas

1. Main Idea and Details On a separate piece of paper, fill in the missing details.

> During the Late Stone Age, complex cultures developed.

2. What is culture?

3. What encouraged the development of culture in the Americas?

4. What artifacts tell us the most about prehistoric cultures?

5. Critical Thinking: *Make Inferences* How did landforms and climate influence cultures?

Link to ⚯ **Art**

Draw a Picture Use what you have learned about daily life in the Stone Age to draw some cave art of your own. Look at some of the images in this lesson to help you.

11,000 years ago   9,000 years ago

11,000 years ago
Clovis culture in
the Americas

10,000 years ago
Early agriculture began.
Last Ice Age ended.

about 9,000 years ago
Earliest date Cave of the
Hands could have been
painted

Chapter Summary

Sequence

On a separate piece of paper, make a time line for these events.

- Beringia forms a land bridge from Asia to North America.
- People begin to domesticate plants and animals.
- Bands of people begin to live in villages and form communities.
- People eat plants they gather and animals they hunt.

Vocabulary

Write a sentence with the correct definition or description of each vocabulary word.

1. **culture** (p. 27)
2. **diverse** (p. 27)
3. **technology** (p. 19)
4. **domesticate** (p. 19)
5. **surplus** (p. 21)
6. **prehistory** (p. 11)
7. **archaeology** (p. 11)
8. **archaeologist** (p. 11)
9. **artifact** (p. 11)
10. **glacier** (p. 12)
11. **migrate** (p. 12)
12. **agriculture** (p. 21)

Places and Terms

Write a sentence explaining why each of the following places or terms is important in the study of ancient people.

1. Beringia (p. 14)
2. Ice Age (p. 12)
3. Stone Age (p. 19)
4. Clovis (p. 12)
5. New Stone Age (p. 19)
6. Skara Brae (p. 18)
7. Chauvet (p. 29)
8. Lascaux (p. 28)
9. Altamira (p. 28)
10. Tassili (p. 13)

about 5,300 years ago
The Iceman lived in the Alps.

5,000 years ago
New Stone Age ended.

Facts and Main Ideas

1 Describe one way in which ancient people might have migrated to the Americas.

2 What part do artifacts play in the study of ancient people?

3 How might glaciers have impacted the migration of early people?

4 **Time Line** What events happened at least 10,000 years ago?

5 **Main Idea** How does archaeology help us learn about early people and cultures?

6 **Main Idea** How did people's lives change during the Stone Age?

7 **Main Idea** Describe some of the different cultures that existed in the Late Stone Age.

8 **Critical Thinking:** *Make Inferences* What do you think was the greatest advancement in culture during the Stone Age?

Apply Skills

Use Parallel Time Lines
Read the time lines below. On the first time line are approximate dates of cave art paintings. Then answer the questions.

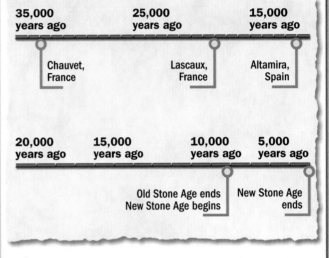

| 35,000 years ago | 25,000 years ago | 15,000 years ago |

Chauvet, France

Lascaux, France

Altamira, Spain

| 20,000 years ago | 15,000 years ago | 10,000 years ago | 5,000 years ago |

Old Stone Age ends
New Stone Age begins

New Stone Age ends

1 Compare both time lines. Where was cave art painted during the Old Stone Age?

2 How long did the New Stone Age last?

Write About History

1 **Write a journal entry** You are an archaeologist who has just discovered 15,000-year-old artifacts near the Great Lakes. How will your find compare with the Clovis points discovery?

2 **Write a news bulletin** describing farming and what effect it has on prehistoric village life.

3 **Write a magazine article** telling people about the newest discovery of cave art. Describe the art and any other artifacts that were found in the cave. Explain how you would estimate the age of the art and artifacts.

Internet Activity

To get help with vocabulary, people, and terms, select dictionary, encyclopedia, or almanac from *Social Studies Library* at **www.sfsocial studies.com.**

Early Civilizations

Lesson 1

c. 3500 B.C.
Uruk
One of the first civilizations develops.

1

Lesson 2

c. 2334 B.C.
Sumer
Sargon forms the world's first empire.

2

Lesson 3

c. 1750 B.C.
Babylon
Hammurabi builds the first Babylonian Empire.

3

Lesson 4

1000 B.C.
Jerusalem
David establishes a capital at Jerusalem.

4

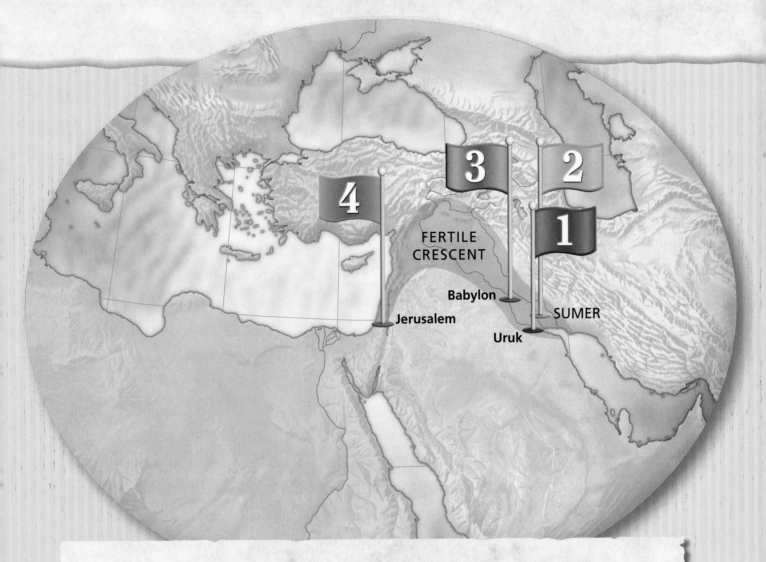

FERTILE
CRESCENT

Babylon

Jerusalem

Uruk

SUMER

Why We Remember

You say the Pledge of Allegiance. You send an email to a friend. You make sure that you follow your school's rules. Have you ever thought about the ideas behind these activities, when they first developed, or where? The basic principles of nationhood, writing, and law were developed by groups of people who lived thousands of years ago. They lived in a gracefully curved region in southwestern Asia and northeastern Africa known as the Fertile Crescent. Some of the peoples of this area also founded and established Judaism, one of the world's major religions, and were pioneers of international trade.

MESOPOTAMIA

Kish
Nippur
Babylon • • Lagash
Uruk
Ur

7000 B.C. — **3000 B.C.**

c. 7000 B.C.
Farmers arrive in the
Fertile Crescent.

c. 3500 B.C.
The first civilizations emerge
in the Fertile Crescent.

The Fertile Crescent

PREVIEW

Focus on the Main Idea
One of the first civilizations developed in the Fertile Crescent.

PLACES
Fertile Crescent
Mesopotamia
Uruk
Kish
Lagash
Nippur
Umma
Ur

VOCABULARY
civilization
fertile
plain
plateau
irrigation
city-state
region
artisan

▶ Barley plants still grow
in what is today known as
the Fertile Crescent.

You Are There

3500 B.C.: You try not to complain, but for days now you've been trailing along behind your family's herd of goats. You've breathed in more than your share of the dust they kick up. You and your family are walking south along the Euphrates (yoo FRAY teez) River in search of good farmland and a new home. Loaded on the back of a donkey are a few possessions—farming tools, clay pots, and two baskets of barley, a kind of grain that the family hopes they'll soon be able to plant. Suddenly, you notice several patches of green, and what looks like a small city. You run ahead and reach a small field. Tender green shoots of barley are just starting to sprout out of the soil. Here it is! The area where you will plant your barley. You hope that it grows well enough to make a surplus.

Cause and Effect
As you read, think of how the climate of the Fertile Crescent made it a good area for civilizations to rise.

Where Civilization Began

As you learned in Chapter 1, people have been living and working together since prehistory. But it was not until about 3500 B.C. that one of the first civilizations began to develop. **Civilizations** are groups of people who have a complex and organized society within a culture. Each has its own customs, food supply, social divisions, government, religion, and technology.

Civilizations first developed in southwestern Asia in a crescent-shaped area. (Look at the map below.) This region stretched from the eastern shores of the Mediterranean Sea between the Tigris and Euphrates Rivers to the mouth of the Persian Gulf. Because of the region's **fertile,** or rich, soil and its curved shape, we call it the **Fertile Crescent.** Today, the land of the Fertile Crescent is part of the countries of Iraq, Jordan, Syria, Lebanon, and Israel. Some scholars include part of Egypt in northeastern Africa in the Fertile Crescent. Other scholars do not.

Near the Mediterranean Sea were forests of cedar, oak, and pine. These trees provided a habitat for deer, sheep, and goats. A wild variety of barley also grew here. Farther south, the land of the Fertile Crescent consisted of grasslands, where wild pigs, oxen, and lions lived. The Zagros Mountains rose on the eastern part of the region. To the west lay deserts. In the central area was a **plain,** or area of flat land, bordered by the Tigris and Euphrates Rivers. The area between the two rivers became known as **Mesopotamia** (meh suh puh TAY mee uh), or "the land between the rivers." It was in Mesopotamia that one of the first civilizations emerged, or rose up.

REVIEW When did one of the first civilizations begin to develop? Sequence

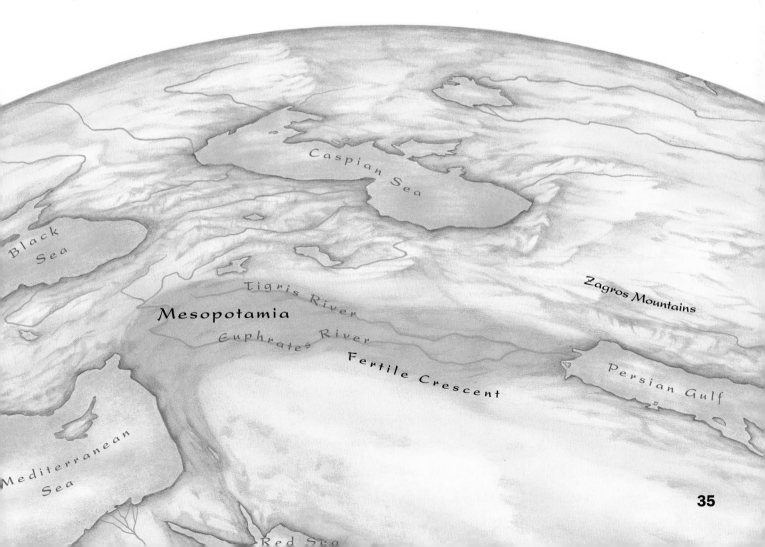

35

Climate and Rivers

The climate of the area is far from ideal for farming. Summers are long, hot, and dry, with temperatures reaching nearly 120°F. In many areas not a drop of rain falls from May to October. When rain falls from November to April, it varies from a brief sprinkle to a huge downpour. Heavy rains cause the riverbanks to overflow and flood the plain. In many parts of the Fertile Crescent, there is not enough rain for crops to grow. The early people of southern Mesopotamia needed to find a solution.

Beginning about 5000 B.C., farmers from the northern part of the Fertile Crescent probably began moving south in search of more fertile land. They moved from a plateau, or area of high, flat land, to the plain between the Tigris and Euphrates Rivers. The rivers provided a permanent source of fresh water, which was essential for human settlement. The rivers also were full of fish that could be eaten. The soil was very rich for growing crops because the rivers overflowed their banks on a regular basis.

Before they could start farming, the people needed to solve the problem of low rainfall. The rivers provided a solution. Farmers built trenches and ditches that brought the water from rivers to their fields. Such methods as these for watering crops are known as irrigation systems. Irrigation helped the people to control when and how much they watered their crops.

REVIEW What problem did people have to solve before they could start farming in southern Mesopotamia? **Sequence**

▶ **Rivers made early farming and settlement possible. However, floods were sometimes so bad that they destroyed crops and washed away entire villages. As irrigation systems and farming methods improved, flooding became less of a problem.**

The People

The people of southern Mesopotamia were problem solvers. They had to be, as the only real natural resources they had were water and soil. If lack of rain was not going to keep them from farming, then the fact that trees and stone were scarce was not going to keep them from building. From the marshy areas near the rivers, they cut reeds and built huts. Later they began making bricks by mixing mud with straw. They then dried these mud bricks in the sun, which made them very sturdy for building. People used these bricks to build homes, temples, and palaces.

For some time, most people worked as farmers or herders of domesticated goats, cattle, and sheep. Farmers planted crops such as barley, millet, wheat, dates, lentils, onions, garlic, turnips, lettuce, cucumbers, and apples. They made better tools for farming. Soon, the Mesopotamians were transporting food and goods on the rivers. Over time, the Mesopotamians developed their farming techniques to a very high level, as described in this farming handbook:

▶ Mud bricks were cut to the same size, using a mold. After the mud bricks dried, they were fitted together to make walls.

> *"Keep your eye on the man who puts in the barley seed. Let him drop the grain uniformly [in the same way] two fingers deep. . . . If the barley seed does not sink in properly, change your share [plow]. . . ."*

Such careful attention resulted in surpluses of food crops. The production of surplus food was a major step toward the rise of civilization in southern Mesopotamia.

REVIEW What kind of building materials did Mesopotamians use before they began using mud bricks? ↻ Sequence

Map Adventure

You're a Mesopotamian Trader

A messenger from the metalsmith's workshop in Ur tells you that his boss is running low on copper. He needs a new supply as soon as possible.

1. Look at the map. Locate the sources of copper that seem nearest to Ur.

2. If your boss gives you a donkey, which is the best land route you can take?

3. If your boss gives you a boat and a donkey, which is the best route you can take?

4. Would your journey take longer going to or returning from the copper sources? Keep in mind that the river runs from north to south.

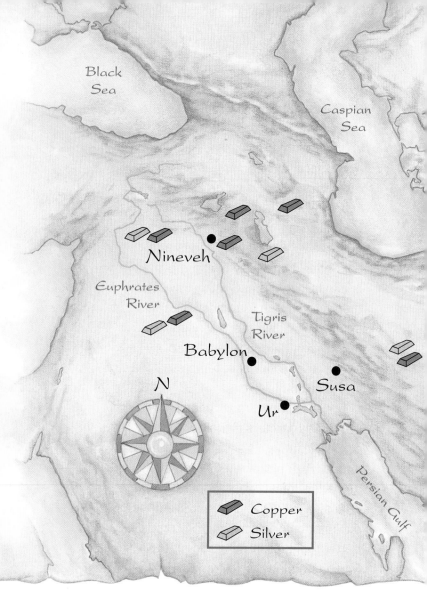

Black Sea

Caspian Sea

Nineveh

Euphrates River

Tigris River

Babylon

Susa

N

Ur

Persian Gulf

Copper
Silver

Growth of City-States and Trade

Once farming techniques had been improved in southern Mesopotamia, families thrived and the population grew. New settlers soon arrived from the northwestern and western parts of the Fertile Crescent. By 3500 B.C. several villages, including Uruk, Kish, Lagash, Nippur, Umma, and Ur, had grown into city-states. A city-state is a city that is an individual unit, complete with its own form of government and traditions. Mesopotamia is a region, or an area on Earth with common physical features. No one single power controlled all the city-states.

Because there was plenty of surplus food, it was no longer necessary for all of the people to work as farmers and herders. Some people helped govern the city, while others were religious leaders or soldiers. Some were artisans, or craftspeople, such as potters and weavers. In exchange for the services they provided, these workers were paid in food.

► The Standard of Ur is a war-peace plaque. This panel shows the peace side.

British Museum

▶ **These soldiers are part of the war side of the Standard of Ur.**

British Museum

Some people also became traders. Traders packed up donkeys with goods like barley and woven cloth. They then set out on long trading journeys. They returned with copper, stone, wood, and other raw materials that Mesopotamia lacked. Traders also used reed boats to trade with other Mesopotamian city-states along the river. The nearby Persian Gulf, however, was the real gateway to the wider world. For these journeys, the Mesopotamians built large wooden ships. They traded with faraway places. Through trade, the Mesopotamians met other peoples. This contact made their culture richer. It also helped them to spread Mesopotamian culture to other parts of the world.

REVIEW After some villages grew into city-states, what new kinds of jobs developed?
⟳ **Sequence**

Summarize the Lesson

- **7000 B.C.** Farmers arrived in the Fertile Crescent.

- **3500 B.C.** One of the first civilizations emerged in the Fertile Crescent.

- **3500 B.C.** The city-states of Mesopotamia rose.

LESSON 1 REVIEW

Check Facts and Main Ideas

1. Cause and Effect On a separate piece of paper, fill in the missing effects.

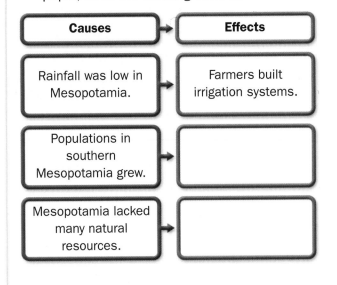

Causes	→	Effects
Rainfall was low in Mesopotamia.	→	Farmers built irrigation systems.
Populations in southern Mesopotamia grew.	→	
Mesopotamia lacked many natural resources.	→	

2. Where did the first civilizations arise?

3. How did Mesopotamian farmers use the Tigris and Euphrates Rivers to solve the problem of low rainfall?

4. What was one of the major steps toward the rise of civilization in southern Mesopotamia?

5. **Critical Thinking: *Make Inferences*** Why do you think settlers from other parts of the Fertile Crescent came to southern Mesopotamia?

Link to ⟨⟩ **Science**

Research on Your Own Fertile soil was one of the Mesopotamians' greatest resources. Research and make a list of some of the characteristics of fertile soil.

39

3200 B.C.
Invention
of writing
in Sumer

2334 B.C.
Sargon of Akkad unites
much of Mesopotamia.

2100 B.C.
Sumerian city-state of Ur controls
much of Mesopotamia.

MESOPOTAMIA

SUMER
Akkad
Uruk

Mesopotamia

PREVIEW

Focus on the Main Idea
The Mesopotamian civilizations of Sumer and Akkad flourished from about 3500 B.C. to 2000 B.C.

PLACES
Sumer
Akkad
Uruk

PEOPLE
Gilgamesh
Sargon
Enheduanna
Ur-Nammu
Shulgi

VOCABULARY
ziggurat
society
polytheism
scribe
cuneiform
conquer
empire
dynasty

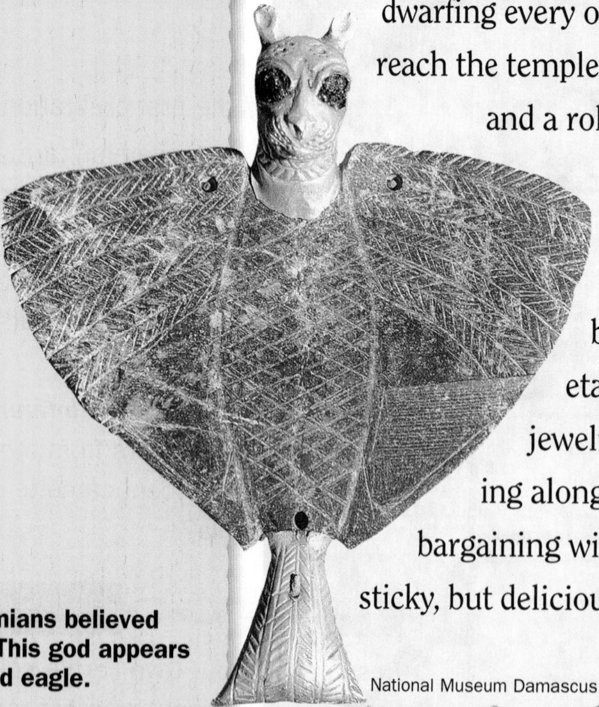

▶ **The Mesopotamians believed in many gods. This god appears as a lion-headed eagle.**

You Are There

It's payday for your father, a sculptor in the city-state of Akkad (AH kahd). He's just finished some statues for a temple. He wants you to come with him when he gets paid. You walk with him through the narrow alleyways, passing a few pigs that are nibbling on food scraps. When you emerge on the main street, the temple looms into view, dwarfing every other building in sight. When you reach the temple, your father receives some barley and a roll of cloth. A young man marks down the payment on a wet clay tablet. You then head straight for the market. You gaze at all of the booths displaying tools, baskets, vegetables, fruits, clothing, and colorful jewelry. Your father thanks you for coming along with him. He does some quick bargaining with a fruit seller and hands you some sticky, but delicious, dates. What a treat!

National Museum Damascus Syria/Dagli Orti/Art Archive

Main Idea and Details As you read, look for examples of ideas and inventions that shaped Mesopotamian civilization.

Sumer and Akkad

Early on, Mesopotamia consisted of the city-states of **Sumer** in the south and the region of **Akkad** in the north. It later included a larger region outside of Sumer and Akkad. The people of Sumer, the Sumerians, and of Akkad, the Akkadians, were actually quite alike. They practiced similar farming and business methods and had similar customs. People went to the market to buy and sell goods like the father you just read about.

The main difference between the two peoples was the language they spoke. People living in Sumer spoke Sumerian. In Akkad people spoke Akkadian, a language related to Hebrew. War between the city-states over control of land and water occurred frequently. But from 3500 B.C. to about 2330 B.C., the city-states of Sumer were more powerful.

Uruk was a large Sumerian city-state. As many as 50,000 people might have lived in Uruk by about 2800 B.C. Outside of the cities were vast, irrigated farm fields that supplied the city with food. A mudbrick wall surrounded most city-states. The wall protected the city from unfriendly nomads and the armies of enemy city-states.

People in Uruk lived in mudbrick houses of one or two stories. The houses were painted white to keep them cool. At the highest point of each city was the city's temple complex. The largest and most impressive temple structures were the ziggurats (ZIH guh rahts). A **ziggurat** consisted of a series of stacked rectangular platforms that formed a huge pyramid-shaped structure. Reaching heights up to 290 feet, ziggurats were believed by Mesopotamians to link the heavens and Earth.

REVIEW Why were most city-states surrounded by a wall? *Cause and Effect*

▶ **This illustration is a model of the reconstructed Ziggurat at Ur. The stairs leading up to the temple at the top were not very deep. Ancient worshippers were forced to climb them slowly.**

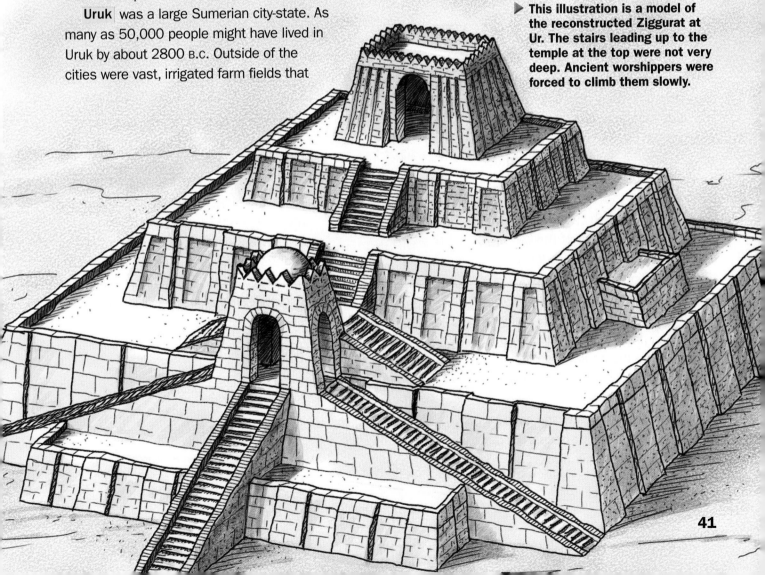

▶ **Representations of Sumerian gods have been found throughout Mesopotamia. In this carving Gula, the goddess of healing, is shown with stars and her dog.**

British Museum

Religion and Government

Temples in both Sumer and Akkad were built as earthly homes for the gods. The size and magnificence of these structures reflect the importance of religion to society, or an organized community with established rules and traditions. The Sumerians and Akkadians practiced polytheism, or the worship of many gods. They believed that the gods and goddesses were responsible for the well-being of the people and the fertility of the land. The chief gods were Anu, the god of the heavens; Enlil, the god of wind; Enki, the god of water; and Ninhursag, the mother of the gods. They also believed in many lesser gods, including a god of the plow and a god of the mudbrick.

If the people of a city were enjoying peace and prosperity, they believed it was because the gods were pleased. Each city-state worked hard to keep their gods happy. Each day temple priests made offerings to the gods by burning incense. They also provided the gods with food and drink.

Religion and government were closely linked. Each city was believed to be under the protection of a particular god who looked after its interests. The Sumerians believed that kings were chosen by the gods to carry out the gods' wishes. This idea of divine kingship—that the right to rule was god-given—was first practiced by the Sumerians. They also believed that the right to rule could be passed from father to son. Their ideas about kingship would have a huge impact on later civilizations.

In Sumer there was a class system. Below the king, society was divided into several classes: wealthy business-people, landowners, and government workers; artisans and farm workers; and slaves. This kind of class system also appeared in later civilizations.

REVIEW What is polytheism?
Main Idea and Details

Baghdad Museum

▶ **This vase was discovered at the temple of Uruk.**

Writing

The Sumerians participated in a great many business activities. They were active within their own city-states and as traders in lands hundreds and even thousands of miles away. About 3200 B.C. the Sumerians invented a writing system to keep track of these business dealings. The earliest examples of Sumerian writing are simple pictures that stood for objects or actions. For example, a drawing of a fish meant "fish."

By about 2400 B.C., this picture writing was simplified. A professional writer, or **scribe**, pressed a reed into a wet clay tablet, leaving groups of wedge-shaped markings. These marks stood for objects, activities, or sounds. The tablet then dried, creating a permanent record. This form of wedge-shaped writing is known as **cuneiform** (kyoo NEE uh fawrm).

Writing was a giant leap forward in the development of civilization. People also could point to a written record if an argument arose.

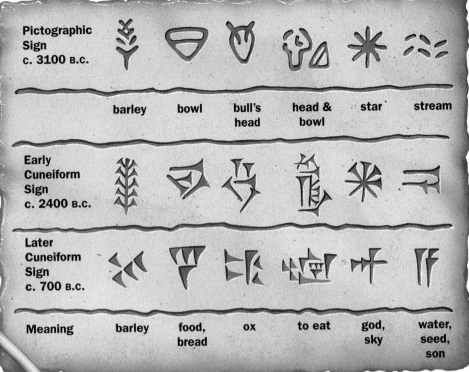

Development of Cuneiform

	barley	bowl	bull's head	head & bowl	star	stream
Pictographic Sign c. 3100 B.C.						
Early Cuneiform Sign c. 2400 B.C.						
Later Cuneiform Sign c. 700 B.C.						
Meaning	barley	food, bread	ox	to eat	god, sky	water, seed, son

British Museum

▶ This cuneiform tablet from about 1125 B.C. gives information about land or property.

Many neighboring peoples, such as the Akkadians, adopted cuneiform. Cuneiform was used for centuries to come.

Many tablets have been decoded, or translated, and appear to be records of the exchange of goods. However, not all Mesopotamian writings were clay versions of cash register slips. Archaeologists have uncovered literature such as the *Epic of Gilgamesh,* the tale of the adventures of the legendary Sumerian king **Gilgamesh.** Read more about Gilgamesh in the biography on page 44. Archaeologists have also found medical texts, law codes, letters, arguments and debates, and wise sayings—all of which help us learn a great deal about the Mesopotamians. This letter is from a father to a son:

> *"You who wander about in the public square, would you achieve success? Go to school, it will be of benefit to you."*

REVIEW Which came first, picture writing or cuneiform? ⟳ Sequence

43

Gilgamesh

c. 2700 B.C.

Gilgamesh may or may not have been a real person. Some historians believe he lived about 2700 B.C. and was the fifth king of Uruk, a city in Mesopotamia. By 2000 B.C., so many stories had been told about Gilgamesh that he became a mythical figure, said to be two-thirds god and one-third human. These tales were eventually written down. A set of 12 clay tablets dating from the 600s B.C. gives the best-known version of the Gilgamesh epic, or long heroic poem. It is doubtful that much, if any, of the epic is based on historical fact.

Perhaps the reason the Gilgamesh story has lasted for so many centuries is because of its themes. The themes include many human experiences: friendship, love, happiness, and, in particular, death.

In the epic, Gilgamesh wants to find out how to live forever. He travels to the ends of the earth to visit a wise man, who is immortal. The king offers Gilgamesh everlasting life if he can stay awake for seven days. Gilgamesh falls asleep almost immediately and loses his chance for immortality. The epic ends with Gilgamesh finally accepting that he is fated to die.

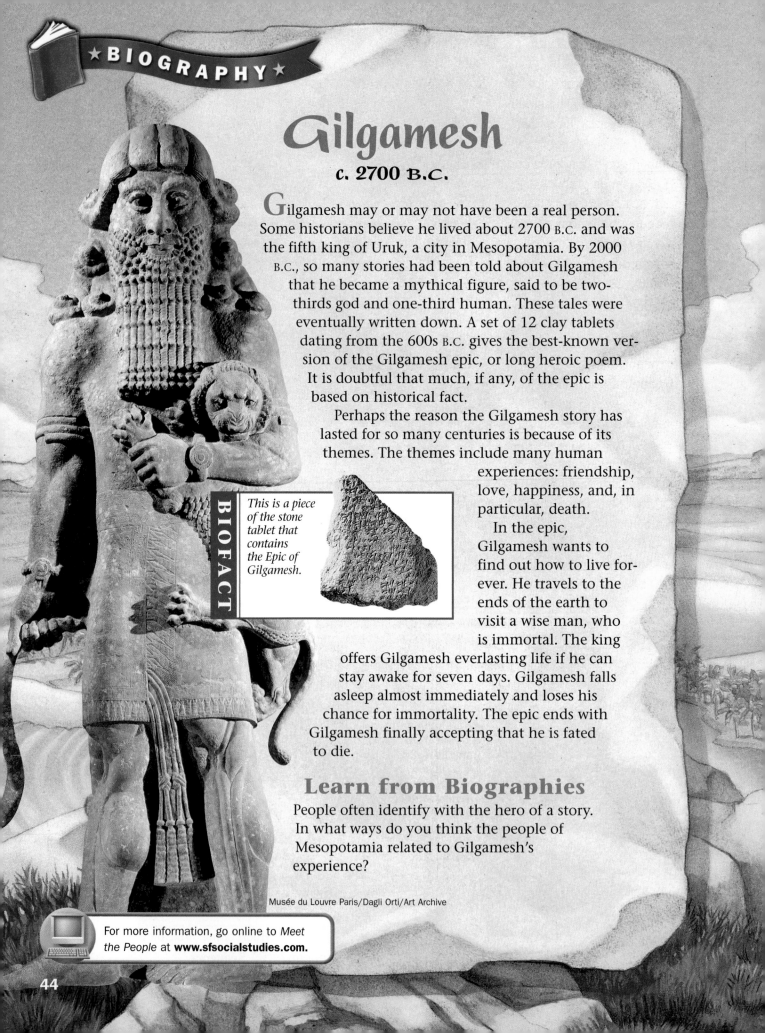

BIOFACT

This is a piece of the stone tablet that contains the Epic of Gilgamesh.

Learn from Biographies

People often identify with the hero of a story. In what ways do you think the people of Mesopotamia related to Gilgamesh's experience?

Musée du Louvre Paris/Dagli Orti/Art Archive

For more information, go online to *Meet the People* at **www.sfsocialstudies.com.**

The Rise and Fall of the Akkadian Empire

About 2334 B.C. an Akkadian ruler, later known as **Sargon**, and his armies thundered southward through Sumer. Read more about Sargon in the biography on page 47. The Akkadians **conquered**, or defeated, one city-state after another, over-throwing many kings. Sargon united all the city-states of Mesopotamia under his rule, forming the world's first empire. An **empire** is a large territory—consisting of many different places—all under the control of a single ruler. Sargon's empire extended far beyond Mesopotamia. Later legends claimed his empire stretched from "the sunrise to the sunset"—meaning that he ruled the whole world.

Sargon gave his daughter, **Enheduanna** (en HAY do wahn ah), the title of high priestess in the city-state of Ur. She was in charge of making offerings to Nanna, the moon god. She also composed songs dedicated to the goddess of the morning and evening star, Inanna. Later kings followed Sargon's practice of appointing their daughters as high priestesses at Ur.

Sargon passed his empire on to his son. But the Akkadian **dynasty**, or ruling family, was constantly threatened by revolts. It remained in power only about 150 years. By 2100 B.C., Ur rose up once again.

REVIEW What is an empire? Main Idea and Details

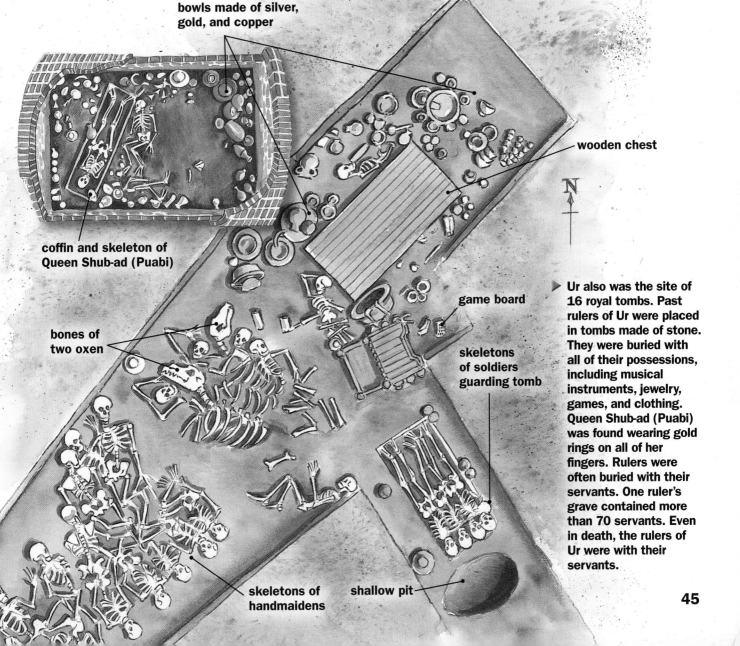

bowls made of silver, gold, and copper

wooden chest

coffin and skeleton of Queen Shub-ad (Puabi)

bones of two oxen

game board

skeletons of soldiers guarding tomb

skeletons of handmaidens

shallow pit

► Ur also was the site of 16 royal tombs. Past rulers of Ur were placed in tombs made of stone. They were buried with all of their possessions, including musical instruments, jewelry, games, and clothing. Queen Shub-ad (Puabi) was found wearing gold rings on all of her fingers. Rulers were often buried with their servants. One ruler's grave contained more than 70 servants. Even in death, the rulers of Ur were with their servants.

Sumer's Final Days

From about 2100 to 2000 B.C., the city-state of Ur in Sumer held control of Mesopotamia. The last and most successful dynasty in Ur was founded by the Sumerian king **Ur-Nammu.** Under Ur-Nammu and his son **Shulgi,** farming, business, literature, and the arts flourished. Pieces of the oldest known written law code date from the period of Ur-Nammu's reign.

Some very impressive structures were built during this period. One was the Ziggurat of Ur, believed to be one of the largest ever built. The many staircases on the ziggurat led to a shrine, or a sacred altar. Ruins of this ziggurat can still be seen. About 2000 B.C., Ur fell to invaders from the northeast.

Sumerian civilization declined but its contributions helped other civilizations to advance. Cuneiform, ziggurats, and the wheel were borrowed or adapted by other and later

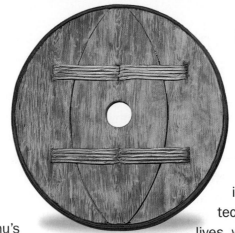

▶ **The first wheel appeared in Mesopotamia more than 5,000 years ago.**

peoples. The Sumerians used writing, religion, and technology in their daily lives, which helped them advance their civilization.

REVIEW What contributions did the Sumerians make to advance their civilization? **Summarize**

Summarize the Lesson

- **3200 B.C.** Writing was invented in Sumer.
- **2334 B.C.** Sargon of Akkad united much of Mesopotamia, establishing the world's first empire.
- **2100 B.C.** The Sumerian city-state of Ur took control of much of Mesopotamia.

LESSON 2   REVIEW

Check Facts and Main Ideas

1. **Main Idea and Details** On a separate piece of paper, fill in the missing main idea and detail below.

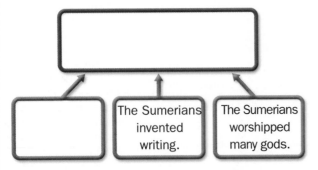

The Sumerians invented writing.

The Sumerians worshipped many gods.

2. How were Sumerian religion and government connected?

3. How did the Sumerian writing system develop and change?

4. Describe an example of an idea or invention that shaped Mesopotamian civilization and influenced other civilizations.

5. **Critical Thinking:** *Recognize Point of View* After Sumer rose again, does it seem that the Mesopotamians continued to make important advances? Explain.

Link to ⊙—⊙ Art

Picture Writing Design a system of picture writing like that of the Sumerians. Write a sentence using your new system and challenge a classmate to decode it.

Sargon

reigned c. 2334–2279 B.C.

Mystery surrounds the life and reign of the Mesopotamian king, Sargon. We do know that he was the first empire builder and founder of the Akkadian dynasty. What is known about him comes from documents and legends written long after his death.

According to legend, Sargon was an abandoned baby. He was placed in a basket that was thrown into a river. A gardener rescued him and became his adopted father. As a young man, Sargon worked as a servant to the ruler of the Sumerian city of Kish. He quickly rose through the ranks.

Sargon came to power in about 2334 B.C., following the defeat of the city-state of Uruk. He soon took control of all of the other city-states in southern Mesopotamia. However, Sargon was an outsider. He was not a Sumerian but an Akkadian from the lands north of Sumer.

Nevertheless, he gave himself the name Sharru-kin, which means "Rightful King." Some historians believe that the Sumerians accepted him as their ruler, and he seemed to have been a just king.

Sargon is said to have ruled some 65 cities. His conquests enabled him to expand trade opportunities and enrich his kingdom. Sargon held power for about 56 years—an unusually long time.

BIOFACT

Sargon once traveled to distant Anatolia (present-day Turkey) on a chariot like the one pictured above. He went there to settle an argument that had lasted for years. He so impressed (or frightened) the quarreling parties that they settled their argument immediately.

Learn from Biographies

How did Sargon encourage the Sumerians to accept him as king?

For more information, go online to *Meet the People* at **www.sfsocialstudies.com**.

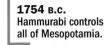

1800 B.C.	1200 B.C.	600 B.C.

1754 B.C.
Hammurabi controls
all of Mesopotamia.

668 B.C. to 627 B.C.
The Assyrian Empire is at its height.

605 B.C.
Nebuchadnezzar II is king of Babylon.

Babylonia and Assyria

PREVIEW

Focus on the Main Idea
New empires in the Fertile
Crescent advanced by adopting
earlier Mesopotamian culture.

PLACES
Babylon
Babylonia
Assyria
Nineveh

PEOPLE
Hammurabi
Ashurbanipal
Nebuchadnezzar II

VOCABULARY
conquest

TERMS
Code of Hammurabi

▶ The Ishtar Gate
was built about
580 B.C. It was
the main entryway
into Babylon.

You Are There

Babylon (ba buh LOHN), 580 B.C.:
Babylon is under construction—again!
Each year it seems the king orders a
new building project. But you have to admit, the city has
never looked better. The city walls are stronger than ever.
You enter the city through a magnificent gateway. It's
made of deep blue glazed brick and decorated with pictures of fierce animals. Inside the walls, work continues
on the ziggurat. The king orders the builders to raise the
top of the tower so that it might rival
heaven. The "hanging gardens," however, are your favorite new sight.
They're amazing! There's not
much greenery around Babylon,
so the king built these rooftop gardens. To keep the gardens lush
and green, builders set up an irrigation system. Water is pumped
from the Euphrates River to the
gardens that overlook the city.

Sequence As you read, keep events in their correct
time order.

The Rise of Hammurabi and Babylonia

Why was there so much construction going on in the city-state of **Babylon?** Following the fall of Ur in about 2100 B.C., people from the surrounding areas began to arrive in Mesopotamia. They remained there for centuries and adopted Mesopotamian customs, law, religion, and art styles.

In 1792 B.C. **Hammurabi** (hah muh RAH bee) became king of Babylon, located between the Tigris and Euphrates Rivers. Read more about Hammurabi in the biography on page 51.

Hammurabi was a shrewd, or clever, leader who sought great power. By 1754 B.C. he controlled all of Mesopotamia, in addition to a number of neighboring city-states. His empire was known as **Babylonia** (ba buh LOH nyah). (Look at the map below.) It spread from the Persian Gulf northward and east to the Zagros Mountains. Hammurabi sent officials throughout the empire to carry out his orders and to collect taxes. Taxes paid on property often went to support Hammurabi's large army and pay for the construction projects you have read about.

REVIEW Why did Hammurabi need tax money, and how did he collect it? **Draw Conclusions**

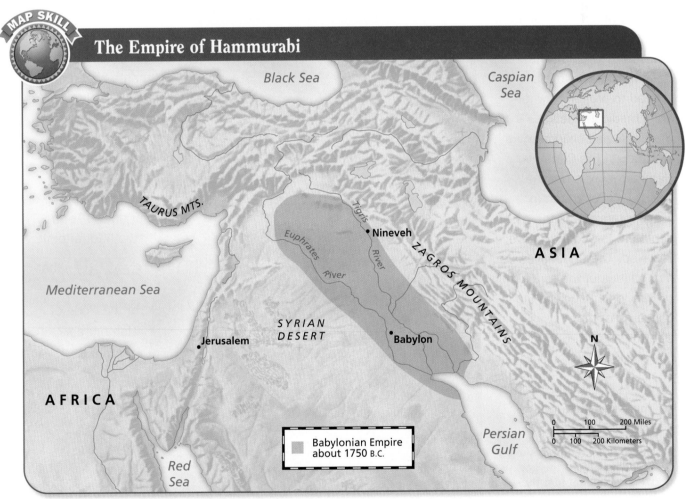

The Empire of Hammurabi

▶ Hammurabi greatly expanded the Babylonian Empire.

MAP SKILL Use Map Scale *About how many miles did the Babylonian Empire extend?*

Babylonian Civilization

Daily life did not change much under Hammurabi. The Babylonians continued to rely on irrigation for farming and on trade. Their religious beliefs were similar. Babylonia also had a strict class system. However, the Babylonians spoke their own version of the Akkadian language.

Under Hammurabi the capital city of Babylon grew. A small village during Sumerian civilization, Babylon became a center of culture and learning. Clay tablets tell archaeologists that many advancements were made in mathematics, literature, and law.

Hammurabi is best known for a set of laws he established. These laws helped him to govern his empire in a new way. This set of 282 laws is known as the **Code of Hammurabi.** Some of the laws were based on earlier Sumerian and Akkadian laws. Many of them dealt with business practices. Others related to property ownership, medical practice, marriage, and childcare.

Although the Code of Hammurabi was not the first law code written in Mesopotamia, it is the most complete law code to have survived. The Code gives us a good idea of the structure of Babylonian society and concerns of the Babylonians.

▶ **This stone stele, or slab, contains the Code of Hammurabi. Above the Code, Hammurabi is shown standing before the god who is handing him the laws.**

Hammurabi explained his purpose for the law code:

> "*. . . to render [give] good to the people, to make justice shine in the land, to destroy the evil and wicked, that the strong do not oppress [mistreat] the weak.*"

The belief that the strong should not oppress the weak is illustrated in some of the laws. For example, there were laws that tried to protect people with little political power, such as children and widows. However, some of the laws were quite harsh. Sometimes a wrongdoer would have to pay a fine.

Hammurabi's Code called for different punishments based on the class of the lawbreaker and the victim of the crime. In the Code, punishments often fit the crime by demanding an "eye for an eye" or a "tooth for a tooth."

REVIEW What was the purpose of the Code of Hammurabi? Summarize

Hammurabi

c. 1810 B.C.–1750 B.C.

Hammurabi became king of the city-state of Babylon in 1792 B.C., when he was a young adult. Other kings ruled the 30 or so other Mesopotamian cities. Rivalry among these rulers was great. To increase their power, rulers formed partnerships with each other.

Hammurabi, with the help of his allies, began conquering neighboring cities. One of his main goals was to gain control of the Euphrates and Tigris Rivers. This meant he would have control of irrigation systems and the farming economy. By 1754 B.C. Hammurabi had conquered more than 20 cities. All of Mesopotamia came under Hammurabi's rule.

Hammurabi was a brilliant warrior, but his military tactics could be brutal. One strategy he probably used was damming a waterway and then releasing it to flood a city.

The crowning achievement of his final years was his code of laws, which he had engraved on a towering stone monument. It is clear from the words on the monument that Hammurabi wished to be remembered as an able ruler and a just lawgiver:

BIOFACT

Some women held high positions during Hammurabi's reign. Hammurabi's sister Iltani handled business matters for the gods Shamash and Aja. British Museum

> *"Hammurabi is a ruler, who is as a father to his subjects . . . who has achieved conquest for Marduk [the chief god of Babylon] over the north and south . . . and has established order in the land."*

Learn from Biographies

Why do you think Hammurabi had his code of law "set in stone"? How might this have helped him rule his empire successfully?

British Museum

For more information, go online to *Meet the People* at **www.sfsocialstudies.com.**

The Assyrians

While the Babylonian Empire flourished under Hammurabi in southern Mesopotamia, a people known as the Assyrians (us SIR ee uhns) began to gain strength in northern Mesopotamia. Their heartland lay in the valley of the Upper Tigris River. From about 1900 B.C. to 600 B.C., Assyria expanded its territory.

Assyrian culture was greatly influenced by Babylonian culture, but the Assyrians placed higher value on war and conquest, or defeat, of another group. The Assyrians were known as great and sometimes merciless warriors. Their heavy, wheeled battering rams quickly reduced a city wall to rubble. The soldiers then stormed the city, forcing the people to surrender. One observer said of the Assyrians:

> *"Their arrows are sharp . . . their bows bent, their horses' hoofs are as hard as flint, and their wheels like the whirlwind. They growl and seize their prey; they carry it off and none can rescue it."*

From 688 B.C. to 627 B.C., the Assyrian Empire was at its largest and most powerful under King Ashurbanipal (ah soor BAH nuh pahl). During his reign, the Assyrians controlled nearly all of the Fertile Crescent. Like other Assyrian kings, Ashurbanipal personally led his armies into battle. However, he also was a very educated man. He could read and write ancient Sumerian as well as Akkadian. He built a great library at

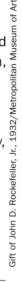

▶ **This statue of a winged lion is from Ashurbanipal's palace.**

Nineveh (NIN uh vah), his capital. There he collected many Sumerian, Akkadian, and Babylonian writings. His library contained works of literature, as well as writings on history, mathematics, and astronomy. Tablets from Ashurbanipal's library have helped historians learn about the peoples of Mesopotamia.

Gift of John D. Rockefeller, Jr., 1932/Metropolitan Museum of Art

REVIEW When did the Assyrians expand their empire? ↻ **Sequence**

Babylonia Grows

After 627 B.C., Babylon again began to expand its influence and wealth. In 605 B.C., Nebuchadnezzar II (neh buh kuhd NEHZ uhr) was crowned king of Babylon. He took over much of the former Assyrian Empire and the desert land west of Babylon. Nebuchadnezzar II ordered massive building projects to make Babylon great and glorious once again. He built walls to protect the great temples of Babylon. He also finished building the great ziggurat.

Several of his projects have become legendary. Some historians think that the enormous ziggurat at Babylon might have been the inspiration for the Tower of Babel, which is mentioned in the

▶ **The Hanging Gardens of Babylon are considered one of the Seven Wonders of the World.**

▶ **This reconstructed glazed brick bull is on the Ishtar Gate of the city of Babylon.**

example, they determined that place value refers to the position of numerals. The numerals 5, 55, and 555 all have different values. Babylonian astronomers, or scientists who study the sun, moon, stars, and planets, made important advancements. They were able to accurately predict, or estimate, when eclipses of the sun and moon would occur. When Nebuchadnezzar II died about 562 B.C., the new Babylonian Empire declined. In 539 B.C. the Persians invaded and conquered Babylon.

REVIEW What was Babylon like during Nebuchadnezzar's reign? **Summarize**

Bible. Some historians believe that Nebuchadnezzar II built the Hanging Gardens you read about earlier in this lesson. Others believe that they were the project of Queen Sammuramat, who reigned about 200 years earlier.

Babylon was a wealthy trading city and an important center of learning. The Babylonians made great advancements in mathematics. For

Summarize the Lesson

- **1754 B.C.** Hammurabi formed the first Babylonian Empire.

- **668 B.C. to 627 B.C.** The Assyrian Empire reached its height.

- **605 B.C.** Under King Nebuchadnezzar II, Babylon became the center of a wealthy and powerful empire.

LESSON 3   REVIEW

Check Facts and Main Ideas

1. ⟳ Sequence The following events are not in the correct order. On a separate piece of paper, list them in the correct order.
   - Nebuchadnezzar II starts a series of building projects in Babylon.
   - Hammurabi establishes his code of law.
   - Ashurbanipal builds his library at Nineveh.

2. Who was Hammurabi?

3. What was the Code of Hammurabi?

4. How did Assyrian culture differ from Babylonian culture?

5. **Critical Thinking:** *Make Generalizations* What contributions did the Babylonians make to civilization?

Link to 🔗 Reading

Read Up on a Ruler Which one of the rulers you have read about in this lesson most interests you? Go to the library or use the Internet to read more.

ISRAEL
Jerusalem •
JUDAH

| 1800 B.C. | 1200 B.C. | 600 B.C. |

1800 B.C.
According to the Hebrew Bible, Abraham forms an agreement with God to worship only Him.

1400 B.C.
Development of an alphabet in Phoenicia

1000 B.C.
David unites the Hebrews.

By 500 B.C.
Lydians mint the region's first coins.

Hebrews, Phoenicians, and Lydians

PREVIEW

Focus on the Main Idea
Judaism became one of the first religions in the world to worship only one God.

PLACES
Canaan
Israel
Jerusalem
Judah
Carthage

PEOPLE
Abraham
Moses
Deborah
David
Solomon

VOCABULARY
covenant
monotheism
slavery
descendant
synagogue
barter

TERMS
Judaism
Ten Commandments
Torah

▶ This illustration from a Hebrew book shows a reconstruction of Solomon's Temple at Jerusalem.

You Are There

On your visit to Jerusalem, you and your family arrive at the First Temple. You have read in your guidebook about how this temple is mentioned in the Hebrew Bible. David chose the site for the temple, but it was completed by his son Solomon, the greatest king of Israel, in 957 B.C.

You have learned a lot about Judaism from your tour guide. You have learned that Solomon inherited a kingdom. He had a good trading partnership with the Phoenicians. The Phoenicians were excellent sea traders. Your tour guide tells you that Solomon even used Phoenician sailors for his own merchant fleet. He traded with other people for cedar wood to build his temple. Before you continue your tour of Jerusalem, you decide to read more about Judaism.

Main Idea and Details Consider how the ideas developed by the groups you read about influence us today.

The Hebrews

According to the Hebrew Bible, **Abraham** was a shepherd who lived in Ur. He is considered by Jewish people today to be the first Jew. The Hebrew Bible says that God spoke to Abraham and told him to leave his homeland and resettle in a new land. According to the Hebrew Bible, when he arrived in this new land, **Canaan** (KAY nuhn), God told Abraham:

> *"The whole land of Canaan . . .*
> *I will give as an everlasting*
> *possession to you and your*
> *descendants after you; and*
> *I will be their God."*

With this **covenant,** or agreement, which occurred about 1800 B.C., Abraham promised to worship only one God. The Hebrew Bible says that God agreed to look after the welfare of Abraham and his people—later known as the Hebrews. **Monotheism,** the worship of only one God, is the key principle of the religion of **Judaism.** Abraham is viewed as the founder of Judaism, one of the first monotheistic religions.

The Hebrews lived in Canaan for some time before moving to Egypt. The Egyptians forced the Hebrews into slavery.

Slavery is the practice of one person owning another person. The Hebrew Bible says that God chose **Moses** to lead the Hebrews out of Egypt across the Sinai Desert to freedom. This probably happened between about 1200 B.C. and 1400 B.C.

The Hebrew Bible says that God gave Moses a set of laws known as the **Ten Commandments.** The Ten Commandments were unlike earlier law codes. Codes such as Hammurabi's listed a series of crimes and punishments. But the Ten Commandments provided guidance for the worship of God. It also set down rules for moral behavior. According to the Hebrew Bible, God expanded the covenant to include those people who were escaping from Egypt, as well as Abraham's **descendants,** or people who are born later into the same family.

REVIEW According to the Hebrew Bible, did Abraham form a covenant with God before or after Moses received the Ten Commandments?

🔄 Sequence

The Ten Commandments

1. I am the Lord your God.

2. You shall have no other gods before me. You shall not make for yourself a graven image.

3. You shall not take the name of the Lord your God in vain.

4. Remember the Sabbath day [day of rest] to keep it holy.

5. Honor your father and your mother.

6. You shall not kill.

7. You shall not commit adultery.

8. You shall not steal.

9. You shall not bear false witness against your neighbor.

10. You shall not covet [desire] your neighbor's wife; and you shall not desire anything that is your neighbor's.

The Hebrew Bible

The Hebrew Bible states that God gave Moses five books at the same time as the Ten Commandments. We know about Abraham and the early development of Judaism from the Hebrew Bible, or the Torah (TAWR uh). The word, *Torah,* comes from a Hebrew word that means, "to teach." The Torah contains the first five books of the Hebrew Bible. These books provide guidance and laws for the Jewish people. The Torah is a very sacred, or holy, Hebrew text. The rollers and coverings that contain the Torah often are decorated.

However, it is against Jewish law to decorate the Torah scrolls themselves. The Torah scrolls are handwritten. Scribes use special animal parchment paper and ink. It is against Jewish law to touch the parchment when reading from the Torah. One must use a pointer to follow the lines of text.

In addition to being a set of moral codes, or laws, the Torah also describes events. The early Hebrews recorded this information and stories for later Hebrews to study.

REVIEW Why do you think the Hebrews consider the Torah to be a sacred text?
Draw Conclusions

The Jewish Museum, NY/Art Resource

▶ **The Torah is kept in an ark that is often decorated.**

Israel and Judah

According to the Torah, the Hebrews settled in Canaan and lived in about a dozen various groups, or tribes. They won several victories over the Canaanites, the people who lived in that region.

According to the Torah, an important victory was inspired by **Deborah,** who was a judge. In the Torah it says that God chose judges who were used in times of trouble. Judges offered guidance and leadership. Women had little power in Hebrew society. Deborah had an unusual role. She encouraged a military leader to gather the tribes of Israel to attack the Canaanites. She predicted that a woman would win the war.

Between 1200 B.C. and 1125 B.C., the war began in response to the oppressive, or harsh and cruel, rule by the Canaanite king. The Torah says that when the Hebrews attacked, the king of the Canaanites escaped. The military leader tried to catch the king, but a woman named Jael from one of the tribes killed him first. From this story in the Torah, Deborah was right, a woman did triumph in this great battle against the Canaanites. Deborah was then viewed as a national leader among the Hebrews.

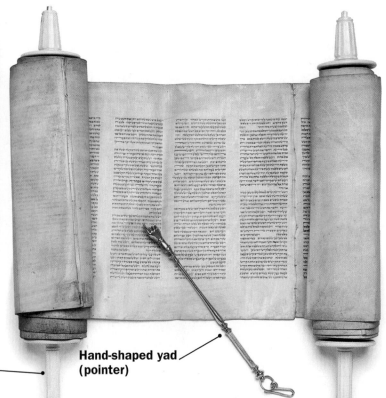

The Torah scroll is considered too sacred to touch, so it is held by handles and a pointer is used to keep the place.

Hand-shaped yad (pointer)

▶ Deborah was a prophet, as well as a judge. Prophets predict what will happen in the future.

In about 1000 B.C., King **David** united the tribes and founded a new kingdom called **Israel.** Its capital was **Jerusalem.** David's son **Solomon,** built a temple in Jerusalem to house the Torah and to serve as a place of worship. Solomon was known as a wise ruler. During his reign there was peace, and the kingdom prospered. After Solomon's death, the kingdom split into Israel in the north and **Judah** in the south. The kingdom of Israel fell to the Assyrians in 722 B.C., and its people fled and scattered. In 587 B.C. Nebuchadnezzar II conquered Judah and forced many of the people to live in Babylonia. Even so, the people of Judah continued to practice their religion and eventually returned to Jerusalem.

REVIEW Why did Deborah have a more powerful role in society than other Hebrew women?
Draw Conclusions

Judaism Today

Judaism is practiced by millions of people today. Jewish people still read the Torah. They gather in **synagogues,** or Jewish houses of worship. They celebrate Jewish holidays such as the festival of Passover, which honors the escape of the Hebrews from Egypt.

Rabbis teach Jews how to read the Torah. In Hebrew, the official language of Israel, *rabbi* means "master" or "teacher." You will read more about the Jews in Unit 4.

REVIEW What is a synagogue? **Main Idea and Details**

▶ Foods on the seder plate are symbolic of an ancient Hebrew story.

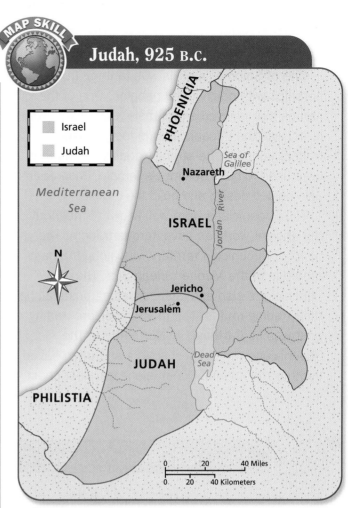

MAP SKILL

Judah, 925 B.C.

Israel
Judah

PHOENICIA

Mediterranean Sea

Sea of Galilee

Nazareth

ISRAEL

Jordan River

N

Jericho

Jerusalem

JUDAH

Dead Sea

PHILISTIA

0   20   40 Miles
0   20   40 Kilometers

▶ After Solomon's death, the kingdom split into Israel and Judah.

MAP SKILL Understand Borders and Capitals
Jerusalem became the capital of what ancient kingdom?

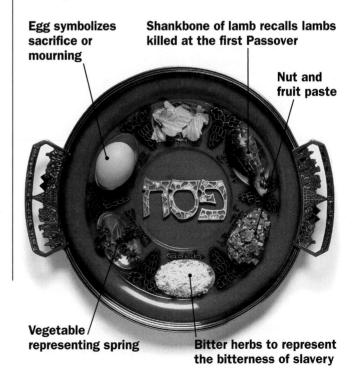

Egg symbolizes sacrifice or mourning

Shankbone of lamb recalls lambs killed at the first Passover

Nut and fruit paste

Vegetable representing spring

Bitter herbs to represent the bitterness of slavery

Phoenicians and Lydians

One of Solomon's skills was forming trade partnerships with neighboring peoples. One of the groups that enjoyed a profitable relationship with Israel was the Phoenicians. In fact, Phoenician traders supplied the strong wooden beams that were used to build Solomon's Temple. Phoenicians also helped design and build the temple.

The Phoenicians were well known throughout the ancient world as adventurous traders. The heart of Phoenician territory was along the eastern edge of the Mediterranean Sea. The Phoenicians also established trading posts along their trading routes. The most important trading post was at **Carthage** in North Africa. The Phoenicians were expert sailors and often sailed out into the Atlantic Ocean along the west coast

▶ **This Phoenician coin shows the importance of ships and trade in this society.**

National Geographic Image

of Africa. They may have traded with places as far north as Europe. (Look at the map below.) It was not the Phoenicians' goal to build an empire. Through their trading activities, however, they linked various parts of the ancient world. Trade promoted the exchange of new ideas, as well as the exchange of goods.

One of the Phoenicians' most important contributions was to help to develop what in time became the modern alphabet. Early on, the

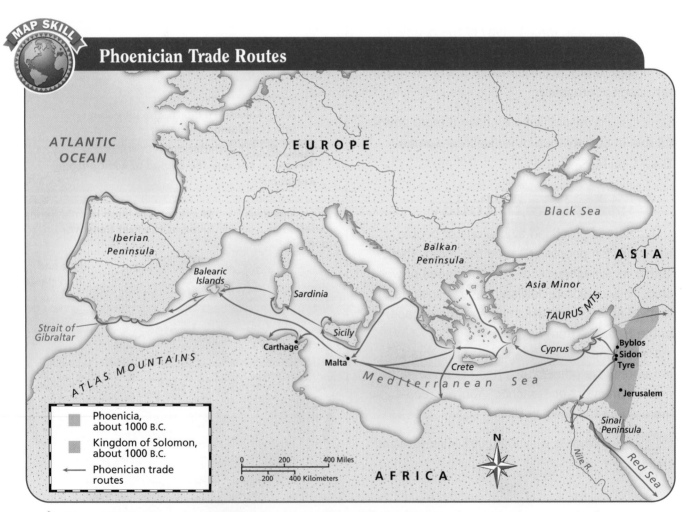

MAP SKILL

Phoenician Trade Routes

ATLANTIC OCEAN

EUROPE

Black Sea

Iberian Peninsula

Balkan Peninsula

ASIA

Asia Minor

Balearic Islands

Sardinia

TAURUS MTS.

Strait of Gibraltar

Sicily

Cyprus

Byblos
Sidon
Tyre

ATLAS MOUNTAINS

Carthage

Malta

Crete

Mediterranean Sea

Jerusalem

■ Phoenicia, about 1000 B.C.

■ Kingdom of Solomon, about 1000 B.C.

← Phoenician trade routes

Sinai Peninsula

0   200   400 Miles
0   200   400 Kilometers

N

AFRICA

Nile R.

Red Sea

▶ **Phoenician trade routes brought goods and culture to many lands.**

MAP SKILL Use Routes *Why are most of the Phoenician trade routes located in the Mediterranean?*

Phoenicians, like many other peoples, used cuneiform. By this time it consisted of about 700 symbols that stood for words or syllables. By about 1400 B.C., the Phoenicians had developed 22 simple characters for their entire writing system. Each character stood for a consonant. Later, the Greeks added vowels to the Phoenician alphabet.

As traders, the Phoenicians faced difficulties in dealing with payment. People usually **bartered,** or exchanged goods and services for others. Some paid with bars or rings of silver. The Lydians, who lived in western Asia, probably

► **The Lydians minted the region's first coins.**

American Numismatic Association

invented the region's first coins by 500 B.C. The coins had images and markings stamped on them to show their value. This value was guaranteed by the Lydian king. Coins made trading simpler and easier. Soon other peoples, such as the Greeks, began making their own coins.

REVIEW What advantage do you think the Phoenicians' form of writing had over cuneiform? **Compare and Contrast**

Summarize the Lesson

- **about 1800 B.C.** According to the Bible, Abraham formed a covenant with God that he would worship only Him.

- **about 1400 B.C.** The Phoenicians developed an alphabet.

- **about 1000 B.C.** David united the Hebrews.

- **by about 500 B.C.** Lydians had minted the region's first coins.

LESSON 4   REVIEW

Check Facts and Main Ideas

1. **Main Idea and Details** On a separate piece of paper, fill in the main idea below.

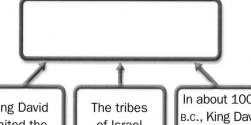

| King David united the tribes of Israel. | The tribes of Israel defeated the Canaanites. | In about 1000 B.C., King David founded the kingdom of Israel. |

2. What was one of the first monotheistic religions?

3. What was the purpose of Solomon's temple?

4. What did the Lydians invent that we use today?

5. **Critical Thinking: *Make Generalizations*** How did the Phoenicians help spread new ideas from one part of the ancient world to another?

Link to ⚭ Art

Design a Coin Suppose you are a ruler of an ancient empire. You've just seen a new Lydian coin and decide it would be great to have your own coins. What will they be made of? What shape will they be? How will people know their value and to which empire they belong?

59

Thinking Skills

Make Inferences

What? Inferences are logical guesses that people make to explain something when all the facts are not available. For example, suppose an archaeologist discovers a small piece of a clay tablet with the cuneiform words "he shall pay" on it. She knows the writing is in the Sumerian language and that Sumerian law codes often called for wrongdoers to be fined. She makes an inference that what she has found is a fragment of a Sumerian law code.

Her inference seems logical based on the facts and knowledge available to her. However, inferences are not always correct. For example, suppose she then finds another fragment that fits next to the other fragment. It contains the words "ten sheep in exchange for one ox." If she places the two fragments next to each other, they read, "he shall pay ten sheep in exchange for one ox." Now her previous inference seems wrong. With this new information, she might now infer that the tablet fragments are part of a Sumerian sale agreement.

▶ At an excavation in the 1930s in Khorsabad, Iraq, an archaeologist poses beside an artifact from King Sargon II's reign. (right) In 2001 workers excavate a Sumerian temple and what could be the world's oldest cemetery.

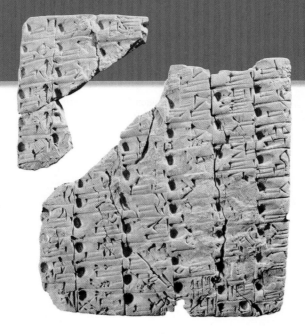

▶ Archaelogists made an inference that this Sumerian cuneiform tablet dates to about 3200 B.C.

Why? Making inferences can help you better understand the people, events, and circumstances of the history you read about. Often information is not directly stated. Sometimes you must "read between the lines" to gain a deeper understanding of what you read.

How? To make an inference when reading history, think carefully about the facts stated in the text. Next think about whether you have ever read about or experienced something similar. Then relate the facts from the text to your own knowledge and experience to come up with a logical explanation.

Read the following passage about a young student scribe's preparation and arrival at school. Then make an inference about why the student bows respectfully to his teacher.

> *"My mother gave me two rolls . . . and I went to school. In school, the fellow in charge of punctuality said: "Why are you late?" Afraid and with pounding heart, I entered before my teacher and made a respectful [bow]."*

Think and Apply

1. What does the student scribe learn when he arrives at school?

2. What happens at your school when students are late?

3. What inference can you make about why the student bows to his teacher?

4. Suppose you later found out that the scribe was doing very poorly at school. Would you want to change your inference? Why or why not?

5. Why is it sometimes necessary to make inferences?

CHAPTER 2
REVIEW

3500 B.C.   3000 B.C.

3500 B.C.
Civilization
developed
in Mesopotamia.

3200 B.C.
Writing was
invented in Sumer.

2334 B.C.
Sargon of Akkad united
much of Mesopotamia.

Chapter Summary

Sequence
The following events are not in correct order. Copy the diagram on a separate piece of paper and write the events in chronological order.

- Sumerians invented a system of writing.
- The first civilization arose in Mesopotamia.
- Israel was founded.
- Hammurabi established the Babylonian Empire.

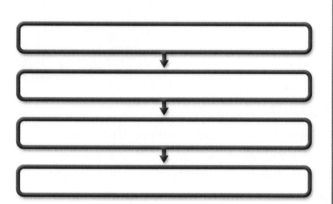

Vocabulary

Match each word with the correct definition or description.

1. **civilization** (p. 35)

2. **cuneiform** (p. 43)

3. **empire** (p. 45)

4. **irrigation** (p. 36)

5. **monotheism** (p. 55)

a. group of people who have formed an advanced, organized society

b. large territory under one ruler

c. watering system

d. wedge-shaped writing

e. worship of many gods

f. worship of one God

People and Terms

Write a sentence explaining why each of the following people or terms was important in shaping the development of civilization in the Fertile Crescent.

1. Sargon (p. 45)

2. Enheduanna (p. 45)

3. Hammurabi (p. 49)

4. Code of Hammurabi (p. 50)

5. Deborah (p. 56)

6. Nebuchadnezzar II (p. 52)

7. Abraham (p. 55)

8. David (p. 57)

9. Judaism (p. 55)

10. Ten Commandments (p. 55)

2500 B.C.　　2000 B.C.　　1500 B.C.　　1000 B.C.　　500 B.C.

2100 B.C. Sumerian city-state of Ur gained control of Mesopotamia.

1800 B.C.
According to the Hebrew Bible, Abraham formed an agreement with God.

1754 B.C.
Hammurabi controlled all of Mesopotamia.

1400 B.C.
Phoenicians developed a new form of writing.

By 500 B.C.
Lydians minted the region's first coins.

Facts and Main Ideas

1 What are the characteristics of a city-state?

2 Why did the Mesopotamians make daily offerings to the gods?

3 **Time Line** Did the Phoenicians develop a writing system before or after the Sumerians?

4 **Main Idea** How did the climate of southern Mesopotamia lead to the development of a new farming technique?

5 **Main Idea** What effect did the invention of cuneiform writing have on other cultures?

6 **Main Idea** How was the Code of Hammurabi different from earlier Mesopotamian laws?

7 **Main Idea** According to the Hebrew Bible, what did Abraham and God agree on in their covenant?

8 **Critical Thinking:** *Make Generalizations* What Mesopotamian invention contributed to the development of civilizations?

Write About History

1 **Write a menu for a meal** a Mesopotamian might have eaten. If necessary, review page 37.

2 **Write a dialogue** in which two Mesopotamians complain about the weather.

3 **Write a riddle** about one of the rulers you read about. Exchange riddles with a class-mate and try to solve each other's riddle.

Apply Skills

Make Inferences

Use what you have learned in the chapter and the information in the quotation below to make an inference about which ruler is being quoted.

"[S]eek out and send to me any rare tablets which are known to you and are lacking in Assyria."

1 Which facts help you make your inference?

2 Which ruler did you name?

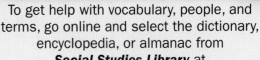

To get help with vocabulary, people, and terms, go online and select the dictionary, encyclopedia, or almanac from *Social Studies Library* at **www.SFsocialstudies.com**.

End with Literature

THE EPIC OF GILGAMESH

Many stories were told about the Mesopotamian king, Gilgamesh. These stories and myths were retold for hundreds of years. From the passage on page 65, do you think that the people who told the stories respected Gilgamesh?

I will proclaim to the world the deeds of Gilgamesh.
This was the man to whom all things were known;
this was the king who knew the countries of the world.
He was wise, he saw mysteries and knew secret things,
he brought us a tale of the days before the flood. He went
on a long journey, was weary, worn-out with labour,
returning he rested, he engraved on a stone the whole story.

When the gods created Gilgamesh they gave him a perfect
body. Shamash the glorious sun endowed him with beauty,
Adad the god of the storm endowed him with courage,
the great gods made his beauty perfect, surpassing all
others, terrifying like a great wild bull. Two thirds
they made him god and one third man.

Source: *The Epic of Gilgamesh*, translated by N.K. Sandars

Review

Main Ideas and Vocabulary

TEST PREP

Read the passage below and use it to answer the questions that follow.

Many scholars believe that at least 130,000 years ago, glaciers covered much of the Americas. About 11,000 years ago people may have begun to migrate across Beringia to the Americas. They hunted and gathered food and made simple stone and pebble tools. Later people began to domesticate plants and animals. Groups of people began to live in villages. People could divide up work once they had a surplus of food. Soon came the beginning of <u>civilizations</u>.

In Mesopotamia in the Fertile Crescent, there was little rainfall. To grow crops, farmers began to irrigate fields. By about 3500 B.C., a number of small Mesopotamian villages had grown into city-states.

One of the first civilizations was in Sumer. The Sumerians based wealth on farming and trade. They invented cuneiform writing. In about 2330 B.C., Sargon conquered Mesopotamia and built the world's first empire.

In the 1750s B.C. the Babylonian ruler Hammurabi also built a great <u>empire</u> in Mesopotamia. He governed his empire with a set of written laws.

In the Fertile Crescent the Hebrews developed a new religion called Judaism. It was based on the worship of only one God. The Phoenicians made important contributions as traders and in writing. The Lydians invented the use of coins to make the payment for goods and services easier.

1 According to the passage, what made it possible for people to divide up work?
 A farming   **C** food surplus
 B culture   **D** tools

2 In the passage the word *civilizations* means—
 A groups of people
 B organized societies
 C city-states
 D writing and trade

3 In the passage the word *empire* means—
 A powerful   **C** generous
 B a small   **D** a large area under
    territory   one ruler

4 What is a main idea of this passage?
 A Civilizations are found only in Mesopotamia.
 B Farming, trade, and writing are aspects of civilization.
 C The Assyrians traded goods with the Lydians.
 D Hammurabi developed Judaism.

People and Terms

Match each person and term to its definition.

1 Hammurabi (p. 49)

2 Moses (p. 55)

3 Gilgamesh (p. 44)

4 Solomon (p. 57)

5 Old Stone Age (p. 19)

6 Albert Goodyear (p. 7)

a. archaeologist

b. built temple at Jerusalem

c. slow period of progress

d. established Babylonian Empire

e. led Hebrews out of Egypt

f. king of Uruk

Write and Share

A Public Meeting Divide the class into three equal groups. One group will represent the government, one will represent the archaeologists, and one group will represent citizens. The archaeologists want to excavate a site where the citizens live. They need money and permission from the government to carry out their project. The citizens do not want the site to be disturbed and refuse to have their taxes pay for the excavation. Have students prepare their arguments in advance. Encourage research.

Read on Your Own

Look for books like these in your library.

Apply Skills

Create Time Lines Use events from your own life on one time line and public events on the other. Public events might include national and international events such as elections, peace and trade agreements, or weather events.

FEB — my birthday
JUNE — Lacy the cat has kittens
SEPT — Win Safety Poster Contest
NOV — Vacation in Florida
DEC — Move to new house

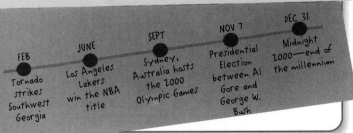

FEB — Tornado strikes Southwest Georgia
JUNE — Los Angeles Lakers win the NBA title
SEPT — Sydney, Australia hosts the 2000 Olympic Games
NOV 7 — Presidential Election between Al Gore and George W. Bush
DEC 31 — Midnight 2000—end of the millennium

Future World

Create a documentary about life today for people living a hundred years from now.

1 Form a group to write a script for a documentary about life today. Include discussion of common objects from school or home. Consider what clues the objects give about people's activities.

2 Choose objects that will survive for a long time.

3 Describe the objects and how people today use them. Tell what it is that people in the future might learn from the objects.

4 Present your documentary to the class.

Internet Activity

Explore early civilizations on the Internet. Go to **www.sfsocialstudies.com/activities** and select your grade and unit.

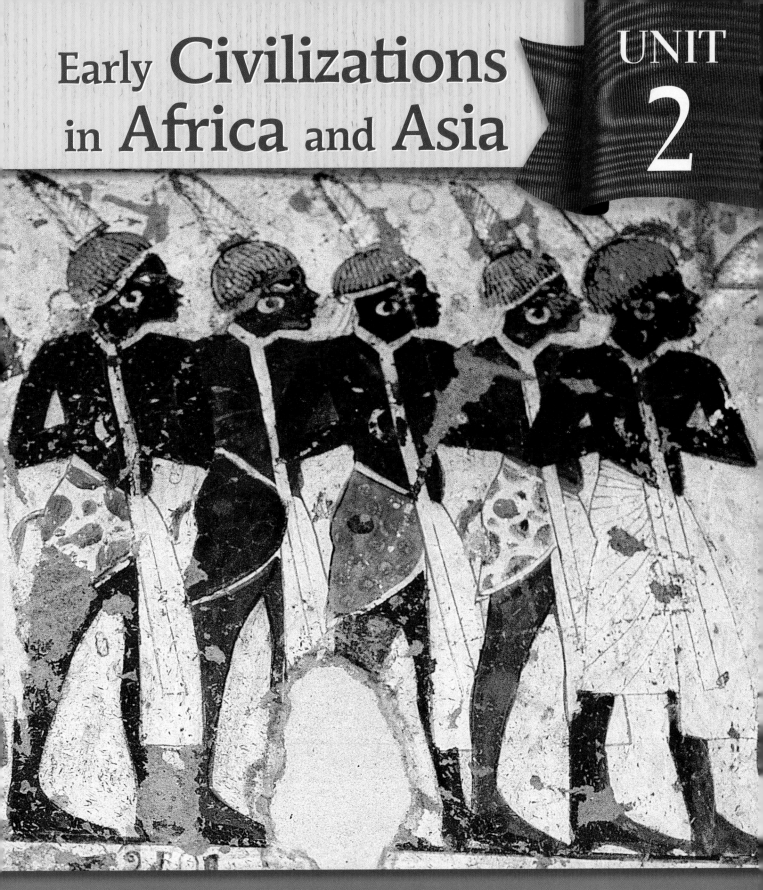

How does interaction among cultures spread ideas and inventions?

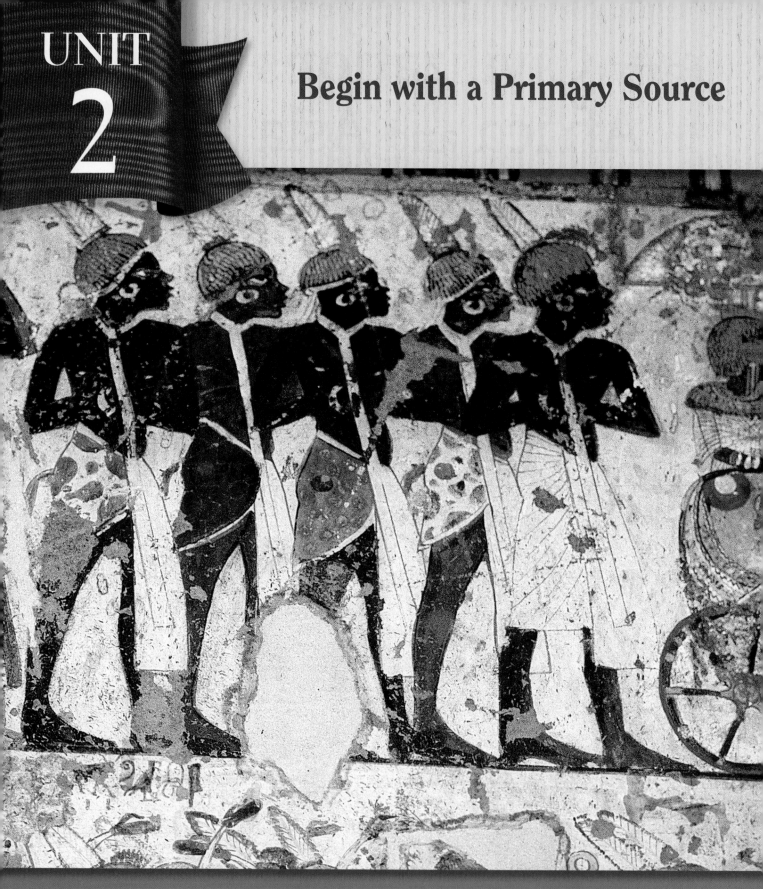

5000 B.C.   4000 B.C.   3000 B.C.

5000 B.C.
Early civilizations rise
in the Nile River Valley.

3500 B.C.
Early civilizations rise in
the Indus River Valley.

3000 B.C.
Rise of early
civilizations
in China

about 2600 B.C.
Construction begins
on the Great
Pyramid.

> *"I will lead the army on water and on land, to bring marvels from God's-Land."*
>
> —Probably said by Queen Hatshepsut of Egypt

On a tomb painting, Nubians bring gold to the Egyptians about 1525 B.C.

2000 B.C.　　　　　1000 B.C.　　　　　A.D. 1

2500 B.C.
Height of Harappa and Mohenjo-Daro civilizations

about 1760 B.C.
The first Chinese dynasty, the Shang, begins.

Meet the People

Khufu

reigned sometime between 2575 B.C. and 2465 B.C.
Birthplace: Memphis, Egypt
Pharaoh
· Ruled Egypt
· Built the Great Pyramid of Giza, one of the Seven Wonders of the Ancient World

Queen Hatshepsut

reigned c. 1498 B.C.– 1483 B.C.
Birthplace: Egypt
Queen of Egypt
· Wore a fake beard to look like a pharaoh
· Built many temples throughout Egypt and Nubia
· Sent trade expeditions to Punt

Chandragupta

reigned c. 320 B.C.– 297 B.C.
Birthplace: India
Emperor
· First emperor of Mauryan dynasty
· Lived a life of luxury before becoming a monk

Ashoka

reigned c. 265 B.C.– 238 B.C.
Birthplace: India
Emperor
· Expanded and strengthened Mauryan Empire
· Became a Buddhist monk

3000 B.C.	2500	2000	1500 B.C.

Khufu
reigned sometime between 2575 B.C. and 2465 B.C.

Queen Hatshepsut
reigned c. 1498 B.C.–1483 B.C.

Shi Huangdi

c. 259 B.C.–210 B.C.
Birthplace: Qin, China
Emperor
- First Chinese emperor
- Unified states of China into one empire
- Put a ban on books that opposed him

Wu Di

c. 156 B.C.–87 B.C.
Birthplace: China
Emperor
- Chinese Emperor during the Han dynasty
- Built roads, increased trade, and started civil service exams
- Encouraged writing of the first complete Chinese history book

Amanirenas

reigned c. 30 B.C.–18 B.C.
Birthplace: Kush
Queen
- Led Kush into battle against the Romans
- Fought against taxes imposed on her people

Ban Zhao

c. A.D. 45– A.D. 115
Birthplace: Anling, China
Writer, scholar, historian
- Prominent historian during Han dynasty
- Helped write "The Book of Han"
- Wrote poems and essays for the empress

1000   **500**   **A.D. 1**   **A.D. 500**

Chandragupta
reigned c. 320 B.C.–297 B.C.

Ban Zhao
c. A.D. 45–A.D. 115

Ashoka
c. 265 B.C.–238 B.C.

Amanirenas
reigned c. 30 B.C.–18 B.C.

Shi Huangdi
c. 259 B.C.–210 B.C.

Wu Di
c. 156 B.C.–87 B.C.

The Nile River

 Summarize

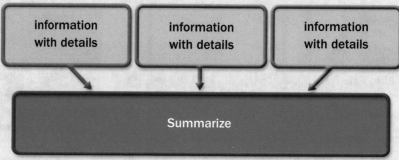

- After you read something, you will want to remember it for yourself or maybe later for a test.

- Write down the main ideas as either complete sentences or as a list.

- Write down the main ideas in your own words to show that you understand what you have read.

Read the following paragraph. The **details** of the summary are highlighted in yellow. The **summary** has been highlighted in blue.

The Egyptians were very curious about how the Nile River was able to flood so regularly. They thought of ways to predict when the Nile would flood. The Egyptians made devices to help them record information about the Nile. Many people in the past have been interested in the Nile River.

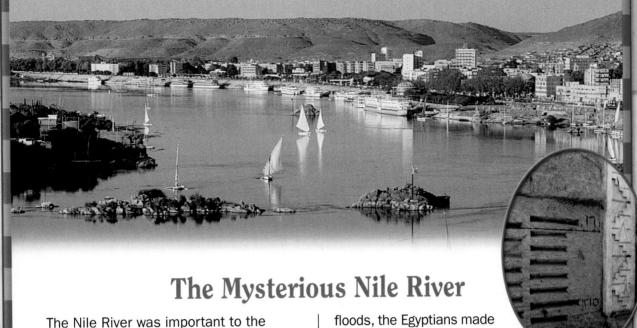

The Mysterious Nile River

The Nile River was important to the ancient Egyptians because it provided water. Without water, Egyptian civilization could not have survived. For this reason, the Egyptians celebrated the flooding of the Nile every year. They kept track of the level of flooding by using a nilometer, which measured the level of the Nile as the water rose higher and higher. We know about nilometers because archaeologists have found some in their excavations.

At first, the Nile was mysterious to the Egyptians. Not knowing when it flooded meant that the Egyptians could not prepare for too much or too little water. The Egyptians decided to keep track of when the Nile flooded. They watched the position of the sun in the sky during the day and Sirius, the brightest star in the sky, at night. After recording the number of days between floods, the Egyptians made a calendar. The calendar helped them keep track of when the Nile would flood. The Egyptians discovered that the flood season lasted about four months. Now they could be better prepared.

▶ **A nilometer had slots or steps to measure the level of the Nile.**

Celebrating the annual flooding became part of the Egyptian way of life. This special time of the year was called *Inundation*. According to the Egyptian calendar, Inundation was the first of three parts. The other two were Emergence and Harvest.

What the Egyptians learned about the Nile helped them in their everyday lives. The technology they developed helped the Egyptians understand the Nile. It was also used by other cultures.

Use the reading strategy of summarize to answer these questions.

1 Why was the Nile important to the Egyptians?

2 How did technology help the Egyptians understand the Nile?

3 Summarize how the Nile was mysterious to the Egyptians at first.

CHAPTER 3

Ancient Egypt and Nubia

Lesson 1

5000 B.C.
Nile River Valley
Egyptian civilization emerges in the Nile River Valley.

1

Lesson 2

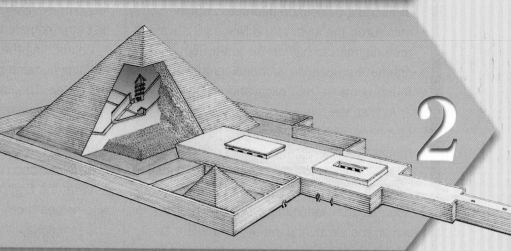

c. 2600 B.C.
Giza
The Great Pyramid is built.

2

Lesson 3

591 B.C.
Meroë
The Nubians build a capital.

3

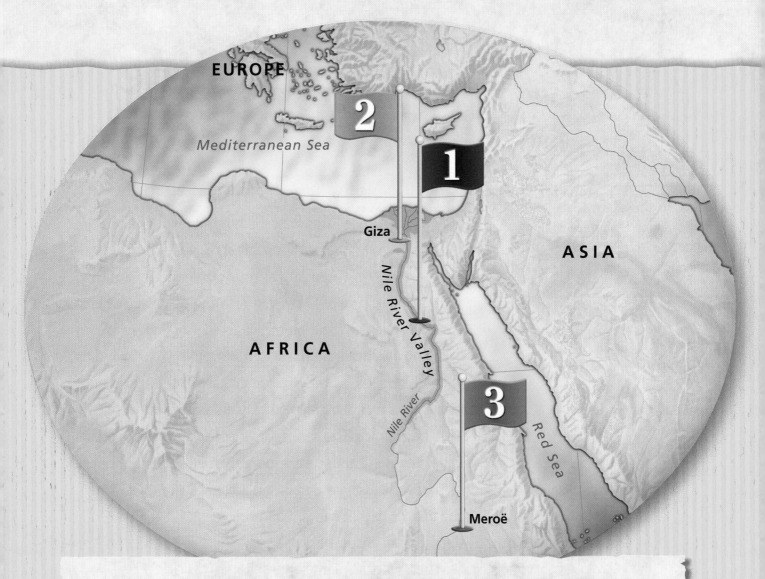

Why We Remember

We know about the lives of the ancient Egyptians from artifacts that archaeologists have found. From the writings they left behind, we understand more about their civilization. Writings from other civilizations also tell us about the ancient Egyptians. From the enormous stone structures they built, we are reminded that the ancient Egyptians were there. The ancient Egyptians influenced the lives of many cultures and civilizations all over the world—then and now. How do you think that people in the future will interpret our civilization?

3.5 million years ago

3.5 million years ago
Early humans may exist in Africa.

7,000 years ago

7,000 years ago
Early civilizations emerge
in the Nile River Valley.

Nile River Valley

Nile River

PREVIEW

Focus on the Main Idea
The Egyptians have depended
on the Nile River to survive for
thousands of years.

PLACES
Egypt
Nile River Valley
Nile River
Lower Egypt
Upper Egypt
Memphis

VOCABULARY
delta
silt
papyrus
cataract

The Lifeline of the Nile

You Are There
You've been chosen to work on an excavation site in Egypt in northeastern Africa. Your experience in South Carolina sure paid off! Now you're going to a place where early Egyptian civilization began about 7,000 years ago.

Flying overhead the Nile River looks like a long, winding snake. The banks of the Nile are lined with palm trees and crops. However, the green quickly disappears into a sea of sand and stones. The desert, or what the ancient Egyptians called the Red Land, covers more than 90 percent of Egypt.

You wonder if you'll make an amazing discovery that will reveal more about life in ancient Egypt.

When your airplane lands at the airport in Cairo (KY roh), modern Egypt's capital city, you prepare for the adventure ahead.

▶ **Egyptian pots such as this one were used to store food.**

Summarize As you read about the geography of ancient Egypt, combine the main ideas.

The Nile River Valley

You read in Chapter 1 about how archaeologists have been searching for the first Americans. Then you read about the first civilizations in southwest Asia. In the 1970s, a skeleton was uncovered in East Africa. Some archaeologists believed it could be 3.5 million years old. They continue to search for more evidence about the first Africans. However, until now they have found only enough artifacts to piece together the first African civilizations from about 5000 B.C.

The Nile River Valley was an ideal place for civilizations to thrive in northeastern Africa. Since ancient times, life in Egypt has depended on agriculture. Egypt gets little rain. Surrounded by hot, sandy deserts, the Nile River brought life to the people who lived by it. The Nile is the longest river in the world. It extends more than 4,000 miles in length. Look at the map on the right. The Nile begins in East Africa and flows northward into Egypt.

The Nile flows through a delta, a triangular-shaped area of soil at the mouth of a river that looks like fingers spread out. Water flowing northward used to carry silt, a mixture of soil and small rocks, as it surged from south to north into the Mediterranean Sea. Soil was deposited near the mouth of the river. In ancient Egypt, the delta was located in Lower Egypt, which lies to the north of Upper Egypt.

In ancient Egypt, the Nile irrigated land that stretched about five miles on both sides of the river. This is where Egyptian civilization began, and agriculture thrived. In the fifth century B.C., the Greek historian Herodotus called Egypt the "gift of the Nile."

REVIEW Why was the Nile River Valley important to the development of civilization in Egypt? Summarize

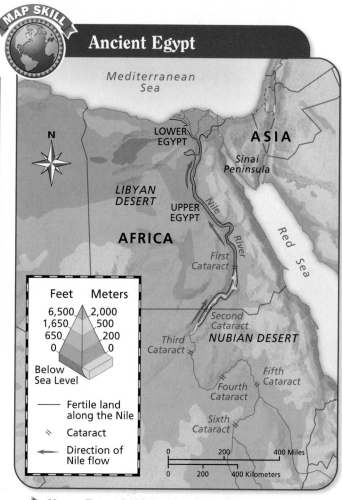

Ancient Egypt

▶ Upper Egypt is higher in elevation than Lower Egypt. The Nile flows to the north.

MAP SKILL Use an Elevation Map *What is the difference in elevation between Upper and Lower Egypt?*

▶ This tomb painting shows an ancient Egyptian family hunting along the Nile.

Giver of Life

The Nile overflowed because of heavy rains in East Africa. People living near the Nile, in places such as Memphis, planted seeds after the floods and harvested in late summer. They called this area "black land," because the land was very fertile. Then the cycle began again. The ancient Egyptians sang a hymn, or song, about the Nile. As the *Hymn of the Nile* goes:

> ### *"When he [the Nile] arises earth rejoices and all men are glad."*

Not far from the banks of the Nile is dry, desert land, or what the Egyptians called "red land." No crops could grow here. Without the Nile, people would not have been able to grow crops and get water to survive. The *Hymn of the Nile* reveals the importance of the Nile:

> ### *"That givest drink to the desert places which are far from water."*

Wheat and barley were the most important crops in ancient Egypt. Farmers also grew vegetables. Papyrus (puh PY ruhs) was another valuable crop. The Egyptians used its stems to make paper. The papermaking process involved cutting thin strips

▶ **This ancient model of an Egyptian boat has a mast from which sails used to hang.**

from the plant's stem and pressing them together. When the pressed strips dried, they produced a smooth surface. Papyrus became widely used for record keeping.

The Nile also was a means of transporting goods. However, the geography of the Nile caused some roadblocks for travelers. Six cataracts, or waterfalls, break up the flow of the Nile. The cataracts made it impossible to sail directly from the Nile Delta south to East Africa without taking a boat out of water and carrying it. Because the river flows from south to north, a boat also needed sails to move it upstream.

The Nile gave the Egyptians many gifts to help their civilization develop. However, you will read about how the Nile also caused problems for the Egyptians.

REVIEW What made the Nile River an important resource to people living near it?

↻ Summarize

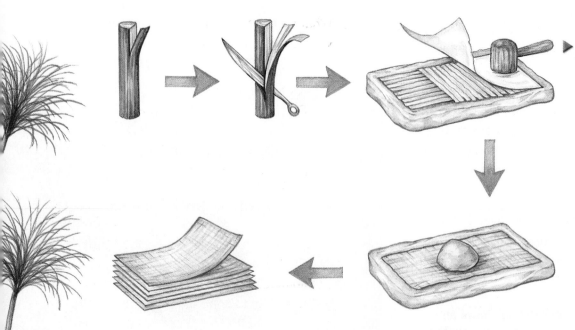

▶ **The Papyrus plant was cultivated in Egypt for thousands of years. Egyptians used its stalk or stem to make papyrus paper. By cutting the stem into strips and pressing two layers together, Egyptians got the smooth surface needed for writing. The sheet was then hammered and dried in the sun.**

Taker of Life

Although the Nile did flood regularly, it did not always do so in the same way. Sometimes heavy rains caused too much water to overflow. Crops would be destroyed, and people lost their lives. Other times, the Nile did not flood enough and crops could not grow. When this happened, the Egyptians used the food they stored from surplus harvests.

The Egyptians needed to investigate why the Nile flooded in a different way from year to year. Like the Mesopotamians, the Egyptians built irrigation canals to transport water to their crops.

The Egyptians were polytheistic, or believed in many gods, just like the Mesopotamians. They used stories about their gods to explain the natural world, including the Nile. Their main god, Amon-Ra, or Ra, was represented by the sun. The Egyptians observed that over time the sunrise and sunset changed. They also understood that the moon's appearance changed slightly every evening.

The Egyptians then used these observations to make predictions about when the Nile would flood.

▶ Ra (left) was the Egyptian sun god. Horus (below) was god of the sky.

As you read earlier, they used a calendar to keep track of the number of days between flooding cycles. They determined that the Nile would flood sometime between May and September. The use of irrigation canals and the calendar helped the Egyptians solve their problems with the Nile.

REVIEW Why did the Egyptians consider the Nile a taker of life? Summarize

Summarize the Lesson

- **3.5 million years ago** Humans may have existed in Africa.

- **7000 years ago** Early civilizations appeared along the Nile River.

LESSON 1   REVIEW

Check Facts and Main Ideas

1. Summarize On a separate piece of paper, fill in the missing detail below.

| | | The Egyptians made calendars to keep track of when the Nile would flood. |

| Sometimes the Nile flooded too much or not enough. |

→ Even though the Nile flooded, it was important to the Egyptians.

2. Describe the route of the Nile River.

3. What solutions did the Egyptians come up with to deal with the flooding of the Nile?

4. How was the Nile a giver and taker of life?

5. **Critical Thinking:** *Make Inferences* Suppose the Egyptians had not tried to predict when the Nile would flood. Do you think their civilization would have lasted very long? Explain your answer.

Link to — Writing

Write a Poem Write four to eight lines about the annual flooding of the Nile. Think about what information you would include in your poem to remind you when the Nile would flood.

Map and Globe Skills

Compare Maps at Different Scales

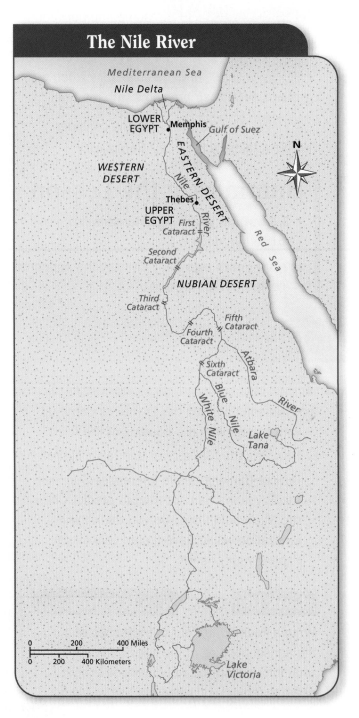

The Nile River

Mediterranean Sea

Nile Delta

LOWER EGYPT

Memphis

Gulf of Suez

WESTERN DESERT

EASTERN DESERT

Nile River

Thebes

UPPER EGYPT

First Cataract

Second Cataract

NUBIAN DESERT

Red Sea

Third Cataract

Fifth Cataract

Fourth Cataract

Atbara

Sixth Cataract

Blue Nile

White Nile

River

Lake Tana

N

| 0 | 200 | 400 Miles |
| 0 | 200 | 400 Kilometers |

Lake Victoria

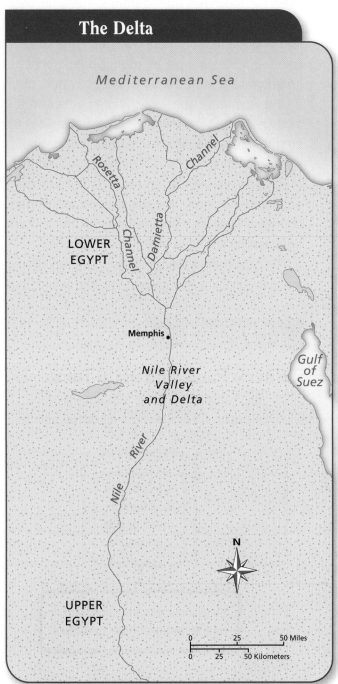

The Delta

Mediterranean Sea

Rosetta Channel

Damietta Channel

LOWER EGYPT

Memphis

Nile River Valley and Delta

Gulf of Suez

Nile River

N

UPPER EGYPT

| 0 | 25 | 50 Miles |
| 0 | 25 | 50 Kilometers |

▶ **Lush greenery outlines the east bank of the Nile near the First Cataract.**

What? Maps help you see where places are located. However, not all maps are the same. Some maps show you a lot of territory such as a whole continent or the whole world. Others show just a part of a country.

The Nile River map on page 82 shows the Nile River past the Sixth Cataract. The Delta map on page 82 shows the entire Nile River Valley in Egypt.

Why? Maps help you see where places are located. They show you where a place is in relation to other places. They can show one place such as a city or a section of the Nile in great detail. They also can show you a larger area such as the entire Nile River, from where it starts in East Africa to where it ends at the Mediterranean Sea. Maps can do this because they have different scales.

A map with a large scale shows a small area, but it can show the area in greater detail. It illustrates greater detail of smaller cities and waterways. For example, you can see a lot of detail of the Nile Delta on the second map on page 82.

Maps with a small scale show a larger area, but they show less detail. They will show only general features of an area.

How? Look at The Nile River map again. This is a map of the Nile River from the Mediterranean Sea to beyond the Sixth Cataract. This map shows a large area. Now look at The Delta map. This map shows a much smaller area than the first map does.

Look at the city of Memphis on The Nile River map. Next, look for the city of Thebes on the same map. Now look at The Delta map. You should be able to see the Nile Delta and the city of Memphis but not the city of Thebes. Finally, look at the scale on both maps. The scale will tell you how many inches equal how many miles on the map.

Think and Apply

1 How many miles are between Memphis and Thebes?

2 How does the Nile look on The Nile River map compared to The Delta map?

3 What other features appear on one map that do not appear on the other?

Internet Activity

For more information go online to the *Atlas* at **www.sfsocialstudies.com.**

3500 B.C.   2500 B.C.   1500 B.C.

3150 B.C.
King Menes unites Lower and Upper Egypt.

c. 2600 B.C.
Construction begins on the Great Pyramid at Giza.

c. 2575 B.C.
The Old Kingdom begins.

c. 1570 B.C.
The New Kingdom begins.

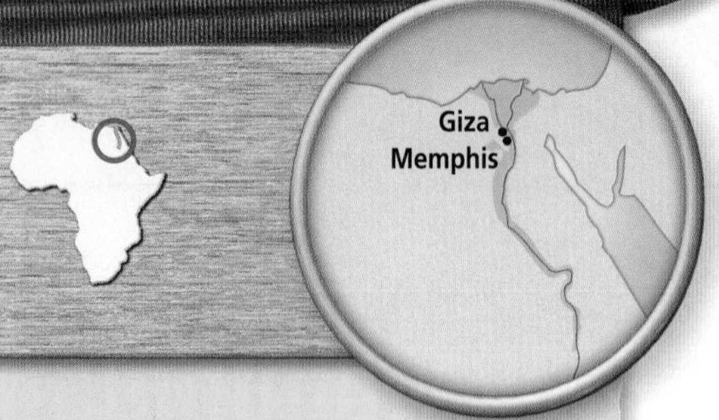

Giza
Memphis

Life in Egypt

PREVIEW

Focus on the Main Idea
The first civilizations in ancient Egypt were great and complex.

PLACES
Giza
Deir el-Medina

PEOPLE
Menes
Manetho
Khufu
Hatshepsut
Akhenaten

VOCABULARY
unify
pharaoh
hieroglyphics
pyramid
mummy
economy

TERMS
Rosetta Stone

You Are There

You're waiting for your brother to return home from school. He is learning to be a scribe, a person who keeps written records. He is older than you are, and your parents have only enough money to send one of you to school. You cannot wait for him to share with you what he learned today. You look forward to the day when you and maybe your older sister will be scribes.

When your brother arrives, he bursts out with the latest news in the kingdom. Upper Egypt, where you live, is being united with Lower Egypt! This means that the king will have an even bigger responsibility. The streets in your village are buzzing. You hear rumors that the king will be given a new, special title.

▶ **Scribes were often shown sitting cross-legged. Few ancient Egyptians could read or write.**

Summarize As you read, summarize the main points about life in ancient Egypt.

Unifying Egypt

As you read in Lesson 1, farming emerged in the Nile River Valley in Upper and Lower Egypt. Both kingdoms had their own kings. These kings even wore their own special crowns. The king of Upper Egypt wore a white crown, and the king of Lower Egypt wore a red one. When the two kingdoms were **unified,** or united, into one country, the two different-colored crowns were united into one crown. Look at the diagram to see how the single crowns became a double crown after Egypt was unified.

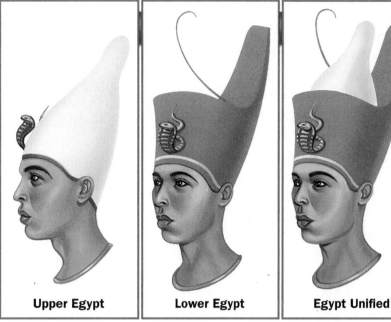

| Upper Egypt | Lower Egypt | Egypt Unified |

▶ The crown of Lower Egypt was placed on top of Upper Egypt to make the double crown that King Menes wore.

DIAGRAM SKILL *Why were the crowns of Upper and Lower Egypt combined?*

Legend says that in about 3150 B.C., King **Menes** (MEE nees) led his army north into Lower Egypt, wearing the double crown. No one is certain if this is true. Some historians believe that other kings named Scorpion or Narmer could have united the two kingdoms. It is hard to know exactly what happened because archaeologists have found few records from the period.

During the first dynasty, or period of time during which members from the same family ruled, Memphis was made Egypt's capital city. However, we do not know much about kings and life in Egypt until the third dynasty. That is when **Manetho,** who was a priest and an advisor, began to keep records. He divided the kings into differ-

ent dynasties. Later, historians made three main divisions in ancient Egypt: the Old Kingdom (c. 2575–2181 B.C.), the Middle Kingdom (c. 2040–1782 B.C.), and the New Kingdom (c. 1570–1070 B.C.).

During the New Kingdom, people began to refer to a king as a god-king or **pharaoh,** which means "great house." As described on a tomb,

> *"[A pharaoh] is a god by whose dealings one lives, the father and mother of all . . . without an equal."*

The Egyptians considered the pharaoh to be related to Amon-Ra, the sun god. They worshipped the pharaoh as a god.

REVIEW Why do we not know for certain who united Upper and Lower Egypt? *Main Idea and Details*

▶ In this tomb painting, the sun god Amon–Ra is shown on a journey to another world.

Egyptian Records

We know about the pharaohs because of the records Egyptians kept. Like the Sumerians, the Egyptians developed a form of writing—based on pictures—called **hieroglyphics** (hy ruh GLIH fiks), or "sacred carvings." Unlike Sumerian cuneiform writing, these hieroglyphics represented objects or ideas but also stood for sounds. They could be carved into a clay or stone tablet or written on paper.

Archaeologists did not know how to read the hieroglyphics they found on Egyptian buildings and artifacts for a long time. The discovery, and later decoding, of the Rosetta Stone in 1799 solved the mystery! On the stone was a passage written in Greek, Egyptian hieroglyphics, and a form of Egyptian cursive writing. By comparing Egyptian hieroglyphics to Greek words, the Rosetta Stone could be read. Now we know that the Egyptians

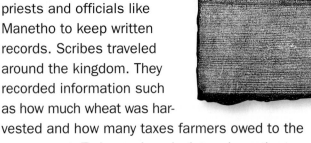

► **The Rosetta Stone was decoded in 1822 by French scholar Jean Champollion.**

used at least 700 different hieroglyphic symbols.

Pharaohs depended on priests and officials like Manetho to keep written records. Scribes traveled around the kingdom. They recorded information such as how much wheat was harvested and how many taxes farmers owed to the government. Today, archaeologists rely on these records to understand ancient Egyptian civilization.

REVIEW What are Egyptian hieroglyphics, and how are they different from Sumerian picture writing? **Compare and Contrast**

 DORLING KINDERSLEY EYEWITNESS BOOK

Egyptian Writing

Scribes used about 700 different signs or pictures in hieroglyphic writing. The ancient Egyptians made sure that their writing system was difficult so that few people could learn it. Hieroglyphs could be written from left to right, right to left, or top to bottom. Why do you think the Egyptians wanted only a few people to learn how to write?

Label
Scribes used tags to label their scrolls. A translation of this tag from about 1450 B.C. explains that the papyrus scroll told a story about a fig tree.

Script
Scribes usually wrote religious or official documents on papyrus in a fast form of writing called hieratic. On this papyrus, hieratic appears as script. Hieroglyphs appear above the picture.

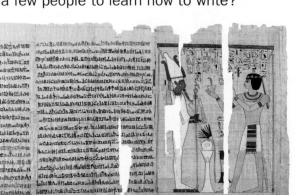

Pyramid Building

Egyptian kings in the Old Kingdom are best known for the huge structures they built— **pyramids.** These large stone buildings served as houses or tombs for the dead.

The Egyptians believed that kings (pharaohs) remained gods even after death, and that pyramids were like palaces. Kings were buried with their possessions. The Egyptians thought that kings took their possessions with them to the afterlife, or life that continued after death.

Because the afterlife was more important than life on Earth, the Egyptians took great care in preparing kings for burial. They believed the bodies of the pharaohs needed to be preserved. They used a process called mummification. Mummification took 70 days. First, the Egyptians removed all organs except for the heart from the body. Then, they rubbed oils and perfumes over the body. Next, they wrapped the body in linen bandages. Finally, the **mummy,** or preserved body, was placed in a coffin and put into a tomb.

▶ Coffins were made to look like humans. The face was often a portrait of the person inside.

Before the Egyptians built pyramids, they constructed mastabas (MAS tuh buhz), or "benches," as tombs. However, when King Zoser became king, he hired an advisor, much like an architect, to build a step pyramid. Kings continued to follow this custom of pyramid building.

The building of Egypt's largest pyramid began about 2600 B.C. at **Giza** (GEE zuh). It is called the Great Pyramid, built for the pharaoh **Khufu.** Archaeologists and historians estimate that this pyramid took about 20 years to build and that slave labor was not used. Until the 1800s, the Great Pyramid was the tallest structure in the world made by people.

When the Nile was flooding, farmers could not work in their fields. They were then available to work on the pyramid. Perhaps as many as 20,000 workers used more than two million blocks of heavy stone to build it! They cut the gigantic blocks of granite from cliffs to the south. Then, some believe, they dragged the stones with rope to ramps that led to the building site.

REVIEW Why and how did the Egyptians build pyramids? **Main Idea and Details**

▶ A cutaway diagram of King Khufu's Great Pyramid shows the inside details of many pyramids that were built in the Old Kingdom.

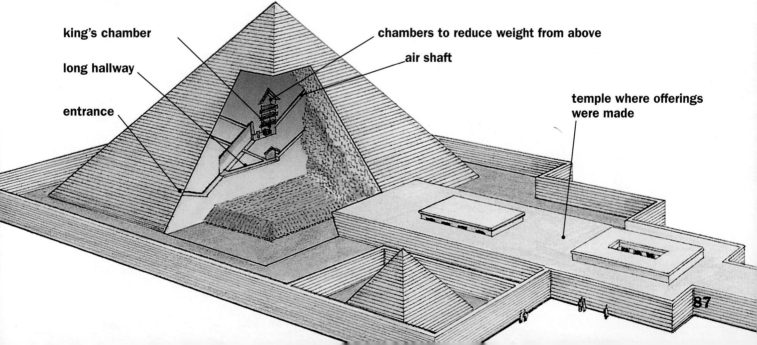

king's chamber

long hallway

entrance

chambers to reduce weight from above

air shaft

temple where offerings were made

BUILDING
CITIZENSHIP

Caring
Respect
Responsibility
Fairness
Honesty
★ Courage

The Tomb Builders

In the New Kingdom, tombs were built into solid rock in the Valley of the Kings. Construction of a tomb would begin the moment the pharaoh took the throne. Tomb building was dangerous work.

Because of the constant need for workers to remain at the work site, a workers' village was built at **Deir el-Medina,** on the west bank of the Nile across from Thebes. Workers labored eight hours every day for ten days in a row. Then they received one day of rest and began the work cycle again. They had their families living with them to avoid the long journey from work to home. Their houses were made of mud bricks. Wives were in charge of the household. They took care of the children and the house when their husbands were working.

The workers were paid with food. They received mostly grain. Sometimes this was not enough to live on, so workers had to find additional work. Some worked as scribes, decorating the tombs of wealthy Egyptians.

Building the tombs was important and hard work. Many people died because the labor was difficult and dangerous. The pharaohs counted on the tomb builders and their families to be committed and courageous. They trusted that the workers would be on time and prepared to work. Because no one really knew how long the pharaoh would live, they had to work quickly and accurately.

Courage in Action

Link to Current Events Research someone who has done courageous work or has shown courage in his or her lifetime.

Social Life

As you have read, the Egyptians had many different jobs. Some were farmers and pyramid builders; others were scribes or priests. When trade expanded during the Middle Kingdom, more people became merchants and craftspeople. This caused a new middle class to emerge, made up of artisans and scribes. In the Old Kingdom, there were two levels: kings (pharaohs) and farmers. With this new middle class, the social class structure changed.

The king was at the top. Nobles and priests were next. Merchants, craftsmen, and scribes followed them. Then came farmers and unskilled workers. Another class level was added later in Egypt. When prisoners were captured in battle, they were brought to Egypt as enslaved people. An enslaved person has lost his or her freedom and is owned by another person. The Egyptians could move between classes if they worked hard. If they were born into one class, they did not have to stay there.

Egyptian women had more rights than women in many other ancient civilizations. Like Sumerian women, they could inherit land and handle business transactions. Some Egyptian women may have even been scribes and merchants. Archaeologists have found an Egyptian word for a female scribe. However, most women were not taught how to read and write.

REVIEW How were the social class structures similar and different in Sumer and Egypt?
Compare and Contrast

▶ **Egyptian society was structured like a pyramid.**

Trade and Technology

During the Middle Kingdom, Egypt's power began to grow. By about 2040 B.C. Egypt's empire had expanded greatly.

The Egyptians had been trading with people from other lands to the north and south. Trade increased during this period and made the Egyptian economy more prosperous, or profitable. An **economy** is the way people use and manage resources. The Egyptians went on expeditions to southwest Asia to trade goods such as wheat, gold, and linen with other peoples. To improve transportation, they dug a canal from the Nile River to the Red Sea, which became a trade route.

Groups of people began to invade and take control of Egypt. One group was called the Hyksos (HIHK sahs), which means "desert princes." The Hyksos came from western Asia and brought new technology and ideas. They rode chariots that were pulled by horses. About 1660 B.C., the Hyksos took power in Egypt. About 100 years later, Egyptian kings again took power. This was the start of the New Kingdom, a period of even greater change and growth.

▶ **This model of a chariot is made of clay.**

REVIEW How did the growth of trade in the Middle Kingdom affect Egypt's economy?
Cause and Effect

king

nobles and priests

merchants, craftsmen, scribes

farmers and unskilled workers

enslaved people

New Kingdom Pharaohs

A tradition that began during the Middle Kingdom continued during the New Kingdom. Pharaohs ruled with their sons or wives. For example, Queen Sobeknefru (so bek NAY froo) ruled Egypt after the death of her husband. About 1498 B.C. a very powerful woman, **Hatshepsut**, (hat SHEP soot), took power. During her reign, trade expeditions brought back many valuable goods. She also started and finished several building projects. Read more about Hatshepsut in the biography on page 91.

Egypt continued to expand its borders during the New Kingdom. About 1350 B.C. Amenhotep IV (ah muhn HOH tep) became pharaoh. He and his wife, Nefertiti (nef er TEET ee), started

▶ **Ramses II was a New Kingdom pharaoh who built more statues and temples than any other pharaoh.**

to worship a new sun god, Aton. Amenhotep even changed his name to **Akhenaten** (ahk NAHT uhn), which means "servant of Aton." Many Egyptians thought it was wrong to worship a sun god other than Ra. Akhenaten became so focused on Aton that he neglected his duties as pharaoh. His advisors took control.

After Akhenaten's death, a young boy became pharaoh. His name was Tutankhamen (too tahng KAH muhn). During his rule, order was restored. The worship of Aton was forgotten. Tutankhamen died young. However, we know about his life from the discovery of his tomb in the twentieth century.

REVIEW What was different about how some pharaohs ruled during the New Kingdom? **Compare and Contrast**

Summarize the Lesson

- **3150 B.C.** Menes united Lower and Upper Egypt into one country.
- **c. 2575 B.C.** The Old Kingdom began.
- **c. 1570 B.C.** The New Kingdom began.

LESSON 2   REVIEW

Check Facts and Main Ideas

1. 🔄 **Summarize** On a separate piece of paper, fill in the missing detail in the blank box below.

```
┌──────────────┐  ┌──────────────┐  ┌──────────────┐
│ Pharaohs were│  │ The Egyptians│  │              │
│ considered   │  │ built pyramids│ │              │
│ god-kings.   │  │ for the      │  │              │
│              │  │ pharaohs.    │  │              │
└──────┬───────┘  └──────┬───────┘  └──────┬───────┘
       │                 │                 │
       └─────────────┐   │   ┌─────────────┘
                 ┌───▼───▼───▼───┐
                 │ Pharaohs were very important │
                 │ to the Egyptians. │
                 └───────────────┘
```

2. According to legend, how was Egypt unified?

3. What are hieroglyphics and how do we know what they mean?

4. How was Egyptian culture similar to and different from Sumerian culture?

5. **Critical Thinking:** *Evaluate Information* Why was trade important to the Egyptians?

Link to 🔗 **Art**

Develop a Plan Put yourself in the position of an architect in ancient Egypt. Make a diagram to show the pharaoh how the pyramid will look. Tell how many workers you will need, when the project will begin, and how long the project will last. Make a list of the materials needed to build the pyramid.

Hatshepsut
reigned c. 1498 B.C.–1483 B.C.

Hatshepsut was the daughter of a pharaoh. She also was married to one, King Thutmose II. When he died, she became a regent, or a ruler in the place of a young king. She ruled in place of her nephew while he went on military expeditions. Later, Hatshepsut took complete control. She supported her claim by creating a garden in a temple for the sun god Ra, who she claimed was her real father. The wall of the temple read:

"I [Hatshepsut] shine forever in your faces through that which my father hath desired . . . . I have entered into the qualities of the august god . . . . He hath recognized my excellence."

Hatshepsut was often portrayed wearing the clothing of a pharaoh, including a false beard. On the walls of her tomb, she is often described with a male pronoun. This was because the Egyptians believed that all kings were males.

There were not many military campaigns during her reign, which lasted until her death in 1483 B.C. However, she sent several trading expeditions in search of riches. One of these expeditions was to Punt on the northeastern coast of Africa. Myrrh [mer], which was used to make perfume, was one item the Egyptians brought back with them.

BIOFACT

Hatshepsut liked perfumes. She had traders bring back myrrh trees from Punt and plant them around her temple at Dayr al-Bahri.

Even though her reign was peaceful, later Egyptians did not like that she was king. They eventually took her name off the list of Egyptian kings.

Learn from Biographies

The Egyptians were not accustomed to women pharaohs. Some officials supported Hatshepsut, while others did not. How would this have made ruling difficult for her?

For more information, go online to *Meet the People* at **www.sfsocialstudies.com.**

3000 B.C. 2000 B.C. 1000 B.C.

3200 B.C.
First civilizations
rise in Nubia.

1800s B.C.
Egypt expands its
borders into Nubia.

c. 750 B.C.
Kashta conquers
Upper Egypt.

EGYPT

NUBIA
Napata •Meroë

Nubia and Egypt

PREVIEW

Focus on the Main Idea
The Egyptians and Nubians
interacted with each other and
with other peoples.

PLACES
Nubia
Meroë
Kush
Napata

PEOPLE
Thutmose III
Kashta
Piankhi
Amanirenas

VOCABULARY
independent

You Are There

Your father has returned from a country in the north called Egypt. You are so happy to see him. He has been gone for two years, working as an archer in the pharaoh's army. The pharaoh thinks that Nubian archers are superior to other archers in battle. As a Nubian archer, your father has fought in many battles for the pharaoh.

Your father tells you about the large stone buildings and statues that he saw in Egypt.

You are curious about Egypt. You have never left your country. What is it like to live in Egypt? Is it the same as Nubia (NOO bee uh)? You hope to learn more about this far-away land from your father's stories.

▶ Skilled Nubian archers,
with bows and arrows,
helped fight with the
Egyptians in battle.

Summarize As you read, summarize the main points about Nubian civilization.

Lands South of Egypt

Nubia was a kingdom to the south of Egypt. Today, part of Nubia makes up an African nation, the Sudan. The Egyptians knew that people were living there even before Egypt was unified. Archaeologists have found evidence that people have been living in Nubia since the Old Stone Age. Some archaeologists believe that civilizations emerged in Nubia about 3200 B.C.

Nubia's borders began at the First Cataract on the Nile River. Unlike Egypt, Nubia had tall cliffs of granite rock surrounding the land from the First to the Second Cataract.

The Egyptians cultivated crops by using wooden digging sticks. However, the Nubians had to work harder because the soil was rocky. They used sturdier farming tools. To transport water from the Nile to the crops, the Nubians built irrigation canals similar to those in Egypt.

The Nubians developed their own culture. They had their own art, architecture, and beliefs. However, both the Egyptians and Nubians borrowed from each other's culture.

The Nubians had a written language called Meroitic (MAIR oh EE tick), which was named for one of the capital cities, Meroë (MAIR oh EE). Although Meroitic is similar to Egyptian hieroglyphics, no one has yet been able to decode it. Most of what we know about the Nubians comes from Egyptian sources.

The Egyptians and Nubians both believed in many gods. Some archaeologists think that the Nubians also worshipped Egyptian gods. The Nubians believed in the afterlife. Like the Egyptians, the Nubians built pyramids. However, they were much smaller and had a distinctive style.

REVIEW How do archaeologists know that a different civilization lived to the south of Egypt? ⟳ **Summarize**

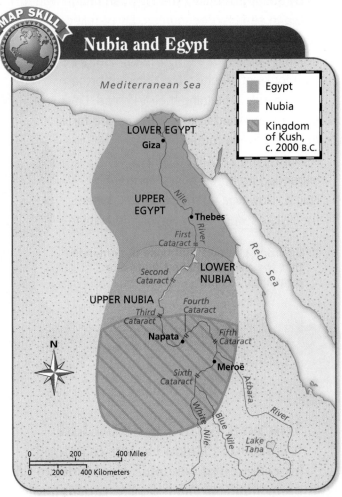

MAP SKILL Nubia and Egypt

▶ The borders of Nubia extended to the Sixth Cataract.

MAP SKILL Use a Compass Rose *Was Upper Nubia north or south of Lower Nubia?*

▶ Nubian pottery was often red and black. It was a valuable trade good.

93

Interaction

By about 2575 B.C., the Egyptians had invaded Nubia in search of resources. Egypt relied on Nubia for trade goods such as gold, ivory, cattle, and ostrich feathers. The Egyptians also cut blocks of granite from Nubia's northern cliffs to use in building their temples. Egypt soon established trading centers and forts to protect trade routes in Nubia.

During the 1800s B.C., Egypt expanded its borders into northern Nubia. However, about 1650 B.C., when the Hyksos were ruling Egypt, the Nubian kingdom of **Kush** became **independent**, or free. After the New Kingdom pharaohs regained power, **Thutmose III** retook Nubia in the 1400s B.C. However, when the New Kingdom ended, Egypt became weak, and Kush regained its independence.

By 750 B.C., King **Kashta** of Kush had conquered Upper Egypt. His son, **Piankhi** (pee AHN kee), conquered the rest of Egypt. Kushite kings then became pharaohs of Egypt.

▶ **Egyptian pharaoh Thutmose III demanded that the Nubians make tributes, or payments, to him.**

REVIEW Why did Egypt invade Nubia?
Draw Conclusions

Egyptian Museum Cairo/Dagli Orti (A)/Art Archive

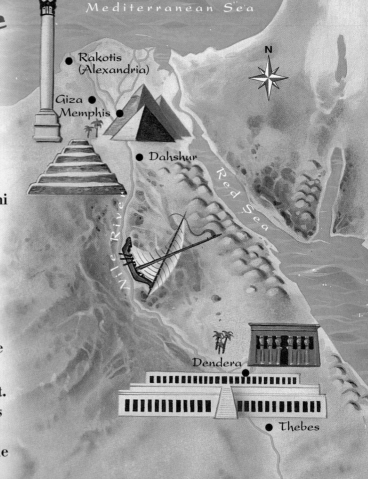

Map Adventure

You're a Guide for Piankhi

It is 720 B.C. Piankhi has just completed his conquest of Memphis. He decides to take a trip south up the Nile. You are his guide. Piankhi is counting on you to answer any of his questions.

1. You leave from the Egyptian village of Rakotis and travel toward Dahshur. Piankhi asks you if Dahshur is in the Nile Delta. What is your response?

2. At Dahshur, you get off the boat to look at the pyramids of the Old Kingdom. How many do you see?

3. You return to the boat and head toward Dendera. Are you traveling up or down the Nile?

4. In Dendera, Piankhi climbs out of the boat. He explores the Temple of Hathor, goddess of the sky. You both return to the boat so you can head for your last stop. The Temple of Hatshepsut is located in Thebes. Does it lie north or south of Dendera?

Mediterranean Sea

Rakotis (Alexandria)

Giza
Memphis

Dahshur

Nile River

Red Sea

N

Dendera

Thebes

Kush Rises

The Kushite kings completed many building projects during their reign. However, they were soon challenged by invaders from the east.

About 670 B.C., the Assyrians attacked Egypt, and the Kushites moved south to their capital at Napata. After 600 B.C., the Egyptians regained some power and invaded Kush, destroying Napata. The Kushites founded a new capital in Meroë, where trade flourished. In Meroë, iron was plentiful. Traders from other lands wanted tools and

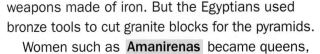
British Museum

▶ **This stone with Meroitic writing was made during the reign of Queen Amanirenas.**

weapons made of iron. But the Egyptians used bronze tools to cut granite blocks for the pyramids.

Women such as Amanirenas became queens, as they did in Egypt. They led military expeditions and built great monuments. Queen Amanirenas opposed taxes that were imposed on her people. As a result, she led Kush into battle against the Romans in the first century B.C.

As Egypt grew weaker, its influence on Kush faded. However, Meroë remained a great trade center until A.D. 350.

REVIEW How did Egypt's decline affect Kush?
Cause and Effect

Summarize the Lesson

- **3200 B.C.** First civilizations arose in Nubia.

- **1800s B.C.** Egypt expanded its borders into Nubia.

- **about 750 B.C.** King Kashta conquered Upper Egypt.

LESSON 3 REVIEW

Check Facts and Main Ideas

1. ⟳ **Summarize** On a separate piece of paper, fill in the missing detail in the blank box.

```
┌──────────────┐  ┌──────────────┐  ┌──────────────┐
│ The Egyptians│  │              │  │ The Egyptians│
│ and Nubians  │  │              │  │ invaded Nubia│
│ shared some  │  │              │  │ and set up   │
│ aspects of   │  │              │  │ trade and    │
│ culture.     │  │              │  │ military posts│
│              │  │              │  │ to protect   │
│              │  │              │  │ resources.   │
└──────────────┘  └──────────────┘  └──────────────┘
        │                │                  │
        └────────────────┼──────────────────┘
                         ▼
              ┌─────────────────────┐
              │ The Nubians and     │
              │ Egyptians           │
              │ interacted.         │
              └─────────────────────┘
```

2. How was the geography of Nubia different from Egypt?

3. Why did the ancient Egyptians and Nubians interact?

4. Why did other groups of people want to conquer Egypt? What impact did this have on Nubia?

5. **Critical Thinking:** *Make Inferences* Why do you think that the peaceful relationship between the Egyptians and Nubians changed over time?

Link to 🔗 Writing

Write a Paragraph Write a paragraph about what the Nubians might have written down after seeing the Egyptians for the first time. Keep in mind that the Egyptians were in search of gold and other resources.

CHAPTER 3 REVIEW

5000 B.C. — 4000 B.C.

5000 B.C.
Early civilizations emerged in the Nile River Valley.

Chapter Summary

Summarize

Target Skill

On a separate piece of paper, copy the diagram below. Fill in the details that combine to form the summary.

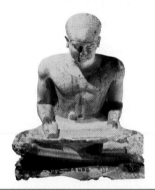

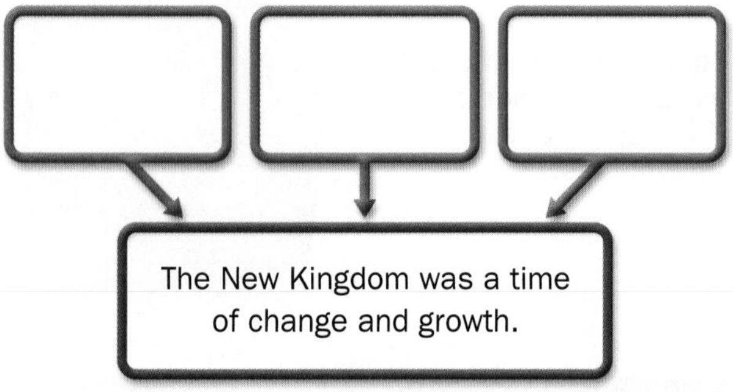

The New Kingdom was a time of change and growth.

Vocabulary and Terms

Write a sentence defining or describing the meaning and importance of each word or term below.

1. **unify** (p. 85)
2. **pyramid** (p. 87)
3. **cataract** (p. 80)
4. **delta** (p. 79)
5. **independent** (p. 94)
6. **mummy** (p. 87)
7. **pharaoh** (p. 85)
8. **hieroglyphics** (p. 86)
9. **economy** (p. 89)
10. **Rosetta Stone** (p. 86)

Places and People

Write a sentence explaining why each of the following places or people is important in the study of Egypt and Nubia. You may use two or more in a single sentence.

1. Manetho (p. 85)
2. Deir el-Medina (p. 88)
3. Khufu (p. 87)
4. Kashta (p. 94)
5. Hatshepsut (p. 90)
6. Akhenaten (p. 90)
7. Nubia (p. 93)
8. Kush (p. 94)
9. Menes (p. 85)
10. Meroë (p. 93)

3000 B.C.	2000 B.C.	1000 B.C.	A.D. 1

3200 B.C.
First civilizations arose in Nubia.

3150 B.C.
King Menes united Lower and Upper Egypt.

about 2600 B.C.
Construction began on the Great Pyramid at Giza.

about 1800 B.C.
Egypt expanded its borders into Nubia.

about 750 B.C.
Kashta conquered Upper Egypt.

Facts and Main Ideas

1. What is the importance of the Nile River?

2. How is the geography of Nubia different from that to Egypt?

3. What changes occurred during the Old Kingdom, the Middle Kingdom, and the New Kingdom?

4. **Time Line** How much time passed between the beginning of Nubian civilization and Egyptian expansion into Nubia?

5. **Main Idea** How did religious beliefs of the ancient Egyptians affect the way they lived their lives?

6. **Main Idea** How were pyramids built?

7. **Main Idea** How did the relationship between Egypt and Nubia change over time?

8. **Critical Thinking:** *Evaluate Information* What do you think was the greatest contribution of the ancient Egyptians?

Write About History

1. **Write a journal entry** as an archaeologist who has just found the tomb of a pharaoh. What kinds of things do you think you would find in the tomb?

2. **Write a news bulletin** about King Menes unifying Upper and Lower Egypt.

3. **Write a magazine article** about everyday life for a tomb builder and his family.

Apply Skills

Compare Maps at Different Scales

Using the map of Nubia and Egypt on page 93, answer the following questions.

1. On the map scale, if 1 inch = 100 miles, would the map show a smaller or larger area?

2. On the map scale, if 1 inch = 50 miles, would the map show a smaller or larger area?

Internet Activity

To get help with vocabulary, people, and terms, select the dictionary, encyclopedia, or almanac from *Social Studies Library* at **www.sfsocialstudies.com.**

97

CHAPTER 4

Ancient China

Lesson 1

c. 3000 B.C.
Huang River Valley
Farmers plant crops
in terraces.

1

Lesson 2

1250 B.C.
Anyang
Bones and shells are
used in ceremonies.

2

Lesson 3

551 B.C.
Lu Province
The teacher Confucius
is born.

3

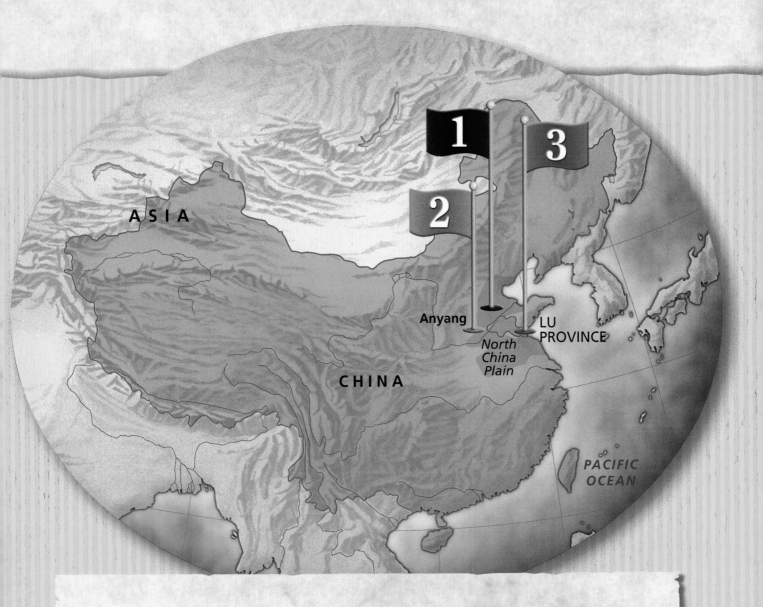

ASIA

1

3

2

Anyang

North China Plain

LU PROVINCE

CHINA

PACIFIC OCEAN

Why We Remember

Nearly 5,000 years ago, farmers settled in the Huang River Valley on the North China Plain. China's civilization began. The ancient dynasties were times of much growth and change. Over time, new technologies—from bronze crafting and silk making to porcelain and paper—were born. Religious practices and new ways of thinking flourished. By 100 B.C., traders were actively transporting goods along a trade route called the Silk Road. They brought Chinese goods—and culture—to the rest of the known world.

Beijing

Huang River

North China Plain

The Geography of China

PREVIEW

Focus on the Main Idea
A tour of China reveals great diversity in the land, water, and ways of life.

PLACES
North China Plain
Beijing
Huang River
Huang River Valley
Guangxi Zhungzu
Tibetan Plateau
Himalayas

VOCABULARY
loess
terrace
levee
double cropping

You Are There

You're flying over Asia as a passenger on an airplane. As the airplane heads east, you look out the window. Below you is a vast land area of green, brown, black, and white. All of this is surrounded by the rich blue of the ocean. It all looks close enough to touch! You make out the rocky surface of tall mountains, topped by silvery snow. Reddish plateaus, or raised areas of flat land, separate the sharp mountain ranges.

Some areas seem dry like sandy deserts. From mountainous areas in the west, long winding rivers begin. Small streams lead to rivers as they flow eastward to the ocean. Lowland areas near the coasts in the south are lush and green. Land surrounded by water juts out into the sea. Islands look like dots in the deep, dark water.

Welcome to China.

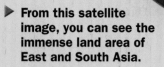

▶ **From this satellite image, you can see the immense land area of East and South Asia.**

Summarize As you read, combine the most important facts about China's geography.

Target Skill

A Land of Differences

You are going to explore a land where civilizations emerged about 3000 B.C. In Lesson 2, you will read about its history. Unlike ancient Egypt and Nubia, which are now several African countries, ancient China developed into modern China. China's borders have changed during its history, as well as its name. You will read more about these changes in Units 5 and 7.

China is the largest country in Asia, and the third largest country in the world. Its landmass is almost as large as the entire continent of Europe! More people live in China than in any other nation. With its geographic size and the way it spreads across Earth, China is a land of contrasts—in landforms, climate, and the ways of life of the people who live there.

REVIEW Did civilization emerge in China before or after it did in Egypt? **Sequence**

The North China Plain

Historians trace human settlement and culture in China to the **North China Plain.** Look at the map below. Today, this plain is heavily populated. It is a center of agriculture and industry. A large portion of China's food comes from this region.

Land is fertile on the plain because it is enriched by **loess,** or a yellowish brown soil that blows in from the desert. Winters are cold and summers are hot on the plain. Soybeans, wheat, and cotton are grown here. From the air you might see miles of crops on broad **terraces,** or platforms of earth that look like stairs.

Beijing (BAY JING), the country's capital, is located on the northern tip of the plain. About 12 million people live there. Beijing has been a center of culture and government since the thirteenth century!

REVIEW Why is the North China Plain a good place to grow crops? **Summarize**

MAP SKILL

China

Legend:
- Huang River Valley
- Guangxi region
- Present-day boundaries

RUSSIA, KAZAKHSTAN, ASIA, KYRGYZSTAN, MONGOLIA, TAJIKISTAN, AFGHANISTAN, PAKISTAN, GOBI, TAKLIMAKAN DESERT, Beijing, ORDOS DESERT, NORTH CHINA PLAIN, NORTH KOREA, SOUTH KOREA, JAPAN, PACIFIC OCEAN, 150°E, PLATEAU OF TIBET, HIMALAYA MOUNTAINS, CHINA, Huang River, Yellow Sea, NEPAL, Chang Jiang, East China Sea, INDIA, BHUTAN, 40°N, 30°N, 20°N, Xi River, MYANMAR (BURMA), VIETNAM, TAIWAN, LAOS, Gulf of Tonkin, South China Sea, PHILIPPINES, 90°E, 110°E, 120°E, 130°E, 140°E

0 250 500 Miles
0 250 500 Kilometers

▶ China is the largest country in Asia and has a diverse landscape.

MAP SKILL Use a Locator Map *What region of Asia does this map show?*

▶ Over many years, higher and higher levees became necessary on the Huang.

China's Sorrow

The Huang He (HWAHNG HUH), or **Huang River,** cuts through the North China Plain. Follow the course of the Huang River in northern China on the map on page 101. From start to finish, you have nearly 3,400 miles to go. About 3000 B.C., early civilizations in China made their homes near the **Huang River Valley.**

Begin in the mountains of western China, south of the Gobi, a desert that stretches across parts of Mongolia and China. Follow the Huang River east through desert lands and then turn sharply to the south.

The great river picks up and carries a large amount of yellow silt, dissolved in the water. The river takes on a distinctive yellow color, which is why it is called the Huang, or "yellow," River in Chinese.

When the Huang flows onto the North China Plain, it changes from a swift river to a sluggish one. Dikes, or **levees,** wall it in within its river-bank. Floods occur when the river rises during heavy summer rains. People built levees in a cen-turies-long effort to control flooding. The Huang has been called "China's Sorrow" because for centuries floods have wiped out crops and left people homeless.

REVIEW What facts are important to know for people who live by the Huang River?

🔁 Summarize

Guangxi Zhungzu

Look to the south and east on your map. You are now traveling to the region called **Guangxi Zhungzu** (gwahng shee DZUHNG JOOH). Warm waters of the Gulf of Tonkin in the South China Sea wash the land's southern shoreline. The country of Vietnam lies to the southwest. Here the warm and moist winds blow in from the sea, and the weather often feels hot and steamy. There is plenty of rain and sun throughout the year.

The Guangxi Zhungzu has one of the best climates for farming in China. The growing season is long in these lowlands. Farmers in this region use a cultivation system called **double cropping,** in which two crops are grown on the same land in the same year. They can double-crop rice and a veg-etable or rice and sugar cane. Access to the sea makes fishing an important industry in this coastal region. People can rely on both farming and fishing.

As you travel the Guangxi Zhungzu you may come across sinkholes, where rainwater collects, and caves. Rugged peaks rise before you. Small streams suddenly flow underground. The region contains much limestone, a sedimentary rock that lies beneath the region's thin soil. Over many years, limestone has eroded into many fantastic shapes.

REVIEW How can you summarize the charac-teristics of the Guangxi Zhungzu that make it different from other areas in China?

🔁 Summarize

▶ The karst hills in Guangxi Zhungzu are landforms made of limestone.

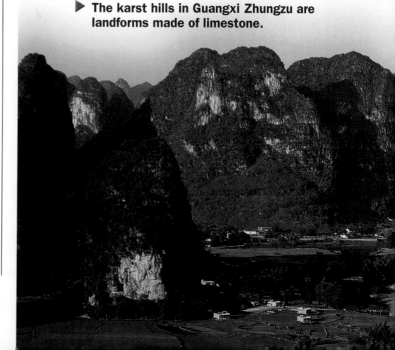

► A group of nomads watches over their yaks, or oxlike mammals, grazing in the landscape of Tibet.

To the Roof of the World

The last stop on your tour of China is a place very different from anywhere else on Earth. The land is very rocky. You see mountain ranges to the north and south. You have reached the **Tibetan Plateau.**

The Tibetan-speaking people who live here are the Zhuang in Chinese. They are the largest minority group in China. They make their living by cultivating barley or herding sheep. Many Zhuang are nomads, who travel and live in tents alongside their livestock. Depending on where they travel, weather and food conditions change.

► A group of nomads watches over their yaks, or oxlike mammals, grazing in the landscape of Tibet.

The Tibetan Plateau is sometimes called the Roof of the World. As you may guess, it is the location of the **Himalayas** (hih muh LAY uhz), a mountain range located on the southern border of the Tibetan Plateau. The tallest peak on Earth is located in the Himalayas. Because the Himalayas stretch so far, they are located in more than one country. In the next chapter, you will read more about them.

REVIEW What challenges do nomadic people face on the Tibetan Plateau? ⟲ Summarize

Summarize the Lesson

- China is a large country and its landforms, climate, and people are diverse.
- People have built levees to control the flooding of the Huang River.
- The Guangxi Zhungzu in the Southeast is a region of farmland.

LESSON 1 REVIEW

Check Facts and Main Ideas

1. ⟲ **Summarize** On a separate piece of paper, fill in the missing fact in the space provided.

```
┌──────────┐   ┌──────────────┐   ┌──────────────┐
│          │   │ The Huang    │   │ The Huang    │
│          │   │ River        │   │ River is     │
│          │   │ irrigates    │   │ controlled   │
│          │   │ land on the  │   │ by using     │
│          │   │ North China  │   │ levees.      │
│          │   │ Plain.       │   │              │
└──────────┘   └──────────────┘   └──────────────┘
      │               │                  │
      └───────────────┼──────────────────┘
                      ▼
        ┌──────────────────────────────┐
        │ The Huang, or "yellow," River│
        │ irrigates land but must be   │
        │ controlled by using levees.  │
        └──────────────────────────────┘
```

2. How has the Huang River affected people living near it?

3. What gives the Huang River its name?

4. How does China's geography show differences within the large country?

5. **Critical Thinking:** *Make Generalizations* Is it possible to make generalizations about the people of China based on where they live? Explain.

Link to ◦◦◦ Writing

Write an Article You are a geographer documenting your recent trip to China. Describe one area of China, using as many details as you can. Consider the land, landforms, and climate.

Chart and Graph Skills

Interpret Climographs

What? A climograph shows a place's average weather over a period of time. It is really two graphs in one—a bar graph shows precipitation, or rain and snowfall, and a line graph shows temperature. When you look at the two graphs together, you can make some conclusions about a place's climate.

A year of weather in Beijing and Hong Kong is graphed in the climographs below. Beijing is in a temperate, or moderate, climate zone. People who live here are ready for four distinct, or different, seasons in a year. The climate in Hong Kong is milder, with a much larger temperature range.

▶ **You can see that both precipitation and temperatures increase in the summer and decrease in the winter in Beijing and Hong Kong.**

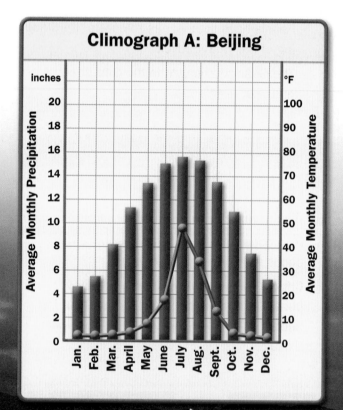

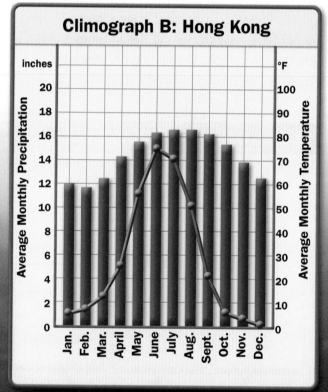

Why? You learned about differences in the land and ways of life in the large country of China. Climate is an important factor in how people live and work. In any place on Earth, climate affects the food people eat and how they grow it. A region's climate also affects its economy. When a quick, "at-a-glance" picture of a place's climate is available, it tells us a lot about what life could be like in that place. A climograph is the tool that provides that picture.

You can plot two graphs for the same year—one for temperature and one for precipitation—on one climograph. The blue bar graphs show the average monthly temperature for the year. The green line graphs show the average monthly precipitation for the same year. Compare the two graphs on each climograph to get a general idea of what the weather is like in any month.

How? What's the easiest way to read a climograph? Start by looking at the three scales that organize its information.

The first one, the horizontal axis, lists the months from January through December from left to right. The vertical axis on the right is a scale for average monthly temperatures, in Fahrenheit, starting at the top with higher temperatures and moving down to lower ones. Parallel to the temperature scale, a scale for precipitation in inches appears on the left side of the graph, again going from high to low amounts, top to bottom.

The bar and line graphs form when the data is plotted on the climograph. You can make comparisons and see overall patterns in a place's weather over a year.

On pages 104–105 there are three climographs: Hong Kong, an island city; Beijing on the North China Plain; and Urumchi in the northwest. Compare the climates in all three locations. What differences and similarities do you notice?

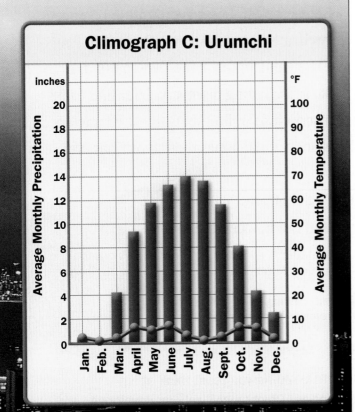

Climograph C: Urumchi

Think and Apply

1 Which two cities of these three in China have climates that are most alike? Which two have climates that are most different?

2 Which city receives the most rainfall during a typical year, and which receives the least?

3 With a group, discuss what conclusions you can make about the climate in Beijing, Hong Kong, and Urumchi. Summarize similarities and differences in your own chart.

c. 1760–1500 B.C.
Shang dynasty

221 B.C.
Shi Huangdi becomes
emperor of China.

2000–1700 B.C.
Xia legendary period

China's Past

PREVIEW

Focus on the Main Idea
China's history, organized by dynasties, includes many inventions and ideas.

PLACES
Anyang

PEOPLE
Shi Huangdi
Gaozu
Wu Di
Sima Qian
Ban Zhao

VOCABULARY
pictograph
oracle bone
province
ancestor
civil service
middleman

TERMS
Shang dynasty
Bronze Age
Zhou dynasty
Qin dynasty
Great Wall
Han dynasty
Silk Road

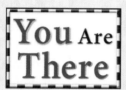

You Are There

One day in 1899 in Beijing, China, you go with your father to an apothecary, or pharmacy, to buy medicine for his friend, Wang. His friend has malaria, later known to be a disease spread by mosquitoes. The cure for malaria is believed to come from tortoise, or land turtle, shells. You and your father watch the shopkeeper begin to grind the shell into a fine powder. Suddenly, you notice something that looks like writing on the larger piece. Curiosity strikes!

When Wang feels better, he and your father go on a mission. They search apothecaries all over Beijing, buying every tortoise shell and animal bone they can find. In the end, they make a fascinating discovery. They find 1,058 old, strange inscriptions written in Chinese characters on tortoise shells and animal bones that no one has ever seen before.

You're thrilled that you were with your father, Lui E, when the first discovery was made.

▶ **About 1250 B.C., a king used this animal bone in a ceremony to make predictions.**

Summarize As you read, think about how ancient Chinese civilizations developed.

Picturing Chinese History

The rich picture of China's past began about 4,000 years ago. In the nineteenth century, people living in the town of Anyang found what they called dragon bones but were actually tortoise shells and animal bones with writing on them. These shells and bones were artifacts from earlier Chinese civilizations. In this lesson, you will read more about how these shells and bones were used.

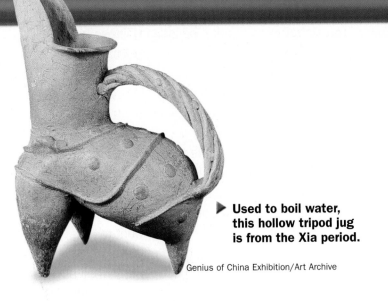

▶ **Used to boil water, this hollow tripod jug is from the Xia period.**

Genius of China Exhibition/Art Archive

Early people in China made their homes in the Huang River Valley. Artifacts of stone tools and pottery tell us they were there, but a full understanding of their lives remains a mystery.

No other civilization is believed to have existed as long as China's has. However, China's culture is not the world's oldest. Civilizations in Mesopotamia, Egypt, and Greece are thought to have begun earlier. What is special about Chinese culture is that it is continuous, or unbroken, from its earliest recorded history to today. Many of the world's oldest civilizations have been greatly changed through time, even destroyed. But in China, writing, art and artifacts, and archaeological remains reveal a culture that remained mostly unified over centuries.

Writing may be a key part of the evidence. The Chinese language is written in pictographs, or pictures that represent words. Many charac-

ters in the Chinese language have been written in similar ways for long periods of time. Scholars who recorded history could read and interpret other writers' works written thousands of years before.

REVIEW What evidence do archaeologists have about China's history? 🔄 Summarize

Ancient Voices

According to Chinese legend, Pangu was the creator of the universe. Later, stories of "superheroes" followed. Legend says that these superheroes invented useful things or taught people how to survive by finding food, clothing, and shelter. One hero named Yu worked for thirteen years to conquer flooding on the Huang River. These legends enriched ancient Chinese life. The stories also reveal how valuable the domestication of animals, agriculture, and inventions were to people of that time.

These stories date to a time known as the Xia (SHEE ah) legendary period, about 2000–1700 B.C. The tales of Xia formed a bridge between prehistory and the time when Chinese history began to be formally recorded.

REVIEW What was the Xia period and how do we know about it? 🔄 Summarize

▶ **These are Chinese characters for sun, moon, star, and water as they are written today.**

The Shang Dynasty

The Xia refers to the first period in Chinese history. However, the first dynasty was the **Shang dynasty.** The Shang dynasty began between 1760 and 1500 B.C. Before the discovery of the tortoise shells in 1899, the Shang people were considered part of another legendary period.

Farming was the way of life for most people in the Huang River Valley at this time. People grew grains such as millet and rice and raised animals. They made cloth from silk and flax, a type of fiber. Warriors, riding horse-drawn chariots, went to war.

During the Shang dynasty, bronze was used for many kinds of tools, cups, and weapons, as well as trade goods. Bronze was made by melting together copper and a small amount of tin. The **Bronze Age** was the period during which tools and weapons were made of bronze.

Remember the man who found writing on the tortoise shell in the beginning of this lesson? People living around Anyang began digging up bones and shells to sell them to merchants in Beijing.

Anyang was the capital of a Shang settlement thousands of years ago. It turned out that the shells and bones were ancient **oracle bones** commonly used during the Shang dynasty to predict the future.

Rituals were important to the Shang people. People wrote questions on turtle and sometimes oxen or deer bones. They asked questions such as what crops to plant or when to travel or hunt. They then heated the shells or bones. Finally, they examined them for any cracks. Cracks helped the Shang people make predictions about future events. After the event that was predicted happened, the date was written down on the shell or bone.

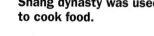

▶ **This bronze vessel from the Shang dynasty was used to cook food.**

Writing on the animal shells and bones led Chinese archaeologists to another discovery. The Shang people were the first people in China to make written records. Besides shells and bones, writing has been found on bronze and stone.

REVIEW How do we know about the Shang dynasty? **Main Idea and Details**

The Longest Dynasty

The Zhou (JOH) people came from west of the Huang's great river bend. In 1027 B.C., a Zhou leader's army conquered the armies of the last Shang ruler, and the **Zhou dynasty** began. Look at the map on page 109 to see the territory changes under the Shang and Zhou dynasties.

The Zhou dynasty was the longest of the Chinese dynasties, lasting more than 800 years. It can be separated into two periods, each with distinct characteristics. The earlier period was called Western Zhou because the government's capital city was in Hao in western China.

In Western Zhou, most people were farmers who grew wheat, rice, beans, and fruit. Some people were slaves who also worked on the land. Society was organized so farmers worked small areas of land and contributed food and valuables to the king. Women most often harvested the crops.

Silk was an important product of the Zhou economy. Women were in charge of producing silk. Silk is made from the cocoons of silkworms, a kind of caterpillar. Women cultivated mulberry trees to feed the silkworms. They boiled the cocoons to get the silk fibers, and then wove cloth from these fibers.

REVIEW What was the role of women in Zhou society? **Main Idea and Details**

▶ **This scroll painting from about the eleventh century B.C. shows women preparing newly woven silk.**

Eastern Zhou Dynasty

The second part of the Zhou dynasty began around 770 B.C. and lasted until 221 B.C. Because its capital city was in Luoyang in the east, it is known as Eastern Zhou. This period of time often is referred to as a "golden age" in China.

A new system of money encouraged trade, and the economy thrived. The government started projects that included flood control, irrigation, and canal building. People built huge walls around some towns along the northern border to keep out nomadic, or wandering, peoples. They began to use iron to make farm tools and weapons.

During this time, the king's power was weakened by warfare between rival states. Traditions were being challenged and new ideas emerged. More people were becoming scholars, teachers, and government officials. This brought new philosophies, or ways of thinking. Some teachings of this period affected life in China for thousands of years to come. You will read more about these important teachers and thinkers in the next lesson.

REVIEW What are some differences and similarities between life in the earlier and later periods of the Zhou dynasty? **Compare and Contrast**

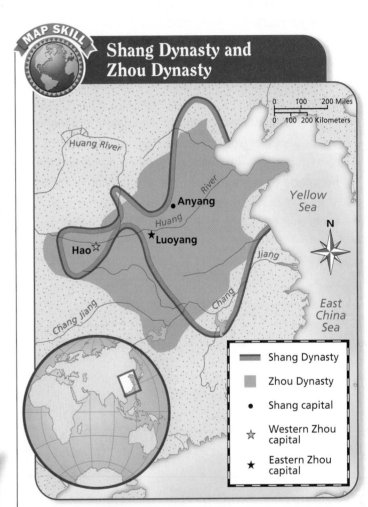

MAP SKILL

Shang Dynasty and Zhou Dynasty

Huang River

Anyang

Huang River

Luoyang

Hao ☆

Chang Jiang

Jiang

Chang

Yellow Sea

N

East China Sea

	Shang Dynasty
	Zhou Dynasty
●	Shang capital
☆	Western Zhou capital
★	Eastern Zhou capital

▶ **How did Chinese territory change from the Shang to the Zhou dynasty?**

MAP SKILL Region *What part of China does this map show?*

▶ **This piece of spade money was used during the Eastern Zhou dynasty. Spade money was often made in the shape of tools.**

109

The First Emperor

Toward the last years of the Zhou dynasty, many states were fighting for control of the government. In 221 B.C., the king of the strongest state, Qin (CHIN), became **Shi Huangdi** (SHEE hwang dee), or "first emperor" under the **Qin dynasty.** (Read more about Shi Huangdi in the biography on page 113.) No leader had been called an emperor since about 1700 B.C., the end of the days of the legends. The title signified a very powerful ruler. Qin was divided into 36 **provinces,** or political divisions. Shi Huangdi made the government more centralized by forming new states to bring all areas under his rule. Systems of money and weights and measures were standardized, which probably helped trade between regions.

Shi Huangdi started one of the biggest engineering projects in world history. Beginning under his rule, hundreds of thousands of laborers worked for hundreds of years to build the **Great Wall** of China. This was done by connecting existing defensive walls that had been built earlier. The Great Wall was built to protect the empire from northern invaders. It was not finished for centuries. Rulers of later dynasties added to the Great Wall and rebuilt parts of it. Follow the route and time line of the Great Wall on the map below.

Shi Huangdi punished anyone who criticized him. He wanted the government to control what people talked about and studied. People felt oppressed, or persecuted, by this form of government. They wanted freedom, and revolts broke out. The Qin dynasty lasted only about 20 years, ending in about 206 B.C., shortly after the emperor died.

► **Bronze mirrors were made in China as early as 500 B.C. This bronze mirror is from the Qin dynasty.**

Asian Art &

REVIEW What do you think may happen in a society where a ruler wants to control what people do and think? **Draw Conclusions**

► **The Great Wall crosses mountains and rough terrain. It stretches for more than 4,300 miles. A new section of the Great Wall was discovered in northwest China in 2001.**

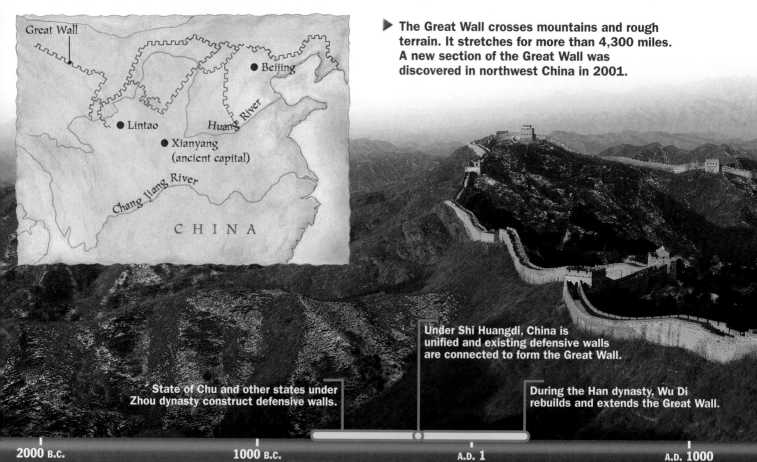

Great Wall

Beijing

Lintao

Huang River

Xianyang
(ancient capital)

Chang Jiang River

CHINA

Under Shi Huangdi, China is unified and existing defensive walls are connected to form the Great Wall.

State of Chu and other states under Zhou dynasty construct defensive walls.

During the Han dynasty, Wu Di rebuilds and extends the Great Wall.

2000 B.C.   1000 B.C.   A.D. 1   A.D. 1000

Han Dynasty

The **Han dynasty** began in 206 B.C. and lasted until A.D. 220. The Han dynasty eventually stretched as far south as what are today the countries of Vietnam and Cambodia.

The first Han ruler was a peasant who called himself Han **Gaozu** (GOW ZOO), meaning "High Ancestor." An **ancestor** is a relative who lived longer ago than a grandparent. He took the throne after joining a revolt against Shi Huangdi.

Some changes were made under Gaozu. He lifted the ban on books imposed by Shi Huangdi. More improvements came under emperor **Wu Di** (WOO DEE), who ruled about 141–87 B.C. Under his reign, China made many changes and advancements. Wu Di divided lands owned by princes and lords. He took away power from those people who challenged him. To benefit the government, he taxed imported and exported trade goods. To improve transportation, Wu Di built new roads.

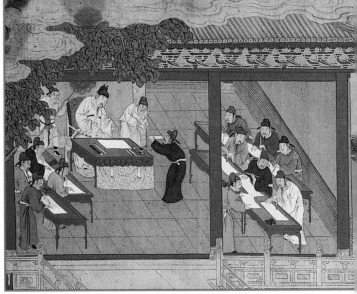

▶ Only a few people passed the civil service exams. Most questions were based on Chinese thought, and memorization of Chinese classics was required.

Wu Di valued the contributions of scholars and teachers. A historian named **Sima Qian** (soo muhn CHIH ehn) wrote the first complete history book on China. The book recorded China's history for about 3000 years. Sima Qian challenged the way history was written from then on. He believed there was more to history than only what kings thought should be written. **Ban Zhao** (ban JOW) continued the work of Sima Qian. Her writing supported education for women. She wrote:

> *"Only to teach men and not to teach women—is that not ignoring the essential relation between them?"*

Another contribution to China under Wu Di was **civil service,** the practice of using skills and talents to work in the government. It was difficult to find people who were capable and committed. Many government officials were not trained for their positions. For the first time, officials had to take civil service exams to work for the government. In the past, people became officials because their families were important. Peasants and anyone else who passed the exams qualified for a government job.

REVIEW What were Wu Di's contributions to Han society? 🔄 Summarize

Ming dynasty strengthens and adds onto the Great Wall for about 200 years.

Under Mao Zedong, sections of the Great Wall are torn down.

Under Deng Xiaoping, groups begin to restore the Great Wall.

2000

Inventions

Many inventions made during the Han dynasty contributed to Chinese culture and civilization. The Chinese practiced new ways of trading and transporting goods. For example, they used **middlemen,** or people who go between buyers and sellers. Important inventions included porcelain and two things you are using right now—paper and ink! Before this time, people wrote on wooden or bamboo slips with a mixture of dust and water. Books could now be made available to more people.

In the second century B.C., China had only one way to connect with the rest of the world on land—the **Silk Road.** This road was actually more than just one route that went

▶ Trade goods such as this decorated bowl from the Han dynasty were carried on the Silk Road.

through northern China and across central Asia to the lands of the Roman Empire. The Chinese exported silk and porcelain to these lands and imported glass, gold, and horses. Middlemen traveled along this route to carry on trade between buyers and sellers. You will learn more about the Silk Road in Unit 5.

The Han dynasty marked a time of great advancements in China. Chinese culture became unified across a vast land.

REVIEW What are some important inventions that were made during the Han dynasty?
Main Idea and Details

Summarize the Lesson

- **2000–1700 B.C.** Xia legendary period

- **221 B.C.** Shi Huangdi became China's first emperor.

- **141–87 B.C.** Wu Di was emperor of the Han dynasty during which many great advancements were made.

LESSON 2 REVIEW

Check Facts and Main Ideas

1. ↻ **Summarize** On a separate piece of paper, fill in the blank spaces with two details from the summary below.

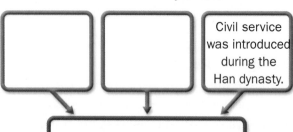

> [blank] →
>
> [blank] →
>
> Civil service was introduced during the Han dynasty. →
>
> The Han dynasty was a period of great change and advancement.

2. Name some of the things that people may have done in their daily lives during the Zhou dynasty.

3. How did Chinese culture become more unified during the Han dynasty?

4. What inventions were made in China's early history?

5. **Critical Thinking:** *Make Inferences* Why do you think that Shi Huangdi wanted to connect the defensive walls into what became the Great Wall of China?

Link to ⌾⌾ Writing

Write an Article Put yourself in the position of a scholar and teacher during the Han dynasty. Write about what you are noticing in your village. Explain why you think that changes are taking place.

Qin Shi Huangdi
259 B.C.–210 B.C.

Qin Shi Huangdi (CHIN SHEE hwang dee) became the ruler of the kingdom of Qin in China in 238 B.C. He began expanding his power immediately. By 221 B.C. he had conquered all of China. As emperor, he proclaimed that his dynasty would rule for 10,000 generations.

Shi Huangdi was a great builder. He ordered the building of three highways to reach all parts of his empire. He used these roads to personally oversee the empire. In 214 B.C. work began on the Great Wall.

The emperor had many achievements, but he was a harsh and strict ruler. For example, his building projects needed the forced labor of hundreds of thousands of his people. Many of them died while working. He also was not open to criticism. He ordered that all books except those about medicine, farming, and his own rule be burned. When some scholars objected to this, legend says that Shi Huangdi had many of them buried alive.

After his death, Shi Huangdi was buried in an elaborate tomb carved into the side of a mountain. Guarding his body was an "army" of more than 6,000 life-sized warrior statues. In the walls were arrows ready to be released if anyone tried to enter the tomb.

British Museum

BIOFACT

No two warrior statues found in the emperor's tomb are alike. This one kneels before the emperor.

Learn from Biographies

Rebellions began soon after Shi Huangdi's death and his empire fell about four years later. What aspects of the emperor's style of rule may have been responsible for the fall of his empire?

For more information, go online to *Meet the People* at **www.sfsocialstudies.com.**

500 B.C.   400 B.C.

551 B.C.
Confucius is born
in Lu Province.

about 350 B.C.
Mencius spreads
Confucianism.

Legacy of Thought

PREVIEW

Focus on the Main Idea
Confucianism is a way of thought that became a way of life in China.

PLACES
Lu Province

PEOPLE
Confucius
Mencius
Laozi

VOCABULARY
nobility

TERMS
Book of
  Documents
Analects
Confucianism
Mandate of Heaven
Daoism

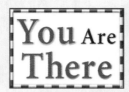

▶ In China robes made of silk cloth were worn by the wealthy.

You Are There

You follow your tour guide through a grove of cypress [evergreen] trees into a passageway. Walls surround you, as do ancient shrines and monuments.

"We are now entering the Great Temple," the tour guide says.

You walk into an enormous temple. Several statues fill the room. Your eyes move to the largest one. It towers above you. Nine brilliantly colored silk robes cover the statue. On the garments are beautifully embroidered symbols. You identify images of the sun, moon, mountains, dragons, pheasants, water lilies, and flames of fire.

"The sun, moon, and mountains were the signs of kings," the tour guide remarks. Surely this man was someone great, you think to yourself. He might have even been an emperor. As you listen to the tour guide, you learn that this man was a teacher, rather than a king.

Summarize As you read, combine the most important facts about Confucianism.

Master Kung

At the Great Temple, you learn more about who this teacher was. You also learn about how his teachings and ideas influenced Chinese culture.

In China, **Confucius** (kuhn FYOO shuhs) is known as Kung Fuzi (KOONG FOO zuh), or Master Kung. He was born in 551 B.C. in the state, **Lu Province.** Because his family was of some **nobility,** or a high-ranking social class, Confucius was able to be educated as a scholar. He gradually gathered around him a group of fellow scholars as disciples, or followers. Many scholars like Confucius traveled during that time. With his disciples, Confucius set off one day in search of a ruler who would welcome him as an advisor.

Confucius lived in the later years of the Zhou dynasty, a time of much conflict. Traditional society had broken down. Confucius found signs of this chaos on his travels. Many people were greedy, cruel, and insensitive toward the needs of others. Confucius was a teacher of morals, or deciding what is right and wrong, and a disciplined thinker. He valued order, harmony, and ways of making the world right.

▶ Built in 1724, the Great Temple of Confucius is located in Qufu, Shandong Province, China.

▶ Confucius was not an emperor or a king, but his ideas greatly influenced Chinese culture and civilization.

Confucius found a place in the court of a king and stayed for several years. His reputation as a great teacher grew, and many people went to him for advice. When he was older, Confucius returned to his home state of Lu, where he did much writing. He interpreted and revived older Zhou texts as well, such as the *Book of Documents.* It is said that Master Kung had some 3,000 followers by the time of his death in 479 B.C.

REVIEW What are some of the morals that Confucius valued? ↻ **Summarize**

The Master's Work

The **Analects** is a collection of sayings by Confucius that were written down by his students. It is the main printed work of Confucius. In it he gives advice to people who want to do the right thing. Confucius tried to give examples that were relevant to the daily lives of people. Respect for all people is probably his first principle:

> *"When you go out, treat everyone as if you were welcoming a great guest. Do not do unto others what you would not have them do unto you."*

These virtues—a sense of humanity, respect for the family, and humility, or modesty—are at the core of **Confucianism.** This way of thinking and living continued to develop centuries after Confucius died.

Confucianism teaches the middle way, which means that people should make balanced decisions. For example, a person should think twice before fighting. The middle way between being a coward and being a reckless person is bravery.

▶ **These figures are from a cave at Luoyang in Henan Province. Confucius strongly approved of the growing practice of placing statues, such as those pictured below, in tombs.**

▶ **Some Chinese thinkers tried to explain the universe in terms of five elements—water, fire, wood, metal, and earth.**

Confucianism teaches that each person should accept his or her role in society: ruler, subject, teacher, student, noble, or peasant. Confucius taught the central value of parents' love for their children. He also taught that children must obey, respect, and honor their parents and teachers. Confucius found greater peacefulness and social order in the earlier years of the Zhou dynasty. He wanted to revive what he thought was good and get rid of what was bad.

In Confucianism, a ruler was seen as a great authority, the "son of heaven." Rulers should have the **Mandate of Heaven,** or the divine right to govern for the good of all people. A good ruler brought times of prosperity and peace. But a harsh or unwise ruler could be pushed off the throne by the people, losing the Mandate of Heaven. Confucius also thought that the people needed to respect their ruler. He warned kings:

> *"Lead the people by means of government policies and regulate them through punishments, and they . . . have no sense of shame. Lead them by means of virtue . . . and they will have a sense of shame and moreover have standards."*

REVIEW Name three important Confucian principles. **Main Idea and Details**

116

Beyond Confucianism

Confucius was not the only scholar who had influence on China during this time. This period was called the "hundred schools of thought."

One of its thinkers was a follower of Confucius. His name was **Mencius** (MEHN shee uhs). Mencius declared that people were good by nature. His work supported the Confucian belief of respect for humanity and strong, honest rulers. By about 350 B.C., Mencius began to spread Confucianism.

Daoism (DOW ih zuhm) is the belief in finding the "way," or the dao, of the universe. Daoism had almost as much influence on Chinese culture as did Confucianism. However, it did not focus on order like Confucianism did. **Laozi** (LAOW dzuh) was the first great teacher of Daoism and taught before Confucius. He and other Daoists believed that people should live in harmony with nature, not apart from it.

Réunion des Musées Nationaux/Art Resource

▶ The yin and yang show that all forces have a complementary force: good and evil, sun and moon, heaven and earth.

REVIEW What are some similarities among Confucianism and other ways of thinking in China?
Compare and Contrast

Summarize the Lesson

- **551–479 B.C.** Confucius was a teacher who lived at the end of the Zhou dynasty in a time of conflict.

- **about 350 B.C.** Mencius began to spread Confucianism.

LESSON 3   REVIEW

Check Facts and Main Ideas

1. ↻ **Summarize** On a separate piece of paper, fill in the missing detail in the blank below.

| The teachings of Confucius are important to understanding China's history. | | The "hundred schools of thought" influenced Chinese culture. |

↓

Confucianism, Daoism, and the "hundred schools of thought" influenced Chinese culture and history.

2. Briefly explain three Confucian principles.

3. What are the *Analects*?

4. Besides Confucianism, what other way of thinking has had much influence in China?

5. **Critical Thinking: *Make Generalizations*** How have Confucianism and Daoism influenced Chinese culture?

Link to ⚭ Writing

Write an Article Write an article explaining how a follower of Confucius might answer this question: "Should we honor our rulers?"

2000 B.C.

about 2000–1700 B.C.
Xia lengendary period

about 1760–1500 B.C.
Shang dynasty

Chapter Summary

 Target Skill

Summarize

On a separate piece of paper, write in the missing detail in the middle box.

| Advancements made by China's dynasties influenced its civilization. | | Confucianism has been a major influence in Chinese civilization. |

Chinese civilization was influenced by its dynasties, geography, and Confucianism.

Vocabulary

Match each word with the correct definition or description.

1 loess (p. 101)

2 double cropping (p. 102)

3 terrace (p. 101)

4 levee (p. 102)

5 province (p. 110)

6 pictograph (p. 107)

a. rich, loose soil

b. political division

c. dike that holds back river

d. two crops on same land in one season

e. stepped farmland

f. symbol or picture that represents words

People and Terms

Write a sentence explaining why each of the following people or terms is important in the study of China's history. You may use two or more in a single sentence.

1 Shang dynasty (p. 108)

2 Zhou dynasty (p. 108)

3 Book of Documents (p. 115)

4 Han dynasty (p. 111)

5 Wu Di (p. 111)

6 Sima Qian (p. 111)

7 Confucius (p. 115)

8 Mencius (p. 117)

9 Great Wall (p. 110)

10 Shi Huangdi (p. 110)

1500 B.C.   1000 B.C.   500 B.C.   A.D. 1

1027–221 B.C.
Zhou dynasties

551 B.C. Confucius was born.

c. 350 B.C.
Mencius began to spread Confucianism.

221–206 B.C.
Qin dynasty

Facts and Main Ideas

1. Describe the North China Plain and its importance to China.

2. Why is writing important to the way Chinese history is told?

3. How is Confucianism different from Daoism?

4. **Time Line** Which of the early dynasties is China's longest and which is the shortest?

5. **Main Idea** How does geography contribute to differences in how people in China live and work?

6. **Main Idea** How did life change for people from 2000 B.C. to 221 B.C.?

7. **Main Idea** What are three aspects of Confucianism that have influenced China?

8. **Critical Thinking:** *Recognize Point of View* What do you think Chinese history would be like if it were not told from the written point of view of rulers and scholars?

Apply Skills

Interpret Climographs
Answer the following questions using the climographs on pages 104–105.

1. Compare spring and fall in Hong Kong and Urumchi.

2. During which month does the most precipitation fall in all three cities?

3. What is summer like in Beijing compared with summer in Urumchi?

4. Collect data on average monthly temperatures and precipitation in your city. Plot that information on a climograph. Compare your climograph with those on pp. 104–105.

Internet Activity

To get help with vocabulary, people, and terms, select the dictionary, encyclopedia, or almanac from *Social Studies Library* at **www.sfsocialstudies.com**.

Write About History

1. **Write a journal entry** that would tell more of China's history from different points of view. What would you say about people's lives and jobs in each of the dynasties? You may focus on a variety of occupations, such as scholars, farmers, silk makers, metal workers, or traders.

2. **Write a news bulletin** dated 218 B.C. announcing some of the things local townspeople and farmers have observed Shi Huangdi's army doing.

3. **Write a magazine article** about some of the ways of thinking that came into focus during the "hundred schools of thought."

CHAPTER 5

Ancient India and Persia

Lesson 1

Indus River Valley
People live and work in farming villages.

1

Lesson 2

**2500 B.C.
Mohenjo-Daro**
Mohenjo-Daro was a well-developed city in the Indus River Valley.

2

Lesson 3

Ganges River
People bathe in the Ganges River to honor the river goddess.

3

Lesson 4

Bodh Gaya
Buddhism takes root in India and spreads throughout the world.

4

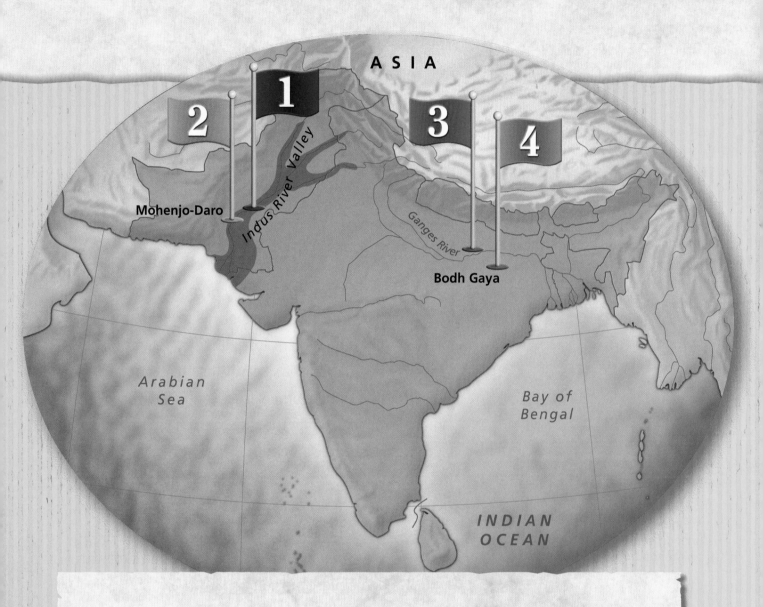

ASIA

2   1   3   4

Mohenjo-Daro

Indus River Valley

Ganges River

Bodh Gaya

Arabian
Sea

Bay of
Bengal

INDIAN
OCEAN

Why We Remember

South Asia is a land of rising and falling rivers flowing through lush plains.
The early people of the Indus River Valley, as well as the Aryans and the
Persians, all contributed crafts, trade, buildings, language, arts, and
science to South Asian peoples. Major religions—Hinduism and
Buddhism—have grown to shape thoughts and lives in South Asia and
around the world. South Asian culture is diverse, complex, and changing
still today.

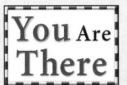

Indus River Valley • Harappa

Geography of South Asia

PREVIEW

Focus on the Main Idea
South Asia is home to different peoples making homes across magnificent landscapes, from mountains to islands.

PLACES
Mount Everest
Indo-Ganges Plain
Indus River Valley
Harappa
Deccan Plateau
Western Ghats
Eastern Ghats

VOCABULARY
subcontinent
monsoon season
subsistence farming

▶ During the monsoon, or rainy, season, temperatures can drop from 110°F to near 70°F when the rain begins.

You Are There

Scorched—that's how you've felt since March. At dawn when you rise there are only a few cool moments. Fields are dry and brown. Roads to school and town are rivers of dust. Now, one afternoon in June, it is all going to change. A friend tells you what she's heard. Together you walk across the street where others from your village have gathered. You look out at the sky, expecting something to happen. Suddenly the air chills, the sky turns gray. The first raindrop falls. You lift your head up and smile. Your friend throws back her head and laughs. Raindrops dance on your face. You and your friend link arms and begin to twirl around in circles. You dance and sing with other children in your village. Welcome to South Asia.

Summarize As you read, summarize the main facts about South Asian geography.

Target Skill

A Diamond Breaks Away

South Asia seems to stand alone as a solitary diamond-shaped land. Look at the map on page 124. From the continent of Asia, it extends far into the Indian Ocean. South Asia is also home to the world's tallest mountains, the Himalayas.

Because this region is so large and separated by water from other land areas, it is called a **subcontinent.** Much of this subcontinent may have formed in a spectacular way about 50 million years ago.

According to a theory called plate tectonics, Earth's surface is made of several slowly moving plates. The movement of plates may cause changes such as the development of mountain ranges, basins, and bodies of water. The subcontinent may have once been part of a huge landmass that included the continents of South America, Africa, Australia, and Antarctica. Its plate may have broken off and moved very slowly northward until it collided with, or pushed into, a larger plate. This bigger plate may have contained the rest of the European and Asian landmass.

The smaller plate pushing up under the larger plate formed the Himalayas. Even today, the Himalayas are still rising! **Mount Everest,** its highest peak, was remeasured in the late 1990s. It reaches 29,035 feet into the sky. Tibetans call Mount Everest "Goddess Mother of the World."

Think of the Earth's plates as constantly in motion. It is almost as if the land is a passenger on them. In some areas on Earth, moving plates cause earthquakes. South Asia is a location that is likely to have earthquakes. In 2001, earthquakes caused a lot of damage and many deaths in several cities in South Asia.

▶ **The government of India discovered that Mount Everest was the highest point on Earth in 1852.**

REVIEW How did the South Asian subcontinent form? ↻ **Summarize**

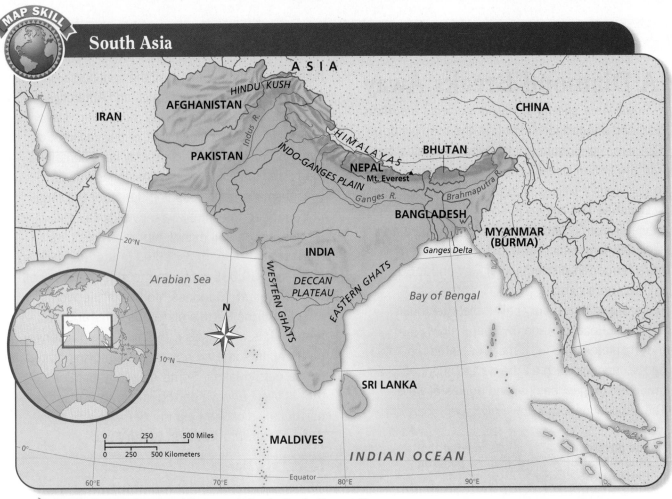

▶ **South Asia is bordered by mountain chains in the north.**

MAP SKILL Understand Borders *What countries border India?*

Snow to Monsoon

Eight countries are part of South Asia: India, Pakistan, Nepal, Bhutan, Afghanistan, Bangladesh, Sri Lanka, and the Maldives Islands or Maldives. These countries have many different landforms. Look at the map above. The Hindu Kush mountain range in the northwest and the snowcapped Himalayas in the northeast separate South Asia from the rest of the continent. Both mountain chains formed at about the same time.

▶ **Lush green rolling hillsides are common landforms near the mountainous regions of South Asia.**

Pakistan lies in the northwestern region of South Asia. It is home to the world's second tallest mountain, the K2. A huge desert stretches across part of Pakistan and northwestern India. To the east and north are mountainous Nepal and Bhutan. To the south, a large river delta cradles Bangladesh. Extending southward is India, which makes up about three-fourths of the subcontinent. South of the Himalayas, India's land flattens into a lush green plain. In the middle and toward the tip of India, the land rises into a wide, dry plateau. Surrounding the subcontinent is the Indian Ocean. The island nations of Sri Lanka and the Maldives are located here.

▶ **Women do much of the harvesting in South Asia. In Nepal, women are shown gathering grain.**

Despite the differences in landforms, much of South Asia has a similar climate. There are three seasons. Temperatures are mild to cool from October through February. They shift to very hot from March through May. Then comes the **monsoon season,** or the rainy season, which lasts from June through September.

Nearly all of the yearly precipitation, or rain and snowfall, falls during the monsoon season. After the monsoon season, the land is refreshed and full of life again. The monsoon season is very important to farmers, who depend on the rains for crops. The region's economy is closely tied to the monsoon.

REVIEW Why do you think the monsoon is important to people in South Asia?
Draw Conclusions

▶ **In Bangladesh, a village may be built on stilts to protect against regular flooding.**

Great Rivers, Great Plain

Three great rivers flow through the subcontinent—the Indus, the Ganges (GAN jeez), and the Brahmaputra (bruh muh POO truh). From sources in the Himalayas, they fan out to the east and west through the wide, flat plain called the Indo-Gangetic Plain or the **Indo– Ganges Plain.** The rivers carry water and silt into farmlands to irrigate and enrich the fields. Monsoon season rains cause flooding, which spreads out more silt. This keeps the soil rich for the next year. Crops grown on the plain include barley, wheat, rice, peas, beans, and other vegetables.

Many families grow food just for themselves. Sometimes, they trade food with small groups of people in their villages. This process is called **subsistence farming,** because people subsist, or live on, the food they grow. They do not sell much of their crops.

India and Pakistan are very heavily populated countries. Almost one billion people live in India, which is about three times smaller in land area than the United States. Much of the population lives in crowded farming villages on the Indo-Ganges Plain. The **Indus River Valley** lies on the plain in Pakistan. It is the site of one of the world's oldest civilizations.

REVIEW Why is the Indo-Ganges Plain a good place for farming?
Summarize

Then and Now

Harappa and Sahiwal, Pakistan: Land of Cotton

Sahiwal (suh EE wul) is a town of about 150,000 people. It is in a densely populated area of east-central Pakistan. The town is a center of the cotton industry, where workers use cotton to weave carpets. Cotton has been an important product here since ancient times. Sahiwal is practically on top of **Harappa** (huh RA puh), one of the earliest sites of civilization in South Asia. The Harappan culture dates from 3500 B.C. Workers in Harappa were probably the first people to cultivate, or grow, cotton for cloth.

▶ In Pakistan, a man weaves a rug out of wool and cotton. Cotton has been cultivated in this area for thousands of years.

Plateau, Coast, and Islands

South of the Indo-Ganges Plain, the land begins to rise. At this point, the land narrows toward the point of a "diamond." This region is called the **Deccan Plateau.** It lies between the Arabian Sea and Bay of Bengal. The climate is dry in this area, and more irrigation for farming is needed. However, the plateau has rich volcanic soil. In the northwestern part, the plateau is made up of lava flows that produce thick black soil. Cotton crops thrive in the region. Farms also produce peanuts.

The Deccan Plateau is framed on the west and east by rugged mountains, the **Western Ghats,** and rolling mountains, the **Eastern Ghats.** Each of these mountain chains extends about 1,000 miles in length. Locate them on the map on page 124. Forests in the hills and mountain areas are home to wildlife, including elephants, monkeys, and tigers.

▶ Fishing is a major industry in southern India. These fishermen pull in their nets at the end of the day.

126

Most people work as farmers in India. People fish and farm along southern India's heavily populated coasts too. The island nations of Sri Lanka and the Maldives Islands export tea, coconuts, fish, and rubber. Manufacturing is another important industry in the coastal areas and Indian Ocean islands. Many people work in the clothing and textile industries here too.

However, Bangladesh, the most densely populated country in the region, has the most garment factories.

REVIEW Why is irrigation necessary for farming on the Deccan Plateau? *Main Idea and Details*

Summarize the Lesson

- South Asia is a subcontinent that may have been formed by a spectacular land collision 50 million years ago.

- The Indo-Gangetic, or Indo-Ganges, Plain is a heavily populated region of rich land worked by subsistence farmers.

- The Deccan Plateau has a dry climate and some rich farmland. People fish, farm, and manufacture textiles in the coastal areas and Indian Ocean islands.

▶ This tailor, or person who makes or alters clothing, works on a cotton shirt in Sri Lanka.

LESSON 1 REVIEW

Check Facts and Main Ideas

1. ⟳ **Summarize** On a separate piece of paper, fill in the missing detail below.

| Mount Everest rises in South Asia. | The Indo-Ganges Plain provides good farmland in South Asia. | |

↓

South Asia has various physical features and landforms.

2. Why is South Asia called a subcontinent?

3. How do many people farm on the Indo-Ganges Plain?

4. What does the geography of South Asia reveal about the many differences within the subcontinent?

5. **Critical Thinking:** *Make Generalizations* What generalizations can you make about the ways of life of South Asian peoples by looking at pictures showing their environments, homes, and work?

Link to ☞☜ Writing

Write a Journal Entry Think about what it would be like to stay with a family in one area of South Asia for a week, such as a farming family on the Indo-Ganges Plain. Set your journal in a time of year, such as early summer, when everyone is waiting for the monsoon season.

Harappa
Mohenjo-Daro

3500 B.C.   **1500 B.C.**   **500 B.C.**

2500 B.C.
Height of
civilization in
Harappa and
Mohenjo-Daro

c. 1500 B.C.
Aryan migration
begins.

550 B.C.
The Persian Empire spreads
to the Indus River Valley.

c. 320 B.C.
The Mauryan Empire unites much of the Indian subcontinent.

India and Persia

PREVIEW

Focus on the Main Idea
Indian civilization developed
with influences from the Aryans
and Persians.

PLACES
Harappa
Mohenjo-Daro

PEOPLE
Cyrus II
Darius I
Chandragupta Maurya
Ashoka

VOCABULARY
brahmin
sudra

TERMS
Sanskrit
Vedas
Zoroastrianism

▶ The uncovering of seals with
markings and pictographs
like this one led to the
discovery of the first
civilizations in South Asia.

You Are There
During your travels to South Asia,
you come across a tall, polished column of rock. You stop for a moment,
have a drink of water, and then squint your eyes. The
hot sun is almost blinding. You notice several inscriptions on the column but cannot make out the writing.
You read in your guidebook that these writings were
the proclamations of a king.

As you continue sightseeing, you come across ruins
of brick buildings. They are in the form of what used to
be a grid-shaped pattern. Your guidebook tells you that
the civilization that lived here
disappeared suddenly. No one
really knows why or how.

You think about your travels in
China. While loading your camera
with film, you wonder if South Asia
will be very different from East Asia.
You snap a photo and run to catch
up with the group.

Summarize As you read, summarize the main
ideas about early civilizations in the Indus River
Valley.

Indus River Valley Civilization

▶ This decorative pin made of gold and silver was discovered at Harappa. It is more than 4,000 years old.

People began to settle in the Indus River Valley about 3500 B.C. However, the civilization began about 2500 B.C. At the center of this civilization were people very much like the cotton workers in Pakistan you read about in Lesson 1. In the 1920s and 1930s, archaeologists uncovered several ancient cities in the Indus River Valley in Pakistan. Two of these cities, **Harappa** and **Mohenjo-Daro** (moh HEN joh DAR oh), were home to thousands of people. Look at the map on page 128 for a locator map of this area.

Artifacts tell us about how these people lived. We know that they had a system of writing. However, like the writing system of the ancient Nubians, we have not been able to decode it. Archaeologists also know that people farmed and stored grain, worked with metal crafts and pottery, wove cotton, and traded and sold goods. Statues that may represent gods and goddesses suggest that they had religious beliefs. People made toys and beads for jewelry. By 2500 B.C. the Harappan civilization was thriving. Its culture had spread through much of the Indus Valley.

Remains found at Mohenjo-Daro reveal complex architecture and city planning. The people used a system of weights and measures to construct buildings and roads. Brick homes were laid out in a grid system, like many modern cities are. People enjoyed a large public bath and even garbage collection.

The Harappan civilization vanished suddenly sometime about 1700 B.C. Many archaeologists suspect this was because of a natural disaster, such as a monsoon, flood, or earthquake. The region's river location and physical geography could have made these disasters very possible.

REVIEW What do we know about Harappan civilization in the Indus River Valley? ⟳ Summarize

▶ Mohenjo-Daro was organized into upper and lower levels. This building probably was the center of government and may have been a spiritual center too.

The Aryans Arrive

About 1500 B.C., another group of people, the Aryans (AIR ee uhnz), migrated to the Indus River Valley. They crossed the Hindu Kush Mountains from the north and went through the Khyber Pass before arriving in the Indus River Valley.

The Aryans spoke **Sanskrit,** a different language from other people who were living in the valley. In the valley, the Aryans continued their nomadic way of life, herding cattle, sheep, and goats. The Aryans brought new technology. Like the Hyksos who took power in Egypt in about 1650 B.C., the Aryans rode chariots drawn by horses. The Aryans soon developed villages and towns where they farmed and traded.

The Aryans left behind few objects for archaeologists to find, such as pottery, jewelry, or ruins of buildings. What they did leave was literature and their main language, Sanskrit. For hundreds of years before their stories and songs were written down, they were recited from memory. The **Vedas** (VAY duhz), or "Books of Knowledge," contain these writings. According to the Vedas, the Aryans waged many wars among their groups or tribes. The Vedas also describe contests between gods and humans.

REVIEW What did the Aryans leave behind that tells us about their culture? ⟳ Summarize

▶ **The Vedas contain writings by the Aryans. This book is a collection of hymns.**

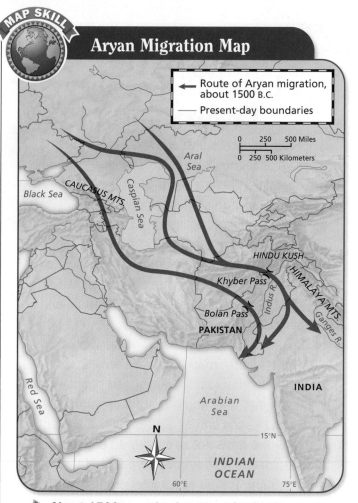

Aryan Migration Map

← Route of Aryan migration, about 1500 B.C.
— Present-day boundaries

0   250   500 Miles
0   250   500 Kilometers

Aral Sea

Black Sea

CAUCASUS MTS

Caspian Sea

HINDU KUSH

Khyber Pass

HIMALAYA MTS.

Indus R.

Bolan Pass

Ganges R.

PAKISTAN

INDIA

Red Sea

Arabian Sea

N

15°N

INDIAN OCEAN

60°E   75°E

▶ **About 1500 B.C., the Aryans arrived in the Indus River Valley.**

MAP SKILL Movement *From which direction did the Aryans come?*

Aryan Culture Spreads

The Aryans formed groups that were headed by a rajah (RAH juh), or priest leader. Councils advised the rajah. The groups traded with each other, using cattle and gold for money. As the Aryan society became more prosperous, many conflicts arose among the groups. In the Battle of the Ten Kings, one group was victorious over other groups. *Mahabharata* (muh HAH BAHR ah tuh) and *Ramayana* (rah MAH yuhn uh) are two popular tales. They describe these battles, as well as many other stories.

The Aryans believed that what a person did in life had much to do with who he or she was. Their society was organized according to these beliefs. Priests and teachers, or **brahmins,** held the highest position in society. Warriors, kings, and other rulers took the next position, followed by a group called the cultivators—artisans, traders, and merchants. The **sudras,** or serfs, were given the lowest position in society. They were ordered to farm the land and serve others.

By about the sixth century B.C., Sanskrit was in written form. Sixteen states had been formed. The Aryan culture had spread east to the Ganges River

Victoria & Albert Museum, London/Art Resource

▶ This nineteenth century scene is from an Aryan epic about two brothers, Rama and Lakshmana.

Valley. Another group of people from the north—the Persians—then began to arrive in the Indus River Valley. News about riches in the valley encouraged people in Persia to migrate south. Armies sent by Persian kings moved into two regions in the Indus River Valley.

REVIEW How did the Aryans organize themselves into different positions in society? **Main Idea and Details**

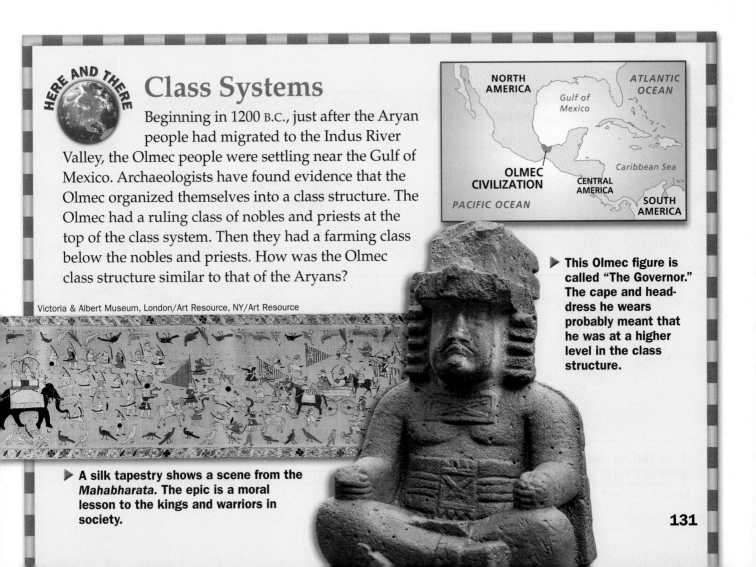

HERE AND THERE

Class Systems

Beginning in 1200 B.C., just after the Aryan people had migrated to the Indus River Valley, the Olmec people were settling near the Gulf of Mexico. Archaeologists have found evidence that the Olmec organized themselves into a class structure. The Olmec had a ruling class of nobles and priests at the top of the class system. Then they had a farming class below the nobles and priests. How was the Olmec class structure similar to that of the Aryans?

Victoria & Albert Museum, London/Art Resource, NY/Art Resource

NORTH AMERICA — Gulf of Mexico — ATLANTIC OCEAN — Caribbean Sea — CENTRAL AMERICA — SOUTH AMERICA — PACIFIC OCEAN — OLMEC CIVILIZATION

▶ This Olmec figure is called "The Governor." The cape and headdress he wears probably meant that he was at a higher level in the class structure.

▶ A silk tapestry shows a scene from the *Mahabharata.* The epic is a moral lesson to the kings and warriors in society.

131

The Persian Empire

Cyrus II is said to have been the founder of the Persian Empire. Look at the map below. From about 550 to 320 B.C., the empire stretched from the Mediterranean Sea to the Indus River Valley. Persian culture was united with the culture of the Babylonians, Lydians, and the Egyptians.

The Persian Empire was constructed after the Persians invaded the lands of these people. At its height, the Persian Empire ruled 20 provinces linked together with a system of roads. King Darius I, who followed Cyrus, brought the Persian Empire to India.

Although war and bloodshed helped build this empire, historians suggest that Cyrus may have been a tolerant ruler. For example, it is believed that he freed the Jewish people from slavery in Babylon and ordered that their temple be rebuilt in Jerusalem.

▶ **In this tapestry, Cyrus II is shown capturing the city of Jerusalem.**

The development of roads and trade by the Persians connected India with other lands in Central Asia. India was no longer cut off by its northern mountains. South Asian culture, technology, and people began to spread to the rest of the world.

One aspect of Persian culture that can be found in South Asia today is Zoroastrianism (zohr uh WASS tree uh nih zuhm). **Zoroastrianism** is a religion founded by the Persian prophet Zoroaster (zoh roh AS tuhr) in what is today known as Iran. Although Persian religion recognized many gods, Zoroaster identified one god as supreme and the enemy of evil. People who follow the teachings of Zoroaster today are known as Parsis because their ancestors came from Persia.

REVIEW How did the Persians influence Indian civilization? **Cause and Effect**

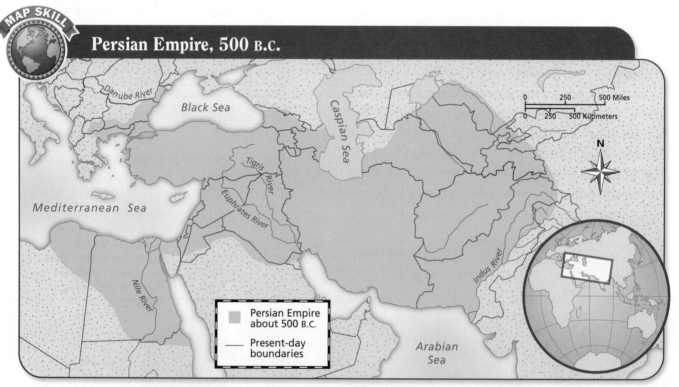

MAP SKILL

Persian Empire, 500 B.C.

Danube River

Black Sea

Caspian Sea

Tigris River

Euphrates River

Mediterranean Sea

Nile River

Indus River

Arabian Sea

0 250 500 Miles
0 250 500 Kilometers

N

- ▢ Persian Empire about 500 B.C.
- — Present-day boundaries

▶ In 500 B.C. the Persian Empire extended from the Mediterranean Sea to the Indus River Valley.

MAP SKILL Use Intermediate Directions *From the Indus River Valley, which direction did the Persian Empire spread?*

The First Indian Empire

About 320 B.C., a soldier named **Chandragupta Maurya** (chuhn druh GUP tuh MOW ree uh) seized power in India. He started the Mauryan Empire, the first Indian empire, and extended it to the borders of Persia. Chandragupta lived a life of luxury. But he soon got tired of that life and became a monk, a person who devotes his life to a religious order or group. Read more about Chandragupta's life in the biography on page 135.

His grandson, **Ashoka** (uh SHOH kuh), took power in about 270 B.C. By that time, the Mauryan Empire stretched southward across the Deccan Plateau. The government was highly organized. It controlled many aspects of life, such as how artisans worked and how doctors treated their patients. India had a strong group of civil service workers, a powerful army, and even an army of spies to keep an eye on what was going on in the empire.

Ashoka had a special way of communicating with his people. Remember the stone column you read about at the beginning of the lesson?

Ashoka used these columns to mark the territory of the empire or religious sites. He also had proclamations, or announcements, and news of the empire inscribed on them. These "rock markers" explained Ashoka's policies of tolerance and nonviolence.

Rulers after Ashoka were less successful at keeping the empire under control, and the Mauryan Empire ended about 185 B.C. Conflicts between regions broke out in India. These regions ruled themselves until A.D. 320, when the Guptas (GUP tuhz) finally took control.

REVIEW How would Ashoka's rock markers encourage regions of his empire to be unified? **Draw Conclusions**

▶ The column of Ashoka marked the emperor's power throughout the empire. Today, it is an Indian national symbol.

▶ This is the Great Stupa at Sanchi, which was built under Ashoka. The four lions on the top of the pillars symbolize the religion he followed reaching out to the four corners of the Earth.

Arts and Sciences

The Gupta Empire lasted for about 200 years. During this time India made great achievements in science such as astronomy. Mathematics expanded with the development of the number system we use today. This system includes nine digits, zero, and the decimal.

Literature, poetry, and art flourished. Sculptures made during this period set the style for Indian art that followed. Architects designed elaborate temples made of stone instead of wood. Higher education became available, but only to men. Sanskrit became the language of the wealthy.

India's economy began to improve along with trade. Textiles—silk, cotton, and linen—became especially valuable exports. By the fifth century, more people from the north arrived—the Huns.

British Museum

▶ **Music flourished during the Gupta Empire, as represented by this tile of a musician.**

By the mid-sixth century, the Huns had taken power from the Guptas and seized much of India. The Gupta Empire came to an end.

REVIEW List some of the developments of the Gupta Empire in India. **Main Idea and Details**

Summarize the Lesson

- **c. 1500 B.C.** Aryan people migrated to the Indus River Valley from Central Asia.
- **550 B.C.** The Persian Empire spread from the Mediterranean Sea to the Indus River Valley.
- **c. 320 B.C.** India's first empire, the Mauryan Empire, united almost the entire Indian subcontinent.

LESSON 2   REVIEW

Check Facts and Main Ideas

1. ⟳ **Summarize** On a separate piece of paper, copy the diagram below. Fill in the missing detail that completes the summary.

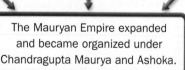

| Chandragupta Maurya extended the empire to the Persian border. | Ashoka organized the government of the Mauryan Empire. | |

↓ ↓ ↓

The Mauryan Empire expanded and became organized under Chandragupta Maurya and Ashoka.

2. What was the Aryan migration?

3. How did the Persian Empire influence Indian civilization and culture?

4. What are the most important stages in the development of Indian culture from 2500 B.C to A.D. 300 ?

5. **Critical Thinking:** *Evaluate Information* How do the Vedas, poems, and epics of the Aryan people reflect their culture?

Link to ⟨⟩ Writing

Write a Proclamation Would you like to be an emperor or empress with something to proclaim? Outline how you would rule fairly, what you would like people to know, and what you believe in as a ruler.

Chandragupta Maurya
c. 360 B.C. – 297 B.C.

Traditional stories tell us that Chandragupta Maurya was the son of the king of Magadha. The king died in battle before Chandragupta was born. Chandragupta grew up as a servant to a hunter. One day a politician noticed the boy's leadership skills and decided he should be trained to be a soldier.

As a young commander, Chandragupta organized a successful rebellion against the Greeks. Several years later, he led an army of 600,000. His empire soon stretched across most of India.

BIOFACT

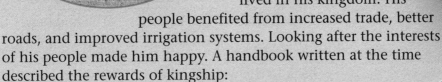

Chandragupta exchanged 500 elephants for territory in present-day Afghanistan.

As emperor, Chandragupta lived a life of luxury in his palace. But Chandragupta did not ignore the people who lived in his kingdom. His people benefited from increased trade, better roads, and improved irrigation systems. Looking after the interests of his people made him happy. A handbook written at the time described the rewards of kingship:

"In the happiness of his subjects lies his happiness; in their welfare his welfare . . . whatever pleases his subjects he shall consider as good."

According to legend, Chandragupta eventually gave up his life of wealth and glory. He lived his last years as a monk and died as the result of a long fast, a period in which a person eats little or no food.

Learn from Biographies

Chandragupta's rebellion against Greek rule took a group effort. He gathered local rulers, who set aside their differences to fight against the Greeks. How do you think Chandragupta convinced local rulers to join in a group effort?

For more information, go online to *Meet the People* at **www.sfsocialstudies.com.**

Ganges
River

Hinduism

PREVIEW

Focus on the Main Idea
Hinduism combines spiritual beliefs, gods, and practices.

PLACES
Ganges River

VOCABULARY
reincarnation
caste

TERMS
Hinduism
Rig Veda
Brahman
dharma

You Are There
In the chilly darkness before dawn you watch a young man walk sleepily down the alley. He meets up with a friend, and they walk side-by-side through narrow streets to the river. You shiver as you follow them down the alley. Before heading down the stone steps, one of the men stops to buy a small lamp made of a curled, dry leaf. The two of them slip off their shoes and head down to the water where other men are already bathing. It's so cold you can hear their teeth chatter. The two men bathe and head out, shivering. Now they bow their heads to pray. They walk back to the water, and one of them lights the leaf lamp. Together they praise Ganga, the river goddess. They sing to Surya, the source of all energy, who is also the sun.

▶ **People call the Ganges Ganga Mai, or Mother Ganges. Bathing in its waters is a sacred Hindu ritual.**

Summarize As you read, think about how you would summarize the main beliefs of Hinduism.

Target Skill

Seeds of Belief

Hinduism is the main religion in India. It is one of the world's oldest religions. Thousands of people in Nepal, Malaysia, and other parts of the world also follow this religion. Hinduism is different from many other religions because it has no founder.

You read in Lesson 2 about the Aryans who wrote the Vedas. Hinduism probably started with the religious beliefs of the Aryans and the first people who lived in the Indus River Valley.

▶ This Hindu boy is reciting the Vedas.

There are four Vedas, the oldest of which is the Rig Veda. It is a collection of more than 1,000 hymns that priests recited at ceremonies and during rituals. The hymns are all dedicated to Aryan gods. The themes of the Rig Veda include spiritual beliefs in the power of nature. Faithful Hindus recite verses from the Vedas every day. Here is part of a verse from the Rig Veda describing the light of dawn:

> *"The goddess Light has looked abroad*
> *With her eyes, everywhere drawing near . . . .*
> *Her radiance drives out the dark."*
> —*Rig Veda X. 127*

The Aryan people believed that for the hymns to be effective, they had to be recited precisely. Committing these hymns to memory also helped them record the hymns accurately. Today, Hindus still sing hymns from the Rig Veda at ceremonies such as weddings and funerals. However, some of the beliefs and practices of Hindus have changed over time.

REVIEW How is the Rig Veda important to people who practice Hinduism? **Main Idea and Details**

▶ Brahma, the creator, has four heads facing four directions, seeing all.

▶ Shiva, the destroyer, represents forces that destroy what is old and begin what is new.

▶ Vishnu, the preserver, maintains the order of all things.

▶ Images of Hindu gods are important to people who follow Hinduism. People offer prayers and songs at temples. More commonly, they keep small shrines in their own homes where they can offer prayers in private. These rituals show respect for the spiritual belief the god or goddess represents.

Reunion des Musées Nationaux/Art Resource

Musée Guimet Paris/Dagli Orti (A)/Art Archive

Spread of Hinduism

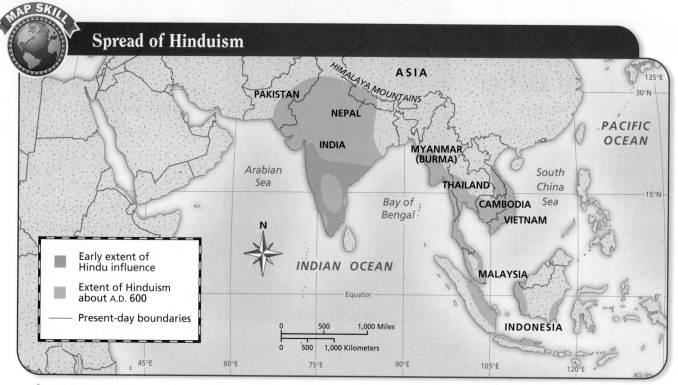

▶ Hinduism spread to other areas outside of India, such as Nepal, Myanmar (Burma), Thailand, and Cambodia.

MAP SKILL Location *From where did Hinduism originate?*

Gods and Goddesses

Hinduism is often thought of as a religion with many gods, but it is also a religion of many beliefs. Some Hindus recognize only one universal being, **Brahman**, that is the source and final destination of everything.

Three of the principal forms of Brahman are the gods Brahma, the creator; Vishnu, the preserver; and Shiva, the destroyer. Hindus believe that Vishnu maintains **dharma** (DAHR muh), which is the order of the universe.

Other Hindu gods and goddesses are aspects of Brahman. For example, Krishna is a form of Vishnu who came to live on Earth. Gods and goddesses based in nature include the **Ganges River** goddess, Ganga Mai, who gives water the power to clean and purify.

REVIEW Is Hinduism a monotheistic or a polytheistic religion? **Main Idea and Details**

Seven Truths and Reincarnation

Seven essential doctrines, or truths, are important Hindu beliefs. These doctrines include peaceful living, freedom of thought, respect for nature and animals, becoming one with Brahman, and the belief that good and bad actions will one day affect us.

Reincarnation is the process through which a person goes from one life to the next. Hindus believe that after a person dies, he or she is reborn into a new life.

If Hindus live good lives, according to truthful principles, then their karma, or the lifetime actions of a person, is good. With good karma, a Hindu's rebirth on Earth is good. Although good rebirth is desirable, the end of rebirth by becoming one with Brahman is the goal of a good life for a Hindu.

REVIEW What are some conclusions you can make about the Hindu beliefs? **Draw Conclusions**

Way of Life

In India every Hindu is traditionally a member of a caste, a lifelong social group into which he or she is born. From the time of the Vedas, the castes were strictly ranked according to birth. Castes also determined for which job each caste member was qualified. Marriages were permitted only between persons of the same caste. The ranked order of the castes was an important part of dharma.

The highest caste was that of the priests and teachers. Rulers and warriors came next, and then farmers and merchants. The lowest castes were supposed to be the servants of all the others. Some jobs, which no one else was willing to do, were assigned to castes that were treated as "untouchables." Since 1950 the discrimination, or mistreatment, of castes is illegal in India. But the caste system is still a part of daily life there.

Many members of the highest castes are vegetarians. This is part of the way of life based on the respect for other living things. Vegetarian Hindus get their protein needs from beans and other legumes, as well as from dairy products.

► **At a Hindu wedding, Indian men and women bless the bride and groom.**

REVIEW How is India's caste system different from the Aryan social class system? **Compare and Contrast**

Summarize the Lesson

- Hinduism is one of the oldest religions in the world.
- The Hindu way of life is based on the writings of the Vedas.
- Hindus follow seven essential truths.

LESSON 3 ⟩ REVIEW

Check Facts and Main Ideas

1. ↻ **Summarize** On a separate piece of paper, fill in the missing detail about Hindu beliefs below.

| Hindus recite verses from the Vedas. | | Hindus believe in reincarnation. |

↓ ↓ ↓

The Vedas, Hindu gods and goddesses, and reincarnation are important to followers of Hinduism.

2. What are Hinduism's roots?

3. What are the three main forms of Brahman, the universal truth?

4. What are the main points of Hindu beliefs?

5. **Critical Thinking:** *Fact or Opinion* The caste system is still part of daily life in India.

Link to ⚭ Science

Make a Menu As you learned in this lesson, many Hindus do not eat meat for religious reasons. Put together a vegetarian menu for a Hindu dinner guest. Remember to include a protein source.

Bodh Gaya

Buddhism

▶ Buddhists come to pray at Maha Bodhi, or the Buddha Gaya Temple. This shrine was built by Ashoka in the third century B.C.

You Are There

The barefoot man before you wears an orange robe. You watch him walk to the top of a hill. There is no one else around. He sits silently and closes his eyes. He looks so serious, yet so peaceful. You're not sure what he is doing. He continues to sit on the grass with crossed legs. He seems so at ease and comfortable. You wonder what he could be thinking about. His hands are together in front of him. You look at his shaven head. The winds start to pick up, but the man doesn't move. Later that day you pass the same hill. The man is still sitting there in the same position. Has he been there all this time? He rises and walks back down the hill. There he meets other men who are dressed just like him. All of them are barefoot and have shaven heads. They walk silently together through the village.

Summarize
As you read, combine the main facts about Buddhism.

Who Was the Buddha?

The sixth century B.C. was a time of conflict and religious questioning in Asia. According to Buddhist tradition, the man who became **the Buddha** was born during this period. The religion he founded was established in India in the fourth century B.C. In the next century, Emperor Ashoka spread **Buddhism** throughout South Asia. From India, Buddhism spread throughout East and Southeast Asia.

Siddhartha Gautama (sih DAHR tuh GOW tah muh), the man who came to be known as the Buddha, or "The Enlightened One," was born about 563 B.C. He was born just south of the Himalayas. His father, who was a wealthy ruler, was told that his son would be a great king if he stayed at home or a great teacher if he left. When Siddhartha was born, his father protected him from the world, keeping him within the palace walls.

When Siddhartha was an adult, he left the palace. For the first time in his life, he saw a sick person in a nearby

▶ **Ashoka built thousands of Buddhist temples and shrines and wrote Buddhist sayings on rocks and stone pillars.**

village. Then he saw a monk, who had no possessions and seemed to be calm and free from suffering. After thinking about these experiences, Siddhartha left his comfortable life in the palace and began his lifelong journey.

REVIEW How would you summarize the early life of Siddhartha according to Buddhist tradition?
🔄 **Summarize**

Literature and Social Studies

The Jataka Tales

The Jatakas include some 500 stories the Buddha might have told. They are popular among many Buddhists. Animals are characters in a number of the tales. What message does the verse below give?

When you are made responsible,
The job is up to you,
And if you give that job to others,
You're to blame for what they do.

—*From* Jataka Tales, *edited by Nancy DeRoin*

141

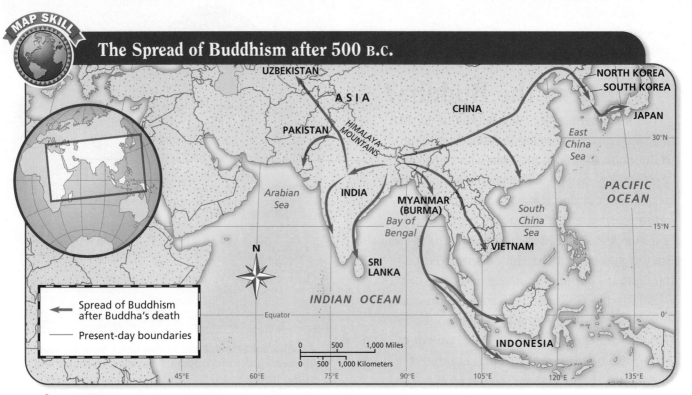

The Spread of Buddhism after 500 B.C.

UZBEKISTAN

ASIA

NORTH KOREA
SOUTH KOREA

PAKISTAN

CHINA

JAPAN

HIMALAYA MOUNTAINS

East China Sea

30°N

Arabian Sea

INDIA

MYANMAR (BURMA)

PACIFIC OCEAN

Bay of Bengal

South China Sea

15°N

N

VIETNAM

SRI LANKA

INDIAN OCEAN

Equator

0°

Spread of Buddhism after Buddha's death

Present-day boundaries

INDONESIA

0 500 1,000 Miles
0 500 1,000 Kilometers

45°E   60°E   75°E   90°E   105°E   120°E   135°E

▶ Buddhism spread to many parts of the world.

MAP SKILL Understand Continents and Oceans *Where did Buddhism spread?*

The Buddha's Travels

Siddhartha joined a group of men who also sought understanding and simple living. For six years they fasted, living on very little food. The monks believed that by giving up what the body needs, they might better understand what the spirit needs. They practiced **meditation,** a way of clearing the mind. Siddhartha felt weak and left the group. He ate, was refreshed, and began his journey again.

▶ According to Buddhist tradition, the Buddha is said to have reached enlightenment at a tree like this near Bodh Gaya, India.

According to Buddhist tradition, sitting silently under a tree near the town now called **Bodh Gaya,** Siddhartha meditated for awhile. When he saw a beautiful morning star, he realized that he had never lost what he was looking for:

> *"Wonder of wonders, this very enlightenment is the nature of all beings, and yet they are unhappy for lack of it."*

All people, he realized, had the power within them to be free from suffering. He then became enlightened and became known as the Buddha.

For nearly fifty years he traveled and taught. His followers believe that he spoke to all people, using a language that everyone could understand. The Buddha stressed that people, not just priests, could achieve **enlightenment,** or a state of pure goodness. His words showed a peaceful and tolerant way of looking at the world.

REVIEW How are Buddhist beliefs different from Hindu beliefs? **Compare and Contrast**

Four and Eight

Buddhism is based on Four Noble Truths about human suffering. The Buddha used these truths to understand his enlightenment.

The Four Noble Truths:
1. Suffering is part of life for all people.
2. People suffer because they want so many things in life.
3. If people can free themselves from wanting so many things, they will not suffer.
4. People can free themselves from wants and from suffering by following the Eightfold Path.

Buddhists also believe in the Eightfold Path, a way of living that can help them find relief from their suffering. According to Buddhists, the Eightfold Path recommends that people develop three qualities: wisdom, morality, and meditation. The Eightfold Path recommends actions, efforts, or ways of thinking that will help Buddhists develop these qualities.

REVIEW What are the Four Noble Truths of Buddhism? **Main Idea and Details**

▶ **Buddhist prayer flags are often used during ceremonies. Here, a fruit offering is made near the Maha Bodhi Temple in Bodh Gaya.**

Summarize the Lesson

- According to Buddhist tradition, Buddhism was founded by Siddhartha Gautama.
- The main Buddhist beliefs include the Four Noble Truths and the Eightfold Path.
- Buddhism gradually spread to other parts of Asia.

LESSON 4 REVIEW

Check Facts and Main Ideas

1. **Summarize** On a separate piece of paper, copy the diagram below. Fill in the blank with a main belief of Buddhism.

```
Buddhism is          Buddhists
based on the         follow the
Four Noble           teachings of
Truths.              the Buddha.
          ↓      ↓      ↓
     The Four Noble Truths, the
     Eightfold Path, and the teachings of
     the Buddha are important to Buddhists.
```

2. According to Buddhist tradition, who was the Buddha?

3. How are the Four Noble Truths and the Eightfold Path connected in Buddhism?

4. Why could Buddhism be considered a peaceful philosophy and why might it appeal to people?

5. **Critical Thinking:** *Make Generalizations* How do the ideas of Buddhism attempt to solve some of life's difficult problems?

Link to Writing

Write a Paragraph Describe the spread of Buddhism to other parts of the world after 500 B.C.

Research and Writing Skills

Gather and Report Information
A Research Report

What? A research report is a paper that presents information you have gathered on one topic in a well-organized way. In the report you may give your own opinion or point of view on the topic.

There are two parts to your assignment. First, you must collect information on your topic from source material available at the library or on the Internet. Second, you must organize the information and summarize it in a written report. The information will document and support your point of view.

Your assignment is a report on the geography of South Asia. Source materials may include maps from atlases, articles from magazines, chapters from books, entries from encyclopedias, statistics from almanacs, and information from Internet sources.

As you read about South Asia you notice that much information—about farming and people's ways of life—has to do with climate. The distinguishing aspect of the subcontinent's climate is the monsoon season. You have your topic! State it as a question so it is researchable.

Why? To really discover how the monsoon affects people in South Asian countries, you probably need more information than what's available in your textbook. Articles written by weather forecasters, agricultural specialists, and maybe even economists can provide much information, as well as different perspectives. Visuals such as maps, diagrams, and photographs also can provide information.

How? First, form a hypothesis, or educated guess, to help guide your research. Then, begin to gather information from a general reference source at the library. Look up *Asia, South Asia, monsoon, climate,* and *subsistence farming.* Try looking up specific countries. What other topics might you want to read about? (meteorology, weather, agriculture) What other library materials could you try? (books, almanacs, magazines, atlases). Try searching on the Internet. Are there any people you could interview who know about the monsoon season? Do not forget to evaluate the sources you have chosen. Could any of them be biased?

Next, begin reading and selecting the most important information from your notes, photocopies, and printouts. Make an outline for the paper. Refine the sections so that they relate to your main topic. Is your topic of the monsoon too broad, too narrow, or just right? What facts will answer the question you ask? Be open to making adjustments. Make a checklist with the following items:

- Draft your paper by writing down your ideas and summarizing your information.
- Look for places where you do not have enough information. Perhaps you would like to discuss South Asia's economy, but you realize you need more facts.

Describe how when the monsoon season comes, people are happy.

Research Report
Topic: Why is the monsoon season important to the people of South Asia?

   I. Introduction
  II. Helps crops grow   *maybe not!*
      A. people are subsistence farmers
      B. irrigation
      C. examples
         1. vegetables in north
         2. rice in south
 III. Relieves heat   *describe how hot it is*
 IV. Important to economy *find out more*
      A. imports
      B. exports
  V. Conclusion

- Revise your paper.
- Make sure you have a topic sentence in each paragraph and a beginning, middle, and end to your paper.
- Check that information on the same subject is in the same paragraph.
- Be concise and clear.
- Proofread for errors and omissions.
- List your sources alphabetically by the author's last name in a bibliography.
- Type your paper or rewrite it neatly.

Think and Apply

1 What are the two phases of writing a research report?

2 Name some types of research sources.

3 What are the main writing checkpoints when you can assess and shape your work?

CHAPTER 5
REVIEW

3500 B.C.

2500 B.C.

3500 B.C.
People made settlements in the Indus River Valley.

2500 B.C.
Height of civilization in Mohenjo-Daro and Harappa

Chapter Summary

Summarize

On a separate piece of paper, fill in the missing blank to complete the summary about South Asia's culture.

Hinduism is the main religion in India.

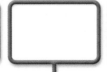

The Persians influenced Indian culture.

South Asia is a land of diverse cultures.

Vocabulary

Write a definition for each vocabulary word.

1. **subcontinent** (p. 123)
2. **monsoon season** (p. 125)
3. **reincarnation** (p. 138)
4. **meditation** (p. 142)
5. **caste** (p. 139)
6. **enlightenment** (p. 142)
7. **brahmin** (p. 131)
8. **subsistence farming** (p. 125)
9. **sudra** (p. 131)

People and Terms

Write a sentence explaining why each of the following people or terms is important in the study of South Asia's history and religions. You may use two or more in a single sentence.

1. Darius I (p. 132)
2. Cyrus II (p. 132)
3. Buddhism (p. 141)
4. Chandragupta Maurya (p. 133)
5. Ashoka (p. 133)
6. the Buddha (p. 141)
7. Hinduism (p. 137)
8. Vedas (p. 130)
9. Sanskrit (p. 130)
10. Brahman (p. 138)

146

| 1500 B.C. | 500 B.C. | A.D. 500 |

1500 B.C.
Aryans migrated into South Asia.

550 B.C.
The Persian Empire spread to the Indus River Valley.

about 320 B.C.
The Mauryan Empire began.

A.D. 320
The Gupta Empire began.

Facts and Main Ideas

1 What are the main beliefs and practices of Hinduism?

2 What are the main beliefs and practices of Buddhism?

3 **Time Line** About how much time passed between the earliest known settlers in South Asia and the formation of the first Indian empire?

4 **Main Idea** What are the major landforms, climates, and water systems in South Asia?

5 **Main Idea** What contributed to cultural and political changes in South Asia between about 2500 B.C. and A.D. 400?

6 **Main Idea** How does Hinduism incorporate many beliefs and practices into one religion?

7 **Main Idea** How would a Buddhist focus inward to find peace and happiness?

8 **Critical Thinking:** *Make Generalizations* What generalizations can you make about how Hinduism and Buddhism are alike and different?

Write About History

1 **Write a "what if" story** about Indus River Valley cities Mohenjo-Daro and Harappa in 1500 B.C. What if these cities did not disappear by 1700 B.C.? Would they still be thriving, or would they have disappeared at another time?

2 **Write a letter** to a friend telling him or her about some of the advancements made during the Gupta Empire.

3 **Write a public announcement** to inform people about some of the diverse geography of South Asia.

Apply Skills

Gather and Report Information
Go to the library or on the Internet to research one of the following topics. Write a short report on the information you gather.

1 Religions of South Asia

2 People of South Asia

3 Climate of South Asia

Internet Activity

To get help with vocabulary, people, and terms, select the dictionary, encyclopedia, or almanac from *Social Studies Library* at **www.sfsocialstudies.com**.

147

End with a Song

A Boat on the Lake

In the Yangtze Kiang region in China, southwest of Shanghai, are many lakes. The lakes supply water for irrigation so that soil can be used for agriculture. Lakes also are a place where people go to meditate and relax. The sound and sight of the water is soothing. "A Boat on the Lake" is an ancient Chinese folk song. As you read and sing along, think about how people who are trying to meditate might find this song useful.

Folk Song from China
Collected by Shao-Mei Ting

Wind is blow-ing a-cross the __ lake, Qui-et-ly __ the
Shan qing shui __ ming you jing __ jing, hu xin piao __ lai
shahn cheeng shweh __ meeng yoh jeeng __ jeeng hoo shin pyow __ lī

rip-ples __ play; We row and __ row, we row and __ row.
feng yi __ zhen a xing a __ xing a jin a __ jin,
fung yee __ jen ah sheeng ah __ sheeng ah jeen ah __ jeen

Few there are who walk by the shore, Where the lake __ re-
huang hun shi hou ren xing __ shao, ban kong yue __ ying
hwahng hwehn sher hoh ren sheeng __ shah ow bahn kong yweh __ yeeng

flects the __ moon; We row and __ row, we row and __ row.
shui mi-an yau, a xing a __ xing a jin a __ jin.
shweh mee-an yow ah sheeng ah __ sheeng ah jeen ah __ jeen.

149

Unit Review

Test Talk

Find key words in the text.

Main Ideas and Vocabulary

TEST PREP

Read the passage below and use it to answer the questions that follow.

The Nile River Valley was an ideal place for civilization to thrive. The ancient Egyptians used the yearly overflowing of the Nile to irrigate crops. They kept records using calendars and hieroglyphics. The Egyptians built great pyramids for the dead. Their achievements in technology influenced future civilizations.

Great geographical differences characterize the vast lands of East and South Asia. Early civilizations were shaped by how lands and people have interacted. In China, people first lived along river valleys where land was fertile. Through ancient dynasties, culture and trade grew along with technology to control flooding. In South Asia ancient cultures faded and new ones arose as people from Persia and Central Asia migrated to the Indus and Ganges River Valleys. Indian empires arose that made advancements in the arts and sciences.

Spiritual meaning underlies Hinduism. Hindus honor gods as part of their daily lives and respect nature and all living things. Buddhism rose from the need to understand suffering and overcome it. Buddhists practice meditation to achieve peace and happiness. These religions remain alive today in many parts of the world.

1 According to the passage, why did the Egyptians build pyramids?
  A to honor gods
  B to store goods
  C to advance technology
  D to bury the dead

2 In the passage the word *dynasties* means:
  A landforms
  B periods of rulers from the same family
  C urban developments
  D times

3 In the passage the word *meditation* means:
  A worship gods through song
  B exercise and breathe
  C clear the mind and focus inward
  D study religions and beliefs

4 What is the main idea of the passage?
  A Developments in ancient civilizations paved the way for life today.
  B People of ancient civilizations were diverse.
  C World religions have many of the same ideas.
  D The ancient Egyptians lived in the Nile River Valley.

People and Terms

Write a sentence to describe or define each person or term.

1 Thutmose III (p. 94)

2 Amanirenas (p. 95)

3 Silk Road (p. 112)

4 Gaozu (p. 111)

5 Rig Veda (p. 137)

6 the Buddha (p. 141)

7 Zoroastrianism (p. 132)

8 Ban Zhao (p. 111)

9 *Analects* (p. 116)

10 Daoism (p. 117)

Apply Skills

Compile a Web Site Resource List Search the Internet for geography and history sites that will be resources for a research report. Use key words to find interesting sites on ancient Eygpt, China, and India. Bookmark them and then file them into a special folder. Print out and distribute your list.

Web Site Resource List

Egypt
 Daily Life
  www.hijkl.edu
  www.mnop.org
 Pharaohs
  www.hijkl.edu
  www.mnop.org

India
 Religion
  www.mnop.edu
 Empires
  www.hijkl.gov

China
 Dynasties
  www.mnop.edu

Write and Share

Make a Travel Presentation Form three groups to collect information on travel in Egypt, China, and India. Each group should consult books, magazines, and travel brochures. Choose three or four sites a traveler might want to visit. Highlight what a traveler might want to see in mountain and farming areas, in cities, or boating down a river. Write brief descriptions of these interesting places, and present them in a travelogue to the class. Put together and hand out maps with the sites marked.

Read on Your Own

Look for books like these in your library.

A Place in the Sun by Jill Rubalcaba

SHOWER OF GOLD Girls and Women in the Stories of India Retold by Uma Krishnaswami Illustrated by Maniam Selven

Stories from The Silk Road retold by Cherry Gilchrist illustrated by Nilesh Mistry

UNIT 2 Project

All About a Pyramid

Take visitors on a video tour of an Egyptian pyramid. What mysteries will it reveal?

1 Form a group and choose an Egyptian pyramid to research.

2 Think of interesting aspects of the pyramid, such as which pharaoh it was built for, how it was built, or how long it took to build.

3 Draw a poster of the pyramid, showing it inside and out, or create a model of the pyramid. Label important parts and features.

4 Take the class on a tour of your pyramid, using the poster or model as a visual reference. Describe the features you researched as if you were in a video.

Internet Activity

Explore the Ancient World on the Internet. Go to **www.sfsocialstudies.com/activities** and select your grade and unit.

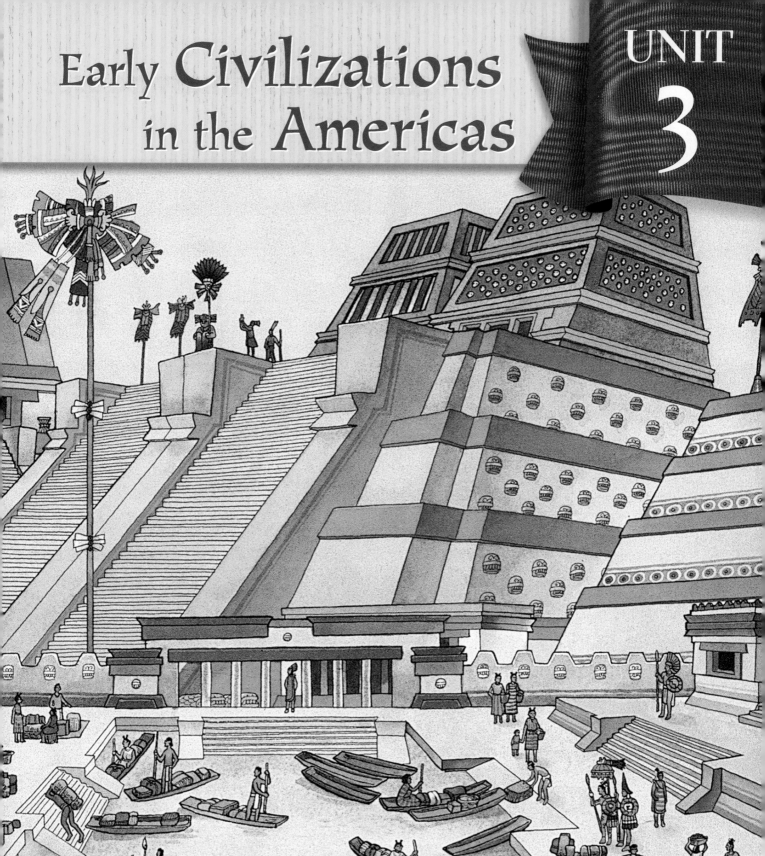

Early Civilizations in the Americas

How do civilizations become empires?

Begin with a Primary Source

1200 B.C.	800 B.C.	400 B.C.	A.D. 1
about 1200 B.C. Olmec civilization arises.	**about 900 B.C.** Chavín culture appears.		**about A.D. 100** Mochica culture appears. / **A.D. 100** Anasazi culture appears.

"With such wonderful sights to gaze on we did not know what to say, or if this was real that we saw before our eyes."

—Account given by Spaniard Bernal Díaz on seeing Tenochtitlan, c. 1560

Tenochtitlan, the capital city of the Aztec Empire, is depicted in this painting by Felipe Davalos.

A.D. 400   800   1200   1600

about A.D. 250
Mayan civilization reaches its peak.

about A.D. 1200
Inca culture appears.

A.D. 1325 Tenochtitlan founded

A.D. 1521
Spain conquers the Aztec Empire.

Meet the People

Manco Capac

c. 1100

Birthplace: Northwest South America

Inca ruler

- Legendary founder of the Inca Empire
- Founded the city of Cuzco

Pachacuti

c. 1391–1473

Birthplace: Inca territory, Northwest South America

Inca ruler

- Saved Inca from Chancas attack
- Built the mountaintop city of Machu Picchu
- Greatly expanded Inca Empire

Moctezuma II

1466–1520

Birthplace: Aztec Empire

Emperor

- Last Aztec emperor
- Was defeated by Cortés
- As a young man proved himself to be an exceptional warrior

Topa Inca

reigned c. 1471–1493

Birthplace: Inca Empire

Inca ruler

- Son of Pachacuti
- Led Inca army
- Nearly doubled the size of the Inca Empire

1100　1150　1200　1250　1300　1350　1400　1450　1500

c. 1100 • Manco Capac

c. 1391–1473 • Pachacuti

1466–1520 • Moctezuma II

reigned c. 1471–1493 • Topa Inca

c. 1475–1541 • Francisco Pizarro

1485–1547 • Hernando Cortés

Francisco Pizarro

c. 1475–1541

Birthplace: Trujillo, Spain

Conqueror

- Conquered the Inca Empire
- Founded the city of Lima, Peru
- Fought with other Spanish conquerors for control of Peru

Hernando Cortés

1485–1547

Birthplace: Medellín, Spain

Explorer and conqueror

- Conquered the Aztec Empire
- Claimed Mexico for Spain
- Served as mayor of Santiago, Cuba

Deganawidah

c. 1550–1600

Birthplace: Ontario, Canada

Peacemaker

- Founded the Iroquois Confederacy
- Convinced different Native American peoples to settle their disagreements peacefully

Alfonso Caso

1896–1970

Birthplace: Mexico City, Mexico

Archaeologist, lawyer

- Created a law that protects archaeological sites in Mexico
- Led the excavation of Monte Albán, 1931–1943
- Cared about preserving and protecting Mexican culture and history

1550 1600 1650 1700 1750 1800 1850 1900 1950 2000

c. 1550–1600 • Deganawidah

1896–1970 • Alfonso Caso

Early Civilizations in the Americas

Compare and Contrast

Item A	Both	Item B
Write what makes Item A different from Item B:	Write what makes Item A and Item B similar.	Write what makes Item B different from Item A.

- When comparing two items, tell how they are alike. When contrasting them, tell how they are different.

- Clue words and phrases such as similar, like, all, both, in the same way, or as well as signal comparisons.

- Clue words and phrases such as different, unlike, in a different way, or in contrast signal contrasts.

Read the following paragraph. The compared items are highlighted in blue. The contrasted items are highlighted in yellow.

In Chapter 5, you read about Hinduism and Buddhism. Both Hinduism and Buddhism have their roots in South Asia. Both include the idea of enlightenment. In contrast, Hinduism did not spread to as many other peoples as Buddhism did. Unlike Buddhism, Hinduism remained dominant in South Asia.

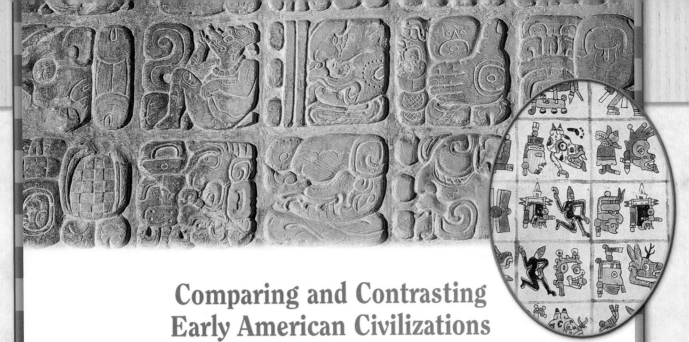

Comparing and Contrasting Early American Civilizations

The Americas include two continents, North America and South America. The continents are connected by a narrow stretch of North America called Central America. Mesoamerica is a region that extends from southern North America to the middle part of Central America. The Americas are home to many different types of landscapes and different civilizations.

In Mesoamerica three major civilizations developed: the Olmec, the Maya, and the Aztecs. All of them were based on agriculture. All of them built stone cities and temples. In addition, all three left us written records in hieroglyphics. However, one was unlike the others in that it built a great empire.

Civilizations developed in South America as well. One of these civilizations, the Inca, built the richest empire the Americas had ever seen. Like the civilizations of Mesoamerica, those of South America were also based on agriculture.

Farming was important to civilizations in other parts of North America too. Many of them developed irrigation techniques. Unlike the civilizations in Mesoamerica, they did not build stone cities. But some of them built great mounds of earth for religious purposes.

By looking at ruins, hieroglyphics, and artifacts, archaeologists have learned that the Americas have been home to some of the greatest civilizations the world has ever seen.

Apply it!

Use the reading strategy of compare and contrast to answer these questions.

1 How were the early civilizations of Mesoamerica similar to each other?

2 How are all of the early American civilizations alike?

3 What makes the civilizations different from each other?

159

CHAPTER 6
Mesoamerican Civilizations

Lesson 1

Mesoamerica
A rugged landscape and long, lush coasts help mold unique cultures.

Lesson 2

about A.D. 250
Tikal
Mayan civilization builds on the accomplishments of the Olmec.

Lesson 3

about A.D. 1350
Tenochtitlan
The Aztecs build a civilization based on agriculture.

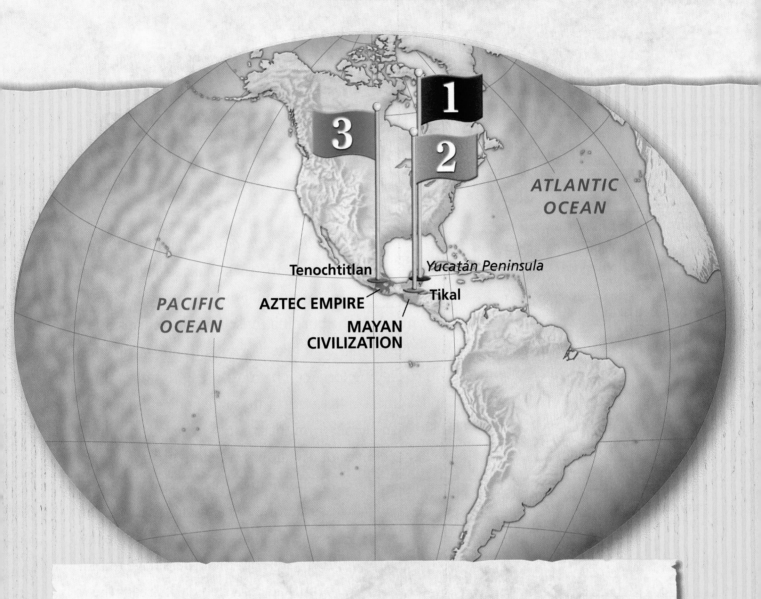

PACIFIC
OCEAN

ATLANTIC
OCEAN

Tenochtitlan

Yucatán Peninsula

Tikal

AZTEC EMPIRE

MAYAN
CIVILIZATION

Why We Remember

Every year, tens of thousands of people travel to Mexico and Central America. They come from all over the world to marvel at the remains of great civilizations. Why do so many people travel so far to see things built so long ago? You can find the answer in the stunning cities and beautiful artwork that these civilizations left behind. They understood the movements of the planets and stars. They understood mathematics and created calendars that are still accurate today. Even though these civilizations are long gone, their achievements are timeless.

Yucatán Peninsula

Geography of Mesoamerica

PREVIEW

Focus on the Main Idea
Early civilizations in Mesoamerica used the rich natural resources of the region.

PLACES
Mesoamerica
Sierra Madre Occidental
Sierra Madre Oriental
Plateau of Mexico
Central Plateau
Gulf of Mexico
Yucatán Peninsula

VOCABULARY
peninsula
cenote

▶ Ancient peoples of Mesoamerica often carved statues from jade, a green stone found in the region.

 **You Are There**

Clink-clink-clink. The noise of your ax on the rock makes an almost musical sound. For a moment, it takes your mind off the burning muscles in your arms and your sweaty hair. You take a break, but only a short one. You're digging for jade, the most precious gift of the land. Your people carve it into sacred objects. They also trade with people from the coast. A little jade can be exchanged for a lot of salt, or even honey. *Clink-clink-clink.* Suddenly, a piece of gray rock breaks away. You stare in disbelief. You have struck jade! But this isn't the light green jade that the others have found. Your jade is a rich dark green, the rarest and most valuable kind. Your father sees it too and rushes to your side. You are proud, and so is he.

 Compare and Contrast
As you read, think about how the peoples of Mesoamerica used natural resources in ways similar to other civilizations.

Museum of Mankind London/ Eileen Tweedy/ Art Archive

A Land of Rugged Mountains

Mesoamerica extends from about the middle of present-day Mexico to the central part of Central America. Besides jade, the land also provides basalt, a black rock formed when lava from a volcano cools slowly. Some people of Mesoamerica carved basalt into huge statues. Obsidian (ub SIHD ee un) is a natural glass formed when lava cools quickly. Some Mesoamerican peoples thought obsidian was a sacred stone formed by lightning strikes. Obsidian is black and brittle. Chipped obsidian made excellent arrowheads and knives.

Jade, basalt, and obsidian are beautiful, but they come from a rugged, varied land. In northern Mesoamerica, the two main mountain ranges, the **Sierra Madre Occidental** (see AIR uh MAHD ray oks see den TAHL) and the **Sierra Madre Oriental** (o ree en TAHL) frame the huge **Plateau of Mexico.** A plateau is a high, flat area. The **Central Plateau** lies at the center of the plateau.

Volcanoes lie to the south of the Plateau of Mexico. They produce basalt and obsidian, as well as fertile soil for farming. Farther south is a region of highlands. This is a rugged land of steep ridges and gorges, or deep, narrow valleys.

The climate of Mesoamerica can be as varied as the landscape. In some places, the lack of rain has created desert conditions. In other places, enough rain falls to grow crops. In these areas, maize (corn), beans, squash, and other crops have been grown for thousands of years. In fact, the land of Mesoamerica, with its forests and trees, hid the ruins of ancient civilizations for centuries.

REVIEW How did the people of Mesoamerica use basalt and obsidian? ↻ **Compare and Contrast**

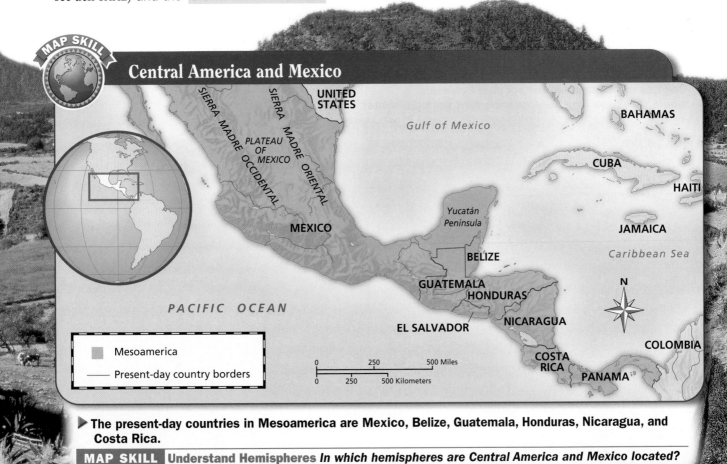

MAP SKILL

Central America and Mexico

SIERRA MADRE OCCIDENTAL

SIERRA MADRE ORIENTAL

PLATEAU OF MEXICO

UNITED STATES

Gulf of Mexico

BAHAMAS

CUBA

HAITI

Yucatán Peninsula

JAMAICA

MEXICO

Caribbean Sea

BELIZE

GUATEMALA

HONDURAS

PACIFIC OCEAN

N

EL SALVADOR

NICARAGUA

COLOMBIA

COSTA RICA

PANAMA

Mesoamerica
— Present-day country borders

0   250   500 Miles
0   250   500 Kilometers

▶ The present-day countries in Mesoamerica are Mexico, Belize, Guatemala, Honduras, Nicaragua, and Costa Rica.

MAP SKILL Understand Hemispheres *In which hemispheres are Central America and Mexico located?*

A Land of Lush Coasts

The interior of Mesoamerica is a land of rugged mountains and plateaus. However, a glance at the map on page 163 will show you that Mesoamerica is a land of long coastlines as well. No place in Mesoamerica is more than about 200 miles from the coastline. People can walk this distance in about two weeks. In fact, many people from the mountains did travel to the coasts.

Traveling north, they would reach the **Gulf of Mexico,** a part of the Atlantic Ocean. The land along much of the gulf is lush, tropical rain forest. There are also stretches of grasslands, rivers, swamps, and even pine forests. The climate here is hot and humid.

The huge **Yucatán** (yoo kuh TAN) **Peninsula** forms the southeastern border of the Gulf of Mexico. A **peninsula** is an arm of land sticking into the sea so that it is nearly surrounded by water. There are few rivers on the Yucatán Peninsula because the Yucatán is a plateau made up of limestone. Rainfall dissolves the limestone. Over time, the action of rainwater on the limestone has created many underground streams and caves. In many places, the roofs of these underground streams have collapsed, creating sink holes, or natural wells. They are called **cenotes** (se NOO teez). In a land with few major rivers, these natural wells provide drinking water. Many people believed that these natural wells were sacred gifts of the gods.

Traveling south and west, people would come to the coast of the Pacific Ocean. Unlike the land near the northern coast, the land near the southern coast is mountainous. The highlands nearly reach the beach.

REVIEW How do Mesoamerica's northern and southern coasts differ? ⟳ **Compare and Contrast**

A Land of Many Peoples

Many peoples flourished in the rugged, varied environments of Mesoamerica. Some lived in the highlands. Others lived on the coasts. The differences in the landscapes helped these peoples develop unique cultures. In the next two lessons, you will read about three of these groups: the Olmec, the Maya, and the Aztecs.

▶ **Cenotes are common in the Yucatán Peninsula, where they have long been an important source of water.**

Even so, the cultures of the peoples of Mesoamerica had many things in common. They had an advanced form of agriculture, growing crops such as beans, maize, chili peppers, and squash.

While many people lived in rural areas, many others lived in cities and towns. The cities contained temple-pyramids and large, public works of art such as stone monuments. The people used their knowledge of astronomy, or the study of outer space, to develop complex, highly accurate calendars. They used a system of hieroglyphic writing unlike that of any other civilization.

▶ **Carrying on the tradition of their ancestors, these women weave clothing by hand in Mesoamerica.**

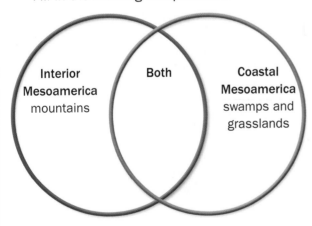

Many archaeologists believe that at least some of these similarities can be traced to a single advanced civilization. You will read about that civilization in the next lesson.

As you read about these ancient peoples, think about how these influences endured through time. You should also note the differences among these peoples and the civilizations they built.

REVIEW How were the peoples of Mesoamerica alike? ⟳ Compare and Contrast

Summarize the Lesson

- Mesoamerica extends from southern Mexico to the central part of Central America.
- The interior of Mesoamerica is a rugged land of mountains and plateaus.
- The northern coastal area of Mesoamerica is a region of lowlands. The southern coastal area of Mesoamerica is a region of highlands.

LESSON 1   REVIEW

Check Facts and Main Ideas

1. ⟳ **Compare and Contrast** On a separate piece of paper, copy the diagram below. Fill in the missing comparisons.

Interior Mesoamerica
mountains

Both

Coastal Mesoamerica
swamps and grasslands

2. Where is Mesoamerica?

3. What were three crops the Mesoamericans grew?

4. How did the early peoples of Mesoamerica use the natural resources of the region?

5. **Critical Thinking: Make Inferences** How do you think the environments described in this lesson would influence the Mesoamerican peoples?

Link to ∞ Mathematics

Plan a Journey The shortest distance between the Gulf of Mexico and the Pacific Ocean in Mesoamerica is about 140 miles. How long would it take to walk that distance, traveling ten hours a day, at an average speed of two miles per hour?

Map and Globe Skills

Use Map Projections

What? Map projections are the different ways that the curved surface of Earth can be projected, or shown, on a flat surface, such as paper.

Suppose you have an orange. The surface of the orange is curved, just like Earth's surface. If you want to lay the skin of the orange flat, you would have to tear it and stretch it in different places. Every map projection "tears" or "stretches" Earth's curved surface in a different way to show it on a flat surface.

The illustration of Earth on the left appears as an orange. The surface of Earth is torn at the dashed lines. The result would be similar to the Interrupted Projection shown below. It is one of several different map projections. The continents are very accurate in shape and size, but the oceans are distorted, or altered.

▶ **If Earth, like an orange, could be peeled along the white dashed lines, the result would be the interrupted map projection shown below.**

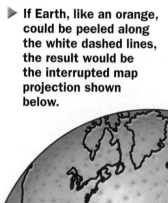

Why? Every type of flat map distorts Earth's curved surface in a different way. Some map projections distort distances. Some distort directions. Some even distort the shape and size of the land. You need to know what projection a mapmaker used so you will know which kind of distortions appear on the map.

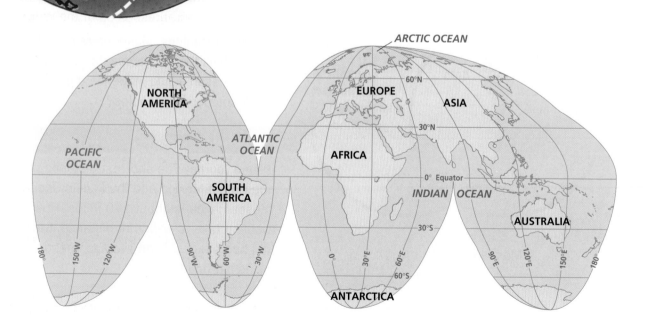

How? Many maps make it easy to determine the map projection. They tell you which projection is being used, right on the map! Usually, the projection will be one of three basic types. These are described below.

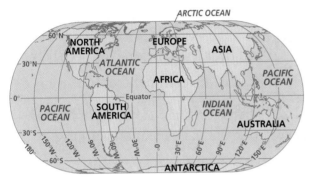

Equal-Area

- true only at the center point; distortion generally is worst at the edge of the map
- often used for comparing the size (but not the shape) of land masses.

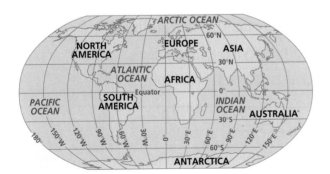

Robinson

- true along a line between the equator and a pole; distortion increases away from this line
- often used for maps of the United States

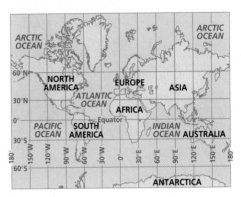

Mercator

- true at the equator; distortion increases toward the poles
- often used for navigation charts

Think and Apply

1. Why must every flat map contain some distortion?

2. What are the three basic types of map projections?

3. Why do you think a mapmaker might choose to use one type of projection over another?

Internet Activity

For more information, go online to the *Atlas* at **www.sfsocialstudies.com**.

1200 B.C.	600 B.C.	A.D. 1	A.D. 600

c. 1200 B.C.
Olmec civilization rises
in Mesoamerica.

c. 300 B.C.
Olmec civilization declines.

about A.D. 250
Mayan civilization
reaches its peak.

about A.D. 900
Mayan civilization
declines.

Chichén
Itzá

Gulf of
Mexico

**MAYAN
CIVILIZATION**

Tikal

PREVIEW

Focus on the Main Idea
The Olmec and the Maya
developed complex civilizations
in Mesoamerica.

PLACES
Tikal
Chichén Itzá

VOCABULARY
theocracy
aqueduct
codex

▶ The Olmec left behind ceramic
and stone figurines such as
this bald-headed baby.

The Olmec and the Maya

You Are There

You hear them before you see them.
First is the command of the group
leader—*"PULL!"* This is followed by
the unmistakable sound of dozens of men working
together. The command is repeated, as are the
grunts of the men. The sound is coming from up
the river. The only other sounds are the buzz of
insects and the soft rushing of the current.
Another command, another collective groan, and
they come into sight. You see men on both sides of
the river, pulling on huge ropes. Another
"PULL!" and you see what they are pulling.
It is a wooden raft, carrying a great black
shape far larger than any house in your
village. You know it is a huge chunk of
basalt, which will be carved into a giant
figure. You wonder if the stone will be
carved into an image of your king.

Compare and Contrast
As you read, think about
how the Olmec and the
Maya were similar and different.

Target Skill

A Mother Civilization

The sight of dozens of people pulling a huge rock down a river is more than an amazing scene. It is a sign of civilization.

The Olmec civilization was the first great civilization of Mesoamerica. It lasted from about 1200 B.C. to about 300 B.C. The Olmec people lived along the hot, humid coast of the Gulf of Mexico. They were surrounded by rain forests, grasslands, and swamps.

Most Olmec were farmers. Like the other peoples of Mesoamerica, they raised corn, beans, squash, and other crops. They also hunted and fished. They lived in small houses with thatched roofs. These small houses surrounded small villages. Much of the farmers' crops went to feed the people who lived in the villages.

The Olmec people were divided into social classes based on wealth and power. Olmec government was a **theocracy.** In a theocracy, the leader and the ruling classes are believed to represent the will of the gods. The priests and government officials were the most powerful classes in Olmec civilization.

Other social classes were made up of merchants and craftspeople. The lowest social class was made up of farmers.

Olmec communities were connected by roads. These roads fanned out to the villages of other peoples, especially those in the highlands of Mesoamerica. The Olmec traded honey and salt for jade, obsidian, and basalt from the mountains.

Olmec civilization is often called the "Mother Culture" or "Mother Civilization" of Mesoamerica. This is because the Olmec directly influenced all of the Mesoamerican civilizations that followed.

REVIEW What were the differences among the social classes in Olmec civilization?
🔁 Compare and Contrast

▶ **At the ruins of El Tajín in present-day Mexico lies the Pyramid of the Niches, built by the Totonac people of Mesoamerica.**

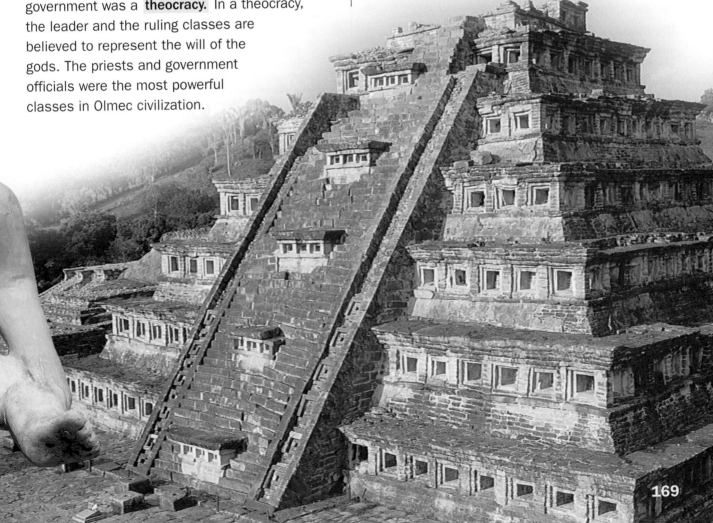

Olmec Accomplishments

Today, the Olmec people are most famous for the giant stone heads they constructed. These huge sculptures represented Olmec rulers. They were carved from basalt and weighed as much as 40 tons. This is about one-half the weight of a large tractor-trailer.

Other sculptures show gods that are half human and half animal, or combinations of two animals. These were animals that the Olmec were very familiar with, including jaguars, eagles, snakes, and sharks. The Olmec worshipped hundreds of gods. One Olmec god, the winged serpent, would appear later in other Mesoamerican cultures.

The Olmec developed a number system, a calendar, and a form of writing. Later Mesoamerican civilizations would learn from these developments. Some would improve on them.

No one knows what became of the Olmec. Some archaeologists think that they migrated east. They may have been the ancestors of another important civilization in Mesoamerica: the Maya.

REVIEW What did the Olmec develop that would be used by later Mesoamerican civilizations? **Main Idea and Details**

▶ **Heads made of basalt were left behind by the Olmec. Some archaeologists believe that the heads were of gods or rulers.**

170

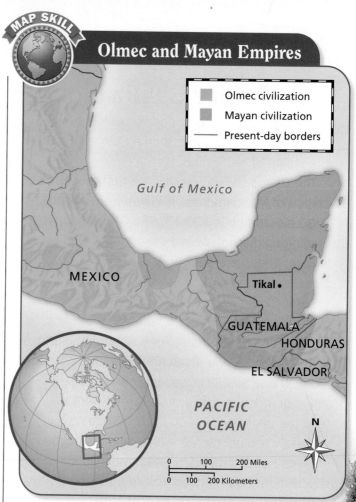

- Olmec civilization
- Mayan civilization
- Present-day borders

Gulf of Mexico

MEXICO

Tikal •

GUATEMALA
HONDURAS

EL SALVADOR

PACIFIC OCEAN

N

0   100   200 Miles
0   100   200 Kilometers

▶ **The Olmec and Mayan civilizations lived in parts of present-day Mexico, Guatemala, Honduras, and El Salvador.**

MAP SKILL Use a Map Key *Did the Olmec or the Mayan civilization cover more land area?*

The Maya

Tikal (tee KAHL) is one of the more than 100 locations of the Maya (MAH yuh) in Central America and Mexico. This city was once home to nearly 100,000 people. The people who lived there built more than 3,000 structures in Tikal. The sheer number of structures is impressive. Today there are ruins of observatories, palaces, plazas, baths, reservoirs, or artificial lakes, and **aqueducts,** or structures that carry flowing water. There are also pyramids more than 200 feet high—higher than a 20-story building.

But Tikal was more than a city. Like other Mayan settlements, it was a city-state. As you have learned, a city-state is an independent city. City-states such as Tikal grew and prospered. Mayan civilization reached its peak about A.D. 250. It flourished for another 650 years.

Did you remember that the Yucatán Peninsula is dotted with cenotes? These cenotes collect water. As a source of water, the cenotes were sacred to the Maya. With two large cenotes, the Mayan city of Chichén Itzá (chee CHAYN it SAH) served as the only source of water in the region. The Maya believed the cenotes were a way to communicate with the gods. Mayan priests made sacrifices to them. Today, the bottom of some cenotes are archaeological gold mines. From cenotes, archaeologists have recovered such objects as textiles, wood baskets, rubber, copper bells, spears, carved sticks, benches, jewelry, beautiful works of jade and gold, and a sacrificial knife made of stone.

Archaeologists have learned a great deal about the Maya from the artifacts found at these locations. Like the Olmec before them, the Maya developed a form of writing. However, the Mayan writing system was more complex. From artifacts and writing we know that the Maya grew vast fields of maize (corn), beans, and squash. Like the Olmec, the Maya lived in a theocracy. Like Olmec cities, Mayan cities were designed and constructed to pay tribute to the gods. The Maya believed the gods ruled Mayan life.

REVIEW When did Mayan culture flourish? Sequence

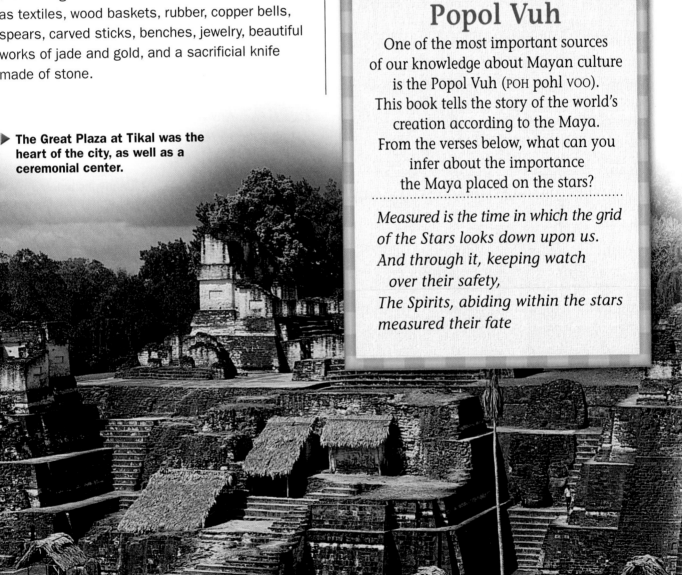

▶ **The Great Plaza at Tikal was the heart of the city, as well as a ceremonial center.**

Literature and Social Studies

Popol Vuh

One of the most important sources of our knowledge about Mayan culture is the Popol Vuh (POH pohl VOO). This book tells the story of the world's creation according to the Maya. From the verses below, what can you infer about the importance the Maya placed on the stars?

Measured is the time in which the grid of the Stars looks down upon us. And through it, keeping watch over their safety, The Spirits, abiding within the stars measured their fate

Time and Numbers

The Maya were very interested in keeping track of time and numbers. They used this information in their everyday lives and for religious customs.

Calendars served a variety of purposes, including recording birth dates, marriages, and the military victories of their leaders. The Maya also used calendars to make sure they were honoring their gods on the right dates.

The Maya actually used two different types of calendars, one for the solar seasons and the other for sacred rites. Without the benefit of telescopes, the Maya kept very accurate records of the length of the year and of the movements of the moon and planets. The Mayan year was divided into 365 days based on Earth's orbit around the sun, which did not become part of European knowledge until centuries later!

The **codex,** or folding-screen book, contained information about predicting the future and religious rituals for the priests. Each codex was written or painted on fig leaf bark or on animal skin, a preparation similar to Egyptian papyrus-making. The Maya used fine brushes and covered the bark or skin

▶ **Now in ruins, Chichén Itzá served as a center of trade and commerce for the Maya.**

with a protective layer made from a pasty substance. Like the Egyptians, the Maya used a system of hieroglyphic writing. Unfortunately, archaeologists have not been able to read many Mayan hieroglyphics.

The Maya were also excellent mathematicians. They created a unique counting system, based on the unit of 20. They are believed to have been the first people in the world to use the idea of zero in calculations.

REVIEW Why were the Maya so interested in telling time? **Main Idea and Details**

bars and dots representing numbers

hieroglyphs showing five gods

hieroglyphs painted onto protective layer

▶ **This copy of the Codex Tro-Cortesianus can be read from top to bottom and from left to right.**

Daily Life

Family life was very important to the Maya. Entire families, including grandparents, lived together. Except for very young children, everyone in the household had daily chores to do. Men plowed and planted fields, tended crops, and hunted and fished. Maize was the main crop, but beans, tomatoes, avocados, and fruits also were grown.

Women and older girls were responsible for all housekeeping chores, making clothes, supplying the home with firewood and water, and caring for the younger children.

Young children learned about farming and housekeeping chores but spent much of their time playing. While some of their toys had wheels, the Maya did not use wheels to help with labor.

Houses were small, with courtyards, kitchens, and small shrines to the gods. The houses usually were made of adobe, or dried mud bricks. Thatched roofs were made of palm leaves or grass. Furniture was simple: a few beds made of thick reed mats along with low tables and reed chests for clothing.

About A.D. 900, the Maya began to abandon many of their cities. Descendants of the Maya continued to live in Mesoamerica. In fact, the Maya live in Mexico and Guatemala to this day. What became of the great Mayan civilization remains a mystery. Some scholars believe that Mayan civilization may have disappeared as a result of invasion, crop failures, or even civil war.

REVIEW How were daily chores divided among members of Mayan families? **Main Idea and Details**

Summarize the Lesson

- **c. 1200 B.C.** The Olmec civilization arose.
- **c. 300 B.C.** The Olmec civilization declined and its people may have migrated east.
- **about A.D. 250** The Mayan civilization flourished on the Yucatán Peninsula.
- **about A.D. 900** The Mayan civilization declined.

LESSON 2   REVIEW

Check Facts and Main Ideas

1. ⟳ **Compare and Contrast** On a separate piece of paper, copy and complete the diagram below to compare and contrast the Olmec and the Maya.

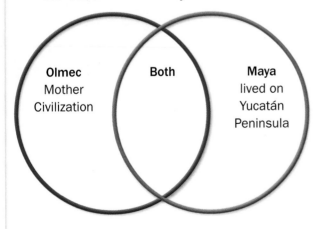

Olmec
Mother Civilization

Both

Maya
lived on Yucatán Peninsula

2. Why is the Olmec culture called a "Mother Civilization"?

3. Why were cenotes important to the Maya?

4. How were the Olmec and Mayan civilizations organized?

5. **Critical Thinking:** *Make Inferences* Do you think it is likely that the Olmec were the ancestors of the Maya? Why or why not?

Link to ⛓ **Science**

Explain the Connection Write a paragraph in which you explain why knowledge of astronomy was necessary for the Maya to create calendars.

AZTEC EMPIRE · Tenochtitlan

1200	1300	1400	1500	1600

A.D. 1200s
The Mexica migrate into the Valley of Mexico.

c. 1325
Tenochtitlan founded.

1440
Moctezuma I becomes ruler of the Aztecs.

1521
Spanish conquer the Aztec Empire.

The Aztecs

PREVIEW

Focus on the Main Idea
The Aztecs built a great empire in Mesoamerica.

PLACES
Valley of Mexico
Lake Texcoco
Tenochtitlan

PEOPLE
Moctezuma I
Moctezuma II
Hernando Cortés

VOCABULARY
mercenary
chinampa
causeway
alliance

▶ The Aztec athletes are shown playing a game that had also been popular with the earlier Olmec and Mayan civilizations.

You Are There

A feeling of triumph wells up inside you. A player on your team has just stolen the ball from the opponents. You're not old enough yet to play, but you've watched this ball game since you were little. You sit high atop a brick wall and watch the fast-paced game in the stone court beneath you. The rules are simple: each team tries to knock a rubber ball through a stone ring. The ball is heavy. It is about the same size as a human head. The players must get the ball through the hoop without letting it touch the ground—or their hands. The players are heavily padded. They use their elbows, shoulders, and hips to knock the ball. The game is so difficult that the first team to score wins the game. The winning team will be showered with honors. The losing team will receive an honor of a different sort: they will be sacrificed to the gods.

Main Idea and Details As you read, think about how the Aztec civilization built a great empire.

A Mesoamerican Civilization

The ball game of ulama (YU lah muh) was invented by the Olmec about 3,000 years ago. Like many Olmec inventions, it became part of other civilizations in Mesoamerica. The word *Olmec* means "the rubber people." This name was given to the Olmec people because rubber grew well in the region where they lived. You have read that the Olmec was "the Mother Civilization" of Mesoamerica, and that they influenced the Maya and others. There also were Olmec influences in the Aztec civilization, the last great civilization of ancient Mesoamerica.

Like the Olmec, the Maya, and other Mesoamerican civilizations, the Aztecs based their economy on farming. They grew maize, beans, and other crops. Like other regional civilizations, the Aztecs were great builders in stone. They constructed monuments, ceremonial

▶ **In this carving, the Mesoamerican winged-serpent god is in the center, surrounded by symbols representing years.**

Werner Forman/Museum fuer Voelkerkunde, Hamburg, Germany

centers, and pyramids. They were astronomers, mathematicians, priests, and farmers. Like the Egyptians, they left us a record in hieroglyphics. Like other civilizations in Mesopotamia, ancient Egypt, and Mesoamerica, they were polytheistic, or worshipped many gods. But the Aztecs did something the other Mesoamerican civilizations did not: they built a great empire.

REVIEW What is one important way the Aztecs differed from other Mesoamerican civilizations?

🔄 **Compare and Contrast**

MAP SKILL

Aztec Empire

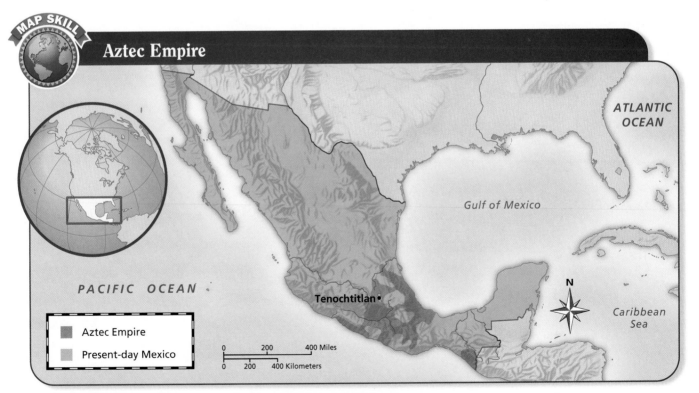

ATLANTIC OCEAN

Gulf of Mexico

PACIFIC OCEAN

Tenochtitlan •

Caribbean Sea

N

Legend:
- ▪ Aztec Empire
- ▪ Present-day Mexico

0   200   400 Miles
0   200   400 Kilometers

▶ **The Aztec Empire covered part of present-day Mexico.**

MAP SKILL Compare Maps *Compare this map with the map on page 170. Did the Mayan and Aztec Empires overlap?*

Early Aztec History

At one time, the Aztecs were just one of many Mesoamerican peoples. They called themselves the Mexica (me CHEE ka). They had migrated from the north. In the 1200s, the Mexica reached the **Valley of Mexico.** For generations, they lived on the fringes of land settled by other Mesoamerican peoples. Sometimes they served as **mercenaries,** or hired soldiers, for them. At other times, they had no choice but to live under the rule of others.

In the mid-1300s, the Mexica ended their wandering and started a city. All of the good land had been taken, so they settled on two swampy islands in **Lake Texcoco** (tay SKOH koh). The Mexica built their city, which they named **Tenochtitlan** (te noch tee TLAHN), after an ancestor named Tenoch.

As the population grew, Tenochtitlan and the island became overcrowded. To make more room, the Mexica built islands called **chinampas** (chin AHM phahz). How do you build an island? First, it helps if the water is not very deep. The Mexica started by anchoring wicker baskets to the shallow bottom of Lake Texcoco. Then they filled the baskets with cut plants and mud from the lake. The mud and vegetation were piled, layer upon layer, until they broke the surface of the water. The chinampas made excellent farmland. The Europeans later called the chinampas "floating gardens."

The Mexica built many artificial islands in the lake. They connected them with **causeways,** or raised bridges made of land. Causeways also connected the islands to the mainland.

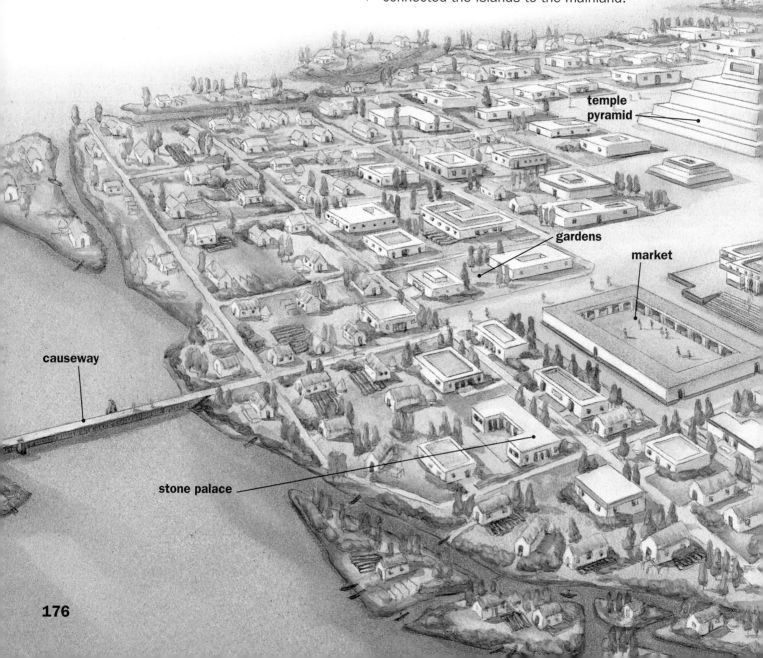

temple pyramid

gardens

market

causeway

stone palace

Tenochtitlan continued to grow. By the early 1400s, it was a powerful city-state, controlling the region around Lake Texcoco. The Mexica formed **alliances,** or agreements to work with other city-states. This helped their power grow far and wide.

As the Mexica grew in strength and power, they conquered neighboring city-states. They began to call themselves the Aztecs, after their legendary homeland of Aztlán (AHZ tlahn). The Aztec Empire had begun.

REVIEW Why did the Mexica build their city on a swampy island in Lake Texcoco? **Cause and Effect**

▶ **Tenochtitlan was the capital of the Aztec Empire.**

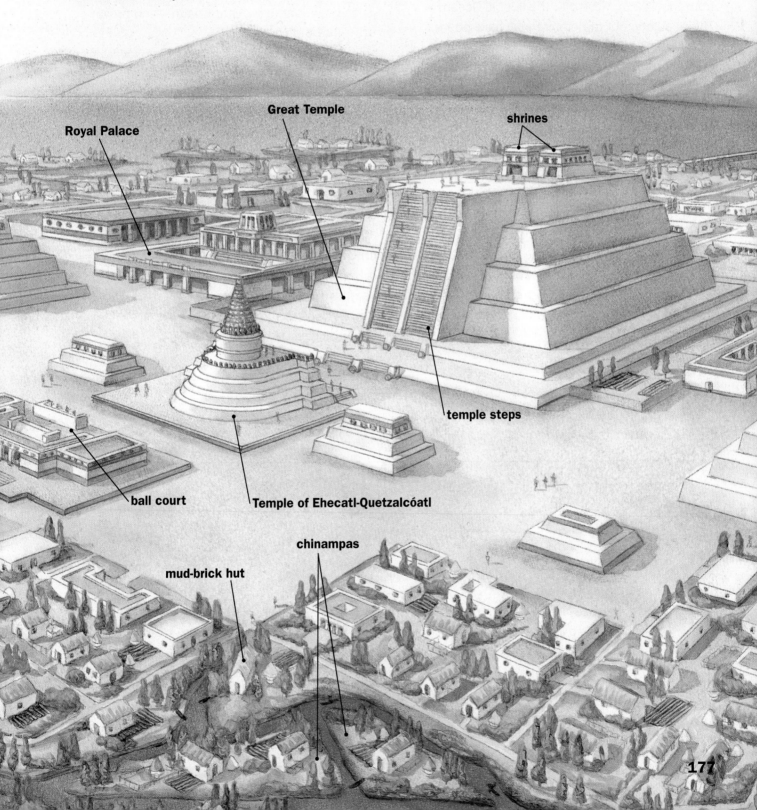

Royal Palace

Great Temple

shrines

temple steps

ball court

Temple of Ehecatl-Quetzalcóatl

chinampas

mud-brick hut

The Aztec Empire

The center of the Aztec Empire was always Tenochtitlan and the Valley of Mexico. At its peak, Tenochtitlan grew to a magnificent city with a population of 300,000. Tenochtitlan became the most densely populated city that had ever been seen in Mesoamerica up to that time. The Aztec Empire controlled many city-states from the Gulf of Mexico to the Pacific Ocean. The population of the empire may have been as high as 5 million people.

Moctezuma I (mahk tuh ZOO muh) ruled the empire from 1440 to 1469. He expanded the empire east and south. His successors continued the conquests.

The Aztecs often forced conquered city-states to pay tribute, or taxes, in gold. As the empire grew in size, it also grew in wealth.

How did the Aztecs gain such a large empire? Warfare was a normal part of life for them. All young men had to receive intensive training. The Aztecs encouraged a fighting spirit. To those who showed great courage in battle came fame and honor, as well as social advancement. Success in battle brought wealth—and prisoners—into the Aztec Empire.

REVIEW How did the Aztecs build a large empire? **Main Idea and Details**

HERE AND THERE

The Age of European Exploration

At the same time the Aztecs were building their empire, the Europeans were expanding their horizons. The Europeans wanted to find a sea route to Asia. Improvements in sailing ships and navigation led them into a great age of exploration. In 1487 the Portuguese explorer Bartolomeu Dias (bahr tu lu MAY u DEE ush) sailed east around the southern tip of Africa. Others sought a western sea route to Asia. One of these explorers was Christopher Columbus. In 1492 he attempted to take a western route to Asia. His voyage was interrupted when he ran into the Americas. Within just a few decades, the Europeans would change life forever in the Americas.

► **Bartolomeu Dias became the first European to round the Cape of Good Hope at the southern tip of Africa.**

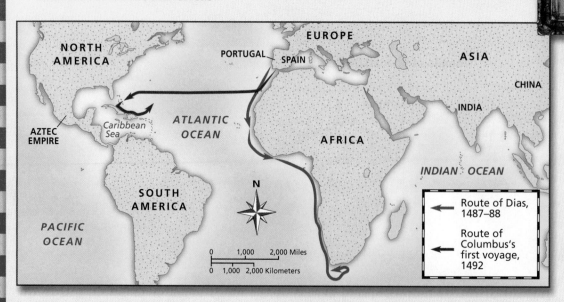

NORTH AMERICA
EUROPE
PORTUGAL SPAIN
ASIA
CHINA
INDIA
Caribbean Sea
ATLANTIC OCEAN
AFRICA
AZTEC EMPIRE
SOUTH AMERICA
INDIAN OCEAN
PACIFIC OCEAN
N

| 0 | 1,000 | 2,000 Miles |
| 0 | 1,000 | 2,000 Kilometers |

Route of Dias, 1487–88

Route of Columbus's first voyage, 1492

Life

Agriculture formed the base of the Aztec economy. The Aztecs grew maize, beans, squash, tomatoes, and cacao beans, which were used to make chocolate.

As important as agriculture was, religion was even more important. In the Aztec Empire, every aspect of life was touched by religion. Like other Mesoamerican peoples, the Aztecs worshipped hundreds of gods and goddesses. Do you remember reading in Lesson 2 about the Olmec god that was a winged serpent? The Aztecs also worshipped this god. They called him Quetzalcóatl (khet zahl koo WAH tahl), which means "feathered serpent." To the Aztecs, Quetzalcóatl was a god of creation. He influenced the wind, rain, and clouds.

▶ The Aztec god of springtime and vegetation was also the patron of metal workers. To honor him, the Aztecs often sacrificed people.

Many Aztec religious ceremonies were based on agricultural events, such as planting and harvesting. The Aztecs worshipped gods that represented certain crops and seasons.

One aspect of Aztec religion that has troubled people who study them today is the Aztec practice of human sacrifice. The Aztecs believed that they needed to perform sacrifices to honor their gods. Even the sun needed to be fueled by human sacrifice so that it would continue moving across the sky.

The Aztecs believed that the human heart was the most precious gift they could offer their gods. The Aztecs mainly sacrificed prisoners of war. However, they also sacrificed their own people, slaves, and even children. One estimate puts the number of people sacrificed by the Aztecs each year at about 250,000.

REVIEW Why did the Aztecs believe that they needed to practice human sacrifice? **Main Idea and Details**

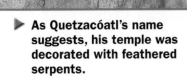

▶ As Quetzacóatl's name suggests, his temple was decorated with feathered serpents.

179

A Violent End

The Aztecs built their empire through the violent conquest of other city-states. Being a soldier was even considered a religious duty. However, the Aztec Empire itself was soon to fall victim to a violent conquest.

In 1502 **Moctezuma II** became emperor. For the next two decades, the Aztecs would enjoy their greatest period of power and wealth. Then, in 1519, Spanish explorers, led by **Hernando Cortés**, (er NAHN doh kawr TEZ) marched into Tenochtitlan. Moctezuma II did not fight his advance. Why? He may have believed that Cortés was Quetzalcóatl. According to an Aztec legend, the god had sailed away long ago, but would someday return. We do not know whether or not Moctezuma II believed Cortés was the fulfillment of this legend. However, we do know that the Spanish took Moctezuma II prisoner. The Aztecs rebelled when they realized that Cortés's goal was to conquer them. But they were unsuccessful. By 1521 the Spanish conquest was complete. The Aztec Empire was no more.

REVIEW What caused the end of the Aztec Empire? **Cause and Effect**

▶ In this sixteenth-century illustration, local enemies of the Aztecs make peace with Cortés and offer to lead him to Moctezuma II.

Summarize the Lesson

- **A.D. 1200s** The Mexica migrated into the Valley of Mexico.
- **c. 1325** The Mexica founded the city of Tenochtitlan.
- **1440** Moctezuma I became the ruler of the Aztecs.
- **1521** The Spanish, under Hernando Cortés, conquered the Aztec Empire.

LESSON 3 REVIEW

Check Facts and Main Ideas

1. Main Idea and Details On a separate piece of paper, complete the diagram below.

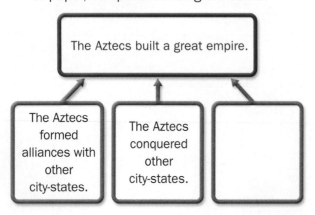

The Aztecs built a great empire.

The Aztecs formed alliances with other city-states.

The Aztecs conquered other city-states.

2. What was Tenochtitlan?

3. How did the Aztecs use alliances to build their empire?

4. What became of the Aztec Empire?

5. **Critical Thinking:** *Make Inferences* Do you think the Aztec Empire would have continued without the arrival of the Spanish?

Link to ∞ Art

Design a Picture Sketch, draw, or paint a picture in the Aztec style of art, based on the Aztec artwork on pages 175 and 179.

Moctezuma II

1466–1520

Moctezuma II was not always in line to be emperor of the Aztec Empire. As a young man, Moctezuma proved to be an exceptional warrior. When his uncle died in about 1502, Moctezuma became the new leader of the Aztecs.

Moctezuma was said to be quite superstitious. Dreams often influenced his actions and decisions. When news came that "light-skinned men" had arrived in the empire, Moctezuma may have believed that they were ambassadors of the light-skinned god, Quetzalcóatl. According to a legend, Quetzalcóatl would one day arrive and take over the empire.

Moctezuma sent gifts of gold to the Spanish but warned them to keep away from the capital. The Spanish ignored this warning and entered Tenochtitlan. Moctezuma met with Cortés and told him:

"I do not doubt the goodness of the god whom you worship . . . our gods are equally good for Mexico."

BIOFACT

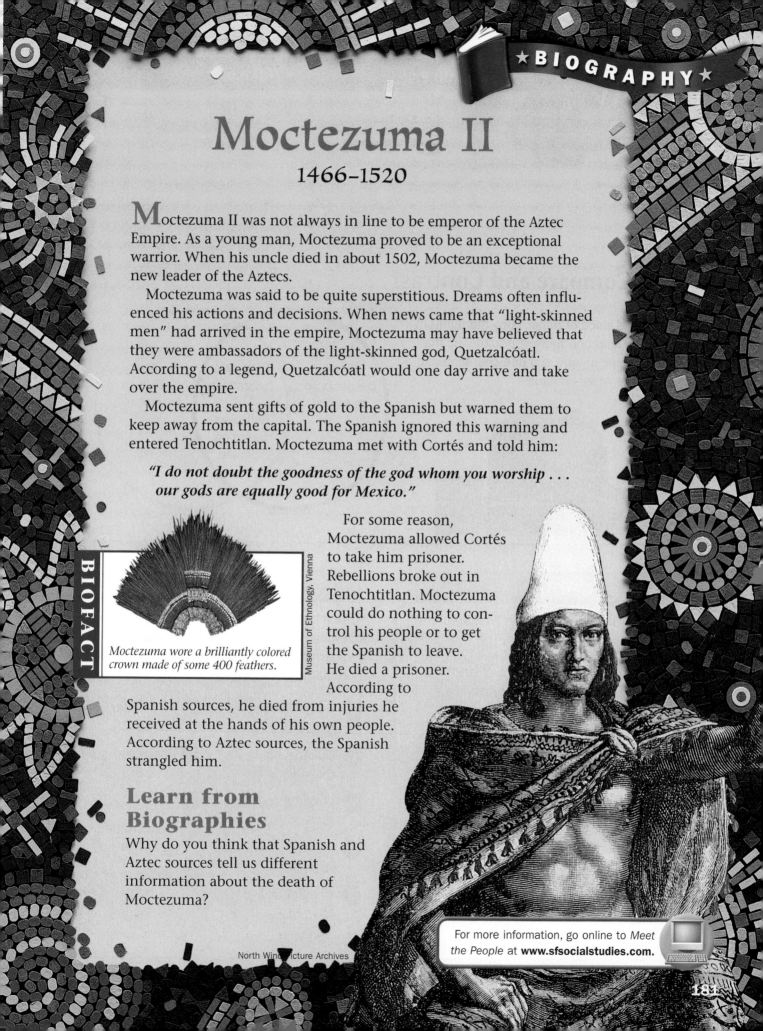

Moctezuma wore a brilliantly colored crown made of some 400 feathers.

Museum of Ethnology, Vienna

For some reason, Moctezuma allowed Cortés to take him prisoner. Rebellions broke out in Tenochtitlan. Moctezuma could do nothing to control his people or to get the Spanish to leave. He died a prisoner. According to Spanish sources, he died from injuries he received at the hands of his own people. According to Aztec sources, the Spanish strangled him.

Learn from Biographies

Why do you think that Spanish and Aztec sources tell us different information about the death of Moctezuma?

North Wind Picture Archives

For more information, go online to *Meet the People* at **www.sfsocialstudies.com.**

1200 B.C.   700 B.C.   200 B.C.

c. 1200 B.C.
Olmec civilization arose
in Mesoamerica.

c. 300 B.C.
Olmec civilization declined.

Chapter Summary

Compare and Contrast

On a separate piece of paper, copy the diagram
to the right. Fill in one more characteristic that
made the Olmec unique and one characteristic
that made the Aztecs unique.

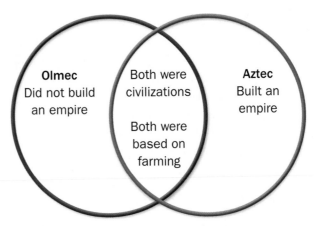

Olmec
Did not build
an empire

**Both were
civilizations**

**Both were
based on
farming**

Aztec
Built an
empire

Vocabulary

Match each vocabulary word with its correct
definition.

1. **peninsula**
   (p. 164)

2. **cenote**
   (p. 164)

3. **theocracy**
   (p. 169)

4. **alliance**
   (p. 177)

5. **chinampa**
   (p. 176)

a. a long arm of land
   reaching out to sea

b. an artificial island

c. an agreement

d. sacred well

e. a form of government in
   which the rulers are
   believed to know the
   will of the gods

Places and People

Write a sentence explaining why each of the
following people and places are important to
Mesoamerican civilization. You may use two or
more names or places in a single sentence.

1. Gulf of Mexico
   (p. 164)

2. Moctezuma I
   (p. 178)

3. Lake Texcoco
   (p. 176)

4. Plateau of Mexico
   (p. 163)

5. Chichén Itzá
   (p. 171)

6. Hernando Cortés
   (p. 180)

7. Moctezuma II
   (p. 180)

8. Tikal (p. 170)

9. Tenochtitlan
   (p. 176)

10. Valley of Mexico
    (p. 176)

A.D. 200   900   1600

about A.D. 250
Mayan civilization reached its peak.

about A.D. 900 Mayan civilization declined.

1200s Mexica migrated into the Valley of Mexico.

c. 1325 Tenochtitlan was founded.

1440 Moctezuma I became ruler of the Aztecs.

1521 The Spanish conquered the Aztec Empire.

Facts and Main Ideas

1. What are two bodies of water that border Mesoamerica?

2. Why were calendars important to the Maya?

3. Why did the Aztecs settle on swampy islands in Lake Texcoco instead of on more productive land?

4. **Time Line** About how many years passed between the rise of civilization in Mesoamerica and the Spanish destruction of the Aztec Empire?

5. **Main Idea** What is the interior of Mesoamerica like?

6. **Main Idea** Why are the Olmec called the "Mother Civilization" of Mesoamerica?

7. **Main Idea** How did the Aztecs build their empire?

8. **Critical Thinking:** *Make Generalizations* Did the Olmec, Maya, and Aztecs all have the characteristics of a civilized society? Explain your answer.

Write About History

1. **Write a postcard** as if you were visiting the ruins at Tikal. Tell the people back home what you see.

2. **Write a letter** explaining why you would or would not like to live in a theocracy.

3. **Write a description** of what you think it would be like to dive to the bottom of a cenote in search of Mayan artifacts.

Apply Skills

Use Map Projections
Study the map of the North Pole below. Then answer the questions.

1. If the map of the North Pole is true only at its center point, what kind of projection is it?

2. Can this map be used to determine the shape of the continents? Explain your answer.

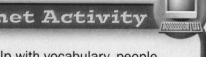

Internet Activity

To get help with vocabulary, people, and terms, select dictionary, encyclopedia, or almanac from *Social Studies Library* at **www.sfsocialstudies.com.**

The Early Peoples of South America

Lesson 1

Andes Mountains
Rising in South America, the Andes are home to many people.

1

Lesson 2

A.D. 100
Chavín
Two ancient civilizations rise in Peru.

2

Lesson 3

A.D. 1471
Cuzco
The Inca people build the largest and richest empire in South America.

3

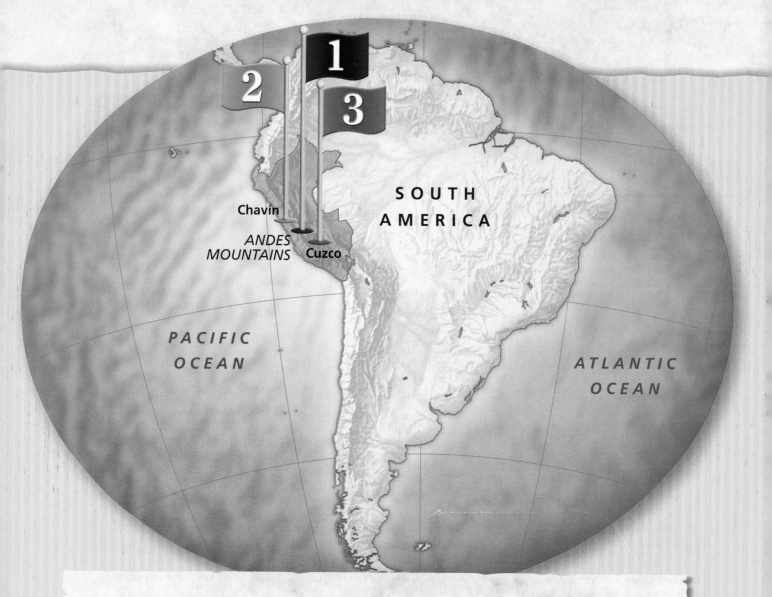

PACIFIC OCEAN

SOUTH AMERICA

ATLANTIC OCEAN

Chavín

ANDES MOUNTAINS

Cuzco

Why We Remember

The South American country of Peru is a rugged land. Visitors to the country are often stunned by a climate that can be harsh and a landscape that can be even harsher. Deserts and mountains rule here. Yet people have lived here for centuries. In fact, one of the greatest empires the world has ever known thrived in this landscape. How did these people build a great civilization in such a harsh environment? The early peoples of Peru teach us that civilizations can flourish in many different places.

Geography of South America

PREVIEW

Focus on the Main Idea
South America is a large continent of many landscapes.

PLACES
Amazon River
Amazon rain forest
Pantanal
Andes Mountains
Altiplano
Lake Titicaca
Guiana Highlands
Pampas

VOCABULARY
wetland
biome
scrub land
archipelago

▶ Llamas belong to the camel family. For centuries, they have provided food, wool, and hides for the South American peoples.

You Are There

You have to tilt your head back to see the tops of the mountains. You see their snow-capped peaks glistening in the late day sun. Could anything else in the world be so tall? You think that no human will ever reach the tops of the tallest peaks. Yet, when the air is clear, you sometimes feel as though you could almost reach out and touch them. Looking to the left, and then to the right, you see the great mountain chain stretch across the horizon. Your mother told you that she once met a man, a government official, who had been to the edge of the empire. Even there, the mountains stretch out to the horizon. Behind you the surf from the great sea rumbles on the shore. It is as vast, you think, as the mountains are high. This is truly a great land. You are proud to be a member of a great empire.

Compare and Contrast As you read, think about how various regions of South America are different from each other.

A Land of World Records

Rugged mountains are just one of the wonders of South America. In fact, you can think of the continent as a land of world records. Here, you can gaze at the world's highest waterfall, Angel Falls. You can travel the world's second longest river, the **Amazon River.** You can hike through the world's largest rain forest, the **Amazon rain forest.** You can see the world's largest wetland, the **Pantanal** (pahn teh NAHL). A **wetland** is an area of very moist soil, such as a swamp.

South America stretches nearly 5,000 miles north to south, and more than 3,000 miles east to west. If you could stretch its more than 15,000 miles of coastline into a straight line, it would reach more than 60 percent of the way around the world.

All along South America's western edge lie the stunning **Andes Mountains.** This mountain range sets another world record: at 4,500 miles in length, it is the longest chain of mountains in the world. The Andes are rough, snow-capped mountains. There are glaciers among its peaks. At lower elevations, or the height of the land above the sea, are steep slopes and many miles of grassy plateaus. People have made the harsh Andes their home for thousands of years.

One place they lived was on the **Altiplano,** a region of plateaus and plains high in the mountains. Early peoples discovered that the cold, dry air was suitable for farming grains, potatoes—an important crop native to the region—and maize (corn). It was also on the Altiplano that ancient peoples first domesticated the llama and alpaca, both members of the camel family. These animals served as beasts of burden and sources of meat and wool. The people used the wool to make cloth and rope. The cloth helped protect people from the harsh, cold winds that sweep down from the mountains across the Altiplano.

REVIEW How is the Altiplano different from the other parts of the Andes Mountains?
 Compare and Contrast

▶ **The Pantanal**

▶ **The Andes Mountains**

Guiana Highlands
Atlantic Ocean
Amazon River
Amazon Rain forest
Pacific Ocean
Andes
Altiplano
Atacama Desert
Lake Titicaca
Pantanal
Brazilian Highlands
Andes
Pampas
Tierra del Fuego

Rain forest
Mixed forest
Grassland
Shrub
Water

▶ **Amazon rain forest**

▶ **Altiplano**

187

Lake Titicaca

Lake Titicaca lies in the Altiplano between the present-day countries of Bolivia and Peru. No one knows what "titicaca" means for sure, but it may mean "Rock of the Puma." Some ruins at Lake Titicaca are more than 2,000 years old—among the oldest in South America. Ancient peoples who lived there knew the advantages of life by the lake.

One advantage is that many rivers flow into the lake. These rivers provide fresh water and fish. Lake Titicaca has a somewhat moderate, or mild, climate. However, nights can be very cold and days quite warm.

The land near Lake Titicaca can support crops such as maize and potatoes. Barley grows here as well. However, the weather and elevation are too harsh for the barley to ripen. Barley is grown to provide food for the llamas and alpacas.

Lake Titicaca also provides a means of transportation. Reeds grow at the edge of the lake. Ancient peoples wove them to make small boats. Today, these boats are called balsas. The people of this region still make and sail balsas.

REVIEW What are some of the advantages of living near Lake Titicaca? **Main Idea and Details**

▶ **The Aymara culture built these tombs at Lake Titicaca about A.D. 1000.**

Many Landscapes

The landscapes of South America are diverse and contain many **biomes.** Biomes are places that have distinct climates and types of plants and animals.

The Andes Mountains dominate the western edge of South America. Tiny streams in the Andes merge to form the Amazon River in the northern half of South America. The Amazon River flows nearly 4,000 miles eastward to its mouth on the Atlantic Ocean. It drains the Amazon rain forest, the largest rain forest on Earth.

Farther east, the mighty Amazon River cuts through a region of mountains. These mountains are called the Eastern Highlands. To the north of the river are the **Guiana Highlands** (gee AHN ah), a land of vast tropical forests.

Much of central and southern South America is quite different from the mountains and forests of the north. The Atacama Desert is in the northern part of present-day Chile, in west-central South America. The Atacama Desert is one of the driest regions on Earth.

Central and southern South America is a land of plains. Much of it is **scrub land,** or areas of low-growing vegetation. At the southern part of the plains lie the **Pampas,** a vast grassland. Even farther south, the land turns drier and becomes the scrub land of Patagonia. The tip of South America is made up of an **archipelago,** or group of islands, called Tierra del Fuego (tee AIR ah del FWAY goh).

Grasslands, deserts, and rain forests are all types of biomes.

REVIEW How does the southern part of South America differ from the northern part of the continent?
↻ **Compare and Contrast**

The Peoples of South America

People have lived throughout the diverse landscapes of South America. They have lived in forests and in deserts, in the mountains and on the plains for thousands of years. However, only a few early peoples created large-scale, complex civilizations. This was probably due in part to the rugged landscape of the continent. It is difficult to unite people

▶ **In traditional dress, this Quechua (KEHCH wuh) boy is a descendant of the early peoples of Peru.**

who are separated by high mountains, dense forests, and great distances. Yet it was accomplished in a surprising place: the most rugged part of South America, the Andes Mountains.

REVIEW What is one important way the early peoples of South America differ from one another? ↩ Compare and Contrast

Summarize the Lesson

- The Andes Mountains are the longest mountain chain in the world.
- The Altiplano and Lake Titicaca were settled by people thousands of years ago.
- The northern half of South America is dominated by the Amazon River, the Amazon rain forest, and highlands.
- The central and southern parts of South America are dominated by scrub land and grasslands.

LESSON 1   REVIEW

Check Facts and Main Ideas

1. ↩ **Compare and Contrast** On a separate piece of paper, copy and complete the diagram below.

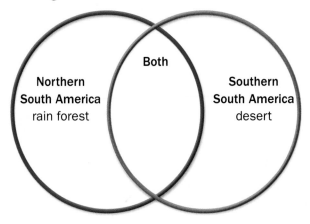

Northern South America
rain forest

Both

Southern South America
desert

2. What world record is held by the Andes Mountains?

3. Why did ancient peoples settle near Lake Titicaca?

4. What are several types of landscapes that can be found in South America?

5. **Critical Thinking:** *Make Generalizations* In which part of South America do you think it would be easiest for people to live? Why?

> ### Link to ⬤—⬤ Science
>
> **Life at the Lake** You have read that Lake Titicaca has a moderate climate. Explain what effects you think this would have on the surrounding area.

900 B.C.　　　　　　　A.D. 1　　　　　　　A.D. 900

about 900 B.C.
Chavín culture appears.

about A.D. 100
Mochica culture appears.

about 200 B.C.
Chavín culture disappears.

about A.D. 800
Mochica culture disappears.

The Chavín and the Mochica

PREVIEW

Focus on the Main Idea
The Chavín and Mochica developed civilizations in ancient Peru.

PLACES
Peru
Chavín
Moche Valley

You Are There

You turn the vessel in your hands. The bottle has a beautiful shape. You are especially pleased with the way you've molded the hollow handle and its protruding sprout. This was the most difficult part of the job. You have done it well. The main part of the bottle shows warriors in battle. You worked hard to make the warriors' faces appear fierce and courageous. You are almost finished. Now comes the delicate design work. You prepare to paint the vessel carefully. You know your handiwork will be buried with a great warrior. You're proud and wonder what color paint you will use.

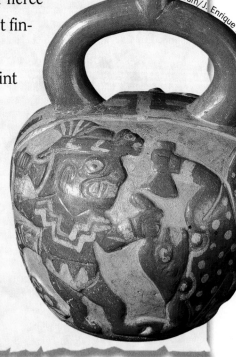

Album/ J. Enrique N

▶ **This Mochican ceramic vase portrays warriors fighting.**

Main Idea and Details As you read, think about why the Chavín and Mochica are considered important ancient civilizations.

The Chavín

About 900 B.C., a civilization took root in the Andes Mountains of South America, in the present-day country of **Peru.** Peru is a rough land. Its coastal area is one of the driest in the world. The Andes Mountains soar more than two miles into the sky. Their snow-capped peaks are within 50 miles of the dry coast. However, an early civilization still was able to flourish in this region. The people in this civilization lived in the narrow valleys formed by rivers that flowed from the peaks to the desert floor.

This civilization lived here until about 200 B.C. We know about it from ruins, especially from the city of **Chavín** (chah VEEN). It is the ruins of Chavín that give this civilization its name. As with so many other early groups, we do not know what the Chavín people called themselves.

We do know that the Chavín were accomplished artists. They made elaborate textiles, pottery, and stone carvings. In fact, the Chavín are most famous for their art. The Chavín style of art is noted for fantastic images. These images include cats, crocodiles, and serpents. Jaguars were common images. Some people believe that the Chavín worshipped jaguars.

Chavín-style art has been found over a large area. That area covers what is today the northern part of Peru. Because Chavín art is widespread,

► From the art of the Chavín, archaeologists have learned that the Chavín were polytheistic. This wool wrap shows the "Smiling God."

archaeologists believe that the Chavín influenced other peoples. Before the Chavín, there were many different cultures living in the region. The Chavín culture unified these peoples.

About 200 B.C. the Chavín style suddenly disappeared. No one knows why. We do know that the ancient peoples of Peru split into many cultures. They would not be united again for another 500 years. However, the Chavín people left a lasting legacy of beauty in their art.

REVIEW How did the appearance of the Chavín change the cultures that lived in the region? How did their disappearance change the cultures of the region?

Sequence

► Discovered in the temple at Chavín de Huantar in Peru, this stone head probably represented a god.

Archaeological Museum Lima/Dagli Orti

191

The Mochica

About A.D. 100, one of the early cultures of Peru rose up over the other peoples. Like the Chavín long before them, these people were accomplished artists. No one knows where they came from or what happened to them. But their civilization lasted for about 700 years. Because their artifacts have been found in the Moche Valley, we refer to these people as the Moche (MOH cheh), or Mochica (moh CHEE kah). They left behind ceramic vessels, woven textiles, murals, and amazing objects of copper, silver, and gold.

Like the Chavín before them, the Mochica lived in river valleys between the mountains of Peru. Evidence shows that the Mochica probably settled along the dry coast of Peru as well.

The Mochica were farmers. They also were skilled builders. They altered the courses of rivers and streams flowing down from the Andes. They used the water to irrigate their crops. They grew maize, beans, and squash. They were also excellent fishermen.

Mochica city-states had flat-topped pyramids, stone courtyards, and plazas. The ruins of these city-states have taught us most of what we know about the Mochica. Water jars have been another important source of information. Archaeologists have found water jars painted with pictures of people, animals, plants, buildings, and gods. Many contain pictures of Mochica ceremonies, from which we can learn something about their religion.

The disappearance of the Mochica remains a mystery. All we know is that, even though they lived in a harsh environment, they created beautiful objects that have lasted for centuries.

REVIEW How have we learned about the religious beliefs of the Mochica? **Main Idea and Details**

▶ **Many gold and copper artifacts from about A.D. 300 were discovered at the tomb of the Lord of Sipan in Peru.**

Solving a Mystery

In many ways, the Chavín and the Mochica are mysteries. No one knows for sure where they came from, or what happened to them. We do not even know their real names. As you learned earlier in this lesson, the name *Chavín* comes from an archaeological site. The name *Mochica* comes from the modern name of a river valley. It is from their art, artifacts, and ruins that we have been able to learn about them.

Archaeologists are still finding artifacts. Each new group of artifacts tells us a little more about the lives of these ancient peoples. With each new discovery, a little bit of the mystery is uncovered. You have read about the rugged, sometimes harsh environments of South America. The Andes Mountains might not seem to be a promising place for a great empire. However, hundreds of years after the mysterious disappearance of the Mochica, a great empire did emerge in this region. Only further exploration can tell us how great the Chavín and Mochica influence was on that civilization.

REVIEW How have archaeologists learned about the Chavín and the Mochica? **Summarize**

Summarize the Lesson

- **c. 900 B.C.** Chavín culture, with its distinctive style of art, appeared in ancient Peru.
- **c. 200 B.C.** Chavín culture disappeared.
- **c. A.D. 100** Mochica culture appeared in the river valleys and coastal areas of ancient Peru.
- **c. A.D. 800** Mochica culture mysteriously disappeared.

▶ **Also from the tomb of the Lord of Sipan is the reconstruction of the ornaments that decorated the lord. Much of the gold and ornate decorations symbolized power.**

LESSON 2   REVIEW

Check Facts and Main Ideas

1. **Main Ideas and Details** On a separate piece of paper, copy and complete the diagram below.

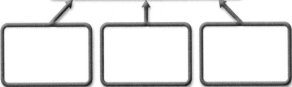

Chavín and Mochica were two important early Andean civilizations.

2. Where did the Chavín and Mochica live?

3. Describe Chavín art and explain how it has helped us learn about Chavín culture.

4. How do we know about the Chavín and the Mochica?

5. **Critical Thinking:** *Accuracy of Information* Do the artifacts that archaeologists have found tell us how the Chavín and Mochica disappeared? Explain your answer.

Link to ⊶ Writing

Take an Archaeological Adventure Write a letter to an archaeologist explaining why you would like to participate in an archaeological dig at a Chavín or a Mochica site.

Map and Globe Skills

Use Latitude and Longitude

What? Latitude and longitude are the names of the imaginary lines that form a grid on a globe or map. Lines of latitude extend east and west. Lines of longitude extend north and south. Lines of latitude and lines of longitude intersect, or meet and cross each other. The pattern they make covers a globe or map with a grid. By referring to this grid, we can name the location of any point on Earth.

Both latitude and longitude are measured in degrees from a base line, or starting point. The base line for latitude is the equator, or 0° latitude. For example, the latitude of New Orleans, Louisiana, is 30° north (30°N).

The base line for longitude is the prime meridian, or 0° longitude, which runs through Western Africa and Europe. For example, the longitude of New Orleans is 90° west (90°W).

If a place is located part-way between degrees of latitude or longitude, you can measure it more accurately by counting minutes. Each minute represents one-sixtieth of a degree. This means that there are 60 minutes in every degree.

▶ **The location of New Orleans is 30°N, 90°W. The location of Guatemala City, Guatemala is 15°N, 90°W.**

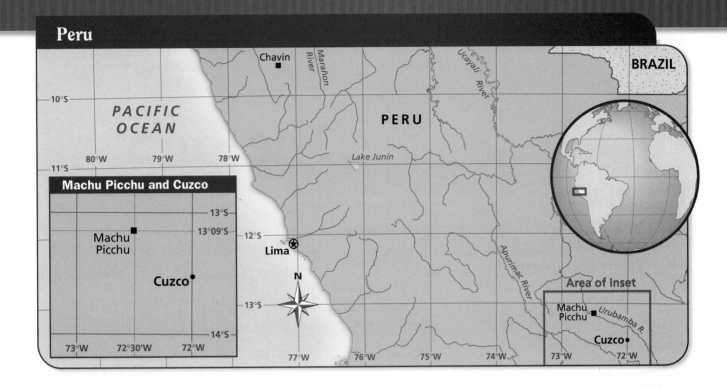

Peru

Machu Picchu and Cuzco

Why?

Navigators of ships and airplanes use the latitude/longitude grid to help plot their courses. Archaeologists use it to pinpoint the locations of their digs. Government officials use it to plan roads and cities.

How?

Follow this three-step process.

1. Determine latitude. The latitude is marked on the left or right edge (or both) of most maps. Set your finger on a place. Then run your finger horizontally toward the latitude markings. Be sure to note whether the latitude is north or south.

2. Determine longitude. Longitude is marked on the top or bottom edge (or both) of most maps. Set your finger on a place. Then run your finger vertically toward the longitude markings. Be sure to note whether the longitude is east or west.

3. Express the location. Always express latitude first, then longitude. Use this format: "00° [north or south], 00° [east or west]." If you are indicating minutes as well as degrees, use "00° 00'."

Another way of determining latitude and longitude is through the use of GPS, or Global Positioning Satellites. GPS is a system of

satellites and ground stations that are used to locate exact points on Earth's surface.

Use the map at the top of this page to answer the following questions. Express your answer using latitude and longitude.

1 What is the location of Lima?

2 What is the location of Cuzco? Estimate the minutes as well as degrees.

3 What is the location of Machu Picchu? Use the inset map to determine the minutes.

For more information, go online to the *Atlas* at **www.sfsocialstudies.com**.

INCA EMPIRE
Cuzco

| 1200 | 1300 | 1400 | 1500 |

about A.D. 1200
Inca culture appears.

A.D. 1438
Inca defeat Chancas.

1471
Topa Inca becomes emperor.

The Inca

PREVIEW

Focus on the Main Idea
The Inca ruled a vast empire in the Andes Mountains.

PLACES
Machu Picchu
Cuzco

PEOPLE
Manco Capac
Inca Viracocha
Pachacuti
Topa Inca
Francisco Pizarro

VOCABULARY
quipu

You Are There

Your breathing is heavy, but not hard. As you run up the hill you find yourself breathing out on every other step. Perfect. You know now that you will complete your journey. Another few paces and you will reach the top of the hill. Then you can enjoy the easy run down the other side to the outpost. There, you will tell the next runner on the route the important orders from the emperor. The next runner should be very easy to spot. This road is used only to deliver messages to and from the emperor. There he is! The next runner stands at the bottom of the long hill. You don't know him, but you are confident that he, like you, knows the important role of an Inca runner.

Main Idea and Details
As you read, think about the major contributions of the Inca Empire to civilization.

▶ Machu Picchu was most likely a religious center of the Inca Empire. It was discovered by explorer Hiram Bingham in 1911.

A Vast Empire

The Inca people of South America built the largest and richest empire the Americas had ever seen. The name *Inca* originally was the title of the emperor. Eventually, it referred to all of the people in the empire.

The Inca Empire stretched down the western side of the Andes. It included dozens of different peoples. The Inca were able to keep this vast empire united for many years.

▶ **The Inca made beautiful artifacts from gold, such as this goblet, or drinking glass.**

Little is known about the origins of the Inca. The Inca themselves had different origin stories, or legends about how they came to be. However, much of what we do know comes from the archaeological site of **Machu Picchu** (MAHCH oo PEEK choo). This mountaintop city of more than 140 granite buildings may have been home to some 1,000 people. Archaeologists have discovered that many of the buildings were temples. They have also uncovered many mummies. As a result, many believe that Machu Picchu was a religious center.

The first Inca ruler was **Manco Capac,** who, according to one origin story, came from Lake Titicaca. Archaeologists believe that the Inca were one of many peoples living in the region. They eventually settled down and built a city, **Cuzco.** Cuzco was to remain the Inca capital for the life of the empire. About A.D. 1200, the Inca civilization was not particularly large. The Inca also were not very powerful. For about 200 years, the Inca fought against local groups of people for dominance. They also formed alliances with some of these groups. One of these alliances would soon make the Inca the rulers of a vast empire. This is similar to what you learned in Chapter 6 about the beginnings of the Aztec Empire. As you will see, the Inca were to meet a similar destiny.

REVIEW Why do many people believe that Machu Picchu was a religious center? **Summarize**

An Empire Is Born

Many historians believe that the eighth Inca ruler was **Inca Viracocha.** In 1438 the Inca were attacked by a powerful people from the north, the Chancas. Viracocha might have abandoned his people because he feared that it was impossible to defeat the powerful Chancas. What we do know is that Viracocha fled Cuzco.

Inca history might have ended then and there if it were not for **Pachacuti** (pah cha KOO tee), one of Viracocha's sons. Read more about Pachacuti in the Biography on page 203. Instead of running, Pachacuti stayed to fight. The Chancas attacked. Even with the help of some foreign soldiers, the Inca were still losing the battle. Pachacuti needed to rally his troops. According to legend, Pachacuti called out to the stones of the battlefield. The stones rose up and turned into soldiers to help the Inca, giving the soldiers the confidence to defeat the Chancas.

Pachacuti then became emperor. Motivated by his great victory, he began to expand the Inca world. He conquered many neighboring peoples and made them part of the Inca Empire. He also ordered that many conquered peoples be resettled, or moved to, other parts of the Inca Empire. The Inca thought that if conquered people were separated from other people in their own group, it would be harder for them to put up a strong resistance.

Men from conquered lands became soldiers in the Inca army. Thus, Pachacuti's army grew. His power increased and his empire expanded greatly. To commemorate, or honor, his victories, Pachacuti became a great builder. It was under his leadership that many great buildings were built in Cuzco, the capital of the empire.

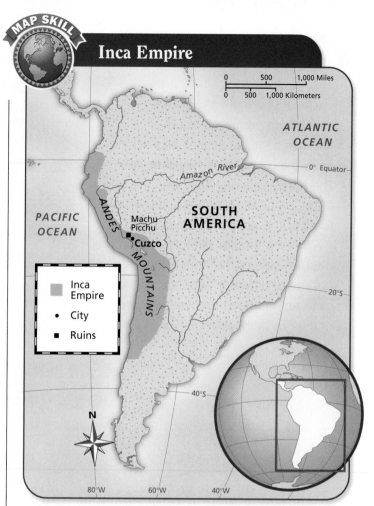

Inca Empire

ATLANTIC OCEAN

Amazon River

0° Equator

PACIFIC OCEAN

ANDES MOUNTAINS

Machu Picchu

Cuzco

SOUTH AMERICA

20°S

- Inca Empire
- City City
- Ruins Ruins

40°S

N

80°W 60°W 40°W

▶ The ruins of Machu Picchu have provided many clues about life in the Inca Empire.

MAP SKILL Use a Map Key *Were the Andes Mountains within the Inca Empire?*

In about 1463, Pachacuti turned control of the ever-growing Inca army over to his son, **Topa Inca.** Like his father before him, Topa Inca became a great conqueror. After his father gave up the throne, Topa Inca became emperor in 1471. During his rule, Topa Inca conquered many other peoples in the region. He nearly doubled the size of the Inca Empire. In just over 50 years, Pachacuti and Topa Inca had turned the Inca into rulers of the greatest empire in the Americas.

REVIEW According to legend, how did Pachacuti defeat the Chancas? **Main Idea and Details**

▶ The Inca often buried their dead with possessions. This Inca burial doll was discovered in present-day Chile.

Empire Builders

How did the Inca emperors manage to keep the vast Inca Empire together? One key was an efficient form of government. When the Inca conquered new peoples and territories, they allowed the old rulers to stay in power. The old rulers could rule as long as they were loyal to the Inca. Because they could stay in power, local rulers often saw little reason to revolt against the Inca.

However, these rulers and their people did pay some taxes in the form of land or services. Most people had to work on government building projects such as roads. Others were required to serve in the army.

The Inca government closely supervised the people in the Empire. The chain of command included the ministers of the Empire, the traveling inspectors, and the governors of the provinces. The governors of the provinces were each responsible for about 10,000 Inca subjects. These officials supervised lesser officials. As a result, when the emperor gave an order, it went down the chain of command to everyone in the Empire.

The Inca never developed a system of writing. However, they could keep records of government orders, taxes, crop production, and almost anything else through their use of quipu (KEE poo). A **quipu** was a rope with various lengths and colors of cords. These cords were knotted together. The length, color, and knots could stand for distances, directions, numbers, and objects. Archaeologists have studied quipu to learn about how the Inca governed the Empire.

▶ This advertisement from about 1620 shows an Inca "accountant" using a quipu.

▶ A quipu was used to record population counts and taxes.

The Inca were fine stoneworkers and builders of great cities. Small villages became thriving cities. The Inca used enormous stones to construct their buildings. These stones were cut into irregular shapes.

The Inca did not need to cement the stones together. The stones were first cut with stone hammers. Then they were polished with wet sand. The blocks of stone fit together so tightly that not even a knife blade could fit between them.

REVIEW How did the Inca make sure that local rulers would stay loyal to the Empire?
Main Idea and Details

Inca Roads

One of the most amazing accomplishments of Inca engineering was their road building. The Inca built more than 14,000 miles of roads to link their empire.

The Inca never developed or used wheels for transport. One result of this is that the roads did not need to be built to a certain width to fit wheeled vehicles. Many of the roads were little more than footpaths. Others were paved in stone and wide enough for whole armies to march along.

Inca roads were built across nearly every type of landscape: across deserts, through rain forests, on plateaus, and in the mountains. The Inca dug tunnels through rock. They built rope bridges across canyons, or narrow, deep valleys with steep walls.

The Inca roads were built to be used by the government and military only. The Inca considered bridges sacred. Anyone who destroyed or damaged one on purpose was put to death. The roads were built so well that, even today, you can still walk some of the very roads the Incas built long ago.

▶ **The Inca Trail can still be traveled on and accessed by the Intipunco Stairway.**

REVIEW Why are we able to walk on some of the Inca roads today? **Draw Conclusions**

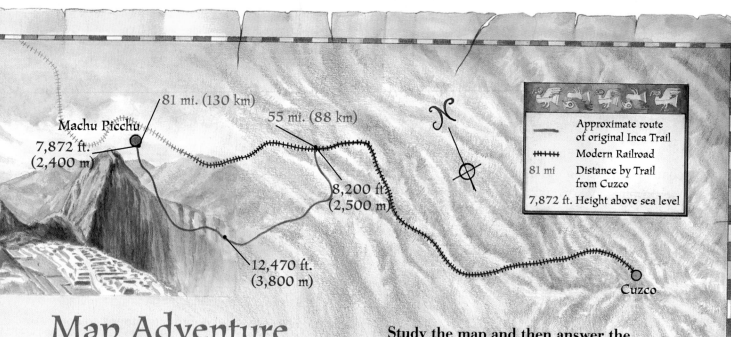

Machu Picchu
7,872 ft. (2,400 m)

81 mi. (130 km)

55 mi. (88 km)

8,200 ft. (2,500 m)

12,470 ft. (3,800 m)

Cuzco

Approximate route of original Inca Trail

Modern Railroad

81 mi Distance by Trail from Cuzco

7,872 ft. Height above sea level

Map Adventure

You're an Inca Runner

From the Inca capital of Cuzco, runners carried the orders from the emperors to all parts of the Empire. One route they took is now known as the Inca Trail. It runs from Cuzco to the famous "Lost City," Machu Picchu. Along the way, runners ran up stone steps, down dirt paths, and across the famous Inca bridges. Their route took them across high-desert plateaus and tropical rain forests.

Study the map and then answer the questions below.

1. About how long is the trail from Cuzco to Machu Picchu?

2. If you begin at Cuzco, in what general direction does the trail run?

3. Describe how the elevation changes as you follow the route between the 55 mile point and Machu Picchu.

4. If you average a nine-minute mile, how long would it take you to complete the journey from Cuzco to Machu Picchu?

The Inca Legacy

The Inca Empire did not last very long. It grew from small to great in less than 100 years. But during that time, it became magnificent. Many Inca cities are impressive today, even as ruins. As you read earlier, Inca stoneworkers could tightly wedge together huge, heavy stones. Even after centuries, it is still impossible to stick a knife blade between the stones.

The Inca, the great conquerors of the Andes, would themselves be conquered. In 1527 civil war broke out in the Inca Empire between two rivals for the title of emperor. The war severely weakened the Inca. Just as the war was ending, the Spanish explorer and conquerer **Francisco Pizarro** (fran SEES koh pee SAHR roh) arrived. He came with only 167 men. However, he had horses and firearms, which helped him defeat the Inca. The Spanish executed the emperor. Lacking leadership, the Inca Empire fell apart—and into Spanish hands. You will read more about the Spanish conquests in South America in Unit 6.

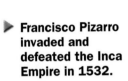
▶ **Francisco Pizarro invaded and defeated the Inca Empire in 1532.**

Réunion des Musées Nationaux/Art Resource

REVIEW What caused the end of the Inca Empire? **Cause and Effect**

Summarize the Lesson

- **about A.D. 1200** Inca culture appeared in the Andes Mountains of South America.
- **A.D. 1438** The Inca, under Pachacuti, defeated the Chancas and began to grow in strength.
- **about 1463** Topa Inca took control of the army and continued to expand the Inca Empire.
- **1471** Topa Inca became emperor.

LESSON 3 REVIEW

Check Facts and Main Ideas

1. **Main Idea and Details** List some of the main accomplishments of the Inca in the boxes below.

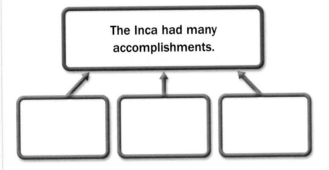

The Inca had many accomplishments.

2. Who was Pachacuti?
3. What was the Inca capital?

4. How did the Inca system of government help hold the Empire together?

5. **Critical Thinking: *Make Inferences*** Do you think the Inca roads would have been built differently if the Inca had used wheels for transport? Explain your answer.

Link to ⚭ Technology

An Archaeological Adventure The Inca managed to move huge stones weighing many tons without using wheels. How do you think the Inca accomplished this? As you think about your answer, consider what you have learned about how the Egyptians built the pyramids.

BUILDING CITIZENSHIP

★ Caring

Respect
Responsibility
Fairness
Honesty
Courage

Caring for Culture

Monte Albán was the ancient mountain capital of the Zapotec people, who began building it in 500 B.C. As many as 50,000 people lived there in A.D. 750. Centuries later, in 1931, a famous Mexican archaeologist, Dr. Alfonso Caso, found the site of this ancient city high in the Sierra Madre del Sur mountain range. He cared enough for his culture and history to work toward protecting these ruins.

Monte Albán was an important political, economic, and culture center in the area. It was one of the first big cities in Mesoamerica.

Centuries had passed since anyone had lived there. Monte Albán was just piles of stones and mounds of grass. Caso thought that ancient places such as Monte Albán deserved protection by the Mexican government. He cared so much about this that when he went to college, he studied to become a lawyer and archaeologist. With his knowledge, he helped to create a Mexican law that granted special protection to archaeological sites. Today, this law preserves historical places in Mexico. People can then continue to visit them. Caso also thought it was very important to preserve Mexican history and culture.

Caso led the excavation at Monte Albán from 1931 to 1943. During that time, he discovered some amazing artifacts. He uncovered a tomb that contained Zapotec treasures of gold jewelry, turquoise, and pottery. In another area, he found large carved stones in the shapes of people. Caso worked carefully to avoid harming these artifacts. Visitors to Mexico can see and learn about many of these treasures in museums.

Caso cared deeply about Mexican history and culture. He wanted everyone to understand how special Mexico was. He dedicated his life to finding and protecting some of Mexico's most important archaeological sites.

Caring in Action

Link to Current Events Research someone who has made a difference because he or she cares for something deeply.

Pachacuti

c. 1391–1473

According to legend the Inca sun god, Inti, singled out Pachacuti for greatness. A story tells us that Inti appeared to the young prince in a dream. Pachacuti's first instinct was to run for his life. But Inti spoke to him:

> *"Come here, my child, have no fear, for I am your father the sun. I know that you will subjugate [conquer] many nations and take great care to honor me. . . ."*

The Inca believed that Pachacuti fulfilled the god's prediction. In 1438 Pachacuti led an army to victory over the Chancas, who were trying to take over Cuzco. Following his triumph, he forced his father and brother from power and named himself ninth emperor of the Inca. He gave himself the name Pachacuti, which in the Quechua language means "earth-shaker" or "reformer."

Pachacuti greatly expanded Inca territory and power. He would send Inca messengers to threaten war unless the people agreed to accept him as their ruler. Many groups feared the Inca army so much that they surrendered without a fight.

Pachacuti allowed local rulers to continue to rule their own people. In addition, he allowed conquered peoples to continue to worship their local gods. However, they also had to worship the chief Inca god.

Pachacuti did several things to further his claim as the ruler of the Inca Empire. He rebuilt Cuzco and built the dazzling mountaintop city of Machu Picchu. Pachacuti had a well-known legend about the discovery of irrigation changed. The reworked legend made Pachacuti the discoverer of irrigation even though it had been developed hundreds of years earlier!

BIOFACT

As a symbol of kingship, Pachacuti wore a multicolored braided crown, decorated with three feather plumes and red wool tassels.

Learn from Biographies

Why do you think Pachacuti did not force people to give up their religion?

For more information, go online to *Meet the People* at **www.sfsocialstudies.com.**

900 B.C.   700 B.C.   500 B.C.   300 B.C.   100 B.C.

c. 900 B.C.
Chavín culture appeared.

c. 200 B.C.
Chavín culture disappeared.

Chapter Summary

Target Skill

Compare and Contrast

On a separate piece of paper, contrast the Inca and the Aztecs.

Inca — both built great cities — Aztec

Vocabulary

Match each word with the correct definition or description.

1. **quipu** (p. 199)
2. **wetland** (p. 187)
3. **archipelago** (p. 188)
4. **biome** (p. 188)

a. Inca method for keeping records

b. group of islands

c. an area of very moist soil, such as a swamp

d. a place that features specific kinds of climate, plants, and animals

Places and People

Write a sentence explaining why each of the following people or places was important to South America or to the development of civilizations in Peru.

1. Lake Titicaca (p. 188)
2. Pampas (p. 188)
3. Manco Capac (p. 197)
4. Inca Viracocha (p. 198)
5. Machu Picchu (p. 197)
6. Moche Valley (p. 192)
7. Pachacuti (p. 198)
8. Cuzco (p. 197)
9. Topa Inca (p. 198)
10. Francisco Pizarro (p. 201)

A.D. **100**   **300**   **500**   **700**   **900**   **1100**   **1300**

C. A.D. **100**
Mochica culture
appeared.

C. A.D. **800**
Mochica culture disappeared.

1200
Inca culture appeared.

1471
Topa Inca became
emperor.

Facts and Main Ideas

1 What mountain chain stretches along the western edge of South America?

2 How did the Chavín affect other cultures in the region?

3 Who used the roads built by the Inca Empire?

4 **Time Line** About how long did Chavín culture last?

5 **Main Idea** Why is South America considered a continent of world records?

6 **Main Idea** What is Chavín art like?

7 **Main Idea** How did the Inca govern their empire?

8 **Critical Thinking:** *Make Inferences* Why were just a few Spanish soldiers able to conquer the whole Inca Empire?

Apply Skills

Latitude and Longitude

Study the map below. Then answer the questions that follow.

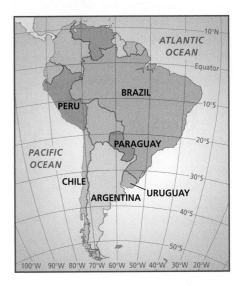

1 Name the countries that lie partially at 30°S.

2 Where are you if you are located at about 10°S, 75°W? 20°S, 50°W?

Write About History

1 Write a **journal entry** from the point of view of a Spanish soldier who has just marched into the Inca Empire. Write about what you see.

2 Write a **paragraph** using the following topic sentence: "The Inca were amazing engineers."

3 Write a **description** of one of the artifacts or ruins pictured in this chapter.

Internet Activity

To get help with vocabulary, people, and terms, select dictionary, encyclopedia, or almanac from *Social Studies Library* at **www.sfsocialstudies.com**.

Early North American Peoples

Lesson 1

Rocky Mountains
The continent of North America features tall mountains, deep valleys, forests, and deserts.

Lesson 2

**about A.D. 300
Snaketown**
The Hohokam and other cultures begin to thrive in the Southwest.

Lesson 3

**about A.D. 700
Great Serpent Mound**
The Adena and other peoples build mounds throughout eastern North America.

Lesson 4

**1997
Nunavut**
Modern descendants of the Inuit people live in Canada's newest territory.

Why We Remember

The United States became a nation less than 235 years ago. Canada is a little younger. To us, they might seem like old, established countries. However, the United States, Canada, and other countries of North America are children compared to the first nations of the continent. Many of the first civilizations of North America lasted more than one thousand years. What made them so successful? By learning about ancient North American civilizations, we might learn how to make our own civilization last centuries into the future.

ROCKY MOUNTAINS

PREVIEW

Focus on the Main Idea
North America is a diverse continent that has been home to many different cultures.

PLACES
Rocky Mountains
Great Basin
Coastal Range
Appalachian Mountains
Interior Plains
Great Plains
Mississippi River
Canadian Shield

VOCABULARY
basin and range
tributary
tundra
arid

▶ North American landscapes range from mountains to forests, plateaus to plains, and arctic to desert.

Geography of North America

You Are There You're riding in an airplane across the country to visit relatives. You talked with the woman in the next seat for a while. But now she has returned to her book. Much more interesting to you is the view through the window. Far below, the land seems to roll by slowly. You're amazed at what you see. Your plane took off from a flat area. First, you flew over mountains and next over a desert. Later, you flew over a vast grassland. Now, below you is a forest. On the horizon you see low hills. Who knew that the land in North America was so varied? You can't wait to tell your relatives about what you've seen.

Compare and Contrast As you read, think about how the early peoples of North America used natural resources in ways similar to other civilizations.

A Diverse Land

If you had to choose just one word to describe the continent of North America, it might be *diverse.* North America has tall mountains, deep valleys, lush forests, and deserts. It has frozen landscapes, sandy beaches, and vast grasslands.

The "backbone" of North America is the **Rocky Mountains,** or "the Rockies." Some Native Americans called them the "Shining Mountains," because they reflected so much sunlight. As you can see on the map on page 210, the Rocky Mountains stretch nearly the entire length of North America. The northern Rockies are forested, while the southern Rockies are more desert-like. Erosion has not yet been able to wear away the tall, sharp peaks of the Rockies.

To the west of the Rocky Mountains lies a region of **basins and ranges,** or low areas alternating with small mountain ranges. This area is often called the **Great Basin.** A mountain range lies to the west of the Great Basin along the Pacific Ocean. This is known as the **Coastal Range.**

The **Appalachian Mountains** lie far to the east. Geologically older than the Rockies, they have eroded much more as well. They are low, rounded mountains, divided by forested valleys.

The Rockies and the Appalachians contrast sharply with each other. They both also contrast with the **Interior Plains,** one of the largest areas of plains in the world. In ancient times, the eastern Interior Plains was a land of great forests. The western part of the plains is called the **Great Plains.** The Great Plains is grassland today, much as it was in ancient times.

The Interior Plains is home to one of the greatest river systems in the world: the **Mississippi River** and its tributaries. A **tributary** is a smaller stream or river that flows into a larger river. Important tributaries of the Mississippi include the Missouri, Ohio, Arkansas, and Red Rivers.

North of the Interior Plains lies a vast area called the **Canadian Shield,** a land that contains some of the oldest rocks on Earth. Evergreen forests cover the Canadian Shield. The climate here brings cold winters and summers that vary from warm to cool.

East and south of the Interior Plains and the Appalachian Mountains lie the Coastal Lowlands. This is a low, humid area. The shore of these lowlands forms a small part of all of North America's nearly 200,000 miles of coastline— the most of any continent. Stretched out, the coastline would circle Earth almost eight times!

REVIEW How are the Rocky Mountains similar to the Andes Mountains you read about in Chapter 7?

 Compare and Contrast

Diverse Climate

The climate of North America also is diverse. Look at the map below. North America has about ten different climate regions. They range from cold and dry to hot and wet. To the north, the climate is subarctic and tundra. **Tundra** is a type of cold, treeless land with only low-lying vegetation.

These climates are cold year-round. Summers are short, and winters are long. Little vegetation grows in arctic regions.

The eastern and southern climates are more tropical and humid. In many parts of the west, the climate is more **arid**, or dry. Summers are longer, and winters are shorter. More vegetation generally grows in these climates.

MAP SKILL
Climate Zones of the United States and Canada

Legend:
- Very cold winter, cool summer, wet
- Very cold winter, cold summer, dry
- Warm all year; wet summer, dry winter
- Cold winter, hot or dry summer, wet
- Mild or warm winter, hot summer, wet
- Mild, wet winter; hot, dry summer
- Mild winter, cool summer, wet
- Highlands; temperature and precipitation vary with elevation
- Semi-dry, temperature varies with latitude
- Dry, temperature varies with latitude

▶ The climate is more diverse in the United States than in Canada.

MAP SKILL Use a Climate Map *Where are the mild climates located in the United States?*

In between the northern and southern regions of North America are more moderate climates. However, moderate climates do not mean that weather is not extreme. Great thunderstorms, blizzards, tornadoes, floods, and hurricanes are not unusual in these climate regions. Temperatures range from more than 100°F to well below zero.

REVIEW How are the climate regions of North America diverse? ↻ **Compare and Contrast**

Many Peoples

Since the land and climate in North America is diverse, it should not surprise you that the peoples who have lived here have been just as diverse.

The original inhabitants of North America were American Indians, or Native Americans. These terms sometimes are used interchangeably. The people the names refer to never called themselves by these names. The native peoples of North America included hundreds of different and distinct cultural groups. Each had its own name.

► **Native Americans in Ontario, Canada, participate in dance ceremonies much like their ancestors did hundreds of years ago.**

Native Americans developed many different, unique cultures. They adapted to the many diverse biomes of North America.

REVIEW Is there a difference between Native Americans and American Indians? Explain your answer. **Summarize**

Summarize the Lesson

- North America is a diverse continent.
- North America is a land of many climates.
- The original inhabitants of North America were peoples of many different cultures.

LESSON 1   REVIEW

Check Facts and Main Ideas

1. ↻ **Compare and Contrast** On a separate piece of paper, complete the diagram below by comparing the Rocky and Appalachian Mountains.

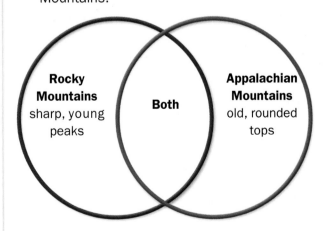

Rocky Mountains
sharp, young peaks

Both

Appalachian Mountains
old, rounded tops

2. How were the eastern Interior Plains different in ancient times?

3. How would you describe the climate of North America?

4. What are several types of landscapes that can be found in North America?

5. **Critical Thinking:** *Make Inferences* How would the diverse landscapes of North America influence the cultures that developed there?

Link to ⊶ Art

Create a Landscape Draw, paint, download, or take a photograph of a landscape to show a part of the diverse continent of North America.

A.D. 1   500   1000   1500

about 300
Hohokam culture appears.

about A.D. 100
Anasazi culture appears.

about 1280
Anasazi abandon many pueblos.

about 1400
Hohokam culture disappears.

Snaketown   •Pueblo Bonito

The Southwestern Peoples

PREVIEW

Focus on the Main Idea
The Hohokam and Anasazi cultures thrived in the Southwest.

PLACES
Snaketown

VOCABULARY
etching
pit house
pueblo
adobe

▶ This imprinted shell portrays a lizard, a common subject in the art of the Hohokam culture of the Southwest.

You Are There

The pieces of cactus you cut have soaked for days. You stir the mixture, and your eyes and nose tell you it's ready. In another pot is the pitch— a black, gooey liquid. The third thing you need is a shell. You pick up a brush made from a desert plant and dip it into the pot of pitch. You then paint the shell, completely covering it with the thick black liquid. Next, you use a twig to draw a design in the pitch on the shell. You take your time—this is careful work. You draw a lizard, and you are pleased with the image. You dip the shell into the pot where the cactus has been soaking. You know that this liquid will eat away at the shell where you removed the pitch to draw the lizard. The image will then be imprinted into the shell forever.

Compare and Contrast As you read, think about how the southwestern peoples were alike and different.

The Vanished Ones

Centuries ago, the process of etching, an imprinted drawing or design, was developed in what is now the southwestern part of the United States. We do not know the name of the person or persons who invented this art. We also do not know the name of the culture or tribe that developed etching. Today, we call these peoples the Hohokam, the name given by a later culture that lived in the region. "Hohokam" was the later culture's word for "the Vanished Ones."

The Southwest is an arid, desert land. There are few large animals and few edible plants here. Temperatures can soar well over 100°F in the day and drop below freezing at night.

The Hohokam lived in present-day south-central Arizona from about A.D. 300 until about 1400. How did they survive in such a harsh climate? The Hohokam turned to farming to provide the food that the landscape did not provide naturally. They grew maize, beans, squash, and other crops. They even grew cotton.

To water their fields, they used irrigation. The sources of their water were the Gila (hee LAH) and Salt rivers. The Hohokam built dams and canals to transport water to their fields. They were able to direct water to farm fields as far away as ten miles from the river. More than 150 miles of Hohokam canals have been located. Some have even been repaired and are being used by farmers today!

Farming made life in villages possible. The Hohokam's largest village is called Snaketown today. It was made up of about 100 pit houses. A pit house was made by digging a pit in the ground and covering it with a framework of logs. The framework was covered with plants and mud to make a roof and walls. Can you think why the Hohokam would build and live in pit houses? The pit gave them relief from the harsh desert sun and kept them cool in the summer.

At Snaketown and other Hohokam settlements, the people made beautiful pottery and human figures from clay. Archaeologists have also found bells made from copper and mirrors made of polished iron.

In about A.D. 1400, the Hohokam abandoned their villages after living there for more than 1,000 years. No one knows why they left.

REVIEW How did the Hohokam survive in the arid Southwest? Summarize

▶ **The Hokokam farmed in the arid climate of present-day south-central Arizona. Despite harsh conditions, the Hohokam lived in this region for more than 1,000 years.**

The Ancient Ones

Another culture that flourished in the Southwest was the Anasazi (ah nuh SAH zee). Anasazi is a Navajo word for "the Ancient Ones." Anasazi culture thrived in the Southwest from about A.D. 100 to about 1280. Some of their descendants live in the region today.

The Anasazi are known for their architecture. In about A.D. 750 they built **pueblos,** structures of stone or adobe bricks. **Adobe** is made from sun-dried mud. One pueblo that still stands today is called Pueblo Bonito (boh NEE toh), which is Spanish for "pretty village." It is a huge structure: as many as five stories tall with 800 rooms. Archaeologists are still studying the pueblos to learn about the Anasazi. In the past decade, some archaeologists have concluded that many pueblos were used as forts for defense.

The Anasazi were excellent farmers who could grow enough to feed the many people of the pueblos. Many of their fields were terraced and watered with complex irrigation systems. Some archaeologists believe that the Anasazi collected water that flowed over cliffs during brief, hard desert showers. The Anasazi also were accomplished artists. They created beautiful pottery, jewelry, and elaborate baskets. They had an advanced knowledge of astronomy. They also could communicate over long distances with signal fires.

The Anasazi began to abandon their pueblos in about 1280. Scientists have discovered that their homeland suffered a great drought that lasted for about 25 years. This is one theory about why the "Ancient Ones" left their homes and moved to other lands.

REVIEW How did the Anasazi survive in the arid Southwest? **Main Idea and Details**

▶ These ruins of Pueblo Bonito are located in Chaco Culture National Historic Park. They may have once been used as a trading or ceremonial center.

MAP SKILL

Hohokam and Anasazi Cultures

- Hohokam culture
- Anasazi culture
- Present-day borders

NEVADA
UTAH
COLORADO
CALIFORNIA
ARIZONA
NEW MEXICO
TEXAS
PACIFIC OCEAN

N

0   100   200 Miles
0   100   200 Kilometers

▶ The Hohokam and Anasazi cultures emerged in the same region of the United States.

MAP SKILL Use a U.S. Map *In what region of the United States did the Hohokam culture thrive?*

Contact Among Peoples

Ancient Native American cultures were connected to other cultures in two ways. First, they were influenced by the cultures of the past. Second, they interacted with neighboring cultures.

These cultures were the descendants of earlier cultures. They were also the ancestors of later cultures. For example, some people think that the Hohokam were descendants of the Mesoamerican peoples you read about in Chapter 6.

Cultures were influenced by the contact they had with other cultures. Sometimes the cultures clashed

▶ **This Hohokam pot and these effigies were probably used for religious purposes.**

with each other. Sometimes contact between them was friendly. For example, some scientists think that the Hohokam traded with Mesoamericans.

The Native American peoples shared their ideas and their cultures. This was true of the Hohokam, the Anasazi, and other cultures of the region. Through interaction, these cultures influenced each other over time.

REVIEW How did Native American cultures influence each other? *Cause and Effect*

Summarize the Lesson

- **about A.D. 100** The Anasazi culture appeared in the Southwest.

- **c. 300** The Hohokam culture appeared in the Southwest.

- **about 1280** The Anasazi began to abandon many pueblos.

- **c. 1400** The Hohokam culture vanished.

LESSON 2   REVIEW

Check Facts and Main Ideas

1. 🔄 **Compare and Contrast** On a separate piece of paper, complete the diagram below by contrasting the Hohokam and the Anasazi cultures.

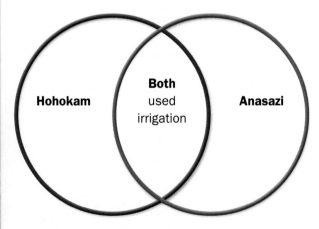

Hohokam — **Both** used irrigation — Anasazi

2. What art technique did the Hohokam invent?

3. What are pueblos?

4. How did the Hohokam and the Anasazi farm desert land?

5. **Critical Thinking: *Evaluate Information*** Which is better suited to life in a hot and arid environment: a pit house or a pueblo? Explain your answer.

Link to ⚭ Art

Make a Model Use clay and other materials to make a model of a Hohokam pit house or an Anasazi pueblo. Find pictures of pit houses or pueblos to use as examples for your own model.

Thinking Skills

Detect Bias

What? *Bias* is a strong opinion or set of opinions based on powerful feelings, rather than careful reasoning. A person who has a bias can be described as *biased*. Because a bias usually cannot stand up to facts, a biased person often will refuse to consider any facts that might change his or her opinion.

One of the most famous biases in the history of North America was the U.S. government's attitude toward the Native Americans. Throughout the 1800s, the population of the United States was growing and spreading westward. There was a widespread belief that the people already living on the land—the Native Americans—were not civilized enough to live among white settlers. In an 1835 speech to Congress, President Andrew Jackson said:

> *"All . . . experiments for the improvement of the Indians have failed. It now seems to be an established fact that they cannot live in contact with a civilized community. . . ."*

The Granger Collection

▶ **This 1821 portrait shows young men belonging to various Native American groups.**

Smithsonian American Art Museum, Washington DC/Art Resource

Why? Understanding bias and knowing how to detect it makes you a better reader, student, and citizen. People try to persuade you to accept their opinions in books and magazines, on TV and radio, on the Internet, and in public speeches. Knowing how to weed out the biased opinions will help you make up your own mind.

How? Read the following warning signs to help you identify bias.

Generalization A sweeping judgment about an entire group of people is an example of generalization. Whenever a person makes a judgmental statement about a whole group of people, you can be certain that bias is involved.

Lack of evidence For any statement or claim that is not clear to the listener, a speaker should provide strong, supporting evidence. Suspect a bias when such evidence is missing.

Strong language Words that show very strong feelings are suitable in some situations. For instance, a storyteller might use words such as *awful* or *magnificent* in a story. However, in a political speech, such words might be clues about a speaker's biases.

Hidden reason Try to understand what the writer's or speaker's personal reason is in trying to persuade you. This hidden, inner reason is sometimes called a "hidden agenda." For instance, when President Jackson claimed the Native Americans were unable to live among civilized people, he had a larger plan in mind. Within three years of making that statement, he had many Native Americans removed from the places they lived so that others could settle those places instead.

Think and Apply

1. Explain why the quote on the previous page is a biased statement.

2. What kind of warning signs could give you clues to the hidden agenda behind President Jackson's quote?

3. Think of a generalization or other example of bias that you have heard. Write it down and share it with the class.

700 B.C.   A.D. 1   A.D. 700

c. 700 B.C.
Rise of Adena
culture

c. 100 B.C.
Rise of Hopewell
culture

about A.D. 100
End of Adena
culture

about A.D. 500
End of Hopewell
culture

Cahokia
Great Serpent
Mound

PREVIEW

Focus on the Main Idea
Native American peoples built burial and ceremonial mounds throughout eastern North America.

PLACES
Great Serpent Mound
Cahokia

VOCABULARY
burial mound
wattle
wigwam
temple mound

The Mound Builders

You Are There

You support the woven basket with your hands. It's getting heavier. You scoop up dirt from the creek bank, deposit it in the basket, and repeat the process. The basket is large, and it takes many handfuls of dirt to fill. Finally, you put the full basket on your back and turn away from the creek. You carry the basket across a small field, then uphill to the top of the mound. There you dump the basket and turn back toward the creek for another load. The mound has grown so much! How many of your ancestors worked to build the mound? How many generations of your people have done what you are doing now? You will carry dirt all day, for many days. The work is hard, but you do it gladly. This is how your people honor the dead.

▶ This picture, engraved on sandstone by an artist of the Mississippian culture, was discovered at Cahokia.

Compare and Contrast As you read, think about how the mound builders were alike.

▶ The people of the Adena culture did some farming, but got most of their food by hunting animals and gathering plants.

The Adena Culture

All across the eastern United States are great mounds of earth. Some are shaped like domes, some like cones, and some are built in the form of huge circles. They are the works of people, not of nature. They were built by different Native American cultures. Together, these cultures are called the mound builders.

One of the first groups of mound builders is called the Adena culture. The Adena culture developed in the Ohio River Valley but spread hundreds of miles in all directions. The Adena thrived from about 700 B.C. to about A.D. 100.

The mounds the Adena built were burial mounds. At first, they were small hills of dirt built over the graves of important people in their culture. Over the centuries, more people were buried in them, and new layers of dirt were added. With each burial, the mounds grew.

Archaeologists have determined that the Adena were hunter-gatherers. However, they did practice

▶ Built by the Adena, the Great Serpent Mound is located in present-day Spring, Ohio.

some agriculture. They did not have to grow many crops because the land was rich with animals and plants. The Adena lived in small circular houses with log frameworks. They smeared a mud-like plaster over a framework of twigs, logs, branches, or vines. This type of framework is called wattle.

One of the most impressive mounds of the Adena is the Great Serpent Mound, which is located in what is now Ohio. This mound of earth ranges from about 4 to 6 feet high, 4 to 20 feet wide, and is as long as a dozen football fields. It is in the shape of a great snake.

The Adena disappeared about A.D. 100. No one really knows why or how.

REVIEW Why did the Adena build large mounds of earth? **Summarize**

The Hopewell Culture

The Hopewell culture was very similar to the Adena culture. Like the Adena, the Hopewell built burial mounds. They were hunters and gatherers. They lived in small houses constructed from materials they found in their environment. The Hopewell lived in houses similar to **wigwams**, dome-shaped frames of branches covered with animal skins or woven mats.

The Hopewell thrived between about 100 B.C. and A.D. 500. Did you remember that these dates overlap the dates of the Adena culture? The Hopewell also lived in some of the same places as the Adena did. This is probably why their cultures were so similar.

However, the Hopewell spread over a far greater area, reaching from the Great Lakes to the Gulf Coast. The Hopewell also farmed much more than the Adena. They built many more mounds. Their mounds were larger and more complex.

One of the most striking differences is that the Hopewell traded over a vast area. Artifacts in Hopewell mounds come from as far away as present-day Florida, Canada, and even the Rocky Mountains.

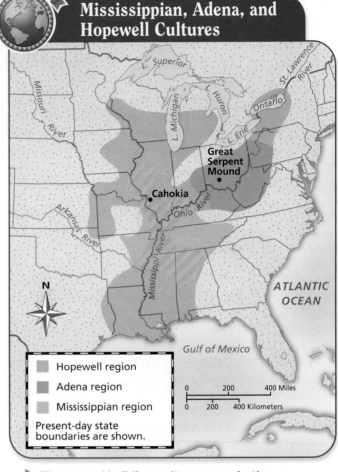

MAP SKILL

Mississippian, Adena, and Hopewell Cultures

Hopewell region

Adena region

Mississippian region

Present-day state boundaries are shown.

▶ The mound-building cultures rose in the eastern central region of the United States.

MAP SKILL Use a Distribution Map *What culture spread near the Great Lakes region?*

▶ Wigwams were built using resources that were abundant in the environment of the Hopewell.

smoke hole

woven mats

Tree branch

Many artifacts have been recovered from Hopewell mounds—many more than from Adena mounds. These artifacts include elaborate figurines, knives, jewelry, and cups. The skill that went into making these artifacts is impressive. Archaeologists believe that the Hopewell civilization was advanced enough to have specialized artists and craftspeople.

The fate of the Hopewell people remains a mystery. They disappeared about A.D. 500. Like the Adena, no one really knows why or how the Hopewell vanished.

REVIEW How were the Hopewell different from the Adena?
🔄 Compare and Contrast

Mississippian Culture

The Mississippian culture flourished after about A.D. 700 in much the same area as the Hopewell. Like the Hopewell before them, the Mississippian culture built mounds. However, they did not build burial mounds. They built **temple mounds.** These mounds were used for religious and ceremonial purposes. Sometimes, high-ranking priests lived on top of them.

Just across the Mississippi River from what is today St. Louis, Missouri, is **Cahokia.** Cahokia is the largest temple mound site. There are 85 mounds built close together at this site. The largest mound took more than 200 years to build. It covers an area the size of 15 football fields and stands more than 100 feet high!

Today, the Cahokia Mounds State Historic Site in Illinois preserves the ancient settlement for visitors. There you can see firsthand the wonders of the Mound Builders of North America.

REVIEW Did the Mississippian culture thrive before or after the Hopewell culture? **Sequence**

Summarize the Lesson

- **c. 700 B.C.** The Adena culture arose in what is now the Ohio River Valley.
- **c. 100 B.C.** The Hopewell culture appeared.
- **about A.D. 100** The Adena culture disappeared.
- **about A.D. 500** Hopewell culture vanished.

▶ The ceremonial mounds built by the Mississippians at present-day Cahokia can be accessed by a staircase.

LESSON 3   REVIEW

Check Facts and Main Ideas

1. ↺ **Compare and Contrast** On a separate piece of paper, complete the diagram below by contrasting the Adena and Hopewell cultures.

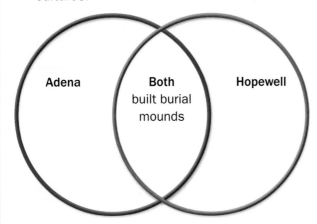

Adena   Both
          built burial
           mounds   Hopewell

2. Why did the Adena people build mounds?

3. Why did the Mississippian people build mounds?

4. Where can some of the remains of mound-building cultures be found today?

5. **Critical Thinking:** *Make Inferences* Cahokia is home to 85 large mounds. What can you conclude about the people who lived in Cahokia based on this fact alone?

Link to ∞ **Technology**

Use Online Resources Use an Internet search engine to find the official Web site for the Cahokia Mounds State Historic Site. Report what you learn from the Web site to your class.

3000 B.C.   A.D. **2000**

about 3000 B.C.
Inuit settle in
northern Canada.

about A.D. 1570
Formation of the
Iroquois Confederacy

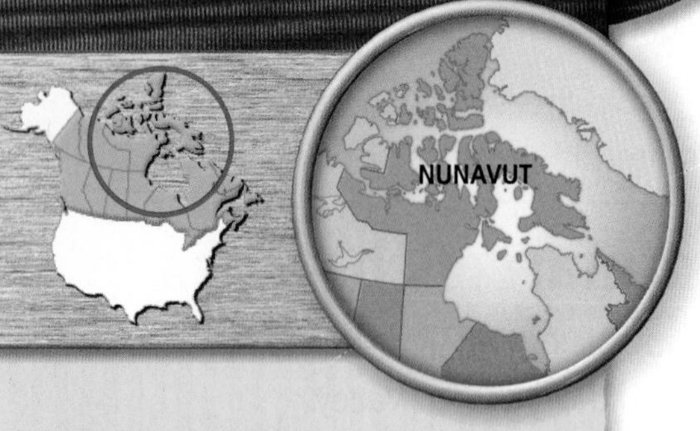

Early Canadians

PREVIEW

Focus on the Main Idea
Early Canadians survived by using what their environment provided them.

PLACES
Canada
Nunavut
Great Lakes

PEOPLE
Deganawidah

VOCABULARY
snowhouse
sod house
long house

▶ This fifteen-hundred-year-old carving of a human figure was made from animal bone.

You Are There

Even though it is summer, the air is bitter cold. So are the water and land. But your pants and coat keep you warm and toasty. They are made from the skin of a caribou, a type of reindeer. The kayak you're in also is made of caribou skin. You paddle along the frozen coast, dodging chunks of ice in the water. You're hunting seal. Like the caribou, its skin will be used to make clothes and to cover kayaks. You will use its blubber as fuel for lamps. From its blood, you will make soup. You will also eat its meat. Your parents and others in your group have taught you the value of using all the parts of an animal. Suddenly, you hear the splashing of seals. You paddle toward them with your harpoon at hand.

Compare and Contrast As you read, think about how the cultures you learn about were alike and different.

Survivors in the Arctic

Northern **Canada** is a land of extreme cold and few natural resources. The early peoples who lived here became experts at living in one of the harshest regions on Earth.

The Inuit were skilled at surviving in present-day northern Canada. Few plants and animals survived on the tundra, so the Inuit relied on hunting and fishing for food. The Inuit hunted polar bears, birds, and even whales.

Most of what they needed came from caribou and seal. Both animals provided meat and blood for food. Their skins and fur were used for clothing, tent covers, and blankets. Their bones were carved into artwork, knives, spear points, and needles. Seal intestines were used for waterproof jackets and boat covers. Caribou horns sometimes were used as the shafts of spears. Almost no part of the animals was wasted.

In their harsh environment, the Inuit could not afford to waste anything.

The Inuit even used the snow and ice of their cold homeland. When traveling, they used a bone knife to cut blocks of snow. The blocks were stacked to make temporary shelters. Some Inuit lived in these **snowhouses,** or igloos, year-round. But most Inuit lived in **sod houses.** These shelters were built from blocks of soil and vegetation cut from the frozen ground. In the warmer summer months, some Inuit lived in tents made of animal skins.

It is thought that the Inuit first came to northern Canada about 5,000 years ago. Even today, some Inuit still live much as their ancestors did. They carry on many of the same traditions.

REVIEW Why did the Inuit make most of their belongings from the animals they hunted?
Main Idea and Details

The Inuit

Then and Now

We know a great deal about how the early Inuit survived in their cold homeland. Even within the last century, many Inuit lived in the same way their ancestors had. The Inuit have perfected the art of arctic survival, and there have been no reasons for them to change their way of life.

Today, most Inuit have adopted modern technology and lifestyles. However, their cultural traditions survive, as they have for thousands of years. Most present-day Inuit live in the Canadian province of **Nunavut,** which was created in 1997. In the Inuit language of Inuktitut, *Nunavut* means "Our Land."

PROVINCE OF NUNAVUT

► **This Inuit woman leader practices a traditional ceremony at the dedication of the Nunavut Legislature.**

The Iroquois and Algonquin

Far to the south of the Inuit lived another important group of early people. The Iroquois were members of the Iroquois-speaking Native American tribes, including the Cherokee, the Huron, and the Mohawk. All of the Iroquois tribes spoke languages of the Iroquois family. They all lived in similar ways around the eastern Great Lakes.

By about A.D. 1000, the Iroquois became skilled at farming and began to live in more permanent settlements.

The Iroquois became famous for living in long houses. These rectangular buildings were typically made of logs covered by bark. Each long house was home for many families. Long houses were built with a door at each end. Some were more than 100 feet long!

Sometimes the Iroquois surrounded their villages with walls made of tree trunks sunk into the ground. They did this for protection in times of war.

The Algonquin peoples lived near the Ottawa River in east-central Canada. The Algonquin, like the Iroquois, belonged to a larger group of Algonquian-speaking Native American tribes made up of several distinct groups.

The Algonquin grew some crops, especially maize, or corn, but they were not a farming people. They were hunters. They organized their tribes by hunting parties. Their forested homeland was rich in deer and moose. They also fished and gathered plants.

The Algonquin lived in lodges made of small logs covered with bark. Like the other early peoples of Canada, they relied on nature to provide them with what they needed to survive.

REVIEW Why did the Iroquois sometimes surround their long house villages with wooden walls? *Cause and Effect*

Summarize the Lesson

- **c. 3000 B.C.** The Inuit settled in what is now northern Canada.

- **about A.D. 1000** The Iroquois began to settle in large, permanent homes.

LESSON 4   REVIEW

Check Facts and Main Ideas

1. **Compare and Contrast** On a separate piece of paper, complete the diagram by contrasting the Inuit and the Algonquin.

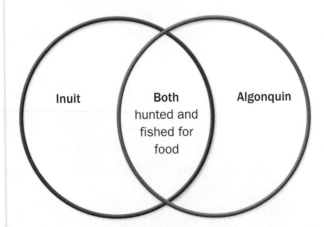

Inuit   Both hunted and fished for food   Algonquin

2. What did the Inuit use seals for?

3. Where did the Iroquois peoples live?

4. How did the Iroquois and Algonquin use forest resources to build their homes?

5. **Critical Thinking: *Make Inferences*** Why do you think the Algonquin peoples did not become dedicated to farming?

Link to ∞ **Writing**

Write a Paragraph Describe the early Canadian people you find most interesting. Explain why you chose to write about them instead of another group.

Deganawidah
c. 1550–1600

Deganawidah was a legendary Native American leader who is credited with founding the Iroquois Confederacy. A legend tells us that he nearly died as an infant. He was born a Huron in what is now Kingston, Ontario, in Canada.

Deganawidah grew up at a time when many neighboring tribes were at war with each other. He believed that disagreements could be settled peacefully. He thought that tribes would be much better off if they banded together. Traveling to New York with his message of peace, Deganawidah met Hiawatha, a Mohawk, who shared his ideas. Deganawidah did not speak clearly, so Hiawatha spoke for him.

Deganawidah and Hiawatha convinced five groups of people—the Cayugas, Mohawks, Oneidas, Onondagas, and Senecas—to put their differences aside and join together to form the Iroquois Confederacy. The purpose of the Confederacy was to end the fighting among the tribes and to fight together against common enemies. The members of the Iroquois Confederacy became powerful. They were a well-organized group.

Deganawidah established a set of rules for the Confederacy. He said that each tribe could vote on actions the Confederacy should take. The Confederacy would not go ahead with any decision unless all tribes agreed to it. Today, a modified form of Deganawidah's rules is still honored by the Iroquois.

BIOFACT

While working on his ideas for the Iroquois Confederacy, Deganawidah was inspired by an eagle perched in a nearby tree.

Learn from Biographies

How is the set of rules established by Deganawidah similar to the form of government of the United States?

For more information, go online to *Meet the People* at **www.sfsocialstudies.com.**

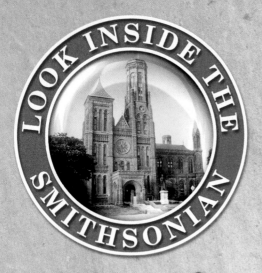

Inuit Artifacts

The Inuit have lived in the northern parts of North America for thousands of years, many of them in present-day Nunavut, a province in Canada. Here are some images and objects that reveal the artistry of this Native American group.

"X-ray" Animal Carvings
The ivory animal carvings created by Inuit artists often show skeleton patterns similar to the ones shown here.

Men's Earrings
Inuit men often wear earrings like the ones shown here. Some of these earings are attached to each other with strands of beads.

POLAR ESKIMO
THE NORTHERNMOST PEOPLE OF THE WORLD

Inuit Hunters
The Inuit people in the display are shown on a seal hunt. Seals provide food, and their hides are used as coverings for the Inuits' warm-weather homes.

Wooden Drum
An owl is depicted on this box drum. Drums similar to this are often used in religious activities.

Inuit Mittens
During some Inuit ceremonies men dance, wearing large sealskin mittens. This pair is adorned with bird beaks.

Inuit Girl's Beaded Coat
This coat is made of caribou skin and is decorated with beads.

Artifacts are from the Smithsonian Institution.

The Future of Rain Forests

Over the last hundred years, logging, farming, and cattle ranching have taken a toll on the rain forests of North and South America. In 1999 alone, a section of Brazil's Amazon rain forest as large as Hawaii was destroyed.

Many people around the world have called for an end to the destruction of rain forests. However, there is no simple solution. Large sections of rain forest are still being cleared of trees because the global demand for wood and other forest products continues. In Central and South America, poverty has forced people out of cities and into the forests. People clear the trees away, then raise crops there that remove nutrients from the soil. Once the nutrients are gone, the forests cannot regrow.

Rain forests contain some of the most diverse collections of plant and animal life on Earth. Forest destruction has resulted in the loss of many species. In addition, many scientists believe that the burning of rain forests affects the climate.

Many people would like to see rain forests managed so that forest products can be harvested while allowing the forest to naturally recover. People living in rain forests for centuries have practiced this kind of method. The Lacandon Maya of the Selva Lacandona rain forest in Mexico use this method of sustainable farming.

"What the people of the city do not realize is that the roots of all living things are interconnected. When a mighty tree is felled [cut down], a star falls from the sky. Before one chops down a mahogany [a type of tree], one should ask permission of the guardian of the stars."

Chan K'in, Lacandon Maya leader, c. 1900–1996

"I never beheld so fair a thing: trees beautiful and green, and different from ours, with flowers and fruits each according to their kind, many birds and little birds which sing very sweetly."

Christopher Columbus, explorer, 1492

"Humanity is cutting down its forests, apparently oblivious to the fact that we may not be able to live without them."

Isaac Asimov, scientist and author, 1988

"We are learning that the forest is not as fragile as we had feared."

Christopher Uhl, scientist, author, and professor, 1998

Issues and You

Conserving rain forests must be a global effort. Search the Internet to find out more information about rain forest conservation as well as rain forest products. Choose three conservation ideas and then write an email explaining how the ideas will or will not help. Email your letter to at least three friends.

CHAPTER 8 REVIEW

1000 B.C.
600 B.C.
c. 700 B.C.
Rise of Adena culture

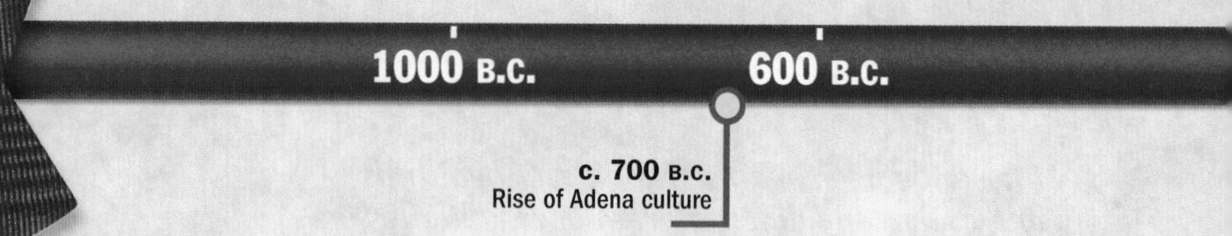

Chapter Summary

Compare and Contrast

Target Skill

On a separate piece of paper, complete the diagram by contrasting the Iroquois and the Algonquin peoples.

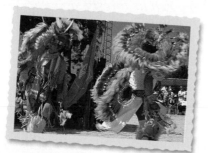

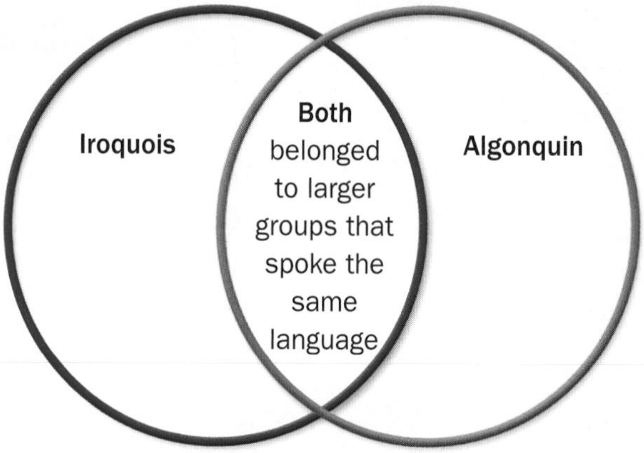

Iroquois
Both
belonged to larger groups that spoke the same language
Algonquin

Vocabulary

Match each word with the correct definition or description.

1. **tributary** (p. 209)
2. **adobe** (p. 214)
3. **wattle** (p. 219)
4. **arid** (p. 210)
5. **pueblo** (p. 214)
6. **etching** (p. 212)

a. Anasazi building
b. stream or river that flows into a larger river
c. dry
d. sun-dried mud brick
e. framework of twigs, logs, branches, or vines
f. an imprinted drawing or design

People and Places

Write a sentence describing each of the following places and people.

1. Canadian Shield (p. 209)
2. Rocky Mountains (p. 209)
3. Great Serpent Mound (p. 219)
4. Snaketown (p. 213)
5. Deganawidah (p. 225)
6. Appalachian Mountains (p. 209)
7. Great Lakes (p. 224)
8. Cahokia (p. 221)
9. Great Plains (p. 209)
10. Nunavut (p. 223)

200 B.C.	A.D. 200	600	1000	1400

c. 100 B.C.
Rise of Hopewell culture

about A.D. 100
Anasazi culture appeared.
Adena culture disappeared.

about A.D. 500
End of Hopewell culture

c. 300 Hohokam culture appeared.

about 1280
Anasazi abandoned many pueblos.

c. 1400
Hohokam culture vanished.

Facts and Main Ideas

1 What are two major mountain ranges of North America?

2 How did the Hohokam manage to grow crops in a desert?

3 **Time Line** About how long did the Anasazi culture last?

4 **Main Idea** What types of climates are found in North America?

5 **Main Idea** How did the Anasazi and Hohokam cultures use resources in their environment?

6 **Main Idea** Why did cultures of eastern North America build mounds?

7 **Main Idea** How did the Inuit survive in a harsh and cold environment?

8 **Critical Thinking:** *Make Inferences* What do the artifacts found in different parts of North America tell us about Hopewell culture?

Write About History

1 **Write a letter** to your teacher explaining why you think a field trip to Cahokia would help the students in your class better understand mound building and Native American history.

2 **Write a paragraph** explaining why some Native Americans practiced agriculture in a desert, while other Native Americans living in areas with plenty of rainfall did not practice agriculture.

3 **Write an essay** on the following topic: "Similarities and Differences of the Adena and Hopewell Cultures."

Apply Skills

Detect Bias

Read the passage below and then answer the questions that follow.

One should group together all early North American peoples as one group. All of these peoples should be called "Native Americans" or "American Indians." They are all the same.

1 What is the bias in this passage?

2 What warning sign helped you identify the bias in this passage?

Internet Activity

To get help with vocabulary, people, and terms, select dictionary, encyclopedia, or almanac from *Social Studies Library* at **www.sfsocialstudies.com.**

UNIT 3

End with Literature

An Inuit Story

The Inuit have a rich cultural tradition of storytelling. Many of their stories are told through songs. Singing the stories made it easier for young people to remember them.

This land of ours
has become habitable
because we came here
and learned to hunt.
Even so, up here where we live
life is one continuous fight
for food and clothing
and a struggle against bad hunting
and snowstorms and sickness

But we know our land is not the whole world.

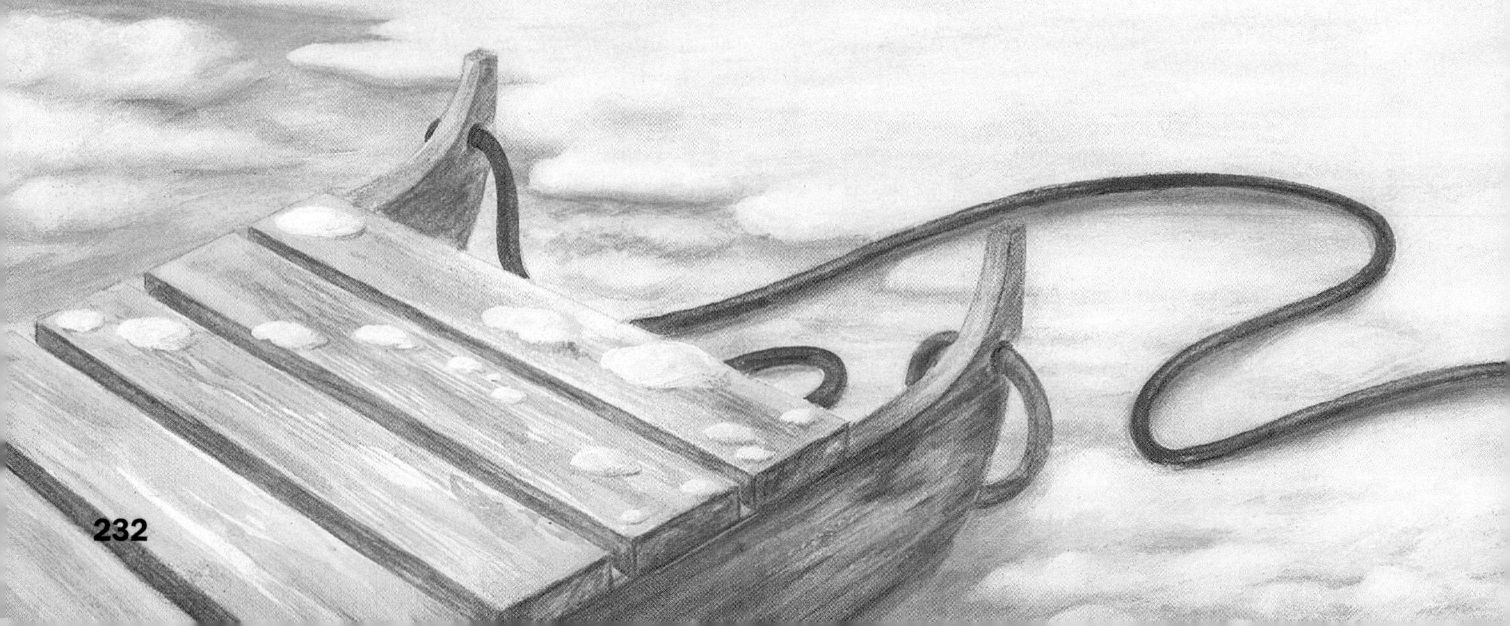

Test Talk

Narrow the answer choices. Rule out answers you know are wrong.

Main Ideas and Vocabulary

TEST PREP

Read the passage below and use it to answer the questions that follow.

Many of the ancient peoples who came to the Americas established civilizations. In Mesoamerica, which includes parts of North America and Central America, the Olmec culture established the first civilization. The Olmec are often called the "Mother Civilization" of Mesoamerica because they influenced later civilizations in the region. The Mayan civilization was one such civilization. Another civilization the Olmec influenced was the Aztec civilization. The Aztec Empire was defeated by the Spanish.

Mesoamerican civilizations had many things in common. They were based on agriculture, especially the growing of maize (corn), beans, and squash. They built city-states. They used hieroglyphics. The government each civilization created was a <u>theocracy</u>, reflecting the importance of religion in their lives.

In South America, the Chavín and the Mochica cultures lived in the river valleys of the Andes Mountains. The Inca was a later culture that thrived in this area. The Inca created an empire along the western edge of South America. Like the Aztecs, they were also conquered by the Spanish.

In North America, many different cultures flourished on diverse landscapes. In the <u>arid</u> Southwest, the Hohokam and Anasazi survived by using irrigation. In the east-central region, mound builders relied less on agriculture because the land was so plentiful. The Adena, Hopewell, and Mississippians built huge mounds as burial centers and places of worship. Farther north, the Inuit survived by learning to use what little resources their cold environment offered them. Farther south, the Iroquois lived in long houses near the Great Lakes. The Algonquin became expert hunters.

1 According to the passage, which three cultures were most closely related?
   A the Inuit, Adena, and Chavín
   B the Olmec, Aztec, and Maya
   C the Iroquois, Hopewell, and Mochica
   D the Anasazi, Iroquois, and Chavín

2 According to the passage, a *theocracy* is—
   A a form of government
   B a kind of building
   C a type of agriculture
   D a social class

3 In the passage, the word *arid* means—
   A rich   **C** dry
   B cold   **D** old

4 What is the main idea of the passage?
   A The Olmec was the "Mother Civilization" of Mesoamerica.
   B Some Native Americans farmed, while others hunted and gathered.
   C The early peoples of the Americas were all great builders.
   D Many different civilizations arose in the Americas.

Places, People and Vocabulary

Match each place, person, and vocabulary word to its definition.

1 peninsula (p. 164)

2 Moctezuma II (p. 180)

3 Altiplano (p. 187)

4 Manco Capac (p. 197)

5 pueblo (p. 214)

6 Francisco Pizarro (p. 201)

a. arm of land sticking out to sea

b. Anasazi building

c. conqueror of the Inca

d. high flat area in Andes Mountains

e. last Aztec emperor

f. legendary founder of the Inca

Apply Skills

Create a Latitude and Longitude Wish List
Mark the location of your home on a world outline map. Label it "Home Base." Write its latitude and longitude next to it. Then make a wish list of ten places you dream of visiting someday. They can be any place in the world! Mark the locations of these places on the map. Record the latitude and longitude next to each place. Decorate the map any way you want, and give it a good title.

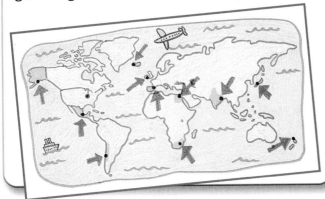

Write and Share

Play a Game Show Choose one of the cultures you read about in this unit. Then write down five sentences about this culture on note cards, one sentence per card. Do not include the name of the culture in the sentences. On the backs of the note cards, write down the names of the culture you have described. Choose one of your classmates to be the host and make teams. The host will shuffle the cards and read the sentences. The teams will earn points for naming the correct culture described.

Read on Your Own

Look for books like these in the library.

UNIT 3 Project

Time Travel

Host a travel program about a historic culture.

1 **Form** a group to choose a historic culture studied in this unit.

2 **Make** a travel brochure about the culture you chose. Include pictures and descriptions of such things as its location, daily life, activities, its leaders, technology, economic system, and natural resources.

3 **Prepare** your travel program. You may choose to make props or bring in costumes from home.

4 **Present** your travel brochure and travel program to the class.

Internet Activity

Explore historic cultures on the Internet. Go to **www.sfsocialstudies.com/activities** and select your grade and unit.

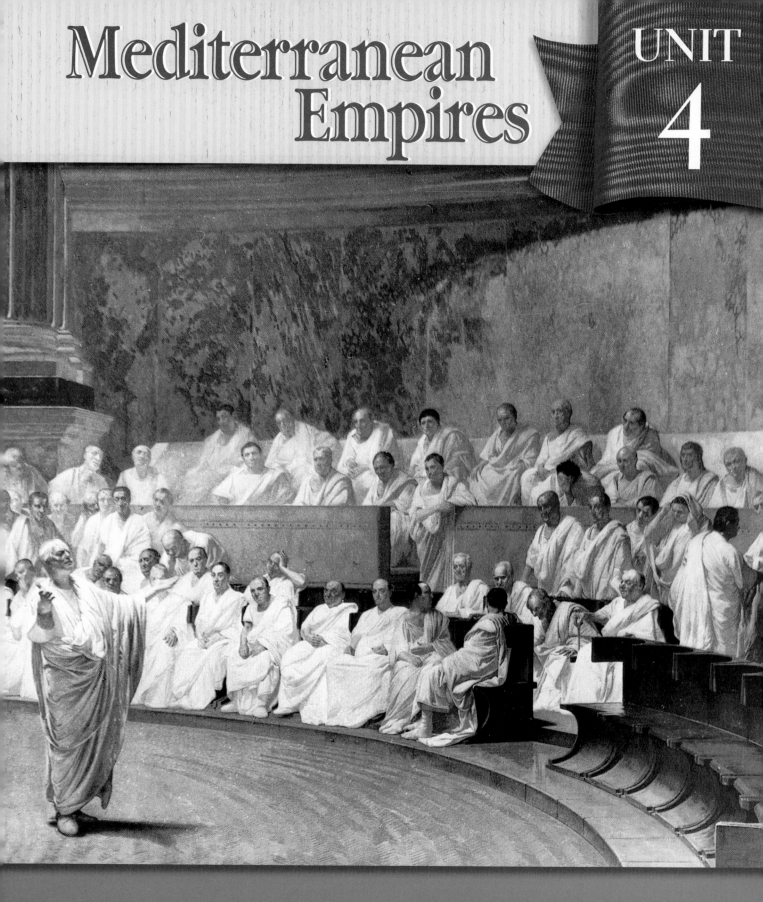

Mediterranean Empires

How do civilizations become empires?

UNIT 4

Begin with a Primary Source

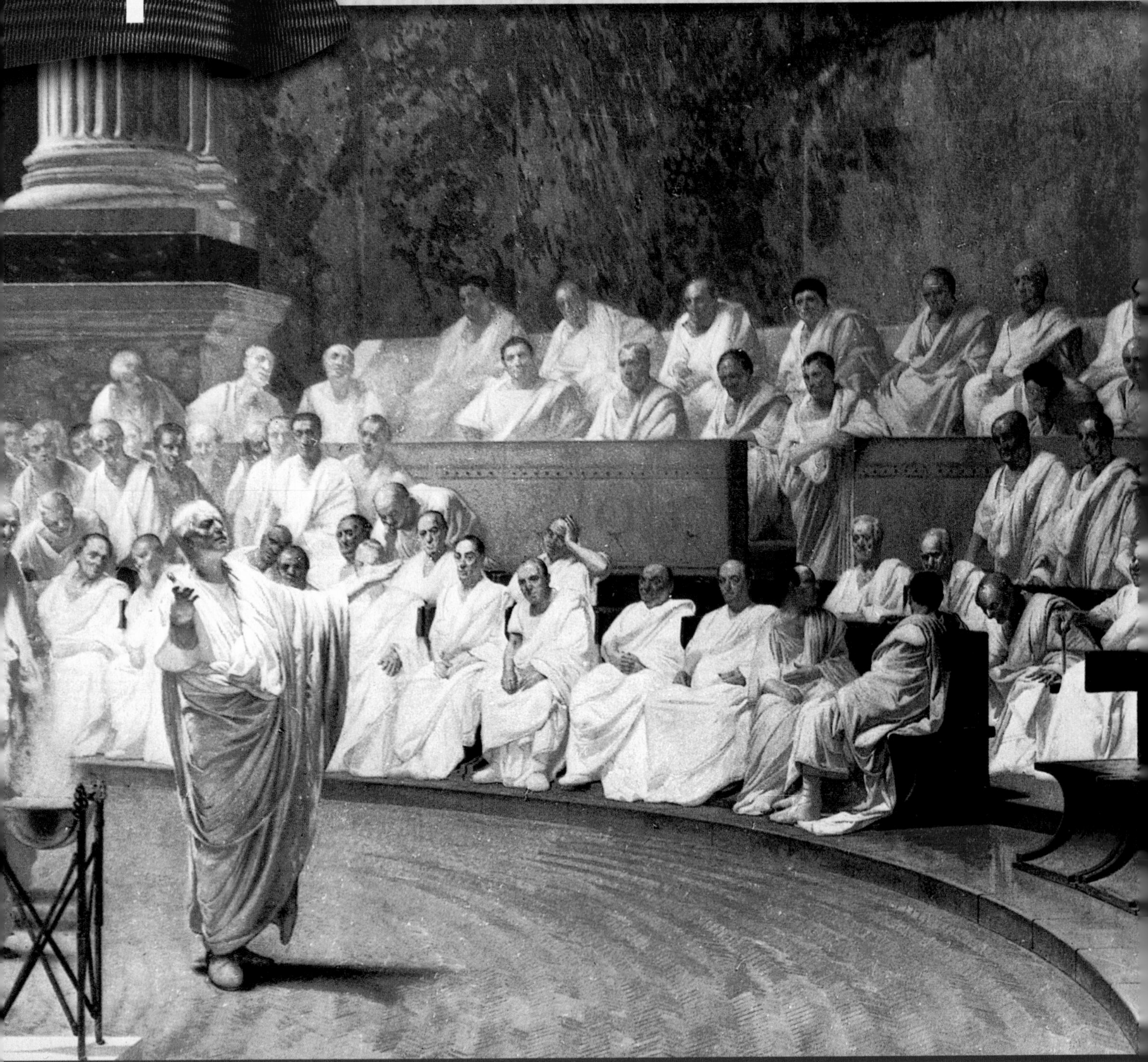

1600 B.C. | 1400 B.C. | 1200 B.C. | 1000 B.C. | 800 B.C. | 600 B.C.

1600 B.C. Minoan civilization at its height

1250 B.C. The Trojan War begins.

500 B.C. Romans set up a republic.

404 B.C. Sparta defeats Athens in battle.

> **"Let them enjoy indeed the title of citizens."**
>
> —Emperor Claudius, as recorded by Tacitus, A.D. 48

The Roman Senate, as painted by Cesare Maccari in the nineteenth century, shows one senator criticizing the conduct of the senator who is seated alone.

400 B.C.	200 B.C.	A.D.1	A.D. 200	A.D. 400	A.D. 600

323 B.C.
The death of Alexander the Great

146 B.C.
Rome destroys Carthage.

27 B.C.
Augustus becomes first Roman emperor.

A.D. 330
Constantinople becomes new capital.

A.D. 476
Last Roman emperor is driven from throne.

Meet the People

Pericles

c. 495 B.C.–429 B.C.

Birthplace: Athens, Greece

Greek statesman

- Made Athens the cultural and political center of Greece
- Embraced democracy
- Rebuilt and beautified Athens

Socrates

c. 470 B.C.–399 B.C.

Birthplace: Athens, Greece

Greek philosopher

- Examined the role of humans in the universe
- Invented the Socratic method
- Influenced all Greek philosophers after him

Alexander

356 B.C.–323 B.C.

Birthplace: Pella, Macedonia

Macedonian general and king

- Conquered the Persian Empire
- Built and ruled a vast empire
- Helped spread Greek culture throughout his empire

Hannibal

247 B.C.–181? B.C.

Birthplace: Carthage, North Africa

Carthaginian general

- Led troops across Alps to invade Italy
- Won several battles against Romans during Second Punic War
- Considered one of the most brilliant military leaders of ancient times

500 B.C.   400 B.C.   300 B.C.   200 B.C.   100 B.C.   A.D. 1

c. 495 B.C.–429 B.C. • Pericles

c. 470 B.C.–399 B.C. • Socrates

356 B.C.–323 B.C. • Alexander

247 B.C.–181? B.C. • Hannibal

63 B.C.–A.D. 14 • Augustus

Augustus

63 B.C.–A.D. 14

Birthplace: near Rome (present-day Italy)

Roman emperor

- Carried out many reforms throughout the Roman Empire
- Supported art and culture
- Established the *Pax Romana*

Marcus Aurelius

A.D. 121–180

Birthplace: Rome (present-day Italy)

Roman emperor

- Ruled Roman Empire from A.D. 161 to A.D. 180
- Wrote a series of philosophy books called *Meditations*
- Founded schools, orphanages, and hospitals

Constantine I

c. 280–337

Birthplace: Naissa (present-day Yugoslavia)

Roman emperor

- Became first Christian Roman emperor
- Granted Christians religious freedom
- Declared Constantinople his capital and made it the political center of the Roman Empire

Eudocia

c. 400–460

Birthplace: Athens, Greece

Roman empress, philanthropist, and writer

- Highly educated daughter of an Athenian Philosopher
- Known for her accepting attitude toward non-Christians
- Paid for the building of churches and hospitals in Jerusalem

A.D. 100   A.D. 200   A.D. 300   A.D. 400   A.D. 500   A.D. 600

A.D. 121–180 • Marcus Aurelius

c. 280–337 • Constantine I

c. 400–460 • Eudocia

241

Mediterranean Empires

Target Skill

Main Idea and Details

> The **main idea** is the most important idea in a reading selection or picture.

| detail | detail | detail |

- Identify the main idea of each paragraph. It is usually found in the topic sentence. The topic sentence is often the first sentence of a paragraph.

- Read the selection carefully. Take note of details that help to make the main idea clearer. Some details explain the main idea. Other details give examples to support the main idea.

Read the following paragraph. The main idea is highlighted in blue. Details are highlighted in yellow.

Geography affected how the way of life in Greece developed. Mountains divided Greece into different regions. Greeks in one region did not often travel to another. For example, the city of Sparta was only 60 miles from the city of Olympia (oh LIM pee yuh). Yet it took people nearly a week to travel the rugged land between the two places.

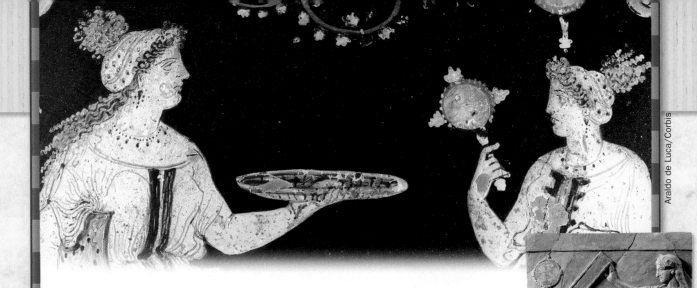
Araldo de Luca/Corbis

Gianni Dagli Orti/Corbis

Greek Women

Unlike the Egyptian women you read about in Unit 2, Greek women did not have many freedoms. Their lives were restricted, or limited.

Some girls from wealthy families learned to read, write, and play musical instruments. However, they could not attend school. A teacher called a tutor would come to the home.

One Greek woman who became a writer was Sappho (SA fo). She lived on a Greek island. Out of the public eye, women on the islands probably had more freedoms than women on the mainland.

Only rarely could women own property or inherit it from their husbands. Women spent their time taking care of the home and children. They wove cloth and cooked the meals. Few Greek homes had running water. Women collected water from public fountains. Women were not allowed to go to social events with their husbands. The fountain gave them a place of their own to be social with other women.

Women did have special religious festivals of their own. One festival was called Thesmophoria. It was just for married women and was held every autumn during the harvest. The festival honored the Greek goddess of agriculture. It usually lasted three days.

Apply it!

Use the reading strategy of main idea and details to answer these questions.

1 What is the main idea of this entire passage?

2 What details do we know about the daily tasks of women?

3 Write a main idea for each of the five paragraphs.

CHAPTER 9

Ancient Greece

Lesson 1

**1600 B.C.
Crete**
Minoan civilization is at its height.

Lesson 2

**500 B.C.
Sparta**
The Spartans rival the Athenians.

Lesson 3

**450 B.C.
Athens**
Athens enjoys a cultural "golden age."

Lesson 4

**331 B.C.
Alexandria**
Alexander the Great conquers the Persian Empire.

EUROPE

3

2

1

ASIA

**ANCIENT
GREECE**

4

Athens

Sparta

Mediterranean Sea

Crete

Alexandria

Why We Remember

We can thank ancient Greece for many of the ideas and values we share today.
Ancient Greece was the birthplace of what we call Western Civilization. More
than 2,000 years ago, Greek civilization made great advances in art and science.
Greek beliefs about learning, beauty, and medicine still affect our lives. Even
more important were Greek beliefs in the freedom and worth of each citizen.
From these beliefs came the idea that people should be free to rule themselves.
This idea led to the creation of a democracy.

3000 B.C.   2000 B.C.   1000 B.C.

3000 B.C.
Minoan civilization
arises on Crete.

1600 B.C.
Minoan civilization
reaches its height.

1400 B.C.
Rise of Mycenae
on mainland

Mycenae•

Aegean Sea

Crete

The Geography of Greece

PREVIEW

Focus on the Main Idea
Surrounded by mountains and water, the ancient Greeks developed communities and traveled on the sea to trade with other peoples.

PLACES
Balkan Peninsula
Mediterranean Sea
Aegean Sea
Asia Minor
Ionian Sea
Crete
Mycenae

PEOPLE
Plato
King Minos

VOCABULARY
agora
plunder

You Are There

1600 B.C. Standing high on a hill, overlooking the sea, there is a huge palace. Inside, the palace has hundreds of rooms—storerooms, bedrooms, workrooms, and bathrooms. Clay pipes carry running water to the people in the palace. Brilliantly colored paintings decorate the walls.

You move into a large courtyard. There, thousands of people are waiting to watch their favorite sport—bull leaping. A teenage girl calmly waits as the bull begins to charge. A split second before the bull strikes, the girl grabs the bull's horns and swings herself over its head. If the girl is lucky, she lands with her feet on the bull's back and then jumps into the arms of another member of the team.

You think to yourself, what is this civilization that lives in such a rugged landscape and enjoys such dangerous sports?

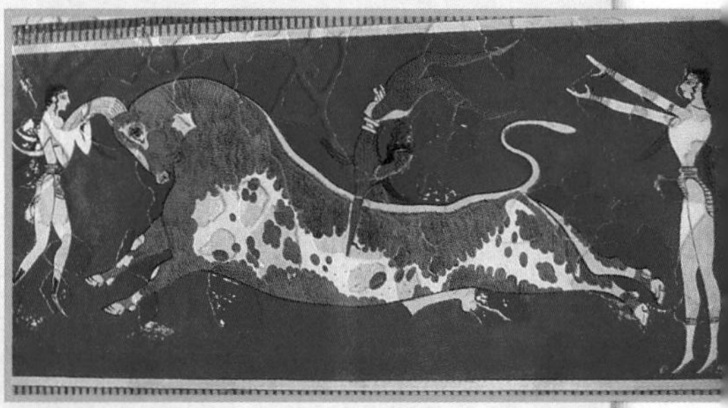

▶ In this fresco from about 1500 B.C., an athlete leaps onto the back of a bull.

Main Idea and Details As you read, think about how the physical geography of Greece influenced the civilizations that thrived there.

A Mountainous Land

In earlier chapters, you read how the first civilizations arose thousands of years ago. Many of these civilizations formed near rivers. The people depended on the rivers to overflow in the spring and flood their fields. This helped make fertile soil.

Greece was different. It did not depend on a river to flood its banks. Greece has no great rivers to form fertile valleys. Instead, it is a mountainous land with deep valleys and rugged highlands. Because of the mountains, it does not have much land that can be used for farming.

Mountains divided the people. In ancient times, Greece was not one united, or unified, country. As you can see from the map on this page, the main part of Greece is located in the southeast corner of the continent of Europe. There, the **Balkan Peninsula** extends outward into the eastern part of the **Mediterranean Sea.** Greece is located on the southern tip of the peninsula. Greek-speaking people also lived on many islands in the **Aegean Sea.** The Aegean (ee JEE un) Sea separates Greece from the western edge of Asia known as **Asia Minor.**

REVIEW What is the land like on the mainland of Greece? ⟳ **Main Idea and Details**

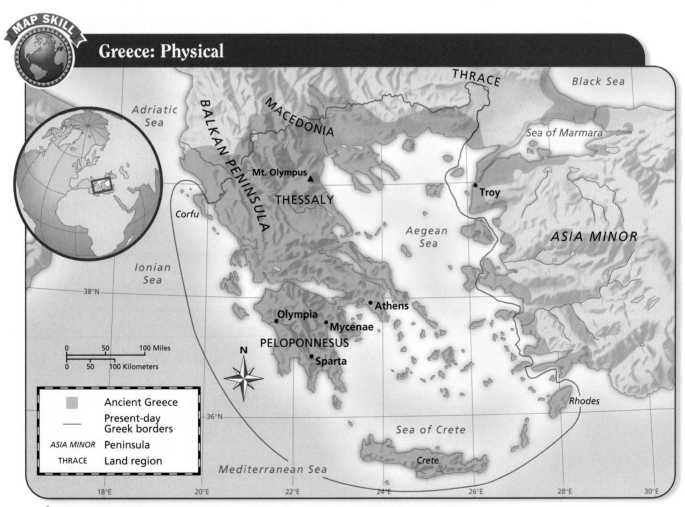

MAP SKILL

Greece: Physical

- THRACE
- Black Sea
- Adriatic Sea
- BALKAN PENINSULA
- MACEDONIA
- Sea of Marmara
- Mt. Olympus ▲
- THESSALY
- Troy
- Corfu
- Ionian Sea
- Aegean Sea
- ASIA MINOR
- 38°N
- Athens
- Olympia
- Mycenae
- PELOPONNESUS
- Sparta
- 0 50 100 Miles
- 0 50 100 Kilometers
- N
- Rhodes
- 36°N
- Sea of Crete

Legend:
- ▨ Ancient Greece
- — Present-day Greek borders
- *ASIA MINOR* Peninsula
- THRACE Land region

- Crete
- Mediterranean Sea
- 18°E 20°E 22°E 24°E 26°E 28°E 30°E

▶ The rugged landscape influenced the development of Greek civilization.

MAP SKILL Use a Map *Besides mountains, what other physical features influenced where cities developed?*

A Land Tied to the Sea

The seas are never far from the people of Greece. The Aegean Sea lies to the east. The Ionian (eye OH nee un) Sea on the west separates Greece from Italy. To the south, the Mediterranean Sea links Greece with Asia, North Africa, and the western part of Europe. This location places Greece squarely at the crossroads of many different cultures.

Although Greece is a small land, it has a long coastline with many bays and inlets. These bays and inlets create many excellent harbors. The sea was a big influence on Greek civilization. A famous Greek thinker named Plato wrote:

> *"Like Frogs around a pool, we have settled down upon the shores of this sea."*

Being so close to these seas helped the Greeks become great sailors and traders.

▶ Grapes, olives, and other produce were both food and trade goods for Greece. Today, they are still important in Mediterranean countries.

In ancient Greece, most people lived along the low coastal areas and in its few short river valleys. Here, the rich soil and mild climate were perfect for raising animals and growing Greece's main crops—grapes, olives, and grains such as barley. The Greeks sold these crops to other lands across the seas.

Trade allowed Greek ideas to spread. It also allowed the Greeks to learn from other cultures. It was through this spread of ideas that the Greeks got their alphabet and began using coins for money.

REVIEW How did living near the sea affect both lives and ideas of the Greeks?
🔁 Main Idea and Details

▶ The Aegean Sea, as seen from the coastline of the island of Santorini.

The Granger Collection

▶ In ancient Greece, the agora, or marketplace, was a center of activity in each city. This is the agora in Athens.

Independent Communities

Geography affected how life in Greece developed. Mountains divided Greece into different regions. In the lowlands, the land was fertile and good for farming. The hills were good for grazing animals.

Uniting the country under one government was very difficult. The people of Greece did speak the same language. They also practiced the same religion. However, mountains physically separated them. People in one region did not frequently travel to another. The people developed many small and independent communities. In time, the communities grew into cities. Each city had its own way of doing things.

Greece has a pleasant climate. Most of the rainfall occurs during the winter months. Summers are hot and dry. This allowed the Greeks to develop an outdoor way of life. Many Greeks spent their time at outdoor marketplaces called **agoras.**

The agora was a common feature in Greek cities. While women filled their pots with water in public fountains, men shopped in the marketplace. Statues of local athletes, important politicians, and, in some cases, gods and goddesses, stood in the marketplace.

Because the climate was so pleasant, the Greeks enjoyed doing activities outside. They watched plays in open-air theaters. Their political meetings and religious celebrations took place outdoors. The Greeks also developed a lasting interest in sports and athletic contests.

REVIEW Why did Greece not develop one strong central government? ⟳ **Main Idea and Details**

Two Early Greek Civilizations

About the same time that people settled in the Nile Valley, settlements developed on islands in the Aegean Sea. By 2500 B.C., the people of **Crete** (creet), an island in the Mediterranean Sea, had developed a written language. They also had learned to weave cloth and make pottery and jewelry. Today, we call this the Minoan (muh NOH uhn) civilization. It is named after **King Minos** (MY nuhs). It was the Minoans who held the dangerous bull-jumping shows.

The wealth of Minoan civilization came from trade. According to Greek historians, the Minoans controlled trade with all the islands in the Aegean Sea and the cities on the coast of the Ionian Sea. We know that they traded with such lands as Syria and Egypt. They traded food grown on the island, as well as beautiful pottery and other crafts made by their artisans.

▶ **Minoan artists frequently painted sea creatures, such as the dolphins in this fresco.**

By 1600 B.C., the Minoan civilization was a powerful influence in the Aegean islands and the part of the Greek peninsula called Peloponnesus (pehl oh puh NEE suhs). Minoan ships patrolled the seas and protected the kingdom from invaders.

HERE AND THERE The Nok of Africa

At the same time the Greek city-states were growing, another culture was developing on a plateau in the central part of present-day Nigeria. There, the Nok people were building their own unique culture. We know very little about the Nok, because they kept no written records. We do know that their culture reached its height between about 500 B.C. and A.D. 200. We also know that they became very skilled at using iron. In fact, the Nok are responsible for the earliest known use of iron in West Africa. Iron tools allowed the Nok to clear the forest and break up the soil. The Nok settled down and built permanent towns. In their settled towns, Nok artisans created artwork from wood and clay. They left behind beautiful clay figurines of elephants and other animals, as well as human heads.

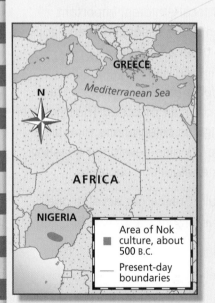

GREECE

Mediterranean Sea

N

AFRICA

NIGERIA

■ Area of Nok culture, about 500 B.C.

— Present-day boundaries

▶ **The people of the Nok culture created wonderfully detailed heads out of terra-cotta. These heads date back more than 2,000 years.**

Then Minoan civilization grew weak. Historians and scientists don't really know why or how. Some believe that earthquakes may have destroyed the Minoan cities. New civilizations soon arose on the Greek mainland.

About 2000 B.C., groups of people migrated to the Greek mainland. Over the centuries, these communities grew into cities. The cities then grew into city-states. Each one developed its own pattern of life.

The greatest of the early city-states was **Mycenae** (my SEE nee). As Mycenae grew, so did its power. It replaced Crete as the center of civilization in the eastern Mediterranean.

Mycenae could defend itself against almost any attack. Walls 20 feet thick surrounded the city. Mycenaean ships left the city to capture ships of other cities. The Mycenaens took **plunder,** or valuables seized in wartime.

▶ **This painting of Minoan ships in the Aegean Sea is from about 1650 B.C.**

The search for plunder probably led Mycenae to launch a war that would be remembered in legends throughout history. You will read more about that famous war in Lesson 2.

REVIEW Which details explain the power of Minoan civilization? Main Idea and Details

Summarize the Lesson

- **3000 B.C.** Minoan civilization arose on the island of Crete.
- **1600 B.C.** Minoan civilization reached its height.
- **1400 B.C.** City of Mycenae grew powerful on the Greek mainland.

LESSON 1 REVIEW

Check Facts and Main Ideas

1. Main Idea and Details On a separate piece of paper, write an appropriate main idea in the box for the three supporting details shown below.

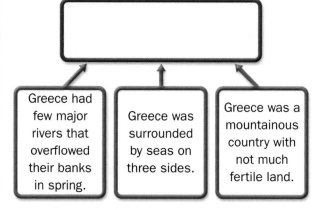

| Greece had few major rivers that overflowed their banks in spring. | Greece was surrounded by seas on three sides. | Greece was a mountainous country with not much fertile land. |

2. What was the Minoan civilization?

3. What are the three seas that border Greece?

4. What effect did mountains have on the peoples in Greece?

5. Critical Thinking: *Make Generalizations* In your own words, describe the importance of the sea to the people of Greece.

Link to ⊶ **Art**

Interpret a Painting The Minoans probably were the first people to use fresco painting. This means that they painted on plaster that was still wet—*fresco* means *fresh*. Look at the fresco paintings on pages 246, 250, and 251. How do you think the Minoans decided what to paint?

1500 B.C.   1000 B.C.   500 B.C.

1250 B.C.
Trojan War
takes place.

about 900 B.C.
Sparta begins
conquering its
neighbors.

500 B.C.
Democracy appears
in Greece.

The Greek City-States

PREVIEW

Focus on the Main Idea
Two very different cultures grew in the city-states of Athens and Sparta.

PLACES
Troy
Mount Olympus
Athens
Sparta

PEOPLE
Homer
Pericles

VOCABULARY
myth
immortal
aristocracy
democracy

TERMS
oral tradition
Assembly
helot

EVENTS
Trojan War
Olympic Games

> You Are There

You feel like it's time for a good action-adventure story. Picking up a book of Greek tales, you begin to read.

For a long time, the battle between the god Zeus (Zoos) and the powerful giants has raged. Armed with thunderbolts, mighty Zeus has finally destroyed his enemies. Now, Zeus rules the gods and goddesses.

As time passes, Zeus becomes father to many new gods and goddesses. The goddess Athena is born when Zeus is struck on the head. She springs from his forehead, full grown, in full armor, and with a loud battle cry.

Athena is known as the goddess of wisdom. However, she is also a warrior goddess. Athena aids the Greeks in the most famous of legendary battles, the Trojan War. Will Athena's power be greater than that of the gods who are helping Troy?

You can hardly wait to read what happens next.

▶ **Athena was the goddess of wisdom. Athens was named for Athena after she won a contest with another god over who would become the patron of the new city.**

Compare and Contrast As you read, think about how Athens and Sparta were different and similar.

▶ **Odysseus had many adventures during his ten-year voyage home. The mythical tale the *Odyssey* includes encounters with monsters, magicians, and giants, such as the one-eyed cyclops.**

The Power of Greek Myths and Legends

In the Trojan War, fought between the Greeks and the people of Troy, gods and goddesses helped heroes on both sides of the battle. In ancient Greece, daily life often focused on trying to keep these gods and goddesses happy.

Troy, a city on the western coast of Asia Minor, really existed. However, the story of the war is a blend of legend and myth. Legends are about heroes and their great deeds. Myths are traditional stories that may include gods and goddesses and that often try to explain events in nature.

Greece's city-states appear in many myths. Sparta was the home of Helen, who was carried off to Troy. This started the Trojan War. Athens was named for Athena, who helped the Greeks during the war. To end the war, the Greeks built a giant, wooden horse. The Trojans thought it was a gift that showed that the Greeks had surrendered. They pulled the horse into the city. At night, Greek soldiers crept out of the horse and opened the city gates to the Greek army.

According to tradition, a blind poet named Homer composed two poems about this war. These poems are the *Iliad* (ILL ee ad) and the *Odyssey* (ODD uh see). The *Iliad* tells about the war itself. One of the heroes in the *Iliad* was Odysseus (oh DIH see uhs). The *Odyssey* tells

of Odysseus, whose ship, while sailing home, was blown off course by gods he had angered.

Before Homer composed the *Iliad* and the *Odyssey*, myths and legends were part of what we call oral tradition. That is, they were passed down, by word of mouth, from person to person. Now they are among the world's most famous stories.

REVIEW Why do we remember the poet Homer today? Draw Conclusions

Literature and Social Studies

The Aeneid

Another hero of the war was the Trojan Aeneas (ih NEE uhs). He survived the destruction of Troy and later founded the town that became Rome. *The Aeneid*, an epic poem by Virgil, tells Aeneas' story. Here, Aeneas speaks of the war. Are these lines more myth or legend?

Wearied of the war,
And by ill-fortune crushed, year after year,
The kings of Greece, by Pallas' [Athena]
* skill divine,*
Build a huge horse, a thing of
* mountain size,*
With timbered ribs of fir.

Forbes Collection, New York City/Bridgeman Art Library, London/Superstock International

The Gods of Mount Olympus

Like most other ancient peoples, the Greeks worshipped many gods and goddesses. The Greeks developed many myths. Like the Egyptians, the Greeks turned to myths to help them understand the mysteries of nature and life. The myths helped them explain birth, death, disease, storms, and victories and defeats in battle.

The Greeks believed that most gods lived on **Mount Olympus** (oh LIM pus), located in northern Greece. The Greeks believed their gods and goddesses were very much like humans. They looked and acted like humans. They argued, fought, fell in love, and were jealous like humans. But, unlike humans, the gods were **immortal**, or able to live forever. They also had special powers.

The Greeks honored their gods and goddesses in many ways. Every four years, the Greeks held athletic contests to honor Zeus, the king of the gods. Because these contests were held in the city of Olympia, they became known as the

► A Greek image of women runners (at left). Below is Joan Benoit Samuelson, winner of the first women's marathon in the modern Olympic Games.

Olympic Games. Boxers, wrestlers, runners, and other athletes came from all parts of Greece to compete in the Olympics. The Greeks began to compete in these games about 3,500 years ago. Our modern Olympics are based on the ancient Greek games.

REVIEW Why might both the Egyptians and Greeks have developed myths? **Draw Conclusions**

FACT FILE

The Greeks believed in many gods and goddesses. The most important, they believed, lived on Mount Olympus. Here are some of them:

Zeus (zoos), king of the gods and ruler of Mount Olympus

Hera (HE rah), wife of Zeus, protector of families, children, and the home

Ares (AIR ees), god of war

Athena (ah THEEN uh), goddess of wisdom

Apollo (uh POHL oh), god of truth, intelligence, music, and poetry

Poseidon (poh SIE dun), god of the sea

Aphrodite (af roh DIE tee), goddess of love and beauty

Hermes (her MEES), god of good luck and wealth

Democracy Begins in Greece

The city-states of Greece developed many different forms of government. In some, a king ruled. In others, the government was controlled by members of wealthy, privileged families. This form of government is known as an **aristocracy.** Around 500 B.C., a new form of government developed in some city-states. This new government became known as a **democracy,** or government by the people.

Demos is a Greek word that means "common people." *Kratos* is a Greek word that means "rule." The Greeks believed that people could think and act for themselves. They proposed that people could rule themselves better than any king could. Democracy arose from these beliefs.

The city-state of **Athens** was the best example of a Greek democracy. At first, Athens was governed by all citizens older than 18. This gathering of citizens was called the **Assembly.** The Assembly soon became so large that it was hard to get anything done. Then, 500 citizens were selected to serve on a council for one year. These citizens were picked by choosing lots, or sticks with numbers on them. Actions of the council had to be approved by the Assembly of all citizens.

Democracy had a very different meaning to the ancient Greeks than it does today. Democracy was limited to citizens. Slaves, women, and workers born outside Athens were not citizens. They did not have the right to vote, own property, or testify in court.

REVIEW What details show that Athens developed a system of democracy?

🔄 **Main Idea and Details**

Rivals: Athens and Sparta

In return for their rights, citizens of Athens had major responsibilities. They were expected to defend the city in times of conflict. They also had to take part in government by serving on juries and participating in political debates on important issues. One of the greatest leaders in Athens, **Pericles** (PEH ruh kleez), described the responsibilities of citizenship:

> *"We do not say that a man who takes no interest in politics is a man who minds his own business; we say that he has no business here at all."*

In many ways, **Sparta,** a city-state located in the southern part of Greece, was the opposite of Athens. The Spartans lived in a strictly ruled military state. Sparta invaded neighboring city-states, taking over farmlands and forcing the local people to become **helots,** or slaves.

Life in Sparta centered on the army. Government officials examined newborn infants to see if they were healthy. Only healthy infants were allowed to live. When Spartan boys turned seven, they were sent to military camps to begin training for a lifetime in the army. Their training was brutal. They were given little food or clothing. They were expected to survive by stealing whatever they needed.

REVIEW What details show that Sparta was governed differently than Athens?

🔄 **Main Idea and Details**

▶ The *dromos* was a running place or race course. The *dromos* in Sparta, shown here, was a place where young people could come and exercise.

Women in Sparta

The state also expected Spartan women to be strong and responsible. They ran, wrestled, and played other active sports. When Spartan women sent their sons off to war, it was with this advice:

> **"Return home with your shield or on it."**

Spartan men spent so much time with the army that their wives did not see them very often. Spartan women spent most of their time with each other. They had more

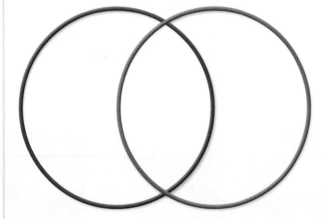

► **A girl is shown exercising in this sculpture made in or near Sparta. Greeks outside of Sparta were usually horrified by the short skirts worn by Spartan women.**

British Museum

personal rights than women in other Greek city-states. They could own property and express opinions on important issues. They managed family estates while men were away at war. However, like the women of Athens, Spartan women could not take part in governing the city-state.

REVIEW Why did the state expect Spartan women to train hard and play active sports?
Draw Conclusions

Summarize the Lesson

- **1250 B.C.** Troy and ancient Greece fought a long war.

- **about 900 B.C.** Sparta began conquering its neighbors.

- **500 B.C.** Democracy began developing in some Greek city-states.

LESSON 2   REVIEW

Check Facts and Main Ideas

1. **Compare and Contrast** On a separate piece of paper, copy the diagram below. Compare and contrast Athens and Sparta.

2. Where did the Greeks believe that most gods lived?

3. What is an aristocracy?

4. What does the story about the Trojan War tell us about the Greek attitudes toward their gods and goddesses?_

5. **Critical Thinking:** *Evaluate Information* If you had the choice, would you rather grow up in Athens or in Sparta? Why?

Link to ⟁⟁ **Reading**

Use a Dictionary You have learned how we got the word *democracy* from Greek words meaning "common people rule." Look in a dictionary to find out what Greek words are used to make the word *aristocracy*.

Pericles

c. 495 B.C.–429 B.C.

When Pericles became a statesman he quickly became a friend to the common people. Pericles often invited poor citizens home to have dinner with him. He was a hard worker and left little time for himself. He is said to have attended only one party in his life, which he left early! He also encouraged a democracy in which all adult male citizens had a voice in government.

However, his policies were sometimes criticized by other Greek states and by his fellow Athenians. For example, Pericles planned to rebuild Athens. He wanted to pay for the project with defense money that was set aside to be used against the Persians. Because Greece was not at war with Persia, Pericles thought the money would be better spent for the building project. Sparta refused to support his plan.

In 447 B.C., an army of Greece's finest builders and craftsworkers began work on the Parthenon and several other splendid buildings. Pericles' rivals complained that the project was too costly:

BIOFACT

Pericles had an oddly shaped head. For this reason, he usually wore a helmet in public.

> *"Greece cannot but resent it . . . when she sees the treasure, which was contributed by her upon a necessity for the war . . . hung round with precious stones and figures and temples, which cost a world of money."*

The Parthenon was completed in 438 B.C. It is considered to be one of the finest achievements in Greek architecture.

Learn from Biographies

Why do you think Pericles thought it was so important to beautify and rebuild Athens after the destruction caused by war?

For more information, go online to *Meet the People* at **www.sfsocialstudies.com.**

Map and Globe Skills

Compare City Maps at Different Scales

What? Different maps can have the same location at their centers, even though the maps are at different map scales. The size of the places shown will appear larger or smaller, depending on the scale. More of the surrounding area will be visible on some maps. Less of the surrounding area will be visible on other maps. The details shown on the maps will be different.

Why? Maps can contain different kinds of details. When choosing the right scale for a particular map, mapmakers consider what types of detail they need to show. To show all the streets of a city on a map, the city will have to appear very large. This makes the streets shown on the map easier to read. However, to show the surrounding land and water, the city will appear smaller on the map. This leaves room for the landforms, bodies of water, and other cities that surround the city.

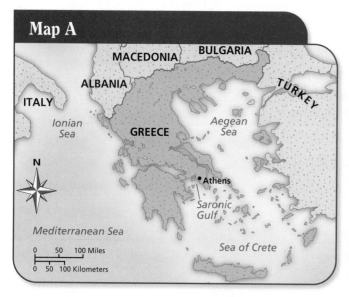

Map A

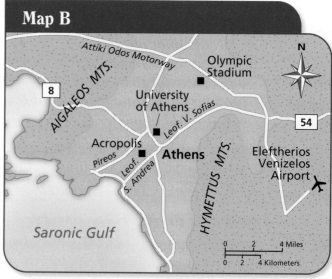

Map B

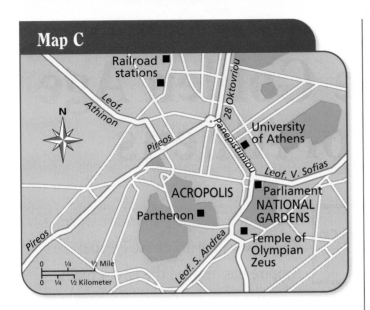

Map C

Railroad stations

N

Leof. Athinon

28 Oktovriou

Panepistimiou

Pireos

University of Athens

Leof. V. Sofias

ACROPOLIS

Parthenon

Parliament
NATIONAL GARDENS

Pireos

Leof. S. Andrea

Temple of Olympian Zeus

0   ¼   ½ Mile
0   ¼   ½ Kilometer

How? These pages contain three different maps. Each is drawn to a different scale. Athens is at the center of each map.

Study Map A. Can you spot Athens on the map? Athens appears small so that there will be room to show the area surrounding Athens. What types of details are being shown on this map? What reasons can you think of for using a map at this scale? What other kinds of details would fit with this particular map?

Now study Map B. More of Athens is visible on Map B than on Map A. Look at the details that appear on Map B but did not appear on Map A. For example, you can see some roads on Map B. Then consider the types of detail that appeared on Map A but do not appear on Map B. For example, you can see in Map A that Italy is nearby. What are the most important facts you can learn about Athens from Map A? What other kinds of details might appear on a map with the scale of Map B?

Compare the two maps. If the word *Athens* were removed from both maps, what details would help you figure out how one map relates to the other?

Now study Map C. This is a detailed street map of Athens. What kinds of details are shown on this map that do not appear on the other two maps? What details appeared on Map B that do not appear on Map C? What other kinds of details would make this map more useful?

Think of a giant telescope out in space. Map A shows you the greatest area. Map B zooms in toward Earth. Map C moves you closest to Earth. It shows the smallest area, but has the greatest detail.

Think and Apply

1. If you were writing a paper on the empire of the Greeks in the ancient world, which map would be most useful?

2. If you were touring downtown Athens, which map would be the most useful?

3. Which map would be most useful if you needed to get to the airport?

4. All three maps are alike in certain ways. Name one way they are alike. The maps are different in certain ways. Name two ways they are different.

Internet Activity

For more information, go online to the *Atlas* at **www.sfsocialstudies.com.**

500 B.C.   400 B.C.   300 B.C.

480 B.C.
Battle of Salamis

404 B.C.
Sparta defeats Athens
in Peloponnesian War.

490 B.C.
Battle of Marathon

The Golden Age of Athens

PREVIEW

Focus on the Main Idea
During the Golden Age of Athens, the Athenians excelled in the arts, philosophy, and government.

PLACES
Athens
Marathon
Salamis
Thebes
Macedonia

PEOPLE
Socrates
Aristotle

VOCABULARY
marathon
philosopher
reason
plague
mercenary

TERMS
Golden Age
Socratic method
Delian League

EVENTS
Peloponnesian War

▶ Sports and physical skill were valued by the Greeks. They were so important that images of athletes were common decorations. Here, runners sprint around a Grecian vase.

You Are There

Your family and neighbors are worried. The powerful army of the Persian Empire has invaded the Greek mainland. At Marathon, a coastal plain northeast of Athens, the Persian army prepares for battle. The Athenian army is outnumbered.

In Athens you worry that your army may not be able to defeat the invaders. The Persian Empire is powerful. Then you hear that the Athenians have attacked the Persians. You wait.

In the distance you see a runner coming toward the city. He is a warrior from the Athenian army.

You can see that he has run a great distance. What news does he have? Reaching the city, the warrior gasps:

Rejoice, we conquer.

Then he collapses.

Main Idea and Details
As you read, think about what made the Golden Age in Athens.

Fine Art Museum, Budapest, Hungary/Bridgeman Art Library, London/Superstock International

The Greeks Clash with the Persians

You have already read about the Persian Empire on page 132. At the time **Athens** was growing more powerful, Persia was the strongest military power in the world. In 490 B.C., Persia attacked the Greek mainland with a huge army. The two armies clashed at a plain northeast of Athens called **Marathon.** According to legend, after the Athenian victory, the Athenian army sent a warrior named Pheidippides (fy DIHP uh deez) back to Athens with the news. He ran the entire distance—25 miles. Today, we remember this legend in the name of the longest Olympic race—the **marathon.**

The Greeks knew the Persians would attack again with an even larger army. To survive, Spartans and Athenians put aside their differences and prepared to fight the Persians together.

In 480 B.C., a Greek army held off a much larger Persian army for three days at a mountain pass north of Athens. A small force that included 300 Spartans stood its ground until almost all its soldiers were killed.

Then, in a mighty sea battle at **Salamis** (SAL uh mihs), Athenian ships trapped and destroyed the Persian fleet. The Persian invasion ended soon afterwards, in 479 B.C. Athens and Sparta, working together, had defeated the most powerful empire of its time.

REVIEW Why did the Spartans cooperate with the Athenians? ⟳ **Main Idea and Details**

Map Adventure

You're Leading the Spartans

You stand at attention before Leonidas, king of Sparta and commander of the army. The Persians are advancing. You must get your troops to Athens in four days or all will be lost.

You consult your map of Greece.

1. Using the map scale, how many miles in a straight line are between Athens and Sparta?

2. By land, your army must march from Sparta to Mantinea, then to Corinth and Megara, and finally to Athens. How many total miles will this march be?

3. If your army can travel 30 miles a day, how long will it take you to get to Athens?

4. Your ships can travel about 6 miles an hour. Instead of marching the whole way, would it be quicker to march to Argos, go to Piraeus by ship, and then march to Athens? Explain your answer.

261

The Golden Age

After the defeat of the Persians in 479 B.C., Athens entered a period known as the **Golden Age.** During this time, the people of Athens built magnificent new temples. Artists created statues and monuments of breathtaking beauty.

During the Golden Age, Greek **philosophers** extended human knowledge. Philosophers study truth and knowledge. Greek philosophers such as **Socrates,** Plato, and **Aristotle** (see the Fact File on this page) searched for beauty and order in the world. They tried to find natural laws that explained actions in the world.

Followers of the great philosophers developed a respect for the power of **reason,** or logical thinking. They believed that it was possible to figure out an explanation for why things happened in nature. It was not just the whims of gods or goddesses. For example, the Greeks were among the first people to study the causes of sickness. Earlier societies had blamed illness on the gods' displeasure. Greek physicians tried to find natural, predictable explanations for the workings of the human body.

REVIEW Why is the period after the defeat of the Persians considered a "golden age" for Athens? **Summarize**

▶ **The Parthenon, at right, was a temple built to honor Athena. It once housed a fabulous gold and ivory statue of the goddess. The Parthenon sits on the acropolis, or high point of the city, in Athens. It is considered the ideal of Greek architecture.**

FACT FILE

The Greek Philosophers

Socrates (SOK ruh teez) tried to teach people to think by asking them questions. Each question was designed to take a person step-by-step to a final conclusion. Today, this approach to teaching is known as the **Socratic method.**

Plato did not believe that democracy was the best kind of government. Rather, he proposed that a small group of wise men should run the government. He thought they could make better decisions than most people. Plato also believed that, if humans applied reason, they could create a perfect world.

Aristotle was Plato's student. He wrote more than 170 books on astronomy, physics, politics, art, and other subjects. He established a school in Athens for the study of all branches of knowledge. This school became a model for the modern university.

The Greeks Fight Against Each Other

During its Golden Age, Athens became the most powerful Greek city-state. After the defeat of the Persians, the leaders of Athens began to act unwisely. They formed an alliance, an agreement to work together, called the **Delian League.** Athens forced some city-states to join the alliance. It used the League's funds to put up public buildings in Athens. Athenian generals began interfering in the affairs of other city-states. Other Greeks became angry and resentful.

Sparta became the leader of the city-states opposed to Athens. In 431 B.C., war broke out between Athens and Sparta. It was called the **Peloponnesian** (pel uh puh NEEZH un) **War** after the area of Greece where most of the fighting took place.

Athens' great strength was as a sea power. Sparta was more of a land power. At first, this made it hard for either Athens or Sparta to gain a real advantage.

In this vase painting, Greek warriors prepare for battle.

Réunion des Musées Nationaux/Art Resource

For example, the Spartans and their allies attacked by destroying farms and homes around Athens. By doing this, the Spartans hoped to starve the Athenians into surrendering. However, the Athenian navy was able to get food to the citizens.

A **plague,** or a fast-spreading, often deadly disease, broke out in Athens. It killed thousands of people, including Pericles. After Pericles' death, the government of Athens became unstable. Finally, in 404 B.C., an exhausted Athens surrendered.

REVIEW In what way did the Athenians act unwisely in dealing with their allies in the Delian League? **Main Idea and Details**

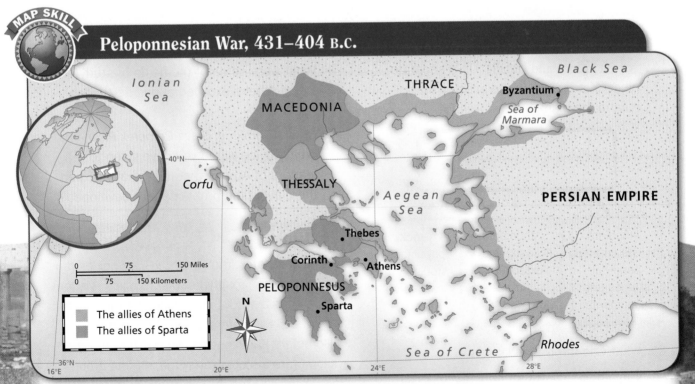

MAP SKILL

Peloponnesian War, 431–404 B.C.

Ionian Sea

THRACE

Black Sea

MACEDONIA

Byzantium

Sea of Marmara

40°N

Corfu

THESSALY

Aegean Sea

PERSIAN EMPIRE

0   75   150 Miles
0   75   150 Kilometers

Thebes

Corinth   Athens

PELOPONNESUS

N

The allies of Athens
The allies of Sparta

Sparta

Sea of Crete

Rhodes

36°N
16°E   20°E   24°E   28°E

▶ Sparta defeated Athens after years of fighting in the Peloponnesian War.

MAP SKILL Use a Map Key *Which city had the most allies?*

263

Decline of the Greek City-States

By the end of the Peloponnesian War, Greece had fallen on hard times. Unemployment was high. When the brother of the king of Persia rebelled against the king, many young Greek men joined his army as **mercenaries,** or hired soldiers.

After so many years of war and plague, Athens was still able to regain its strength in trade. Two of Athens' greatest philosophers—Plato and Aristotle—taught and wrote during the century following the war. However, all of Greece was weakened by the war. Even Sparta had lost

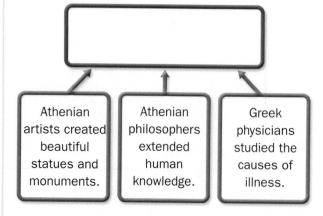

▶ **A coin from Macedonia shows a goat or ram with long horns. Both animals represented kings in this region.**

The Granger Collection

so many of its soldiers in the war that it no longer had the military strength it had once had. In 371 B.C., the Spartan army was defeated in a battle against the Greek city of **Thebes.**

Meanwhile, another power was rising to the north: **Macedonia.** As its army grew and strengthened, Macedonia became a threat to its Greek neighbors to the south. A great leader was soon to emerge from Macedonia.

> **REVIEW** What were the causes of the decline of Athens and Sparta? *Cause and Effect*

Summarize the Lesson

- **490 B.C.** Greeks defeated the much larger Persian army at Marathon.

- **480 B.C.** Athens' fleet destroyed Persian fleet at Salamis, ending Persian threat.

- **404 B.C.** Sparta defeated Athens in Peloponnesian War.

LESSON 3   REVIEW

Check Facts and Main Ideas

1. 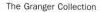 **Main Idea and Details** On a separate piece of paper, fill in the missing main idea in the blank box.

```
┌─────────────────────────────┐
│                             │
│                             │
└─────────────────────────────┘
      ↑         ↑        ↑
```

| Athenian artists created beautiful statues and monuments. | Athenian philosophers extended human knowledge. | Greek physicians studied the causes of illness. |

2. What was the Delian League?

3. Why was the Battle of Salamis important to Greece?

4. What were some of the fields of study in which Athens excelled during its Golden Age?

5. **Critical Thinking:** *Solve Complex Problems* What advice would you have given to the leaders of Athens that might have helped them avoid the problems that developed?

Link to ⚭ Mathematics

Use a Calculator The distance Pheidippides ran from Marathon to Athens was 25 miles. Modern marathons are 26.2 miles long. If 1 mile equals about 1.6 kilometers, calculate how many kilometers Pheidippides ran and how many kilometers athletes today run in a marathon.

Socrates

c. 470 B.C. – 399 B.C.

Socrates was one of the most important ancient Greek philosophers. He looked at the role of humans in the universe. He tried to find the best way for people to live their lives. He attempted to answer questions such as "What is justice?"

We know about his life and philosophical methods from the writings of his students. As a young man, Socrates loved to learn. According to Plato, Socrates said:

> *"I thought it would be marvelous to know the causes for which each thing comes and ceases [stops] and continues to be."*

Socrates used a question-and-answer method of argument, which came to be known as the Socratic method. As you read in the Fact File on page 262, each question was to lead a person step-by-step to a final conclusion. His method showed that many commonly held beliefs were false. However, his methods earned him some enemies. In 399 B.C., Socrates was accused of being a bad influence on young people.

BIOFACT

Socrates was a soldier during the Peloponnesian War. As a Greek warrior, he would have worn a metal chest plate.

At the trial, Socrates served as his own lawyer. He said that he could not be blamed for the actions of his followers. Still he was found guilty and sentenced to death. His friends urged him to escape, but he refused. As a citizen of Athens, he believed it was his duty to obey its laws. Socrates died in jail after being forced to drink a cup of poison.

Learn from Biographies

If Socrates had agreed to escape from jail, do you think he would be viewed differently today? Explain.

Réunion des Musées Nationaux/Art Resource

For more information, go online to *Meet the People* at **www.sfsocialstudies.com.**

Alexandria

400 B.C.   200 B.C.   A.D. 1

323 B.C.
Alexander dies and Hellenistic Age begins.

30 B.C.
Hellenistic Age ends.

336 B.C.
Alexander becomes king of Macedonia.

Alexander the Great

PREVIEW

Focus on the Main Idea
The conquests of Alexander the Great built a new culture that mixed Greek and Asian ways.

PLACES
Alexandria

PEOPLE
Alexander
Hippocrates
Archimedes
Pythagoras
Euclid

TERMS
Hellenistic Age

You Are There

You can't believe it. Your new king, Alexander, is only 20 years old. It's true that he has had the finest education. He has studied in Athens under the great philosopher, Aristotle. He also has proven to be an able warrior. His father, Philip II, king of Macedonia, had been a great leader. He took over many lands and conquered Greece. But he made enemies. One was a young noble who murdered him. What will Macedonia do without the firm hand of Philip? Will Alexander be a good enough leader to continue the conquests of his father?

Will he show the same genius for leadership as his father did?

► Philip II, king of Macedonia (on the left) and his son, Alexander the Great (on the right)

The Granger Collection

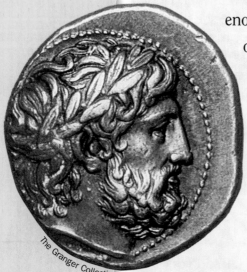
Bettmann/Corbis

Cause and Effect As you read, think about what effects Alexander's conquests had on Macedonia and the world.

Alexander's Conquests

It did not take long for **Alexander** to show his leadership qualities. In 334 B.C., just two years after he became king of Macedonia, Alexander invaded the Persian Empire.

In a battle on the Plain of Issus in Syria, Alexander showed a real genius for leadership. The much larger Persian army rained a storm of arrows down on Alexander's army. However, Alexander did not order a retreat. Instead, he ordered his army to attack.

When the Persians saw their opponents charging at them, they fled in terror. Alexander was triumphant.

Alexander then turned south. He conquered Syria and Phoenicia (fo NEE shuh). In 332 B.C., he invaded Egypt, where the Persians had ruled for 200 years. The Egyptians quickly surrendered, and Alexander was crowned as pharaoh.

Archivo Iconografico, S.A./Corbis

▶ **Alexander rides into battle against the Persians on the Plain of Issus. This picture was created more than 200 years after Alexander's death.**

REVIEW How did Alexander's leadership affect the size of his empire? **Draw Conclusions**

MAP SKILL

Alexander's Conquests

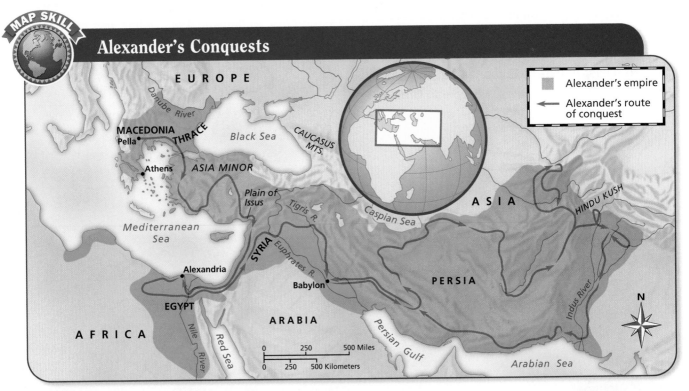

Legend:
- Alexander's empire
- ← Alexander's route of conquest

EUROPE · Danube River · MACEDONIA · Pella · THRACE · Black Sea · CAUCASUS MTS. · Athens · ASIA MINOR · Plain of Issus · Tigris R. · Caspian Sea · ASIA · HINDU KUSH · Mediterranean Sea · SYRIA · Euphrates R. · Alexandria · Babylon · PERSIA · Indus River · EGYPT · ARABIA · AFRICA · Nile River · Red Sea · Persian Gulf · Arabian Sea · N

0   250   500 Miles
0   250   500 Kilometers

▶ **Alexander conquered lands on three continents.**

MAP SKILL Measure Distance *About how far is it from the farthest east to farthest west of Alexander's conquests?*

267

A Great Empire

Alexander's army had to face the Persian army one last time, in 331 B.C. Once again, the Persian forces were larger than Alexander's army. And once again, Alexander's army won the battle.

After defeating the Persians, Alexander led his army eastward. Everywhere he went he was victorious. Finally, he took the army through the rugged mountains of India. Five years after his march started, it ended in the pouring rains of the monsoon. Alexander's soldiers were exhausted. They would go no farther.

Alexander marched his army back toward Greece. However, he fell ill and died before he could return. He was only 33 years old. During his rule, which lasted about 13 years, Alexander created a vast empire in Europe, Asia, and Africa. He founded many new cities. He spread Greek culture to the conquered lands. He also adopted many Asian ways.

▶ In this painting from India, Alexander supervises the building of a defensive wall of fire. The scene was painted more than 1,000 years after Alexander lived. Alexander conquered much of the known world, including northwestern India.

R. Sheridan/Ancient Art & Architecture Collection, Ltd.

A new civilization developed from this blend of Greek and Asian cultures. Historians call this period the **Hellenistic Age.** Hellas was the name the Greeks used for their country. For these accomplishments, the young Macedonian king is known in history as "Alexander the Great."

REVIEW Give two reasons that explain why Alexander has been called "Alexander the Great." 🔄 **Main Idea and Details**

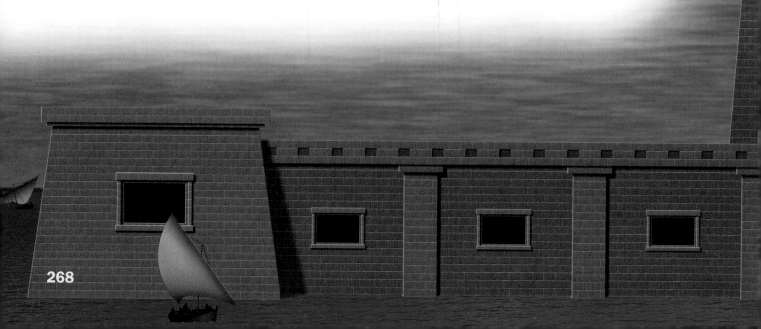

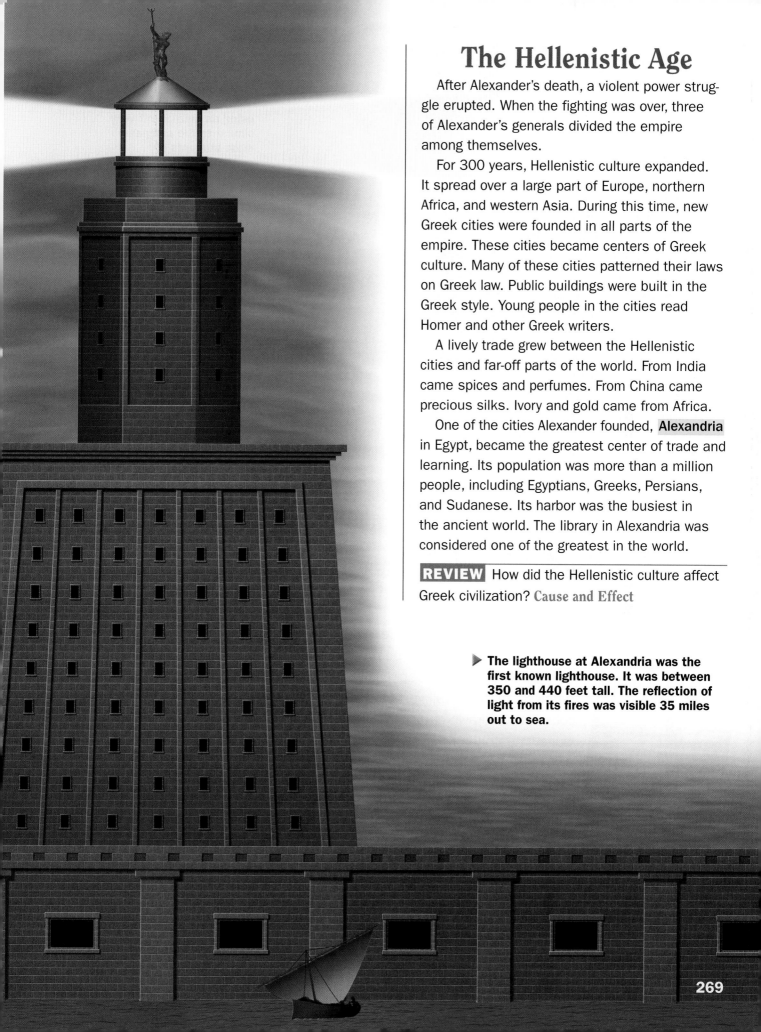

The Hellenistic Age

After Alexander's death, a violent power struggle erupted. When the fighting was over, three of Alexander's generals divided the empire among themselves.

For 300 years, Hellenistic culture expanded. It spread over a large part of Europe, northern Africa, and western Asia. During this time, new Greek cities were founded in all parts of the empire. These cities became centers of Greek culture. Many of these cities patterned their laws on Greek law. Public buildings were built in the Greek style. Young people in the cities read Homer and other Greek writers.

A lively trade grew between the Hellenistic cities and far-off parts of the world. From India came spices and perfumes. From China came precious silks. Ivory and gold came from Africa.

One of the cities Alexander founded, **Alexandria** in Egypt, became the greatest center of trade and learning. Its population was more than a million people, including Egyptians, Greeks, Persians, and Sudanese. Its harbor was the busiest in the ancient world. The library in Alexandria was considered one of the greatest in the world.

REVIEW How did the Hellenistic culture affect Greek civilization? **Cause and Effect**

▶ The lighthouse at Alexandria was the first known lighthouse. It was between 350 and 440 feet tall. The reflection of light from its fires was visible 35 miles out to sea.

Discovery and Invention

Greek science and mathematics reached their peaks during the Hellenistic Age. Doctors in Alexandria made many discoveries about how the human body works. **Hippocrates** (hih PAHK ruh teez) was a doctor who looked for natural causes of diseases. He is often called the "father of medicine." Even today, when people become doctors, the official promise they make to heal is called the Hippocratic Oath. Hippocrates stressed the importance of diet and lifestyle for good health.

Archimedes (ar kuh MEE deez) was the most famous inventor of this time. He was also an

▶ This Dutch painting of Euclid, from the 1400s, shows the mathematician using an instrument very similar to the compass most students of mathematics use today.

important mathematician. His inventions included improved pulleys for moving heavy loads and a screw that carries water. He made discoveries regarding floating objects and described how levers worked. As he proclaimed:

"Give me a place to stand and I will move the Earth."

DORLING KINDERSLEY EYEWITNESS BOOK

Greek Columns

Buildings in ancient Greece are remembered for their great beauty. Many Greek buildings—especially temples—featured tall vertical columns. Ox-drawn carts brought the huge limestone or marble blocks from quarries. Workers carved the stone using hammers and mallets.

The columns were made in cylindrical sections and were held together by metal pegs. They were then lifted into position with ropes and pulleys.

Decorative Ionic style ornament

The Doric style is sturdy and its top is plain.   *The Ionic style is thinner and more elegant.*   *The Corinthian style is more elaborate.*

Columns and Capitals
The columns, capitals (tops of columns), and horizontal lintels (beams) used on Greek buildings may have been inspired by earlier wooden buildings whose roofs were supported by tree trunks.

As a mathematician, Archimedes built on the work of **Pythagoras** (pih THAG ur uhs) and **Euclid** (YOO klid). Pythagoras created some important theories about numbers and music. He also started a school that studied ideas that led to the development of the mathematical field of geometry. The most important mathematician of the period was Euclid. Euclid worked out the system of plane geometry that students still study today.

REVIEW How did the discoveries of scientists in Hellenistic times affect people in later times?
Cause and Effect

▶ **Archimedes' screw was a machine that carried water from a lower to a higher level. Invented more than 2,000 years ago, Archimedes' screw is still used in parts of the world today.**

Summarize the Lesson

- **336 B.C.** Alexander the Great became king of Macedonia upon the death of his father.

- **323 B.C.** Alexander died after building a huge empire in Asia, Europe, and North Africa.

- **30 B.C.** The Hellenistic Age ended.

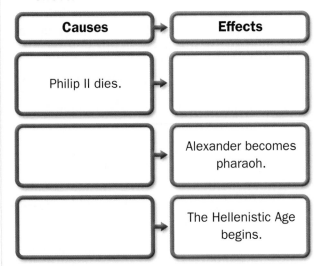

LESSON 4 REVIEW

Check Facts and Main Ideas

1. Cause and Effect On a separate piece of paper, fill in the missing causes and effects.

Causes	→	Effects
Philip II dies.	→	
	→	Alexander becomes pharaoh.
	→	The Hellenistic Age begins.

2. How did Alexander become king of Macedonia?

3. How did Alexander display his leadership qualities?

4. What was Hellenistic culture, and how did it begin?

5. Critical Thinking: *Solve Complex Problems* How might the discoveries made by Hippocrates have changed people's lives during the Hellenistic Age?

Link to ∞ Science

Apply Technology Archimedes demonstrated how levers and pulleys could move a ship without much human strength. How could this invention have helped with building the Egyptian pyramids?

1500 B.C.

1600 B.C.
Minoan civilization at
its height

1250 B.C.
Trojan War between Troy
and ancient Greece

Chapter Summary

Main Idea and Details

On a separate piece of paper, fill in the missing details
that support the main idea shown in the box below.

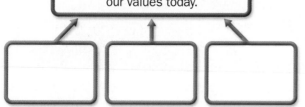

The contributions of the
ancient Greeks have influenced
our values today.

Vocabulary

For each word below, write a sentence with the
correct definition.

1 agora (p. 249)

2 plunder
(p. 251)

3 aristocracy
(p. 255)

4 democracy
(p. 255)

5 myth (p. 253)

6 plague (p. 263)

7 immortal
(p. 254)

8 mercenary
(p. 264)

9 philosopher
(p. 262)

10 reason (p. 262)

People and Terms

Write a sentence explaining why each of the
following people or terms was important in the
development of ancient Greece. You may use
two or more in a single sentence.

1 Crete (p. 250)

2 Mediterranean
Sea (p. 247)

3 Sparta (p. 255)

4 Homer (p. 253)

5 Pericles
(pp. 255, 257)

6 Alexandria
(p. 269)

7 Plato (p. 248)

8 Golden Age
(p. 262)

9 Socratic method
(p. 262)

10 Delian League
(p. 263)

11 Archimedes
(p. 270)

500 B.C.
Democracy began
developing in Greece.

480 B.C.
Battle of
Salamis

404 B.C.
Sparta defeated Athens in Peloponnesian War.

323 B.C.
Alexander the Great died.

30 B.C.
Hellenistic Age ended.

Facts and Main Ideas

1 What responsibilities did citizens of Athens have?

2 What city did Alexander the Great found in Egypt?

3 **Time Line** Which occurred earlier: the beginning of democracy in Greece, or the death of Alexander the Great?

4 **Main Idea** How did the geography of Greece affect the way Greek society developed?

5 **Main Idea** Describe two differences between the cultures of Athens and Sparta.

6 **Main Idea** Who were some of the great philosophers of Athens during its Golden Age?

7 **Main Idea** What effect did Alexander the Great have on Greek Culture?

8 **Critical Thinking:** *Recognize Point of View* The Greeks believed that a person who took part in government needed to be well-educated. Do you agree or disagree? Explain your answer.

Write About History

1 **Write a letter** introducing yourself to one of the people you have read about in this chapter. Tell the person why you think he or she is interesting and ask the person to answer two questions about himself or herself.

2 **Write a plan** of things you would like to see or do during a one-week trip to ancient Greece.

3 **Write a journal entry** about a visit to the court of King Philip II of Macedonia the day he was murdered. Describe the mood of the Macedonians and their opinions about Philip's son, Alexander.

Apply Skills

Compare Maps at Different Scales

Use the maps on pages 258–259 to answer the questions below.

1 Think of a map with a map scale between Maps A and B, or between Maps B and C. Why would this new map be more useful than any of the three maps shown?

2 Describe what a Map D might look like, based on the pattern of the map scales you see.

Internet Activity

To get help with vocabulary, people, and terms, select the dictionary, encyclopedia, or almanac from *Social Studies Library* at **www.sfsocialstudies.com**.

CHAPTER 10

Ancient Rome

Lesson 1

509 B.C.
Rome
The Romans drive out the Etruscans and set up their own republic.

1

Lesson 2

264–146 B.C.
Carthage
Rome defeats Carthage in three wars.

2

Lesson 3

27 B.C.
Rome
Augustus becomes Rome's first emperor.

3

Lesson 4

A.D. 313
Nazareth
Christianity is made equal to other Roman religions.

4

Lesson 5

A.D. 330
Constantinople
Constantinople becomes the capital city of the Eastern Roman Empire.

5

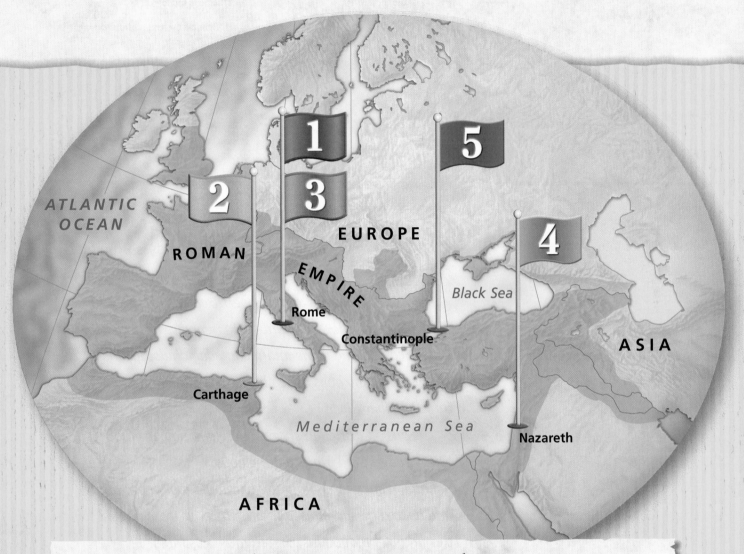

Why We Remember

Three thousand years ago, Rome was a tiny village on the shores of a river on the Italian Peninsula. The Romans were farmers, surrounded by more powerful neighbors. From this modest beginning, the Romans went on to conquer a vast empire.

Today the Roman Empire no longer exists. However, Rome made great contributions to law, language, architecture, and culture. It has influenced nations throughout the world. In addition, many aspects of Roman culture are still part of our lives, from expressions such as *vice versa* and *status quo,* which are still used, to our names for the planets, which come from Roman mythology.

Rome

Tiber River
Rome

1500 B.C.	1000 B.C.	500 B.C.

1600 B.C.
Ancestors of Romans
settle in Italy.

753 B.C.
According to legend,
Rome is founded.

c. 509 B.C.
Romans overthrow Etruscan kings.

Rome's Beginnings

PREVIEW

Focus on the Main Idea
Rome's location helped it grow
from a village into a powerful city.

PLACES
Tiber River
Italian Peninsula
Mediterranean Sea
Rome

PEOPLE
Tarquin
Junius Brutus

You Are There

You wonder if Roman legends are as amazing as Greek legends, so you find a story about the founding of Rome.

According to legend, a man overthrew his brother, the king. He then ordered that his twin nephews be drowned. He feared that the twins might someday challenge his power. The baby boys were placed in a basket and thrown into the Tiber River.

The basket drifted to shore. There a female wolf found it. She cared for and protected the boys.

Later, a shepherd found the twins. He took them home, and he and his wife raised them. The boys were named Romulus (ROHM yoo lus) and Remus (REE mus).

As teenagers, Romulus and Remus discovered who they really were. They killed the evil king and founded the city of Rome in 753 B.C.

Romulus laid out the boundaries of Rome and predicted:

"It is heaven's will that my Rome shall be the capital of the world."

You wonder whether his prediction proved to be true.

Main Idea and Details As you read, think about how Roman civilization began and developed.

A Perfect Location

Historians do not know whether Romulus and Remus ever lived. However, they do know that about 1600 B.C. people came to live along the banks of the **Tiber** (TY ber) **River** on the **Italian Peninsula.**

Look at the map on this page. The Tiber River runs across the center of the peninsula, where there are many plains. Italy is mountainous, much like Greece. The Italian Peninsula has one of the longest coastlines in Europe. It stretches 650 miles southward into the **Mediterranean Sea.** You will notice that Italy looks a lot like a high-heeled boot. The toe of the "boot" looks as if it is about to kick the island of Sicily!

Italy forms a kind of bridge between western Europe, North Africa, and western Asia.

Near the middle of the western coast is the city of **Rome.** It spreads across seven low hills about 15 miles up the Tiber River. The hills offered good protection against attacks. They also offered some safety when the Tiber flooded.

REVIEW What were the advantages of Rome's location? **Main Idea and Details**

▶ Rome was built along the banks of the Tiber River.

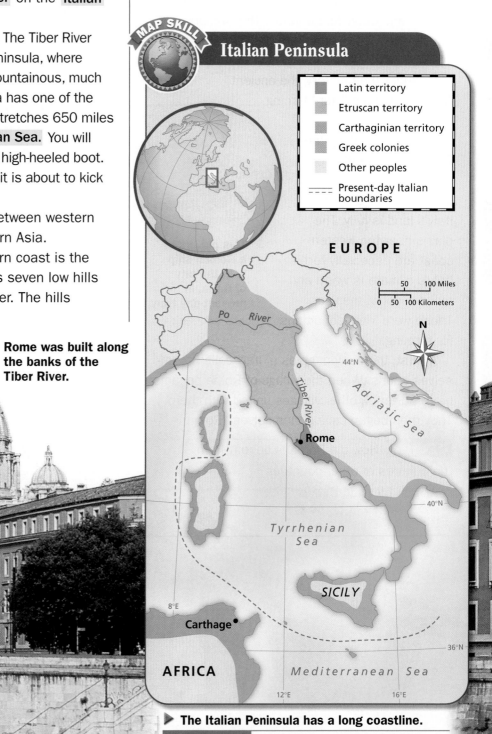

MAP SKILL

Italian Peninsula

- ☐ Latin territory
- ☐ Etruscan territory
- ☐ Carthaginian territory
- ☐ Greek colonies
- ☐ Other peoples
- --- Present-day Italian boundaries

EUROPE

Po River

0   50   100 Miles
0   50   100 Kilometers

N

44°N

Tiber River

Adriatic Sea

● Rome

40°N

Tyrrhenian Sea

SICILY

8°E

Carthage ●

36°N

AFRICA

Mediterranean Sea

12°E   16°E

▶ The Italian Peninsula has a long coastline.

MAP SKILL Place *What is the physical setting of the Italian Peninsula?*

277

The Romans Learn from Other Cultures

In ancient times, ships from all parts of the Mediterranean could sail up the Tiber to Rome. Here, the ships could unload their cargo. Then they could load crops that were growing by the river.

In Rome's harbor, citizens met sailors from Greece and other far-off lands. The Romans studied new ideas about growing crops and learned the stories and legends of other peoples. Throughout their history, the ancient Romans had a gift for learning from other cultures.

The climate along the Tiber was ideal for crops such as grapes and olives. Three-quarters of Italy's land is hilly. The plains near the western coast are especially fertile. Italy's climate is warm and moist most of the year. These were ideal conditions for farming.

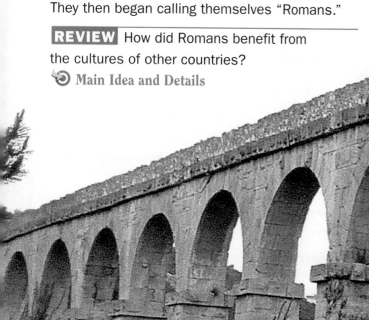

▶ **This picture of a Roman ship is in the city of Ostia, in present-day Italy.**

At first, the early peoples of Italy called themselves Latins. When the village of Rome became more powerful, other villages united with them. They then began calling themselves "Romans."

REVIEW How did Romans benefit from the cultures of other countries?
Main Idea and Details

Etruscan Rule

As Rome grew in size, more Latins and other peoples joined them. Rome prospered. As a result, it attracted the interest of more powerful northern neighbors. These were the Etruscans (eh TRUHS kuhnz). The Etruscans took over Rome about 600 B.C. They soon gained control of nearly all of the Italian Peninsula.

The Etruscans were skilled builders and farmers. They may have taught these skills to the Romans. The Romans learned how to build aqueducts, or structures that carry flowing water to supply water to cities. They also learned how to make better weapons and ships.

However, the Romans resented the Etruscan kings. In 509 B.C., an Etruscan noble named **Tarquin** murdered the king and seized power. The Romans used this as an opportunity to challenge Etruscan rule.

A Roman leader named **Junius Brutus** made a promise to himself: to take the throne from Tarquin. Brutus and his supporters then forced Tarquin and his sons out of Rome. Brutus emerged from this victory as the new leader of Rome.

Rome was about to enter a glorious period. During this time, the Romans would set up a form of government that people continue to study today. Rome's many victories would make Romulus's prediction of Rome's place in the world come true.

REVIEW How did the Romans benefit from the Etruscans? ↻ **Main Idea and Details**

Summarize the Lesson

- **1600 B.C.** Ancestors of the Romans settled in Italy along the Tiber River.
- **753 B.C.** According to legend, Romulus and Remus founded Rome.
- **509 B.C.** The Romans overthrew the Etruscan kings.

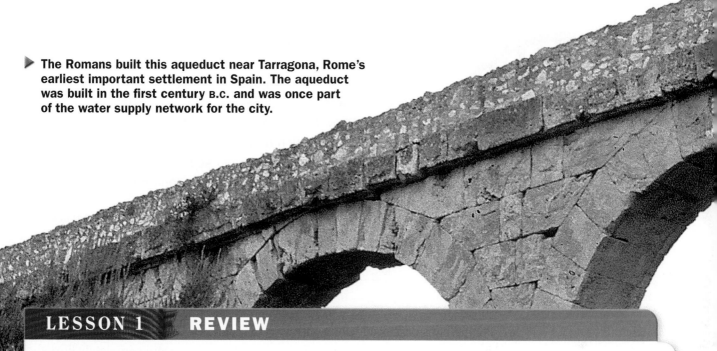

▶ The Romans built this aqueduct near Tarragona, Rome's earliest important settlement in Spain. The aqueduct was built in the first century B.C. and was once part of the water supply network for the city.

LESSON 1 REVIEW

Check Facts and Main Ideas

1. ↻ **Main Idea and Details** On a separate piece of paper, write an appropriate main idea for the three supporting details below.

| Romans learned about farming from other peoples. | Romans studied the legends of other cultures. | Romans learned about building from other peoples. |

2. According to legend, who were Romulus and Remus?

3. Along what river was Rome built?

4. How did a good location help Rome grow from a small village to a powerful city?

5. **Critical Thinking:** *Make Inferences* What does the legend of Rome's founding tell you about how the Romans felt about their place in the world?

| Link to ⦾⦾ | Writing |

Write Newspaper Headlines Look at local or national newspapers and note the style used to write the headlines of articles. Then write three headlines based on the information in this lesson.

Research and Writing Skills

Use Primary and Secondary Sources

What? Primary sources are "snapshots" of history. They are created by people who were there. Primary sources can be in the form of a photograph, painting, letter, recording, or document. For example, the reports Julius Caesar wrote of his battles are primary sources. A textbook that describes Caesar's battles would be a secondary source.

A translation of a primary source is also considered a primary source. The first source shown below is a translation of a letter written by Pliny the Younger to the historian Tacitus. In it, he describes the eruption of Mount Vesuvius in A.D. 79. The letter is a primary source. The second source is an encyclopedia entry about the same event. It is a secondary source.

> *A dense black cloud was coming up behind us, spreading over the earth like a flood . . . . you could hear the shrieks of women, the wailing of infants, and the shouting of men.*

wailing: loud crying

▶ **This profile portrait from Pompeii is made of silver.**

Pompeii was destroyed, along with Herculaneum, by the violent eruption of Mt. Vesuvius on August 24, A.D. 79. Because these cities were completely buried, they were preserved. This makes them a unique document of Greco-Roman life.

▶ **These preserved glass vessels provide a glimpse into the lives of the people of Pompeii.**

Bridgeman Art Library Int'l. Ltd. (U.S.)

▶ This painting is a secondary source. Because it was painted long after the destruction of Pompeii, it is not a primary source. However, it still gives us important information on how the eruption might have looked.

▶ These well-preserved eggs were discovered in the ancient city of Pompeii.

Why? Both primary and secondary sources are valuable. Using both can add to your understanding of a topic. For example, a primary source may give important details or express emotions caused by a situation. A secondary source might include what was happening in several places at once, the outcome, or what we later learned about the causes. By using both kinds of sources, you get a more complete picture. You can also check for errors or bias by using more than one source.

How? To use a primary source or a translation of a primary source, consider the subject matter and point of view. You know that Pliny the Younger wrote this letter, but do you know who he was? Look up his name in an encyclopedia. If you have a subject to study, how do you get ideas for primary sources? Secondary sources will identify people involved, and you can search to find what they wrote. Also, secondary sources often list the primary sources they used.

As with all research, you must also consider the "speaker" in both primary and secondary sources. In looking at letters, you may also want to consider the person to whom the letter was written. If you are not familiar with Tacitus, look up his name in an encyclopedia or Roman history book.

Determine the main idea of the excerpt of the letter. This will help you with the subject matter. Then consider how the encyclopedia entry adds to what you learn from the letter. If any of the words in Pliny's letter are unfamiliar, look them up so that you will understand what he is saying.

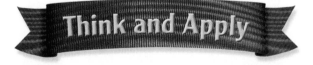

Think and Apply

1 How do we know that Pliny the Younger is describing a terrible event?

2 What is the mood of the letter?

3 How do the two sources create a more complete picture of the event?

500 B.C.   250 B.C.   A.D. 1

about 500 B.C.
Rome sets up a republic.

264–146 B.C.
Rome defeats Carthage in three wars.

44 B.C.
Julius Caesar is killed.

The Roman Republic

PREVIEW

Focus on the Main Idea
Rome's republic became very powerful, but its conquests created major problems.

PLACES
Carthage
Rome

PEOPLE
Regulus
Hannibal
Scipio
Julius Caesar

VOCABULARY
patrician
plebeian
republic
representative
Senate
consul
dictator
tribune
patriotism
caesar

TERMS
Appian Way

EVENTS
The Punic
Wars

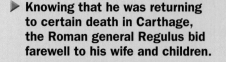

▶ **Knowing that he was returning to certain death in Carthage, the Roman general Regulus bid farewell to his wife and children.**

You Are There
You and your friends gather around the storyteller. It's a story you've heard many times before, but you never get tired of hearing it. It is the story of the brave death of Roman general Regulus.

Regulus fought in the war against Carthage. He was captured in the early stages of the war. The leaders of Carthage sent Regulus back to Rome to convince the Roman leaders to make peace. He was then to return to Carthage.

You and your friends grow quiet when the storyteller comes to the next part of the story. According to the story, Regulus entered the Roman Senate with his head bowed. He told the Senate that he had disgraced Rome by being captured in battle. He then urged the Romans to continue the war against Carthage until they were victorious. He knew that, once he returned to Carthage, he would face certain death.

You know people who don't believe the story of Regulus. You pay no attention to them. To you, Regulus is one of the greatest of Roman heroes.

Main Idea and Details As you read, think about what life was like in the Roman Republic.

The Roman Spirit

Regulus was a real person. He led Roman forces, and he was captured in battle. However, historians are not sure if the story of his release to Rome and return to Carthage really happened. Still, the Romans believed it happened, and that was important. They expected their leaders to be willing to sacrifice their lives to defend Rome.

The Romans were proud of their excellent soldiers. Like Regulus, these soldiers were brave, tough, and loyal to their homeland. The Romans farmed their land in peacetime and defended their country against enemies in war.

Roman citizens were divided into two groups. The wealthiest, most powerful citizens were known as patricians (puh TRISH uhnz). All other citizens were called plebeians (pluh BEE uhnz). About 90 percent of Roman citizens were plebeians. They included farmers, soldiers, and merchants.

All citizens, wealthy or not, were inspired by stories of Roman courage, honor, and loyalty. All citizens were encouraged to think and behave like the heroes these tales praised. These stories defined the Roman spirit.

REVIEW According to these paragraphs, what is "the Roman spirit"? **Draw Conclusions**

How the Romans Governed Themselves

After the Romans drove out the Etruscan king, they established a republic. In a republic, citizens have the right to vote, or choose their leaders. Those who are elected to represent the people are called representatives. Roman representatives served in a governing body called the Senate.

Not everyone who lived in Rome was a citizen. Slaves and most foreigners were not citizens. While Roman women were citizens, they had few rights. They could not vote or hold public office. However, Roman women did have more freedom than Greek women. Roman women had the right to own property and testify in court. Many women played major roles in governing Rome.

At first, only patricians ran the Roman republic. For example, the Senate was made up entirely of patricians. Each year, two patricians were chosen as consuls (KON sulz), or officials who managed the government and the army. Each of the consuls had the power to stop the other consul from taking an action if he did not agree with that action. However, in an emergency, the consuls sometimes named one person to rule. This person was known as a dictator, or someone who has total control over the people.

Rome was growing larger, and getting more crowded. Roman citizens did not have police or fire protection. The plebeians often spoke out against the power of the patricians. Some worried patricians created their own private armies.

REVIEW How was the government in Rome different from the government in Athens? **Compare and Contrast**

▶ The Roman Senate would select two consuls to manage the government and army. This sculpture depicts a procession of Roman consuls and senators.

283

The Tribunes

As time went on, the plebeians began to demand greater rights. They were facing difficult times. As Rome became more powerful, many patricians became very rich. These patricians bought much of the land around Rome. This forced plebeians to rent land from the wealthy landowners. Many plebeians struggled to survive. They threatened to stop serving in the army until the government treated them more fairly.

▶ **Because long togas made movement difficult, plebeians began to wear short togas and tunics.**

To meet their demands, the Senate appointed men to protect the rights of the plebeians. These men were called **tribunes.** Any one of the tribunes could stop an action of the Senate by shouting "Veto!"—a Latin word that means "I forbid." There were only two tribunes at first. Eventually, the number grew to ten tribunes. The tribunes could also make demands on behalf of the plebeians. In time, the tribunes of the plebeians became very powerful.

The wealthy patricians still had far more power than the plebeians. However, some plebeians were able to become wealthy. Being represented by increasingly powerful tribunes made it easier for wealthy plebeians to associate with the patricians.

REVIEW What effect did the tribunes have on the rights of the plebeians?
Cause and Effect

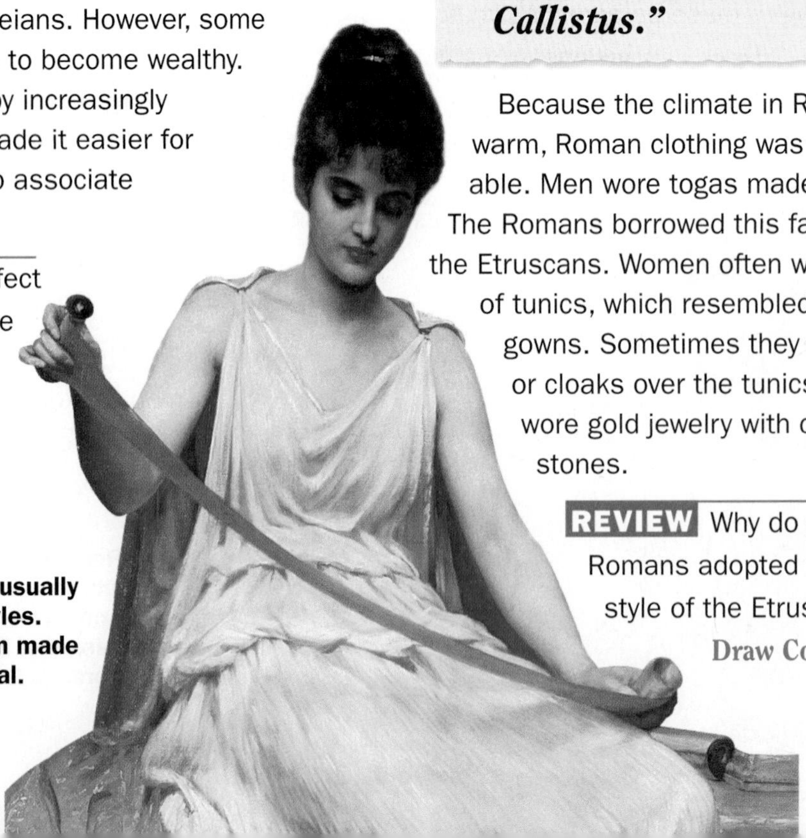

▶ **Women's clothing usually imitated Greek styles. Dresses were often made of very fine material.**

▶ *Fido,* a common name for dogs, is a Latin word meaning *faithful.* However, even faithful dogs got lost, so dog tags were needed in ancient Rome.

Daily Life

What was it like living in ancient Rome? Boys and some girls from wealthy families went to school. Some were taught at home by Greek slaves who served as tutors. Children used abacuses to learn mathematics. They wrote down lessons and learned to read and write on wax tablets or sheets of papyrus. After school, many went home and played. Children played with toys such as marbles, dolls, model chariots, and animals.

The main meal was eaten in the late afternoon. Wealthy people consumed fish, birds, olive oil with herbs, dates, and pork. Poor citizens ate wheat and barley, bread, olives, and meat scraps.

Wealthy citizens had dogs as pets to guard their homes. They also used dogs to hunt small animals and birds. Just like our pets today, some dogs had dog tags. The tags were made of bronze and identified the name of the owner. The dog tag pictured above reads:

> *"Hold me if I run away, and return me to my master Viventius on the estate of Callistus."*

Because the climate in Rome was generally warm, Roman clothing was light and comfortable. Men wore togas made of woolen cloth. The Romans borrowed this fashion idea from the Etruscans. Women often wore two layers of tunics, which resembled long shirts or gowns. Sometimes they would drape robes or cloaks over the tunics. They also often wore gold jewelry with colorful precious stones.

REVIEW Why do you think the Romans adopted the clothing style of the Etruscans?
Draw Conclusions

Wars with Carthage

Carthage (KAR thij) was a city-state located in North Africa. By about 300 B.C., Carthage had become a great power. The city had a large, powerful navy. Its army was one of the strongest in the ancient world.

It was only a matter of time before Carthage and Rome fought against one another. Beginning in 264 B.C., these two powerful city-states fought three destructive wars. These wars were known as the **Punic** (PYOO nik) **Wars.** Altogether, the Punic Wars lasted nearly 120 years. The Romans won all three.

▶ In the second Punic War, the Carthaginian general Hannibal crossed the Alps with his troops and a herd of war elephants.

The second war included one of the most daring adventures in history. A Carthaginian general named **Hannibal** (HAN uh bul) launched an invasion from Spain. Hannibal took his army across the rugged and snowy Alps with a herd of elephants. Hannibal surprised the Romans. A historian, Polybius, wrote of Hannibal:

> *"His best resource . . . [was] the elephants, for the enemy was terrified by their strange appearance."*

Rome was saved when a general named **Scipio** (SKIP ee oh) attacked Carthage. Hannibal had to rush back home. It was too late. Carthage was defeated.

About 50 years later, a third war began between the two cities. This time, the Romans captured and destroyed Carthage.

REVIEW Why is Hannibal remembered as a great general? **Summarize**

Problems at Home

The Romans worked hard to make friends of former enemies. Some of the defeated peoples were granted Roman citizenship. Others were allowed to keep local self-government.

The Romans made improvements in the lands they conquered. They built aqueducts, roads, and buildings. These were meant to make the conquered people feel patriotic toward Rome. **Patriotism** is a sense of pride in one's country.

However, Rome soon faced serious problems that would lead to the end of the republic.

Vast wealth poured into Rome. This made the patricians even wealthier. However, the average Roman gained very little. Slaves taken in wartime took many of the jobs the plebeians had held. The fighting in Italy had destroyed the farmlands and homes of thousands of people. The Romans were becoming poorer even as their armies were taking over new lands.

Rival leaders led armies against each other. Many people died, and poverty grew.

REVIEW Why would the Romans want to make friends of former enemies? **Draw Conclusions**

The Republic Ends

One way to gain great wealth and power in Rome was to lead an army in conquests. One of the most famous generals and caesars, or rulers, was Julius Caesar (JOOL yus SEEZ ur). He was a person of great energy and talent. Between 58 and 51 B.C., he conquered most of present-day France, the British Isles, and Belgium. He also took over parts of present-day Germany and Spain. After one victory, Caesar announced his triumph in three famous Latin words:

> *"Veni, vidi, vici."*
> *("I came, I saw, I conquered.")*

As Julius Caesar won more victories, a power struggle broke out between him and two other Roman generals. Caesar won the struggle and was made ruler for life.

Caesar tried to control the number of slaves in Rome and worked to increase jobs. However, his growing power worried many patricians. They were afraid that Caesar would destroy the republic by taking total power in Rome. In 44 B.C., Caesar was stabbed to death on the floor of the Senate.

With Caesar's death, the struggle for power began. Once again, civil war broke out in Rome, as several leaders fought for power. The Roman Republic, founded nearly 500 years earlier, was at its end.

▶ This Roman coin features a portrait of Julius Caesar.

REVIEW Why did the patricians worry about Caesar's growing power? ⟲ **Main Idea and Details**

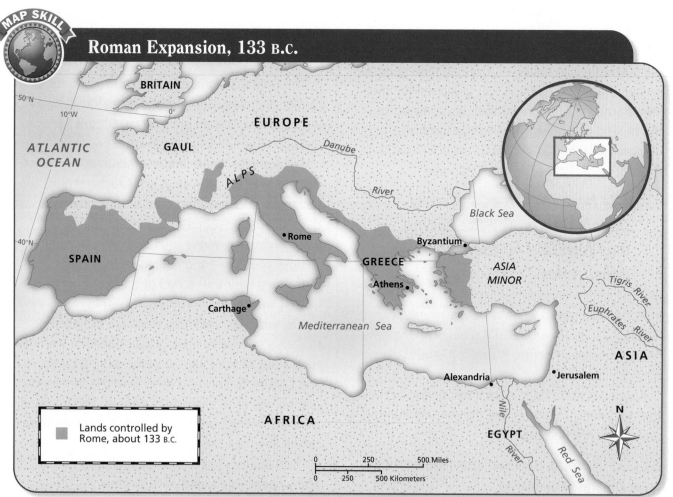

MAP SKILL

Roman Expansion, 133 B.C.

Lands controlled by Rome, about 133 B.C.

▶ By 133 B.C., Rome was already controlling land on three continents.

MAP SKILL Measure Distance *Measuring from the farthest points east to west, how many total miles did the Roman Republic stretch in 133 B.C.?*

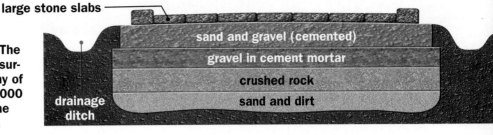

large stone slabs

sand and gravel (cemented)

gravel in cement mortar

crushed rock

sand and dirt

drainage ditch

▶ Roman roads were built to last. The foundations were deep, and the surface was thick, solid stone. Many of these roads lasted more than 1,000 years. A few, including part of the Appian Way, are still used today.

Roads in the Republic

During the period of the republic, the Romans began using concrete to build roads. Concrete is a building material made from a mixture of crushed stone, sand, cement, and water. Once it dries, concrete is very strong. The Roman roads were built over all kinds of surfaces: lakes, deep ravines, and mountains. They were even designed to drain water off the road's surface.

The most famous of these roads is the Appian Way. It stretched for more than 350 miles south and then east of Rome.

Even today, parts of ancient Rome's road system can be seen in many places.

REVIEW Why do you think the Romans used concrete to built their roads? **Draw Conclusions**

Summarize the Lesson

- **c. 500 B.C.** The Romans set up a republic.
- **264–146 B.C.** After three bloody wars, the Romans defeated Carthage.
- **44 B.C.** Julius Caesar was stabbed to death on the floor of the Senate.

LESSON 2   REVIEW

Check Facts and Main Ideas

1. ↻ **Main Idea and Details** On a separate piece of paper, write the appropriate details that support the main idea.

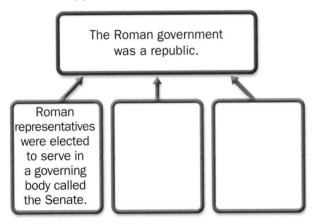

The Roman government was a republic.

Roman representatives were elected to serve in a governing body called the Senate.

2. What is a republic?

3. Who was Hannibal and what was his greatest accomplishment?

4. How did Rome's conquests create major problems for the republic?

5. **Critical Thinking:** *Recognize Point of View* Do you believe the patricians shared enough power with the plebeians? Explain your answer.

Link to ⦻ Reading

Use a Newspaper The verb form of the word *veto* means "to forbid," or "to refuse to agree." In the United States, the President can veto a bill by refusing to sign it into law. Look in a current local or national newspaper. Find a bill that is being debated. Would you want the President to sign this bill into law? Explain.

LESSON 3

100 B.C.   A.D. 1   A.D. 100

27 B.C.
Augustus becomes
first Roman emperor.

A.D. 96
Rule of "Five Good Emperors" begins.

A.D. 120
Roman Empire spreads eastward and westward.

Rome
Colosseum

The Roman Empire

PREVIEW

Focus on the Main Idea
The Roman Empire was one of the world's most powerful empires.

PLACES
Colosseum

PEOPLE
Augustus
Caligula
Claudius
Nero
Marcus Aurelius
Seneca

VOCABULARY
emperor
gladiator

TERMS
Pax Romana

▶ **Many statues show Octavian in armor. The statue to the right emphasizes his Roman citizenship by showing him in the toga of an upper-class Roman man.**

You Are There

Rome is recovering from years of conflict and civil war after the murder of Julius Caesar.

Octavian (ahk TAY vee uhn), the young general and ruler of Rome, marches into the Senate. He tells you and the other members of the Senate that he is restoring the republic. Just as Octavian expects, all of you protest.

The senators know that this is all an act. Octavian has an armed force waiting outside. If Octavian does not get his way, your lives are in danger.

The senators grant him a new title: Augustus (aw GUS tus), or one who is beloved above all other people. Although Augustus has not taken the title of "emperor," he has all the powers of one. Rome is no longer a republic. It is an empire.

Draw Conclusions As you read, think about what impact the Roman Empire had on other cultures.

The Pax Romana

We have witnessed a historic moment in Rome's history. For the next 500 years, **emphasis** **emperors,** or rulers of an empire, would govern Rome. During the first part of this period, Rome was by far the world's most powerful empire.

Augustus ruled from 27 B.C. to his death in A.D. 14. Augustus used his power as emperor to bring order and stability to Rome. He centralized the government and improved the economy. Augustus was responsible for starting Rome's fire brigade and, later, a police force. He continued to increase his own power and added new territories to the Empire.

His rule also saw the beginning of a long period of peace. Trade and business grew. Life improved for most people. Life even improved for many of the peoples that Rome conquered. His efforts made conquered people more loyal to Rome.

The Empire would keep this prosperity and peace for nearly 200 years. Romans called this period "the Roman Peace," or *Pax Romana* in Latin. During this time, people were proud to say:

> ### *"Civis Romanus sum!"*
> ### *("I am a citizen of Rome!")*

The Roman army became the world's most powerful fighting force. Roman soldiers were expertly trained. They could fight, but they could also survive long marches and live off the land. In addition to their weapons, the Roman soliders carried tools. They used these tools to build forts, bridges, and roads and to dig canals. As you can see on the map on page 290, Rome controlled a vast empire on three continents during the *Pax Romana*. By A.D. 120, the Empire began to spread eastward and westward.

REVIEW What did Augustus do to bring order to Rome? ↻ **Main Idea and Details**

The Good Emperors and the Bad

Some of Rome's emperors, such as Augustus, were good rulers. But some were very poor leaders. **Caligula** (kuh LIG yoo luh) became emperor in A.D. 37. Caligula was cruel and mentally unstable. He declared himself a god and tried to have his horse made a senator. His rule ended in A.D. 41 when members of his bodyguard assassinated, or murdered, him.

The emperor **Claudius** (KLAW dee us), who followed Caligula, was a better ruler. Claudius returned artwork that had been stolen by Caligula. Claudius worked hard to improve conditions in the Empire. He granted citizenship to more people in the Empire and made improvements to Rome's laws. Unfortunately for Rome, the emperor who followed Claudius was **Nero.** Nero was as bad an emperor as Caligula. He poisoned his stepbrother and murdered both his wife and his mother. After Nero's death, civil war broke out. In a one-year period, Rome had four emperors.

▶ **Nero was Rome's emperor from A.D. 54 to 68.**

Then, in A.D. 96, Rome entered a more stable period. For the next 84 years, emperors known as the "Five Good Emperors" ruled Rome. Under these rulers, Rome enjoyed a long period of peace and prosperity. Perhaps the greatest of these emperors was **Marcus Aurelius** (aw REE lee uhs). Read more about him in the Citizen Hero feature on page 293.

REVIEW How was Rome affected by good and bad emperors? **Draw Conclusions**

Araldo de Luca/Corbis

Araldo de Luca/Corbis

Government and Law

The Roman Empire covered a huge area with many different groups of people. In time, the Roman Empire stretched from Britain and Spain in the west to Iran in the east. People in the empire spoke many different languages. They followed many different religions.

Yet the Romans were able to unite and rule all of these people. Rome offered citizenship to many of them. In addition to their own language, people throughout the Empire also spoke a common language, Latin. They traveled on Roman roads, used Roman measures, obeyed Roman laws, and were defended by Roman armies.

▶ **Some Roman soldiers would have their citizenship papers copied on pieces of bronze.**

Other nations created vast empires. However, none did a better job of developing a code of laws that all people in the Empire could follow. Rome's laws proved a model for many of today's nations.

Much of the legal system in the United States is based on the principles, or basic rules, the Romans developed:

- All free people have equal rights before the law.
- A person must be considered innocent until he or she is proven guilty.
- Accused people should be allowed to face their accusers and defend themselves.
- Judges must interpret the law and make decisions fairly.
- People have rights that no government can take away.

REVIEW What did all citizens of the Roman Empire have in common? 🔄 **Main Idea and Details**

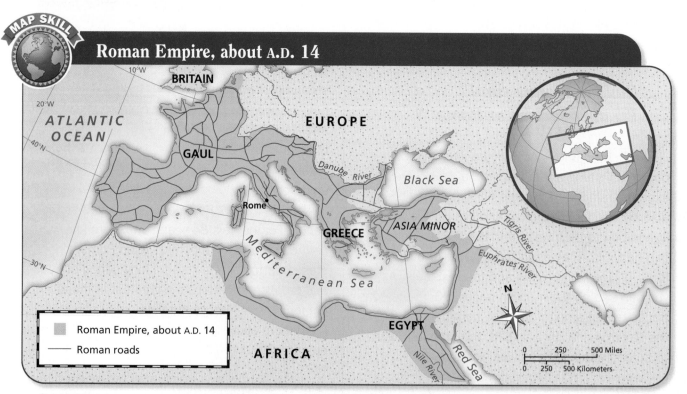

MAP SKILL Roman Empire, about A.D. 14

BRITAIN
10°W
20°W
ATLANTIC OCEAN
40°N
EUROPE
GAUL
Danube River
Black Sea
Rome
ASIA MINOR
Tigris River
GREECE
Euphrates River
30°N
Mediterranean Sea
EGYPT
AFRICA
Nile River
Red Sea

Roman Empire, about A.D. 14
Roman roads

0   250   500 Miles
0   250   500 Kilometers

▶ **The Roman Empire went through a period of growth during the rule of Augustus.**

MAP SKILL Observe Change Through Maps *Compare this map with the map on page 286. How did the borders of Rome change between 133 B.C. and A.D. 14?*

Entertainment

Something was always going on in Rome. The Romans celebrated many holidays. These holidays were marked by plays in the theaters and by religious ceremonies.

Thousands of Romans crowded into sports arenas to see organized battles. The most famous Roman arena is the Colosseum. It could seat 50,000 people. The most popular events involved **gladiators** (GLAD ee AY torz), or professional fighters, most of whom were prisoners or slaves. Sometimes, the gladiators fought animals. Often they fought each other to the death.

▶ Roman gladiators often wore helmets during their fights in the arena.

The gladiators entered the arenas to the cheers of the crowd. They raised their weapons in a salute to the emperor. Then the fighting began. The spectators cheered the victors and booed the defeated. By the end of the day, blood covered the arena.

If a losing gladiator had fought bravely, his life was spared. However, if the spectators disliked the way he had fought, they would stretch out their arms and turn their thumbs toward the gladiator. That signaled a death sentence.

The Roman writer **Seneca** was disgusted by the brutal displays:

> *"The fighters have nothing to protect them. Their bodies are utterly open to every blow. Death is the fighter's only exit."*

REVIEW What did Seneca mean by "Death is the fighter's only exit"? **Draw Conclusions**

Roman engineers used arches and columns to support the weight of the thousands of seats.

The best seats were saved for wealthy or important citizens.

▶ Rome's Colosseum hosted a variety of violent entertainments and could even be flooded for mock sea battles.

The Colosseum was covered in white marble. Statues stood in the outside arches.

Machinery below the arena floor made it possible to lift animal cages or equipment to the surface.

Roman Arts

The Romans took great pride in their skills as builders. Some sports stadiums today resemble the Colosseum.

The Romans also built elevated, or raised, aqueducts. Some of these aqueducts stretched hundreds of miles, bringing fresh water to Roman cities.

Roman rule led to the growth of cities throughout the Empire. As a result, today there are many cities in Europe, Western Asia, and North Africa that were founded during Roman times. Wherever Rome's armies went, Roman style of buildings followed.

Language helped to unite the Roman Empire. When they conquered lands, the Romans brought their Latin language with them. Latin is the basis for many European languages spoken today. These include Italian, French, Spanish, Portuguese, and Romanian.

REVIEW What effect do Roman builders, artists, and writers have on the world today?
Draw Conclusions

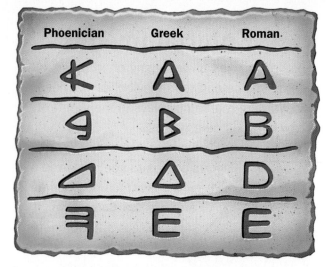

| Phoenician | Greek | Roman |

▶ **The Roman alphabet was influenced by the alphabets of earlier cultures.**

CHART SKILL Use a Table *Which two alphabets share the most similarities?*

Summarize the Lesson

- **27 B.C.** Augustus became emperor.
- **A.D. 96** The rule of the "Five Good Emperors" began.
- **A.D. 120** Rome's rule spread westward and eastward.

LESSON 3 ◢ REVIEW

Check Facts and Main Ideas

1. Draw Conclusions Copy the diagram below on a separate piece of paper. Fill in the missing details that form the conclusion.

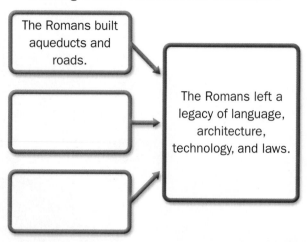

The Romans built aqueducts and roads. → The Romans left a legacy of language, architecture, technology, and laws.

2. Who was Augustus and why is he important?

3. What was the *Pax Romana*?

4. How did wise rule make the Roman Empire very powerful?

5. Critical Thinking: *Evaluate Information* Support the statement that Rome had an advanced civilization.

Link to ⚮ Reading

Use a Dictionary Romance languages include Italian, French, Spanish, Portuguese, and Romanian. Look up the word *romance* in a dictionary. Write a paragraph explaining the origin of the word.

Warrior and Philosopher

In A.D. 161, Marcus Aurelius became the last of Rome's Five Good Emperors. He was an important philosopher and believed that Romans should live simple lives, control their emotions, and be dutiful to the state.

As emperor, Marcus lived simply and was known as a just ruler. He lowered taxes and helped the poor. He even sold his own jewels and property to help ease the effects of famine and plague in the Roman Empire.

He also founded schools, orphanages, and hospitals. He sponsored legal reforms that made criminal laws less harsh and promoted kinder treatment of slaves by their masters. Marcus believed that it was everyone's duty to uphold these laws.

Marcus wrote a series of famous philosophy books called *Meditations.* In the books, he sometimes wrote that he would rather be a simple man than an emperor. However, his most important responsibility was to the people and Roman law. Many people still read his books today.

Marcus thought being emperor was a moral responsibility and not a political responsibility. He thought that living a moral life led to peace and justice. He wrote:

> *"In the morning . . . let this thought be present: I am rising to do the work of a human being."*

In A.D. 180, Marcus died while his army was battling northern invaders. Those who came after him did not rule as well as he had.

Responsibility in Action

Link to Current Events Research the story of a person who has dedicated his or her life to helping other, less fortunate people. What kind of satisfaction does this person get from this work?

A.D. 1   **A.D. 200**   **A.D. 400**

C. A.D. **30**
Jesus is crucified.

A.D. **313**
Christianity is made equal
to other Roman religions.

A.D. **380**
Christianity becomes the official
religion of the Roman Empire.

Nazareth.

The Rise of Christianity

PREVIEW

Focus on the Main Idea
Christianity grew to become
the official religion of the Roman
Empire.

PLACES
Palestine
Nazareth

PEOPLE
Jesus
Peter
Paul
Constantine
Theodosius

VOCABULARY
catacomb
synagogue
disciple
persecute

TERMS
Christianity
New Testament
Gospels
Apostle
Messiah

You Are There
You've heard about a small group of
people who walk silently at dusk to the
hills outside of Rome. One by one, they
climb down dark, damp stairs. Only flickering candles
mark the way. At the bottom, the group enters the catacombs. Catacombs are vast, underground rooms where
the Romans bury their dead.

The people who enter are not frightened. In fact, they
look as though they feel safe. You and other Romans call
these people Christians. They are part of a
new religion taking hold in Rome. Here
in the catacombs, the Christians hold
their religious services.

You wonder who these Christians
are. Why do they practice their religion in secret? What kind of a
future does this new religion have
in the empire?

▶ **In Rome, early Christians often had to
practice their religion in secret. They
used the city's catacombs for this purpose.**

Main Idea and Details As you read,
identify what the basic ideas and teachings
of Christianity are.

Target Skill

294

A New Religion

The people who went into the **catacombs,** or underground burial rooms, were part of a new religion that was spreading throughout the Empire. That religion was **Christianity.** It was started by **Jesus,** a Jewish man born in Judah, or Judea, the southern part of the Roman province of **Palestine.** Palestine included parts of the present-day countries of Israel and Jordan. Jesus grew up in the town of **Nazareth.** You can find Nazareth on the map of Judah on page 57.

Most of what we know about Jesus' life comes from four books in the part of the Bible known as the **New Testament.** These four books are called the **Gospels.** However, Roman historians also wrote about Jesus.

We know very little about Jesus' life before he began traveling and teaching in the towns and villages of Palestine at about the age of 30. Wherever he went, people gathered to listen to him. Sometimes, he spoke to small groups in homes or in what would later become Jewish **synagogues** (SIN uh gogz), Jewish places of worship. Other times, he spoke outdoors to thousands of people.

Jesus gathered a small group of followers, who were known as **disciples** (dih SY puhlz). Jesus chose 12 of these disciples to help him preach. These 12 are known as the **Apostles** (uh PAH sulz).

REVIEW How do we know about Jesus?
⟳ **Main Idea and Details**

What Jesus Taught

Much of what Jesus taught grew out of his Jewish upbringing. He taught that there was only one God. However, the Romans and Greeks believed in many gods. Jesus encouraged people to obey the Ten Commandments, an important part of Jewish law.

Jesus preached that God loved everyone and wanted people to be kind to one another. If people had faith in God and followed his will, Jesus said, they would find peace and joy, and would enter heaven when they die.

Jesus preached about forgiveness and mercy. In the Sermon on the Mount, Jesus said:

> *"Blessed are the meek, for they shall inherit the Earth. . . . Blessed are the merciful, for they shall obtain mercy. . . . Blessed are the peacemakers, for they will be called children of God."*

REVIEW How did Jesus' teaching differ from what the Romans believed? **Compare and Contrast**

▶ *The Last Supper,* by Leonardo da Vinci, was painted on a wall of Santa Maria delle Grazie, a church in Milan, Italy. It is a representation of the last meal Jesus had with his disciples before his death.

Jesus' Message Spreads

Jesus' message and teachings spread through Palestine. Some local leaders feared that Jesus' success would upset their Roman rulers. They arrested Jesus. Though the Romans found him innocent, they wanted to please local leaders. So they sentenced Jesus to be crucified (CROO sih feyed), or put to death on a cross.

According to the Gospels, Jesus rose from the dead. This strengthened the belief among his followers that Jesus was the **Messiah** (muh SIGH uh), or savior, someone who saves or rescues.

After the death of Jesus, some of his disciples traveled widely to spread his teachings. Through the Apostles **Peter**, **Paul**, and others, Jesus' teachings spread throughout the Mediterranean region.

Christianity spread quickly. By A.D. 100, it had gained many followers in parts of the Roman Empire.

REVIEW What effect did the travels of Peter and Paul have? **Cause and Effect**

Toward Acceptance

At first, many Christians were **persecuted**, or punished for their beliefs. Christians refused to worship the emperor as a god. Many Christians were killed for their faith. Some were forced to fight wild animals in the Colosseum.

Despite this persecution—or perhaps because of it—the religion continued to spread. In A.D. 313, the emperor **Constantine** (KAHN stuhn teen) made Christianity equal to all other religions. He also outlawed the persecution of Christians. Before he died in 337, Constantine was baptized a Christian.

In A.D. 380, the emperor **Theodosius** (thee oh DOH see us) made Christianity Rome's official religion.

REVIEW What was the importance of making Christianity equal to other religions? **Draw Conclusions**

▶ **This colossal head of Constantine is more than 8 feet tall.**

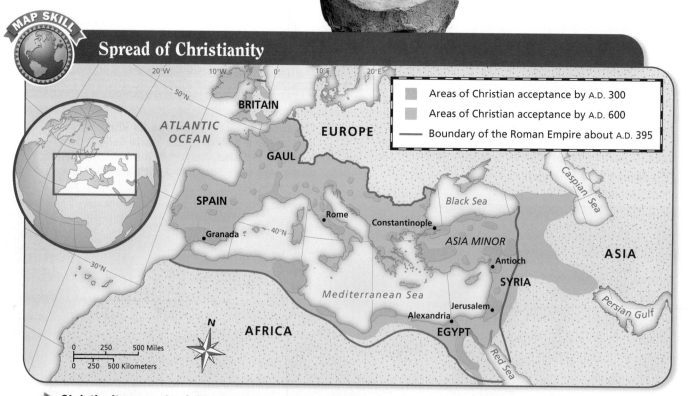

MAP SKILL

Spread of Christianity

Areas of Christian acceptance by A.D. 300
Areas of Christian acceptance by A.D. 600
Boundary of the Roman Empire about A.D. 395

20°W 10°W 0° 10°E 20°E

50°N

BRITAIN

ATLANTIC OCEAN

EUROPE

GAUL

SPAIN

Rome

Granada   40°N

Constantinople

Black Sea

ASIA MINOR

Caspian Sea

ASIA

30°N

Antioch

SYRIA

Persian Gulf

Mediterranean Sea

Jerusalem

Alexandria

N

AFRICA

EGYPT

Red Sea

0   250   500 Miles
0   250   500 Kilometers

▶ **Christianity spread quickly through the Roman Empire.**

MAP SKILL Use a Distribution Map *Which areas accepted Christianity earlier?*

▶ Roman Catholics worship at mass. When Christians celebrate the birth of Jesus, they hold a special Christmas service.

that Jesus was sent to help people reach salvation, or eternal peace in God's presence, when they die. Christians believe that after Jesus was crucified, God's presence remained on Earth in the form of the Holy Spirit. These three elements make up the holy trinity for Christian believers: Father, Son, and Holy Spirit.

Christianity Today

Christianity is practiced throughout the world. The majority of Christians live in Europe and the Americas. Today there are about 1.5 billion Christians.

In Christianity, there are a number of Christian groups. Each group has some different beliefs, customs, and practices. However, all Christians consider Jesus central to their religious beliefs.

Christianity teaches that God sent his son, Jesus, into the world in human form. It teaches

REVIEW In what ways are some groups of Christians different from others? Summarize

Summarize the Lesson

- **about A.D. 30** According to the Gospels, Jesus was crucified.

- **A.D. 313** The emperor Constantine made Christianity equal to other Roman religions.

- **A.D. 380** Christianity became the official religion of the Roman Empire.

LESSON 4   REVIEW

Check Facts and Main Ideas

1. **Main Idea and Details** On a separate piece of paper, write the missing detail that supports the main idea in the top box.

> Christianity started in Palestine and spread throughout the Roman Empire.

> Jesus was from a Jewish family in the Roman province of Palestine.

> Theodosius made Christianity Rome's official religion.

2. Who were Peter and Paul and what was their major accomplishment?

3. Why did the Roman emperors persecute Christians?

4. How do you think the unity of the Roman Empire helped Christianity to become the empire's main religion?

5. **Critical Thinking: *Make Inferences*** Review Chapter 2. How did many Christian teachings grow out of Jewish traditions?

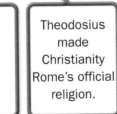

Link to   Writing

Write a Paragraph Write a paragraph explaining why the Romans persecuted the Christians.

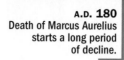

Constantinople

A.D. 1   A.D. 250   A.D. 500

A.D. 180
Death of Marcus Aurelius starts a long period of decline.

A.D. 330
Constantinople officially opens.

A.D. 476
Last Roman emperor is overthrown.

Rise and Fall

PREVIEW

Focus on the Main Idea
Rome fell to invaders, but the Roman Empire continued in the East.

PLACES
Byzantium
Constantinople

PEOPLE
Commodus
Diocletian
Romulus Augustulus

VOCABULARY
auction
pope
pillage
vandal

TERMS
Byzantine Empire
Byzantine Orthodox Church
Roman Catholic Church

▶ The chest plate of a Roman soldier's armor was sometimes decorated with medallions. These often showed images of gods and goddesses.

You Are There
It is bitterly cold tonight. You sit near the banks of the Rhine (ryne) River. It is the border between the Roman Empire and the tribes who live to the north. During the night, about 15,000 of these northern warriors cross the ice-covered river. They bring with them their families, farm animals, and a few possessions.

You wonder why they are here. Why have they left their homeland? Where are they heading?

The warriors tell you that their own land has been invaded. They're heading south. They believe that the Empire will give them access to better farmland and to Roman culture. They also believe that the Empire will offer them protection.

But you have to wonder: how well protected is the Empire?

Cause and Effect As you read, identify the causes and effects of the invasions from the north on the Roman Empire.

The Empire Declines

The emperor Marcus Aurelius died in A.D. 180. After his death, the Roman Empire entered a long period of decline. Most of the emperors who followed Marcus Aurelius cared more about increasing their wealth and power than about the welfare of the Roman Empire.

The trouble started with the emperor who followed Marcus Aurelius. Instead of choosing a capable person, he named his own son, **Commodus,** to lead the empire. Commodus was a violent youth. He even performed as a gladiator in specially staged events. He also loved spending money on himself. Unfortunately, he hated governing and did as little of that as he could.

After 13 years of bad rule, Commodus was murdered by his own bodyguard.

REVIEW Why do you think Marcus Aurelius chose Commodus to succeed him? **Draw Conclusions**

Emperors for Sale

The emperor who followed Commodus tried to cut back on expenses. Roman soldiers did not like that. They murdered him after only three months. There were a few other strong emperors after this, but in 235, the army took control. They **auctioned,** or sold off, the seat of emperor to the highest bidder.

The Roman army began to overthrow emperors. Different groups of soldiers would put their favorites in office. Generals fought for power. Rival armies attacked each other in the cities of the Empire. In the 50 years between the years 235 and 284, there were 23 different emperors. Most were murdered or killed in battle.

As the army battled for power, it grew weaker as a fighting force. Many Romans refused to serve in it. The Romans had to hire foreigners to fight for pay. These soldiers were called mercenaries. Most of them were from the German tribes living on the borders of the Empire. The mercenaries had little loyalty to the Roman Empire.

When German tribes came across the border and raided Roman towns, the German mercenaries did not stop them. Merchants and craftspeople were being attacked. Travel on the roads became dangerous. Trade slowed between cities in the Empire.

REVIEW What caused the powerful Roman army to become weaker as a fighting force? **Cause and Effect**

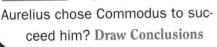

▶ These iron arrowheads and spearhead are from the grave of a German soldier.

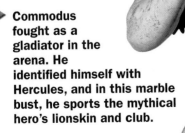

▶ **Commodus fought as a gladiator in the arena. He identified himself with Hercules, and in this marble bust, he sports the mythical hero's lionskin and club.**

The Empire Divides

Rome was facing hard times. In the 100 years after the death of Marcus Aurelius, Roman emperors had become little more than tools of the army. Army units from the east, the north, Africa, and Spain fought one another to put the emperor of their choice on the throne. Finally, a strong ruler came to power.

Emperor **Diocletian** (dy oh CLEE shun) introduced a number of reforms. During his reign from A.D. 284 to 305, Diocletian helped restore order and strengthen the economy.

In order to govern the widespread Empire more effectively, Diocletian divided it into two parts. Diocletian controlled the increasingly wealthy eastern portion. A second "co-emperor" took

▶ **Diocletian created the tetrarchy, the system by which four men ruled the Roman world.**

control of the western half. Six years later, Diocletian added two more co-emperors. Each of them was responsible for a particular part of the Empire. During these years, the people of both Britain and Egypt rebelled against Roman rule. The co-emperors were able to crush these rebellions.

Diocletian decided to retire in A.D. 305. The Empire remained divided for another 19 years.

REVIEW How did Diocletian try to restore order to the empire? ⟳ **Main Idea and Details**

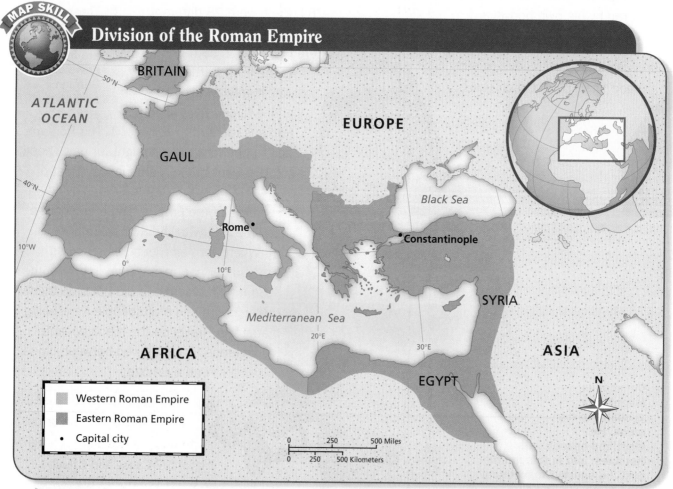

MAP SKILL
Division of the Roman Empire

BRITAIN

ATLANTIC OCEAN

EUROPE

GAUL

Black Sea

Rome •

• Constantinople

SYRIA

Mediterranean Sea

AFRICA

ASIA

EGYPT

N

- Western Roman Empire
- Eastern Roman Empire
- • Capital city

0   250   500 Miles
0   250   500 Kilometers

▶ **The Roman Empire was so large and difficult to govern that it eventually divided.**

MAP SKILL Use Map Scale *Which part of the Roman Empire covers a larger area, the eastern or western part?*

The City of Constantine

In A.D. 324, the emperor Constantine united the Empire again. He built a new capital city in the eastern part of the Empire. The new city was built on the site of an old Greek city named **Byzantium** (bih ZAN tee um). The new city officially opened in A.D. 330.

At first, the city was called New Rome, but it soon became known as **Constantinople,** after Constantine. Constantinople became the center of the **Byzantine** (BIHZ uhn teen) **Empire,** a name that comes from Byzantium.

After Constantine's death, the Empire was again split in two. As the years passed, this division became greater. By the year 400, there were really *two* "Roman" Empires. The weaker one was

The emperor Constantine appears on this Roman coin. Constantine's name in Latin—*Constantinus*—is on the front of the coin. On the back, the word *Senatus* was a reminder that Constantine freed Rome and its Senate and reunited the Empire.

in the west, with its capital at Rome. The stronger one was in the east. Its capital was at Constantinople.

REVIEW What effect did Constantine's reign have on the Roman Empire? **Cause and Effect**

Same City, Different Name

Then and Now

Constantinople remained the capital of the Byzantine Empire for more than 1,000 years. However, the Ottoman Turks targeted the city for conquest. They were from Central Asia, but settled in Anatolia, where they saw the weakening of the Byzantine Empire. Finally, in 1453, the Ottoman Turks captured Constantinople. They renamed it Istanbul. Today, Istanbul is the largest city in present-day Turkey. It is the only city in the world that sits on two continents—it is half in Europe and half in Asia.

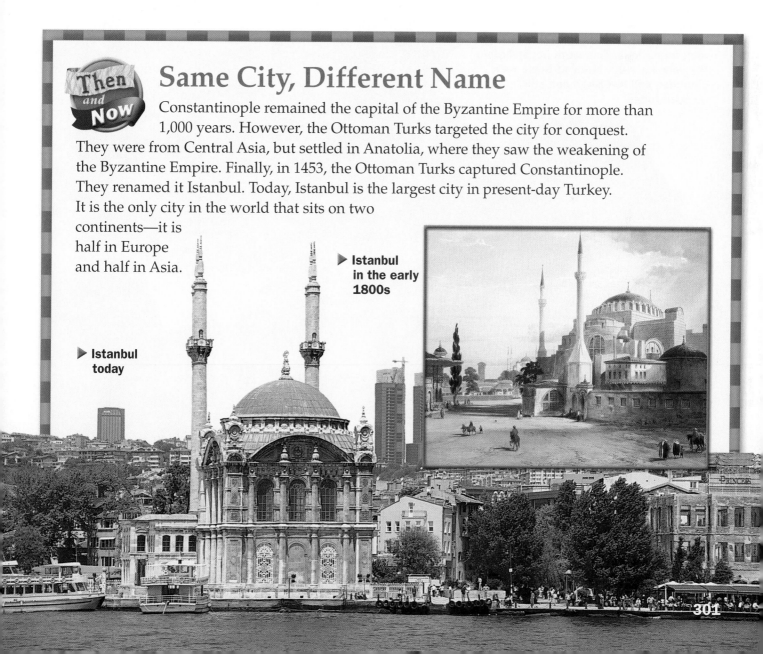

▶ Istanbul in the early 1800s

▶ Istanbul today

Christianity Divides

More than the Empire was splitting in two. During these years, eastern and western Christian churches were developing different traditions. There were many differences, but the most important concerned the role of the emperor. In the east, the emperor also was the head of the church. He claimed to rule directly in the name of Jesus. The emperor appointed all important church officials. The western church claimed that the **pope,** or the leader of the Roman church, had authority over all Christians, including the emperor. Byzantine Christians did not accept this claim.

▶ **Some of the early Christians of the Eastern Roman Empire settled in the region of Cappadocia in present-day Turkey. The Christians began to sculpt beautiful churches and dwellings into the strange rock formations. This work began before the year A.D. 400. Many of these rock churches and dwellings can still be seen today.**

These disagreements would continue until 1054, when the churches officially divided into the **Byzantine Orthodox Church** in the east and the **Roman Catholic Church** in the west.

REVIEW What was the most important difference between the Byzantine Orthodox Church and the Roman Catholic Church? **Compare and Contrast**

The Final Days of Rome

While the eastern half of the Roman Empire was gaining strength, conditions were desperate in the Western Roman Empire. Invaders called "barbarians" by the Romans continued to pour into the Empire. A new enemy, the Huns, a tribe from Central Asia, attacked the German tribes. The German tribes fled south into the Roman Empire. One of these tribes was the Visigoths (VIZ uh goths). They took over a huge area in the eastern part of the Empire. Other tribes attacked Roman cities throughout the northern part of the Empire.

In A.D. 408, the Visigoth leader Alaric (AL uh rik) reached the gates of Rome. His army surrounded the city, cutting off its food supply. However, when

The Granger Collection

wealthy Romans paid him a huge amount of money, Alaric decided not to destroy the city.

In 410, Alaric returned. This time the Visigoths captured the city. For three days, they **pillaged,** or robbed, Rome. Warriors rode their horses into the homes of the wealthy, carrying away riches. What they could not take with them, they burned.

In 455, another German tribe, the Vandals, captured Rome. They also pillaged the city. They took whatever treasures remained. The word *vandal* is now used to describe someone who destroys property.

REVIEW Did the Visigoths attack Rome before or after the Huns attacked the German tribes?
Sequence

▶ **Barbarians are turned back from the gates of Rome in this painting by Raphael.**

Invaders of the Roman Empire

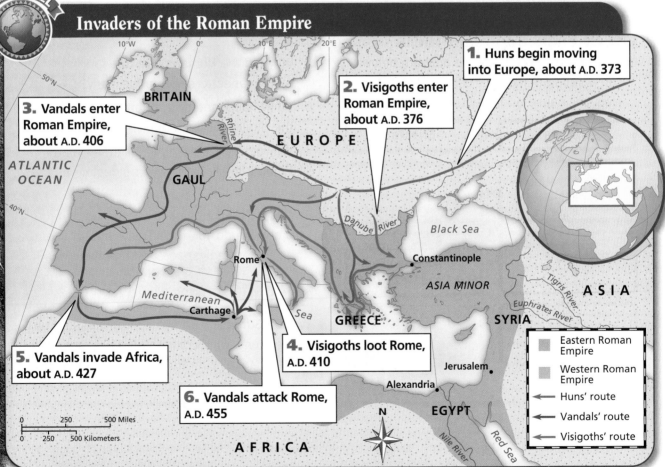

3. Vandals enter Roman Empire, about A.D. 406

2. Visigoths enter Roman Empire, about A.D. 376

1. Huns begin moving into Europe, about A.D. 373

5. Vandals invade Africa, about A.D. 427

4. Visigoths loot Rome, A.D. 410

6. Vandals attack Rome, A.D. 455

BRITAIN
EUROPE
ATLANTIC OCEAN
GAUL
Rhine River
Danube River
Black Sea
Constantinople
ASIA MINOR
ASIA
Tigris River
Euphrates River
SYRIA
GREECE
Rome
Mediterranean Sea
Carthage
Jerusalem
Alexandria
EGYPT
Nile River
Red Sea
AFRICA

0 250 500 Miles
0 250 500 Kilometers

	Eastern Roman Empire
	Western Roman Empire
←	Huns' route
←	Vandals' route
←	Visigoths' route

▶ **Different groups of barbarians invaded the Western Roman Empire.**

MAP SKILL Use a Map Key *From which directions did barbarian invaders come?*

The Fall

The final blow to the Roman Empire came in 476. A powerful soldier named Orestes had his young son, **Romulus Augustulus,** made emperor. A German ruler confronted Orestes and demanded that he be given control of part of the Empire. Orestes refused and was killed. Romulus Augustulus, who was only 12 or 13 years old at the time, was no longer emperor. He had been emperor for less than a year.

Romulus Augustulus was spared because of his youth. He was sent to live with his relatives in southern Italy. No one knows what became of him. Romulus Augustulus was the last emperor of the Western Roman Empire.

As Rome declined, the Byzantine Empire became even more prosperous. When Rome fell, Constantinople became the center of Roman power. It would keep this power for another thousand years after the fall of Rome.

REVIEW Why did Constantinople become the center of Roman power? *Draw Conclusions*

Summarize the Lesson

- **A.D. 180** The death of Marcus Aurelius marked the beginning of a long period of decline for the Roman Empire.

- **A.D. 330** Constantine officially opened the new capital city of Constantinople.

- **A.D. 476** Constantinople became the center of Roman power.

LESSON 5   REVIEW

Check Facts and Main Ideas

1. Cause and Effect Copy the diagram below on a separate piece of paper. Fill in the missing cause and effects.

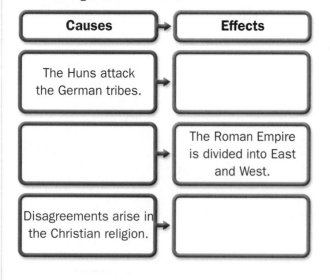

| Causes | → | Effects |

- The Huns attack the German tribes. →
- → The Roman Empire is divided into East and West.
- Disagreements arise in the Christian religion. →

2. Why did the Romans hire foreign mercenaries to serve in the army?

3. What happened to the Roman Empire after the death of Constantine?

4. Why did the eastern half of the Roman Empire not suffer the same decline as the western half?

5. Critical Thinking: *Make Inferences* What problems do you think Rome had by having an army largely made up of mercenaries?

Link to —⬥⬥— Writing

Write a Summary In two sentences, sum up the reasons for dividing the Empire and moving the capital from Rome to Constantinople.

Eudocia
about A.D. 400–460

Empress Eudocia was the wife of Eastern Roman Emperor Theodosius II. She also was the daughter of an Athenian philosopher. Her parents named her Athenais, after the goddess Athena. Athenais studied science, literature, and religion with her father. According to English historian Edward Gibbon, Athenais was not only well-educated but very beautiful.

> *"[She had] large eyes . . . a fair complexion, golden locks . . . [and] an understanding improved by study. . . ."*

As a young woman, Athenais traveled to Constantinople. She converted to Christianity, taking the name Eudocia. She married Theodosius in A.D. 421. As empress, Eudocia is said to have had a great influence over Theodosius. She was a devoted Christian, but was known for her accepting attitude toward non-Christians.

BIOFACT

Eudocia's face is featured on this coin. Many Byzantine emperors had coins made featuring their wives.

She also was a gifted writer. Eudocia wrote a poem that praised Theodosius' army's defeat of the Persians.

In 438, Eudocia visited Jerusalem. She returned to Jerusalem in 443, after quarreling with Theodosius' powerful sister, Pulcheria. Eudocia remained in Jerusalem for the rest of her life. She devoted herself to doing good works. She wrote poetry and paid for the building of several churches and hospitals. She also was known for her support of the city's Jewish population. She died in Jerusalem in 460. She was buried in one of the churches she helped build.

Learn from Biographies

How do you think the events of Eudocia's earlier life influenced the choices she made after moving to Jerusalem?

For more information, go online to *Meet the People* at **www.sfsocialstudies.com**.

1000 B.C.   500 B.C.

753 B.C.
According to legend, Rome was founded.

about 500 B.C.
Rome set up a republic.

Chapter Summary

Target Skill

Main Idea and Details

On a separate piece of paper, fill in the missing details that support the main idea shown in the box at right.

The ancient Romans made important contributions to our ideas and culture today.

The Romans believed in honor and in loyalty to their country.

Vocabulary

Write sentences using each of the vocabulary words.

1 patriotism (p. 285)

2 patrician (p. 283)

3 plebeian (p. 283)

4 republic (p. 283)

5 dictator (p. 283)

6 emperor (p. 289)

7 gladiator (p. 291)

8 catacomb (p. 295)

9 synagogue (p. 295)

10 disciple (p. 295)

11 persecute (p. 296)

12 auction (p. 299)

13 pillage (p. 303)

14 vandal (p. 303)

People and Terms

Write a sentence explaining why each of the following people or terms was important in the development of ancient Rome. You may use two or more in a single sentence.

1 Junius Brutus (p. 278)

2 Regulus (p. 283)

3 Hannibal (p. 285)

4 Julius Caesar (p. 286)

5 Augustus (p. 289)

6 *Pax Romana* (p. 289)

7 Christianity (p. 295)

8 Diocletian (p. 300)

9 Byzantine Empire (p. 301)

10 Romulus Augustulus (p. 304)

A.D. 1

A.D. 500

A.D. 120
The Empire grew eastward and westward.

A.D. 180
Death of Marcus Aurelius began decline of Empire.

A.D. 476
Last Roman emperor was removed.

Facts and Main Ideas

1 What did the Romans learn from the Etruscans?

2 **Time Line** How much time passed between the death of Marcus Aurelius and the rule of the last emperor?

3 **Main Idea** How did the geography of Rome help it to grow into a powerful city?

4 **Main Idea** Who were patricians and plebeians? Why are they important?

5 **Main Idea** What brought about the *Pax Romana*?

6 **Main Idea** How did Constantine change the way Christians were treated?

7 **Main Idea** What weakened the Roman army?

8 **Critical Thinking:** *Make Inferences* How are the principles of government developed by the Romans still important today?

Write About History

1 **Write a newspaper report** describing the change of title given to Octavian. Explain what *Augustus* means and how he had all the powers of an emperor.

2 **Write a persuasive article** urging Roman architects and builders to use concrete, a new building material.

3 **Write an advertising flyer** about a holiday celebration at the Colosseum. Mention the acrobats, magicians, and trained animals as well as other special events.

Apply Skills

Use Primary and Secondary Sources

Read the translation of a primary source below. Then answer the questions.

Description by Livy of the crisis in Rome, 494 B.C.

A great panic seized the City, mutual distrust led to a state of universal suspense. Those plebeians who had been left by their comrades in the City feared violence from the patricians; the patricians feared the plebeians who still remained in the City, and could not make up their minds whether they would rather have them go or stay . . . . What would happen if a foreign war broke out in the meantime?

1 How do you know that this is a translation of a primary source?

2 Why do you think Livy wrote this description?

3 What is Livy's point of view? How do you know?

4 How are translations of primary sources, such as this one, useful?

Internet Activity

To get help with vocabulary, people, and terms, select dictionary, encyclopedia, or almanac from *Social Studies Library* at **www.sfsocialstudies.com**.

End with Literature

THE PERSIAN WARS

Herodotus is known as the "Father of History." The Greek world was filled with myths and legends. Herodotus hoped to separate myth from fact to explain past events and world geography.

"*Thus much, however, is clear: if there are men beyond the north wind, there must also be men beyond the south wind. For my part, I cannot but laugh when I see numbers of persons drawing maps of the world without having any reason to guide them; making, as they do, the ocean-stream to run all round the earth, and the earth itself to be an exact circle, as if described by a pair of compasses, with Europe and Asia just of the same size.*"

—Excerpt from Herodotus, *The Persian Wars*,
translated by George Rawlinson.

Main Ideas and Vocabulary

TEST PREP

Read the passage below and use it to answer the questions that follow.

Greek and Roman civilizations brought a wealth of art, learning, literature, and technology to the world. We know about these civilizations because of great buildings and artifacts they left behind. Both the Greeks and Romans believed in many gods and goddesses. They used legends and <u>myths</u> to describe events. The Romans borrowed much Greek culture in building their civilization. They soon developed their own civilization. However, the Greeks still were a major influence on the Romans.

Because the Romans admired the Greeks, many spoke Greek but wrote using their own language, Latin. In certain things, the Romans did not follow the Greeks. Instead of simple architecture, the Romans built huge palaces and temples. They built <u>elevated</u> aqueducts. They were very skilled road builders. We know this because many of the roads they built are still used today. However, the Romans did not study science like the Greeks did. They did not suggest scientific theories. The Romans studied and borrowed much from Greek philosophy.

Today this blend of Greek, Hellenistic, and Roman tradition is called Greco-Roman civilization. Through trade and travel, people interacted and cultures became richer.

1 According to the passage, why did the Romans borrow aspects of Greek culture?
   A The Romans were not smart.
   B The Romans admired the Greeks.
   C The Romans did not like the Greeks.
   D The Romans did not know how to develop their culture.

2 The word *myth*, used above, means:
   A scientific research about nature
   B a story about gods and goddesses
   C recorded history of people

3 The word *elevated*, used above, means:
   A raised
   B underground
   C solid

4 What is the *main idea* of the passage?
   A The Greeks borrowed much culture from the Romans.
   B The Romans spoke Latin.
   C The Romans borrowed much from Greek culture to develop their civilization.

People and Terms

Write a sentence describing each of these people and terms.

1 Marcus Aurelius (p. 289)

2 Hannibal (p. 285)

3 Julius Caesar (p. 286)

4 Aristotle (p. 262)

5 Constantine (p. 296)

6 Hellenistic Age (p. 268)

7 democracy (p. 255)

8 vandal (p. 303)

9 Alexander (p. 267)

10 Apostle (p. 295)

11 Euclid (p. 271)

12 consul (p. 283)

Write and Share

Present a Skit Use one of the *You Are There* features from a lesson in the unit. In small groups, write a short skit with the information you have from this feature. Act out the skit for the class. You may need to add other characters, depending on the number of students in the class. Use information you have read in the lessons to add characters.

Read on Your Own

Look for books like these in your library.

Apply Skills

Prepare a Primary Source Poster Create a poster about an event in your life, such as a birthday, a trip, or a special occasion. Gather photos, letters, journal entries, and drawings to document the event. Explain how each object is a primary source and what it tells about the event.

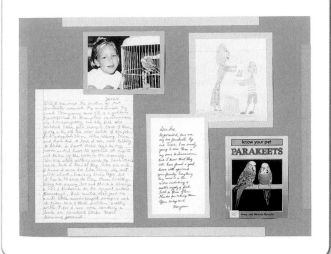

Feature Film

Write a screenplay and bring a myth to life.

1 Form a group to choose a Greek myth.

2 Write a screenplay or script for a short film based on the myth. Write dialogue for the characters and instructions for camera operators. Write about the location and setting of your film.

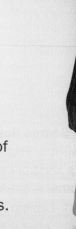

3 Make a backdrop for your screenplay. You may want to include a recording of music and sounds.

4 Perform your Greek myth for the class.

Internet Activity

Explore ancient Greece on the Internet. Go to **www.sfsocialstudies.com/activities** and select your grade and unit.

The Medieval World

How does trade connect peoples, cultures, and ideas?

aquest
de a

500   600   700   800   900   1000

c. 527
The Byzantine
Empire begins
to expand.

c. 622
Islam begins to spread
throughout Southwest Asia.

c. 800
Rise of feudalism
in Europe

about 900
Height of early trading
kingdoms and empires in
East and West Africa

carauana es partida del imi
ta panar aalcatayo :

The Catalan Atlas of 1375
illustrates the caravan
of Marco Polo crossing Asia.

1100   **1200**   **1300**   **1400**   **1500**   **1600**

1206
Genghis Khan
unifies Mongolia.

1215
The Magna Carta is
signed by King John.

1347
The Plague spreads
across Europe.

1526
The Mogul Empire
is established.

315

1095 The beginning of the Crusades

c. 1500
Portuguese invasions begin in Africa.

Meet the People

Justinian
c. 483–565
Birthplace: Illyria (present-day Yugoslavia)
Byzantine emperor
- Became leader of the Byzantine Empire in 527
- Created the Justinian Code, a basis for legal systems
- Built aqueducts, harbors, churches, and public buildings throughout the Empire

Theodora
c. 497–548
Birthplace: Cyprus or Crete
Byzantine empress
- Influenced Justinian's religious and social policies
- Helped Justinian secure absolute power
- One of the first rulers to recognize the rights of women

Wu Hou
625–705
Birthplace: unknown
Chinese empress
- First woman ruler of China
- Favored Buddhism, promoted art and literature
- Installed scholars as government officials

Charlemagne
742–814
Birthplace: Aix-la-Chapelle in present-day Germany
Emperor
- Conquered much of western Europe, forming a great empire
- Protected the Christian Church and helped extend its power
- Instituted reforms and feudalism

450	500	550	600	650	700	750	800	850	900

c. 483–565 • Justinian

c. 497–548 • Theodora

625–705 • Wu Hou

742–814 • Charlemagne

Genghis Khan

c. 1162–1227

Birthplace: near Lake Baikal, Mongolia

Mongol ruler

- Combined tribes into a unified Mongolia
- Ruled an area stretching across central Asia from the Caspian Sea to the Sea of Japan
- Established the first Mongol code of laws

Sundiata Keita

reigned c. 1235–1255

Birthplace: present-day Kangaba, Mali

African ruler

- Founded the Mali Empire
- Built empire into one of the largest and wealthiest in the region
- Defeated the last ruler of the Empire of Ghana

Ibn Battuta

c. 1304–1368

Birthplace: Tangiers, Morocco

World traveler

- Set out on a journey to Mecca in 1325
- Returned from his travels more than 25 years later
- Wrote about his travels around the world

Mansa Musa

reigned c. 1307–1332

Birthplace: Mali Empire

African ruler

- Expanded the Mali Empire, making it the political and cultural leader of West Africa
- Made Timbuktu a center of learning
- Spread Islam throughout the empire

950 1000 1050 1100 1150 1200 1250 1300 1350 1400

c. 1162–1227 • Genghis Khan

reigned c. 1235–1255 • Sundiata Keita

c. 1304–1368 • Ibn Battuta

reigned c. 1307–1332 • Mansa Musa

The Medieval World

Sequence

Events in sequence are listed in the order in which they happened.

| First Event | → | Second Event | → | Third Event | → | Final Event |

- Sometimes writers use words such as _before, initially, after, later,_ and _finally_ to signal sequence.

- Noting the dates of events will help you keep them in the correct sequence.

- Use a time line or a list to help you keep track of the sequence of events.

Read the following paragraph. The words that tell the sequence of events have been highlighted.

As you will read in this unit, the history of a place is often tied to the people living in that location. For example, the Hagia Sophia (ah YEE uh soh FEE uh) is one of the world's greatest buildings. Initially, the Hagia Sophia was a Christian church, built by a Roman emperor. Later, the Ottoman Turks conquered the region, converting the church into a mosque, a Muslim house of worship. Finally, in the twentieth century, it became a museum.

The Many Lives of the Hagia Sophia

In the fourth century, Emperor Constantine ordered that the first Hagia Sophia be built. On the same site where an earlier church that had been burned once stood, Emperor Justinian began the construction of a new church in 532. As the largest church in Constantinople, it was called "The Great Church."

The Hagia Sophia was constructed between the years 532 and 537. Even before the interior was completed, earthquakes rocked the building, cracking the great dome and the eastern half-dome. In 559 earthquakes made the main dome collapse. The church was reconstructed and later reopened by 563.

An earthquake in 869 toppled one of its half-domes. Another earthquake in 989 demolished the great dome. The building was reopened for religious services in 994. Today, periodic earthquakes continue to shake the Hagia Sophia.

Between 726 and 842, all of the church's religious pictures and figures were removed. In 1204 an army of crusaders looted, or robbed, the Hagia Sophia. Many of the holy relics, or remains, are now displayed in European museums.

After the Turkish army conquered the region in 1453, it took over the church. When Sultan Mehmed II entered the city, he was sad to see that the magnificent church was in need of repair.

The Turks converted the Hagia Sophia into a mosque and maintained the building for nearly 500 years. Finally, in 1935, the Hagia Sophia, located in Istanbul, Turkey, was converted into a museum.

Use the reading strategy of sequence to answer these questions.

1 What events took place within the first 300 years of the church's existence?

2 How did the Hagia Sophia change over time?

CHAPTER 11

Byzantine Empire and Ancient Arabia

Lesson 1

500
Constantinople (Byzantium)
Constantinople becomes the center of the Byzantine Empire.

1

Lesson 2

527
Constantinople
Justinian becomes emperor of the Byzantine Empire.

2

Lesson 3

613
Mecca
Islam brings changes to lands in Southwest Asia.

3

Lesson 4

700
Arabian Peninsula
Islamic culture expands outside the Arabian Peninsula.

4

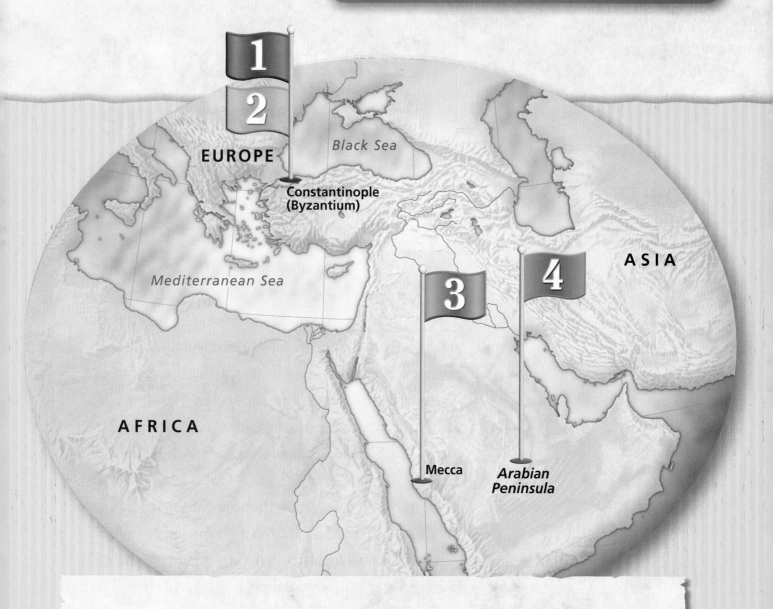

EUROPE

Black Sea

Constantinople
(Byzantium)

Mediterranean Sea

ASIA

AFRICA

Mecca

Arabian
Peninsula

Why We Remember

Some of today's practices and customs have their roots in the Byzantine Empire and in ancient Arabia. For example, parts of the legal codes, or laws, of many countries are similar to the code developed in the sixth century by Emperor Justinian. Islam, founded in the seventh century, is now a major world religion. It spread to other lands through a vast system of trade routes and conquests. Many of the trade routes developed in the seventh and eighth centuries are still used today.

EUROPE ASIA
AFRICA

Black Sea
Constantinople
Bosporus
Sea of Marmara

Geography of the Byzantine Empire

PREVIEW

Focus on the Main Idea
Physical features, climate, and Roman and Greek culture influenced how people lived in the Byzantine Empire.

PLACES
Constantinople
Bosporus
Black Sea
Sea of Marmara
Byzantium
Hippodrome

VOCABULARY
hippodrome

▶ Even today shoppers enjoy strolling through open-air markets and bazaars in what was once the Byzantine Empire.

You Are There

About A.D. 500: You're strolling along Mese—the wide, straight main street of Constantinople (kahn stan tuh NOH pul). The clatter of the metal wheels moving along the paving blocks is loud. Merchants with carts are heading for the marketplace at the public square. The air is filled with many languages: Arabic, Greek, and Latin. The street is crowded. You step aside to let camels with spices and furs pass. It's noon. Jugglers, street musicians, magicians, and fortunetellers entertain the crowd. Customers buy silks, furs, fish, honey, and amber—a brownish, yellowish fossil used in making ornaments and jewelry. At the end of the street is the Imperial Palace. Constantinople (Byzantium) is the capital city of the Byzantine (BIH zan teen) Empire. It's truly the world's marketplace.

Sequence As you read, keep events in their correct time order.

Target Skill

Roots of an Empire

The Byzantine Empire was considered a continuation of the Roman Empire. It stretched across lands that once formed the eastern part of the Roman Empire. At its height, the Byzantine Empire included parts of southern and eastern Europe and the Balkan Peninsula. It also included parts of northern Africa and southwestern Asia.

In the southern and eastern European parts of the empire, the people enjoyed hot, dry summers and cool, wet winters. They raised grapes, olives, and sometimes wheat and barley. The area often supported herds of sheep or goats. Most people lived in villages.

Life was different for people living in northern Africa and across much of southwestern Asia. There the summers were hotter and drier than in southern and eastern Europe. The winters were either mild or warm.

The desert regions received very little rainfall. In the country, people survived as herders, moving from place to place so that their sheep, goats, or camels could find food. In towns and large cities, merchants and artisans sold goods and practiced their trades.

▶ The Byzantine Empire's location and barriers kept out invaders for nearly a thousand years. Today, Turkish women thresh wheat in what was once the Byzantine Empire.

REVIEW Did the Byzantine Empire rise before or after the Roman Empire? ↻ Sequence

ASIA

Bosporus Strait

Byzantium

Black Sea

BALKAN PENINSULA

Sea of Marmara

EUROPE

Mediterranean Sea

ASIA

ATLANTIC OCEAN

Red Sea

AFRICA

Ultimate Location

Constantinople was a perfect location for the capital of the Byzantine Empire. The city stands on a peninsula at the southeastern end of Europe. It serves as a "bridge" between Europe and Asia.

The peninsula itself extends into the Bosporus, a narrow strait linking the Black Sea and the Sea of Marmara. Ships traveling from the Black Sea to the Mediterranean Sea must pass through this 19-mile stretch of water. The waterway and city that controls it are both very important to trade.

People have lived at this location for thousands of years. The ancient city of Byzantium (bih ZAN tee um) was located on these shores. The Roman emperor Constantine I chose this location for his capital. As you read in Unit 4, the city was renamed Constantinople in 330 to honor him.

Because of its location on a triangular peninsula, the city was guarded on three sides by water. For additional protection, leaders built sea walls along the coast. At the western edge of the city stood elaborate walls that were rebuilt and expanded to protect Constantinople from land attacks. Some sections of these walls still stand today.

REVIEW When was Byzantium renamed Constantinople? ⟳ **Sequence**

A Blend of Culture

Isolated from Europe, the Byzantine Empire created an identity of its own. By blending Greek languages and Roman traditions, Byzantine culture flourished.

Based on Roman influence, most houses in Constantinople were made of wood. However, the rich lived in stone mansions. Many of these mansions had enclosed courtyards.

Aspects of Roman culture filled the Byzantine Empire. Based on Roman tradition, the city offered public baths that included steam rooms and swimming pools. Chariot races were a favorite form of entertainment in Byzantium, much as they were in the Roman Empire. They were held in a huge building called the Hippodrome (HIHP uh drohm).

A **hippodrome** is an ancient Greek stadium used for horse and chariot racing. The largest of the time, the Hippodrome in Constantinople was completed by Constantine in 330. With seating for more than 60,000 spectators, the Hippodrome was the center of entertainment. It also hosted other events such as ceremonies and celebrations of military triumphs.

▶ **The word *Bosporus* comes from the Greek words meaning "ox" and "ford." Parts of the strait were once so narrow that cattle could cross, or ford, the water.**

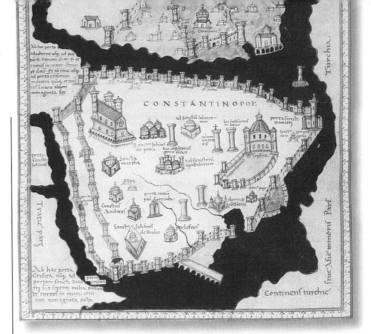

► **Portolan charts, such as this one of Constantinople in the fifteenth century, helped navigators at sea. Notice the high sea walls, details of the coastline, and the city's major attractions.**

Constantinople became the educational center of the Byzantine Empire. The Byzantines called themselves Romans even though they spoke Greek. The ancient Greek language was used for official purposes. However, it differed from the form of Greek spoken by most Byzantines. In the early history of the Empire, Byzantine emperors spoke Latin.

With hundreds of churches and plenty of palaces, mansions, schools, and hospitals, Constantinople thrived. The city's location brought forth a great blend of European and Asian culture. Art, architecture, and learning attracted many people to Constantinople. As the capital prospered, or flourished, so did the Byzantine Empire. All of this prosperity in the eastern part of the Roman Empire began after the western portion of the Roman Empire crumbled.

REVIEW Did Constantinople become a center of trade before or after the western part of the Roman Empire fell? ⟳ **Sequence**

Summarize the Lesson

- The Byzantine Empire was a continuation of the Roman Empire.

- Climate in parts of the Byzantine Empire was hot and dry.

- Constantinople, the capital of the Byzantine Empire, stood along the waterway connecting the Black Sea and the Sea of Marmara.

LESSON 1   REVIEW

Check Facts and Main Ideas

1. ⟳ **Sequence** The following events are not in chronological order. On a separate piece of paper, list them in their correct time order.

   • A city is established at the strait of Bosporus.
   • The Roman Empire weakens.
   • Constantinople is fortified with sea and land walls.

2. Describe how the physical geography and climate of the Byzantine Empire affected the way people lived.

3. What city was the capital of the Byzantine Empire?

4. How was the Byzantine Empire related to the Roman Empire?

5. **Critical Thinking:** *Make Inferences* Why did Constantinople become a center of trade?

Link to ◯═◯ Writing

Write a Letter Suppose you are a member of Constantinople's merchant class. Write a letter to a merchant in another place explaining why Constantinople would be a good place to relocate his or her business.

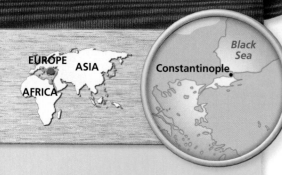

500

1000

527
Justinian becomes emperor of the Byzantine Empire.

537
The Hagia Sophia is completed.

1000
The Byzantine Empire begins to weaken.

PREVIEW

Focus on the Main Idea
Under the rule of Justinian, the Byzantine Empire became great.

PLACES
Hagia Sophia
Constantinople

PEOPLE
Justinian
Theodora

VOCABULARY
cathedral
icon

TERMS
Justinian Code

The Greatness of the Byzantine Empire

You Are There

A.D. 537: The city is buzzing with excitement. Today, after about five years of construction, the great Hagia Sophia [ah YEE uh soh FEE uh] will be opened. It will be the biggest church in the empire! You've sneaked into the church unnoticed as several of the emperor's guests arrive. The multicolored marble walls and columns seem to glow. A ring of 40 arched windows circles a great dome. Looking up at the dome makes you dizzy. How did the architects design such a magnificent building? The procession of animal sacrifices has begun. One hundred oxen, 6,000 sheep, 600 stags, 1,000 pigs, 10,000 hens, and 10,000 roosters are being offered as part of the celebration.

Sequence As you read, keep events in their correct time order.

▶ Outside, the Hagia Sophia is large and massive. Inside, well-placed arches and windows make the gigantic shapes appear to float in space.

Byzantine Glory

Emperor **Justinian** was responsible for rebuilding this magnificent **cathedral**, or large, important Christian church, the **Hagia Sophia**, in **Constantinople.** During his rule, the Byzantine Empire reached its height.

When Emperor Justinian came to the throne in 527, he wanted to restore the Roman Empire and govern it as a whole. To achieve his goal, he began by paying the Persian kings so that they would stop threatening the far western part of Asia. He later expanded the Empire by conquering North Africa, Italy, a small part of southern Spain, and islands in the western Mediterranean.

Justinian's wife, **Theodora** (THEE uh dor uh), became his most trusted advisor. He valued her intelligence and political wisdom. For example, she encouraged him to defend the city of Constantinople when it was attacked in 532. Read more about Theodora's wise advice to Justinian in the biography on page 329.

Justinian told Byzantine scholars to collect and organize the laws of the Romans into a code. This code, called the **Justinian Code,** made the laws clearer. Today, the code is the basis of many legal systems. The Justinian Code allowed the Empire to operate with an efficient and fair central government.

REVIEW What was the Justinian Code?
Main Idea and Details

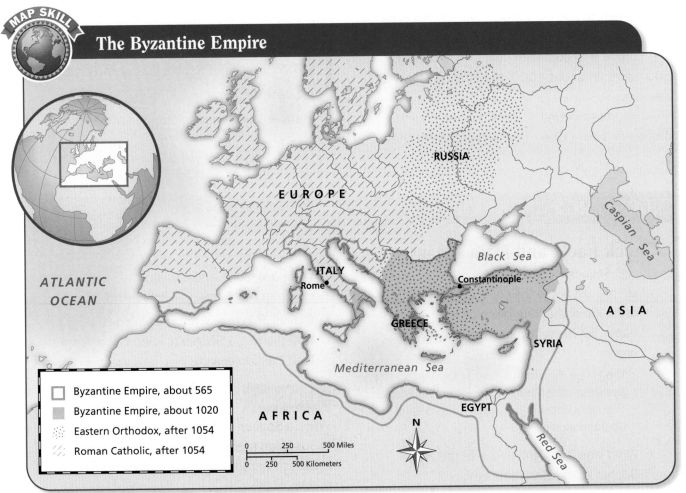

MAP SKILL

The Byzantine Empire

RUSSIA

EUROPE

Caspian Sea

Black Sea

ATLANTIC OCEAN

ITALY
Rome

Constantinople

ASIA

GREECE

SYRIA

Mediterranean Sea

EGYPT

AFRICA

N

Red Sea

Legend:
- ☐ Byzantine Empire, about 565
- ■ Byzantine Empire, about 1020
- ⠿ Eastern Orthodox, after 1054
- ⫽ Roman Catholic, after 1054

0   250   500 Miles
0   250   500 Kilometers

▶ The Byzantine Empire stretched across Southwest Asia, southern and eastern Europe, and northern Africa.

MAP SKILL Understand Borders and Capitals *Which present-day countries were part of the Byzantine Empire in 565?*

The Glorious Church

Art and architecture flourished during Justinian's rule. Justinian called for new harbors, aqueducts, and public buildings throughout the Empire. Many cathedrals were constructed. The interiors of these domed cathedrals were decorated with great detail. The greatest cathedral in the Empire was the Hagia Sophia. On its completion Justinian proclaimed:

> *"My thanks and gratitude to my Lord, for enabling me the means for creating such a glorious temple!"*

Byzantine emperors and the church had strong ties. The Byzantine, or Eastern, Orthodox Church was the official church. It also controlled cultural and political life. Justinian believed that God had chosen him to run the Empire. The church supported this belief and protected the emperor. The Empire that Justinian built lasted almost 500 years. In about 1000, the Empire began to weaken.

As you read in Unit 4, the Christian church divided in 1054. One major disagreement that

▶ The use of religious icons, such as this one of the crucifixion of Christ, divided the Christian church.

led to the split was over the use of icons as part of worship. Religious **icons** are pictures or images of Jesus and saints. After 1054, the Roman Catholic Church and the Byzantine Orthodox Church existed separately.

Ancient Art & Architecture Collection, Ltd.

REVIEW What was the relationship between Justinian and the church? **Summarize**

Summarize the Lesson

527 Justinian began to rule the Byzantine Empire.

537 The Hagia Sophia was completed.

1000 The Byzantine Empire began to decline.

1054 The Christian church split.

LESSON 2 REVIEW

Check Facts and Main Ideas

1. **Sequence** The following events are not in the correct order. On a separate piece of paper, list them in chronological order.

   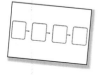

   - The Hagia Sophia was built in Constantinople.
   - Justinian added Italy to the Byzantine Empire.
   - Theodora encouraged Justinian to defend Constantinople.

2. What was the significance of the Hagia Sophia to the Byzantine Empire?

3. Who were Justinian and Theodora?

4. What are icons and explain their significance in the Byzantine Orthodox Church?

5. **Critical Thinking:** *Fact or Opinion* Justinian built the Hagia Sophia to keep close ties with the Christian church.

Link to ━━ **Speech**

Write a Speech Suppose you are a member of Justinian's government. Write and present a speech supporting Justinian's proposal for a code of laws.

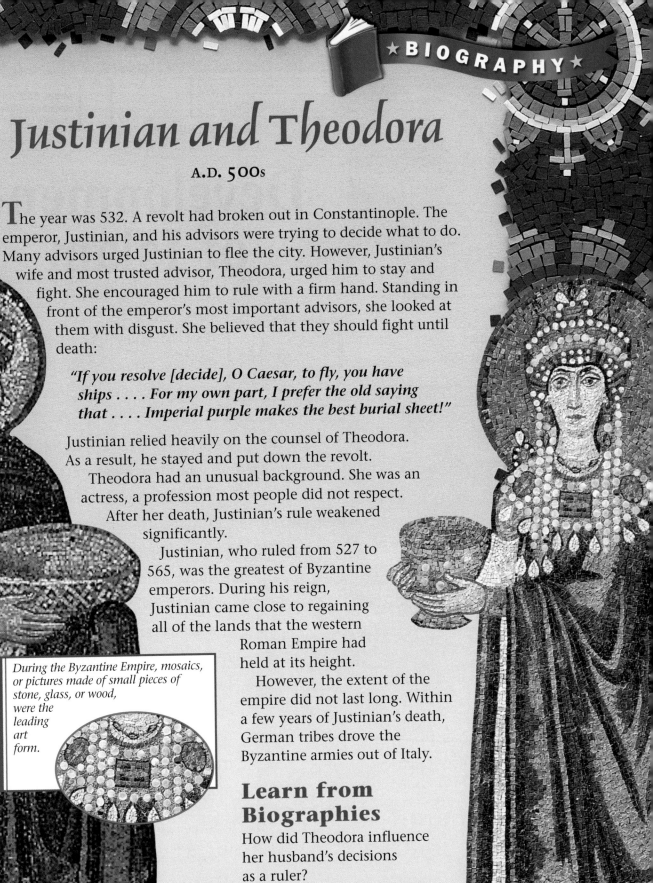

Justinian and Theodora

A.D. 500s

The year was 532. A revolt had broken out in Constantinople. The emperor, Justinian, and his advisors were trying to decide what to do. Many advisors urged Justinian to flee the city. However, Justinian's wife and most trusted advisor, Theodora, urged him to stay and fight. She encouraged him to rule with a firm hand. Standing in front of the emperor's most important advisors, she looked at them with disgust. She believed that they should fight until death:

"If you resolve [decide], O Caesar, to fly, you have ships . . . . For my own part, I prefer the old saying that . . . . Imperial purple makes the best burial sheet!"

Justinian relied heavily on the counsel of Theodora. As a result, he stayed and put down the revolt.

Theodora had an unusual background. She was an actress, a profession most people did not respect. After her death, Justinian's rule weakened significantly.

Justinian, who ruled from 527 to 565, was the greatest of Byzantine emperors. During his reign, Justinian came close to regaining all of the lands that the western Roman Empire had held at its height.

However, the extent of the empire did not last long. Within a few years of Justinian's death, German tribes drove the Byzantine armies out of Italy.

BIOFACT

During the Byzantine Empire, mosaics, or pictures made of small pieces of stone, glass, or wood, were the leading art form.

Learn from Biographies

How did Theodora influence her husband's decisions as a ruler?

For more information, go online to *Meet the People* at **www.sfsocialstudies.com**.

LESSON 3

c. 570
Muhammad is born.

c. 613
Muhammad establishes Islam.

about 622
Islam begins to spread throughout Southwest Asia.

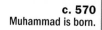

Medina
•Mecca

Development of Islam

PREVIEW

Focus on the Main Idea
Islam brought changes to lands in Southwest Asia.

PLACES
Mecca
Medina

VOCABULARY
pilgrimage
caravan
mosque

TERMS
Islam
Quran
Muslim
caliph

You Are There
It's 1183, and you're watching a small group of men enter Mecca. You see pearls, perfumes, sapphires, and medicines—all for sale.

You've heard Mecca described as a place filled with all kinds of goods. Your mouth waters as you look over the figs and grapes. From Spain merchants have brought fresh foods to sell. Everything looks inviting, especially after traveling across the desert for days. Peaches, lemons, walnuts, watermelons, cucumbers, eggplants, and pumpkins shine in the sun.

A group from another land in the region has come to worship. They have brought wheat, almonds, grains, fruit, and kidney beans. Your eyes focus on the tempting honey and butter. You see that traders make the journey to Mecca even more worthwhile.

▶ **Muslim artists used elaborate artwork and calligraphy to illustrate pages, such as this one from the Quran.**

Main Idea and Details As you read, identify the main beliefs of Islam.

Birth of Islam

A **pilgrimage** is a journey to a place of religious importance. The pilgrimage, or hajj (haj), to **Mecca** is an essential part of **Islam,** the religion revealed to Muhammad (moo HAM uhd). Muhammad, whose name means "Praised One," was born about 570 in Mecca. At an early age, he was orphaned and had to be raised by an uncle. For some time, Muhammad lived with a desert tribe, learning to tend sheep and camels. He eventually married and had a daughter. It is likely that he traveled on caravan journeys through Arabia at this time. **Caravans** are groups of people and animals traveling together.

In Muhammad's time, most people in this region were polytheistic, or worshiped many gods. People prayed to spirits and idols, or images or objects used in worship. This troubled Muhammad, and he went to the desert to pray and meditate alone. In 610, while Muhammad was meditating, according to Islamic beliefs, an angel visited him and said:

> *"Arise and warn, magnify thy Lord . . . wait patiently for Him."*

At first, Muhammad probably told only a few friends and family members about his vision. But according to the **Quran** (kuh RAN), the holy book

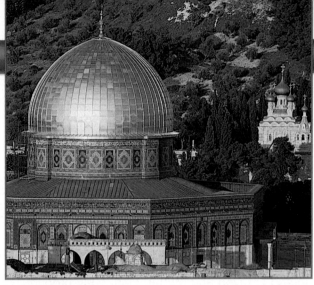

▶ The foundation of the Dome of the Rock, a Muslim mosque in Jerusalem, is holy to Muslims, Jews, and Christians.

of Islam, he had more visions. By about 613, he began to preach in public. Muhammad brought a new message to his people. He taught that there is only one God and that this God requires people to submit to, or obey, him. The Arabic word for submission, *Islam,* became the name of the religion. Believers in Islam are called **Muslims,** and they believe that the words Muhammad heard came directly from God.

In Mecca Muhammad found few people who supported his teachings. Muslims were being persecuted for their beliefs. In 622 Muhammad fled to the town of **Medina,** where he found many people eager to hear his teachings.

REVIEW What is the Quran?

Main Idea and Details

▶ If at all possible, every Muslim makes at least one pilgrimage, or hajj, to Mecca during his or her lifetime. Muslims consider the Ka'ba, a small shrine located near the center of the Great Mosque in Mecca, as the most sacred spot on Earth.

The Message of Islam

After 622 Islam spread quickly throughout Southwest Asia. After Muhammad's death in 632, **caliphs** (KAY luhfs), or successors, carried on his mission. Islam spread to Africa, Europe, and places such as India, the Malay Peninsula, and China. Many different peoples became part of the Islamic world.

All Muslims acknowledge five basic duties. These duties are known as the "Pillars of Islam."

First pillar: The profession of faith: "There is no god but God and Muhammad is his prophet." Muslims believe that God has sent many prophets, or great spiritual teachers. These included Abraham, Moses, and Jesus. They believe that Muhammad was the last and most important prophet.

Second pillar: Five daily prayers are generally offered in a group in a **mosque**, a Muslim place of worship. After a ritual washing, Muslims face in the direction of the holy city of Mecca.

Third pillar: Muslims must give charity to the poor. By giving part of what they own to the poor, Muslims unite the community.

Fourth pillar: Muslims fast during the ninth month of the Muslim calendar, Ramadan. Daily fasting begins at daybreak and ends at sunset. During the day eating and drinking, among other things, are forbidden.

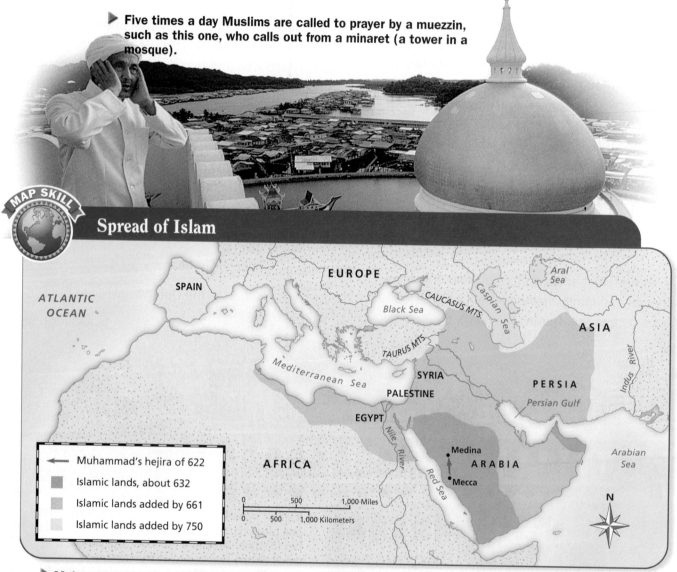

▶ **Five times a day Muslims are called to prayer by a muezzin, such as this one, who calls out from a minaret (a tower in a mosque).**

MAP SKILL

Spread of Islam

EUROPE

SPAIN

ATLANTIC OCEAN

Aral Sea

Black Sea

CAUCASUS MTS.

Caspian Sea

ASIA

TAURUS MTS.

Mediterranean Sea

SYRIA

PALESTINE

EGYPT

Nile River

PERSIA

Persian Gulf

Indus River

AFRICA

Medina

ARABIA

Arabian Sea

Mecca

Red Sea

→ Muhammad's hejira of 622

Islamic lands, about 632

Islamic lands added by 661

Islamic lands added by 750

0   500   1,000 Miles
0   500   1,000 Kilometers

N

▶ **Muhammad fled from Mecca to Medina in what is called the *hejira*.**

MAP SKILL Trace Movement on Maps *In which directions did Islam spread?*

Fifth pillar: A pilgrimage, a hajj, must be made to Mecca. This pilgrimage is required of every Muslim at least once in a lifetime—if at all possible.

REVIEW What are the Five Pillars of Islam? **Main Idea and Details**

Way of Life

Islam is a way of life for most Muslims. In addition to the Five Pillars, Muslims observe certain practices in their everyday lives.

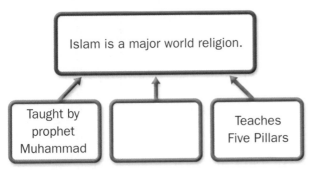

▶ **After noon worship, Muslims leave a mosque in Manama, Bahrain.**

The **jihad** (jee HAD) is a religious duty in Islam. *Jihad* means "struggle." It can refer to a military struggle but can also mean a peaceful struggle—for the good of the Muslim community.

The Quran covers many topics that Muslims face on a daily basis. It tells them what not to eat or drink, such as pork or alcohol. The Quran has a moral code on marriage, divorce, business affairs, and other matters.

Muslims worship in mosques on Friday afternoons. Unlike some other religions, Islam does not have a central religious leader. However, Islam does have religious teachers who study the Quran and the acts of Muhammad and apply them to everyday life.

REVIEW How do Muslims apply Islam to their everyday lives? **Main Idea and Details**

Summarize the Lesson

- **c. 570** Muhammad was born.
- **c. 613** According to Islamic beliefs, Islam was revealed to Muhammad.
- **c. 622** Islam began to spread throughout Southwest Asia.

LESSON 3   REVIEW

Check Facts and Main Ideas

1. **Main Idea and Details** On a separate piece of paper, copy the diagram below. Fill in the missing detail that describes Islam.

```
        Islam is a major world religion.

Taught by          [        ]      Teaches
prophet                            Five Pillars
Muhammad
```

2. What is the relationship between Muhammad and Islam?

3. What is the Quran?

4. What changes did Islam bring to Southwest Asia?

5. **Critical Thinking:** *Make Inferences* Why might a Muslim look at the Quran when faced with a business decision?

Link to 🔗 Geography

Use Maps Using maps from an atlas and the map on page 332, list the present-day countries to which Islam had spread by 750.

1200   1300   1400   1500

1300s
Muslims from Central Asia settle in Anatolia.

1325
Ibn Battuta sets out on his pilgrimage to Mecca.

1453
Constantinople falls to the Ottoman Empire.

Arabian Peninsula

The Islamic World

PREVIEW

Focus on the Main Idea
Trade and conquest helped spread religion and language throughout the Islamic world.

PLACES
Arabian Peninsula
Anatolia

PEOPLE
Ibn Battuta

VOCABULARY
astrolabe

You Are There
You work with your father and uncle at an inn where caravans stop. At night, you clean the rooms and stables surrounding the courtyard of the inn. Many caravans move during the cool of night, stopping at the caravansary, or caravan inn, in the morning. Once they arrive, you help care for the camels. Sometimes there are as many as 10,000 camels in a single caravan! It's hard work. But the animals work hard too. Each camel in a trade caravan may carry as many as 990 pounds. They go for days with little or no food and water, or they may eat only desert scrub—the plants that grow close to the ground. At the inn, you feed them dates, wheat, and oats. You're careful to stay away from the camel's sharp teeth. You recognize that the camel plays an important role in trade in the Islamic world.

▶ **Crossing the desert, travelers often used saddle bags on camels and horses to carry water and transport trade goods.**

Cause and Effect As you read, think about the effects and influence of Muslim trade.

Islamic Culture Spreads

According to the Quran, Muhammad wished to spread the word of God beyond the **Arabian Peninsula** and throughout the world. One way to do this was through trade on caravans. Another way that Islam spread was through war.

From the seventh to the tenth century, Muslim conquests added many lands to the Islamic world. Islam expanded outside of the Arabian Peninsula. In the 1300s, Muslims from Central Asia—called Turks—settled in **Anatolia,** (as Turkey was called in the Byzantine Empire). By 1453 they had conquered Constantinople, which became the capital of their empire, the Ottoman Empire. The Islamic world grew to include much of what was once part of the Byzantine Empire.

The first caliph, Abu Bakr (AH boo BAH kuhr), established a code, or law, for Muslim soldiers:

> *". . . Do not kill an old man, a woman or a child. Do not injure date palms and do not cut down fruit trees."*

Islam also expanded through trade. In addition to trade goods, Muslim traders brought Islam to Southeast Asia, Central Asia and China, North Africa, and sub-Saharan Africa, where they created an international slave trade.

Islam brought with it a system of government, laws, and society. Because the only acceptable version of the Quran was in Arabic, the Arabic language spread along with Islam. Wherever Muslims ruled, there was always a way to distinguish Muslims from non-Muslims. For example, non-Muslims had to pay a special tax. They could not marry Muslim women. Their houses and churches or synagogues could not be out in the open. They could not hold positions of power.

By the end of the tenth century, the Islamic culture, including its religion and language, was known throughout many lands. Muslim traders also brought knowledge about great advancements in mathematics and science in their contacts with Europe, Asia, and Africa.

REVIEW Why did the Arabic language spread with Islam? **Cause and Effect**

▶ **This illustration from a tenth-century book shows Muslims capturing a city in Sicily in the 840s.**

Trading Ideas

Muslim traders carried goods throughout the Islamic world. Through trade and conquest, ideas, the arts, and technology traveled back and forth between cultures.

A great traveler and historian of the time was **Ibn Battuta** (IHB uhn ba TOO tah). He set out on a hajj, or pilgrimage, to Mecca in 1325. Through his many travels, he learned much about different peoples and lands. He traded goods and ideas throughout the Islamic world. He wrote about his adventures, which informed readers about other cultures. You will read more about Ibn Battuta later in this lesson.

The Muslims were the first people to use branch-banking. This means that several different banks functioned as one bank in different locations throughout the Islamic world. Checks, or letters of credit, could be cashed at any of the branch banks. This saved time and made trade safer. Traders no longer had to carry gold and silver on the trade routes, where thieves were waiting.

Muslim engineers built water clocks and made complex irrigation systems. Muslim scientists made important breakthroughs in chemistry. For example, the Muslims were the first to make sulfuric (suhl FYOO rik) acid for use in manufacturing. In an effort to turn some metals into gold, they developed new chemical processes.

The Muslims expanded their knowledge of mathematics after building on ideas from the Hindus and the Greeks. Muslims were among the first people to work with the zero. As you read in Unit 3, the Maya in Central America made this same discovery much earlier. The word *algebra* comes from the Arabic word *al-jabr*, which means "restoring." Algebra was developed by a Muslim, al-Khwarizmi (al KWAR uhz mee).

▶ **Waterwheels, used for irrigation, were introduced and used throughout the Islamic world.**

Algebra had many uses in the Islamic world. With the help of algebra, surveyors could figure out the distance across a river. Algebra also helped determine the distance between objects in the sky. Muslim scientists even used the branch of mathematics called trigonometry to try to measure the distance around the Earth. By using information from the Greeks and trigonometry, Islamic scholars estimated that the distance around the world was about 20,400 miles. The ancient Greek mathematician Ptolemy believed that the distance was about 20,000 miles. (The actual distance is about 25,000 miles.)

Muslims found many other uses for mathematics. They used it to determine the times of day to call Muslims to prayer. They also needed mathematics to learn how to make maps. Accurate maps would help faithful believers of Islam find their way on their pilgrimage to Mecca.

Muslim interest in astronomy, or study of the moon, planets, and stars, was also tied closely to Islam. By looking at the position of the stars with an **astrolabe** (AS truh layb), Muslim astronomers could determine directions and make accurate maps for navigators.

By looking at the position of the moon, Muslim astronomers produced a calendar. Maps were made for navigation and trade. But with calendars, maps could also help other Muslims in the Islamic world know when and in which direction to head toward Mecca. This was useful for pilgrimages and

▶ **Astrolabes were used by astronomers to determine latitude.**

knowing which direction to face when praying.

Muslims made advancements in medicine. One scholar put together an encyclopedia of medicine. He combined the studies and knowledge of Greek, Arabic, and Indian sources. Muslim doctors also discovered that blood circulates throughout the human body.

REVIEW What are some ideas and technology the Muslims spread throughout the Islamic world? **Summarize**

Map Adventure

You're a Navigator Ibn Battuta is relying on your knowledge of the monsoon season for his travels, which begin in 1325 and last more than 25 years. (Refer back to Unit 2 for information on the monsoon season.) Off the coast of China, the summer monsoons blow from southwest to northeast, and winter monsoons blow from northeast to southwest.

1. During which monsoon season will you and Ibn Battuta plan to leave Quanzhou, China, to go to Samudra? Explain why.

2. The trip from Calicut to Zafar will take about 28 days. Will the monsoon winds be blowing during the trip from Calicut to Zafar? How do you know?

3. During which season would it be easiest to make this trip? Why?

Experts at Sea

As you have read, trade expanded throughout the Islamic world. A good transportation network was needed to keep trade moving. While land routes grew, so did sea routes.

Muslim sailors were exceptional navigators. They used many different kinds of instruments to help guide them. By measuring the angle of the North Star above the horizon with astrolabes, navigators could find their position at sea.

The Muslim sailors could travel in all kinds of weather. They made sailing vessels that could sail into the wind as well as with the wind. Astrolabes and triangular sails also gave them the ability to master sailing and expand the Islamic world.

REVIEW What made the Muslim sailors exceptional navigators? *Main Idea and Details*

▶ **The triangular sail, called a lateen sail, was used by Arab merchants and the Ottoman fleet. These sails made it possible for ships to sail well against the wind.**

Summarize the Lesson

- **1300s** Muslims from Central Asia settled in Anatolia.
- **1325** Ibn Battuta began his pilgrimage to Mecca.

LESSON 4 REVIEW

Check Facts and Main Ideas

1. **Cause and Effect** On a separate piece of paper, copy the diagram below. Fill in an effect for each of the following causes.

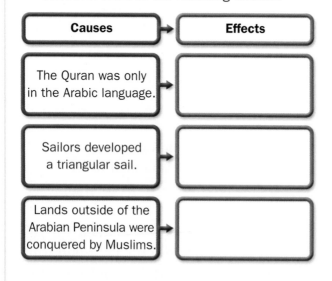

Causes	→	Effects
The Quran was only in the Arabic language.	→	
Sailors developed a triangular sail.	→	
Lands outside of the Arabian Peninsula were conquered by Muslims.	→	

2. How did Islam spread beyond the Arabian Peninsula?

3. In the Islamic world, how were non-Muslims treated differently?

4. What united the lands in the Islamic world?

5. **Critical Thinking:** *Make Generalizations* How did knowledge of the oceans and the development of technology in navigation help expand the Islamic world?

Link to ━━ Speech

Write a News Report Suppose you are a television news anchor in one of the countries the Muslims conquered. Prepare a report on how the lives of Muslims and non-Muslims are different.

CITIZEN HEROES

BUILDING CITIZENSHIP
Caring
★ Respect
Responsibility
Fairness
Honesty
Courage

Respecting Other Cultures

As he grew up, Ibn Battuta studied Arabic and Islamic law, hoping to become a lawyer or a judge. Instead, he became a world traveler and came into contact with many different peoples. He learned to respect other cultures.

In the 1320s, at the age of 21, Battuta set out on a pilgrimage to Mecca and Medina, some 3,000 miles away from his home. He had to cross deserts and mountains, while suffering sickness and risking attacks by thieves. Despite the dangers, Battuta discovered in himself a passion, or strong desire, for travel. He did not return home after his pilgrimage but continued his travels.

Determined to see as much of the world as possible, Battuta tried never to travel the same route twice. Battuta remained on the road for more than 25 years and covered some 75,000 miles. He visited nearly every Islamic kingdom in the world. Battuta was eager to learn about the way people of other lands lived. He was greatly impressed by the West African empire of Mali. Although he found the customs of Mali different from what he knew, he recorded them respectfully:

> "[The] women . . . are shown more respect than men . . . . No one claims descent from his father but from his mother's brother. A person's heirs are his sister's sons, not his own sons."

At the request of the leader of Morocco, Battuta told the story of his life travels to a scribe. The result was the *Rihla (Travels),* one of the most famous travel books ever written.

National Geographic Image Collection

Respect in Action

Link to Current Events Research the story of a person today who has shown respect when coming into contact with different cultures.

Interpret Line Graphs

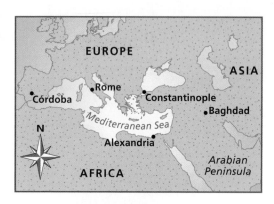

What? Line graphs show how a measurement changes as time passes. They help you understand how a variable, or measured quantity, changes over time.

Why? Line graphs can make it easier to interpret or understand data that changes over time. At a glance, you can see the highs and lows of the data. Line graphs also help you recognize trends. Trends can tell you whether a variable is increasing, decreasing, or staying about the same over time.

How? To use a line graph to answer specific questions, you need to compare the data plot to the horizontal and vertical axes. For example, the graph on page 340 can be used to answer the question, "Which city had the greatest population in A.D. 500?"

► In a line graph, the quantity/amount variable is shown along the vertical axis. For this graph, the vertical axis shows the population (in thousands) in Alexandria, Rome, and Constantinople between A.D. 100 and 622.

1. First find 500 on the horizontal axis.
2. Follow the grid line for 500 until it meets the blue data plot.
3. Next, read across to find out what the population was in 500 for Constantinople. The data plot meets the vertical axis at 400,000. Constantinople had the greatest population in 500.

► The title of a line graph tells you what variable is measured.

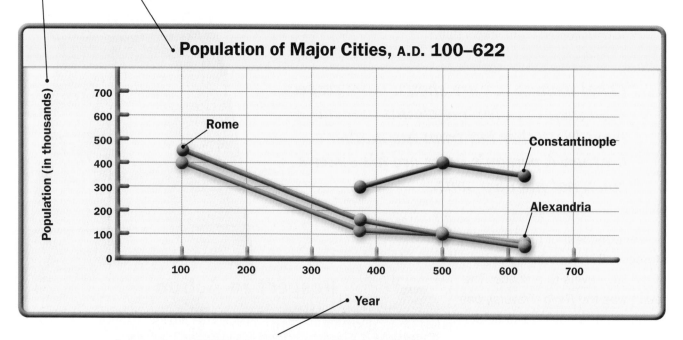

Population of Major Cities, A.D. 100–622

Population (in thousands) / Year

► In a line graph, the time interval, or space between events, is shown along the horizontal axis. For this graph, time is measured in years.

Note that sometimes the data plot will meet the vertical axis between two numbers. In these cases, you will need to estimate the vertical axis number. For example, on the line graph below, the population of Córdoba in A.D. 1150 was 60,000.

Look at the line graphs on pages 340–341, and then answer the questions.

Think and Apply

1 Which city had the greatest population growth?

2 Look at both line graphs on pages 340–341. Which cities had a decline in population between A.D. 500 and A.D. 1150?

3 From what you have learned in this chapter, why do you think Constantinople's population declined after A.D. 1000?

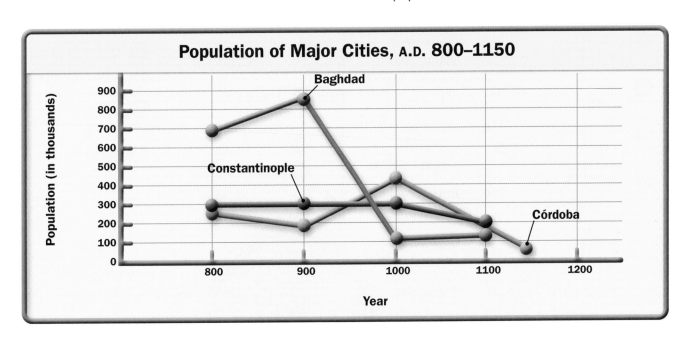

Population of Major Cities, A.D. 800–1150

A.D. **600**

about 500
The Byzantine Empire
began to expand.

about 622
Islam began
to spread.

Chapter Summary

 Target Skill

Sequence

On a separate piece of paper, organize the following events in the correct order.

- Hagia Sophia is completed.
- Emperor Justinian comes to the throne.
- Muhammad is born.
- The Byzantine Empire begins to crumble.
- Islam spreads beyond the Arabian Peninsula.

Vocabulary

Match each word with the correct definition or description.

1 caravan
(p. 331)

2 pilgrimage
(p. 331)

3 cathedral
(p. 327)

4 hippodrome
(p. 324)

5 icon (p. 328)

a. an important Christian church

b. ancient Greek stadium used for horse and chariot racing

c. group of people and animals traveling together

d. journey for religious purpose

e. religious picture of Jesus and saints

People and Terms

Write a sentence explaining why each of the following people and terms is important in the study of the Byzantine Empire and ancient Arabia. You may use two or more in a single sentence.

1 Justinian Code
(p. 327)

2 Theodora
(p. 327)

3 Muslim (p. 331)

4 Caliph (p. 332)

5 Quran (p. 331)

6 Islam (p. 331)

7 Ibn Battuta
(p. 336)

8 Justinian
(p. 327)

1000
The Byzantine Empire began to weaken.

1054
The Christian church split.

1325
Ibn Battuta set out on his pilgrimage to Mecca.

Facts and Main Ideas

1 Why was Constantinople considered a great capital city?

2 What effects did Islam have on countries where it was introduced?

3 **Time Line** Did the Byzantine Empire decline before or after Islam spread?

4 **Main Idea** How are the Byzantine Empire and the Roman Empire related?

5 **Main Idea** How did Theodora influence Justinian's rule of the Byzantine Empire?

6 **Main Idea** What are the main beliefs of Islam?

7 **Main Idea** In what two ways did Islam spread?

8 **Critical Thinking:** *Make Inferences* What part did the dry, arid climate of Arabia play in the spread of Islam?

Write About History

1 **Write a travel brochure** describing travel adventures to such places as Constantinople or Mecca. Include reasons why a person in the Byzantine Empire or Islamic world might wish to travel to these locations.

2 **Write a point-of-view editorial** describing the benefits of trade with people outside of your town or village.

3 **Write a newspaper article** giving a short biography of Justinian and Theodora. Report on where they lived and how they ruled.

Apply Skills

Interpret Line Graphs

Use the line graph below that shows the growth of urban population to answer the questions.

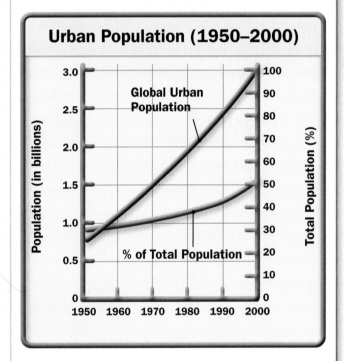

Urban Population (1950–2000)

Global Urban Population

% of Total Population

Population (in billions) — 3.0, 2.5, 2.0, 1.5, 1.0, 0.5, 0

Total Population (%) — 100, 90, 80, 70, 60, 50, 40, 30, 20, 10, 0

1950 1960 1970 1980 1990 2000

1 What generalization can you make about world population in urban areas over time?

2 What was the urban population in 1965?

Internet Activity

To get help with vocabulary, people, and terms, go online and select the dictionary, encyclopedia, or almanac from *Social Studies Library* at **www.sfsocialstudies.com**.

Asian Empires

Lesson 1

1630
Agra
Construction of the Taj Mahal begins.

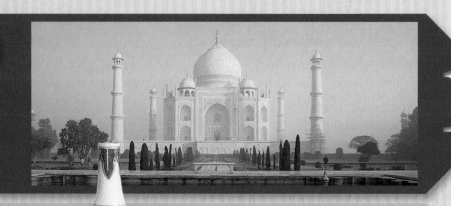

Lesson 2

1368
Beijing
The Ming dynasty develops into one of China's greatest dynasties.

Lesson 3

c. 1120
Angkor
The Khmer build Angkor Wat.

Lesson 4

1603
Edo (Tokyo)
Tokugawa Japan emerges.

1

2

3

4

ASIA

1 Agra
INDIA

2 Beijing
CHINA

3 Angkor
CAMBODIA

4 Edo (Tokyo)
JAPAN

PACIFIC OCEAN

INDIAN OCEAN

Why We Remember

The great expanse of Asia has always been home to a large percentage of the world's population. For many years, the customs and activities of the people were shielded from outsiders. However, through trade, people outside of Asia were able to enjoy some of the goods—such as fine silk and porcelain—of the region. More importantly, ideas and technology that originated in Asia—such as paper money, civil service examinations, and gunpowder—also reached countries far away. Many things we have and use today came from Asia years ago.

400   1000   1600

455
Huns and other groups
begin to invade India.

1526
Babur establishes the Mogul Empire.

about 1630
Construction of the Taj Mahal begins.

•Agra

Empire of Asia

PREVIEW

Focus on the Main Idea
Asia has a variety of climates and landforms that influenced several different cultures.

PLACES
Taj Mahal
Agra

PEOPLE
Babur
Akbar
Shah Jahan

You Are There It's a hot, sunny day in northern India. The sunlight reflecting from the building is so bright that you need to squint to protect your eyes. A few light clouds pass by. You rest your eyes on the white marble building that stands on a red sandstone platform. You're at the Taj Mahal (TAHZH muh HAHL). This magnificent tomb was built by the Indian ruler Shah Jahan (SHAH juh HAHN) in memory of his wife, Mumtaz. Shah Jahan tried to make the tomb as beautiful as the love he and Mumtaz had for each other.

As you step closer, you see that semiprecious stones such as jade and turquoise have been set in the white marble. You also see passages—from what you are told they are from the Quran—that decorate the outside.

Sequence As you read, keep the events in their correct time order.

> The Taj Mahal was constructed over a period of more than 20 years, from about 1630 to 1650. The project employed nearly 20,000 workers from Europe and parts of Asia.

Asia

The Taj Mahal is in Agra, India, which is located in Asia, the largest continent on Earth. Asia covers about one-third of the Earth's land surface. The Arctic Ocean forms Asia's northern boundary, while the Pacific Ocean forms its eastern boundary. To the south of Asia lies the Indian Ocean. On the map below, you can see that Asia's western boundary includes Europe, the Black Sea, the Greek Islands, the Mediterranean Sea, and the Red Sea.

Asia has a great variety of physical features and climates. In Asia there are vast flat lands, as well as the tallest mountains on Earth. Snow covers parts of northern Asia year-round, while tropical rain forests stand tall in southeastern Asia.

The mountain chains of Central Asia supply the continent's great rivers with water. Over time, people have migrated from the dry areas of Central Asia through the mountain passes into South Asia. They have moved from the dry areas of southwestern Asia to Southeast Asia and from the Arabian Peninsula to Indonesia and the Malay Peninsula. Mountain chains gave the Korean, Japanese, and Chinese peoples some protection from other peoples.

Today, most Asians live in river or mountain valleys. Other Asians live near seacoasts where they farm or fish. Agriculture is the most important economic activity in Asia.

REVIEW How did the mountains of Central Asia influence migration? **Cause and Effect**

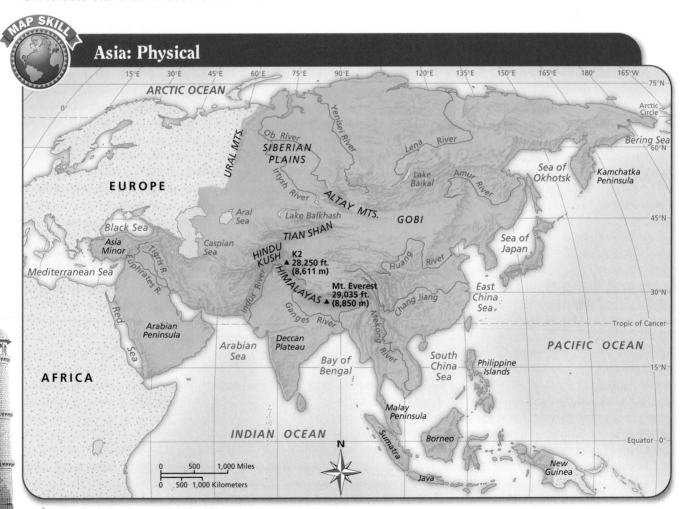

Asia: Physical

▶ The two highest points on Earth are located in Asia.

MAP SKILL Understand Map Symbols **Where are the highest points in Asia located?**

The Mogul Empire

As you read in Unit 2, the Gupta dynasty unified northern India in about A.D. 320. Then different groups of people began to invade India from 455 to the early 1500s. The Huns and Muslims from other parts of Asia were among the invaders who conquered parts of India.

In 1526 a Central Asian leader named **Babur** (BAH ber) seized power in parts of northern India. This marked the beginning of the Mogul (MOH gahl) Empire. During his four-year rule, Babur conquered much of northern India. Babur's son succeeded him, but it was Babur's grandson, **Akbar** (AK bahr), who became the greatest

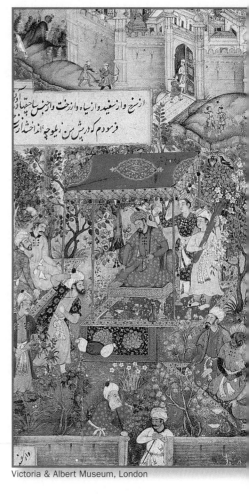

▶ The rise of the Mogul Empire brought Arab and Persian influences to India. In this illustration from 1528, Babur meets with two envoys, or diplomats, in a garden in Agra.

Victoria & Albert Museum, London

Mogul emperor. During his reign from 1556 to 1605, Akbar brought most of the Indian subcontinent under Mogul rule. He made his capital city at Agra.

In order to keep his empire unified, Akbar tried to win the loyalty of his non-Muslim subjects. He reformed and strengthened the central government. Akbar then organized the Empire into provinces, districts, and villages, each with its own administration, or government officials.

Akbar made changes that helped both the nobility and farmers. Nobles were allowed to keep their families' territories. In return, they had to recognize Akbar as emperor, pay taxes to the government, and supply troops on demand.

The most unusual part of Akbar's government was his method of tax collection. Akbar's land tax was equal to one-third of the value of the crops produced on the land each year. The tax was applied to every member of the Empire, including nobles and peasants. This was not a common practice by rulers at this time, as past rulers had only taxed the crops of farmers.

REVIEW How did Akbar govern his empire?
Summarize

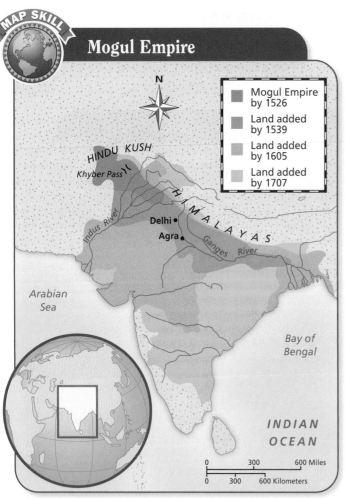

MAP SKILL

Mogul Empire

N

Mogul Empire by 1526
Land added by 1539
Land added by 1605
Land added by 1707

HINDU KUSH
Khyber Pass
HIMALAYAS
Indus River
Delhi
Agra
Ganges River

Arabian Sea

Bay of Bengal

INDIAN OCEAN

0   300   600 Miles
0   300   600 Kilometers

▶ The Mogul Empire expanded until 1707. By 1739 the Persians had massacred much of the population of Delhi, and the Empire weakened.

MAP SKILL Use a Map Key *In what direction(s) did the Mogul Empire expand between 1605 and 1707?*

348

From Rise to Fall

The Mogul emperors were Muslims who ruled a largely Hindu nation. Under Akbar, some Hindus served as Mogul generals and governors. Other Hindus served as administrators and clerks. Hindus and Muslims were working, living, and interacting peacefully. Soon, the Mogul Empire came to be among the richest and most powerful in the world.

Akbar's grandson, **Shah Jahan** (SHAH juh HAHN), ruled from 1628 to 1658. He was responsible for the construction of the greatest building in India, the Taj Mahal. The Taj Mahal was built to honor the memory of Shah Jahan's wife, Mumtaz.

When Aurangzeb (or ANG seb), Shah Jahan's son, took his place, Indians found themselves under a harsh ruler. Aurangzeb forced Hindus, as well as other non-Muslims, to pay a special tax. Hindus held Aurangzeb responsible for destroying many Hindu temples and trying to force Hindus to convert to Islam. Aurangzeb's policies were very unpopular. As a result, the people of western

▶ **Shah Jahan built the Taj Mahal as a large tomb for his wife, Mumtaz Mahal, pictured here.**

India rebelled. Then many local leaders in the south rebelled. The Mogul Empire began to crumble. By the mid-1700s, Mogul control was limited to the area around the city of Delhi in northern India.

REVIEW How did Aurangzeb's policies affect the Hindus in India? *Cause and Effect*

Summarize the Lesson

- **c. 320** The Gupta dynasty unified northern India.
- **455** Huns and other groups invaded India.
- **1526** The Mogul Empire was established by Babur.

LESSON 1   REVIEW

Check Facts and Main Ideas

1. ⟳ **Sequence** On a separate piece of paper, list the following events in correct chronological order. 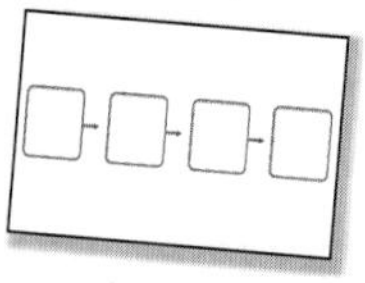
   - Mogul forces control much of northern India.
   - The Mogul Empire crumbles.
   - Babur establishes Mogul Empire.
   - Akbar rules much of India.

2. Why is there a variety of cultures in Asia?

3. Who was the first Mogul ruler of India?

4. What was unusual about Akbar's tax policy?

5. **Critical Thinking:** *Make Inferences* How would cooperation between the Hindus and Muslims help build a rich and powerful Empire?

Link to ⚭ Writing

Write an Announcement You are a member of the nobility in India. Compose a flyer or announcement for a meeting to protest Akbar's tax system. Your announcement will be posted in the village square. Be sure to give reasons for your views.

500   **1000**   **1500**

589
The Sui dynasty
unifies China.

1206
Genghis Khan forms
a unified Mongolia.

1433
China closes
its ports to
foreigners.

1406
Construction begins on the Forbidden City.

MONGOLIA
Beijing •
CHINA

PREVIEW

Focus on the Main Idea
Medieval Chinese dynasties made several significant contributions to trade and technology.

PLACES
Forbidden City
China
Mongolia
Beijing

PEOPLE
Wu Hou
Genghis Khan
Kublai Khan
Zheng He

TERMS
Sui dynasty
Tang dynasty
Song dynasty
Mongol (Yuan)
  dynasty
Ming dynasty

Chinese Dynasties

You Are There

1421: You're standing at the south gate of the Forbidden City. You're excited that your family has sent you here to be a servant to the royal family. You're one of the few people allowed inside the Forbidden City. You can't wait to explore the 9,999 rooms.

You first notice that the walled city is rectangular. After you cross a long, deep moat, you reach the brick walls surrounding the city. The red bricks glow with the color that symbolizes joy. Inside the gate, you see that the buildings—all made of wood—are coated in gold-colored paint, which is reserved for the royal family. Your attention is drawn to the yellow glazed tile roofs. The decorations in the palace are made of gold. Even the bricks on the ground shine! All of these details and ornaments have a special meaning to the history and traditions of China. You feel honored to be chosen to spend your life within the city, serving the royal family.

Main Idea and Details As you read, identify the major contributions of the Chinese dynasties.

Sui, Tang, and Song Dynasties

The **Forbidden City,** which still stands in **China** today, was built by one of the greatest Chinese dynasties. A summary of China's dynasties between the late sixth and mid-seventeenth centuries, along with some of their accomplishments, appears in the table to the right.

Before the **Sui** (SWAY) **dynasty,** China suffered through nearly four centuries of unrest. In 589 the Sui dynasty reunified the country. However, rulers made harsh demands on the people. High taxes and forced labor caused the collapse of the Sui dynasty.

The **Tang dynasty** is considered one of China's greatest dynasties. Empress **Wu Hou** (WOO JOW) came to power in the early years of the Tang dynasty. She was China's first female ruler. Her position was unusual. A Chinese philosopher claimed that having a woman rule would be as unnatural as having "a hen crow like a rooster at daybreak."

But Empress Wu Hou proved him wrong. She strengthened the civil service examinations. Wu Hou even included writing poetry as a requirement for high-ranking government jobs. As a result, literature and fine arts flourished under Tang rule.

Under Wu Hou, trade expanded, and China's contact and interaction with people and cultures of central and western Asia increased. Following the Tang dynasty were more than 50 years of warfare and corruption.

In 960 the **Song dynasty** united warring groups and established a strong central rule. Trade provided a large source of income for the government. The iron plow improved agricultural production. More efficient methods for producing iron were discovered. Iron could now be used as body armor for soldiers and as construction material for bridges.

REVIEW Which dynasty reunified China after 400 years of unrest? **Main Idea and Details**

FACT FILE

Dynasty	Achievements and Advancements
Sui, 581–618	• Canal system connecting waterways is established. Grand Canal eventually will carry water throughout China.
Tang, 618–907	• Civil service examinations bring talented people to government. • Block printing allows pages to be reprinted. • Paper money first printed
Five Dynasties and Ten Kingdoms, 907–960	• Widespread use of block printing helps spread ability to read.
Song, 960–1279 	• First military use of gunpowder • First known use of fractions • Printers use movable type. • First chain-driven mechanism for celestial clock (tells time of day, day of month, and moon movements)
Mongol (Yuan), 1280–1368 	• China leads world in sailing expertise. • Great age of Chinese playwriting • Expert horsemanship skills
Ming, 1368–1644 	• Improvements in ceramic glazes, the potter's wheel, and high-temperature kilns produce high-quality porcelain. • The Great Wall is reinforced and extended to protect against northern invaders.

Mongol and Ming Dynasties

Near the end of the Song dynasty, a warrior leader came to power. His name was Temujin, and he united the nomadic, or wandering, groups of northern Asia to form a unified **Mongolia** in 1206. These groups named Temujin **Genghis Khan** (JEHNG gihs kahn), or universal ruler. Genghis Khan expanded his empire until his death in 1227.

Terror was Genghis Khan's greatest weapon. He ordered his army to give no mercy:

> **"The greatest happiness is to vanquish [conquer] your enemies, to chase them before you, to rob them of their wealth."**

▶ **In this thirteenth-century tapestry, Kublai Khan's army attacks the Chinese near the Chang Jiang River.**

His army, some 110,000 men, was loyal and disciplined. Mongol warriors perfected their horsemanship skills and could shoot arrows even while riding at top speed. Most had as many as four horses so that a fresh and energetic horse was always available.

Genghis Khan defeated the peoples of northern China and Persia. But his sons expanded the empire even more after his death. His grandson, **Kublai Khan,** conquered both southern China and Burma by 1280. This conquest marked the beginning of the **Mongol, or Yuan, dynasty.** It was the first time China had a non-Chinese ruler. By 1294 Mongol power reached its height.

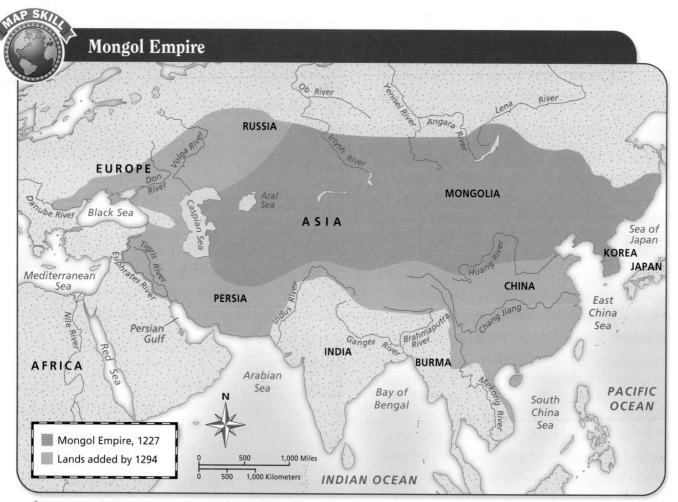

MAP SKILL

Mongol Empire

Legend:
- Mongol Empire, 1227
- Lands added by 1294

0   500   1,000 Miles
0   500   1,000 Kilometers

▶ **The Mongol Empire at the time of the Yuan dynasty was extensive. After Genghis Khan's death, lands he had conquered were ruled by his sons.**

MAP SKILL Use Intermediate Directions *After 1227 in which directions did the Mongol Empire expand?*

Despite the terror that the Mongols used in their conquests, they also made improvements in the lands they conquered. They improved roads and water travel. The Mongols recognized that trade brought wealth and made sure that travel was safe for traders throughout the empire. World traveler Ibn Battuta visited China during the Mongol dynasty. Battuta described the safety of travel in China:

> *"You can travel all alone across the land for nine months without fear, even if you are carrying much wealth."*

After several decades of conflict and natural disasters, the Mongols were overthrown, and the Ming dynasty came to power in 1368. At its height, the Ming dynasty ruled as many as 100 million people. There were great achievements made in the sciences and the arts.

For protection, the Ming dynasty emperors continued to strengthen and add onto the Great Wall. (Look on pages 110–111 to review the time line of the Great Wall.) Construction of the emperor's palace began in 1406. The palace was located in the heart of Beijing. Named the Forbidden City and occupied by the emperor in 1421, the palace was actually a collection of hundreds of buildings, surrounded by walls that were up to 35 feet tall. Only the government's highest officials could enter the Forbidden City.

During the Ming dynasty, people began to believe that China had the greatest civilization in the world. They believed that anything—and anyone—from outside of China should be avoided. As a result, China entered a long period of little contact with foreigners—but not before setting out on great voyages to other countries.

REVIEW How did the Mongol, or Yuan, dynasty show its concern for trade? **Cause and Effect**

▶ The Forbidden City was laid out in the form of a rectangle because the Chinese believed that Earth was square.

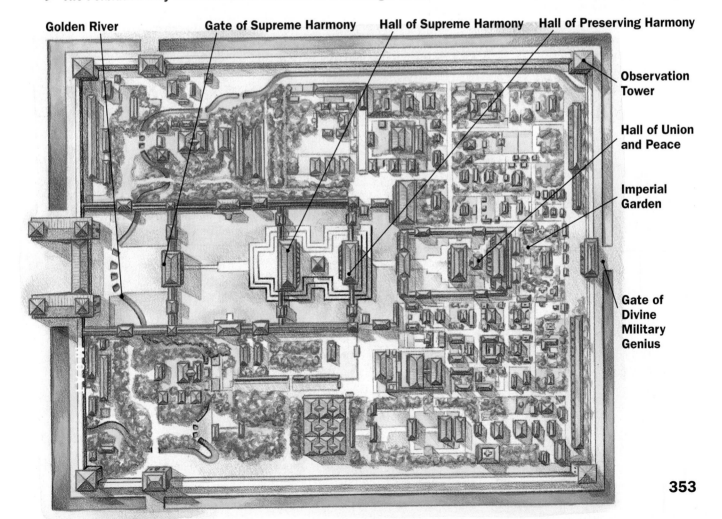

Golden River   Gate of Supreme Harmony   Hall of Supreme Harmony   Hall of Preserving Harmony

Observation Tower

Hall of Union and Peace

Imperial Garden

Gate of Divine Military Genius

Paper, Printing, and Books

Paper and printing were very important Chinese inventions. Credit for the successful manufacture of paper is given to Tsai Lun, an official of the imperial workshops, in A.D. 105. The first paper was made from silk rags. Later, other fibrous materials were used such as bamboo and mulberry bark. During the Han dynasty, there was a great demand for paper from the civil service. Paper was produced in large quantities in government factories. In the ninth century, large-scale woodblock printing was developed, making reading material available to more people.

*Soft, springy
brush tip probably
made of wolf hair*

Woodblock Printing
Since the ninth century, the Chinese printed books from large wooden blocks. The characters were carved in reverse. A print was taken by inking the surface of the block, laying a piece of paper over it, and then rubbing gently with a dry brush.

Seal Prints
Seals were the first form of printing used in China. They were impressed on official documents, personal letters, and artwork.

A Treasured Possession
This decorative writing brush from the Ming dynasty is made of lacquered, or varnished, wood.

*A classical garden
is illustrated in
mother-of-pearl inlay.*

*Book cover with
colorful flowers*

Stylish Notepaper
This collection of illustrative papers is an example of colored woodblock printing. In sixteenth-century China, colored woodblock printing flourished. Scholars used beautifully designed papers for decorative letters. The illustrations were intended to be written over.

China Explores

The Ming dynasty was a time of advancement in exploration. Even before the Europeans set sail to find sea routes to the East, Chinese explorer **Zheng He** (JUNG HUH) went westward. He led the first of seven voyages in 1405. His crews numbered more than 25,000 men. As many as 300 ships went on a single expedition.

Zheng He traveled to Southeast Asia and India. Later, he traveled to Africa and Southwest Asia. The Ming emperor encouraged Zheng He's expeditions. He spent a lot of money filling expedition ships with riches such as gold, silver, and silk. He asked that Zheng He give them as gifts to the people he encountered on his voyages.

The emperor hoped that China would be seen by others as a great and wealthy power. He also hoped that expensive gifts would encourage other countries to send envoys to China. At first,

▶ **During the Ming dynasty, China became a major sea power led by Admiral Zheng He.**

foreign countries began to send envoys. However, the Ming emperor died and the expensive voyages stopped by 1433. Under a new emperor, China soon cut itself off from the rest of the world, welcoming few foreigners.

REVIEW Did Zheng He explore west before or after the Europeans explored east?
⟳ Sequence

Summarize the Lesson

- **589** The Sui dynasty unified China.
- **c. 1206** Genghis Khan formed a unified Mongolia.
- **1406** Construction of the Forbidden City began.
- **1433** China closed its ports to foreigners.

LESSON 2   REVIEW

Check Facts and Main Ideas

1. Main Idea and Details On a separate piece of paper, fill in the missing details below.

> The Mongol dynasty made several improvements in China.

> China was safe for travelers.

> [ ]

> [ ]

2. Identify some of the contributions made by Chinese dynasties.

3. Where and what is the Forbidden City?

4. What was the purpose behind Zheng He's expeditions abroad?

5. Critical Thinking: _Make Inferences_ What benefits might government officials have if positions in China were based on examination results, rather than family ties?

Link to ∞ Writing

Write a Press Release You are the communications director for Empress Wu Hou. Your task is to write a press release, informing the public that civil service examinations must be taken in order to qualify for government jobs.

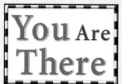

800	1000	1200	1400

802
Jayavarman II reunites the Khmer kingdom.

1113
Suryavarman II takes the throne.

about 1120
Construction begins on Angkor Wat.

1431
Invaders destroy the capital city of Angkor.

The Khmer

PREVIEW

Focus on the Main Idea
For hundreds of years, the Khmer culture dominated the peninsula of Southeast Asia.

PLACES
Cambodia
Laos
Indochina Peninsula
Angkor
Angkor Wat

PEOPLE
Jayavarman II
Suryavarman II

TERMS
deva-raja
absolute power

You Are There
On a mid-winter break, you and your family travel to Southeast Asia. It's the middle of the cool, dry season in Cambodia. What a great day to explore part of Angkor Wat (ANG kwar WAHT), one of the great temples built in the twelfth century! The temple is rectangular in shape. As you walk along the paved main entryway to the temple, you see that it is surrounded by artificial lakes, canals, and moats. These are used for water control and rice irrigation. The central pineapple-shaped tower in front of you stands more than 200 feet tall. Carvings on the walls to your left show scenes of war and legends. To your right are carvings describing everyday life. Everywhere you look, carvings of dancers greet you.

Cause and Effect As you read, identify the causes and effects of the rise and fall of the Khmer.

▶ The centuries-old Angkor Wat is the world's largest religious building. Construction of the temple began about 1120.

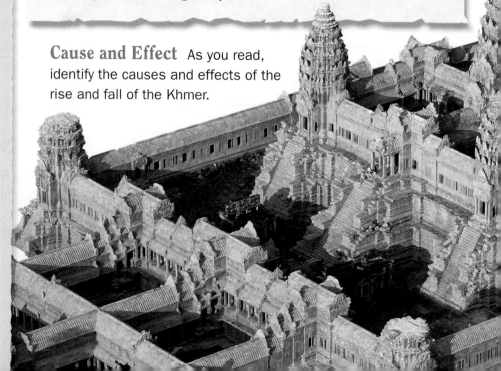

The Khmer Kingdom

The Khmer (kuh MER) kingdom was one of the wealthiest kingdoms in Southeast Asia. *Khmer* is also the name of the people who lived in the kingdom.

In the sixth century, the Khmer ruled the lands we know today as **Cambodia** and **Laos** on the **Indochina Peninsula.** The Khmer civilization was influenced by Indian culture. Buddhism also flourished, along with the worship of Shiva and of other Hindu gods.

Internal conflicts divided the kingdom during the eighth century. But **Jayavarman II** (jah yah VAHR mahn) reunited the kingdom in 802. He was crowned king according to Hindu rites, which declared he was a **deva-raja** (DEE vah RA juh), or god-king. Being a deva-raja allowed Khmer rulers to act with **absolute power,** or the power to control every part of society. They used this power to form large armies that could defend the kingdom, as well as to invade its neighbors. In addition, the kings could force both the Khmer and slaves to work on the extensive irrigation system.

The irrigation system was key to the successful economy. During the monsoon season, the large reservoirs, levees, moats, and ponds helped prevent the farmland from being flooded. They also stored water to be used during the dry season. This irrigation system allowed

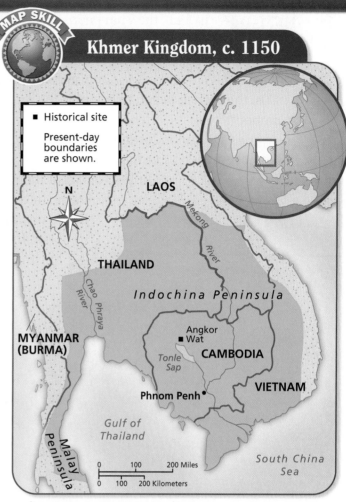

MAP SKILL **Khmer Kingdom, c. 1150**

- ■ Historical site
- Present-day boundaries are shown.

N

LAOS

THAILAND

Indochina Peninsula

Mekong River

Chao Phraya River

MYANMAR (BURMA)

Angkor ■ Wat

Tonle Sap

CAMBODIA

VIETNAM

Phnom Penh •

Gulf of Thailand

Malay Peninsula

South China Sea

0 100 200 Miles
0 100 200 Kilometers

▶ By the twelfth century, the deva-rajas of the Khmer kingdom controlled a vast region of the Indochina Peninsula.

MAP SKILL Region *In what region of the world was the Khmer kingdom located?*

farmers to grow crops as many as two to three times a year.

Agricultural surpluses helped strengthen the kingdom's economy. For more than 500 years, the Khmer kingdom was an important influence in Southeast Asia.

The first royal city was built at **Angkor** in the tenth century. This marked the beginning of the empire's golden age. Under **Suryavarman II** (sur yuh VAHR mun) the empire reached its peak in the early twelfth century. During his rule from 1113 to 1150, he oversaw the construction of the magnificent towers of the temple **Angkor Wat.**

REVIEW How did the position of deva-raja affect expansion of Khmer rule? *Cause and Effect*

The Khmer

In 1431 the Thai people invaded and destroyed the capital city of Angkor. The Khmer kingdom never recovered. In addition, Angkor was ruled by one or another of its neighbors for hundreds of years. In the late 1800s, the French began to colonize the area. But by 1953, Cambodia won its independence. The Khmer, as a people, remained in Cambodia and today make up some 90 percent of the people who live there.

In 1993 a part of the former Khmer kingdom proclaimed itself the Kingdom of Cambodia, or Kampuchea (cam POOH chee uh). Currently, the head of state is King Norodom Sihanouk (SEE ha nook). The government is led by an elected prime minister.

▶ Rice, rubber, cassava, sweet potatoes, corn, soy beans and tobacco are the main agricultural products of present-day Cambodia. This woman is transporting rice stalks.

A Stone Wonder

With some Indian influence on style, the Khmer became very skilled in art, architecture, and sculpture. The earliest known Khmer monuments are isolated towers of brick. They probably date from the seventh century. Later, the Khmer built small temples set on stepped pyramids. Over time, they added more and more covered galleries. The temples became more elaborate. Soon stone replaced brick. Then, carved stone replaced plain stone.

By the end of Khmer dominance in the region, more than 70 huge temple and monument complexes stood at Angkor. Many of the temple walls have scenes of everyday life or battles. Some show men fishing, while others are of markets and entertainment. When French naturalist Henri Mouhot came upon Angkor in the mid-nineteenth century, he considered the ruins of the ancient Khmer capital to be:

> *"Grander than anything left by Greece or Rome."*

Of the dozens of temples, Angkor Wat stands as the finest example of Khmer architecture. It covers nearly one square mile.

The builders of Angkor Wat wanted to honor the Hindu god Vishnu. Later, Angkor Wat became the tomb of the Khmer king who had ordered its construction. Nearly 50,000 artisans, workers, and slaves worked on the temple, which took nearly 40 years to complete. Today, Angkor Wat appears on Cambodia's flag. It is there to remind people of the Khmer culture and its achievements.

▶ Hinduism spread from South Asia to the Khmer kingdom in its early history. This stone statue is of the Hindu god Vishnu, the protector of the world.

Musee National de Phnom Penh, Cambodia/
Bridgeman Art Library Int'l. Ltd. (U.S.)

▶ This Cambodian stamp featuring Angkor Wat was produced after Cambodia won its independence from France.

CAMBODGE 9$ POSTES
ANGKOR VAT

REVIEW What have we learned about the Khmer from the temples and monuments they left behind? **Draw Conclusions**

Summarize the Lesson

- **802** Jayavarman II reunited Khmer kingdom.
- **1113** Suryavarman II took the throne.
- **about 1120** Construction began on Angkor Wat.
- **1431** Invaders destroyed the capital city of Angkor.

LESSON 3   REVIEW

Check Facts and Main Ideas

1. Cause and Effect On a separate piece of paper, copy the diagram below and fill in one cause or effect for each blank.

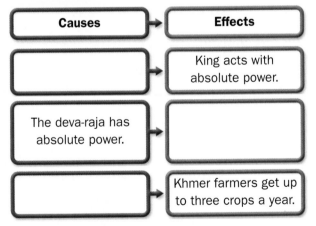

Causes		Effects
	→	King acts with absolute power.
The deva-raja has absolute power.	→	
	→	Khmer farmers get up to three crops a year.

2. Where was the first royal city located?

3. What role did irrigation play in the Khmer economy?

4. Why were the Khmer able to dominate Southeast Asia for centuries?

5. Critical Thinking: *Make Generalizations* Why do you think the Khmer were willing to devote so much time and energy to constructing the temple complex?

Link to 🔗 Art

Make a Poster Suppose you are a member of a team charged with carving a vast expanse of stone for the temple. Make a poster describing the type of artisan you would need. Be sure to describe the work, include job qualifications, and show pictures of designs you would like to see on the temple.

500   1000   1500

1000s
Lady Murasaki Shikibu writes *The Tale of Genji.*

1200s
The Mongols make unsuccessful attempts to invade Japan.

1603
Beginning of rule by the Tokugawa shoguns

JAPAN   Edo (Tokyo)
Kyoto
Osaka
Nagasaki

PREVIEW

Focus on the Main Idea
Japan became isolated, or separated, from most of the world but still carried on some trade.

PLACES
Edo
Kyoto
Osaka
Nagasaki

PEOPLE
Murasaki Shikibu
Toyotomi Hideyoshi
Tokugawa Ieyasu

VOCABULARY
artistocrat
samurai
typhoon
daimyo
shogun

TERMS
Tokugawa dynasty
policy of isolation

▶ Farmers, merchants, warriors, and artisans were stopped at checkpoints along the main road of Japan, as this nineteenth-century woodcut shows.

Japan in Isolation

You Are There

1603: You're a messenger on the *Tokaido,* the main road from Kyoto (kee OH toh) to Edo (modern Tokyo). Although it's early morning, the road is busy. You're pushed and shoved as you move through a crowd of poor farmers and laborers. They're wearing cotton robes, called kimonos, and straw sandals. Ahead of you is a group of wealthy farmers. They're wearing kimonos with fancy designs and wooden sandals. You stop at one of 53 check-points along the road. At each, guards carefully check people for swords or other weapons. Most of the people at the checkpoint carry only turnips, cabbage, and other vegetables. A merchant takes out coins to pay a tax on the goods he plans to sell. The guards then place an official stamp on the goods. When they see that you have no weapons, they point you toward the gate that leads to Edo.

Cause and Effect As you read, identify the causes and effects of isolation on Japan.

Early Japan

Messengers traveled all over **Edo,** one of the major cities in unified Japan. Early in its history, Japan was made up of 100 states that were scattered over four islands. By the early 600s, these states were united under the country's first constitution.

Contact with China and Korea brought Buddhism and the Chinese system of writing to Japan. A unique blend of cultures began to develop toward the end of the eighth century. In the early 1000s, Lady **Murasaki Shikibu** (mer a SA kee shee KEE boo) wrote what is considered to be the world's first novel, *The Tale of Genji.*

Noble families soon occupied an important place in the government. They worked to weaken the emperor's power. For example, they created private estates, or plots of land that were free from the emperor's interference and taxes. The government, as well as the **aristocrats,** or nobles, began to rely on the warrior class for protection. These warriors, called **samurai** (SAM uh rye), defended their land and kept order in society. In 1192 the samurai took away all ruling powers from the emperor.

In the late 1200s, the Mongols in China made two attempts to invade and conquer Japan. During each attempt, the invaders were met by a **typhoon,** a tropical storm with heavy winds and rough seas. Typhoons helped Japan defeat any invaders.

▶ Some people name Lady Murasaki Shikibu as the world's first modern novelist.

These victories led to a feeling of national pride. The Japanese believed that the *kamikaze,* or "divine wind," destroyed the Mongols because the Japanese were a divinely protected people.

The years that followed the Mongol attacks were filled with a series of conflicts. The most powerful samurai became **daimyo** (DY mee oh), or ruling leaders, who controlled many other samurai and governed large areas of farmland. During the 1500s, the daimyo fought one another for power and land. As a result, Japan fell into a long civil war.

In 1590 General **Toyotomi Hideyoshi** (hee day HOH shee) united several warring groups, bringing most of Japan under his control. After his death, an ambitious daimyo, **Tokugawa Ieyasu** (toh kuh GAH wah ee YAY yah soo), rose to power, establishing the **Tokugawa dynasty.**

REVIEW What was the difference between a samurai and a daimyo? **Compare and Contrast**

▶ The Himeji Castle was built by the Akamatsu family in the 1300s. It was reconstructed by Toyotomi Hideyoshi in the late 1500s.

▶ **Tokugawa Ieyasu was the first in a long line of Tokugawa dynasty shoguns who ruled Japan for more than 250 years.**

Bridgeman Art Library Int'l. Ltd. (U.S.)

Tokugawa Rule

In 1603 the emperor gave Tokugawa Ieyasu the title of **shogun** (SHOH guhn), a special, high-ranking military office. This marked the start of 265 years of rule under the Tokugawa dynasty shoguns.

As a result, shoguns of the Tokugawa dynasty controlled foreign trade and operated gold and silver mines. They ruled major cities, including **Kyoto**, **Osaka** (oh SAH kuh), and Edo, the shogun's capital. In addition, shoguns controlled the emperor's land holdings, or about 25 percent of the country's farmland. (See the map to the right.)

The daimyo controlled the remaining 75 percent of Japan's farmland. There were about 270 daimyo, and each governed his own domain. The shogun had to share authority with the daimyo. This meant that the daimyo, not the shogun, issued laws and collected taxes.

During the rule of the Tokugawa dynasty shoguns, there was a strict four-class system. The samurai were at the top of the social system. They were originally warriors, but without wars they became members of the ruling class. Merchants, artisans, and farmers made up the remaining classes.

The divisions between the four social classes were essential to Tokugawa shogun power. Shoguns would make agreements with local daimyo, playing one group against another.

Because the shoguns took control of Japan's international trade, daimyos could not gain too

much wealth and power. Soon, most foreigners were forced out of the country. Only a few Dutch and Chinese traders were allowed to return to Japan to conduct business in one port, **Nagasaki.**

The shoguns outlawed traveling abroad and banned nearly all foreign books. The Dutch, who were from the Netherlands in Europe, brought books for Japanese scholars to read. These books helped scholars learn about studies in Europe and elsewhere. Shipbuilding, mapmaking, astronomy, and medicine were among the subjects of Japanese interest.

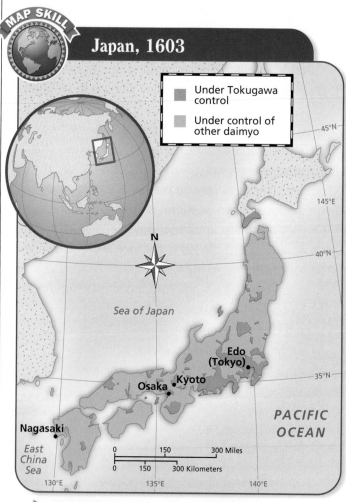

MAP SKILL

Japan, 1603

Under Tokugawa control

Under control of other daimyo

45°N

145°E

N

40°N

Sea of Japan

Edo (Tokyo)

35°N

Osaka · Kyoto

PACIFIC OCEAN

Nagasaki

East China Sea

0   150   300 Miles
0 150 300 Kilometers

130°E   135°E   140°E

▶ **The emperor owned about 25 percent of Japan's farmland.**

MAP SKILL Use a Map Key *Where was most of the emperor's land concentrated?*

362

The **policy of isolation** cut off Japan from the goods and culture of most countries. The only countries Japan still traded with were the Netherlands, China, and Korea, because shoguns wanted some contact with the outside world. In fact, shogun control caused trade to increase. The merchant class grew, and Edo became a large city. Dutchman Engelbert Kampfer commented during an official trade visit in 1691:

> *"The roads are always thronged [crowded] by ordinary citizens on business . . . . It is on most days more crowded than a public street in . . . Europe."*

The shogun government of the Tokugawa dynasty remained in place for about 250 years, but it eventually fell into debt. As the merchant class began to grow wealthier and more powerful, taxes were raised, causing farmers to riot. As a result, the class system began to crumble.

REVIEW How did the Tokugawa shoguns try to isolate Japan? **Cause and Effect**

Summarize the Lesson

- **600s** Japanese culture was influenced by China and Korea.
- **1603** Rule by shoguns of the Tokugawa dynasty began.

▶ **A full suit of samurai armor could weigh up to 40 pounds.**

LESSON 4   REVIEW

Check Facts and Main Ideas

1. **Cause and Effect** On a separate piece of paper, copy the diagram below. Fill in the missing cause or effect.

Causes	→	Effects
The shogun controls all foreign trade.	→	
Japan follows a policy of isolation.	→	
	→	Farmers riot.

2. Which Japanese city was the shogun's capital during the Tokugawa dynasty?

3. What is the difference between a samurai and a shogun?

4. How did Japan's policy of isolation affect Japanese trade and culture?

5. **Critical Thinking:** *Make Inferences* Why did shoguns allow some trade with other countries?

Link to ◖◗ Reading

Detect Bias Otsuki Gentaku wrote this passage in the 1700s after reading a book brought over by Dutch traders during Japan's policy of isolation. What biases has he learned from the Dutch book?

In terms of size, Egypt, a territory of Africa, should be termed the center of the world . . . . China and Japan are at the eastern end of the world, and Holland and the other European nations at the northwest.

363

Gather and Report Information

What? There is a wide variety of resources you can use to gather and report information on a particular subject. Your search for information will be easier if you are familiar with the resources available, as well as the kinds of information they contain. This is true whether you choose an online resource or a bound book.

Your choices for gathering information include primary sources and general resources such as an almanac, atlas, encyclopedia, dictionary, yearbook, thesaurus, guidebook, and telephone directory. In addition, there are specialized resources such as a biographical dictionary, geographical dictionary, and books of famous quotations.

Why? Every day more and more information is available about locations, people, and events. One way to organize the information is to group similar information in a single reference source.

An atlas or a gazetteer gives the exact location of Tokyo, Japan. Look up Tokyo in the alphabetical listing. The location of Tokyo, Japan, is about 35°N, 139°E.

An encyclopedia is a reference book that gives information on many subjects or concentrates on a single topic.

How? To use the reference sources efficiently, you need to gain some familiarity with their contents. Suppose you wanted to learn more about Japan, the country you just studied.

A general encyclopedia will help you learn about the history of Japan. Look for the information under the guideword, or key word, *Japan*. A general encyclopedia will have information about the *samurai* and the *shoguns*.

An almanac might be best to gather current information on how many cell phones are in use in Japan today. Find *cellular telephones* in the almanac's general index. Turn to the page listed and you will find a table giving the number of cell phones in use in several different countries.

Most almanacs are published once a year. They often contain many kinds of information such as a calendar, important dates and events, and facts about governments, history, geography, and weather. An almanac may also give figures on population, industry, and sports.

Gather the following information from at least two sources. Report both on the information you found and the resource you used.

1 How tall is Mount Fuji in Japan? How was it formed?

2 How was the *Tokaido* important to Japan?

3 What are the main exports and imports of Japan today?

▶ **The key to gathering and reporting information is to know which type of resource to use.**

500   700

455
Huns and other groups
began to invade India.

589
The Sui dynasty
unified China.

Chapter Summary

Sequence

On a separate piece of paper, put the following events on a time line
in correct chronological order.

200	700	1200	1700

- Gupta dynasty rules northern India.
- Genghis Khan forms a unified Mongolia.
- Angkor Wat is constructed.
- Taj Mahal is constructed.
- Tokugawa shogun rule begins in Japan.

Vocabulary

Match each word with the correct definition or
description.

1 aristocrat
(p. 361)

2 samurai (p. 361)

3 daimyo (p. 361)

4 shogun (p. 362)

5 typhoon (p. 361)

a. warrior class

b. noble of a high
social class

c. powerful samurai

d. high-ranking
military post

e. tropical storm

People and Terms

Write a sentence explaining why each of the
following terms is important in the study of
Asia. You may use two or more in a single
sentence.

1 Tokugawa Ieyasu
(p. 361)

2 Zheng He
(p. 355)

3 Khmer (p. 357)

4 policy of isola-
tion (p. 363)

5 Suryavarman II
(p. 357)

6 Kublai Khan
(p. 352)

7 Akbar (p. 348)

8 Wu Hou (p. 351)

9 Murasaki
Shikibu (p. 361)

10 Genghis Khan
(p. 352)

11 Shah Jahan
(p. 349)

12 absolute power
(p. 357)

802
Khmer kingdom was reunited.

about 1206
Genghis Khan formed a unified Mongolia.

1433
China closed its ports to foreigners.

1526
The Mogul Empire was established.

1603
Japan began policy of isolation.

Facts and Main Ideas

1. Why did the Khmer, Chinese, and Japanese peoples tend to be isolated?

2. What was the result of early Japan's interaction with Korea and China?

3. **Time Line** Did China follow a policy of isolation before or after Japan?

4. **Main Idea** How was Akbar's tax policy like others of the time? How was it different?

5. **Main Idea** What major changes occurred in China during the Ming dynasty?

6. **Main Idea** How was irrigation linked to the Khmer economy?

7. **Main Idea** How did the Japanese policy of isolation affect Japanese trade?

8. **Critical Thinking: *Detect Bias*** How would the Japanese scholars determine whether the books they received from the Dutch showed biases?

Internet Activity

To get help with vocabulary, people, and terms, select dictionary, encyclopedia, or almanac from *Social Studies Library* at **www.sfsocialstudies.com.**

Apply Skills

Gather and Report Information

Make a chart with the following information on one of the countries you read about in this chapter: country map, population, major languages, exports and imports, and form of government. Document the information you gather by including a bibliography. You may use pictures or drawings from the sources you use. Present your chart to the class.

On a separate piece of paper, answer the following questions.

1. How many sources did you use to make your chart?

2. What kinds of sources did you use?

3. Why did you choose these sources for the information?

Write About History

1. **Write a biography** of a samurai who has become a daimyo. Be sure to research the characteristics of each class.

2. **Write a civil service test** that you would use to screen people who are applying for government jobs, such as postal workers.

3. **Write a magazine article** telling people about Angkor Wat. Describe the temple and explain who built it and when.

CHAPTER 13

African Empires

Lesson 1

c. 2500 B.C.
The Sahara
The Sahara begins to dry up and people migrate to other parts of Africa.

1

Lesson 2

A.D. 1324
Mali
Mansa Musa, the king of Mali, goes on a pilgrimage to Mecca.

2

Lesson 3

1450
Great Zimbabwe
The Shona people complete the stone enclosures of Great Zimbabwe.

3

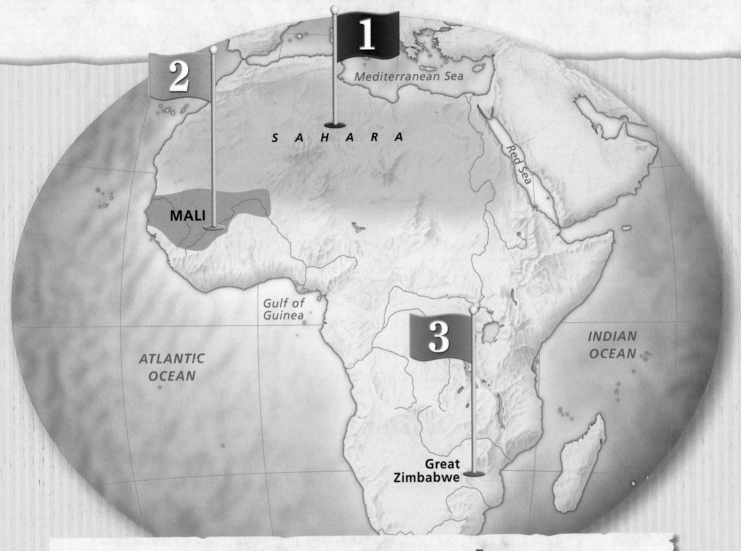

Why We Remember

Powerful African kingdoms were a major source of gold long before they caught the attention of Europeans in the late 1400s. West African states served as middlemen for the gold that came from the south. East African empires and city-states traded gold and iron with the peoples of Europe and Asia. These trade goods made the East and West African empires and city-states wealthy. Trade also helped Islam spread into East and West Africa and Christianity into East Africa. Europeans soon turned their attention to Africa's valuable resources. Today, many of these valuable resources are sold in the United States.

2500 B.C.   1500   500   A.D. 500   1500

c. 2500 B.C.
The Sahara begins to dry up and people migrate to other parts of Africa.

c. 100 B.C.–A.D. 1500
The Bantu people slowly spread across Africa.

SAHARA

PREVIEW

Focus on the Main Idea
People throughout Africa have adapted to a variety of environments.

PLACES
Sahara
Atlas Mountains
Great Rift Valley
Mount Kilimanjaro

VOCABULARY
savanna

TERMS
Bantu

The Geography of Africa

You Are There
You're walking through the desert. One foot sinks into the sand and then the other. A lizard pops its head out of one of the footprints you made in the sand. It dives back in to hide from the sun. You adjust your hat to make sure your head is covered from the scorching sun. Beads of sweat pour down your back. Your clothes are soaked. You look like you've been swimming in a river. How much longer will it be to the next oasis, where you can get a cool drink of water? You feel like you've been walking for days. A few people dressed in blue garments pass you. The men are wearing veils to protect their faces from the blowing sand. All of a sudden, the wind becomes stronger, and the sky turns gray. A sandstorm is coming.

Summarize As you read, summarize the different environments in Africa.

▶ Tuaregs are Berber-speaking peoples who have lived in North Africa since at least 1000 B.C.

370

Climate Zones

The desert that you just read about is in Africa, the second largest continent on Earth after Asia. There are eight climate zones in Africa. The main zones include desert, savanna, rain forest, and Mediterranean.

The desert climate zone is hot and dry. Little vegetation and few animals live in the desert. The **Sahara** is the largest desert in the world. It is located in northern Africa. Look at the map below to see the vast area it covers. Notice that the **Atlas Mountains** separate the Sahara from the Mediterranean Sea. Winds and sandstorms shape the sand dunes that cover about 25 percent of the Sahara.

South of the Sahara lies the **savanna,** or short, grassy plains. About half of Africa is savanna. The soil in the savanna is generally fertile.

▶ **Burchell's zebras graze in the savanna grasslands of a South African nature reserve.**

In areas of the savanna that are drier, people herd cattle.

Tropical rain forest biomes cover a very small area of the continent. Thick vegetation makes farming nearly impossible in this climate region.

The Mediterranean climate on the North African coast and southern tip of Africa is mild. Summers are mostly hot, while winters are generally mild and rainy. Land is fertile in some of these areas, making them suitable for agriculture.

REVIEW How are the climate zones of Africa alike and different? **Compare and Contrast**

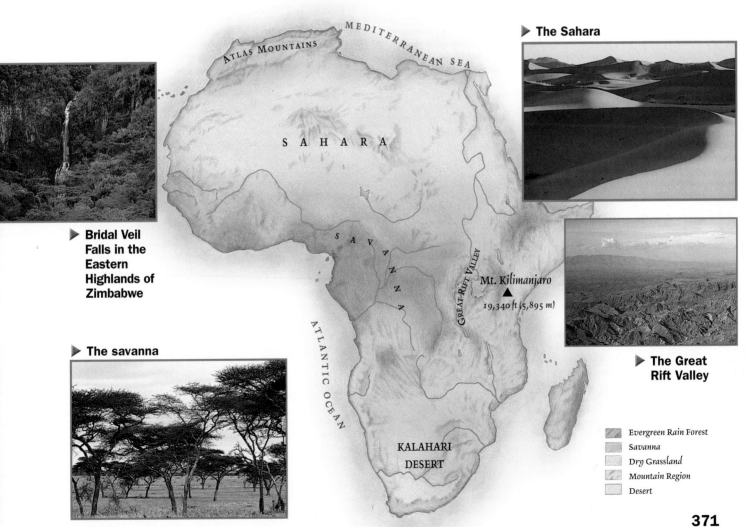

ATLAS MOUNTAINS
MEDITERRANEAN SEA

SAHARA

SAVANNA

GREAT RIFT VALLEY

Mt. Kilimanjaro
▲
19,340 ft (5,895 m)

ATLANTIC OCEAN

KALAHARI DESERT

▶ **The Sahara**

▶ **The Great Rift Valley**

▶ **Bridal Veil Falls in the Eastern Highlands of Zimbabwe**

▶ **The savanna**

Evergreen Rain Forest
Savanna
Dry Grassland
Mountain Region
Desert

371

Mountains and Rivers

The climate in Africa affects the movement of people and goods. As you have read, camel caravans crossed the Sahara in northern Africa. These journeys were dangerous. Traders in the caravans faced sandstorms, high heat, and few water sources. In other parts of Africa, people faced barriers such as mountains, plateaus, and cataracts. Remember how people crossed the cataracts in ancient Egypt and Nubia?

In prehistoric times, a rift, or crack, may have formed in the earth, creating the 4,000-mile-long Great Rift Valley in East Africa. This fertile valley stretches across lakes, highlands, and other, smaller valleys. You can even see it from space! On one of these highlands is Mount Kilimanjaro. At 19,340 feet, it is the highest mountain in Africa.

Plateaus cover much of the interior of Africa. Many rivers flow from the plateaus to the coast. The Zambezi, Congo, and Niger are the major interior rivers in Africa. You have already read about the longest river in Africa and the world, the Nile. Many people used these rivers to move trade goods from place to place. The Red Sea and the Indian Ocean served as ways to transport goods and people to the Middle East.

REVIEW How did people and goods move throughout Africa? **Summarize**

Spread of Peoples

Over time, changes in climate caused people to migrate to other areas of Africa. For example, in ancient times, the Sahara was very different from the way it is today. It contained rivers, grassy plains, and forests. We know this because of prehistoric cave paintings and dried-up riverbeds. Many scientists believe that by about 2500 B.C., the climate began to change. Rain did not fall anymore, and the land dried out.

As the environment changed and resources were used up, people moved to the east and to the south.

▶ Mount Kilimanjaro, the highest mountain in Africa, as viewed from the Great Rift Valley. The Masai people and their herds of cattle live along the Great Rift Valley.

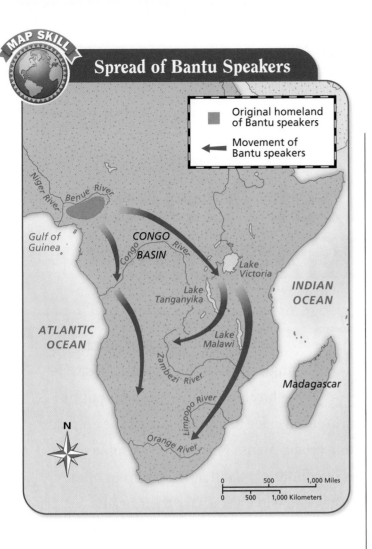

MAP SKILL
Spread of Bantu Speakers

■ Original homeland of Bantu speakers

← Movement of Bantu speakers

Niger River

Benue River

Gulf of Guinea

CONGO BASIN

Congo River

Lake Victoria

Lake Tanganyika

INDIAN OCEAN

ATLANTIC OCEAN

Lake Malawi

Zambezi River

Limpopo River

Madagascar

Orange River

N

0   500   1,000 Miles
0   500   1,000 Kilometers

▶ About 100 B.C., Bantu speakers left the Niger-Benue area.

MAP SKILL Trace Movement on Maps *In which direction did the Bantu speakers move?*

One group of people is considered to be the ancestor of many different African groups today. It is estimated that between about 100 B.C. and A.D. 1500, people living in West Africa began to slowly spread to other parts of Africa. Linguists, or people who study languages, have traced this movement of West Africans by looking at the languages spoken in Africa. The **Bantu** languages are a group of languages spoken in large parts of Africa. Many of the words in these languages are similar. As the Bantu speakers traveled south, their languages spread with them.

REVIEW Why did people move to other parts of Africa? Main Idea and Details

Summarize the Lesson

- **c. 2500 B.C.** The Sahara began to dry up and people migrated to other parts of Africa.

- **c. 100 B.C.–A.D. 1500** The Bantu people slowly moved across Africa.

LESSON 1 REVIEW

Check Facts and Main Ideas

1. **Summarize** On a separate piece of paper, write three short sentences to form the summary below.

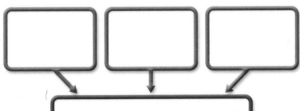

Africa is a diverse continent with many different physical features.

2. Describe the major climate zones of Africa.

3. What are the major rivers of Africa?

4. How did Africans adapt to their environment?

5. **Critical Thinking:** *Make Generalizations* Why do linguists believe that the Bantu speakers spread across Africa?

Link to → Science

Research Climate Zones Research the climate zone that you live in. Go to the library or look on the Internet to help gather information about the climate zone in which you live. Do you live in a type of climate zone that can also be found in Africa?

800	1000	1200	1400	1600

A.D. 900
Height of the empire of Ghana

1324
Mansa Musa sets out on a pilgrimage to Mecca.

1591
Empire of Songhai declines.

Koumbi
Jenne-jenno
Timbuktu
Gao

West African Kingdoms

PREVIEW

Focus on the Main Idea
Many kingdoms developed in the savanna and forested areas of West Africa.

PLACES
Ghana
Koumbi
Mali
Timbuktu
Jenne-jenno
Gao

PEOPLE
Sumanguru
Sundiata
Mansa Musa
Sonni Ali

VOCABULARY
griot

You Are There

You're one of thousands of people traveling with your king, Mansa Musa. He has brought you along on his pilgrimage to Mecca. You travel for many days across the Sahara before reaching Egypt. Mansa Musa pulls out some of the hundreds of pounds of gold that he has brought on the journey. The people in Cairo shake their heads. All this gold means that gold prices will be lowered for years. The king buys the finest clothing for his top officials. Mansa Musa is a generous king. You have even heard that he gives handfuls of gold dust to beggars who come up to him.

As you leave the city, you hear praise singers honoring your king. They sing of his generosity and kindness.

Summarize As you read, summarize the details about the West African kingdoms.

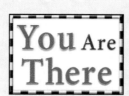

► This Spanish map from the fourteenth century shows Mansa Musa (seated, wearing a crown) during his pilgrimage to Mecca, which began in 1324.

Ghana

Gold was a valuable resource to the empires of West Africa. It made them very wealthy and brought in trade goods from other lands. The ancient kingdom of **Ghana** was so well known that knowledge of its trade in gold had reached as far as Baghdad (modern Iraq) by the eighth century. (The kingdom of Ghana is not to be confused with the present-day country of Ghana in Africa.)

Most of what is known about Ghana comes from the Arabs, who wrote down what they heard about the kingdom from traders and travelers. Ghana had existed since about A.D. 300. It was founded by the Soninke (suhn IHN kay) people who began to act as middlemen for the gold that was mined to the south of Ghana.

People in Ghana probably farmed, fished, and herded cattle. They produced many goods to trade with others. Berber peoples in North Africa led traders across the Sahara. Thieves often attacked camel caravans. But the Berbers still tried to keep the thieves away so that the trade routes would be safe.

Safe trade routes meant that Ghana's capital, **Koumbi,** remained a major center of trade. By the late 900s, Ghana was thriving and had become a great trading empire.

▶ **This person is filling shallow pits with salt water. Once the salt water has evaporated, a cake of dried salt will be retrieved from the pits.**

▶ **These bars of salt are tied together and ready to take to the market.**

Its location between the salt mines in the Sahara and the gold fields in Wangara made the middlemen wealthy and turned Ghana into an empire. Traders in Ghana took gold, copper, and palm oil from the south. From the north, they took salt, glass, and ceramics. Taxes on these goods added more wealth to the empire.

Along with trade goods and wealth came ideas and religion that were brought by Muslim traders. Many of the Soninke people converted to Islam. They also adopted the Arabic system of writing. However, beginning in the 1000s, the Soninke people began to lose control of the empire. Different groups fought for political power. By 1203 King **Sumanguru** defeated the Soninke king and controlled Koumbi. To learn more about Sumanguru, see page 379.

REVIEW How long did the Soninke have control of the empire of Ghana?

↻ **Sequence**

375

Mali

West Africa remained under the control of various smaller states until A.D. 1235. In that year, Sundiata defeated King Sumanguru at the Battle of Kirina and established the empire of Mali. Read more about Sundiata in the biography on page 379. We know about Sundiata's life because of oral stories that are still told today by griots (GREE oats). Griots are professional storytellers.

The empire of Mali was expanded to include more land than had been controlled by the empire of Ghana. People in Mali grew crops such as rice, onions, grains, and yams. They also grew cotton. Although Mali had a strong agricultural economy, it relied on trade for wealth. New discoveries of gold along the Niger River made Mali wealthy. By 1300 Mali had become the most powerful empire in West Africa.

Perhaps the greatest king of Mali to follow Sundiata was his grandson, Mansa Musa. He was a strong Muslim ruler. Many people converted to Islam under his rule.

Mansa Musa is best known for his pilgrimage to Mecca. He took with him thousands of people, hundreds of pounds of gold, dozens of camels, and other supplies. Along the way he stopped in Egypt. His wealth, intelligence, and generosity made a lasting impression on Egyptian writers.

▶ This mosque in present-day Jenné, Mali, was built from mud bricks. The bricks were dried by sunlight. They were then built into walls held together by mud plaster. The wooden sticks are used by people who restore the mosque.

Literature and Social Studies

A Wise Ruler

As you have read, Sundiata was a king of Mali. He made Mali into one of the greatest trading kingdoms in West Africa. We know about him from stories told by griots. This excerpt from *The Royal Kingdoms of Ghana, Mali, and Songhay* by Patricia and Frederick McKissack shows one of the reasons Sundiata was considered a wise ruler.

·····························

Based on experiences learned during his exile, Sundiata set up a system of cultural exchange. His sons and daughters were sent to live in the courts of distant kings, and the princes and the princesses of other rulers were invited to stay at Niani. He wisely reasoned that children who grow up together were less likely to attack one another as adult leaders.

On his return from Mecca, Mansa Musa brought back an Arab architect who built new mosques in **Timbuktu,** one of the major trading cities in Mali. He also brought with him Arab scholars to teach Muslim beliefs and scholarship.

Mansa Musa's pilgrimage to Mecca caught the attention of European mapmakers. The Europeans began to take an interest in the gold and other resources Mali had to offer.

REVIEW What is most significant about the empire of Mali? **Summarize**

Jenne-jenno

Jenne-jenno was an ancient city located southwest of Timbuktu on the Niger River. It was the oldest known city in sub-Saharan Africa. People first settled there about 200 B.C.

The people of Jenne-jenno fished, kept livestock, and grew crops such as rice and sorghum. Archaeologists believe that the people of Jenne-jenno traded with other peoples long before the empire of Mali did.

During the height of the empire of Mali, trade goods were brought by land to Jenne-jenno from the south and west. From Jenne-jenno the trade goods would be shipped up river to Timbuktu.

After A.D. 1200, the city of Jenne-jenno started to weaken. It was completely abandoned by about 1400. No one is certain why the people left. However, some believe that they wanted to live in the newer city of Jenné, which was just next door.

REVIEW Why is Jenne-jenno considered an important city in ancient West Africa? **Main Idea and Details**

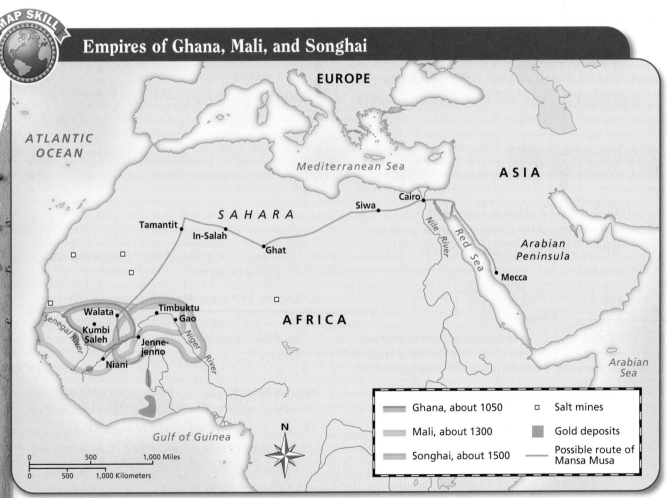

MAP SKILL

Empires of Ghana, Mali, and Songhai

EUROPE

ATLANTIC OCEAN

Mediterranean Sea

ASIA

SAHARA

Tamantit

In-Salah

Ghat

Siwa

Cairo

Nile River

Red Sea

Arabian Peninsula

Mecca

Walata

Timbuktu

Gao

Kumbi Saleh

Jenne-jenno

Senegal River

Niger River

AFRICA

Niani

Arabian Sea

Gulf of Guinea

N

0   500   1,000 Miles
0   500   1,000 Kilometers

Ghana, about 1050	□ Salt mines
Mali, about 1300	Gold deposits
Songhai, about 1500	Possible route of Mansa Musa

▶ In 1324 Mansa Musa set out on his pilgrimage to Mecca.

MAP SKILL Use Routes *Describe the route Mansa Musa took on his pilgrimage to Mecca.*

Songhai

Along the Niger River lived a group of farmers, traders, and warriors called the Songhai. The Songhai people had fought to remain independent from the empire of Mali. The eastern border of the empire of Songhai began at the city of **Gao** (GOW), east of Timbuktu. Gao was under the control of Mali during the rule of Mansa Musa. At first the city was dominated by Mali. However, in about 1375, the Songhai refused to pay tribute to Mali. By about 1464, they began taking over the territory around them.

Under King **Sonni Ali,** Songhai became an even bigger center of trade and learning than Mali had been. Sonni Ali made many changes to the territory he controlled. He divided the land into provinces and had governors oversee them. He created a professional army and navy to protect his kingdom and trade.

While the empire of Songhai was larger than either that of Ghana or Mali, it did not last as long as they did. More and more Muslims poured

▶ **This gold Moroccan coin dates from the empire of Songhai.**

into Gao, Songhai's capital. Fighting among different groups soon led to some states leaving the empire. However, a threat from the north ended the last great empire of West Africa. In 1591 Songhai was attacked by Moroccans from North Africa. The Moroccans were armed with guns. This new form of technology proved successful, and the empire of Songhai was defeated.

REVIEW How was the empire of Songhai different from the empires of Ghana and Mali? **Compare and Contrast**

Summarize the Lesson

— **A.D. 900** Height of the empire of Ghana

— **1324** Mansa Musa made a pilgrimage to Mecca.

— **1591** The empire of Songhai declined.

LESSON 2   REVIEW

Check Facts and Main Ideas

1. **Summarize** On a separate piece of paper, write a summary of the sentences listed below.

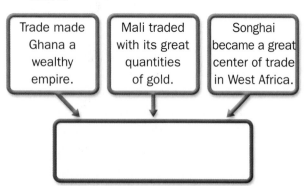

Trade made Ghana a wealthy empire.

Mali traded with its great quantities of gold.

Songhai became a great center of trade in West Africa.

2. What was the role of Ghana in the movement of trade goods across the Sahara?

3. Who was Mansa Musa?

4. How were the West African kingdoms crossroads for trade?

5. **Critical Thinking:** *Make Inferences* Why would European mapmakers include Mali on their maps after hearing about Mansa Musa's pilgrimage to Mecca?

Link to ⚭ **Art**

Draw a Picture What might Mansa Musa's visit to Cairo have looked like? Draw a picture or make a collage from the details you have read about in this lesson.

Sundiata

reigned about A.D. 1235-1255

Most information about Sundiata can be found in oral stories that are still told today by griots, or storytellers. They say that Sundiata was destined to be king. However, Sundiata was sick as a child. He could not speak or walk until he was at least seven years old.

Griots also tell us that the enemy of Sundiata's father was Sumanguru, who had conquered the Kingdom of Kangaba and killed all 11 of Sundiata's brothers. Sundiata outgrew his childhood illness and organized a group of men to rise up against Sumanguru.

According to the griots, at the Battle of Kirina, about 1235, Sundiata fought against Sumanguru. He wanted revenge. Sundiata declared:

"I am the rain that extinguishes the cinder;
I am the boisterous [violent] torrent [outburst]
that will carry you off."

Sundiata was successful and defeated Sumanguru.

Griots say that Sundiata worked to create a stable political structure. The political structure he created lasted hundreds of years after his reign.

After 1240 he moved the capital of his empire to Niani (later known as Mali), which was between the Sankarani and Niger rivers. This site attracted many merchants. It soon became a very important trading point for the entire Sudan region. Sundiata converted to Islam but continued to allow his people to practice their own religion.

BIOFACT

According to legend, Sundiata had special powers. He used these powers to defeat Sumanguru at the Battle of Kirina.

Learn from Biographies

Sundiata ruled over many different people when he created the empire of Mali. What advantage was there in allowing people to practice their own religion?

For more information, go online to *Meet the People* at **www.sfsocialstudies.com.**

379

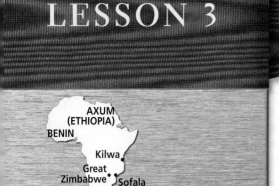

AXUM
(ETHIOPIA)
BENIN
Kilwa
Great
Zimbabwe
Sofala

300   600   900   1200   1500

A.D. 350
The kingdom of Axum invades the former Kush capital of Meroë.

1185–1225
Lalibela builds 11 rock churches in Ethiopia.

1450
Stone enclosures of Great Zimbabwe are completed.

East, Central, and Southern Africa

PREVIEW

Focus on the Main Idea
Trading empires developed in eastern, central, and southern Africa that interacted with Arabia, India, and China.

PLACES
Axum
Ethiopia
Adefa
Sofala
Kilwa
Great Zimbabwe
Benin

PEOPLE
Ezana
Lalibela

VOCABULARY
Swahili
oba

TERMS
Zagwe dynasty
Solomonid dynasty

▶ These bronze bangle bracelets, discovered at Great Zimbabwe, are probably from India.

You Are There

This is the first time your father has taken you on one of his many travels. Your father is a merchant trader. He travels between Sofala and the state of Great Zimbabwe to trade gold and ivory for trade goods such as ceramics from India and China. You want to see for yourself the amazing place he has been describing to you. When you arrive, you see the stone enclosures that rise more than 30 feet in the air. As you take a closer look, you realize that nothing is holding the stones together. They have been cut to fit tightly together, like a giant jigsaw puzzle.

You hear shouts. People are telling you and others in the crowd that you must leave the area because the king is coming. You have heard from your father that the king is a mysterious and powerful person. Most people never get to see him. Your father tells you that the gold and ivory have been loaded and it is time to go. Even after walking several miles, you are still able to see the stone enclosures.

Summarize As you read, summarize information about the civilizations that developed in eastern, central, and southern Africa.

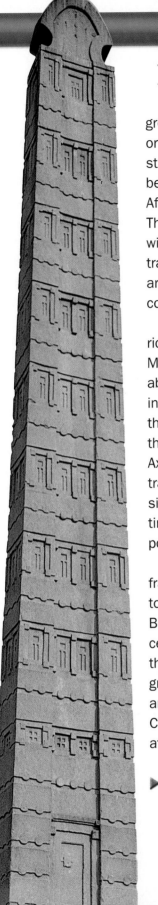

East Africa

What were these great stone enclosures, or walls? They were constructed by people who began to live in eastern Africa about A.D. 300. These people interacted with people living in the trading city-states that arose along the eastern coast of Africa.

In about 350, the iron-rich trade center of Meroë, which you read about in Unit 2, was invaded by forces from the kingdom of **Axum** in the Ethiopian highlands. Axum had begun as a trading settlement in the sixth century B.C. Over time, it had grown into a powerful empire.

Axum exported ivory, frankincense, and myrrh to Greece and Rome. Both myrrh and frankincense were made from the resin of trees that grew in the mountainous areas of Axum. Craftworkers also created luxury goods from brass, copper, and crystal. In exchange for these trade goods, Axum received cloth, jewelry, metals, and steel, which was used to make weapons. Axum traders bartered as a means for the exchange of trade goods.

Christian kingdoms existed in northeastern Africa since about 330, when the king of Axum, **Ezana,** converted to Christianity. To the northwest of Axum were the Christian kingdoms of Noba and Makurra, located between the first and fifth cataracts of the Nile River. The people in these kingdoms converted to Christianity between 500 and 650. After Arabs invaded Egypt in the seventh century, the kingdoms continued to exist.

Arab invasions did not destroy Axum. But changing climatic conditions and trade routes that moved away from the Red Sea forced people to abandon Axum. As a result, many people moved inland.

REVIEW Did Meroë fall before or after Axum became a trading settlement? ⟳ **Sequence**

▶ **The kings of Axum commemorated their glories with stone stelae, or ceremonial stone slabs, sometimes up to 100 feet high, which were built above underground royal tombs. These stone towers could also have been built as symbols of power.**

▶ **The kings of Axum wore elaborate crowns such as this one.**

Ethiopia

Ethiopia replaced the Axum civilization. About 1150 a new dynasty, the **Zagwe dynasty,** took the throne from the old line of Axumite kings. Christianity became firmly established in Ethiopia under the Zagwe. The capital was moved to **Adefa** on the central highlands.

A Zagwe king, **Lalibela,** ruled from about 1185 to 1225. During his rule, he had 11 churches built out of solid rock at the new capital. He built these churches to show his faith and to gain respect for his leadership. The largest church, called Savior of the World, is more than 100 feet long, 75 feet wide, and 35 feet high.

In 1270 the Zagwe dynasty was taken over by the **Solomonid dynasty** (SAW loh moh nihd).

▶ **A modern painting of King Lalibela, who promoted Eastern Orthodox Christianity in his kingdom**

The Solomonid rulers claimed to be descendants of the original rulers of ancient Axum. Their rule of Ethiopia would last until 1974.

The Solomonids stopped building great stone churches and palaces in Ethiopia. The Solomonid kings and their royal courts, which included government and military officials, instead began to live in more modest structures. One result of this was that there was no longer a permanent capital.

The king and his court moved as often as two or three times a year. This was how the king could stay in close contact with all of the regions in the kingdom. As a result, people of the kingdom were more loyal to their king. However, the king's royal court included so many people that every time they moved into a region, they would use up all of its food and fuel supplies.

REVIEW Who was Lalibela and what did he do? **Main Idea and Details**

▶ **The rooftop of the church of St. George, one of the churches carved out of solid rock during the rule of King Lalibela**

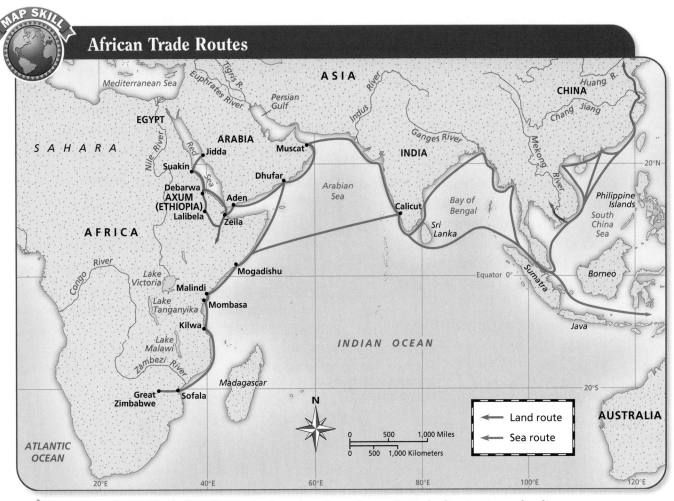

African Trade Routes

▶ **By land and sea, the Indian Ocean trade network exchanged goods, language, and culture.**

MAP SKILL Use a Historical Map *Where were the trading cities located on sea routes?*

Kilwa

As Islam spread in the seventh and eighth centuries, cities along the eastern coast of Africa became more involved in Indian Ocean trade. At first this trade involved northern cities. By the ninth century, more southern cities such as **Sofala** and **Kilwa** were involved in the gold and ivory trade. In 1331 Ibn Battuta visited Kilwa and described its elegance. One Arab trader remarked of Kilwa that:

> *"Their mosques are very strongly constructed of wood. . . it is one of the most beautiful and well-constructed towns in the world."*

The Indian Ocean trade network extended from East Africa to India and China, as well as to Arabia. Arabs settled in East African coastal cities such as Mombasa. Muslim and East African culture mixed, creating a **Swahili** culture and language. *Swahili* is the Arabic word for "people of the coast." Both Arabic and Swahili were used as trading languages to help more traders communicate.

The Portuguese began to attack Kilwa and Mombasa in the early 1500s. They wanted control of Indian Ocean trade. The attacks were successful, but Swahili groups again gained control of many ports along the coast.

REVIEW How did Arab settlement in East African coastal cities affect language and culture? **Cause and Effect**

383

Great Zimbabwe

The stone enclosures of **Great Zimbabwe** were built by the Shona people between 1200 and 1450. *Zimbabwe* means "houses of stone" in the Shona language. The enclosures were not built for defense but to show the power and importance of the king.

Like Kilwa, the city of Great Zimbabwe reached its height about 1400. Great Zimbabwe participated in the gold and ivory trade that eventually made its way to Kilwa. Gold was not actually mined in the region but taxing the trade goods provided a major source of wealth for Great Zimbabwe.

By the early fifteenth century, there were about 11,000 people living in and around Great Zimbabwe. Then, in about 1450, people abandoned Great Zimbabwe. The large population had exhausted resources such as trees for timber, soil for growing crops, and grasses for grazing farm animals. The Portuguese invaded the area about 100 years later and finally conquered the kingdom in the late 1600s.

REVIEW What was Great Zimbabwe?
Summarize

Benin

Near the delta of the Niger River was the forest kingdom of **Benin** (buh NIN). The kings in Benin were called **obas** (OH buhz). They took power about 1300.

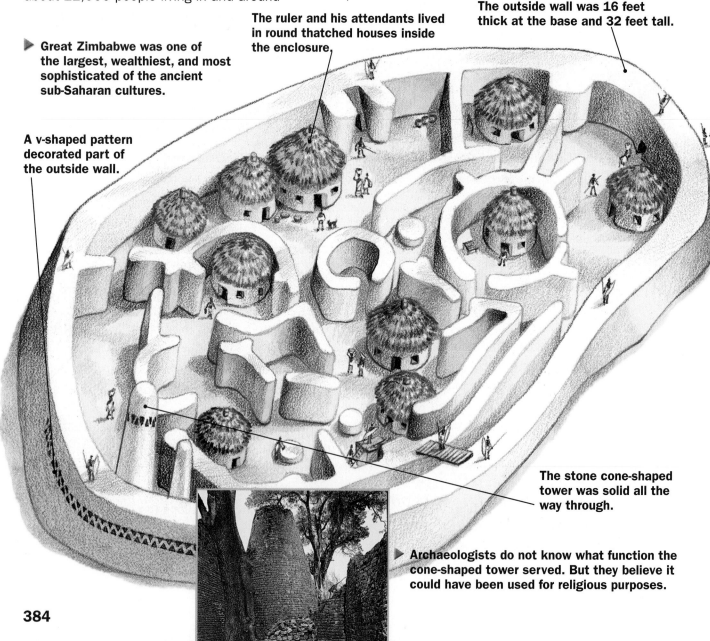

▶ Great Zimbabwe was one of the largest, wealthiest, and most sophisticated of the ancient sub-Saharan cultures.

The ruler and his attendants lived in round thatched houses inside the enclosure.

The outside wall was 16 feet thick at the base and 32 feet tall.

A v-shaped pattern decorated part of the outside wall.

The stone cone-shaped tower was solid all the way through.

▶ Archaeologists do not know what function the cone-shaped tower served. But they believe it could have been used for religious purposes.

In the late 1400s, the Portuguese began to trade coral beads and cloth for ivory, animal skins, and pepper with Benin. By 1500 Benin grew to become a powerful empire. By then Benin was trading its ivory, cloth, spices, and slaves.

This forest region had fertile soil and received lots of rain. People grew crops such as yams and cotton. They lived in Benin City, the capital city, as well as in the country. Houses were made of mud. However, the oba's palace had doors made of metal and had beautiful designs and pictures.

In addition to trade, Benin was known for its great art. Many artists used bronze, ivory, and wood to make sculptures and carvings. Craftspeople made beautiful bronze and brass sculptures to decorate the oba's palace. This was how the artists showed the greatness of the oba.

▶ **Bronze sculptors in present-day Benin still practice the "lost wax" process of casting.**

To protect these riches, high wooden walls were built around the oba's palace.

REVIEW How did contact with the Portuguese affect Benin's growth? *Cause and Effect*

Summarize the Lesson

— **A.D. 350** Axum invaded the former Kush capital of Meroë.

— **1185–1225** Lalibela built 11 rock churches in Ethiopia.

— **1450** The Shona people completed the stone enclosures of Great Zimbabwe.

LESSON 3   REVIEW

Check Facts and Main Ideas

1. Summarize On a separate piece of paper, fill in the missing detail that completes the summary below.

> Axum was abandoned after Arab invasions.

> Ethiopia took over the position of the old kingdom of Axum.

> Axum replaced Meroë in A.D. 350. Later, Ethiopia took over the old kingdom of Axum after it was invaded and abandoned.

2. List goods that were traded in eastern, central, and southern Africa.

3. How were the civilizations that existed in eastern, central, and southern Africa alike and different?

4. How were these civilizations influenced by other civilizations in the Indian Ocean trade network?

5. Critical Thinking: *Make Inferences* What might life have been like in these regions if they had not participated in international trade? Explain your answer.

Link to ⚯ Science

Build a Wall Research how the Shona people would have kept the stones together to build the enclosures at Great Zimbabwe. Use small blocks to build a wall like those in Great Zimbabwe and explain why the blocks stay together.

Research and Writing Skills

Use the Internet

What? The Internet, which you can access through a computer, contains millions of pages on all kinds of topics. In order to find information on a particular topic, you use a search engine. A search engine is a Web site that has directories of information and offers key word searches.

Q? How do I begin my search?

A: Start with a search engine. Then type in a key word or key words for the information you want.

Search Engine

search key word   East Africa

Q? How do I know if a site is dependable?

A: Government and educational sites that end in .gov or .edu, such as museums and colleges, usually have more dependable information than other sites. Also, use what you have learned about telling fact from opinion to judge how dependable a Web site is.

.gov

.org

.edu

Why? The Internet is a tool that students can use to find information on a topic. It was created during the 1960s to allow governments to share information. The Internet allowed researchers in different parts of the world to keep in touch with other researchers.

The World Wide Web was created in the 1990s so that more people could use the Internet. Now, anyone can put information on the Internet. But how can you find the information you are looking for and how do you know it is accurate? Search engines were created to help people find information about specific topics. When you enter key words, or words related to the topic, you are telling the search engine to search the Internet for those key words.

Using search engines to locate information on the Internet does not replace researching a topic by looking at books. However, the Internet may contain more current information than what is available in books.

How? The following steps will help you use a search engine.

- Access the Internet through your computer.
- A teacher or librarian can help you select a search engine that will help you conduct your research.
- Look for the word *search* with a long rectangular box on the first page of the search engine. Type in a topic that you are researching, such as East Africa. You could also type in the name of a more specific place such as Great Zimbabwe.
- After you click on the *search* button, a search engine will return a list of items called "hits." Some of these hits might contain useful information on your topic. Remember, sometimes the information may not be useful. You may need to try narrowing your topic to bring up more specific information.
- Some of the information you find on the Web may not be accurate. Make sure you compare the information from a Web site to at least one other appropriate source.

Think and Apply

1. Try researching the spread of the Bantu languages. What key words or phrases would you type to begin the search?

2. How would you choose which sites to visit from the list created by the search engine?

3. Which Web site gives you more useful information? Why?

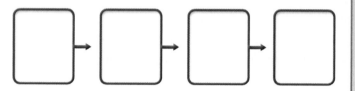

300   500   700

about
A.D. **300–1200**
Empire of Ghana

c. 350
Axum invaded Meroë.

Chapter Summary

Target Skill

Sequence

On a separate piece of paper, put the following events in their correct time order.

· Songhai declines as a great trading empire in West Africa.

· The Sahara begins to dry out.

· Great Zimbabwe is completed.

· The Portuguese invade Kilwa.

☐ → ☐ → ☐ → ☐

Vocabulary and Terms

Match each word with the correct definition or description.

1 **savanna**
(p. 371)

2 **griot**
(p. 376)

3 **Swahili**
(p. 383)

4 **Bantu**
(p. 373)

a. storyteller

b. short, grassy plain

c. language and culture mix of Muslims and East Africans

d. group of languages that was spread by farmers who left West Africa about 100 B.C.

People and Places

Write a sentence explaining why each of the following people and places is important in the study of medieval Africa. You may use two or more in a single sentence.

1 Sundiata
(p. 376)

2 Mansa Musa
(p. 376)

3 Great Rift Valley
(p. 372)

4 Great Zimbabwe
(p. 384)

5 Songhai (p. 378)

6 Ghana (p. 375)

7 Mali (p. 376)

8 Axum (p. 381)

9 Ethiopia (p. 382)

10 Sonni Ali
(p. 378)

900	1100	1300	1500

1185–c. 1225
Lalibela ruled Ethiopia.

1235
Sundiata defeated Sumanguru at the Battle of Kirina.

1270
The Zagwe dynasty was overthrown by the Solomonid dynasty in Ethiopia.

1324
Mansa Musa's pilgrimage to Mecca

1400
Height of Great Zimbabwe and Kilwa

c. 1500
Portuguese invasions begin in eastern and southern Africa.

Facts and Main Ideas

1 How was trade important culturally and economically?

2 With whom did states in East Africa trade?

3 With whom did kingdoms in West Africa trade?

4 **Time Line** What kingdoms in West Africa and East Africa thrived at the same time?

5 **Main Idea** Why did people leave the Sahara after 2500 B.C.?

6 **Main Idea** Why was gold so important to the African kingdoms and empires?

7 **Main Idea** Why were Arabic and Swahili used as trading languages?

8 **Critical Thinking:** *Make Generalizations* What was important about the locations of the trading kingdoms?

Apply Skills

Use the Internet

Use the Internet to find a translation of a primary source from a time period in this chapter. Think about some of the events you have read about in this chapter. Answer the following questions after you have found the appropriate Web site for the event.

1 How do you know that what you have found is a primary source?

2 Is the Web site an appropriate one that would provide accurate information? Explain your answer.

3 Does the Web site lead you to other Web sites with helpful resources and information?

Write About History

1 **Write a journal entry** from the point of view of someone accompanying Mansa Musa on his pilgrimage to Mecca.

2 **Write a news bulletin** describing some trade and travel problems for people traveling on the caravan routes in the Sahara or on the Red Sea.

3 **Write a magazine article** about how trade caused the mixing and blending of cultures in Africa.

Internet Activity

To get help with vocabulary, people, and terms, select dictionary, encyclopedia, or almanac from *Social Studies Library* at **www.sfsocialstudies.com.**

CHAPTER 14

Medieval Europe

Lesson 1

Europe
Europeans farm on the Northern European Plain.

1

Lesson 2

1215
England
England develops a document that limits a ruler's powers.

2

Lesson 3

c. 800
Europe
Feudalism provides protection for kings, lords, knights, and serfs.

3

Lesson 4

1095
Rome
People organize a Crusade to win back control of Palestine.

4

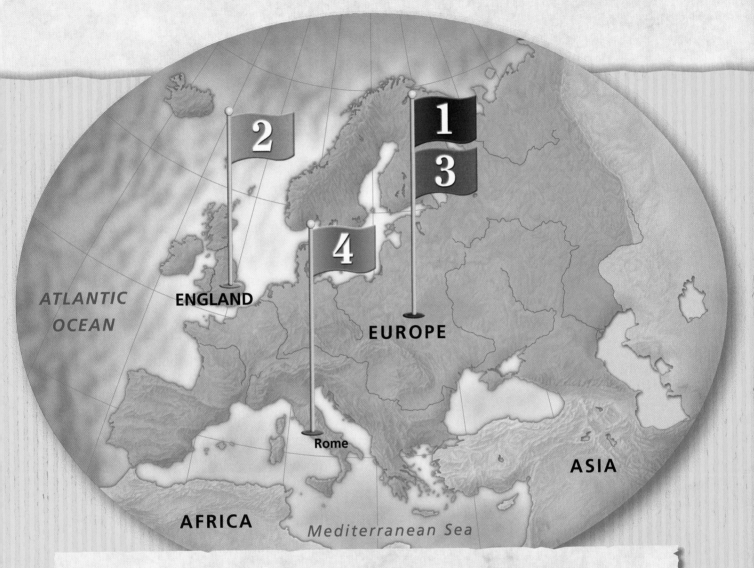

ATLANTIC
OCEAN

ENGLAND

EUROPE

Rome

ASIA

AFRICA

Mediterranean Sea

Why We Remember

Medieval Europe provides a glimpse into one of the ways people organized themselves into a society. People worked together to be self-sufficient. Trade, then towns, began to prosper. Great strides were made in the movement of people and goods in the Middle Ages. During this time, military campaigns moved from Europe to the Holy Land in Southwest Asia. Trade routes began to branch out to even more locations. These routes, which had hugged the European coastline, moved inward. Goods and ideas were traded across different cultures. When Europeans came to America, they brought many goods and ideas that we use today.

EUROPE

PREVIEW

Focus on the Main Idea
The landforms and climate of Europe affect the way Europeans live.

PLACES
Europe
Ural Mountains
North European Plain
Volga River
Danube River
Rhine River

Geography of Europe

You Are There

You're sitting in a room full of desks. Your fingers are cramped. It's winter, so the day is short and cold. Father Abbot fears a fire, so there is no source of heat or light in the room. You and each of the other scribes are copying a text. You write one letter, one word, one line at a time. "Two fingers hold the pen, but the whole body toils [labors]." You've been copying this same text onto paper for weeks. The last book you copied was an account of ancient Rome. When you finish a chapter, your copy is proofread. Corrections will be made. Titles will be added. Then, special pages are sent to an illustrator, who will supply any needed illustrations or art. Finally, the book will be bound. You look out the window for a moment to rest your eyes. The landscape of rolling hills and blowing grass is peaceful. This is Europe, your homeland.

Cause and Effect As you read, consider how the physical geography of Europe affects how people live.

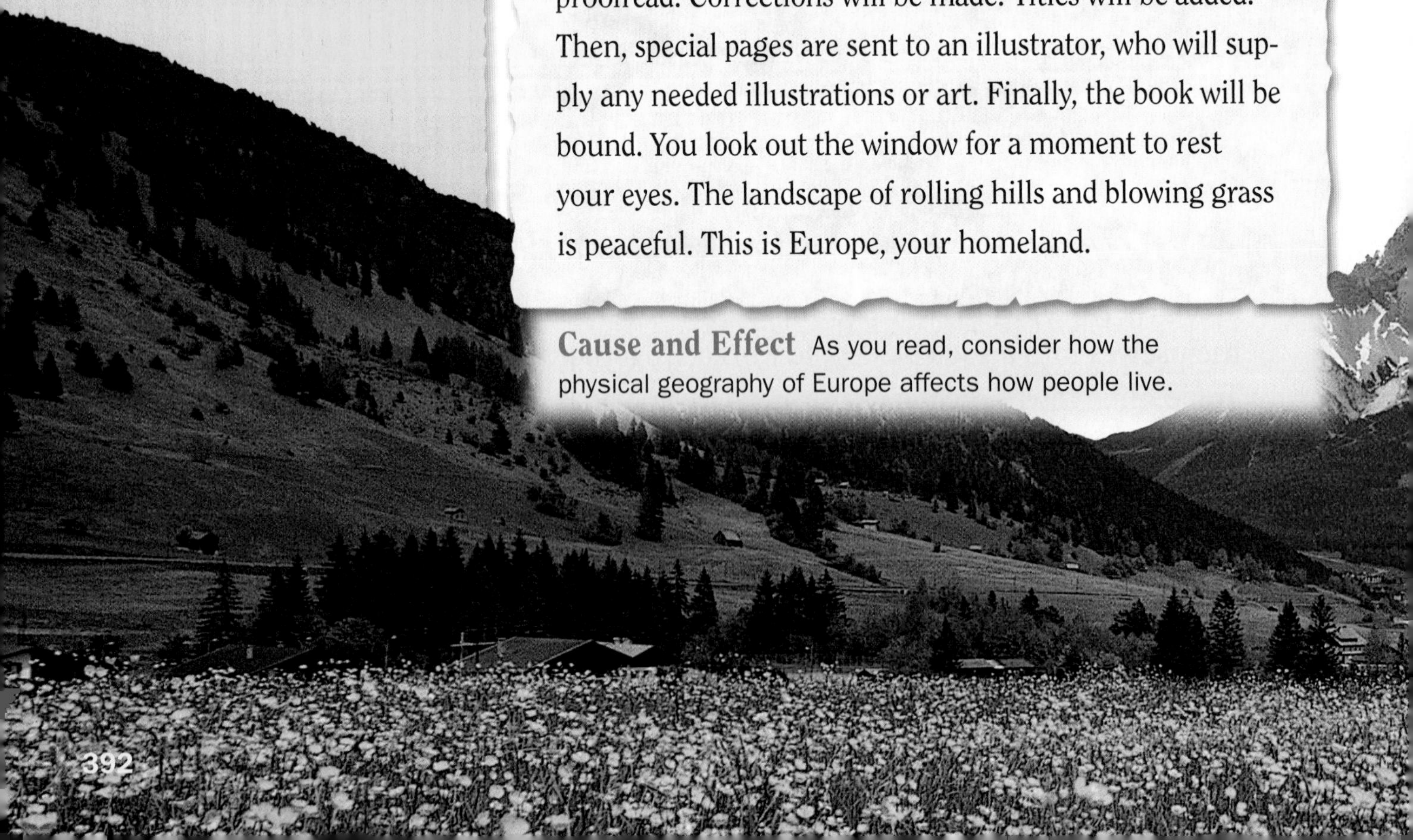

Europe

Europe is the second smallest continent on Earth and extends from the Arctic Ocean in the north to the Mediterranean Sea in the south. Its western boundary is the Atlantic Ocean. In the east, the **Ural** (YOOR ul) **Mountains** separate Europe from Asia. The Urals are old, low mountains.

Europe has four major land regions: (1) the Northwest Mountains, (2) the North European Plain, (3) the Central Uplands, and (4) the Alpine Mountain System. The thin soil and steep slopes of the Northwest Mountain region make it poor for farming. The **North European Plain** is part of the Great European Plain, which covers a vast expanse of Europe, including part of southeast-ern England. The flat and rolling land includes some of the world's most fertile farmland.

The Central Uplands includes low mountains, high plateaus, and forests throughout the central region of Europe. Much of the land is rocky, but some is suitable for farming.

The Alpine Mountain System includes several mountain chains such as the Alps and the Carpathian Mountains. Lower mountain slopes and wide valleys provide good farmland. Heavy forests cover many of the higher slopes. Meadows above the timberline, or where the trees stop growing, are used as pastureland.

REVIEW How would you describe the major land regions of Europe? **Summarize**

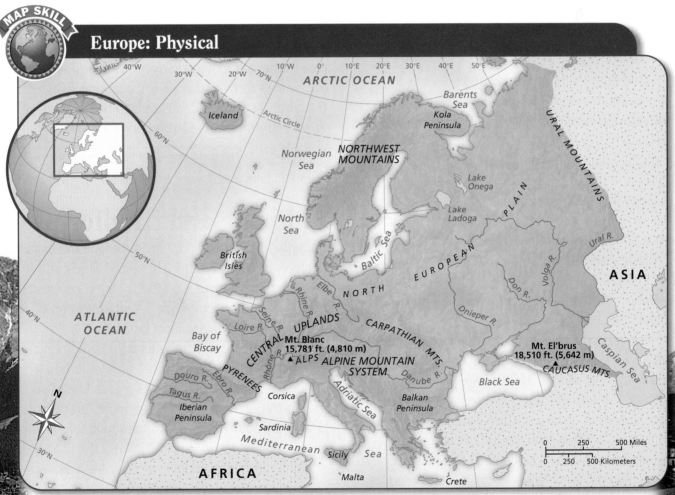

MAP SKILL

Europe: Physical

▶ Europe has four main land regions, an extensive river system, and a coastline with thousands of bays and harbors.

MAP SKILL Use Latitude and Longitude *What is the location of the Alps?*

▶ **The capital city of Budapest, Hungary, sits on both sides of the Danube River.**

Europe's River System

The many rivers of Europe serve as major transportation routes. The Volga (VAHL guh) River is Europe's longest river. It flows through Russia to the Caspian (KAS pih un) Sea. Canals link the Volga with the Arctic Ocean, the Baltic Sea, and the Don River. The Danube River is Europe's second longest river. It is the main water route in the south-central part of the continent. The Rhine River is the backbone of the busiest inland system of waterways in the western part of Europe. The Rhine flows from the Alps through western Germany and the Netherlands to the North Sea.

Europe generally has milder weather than parts of Asia and North America at the same latitude. Europe's mild climate is caused by winds warmed by the Gulf Stream. The Gulf Stream is a powerful ocean current. It carries warm water from the Gulf of Mexico to the western coast of Europe. The winds affect most of the continent because no mountain barrier is large enough to block them.

For more than 2,000 years, European traders have transported goods on the waterways of Europe. Farmers used the power of the flowing water to turn waterwheels to grind grain. Many cities emerged alongside rivers, where their economies thrived. Europeans began to fish in the North Atlantic. Fishing grew to become an important part of Europe's economy.

REVIEW How does the Gulf Stream affect Europe's climate? **Cause and Effect**

Climate and Landforms

During the early Middle Ages, Europeans began to clear the land to farm. This process of cutting down forests to clear the land is called deforestation. Climate and landforms affected how and where people chose to farm crops.

There are different climates across the continent of Europe. However, most of Europe has a temperate, or mild, climate. As you read earlier, the North European Plain is the most fertile farmland in Europe. Wheat and other grains are grown on this plain.

Along the Atlantic coast, winters are mild and summers are cool. This type of climate is good for farming. Crops that are grown in this area include potatoes, cabbage, and onions.

In southern Europe, the climate region is Mediterranean. As you remember from Unit 3, this climate region has hot, dry summers and mild, rainy winters. The ancient Greeks used irrigation to farm. Over time, these lands were overused, and farming declined in the region.

In the Northwest Mountain region, the climate varies. At higher elevations, the climate is cooler. At the lower elevations, people can cultivate

▶ **This farmer plows olive groves in Spain. Today, Spain and Greece are the world leaders in olive production.**

crops because the climate is more moderate. However, many people in these regions also herd animals and cut timber.

Just like Europe's climate, Europeans are diverse in their cultures and the languages they speak. In this chapter, you will learn about how these peoples interacted with each other and with people from other lands.

REVIEW How does location affect people who live and work in the major climate regions of Europe? **Cause and Effect**

Summarize the Lesson

- Europe has four major land regions: the Northwest Mountains, the North European Plain, the Central Uplands, and the Alpine Mountain System.
- Europe has an extensive river and waterway system for transportation.
- Europe's diverse climate affects how people live and work.

LESSON 1 ▷ REVIEW

Check Facts and Main Ideas

1. Cause and Effect On a separate piece of paper, fill in the missing cause and effects.

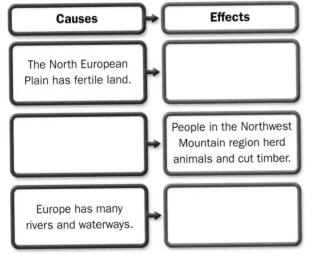

Causes	→	Effects
The North European Plain has fertile land.	→	
	→	People in the Northwest Mountain region herd animals and cut timber.
Europe has many rivers and waterways.	→	

2. What major landform separates Europe from Asia?

3. What are the major rivers of Europe?

4. Identify some ways in which Europeans modified their landscape.

5. Critical Thinking: *Accuracy of Information* If you read in a book that Europe had climate regions that were mostly dry and hot, would that be correct? Explain.

Link to 🔗 Art

Create an Advertisement Create a travel advertisement to attract visitors to Europe. Use photographs or drawings, as well as descriptions, of European geography. Think about what would appeal to people living in other countries.

700	900	1100	1300

768–814
Much of Europe is united under the rule of Charlemagne.

c. 800–1100
Viking warriors and traders invade Charlemagne's empire.

1215
The Magna Carta is signed, limiting royal power.

ENGLAND SCANDINAVIA

Rulers and Invaders

PREVIEW

Focus on the Main Idea
After a series of rulers and invaders, medieval government in Europe experienced a change.

PLACES
England
Scandinavia
Runnymede

PEOPLE
Charlemagne
William the Conqueror
King John

TERMS
Domesday Book
Middle Ages
Magna Carta

> **You Are There**

1086: You're tired. You've ridden on horseback for three hours to reach a small village in the south of England. Yesterday you were in a seaside town. Tomorrow you will be at a lord's castle. You must carry out King William's order that all of England be surveyed. You ask the same questions in every town and village: "Who is the lord of the manor? How much land is here? How many villagers live here? How many sheep? How many pigs? How many fisheries?" There are dozens of other similar questions to ask. Just yesterday some peasants asked what will be done with the Domesday (DOOMS day) Book—for that's what people have been calling it. You're not sure. But you and your fellow workers think that King William will use the information to see if he can get more tax money from the countryside. At the very least you guess that, when it's finished, the Domesday Book will give an accurate picture of life at this time.

▶ The Domesday Book contains specific information about life in England during the Middle Ages. For example, some 6,000 mills were used to grind grain.

Sequence As you read, keep in mind the order in which events happen.

Target Skill

A European Empire

The **Domesday Book** helped keep track of people in **England** during the **Middle Ages,** or the period in Europe from about A.D. 500 to 1500. It also helped the ruler set up a tax system. Before the Domesday Book was put together in 1086, no one really knew how many people lived in England.

During the Middle Ages, rulers in Europe such as **Charlemagne** (SHAHR luh mayn) had to rely on records kept by nobles. In 771 Charlemagne became the sole ruler of his kingdom and, by 800, he had been crowned emperor.

He gave large areas of land to loyal nobles. In return, the nobles gave an oath, or a pledge, of loyalty to him. The nobles were responsible for maintaining roads, bridges, and fortifications, or defense walls, on their estates. Read more about Charlemagne in the biography on page 399.

REVIEW How did Charlemagne strengthen his kingdom? **Main Ideas and Details**

Invaders

Despite Charlemagne's efforts to strengthen his kingdom, it fell apart after his death. First, Vikings, or fierce pirates and warriors from **Scandinavia,** invaded the empire. The Vikings came from the present-day countries of Denmark, Norway, and Sweden.

From about 800 to 1100, the Vikings launched several invasions. They conquered and looted, or robbed, parts of England and France. Then they raided Germany, Ireland, Italy, Russia, and Spain. At first, they raided these areas to steal goods. Later, they set up trading centers and trade routes.

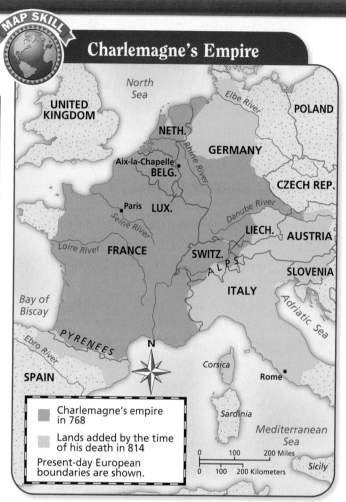

MAP SKILL **Charlemagne's Empire**

Charlemagne's empire in 768

Lands added by the time of his death in 814

Present-day European boundaries are shown.

▶ Charlemagne restored much of the old Roman Empire.

MAP SKILL Use Map Scale *How far west of the Rhine River did Charlemagne's empire stretch?*

In the early 900s, another group of Vikings, the Normans, settled in northern France. There they became Christians and church leaders. They also adopted Frankish customs. Under the leadership of **William the Conqueror,** they marched into England and later advanced into southern Italy.

REVIEW After the Vikings looted the lands they conquered, what did they do? **Sequence**

▶ The Bayeux Tapestry shows William, Duke of Normandy, invading England with an army of well-trained cavalry troops.

Musée de la Tapisserie, Bayeux, France/Bridgeman Art Library Int'l. Ltd. (U.S.)

A Change in Government

From about 1066 through the 1100s, most of the kings who ruled England were strong and governed justly. They followed accepted customs that established both the lords' duties and what was expected of the king. However, there was no real limit on the king's power. **King John,** crowned in 1199, governed with more force than earlier kings did. He demanded more military service and greater amounts of money. He also sold royal positions to the highest bidders.

English lords were angry with John's rule. In 1214 John lost an important battle against France. Then civil war broke out in England. Rather than face defeat, John agreed to a set of promises on June 15, 1215, at **Runnymede.** The document was called the **Magna Carta,** or the "Great Charter."

The Magna Carta contained 63 clauses, or articles. Most of the clauses helped lords and other landholders. Some articles eventually helped all people. For example, the charter stated that the king could make no special demands for money

▶ **King John's Great Seal is attached by string to the Magna Carta.**

without the consent of the lords. The document stated that no free man could be imprisoned, exiled, or deprived of property, except by law. The greatest value of the Magna Carta was that it limited royal power. The king had to obey the law.

REVIEW What was the greatest value of the Magna Carta? **Main Idea and Details**

Summarize the Lesson

— **768–814** Much of Europe was united under the rule of Charlemagne.

— **c. 800–1100** Viking warriors and traders invaded Charlemagne's empire.

— **1215** The Magna Carta was signed.

LESSON 2   REVIEW

Check Facts and Main Ideas

1. ⟳ **Sequence** On a separate piece of paper, put these events in their correct chronological order.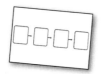

   • King John signs the Magna Carta.
   • Charlemagne is crowned emperor.
   • William the Conqueror invades England.
   • The Vikings invade Europe.

2. What title did Pope Leo III give Charlemagne?

3. How did the Domesday Book help kings rule their kingdoms?

4. How did the Magna Carta limit royal power?

5. **Critical Thinking:** *Fact or Opinion* The Magna Carta indicated that there should be no taxation without the consent of the lords.

Link to ⟨⟩ Writing

Interpret a Law Write a paragraph explaining the excerpt below from the Magna Carta.

No free man shall be taken, or imprisoned . . . except by the legal judgement of his peers, or by the law of the land.

Charlemagne

c. 742–814

Charlemagne was the son of Pepin III. Charlemagne ruled the kingdom of the Franks with his brother. The Franks had invaded the western Roman Empire in the 400s. Charlemagne was educated and raised as a Christian.

In 768 Pepin III died, and Charlemagne and his brother took over their father's kingdom. Charlemagne's brother died in 771, making Charlemagne the sole ruler of the Franks. He immediately set out to conquer neighboring lands and expand his power. Leading his army into battle, Charlemagne at nearly 6 feet 4 inches tall, towered over most men.

Once he conquered a region, Charlemagne forced the people to become Christians. He maintained close ties with the Roman church throughout his reign. At Christmas Mass in 800, Pope Leo III crowned Charlemagne emperor of the former Roman Empire in western Europe. People attending the Mass gave this salute:

> *"To Charles Augustus, crowned by God, great and peace-giving Emperor . . . ."*

Charlemagne ruled much of western Europe, except England and Scandinavia. As ruler of such a large empire, Charlemagne issued a series of legal decrees, or commands, called capitularies. These written laws covered everything from church matters to punishment. Charlemagne also promoted culture and learning in his empire. He invited leading European scholars to his court and asked them to further educate clergy.

BIOFACT

Even after being crowned emperor, Charlemagne could not read or write. He kept writing tablets under his pillows to try to learn but never succeeded.

The scholars also supervised the copying by hand of classic Roman literature. Had these works not been copied, we would not know about many of them today. The originals have been lost.

Learn from Biographies

After Charlemagne conquered a region, what did he do?

For more information, go online to *Meet the People* at **www.sfsocialstudies.com.**

700   900   1100   1300

c. 800
Feudalism begins to rise.

c. 1200
The Manor system starts to decline.

1400
Feudalism starts to decline.

c. 700
Manor system begins.

EUROPE

PREVIEW

Focus on the Main Idea
The church, feudalism, and manor life formed the foundation of European medieval life.

PLACES
Europe

PEOPLE
Christine de Pisan

VOCABULARY
monk
nun
monastery
convent
missionary
monarch
serf
knight
chivalry
guild
lady

TERMS
feudalism
manor system
three-field rotation

▶ The goal of Nine Men's Morris is to get three markers in a row.

Life in the Middle Ages

You Are There

It's September, and the cold night has lasted until morning. You pull the quilt up to your chin to stay warm—Wait! Today is Michaelmas—a holiday! Everyone will be at the fair. You rush to dress, eat, and leave for the commons. As you near the fair, you see stalls offering pottery, saddles, jewelry, fabric, glassware, bread, and even armor for sale. The merchants have come from miles away. You make your way through musicians, acrobats, and candy sellers. You can smell the Michaelmas goose cooking, and you want to make sure to get a taste of it for good luck. Beyond the food, you stop to watch a few wrestling matches, followed by archery contests. On your left are more food stalls. These are full of all things ginger—cake, beverages, cookies, and caramels. You meet a friend and together you play several games of Nine Men's Morris before you head home.

Main Idea and Details As you read, identify details of daily life in medieval Europe.

The Church

The Michaelmas holiday you just read about was one of the many Christian feast days celebrated in medieval **Europe.** During the Middle Ages, Christianity was an important part of daily life.

Not all Europeans were Christians; some were Jews and others were Muslims. But most were Christians. Like Muslims, Christians showed their devotion by going on a pilgrimage—to Rome or Jerusalem, not Mecca. To Jews, Christians, and Muslims, Jerusalem was a holy city. However, Rome was the holy center of Christendom, or "kingdom of the Christians." The Christian leader, or pope, lived in Rome. He was just as powerful as a king was.

Building cathedrals with magnificent stained-glass windows became a major focus of medieval life. Entire towns worked to build these large churches that took decades or even hundreds of years to finish. For example, the construction of the Chartres Cathedral in northwestern France began about 1145. After a fire, Chartres was reconstructed and completed by 1260.

The Christian faith centered around the Christian church. Some young people even devoted their lives to religion. Some men who did this were called **monks,** and women were called **nuns.** Monks studied, prayed, and lived in communities called **monasteries.** Nuns lived in similar communities called **convents.**

Both monasteries and convents served as centers of religion and education. In addition to praying and studying, monks and nuns cultivated crops and helped the poor. Some monks became **missionaries,** or people who teach a religion to people with different beliefs.

REVIEW What role did the Christian church have in medieval Europe? *Summarize*

▶ **Chartres Cathedral has 176 stained-glass windows.**

Feudalism

During the Middle Ages, Europe had few strong central governments. People formed their own system to meet their need for protection and justice. **Feudalism** was a political, social, and economic system that began in the 800s. It provided the needed protection for people.

Feudalism resembled a social structure. At the top was the **monarch,** a king or queen who was the supreme ruler. The next level included lords who pledged their loyalty to the monarch and military support in the event of a war or conflict. In return, the monarch granted the lord an estate.

The lord owned the land. He also received a large percentage of the crops produced on the land and received all the income from the crops. He collected taxes, maintained order, enforced laws, and protected the serfs. **Serfs** were the people who lived on the land and farmed it. A saying of the time was "No land without a lord, and no lord without land."

Many lords had **knights,** or warriors trained and prepared to fight on horseback. Knights had a code of behavior called **chivalry.** According to the code, a true knight had deep faith, was ready to die for the church, gave generously to all, and used his strength to stand against injustice. Between 1100 and 1300, most knights received some land from their lords.

REVIEW Why did a monarch give large estates to lords? **Main Idea and Details**

▶ **During feudalism peasants made up 90 percent of the population. Monarchs, lords, and the church had all the power and wealth.**

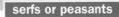

monarch

lords

knights

serfs or peasants

401

Feudalism Declines

Serfs, who are sometimes called peasants, formed the base of the society in the Middle Ages. Unlike kings, lords, and knights, who were bound to be faithful to one another, serfs had no such loyalty to anyone. Serfs were not slaves, yet could not become knights. They could not be bought or sold separate from the land. Even so, serfs were tied to the land they worked and could not leave it without the lord's permission.

As time passed, some lords had many faithful knights, therefore building up much military power. These lords became independent of the monarch, who originally granted the land to them. The lords substituted payment in money for actual military support. By the 1400s, feudalism had begun to decline.

REVIEW What advantages did feudalism provide serfs? Disadvantages? **Main Idea and Details**

The Manor System

Because feudalism was based on holding land, it is sometimes confused with the manor system, which was a way of organizing agricultural labor.

The **manor system,** common from the 700s to the 1200s, was a way to manage feudal lands. Manors usually had four parts: the manor house and village; farmland; meadowland; and wasteland. The manor house or castle was home to the lord of the estate. Gardens, orchards, and farm buildings often surrounded the manor house. Most manors included a church and a mill for grinding grain into flour.

Serfs' cottages were clustered together, forming a small village. The mud brick cottages had reinforced straw walls, dirt floors, and straw thatched roofs. A cottage usually consisted

▶ **The manor system allowed the lord of the manor along with the knights and serfs to be self-sufficient, providing opportunities to grow or make everything they needed.**

castle or manor house

church

knight

of a single room with little floor space and a low ceiling. Many cottages had small vegetable and fruit gardens.

Many serfs shared their cottages with livestock and other animals on the manor. They heated their cottages with wood that they chopped from nearby forests. In addition to working in the fields all day, many serfs worshiped in church. Serfdom was a difficult life. The church offered hope and peace.

After about 1000, serfs worked the manor lands using the **three-field rotation** system.

▶ **The serf's most important tool—the moldboard plow—required a team of four to eight oxen.**

God spede þe ploiȝ:ꝺ sende us kg

Ancient Art & Architecture Collection, Ltd.

In this system, every serf was assigned a strip of land in each of the manor's three fields. In the fall, one field was planted with wheat or rye. In the spring, the second field was planted with oats or barley. The third field was unplanted so that the soil would stay fertile. Each year the fields were rotated.

Fields were divided into long strips about one acre in size. Some of the strips contained good soil, some poor. The best soil was set aside for the lord of the manor. In addition to their own strips, peasants had to work on the lord's land at least three days a week.

The manor's working animals grazed on the meadowland. Meadowlands and wastelands often included ponds and streams for fishing. They provided summer pasture for animals, as well as wood for fuel and building materials. They also provided foods such as nuts, berries, honey, rabbits, and wild fowl.

The manor system generally met all the needs of the lord, knights, and serfs living there. It even allowed for crop surpluses. Serfs could sell the surpluses from the strips to people living in towns and cities. With a surplus, towns and cities began to grow.

REVIEW Name the advantages and disadvantages of the manor system.

Main Idea and Details

lord

serf

403

Guilds

By about 1000, once cities began to flourish, guilds formed. A **guild** was a group of people united by a common interest. A merchant guild included all of the traders in a town. The guild worked together to buy large quantities of goods cheaply and to control the market. A merchant who was not a member of the town's guild could not sell goods in the town. Guilds also guaranteed a fair price for goods.

Workers such as bakers, goldsmiths, tailors, and weavers formed craft guilds. These guilds controlled the quality and quantity of production. Guilds protected the town's merchants and craftspeople from having to compete with those from outside the town.

REVIEW Why would a baker or weaver want to join a craft guild? **Draw Conclusions**

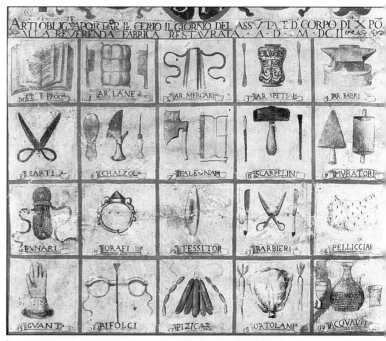

▶ Each guild had its own emblem, or symbol. Emblems were often based on the tools used by the craftspeople.

The Beothuk

HERE AND THERE

At the same time that ancient Europeans were clearing lands for farms, a group of about 1,000 Beothuk (BE ah thuck) were hunter-gatherers living on the island of Newfoundland. The Beothuk ate a rich and varied diet including seals, polar bears, and beavers. They also ate caribou, fish, geese, and many other animals.

In the 1500s, some Europeans sailed to the Newfoundland region to fish. They built fishing structures to use during the summer months. The Europeans left behind a number of items when they moved on. The Beothuk found these objects—nails, fishhooks, and scraps of iron and kettles. They shaped them into arrowheads and spear points. They made harpoon points and animal hide scrapers.

The Beothuk had an unusual opportunity. They acquired these European goods without having to exchange Beothuk goods for them.

▶ The Beothuk often collected metal objects, such as these, by visiting abandoned European fishing locations.

▶ This Beothuk carved bone object was found on the island of Newfoundland.

404

Medieval Women

During the Middle Ages, most women had few rights. Unmarried women who owned some land did have rights. However, when they married they had to give up their rights. A **lady,** or a woman of noble birth, was given little opportunity to make decisions about her own life. Usually a lady's actions were directed by her father or husband. She often had little to do with the estate. Servants managed the lord's affairs, and nurses took care of the children. In contrast, a woman living in a village had more work to do. Wives often worked on the land with their husbands. Unmarried women worked as servant girls or as hired agricultural workers. Women living in towns worked in nearly all the trades. Even though they could participate in the craft, they were kept out of decision-making discussions.

Some women did break out of the common roles led by medieval women. One of these was **Christine de Pisan.** She was one of the few

▶ In this painting, Christine de Pisan is writing at her desk in France.

medieval women to earn a living by writing. She wrote poetry and books protesting the way women were both glorified and insulted by male authors.

REVIEW It has been said that "The greater a medieval woman's wealth and social standing, the lower her status." Do you agree with this statement? **Main Idea and Details**

Summarize the Lesson

- **c. 800s** Feudalism began.
- **c. 1200** The Manor system began to decline.
- **c. 1400** Feudalism began to decline.

LESSON 3   REVIEW

Check Facts and Main Ideas

1. Main Idea and Details On a separate piece of paper, fill in the missing main idea that is supported by the details.

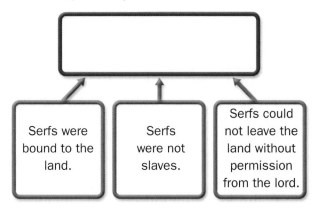

| Serfs were bound to the land. | Serfs were not slaves. | Serfs could not leave the land without permission from the lord. |

2. Name the four levels in feudalism.

3. What was the purpose of a craft guild?

4. Identify some ways in which feudalism and the manor system affected the lives of the nobility.

5. Critical Thinking: *Make Inferences* What feature of the manor system allowed the growth of towns and cities? Explain.

Link to ⚭ Drama

Prepare a Skit Choose the role of a guild member. Prepare a skit in which you explain why the guild is good for your town.

1000   1500

1095
Urban II calls for the First Crusade.

1000
Trade begins to expand in Europe.

c. 1347
A Bubonic plague spreads throughout Europe.

PREVIEW

Focus on the Main Idea
Routes promoted trade, travel, and communication, as well as the Plague, between Europe, Africa, and Asia.

PLACES
Palestine
Rome
Chang'an
Dunhuang
Genoa

PEOPLE
Alexius Comnenus
Urban II
Marco Polo

VOCABULARY
epidemic

TERMS
Crusades
Silk Road
Plague
bubonic plague

▶ This illustration from a twelfth-century tapestry shows a typical full suit of chain mail armor.

Crusades, Trade, and the Plague

You Are There
Hooray! It's your 14th birthday and your parents are sending you to work as a squire to Sir John. You will go on the Second Crusade with him. You will act as his servant much of the time. But, best of all, you will be in charge of Sir John's chain mail armor. It's a great responsibility. Sir John has the latest in armor technology. His chain mail has hundreds of iron rings linked together. It looks like mesh. Even his horse wears some chain mail armor. Sir John's armor weighs about 50 pounds. Sir John will need your help getting in and out of his armor. Once he is in it, you will hand him his weapons. These include a two-edged sword to hang from his waist and a dagger to tuck into his belt. After you help him onto his horse, you will hand him his lance and battle-ax. Then, because of your help, Sir John will be ready for battle.

Cause and Effect As you read, identify the causes and effects of the Crusades, expansion of trade, and the Plague.

The Crusades

After Charlemagne, battles for religion meant that more and more Christian knights were needed to fight. Two hundred years earlier, Islam had spread through North Africa and Asia Minor. Lands to the north and west of the Mediterranean Sea were mainly Christian. Lands along the eastern shores of the Mediterranean were Muslim.

In the mid-1000s, a group of Muslim Seljuk Turks from Central Asia rose up and defeated a Byzantine army. This marked the decline of Byzantine control over Asia Minor. During this time, the Turks conquered many lands, including Palestine. In the first century, Judea had been renamed Palestine by the Romans, who then forced the Jews to leave the region.

Christians considered Palestine the Holy Land. According to the New Testament, this is where Jesus had lived and preached. In the Mediterranean and Black Sea regions, Islam had gradually replaced Christianity, and the Turkish language had replaced Greek. In 1095 Byzantine Emperor Alexius Comnenus asked Pope Urban II in Rome for help. He wanted Christian knights to fight against the Turks. Urban II responded by issuing a plea to free the Holy Land from the Muslims:

> "I, Urban, by the permission of God . . . have come into these parts as an ambassador . . . to you, the servants of God."

Between 1095 and 1214, Christians in western Europe responded by organizing eight major military expeditions called the Crusades. Kings, nobles, knights, peasants, and townspeople became crusaders and set out to win back control of Palestine.

REVIEW What were the Crusades?
Main Idea and Details

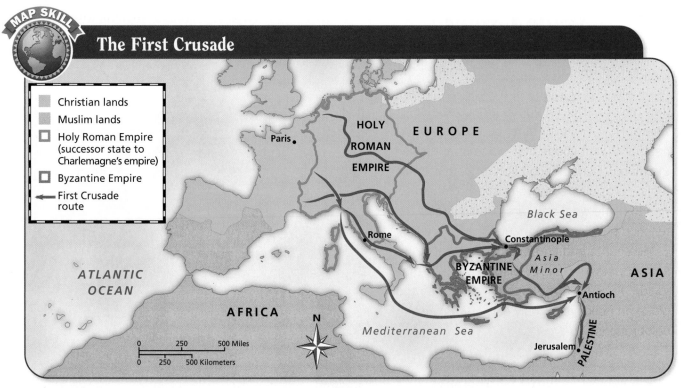

MAP SKILL

The First Crusade

Christian lands
Muslim lands
Holy Roman Empire (successor state to Charlemagne's empire)
Byzantine Empire
First Crusade route

Paris

HOLY ROMAN EMPIRE

EUROPE

Black Sea

Rome

Constantinople

Asia Minor

ATLANTIC OCEAN

BYZANTINE EMPIRE

ASIA

AFRICA

N

Antioch

Mediterranean Sea

0   250   500 Miles
0   250   500 Kilometers

Jerusalem

PALESTINE

▶ While there were many Crusades, the first one produced the most significant results.

MAP SKILL Trace Movement on Maps *Describe the route of the First Crusade.*

407

East and West

The crusaders marched to the East to win control of the Holy Land. Many of the crusaders also fought for themselves. They sought to increase their power, territory, and riches. The Crusades occurred at a time when western Europe's economy was expanding. Its military forces were increasing. The crusaders won some battles. They established crusader states along the eastern shore of the Mediterranean Sea. Although their victories had no permanent effect on the rule of the region, the Crusades increased the contacts between the West and the East. These contacts led to additional trade and commerce.

REVIEW Why would contact between the East and the West lead to increased trade? **Draw Conclusions**

Trade Grows

During the early Middle Ages, in about 1000, people had what they needed to produce their own food, clothing, and shelter. Occasionally they might barter for goods produced else-where. However, over time, people began to need and want goods that were not available on the manor. Serfs needed iron for better farming tools. Lords wanted ways to show off their wealth—fine wool and furs. These goods reached people on the manor by way of a fair.

Merchants and craftspeople in local guilds set up tents or stalls to display and sell their goods. Fairs occurred regularly and often took place on holidays, or holy days, or during celebrations.

▶ **A manuscript by William of Tyre illustrates the First Crusade, the Siege of Antioch.**

A network of European trade routes developed to serve these fairs. Traders developed standard, or regular, trade routes. Along these routes, traders and merchants exchanged local goods for foreign goods. A trader did not need to travel to the markets of Asia. Instead, goods from Asia would reach the trader through a series of middlemen, rather like a relay race.

The European trade routes linked to Muslim trade routes, providing goods from Africa, Asia Minor, and other Muslim lands. For goods from China and the Far East, European trade routes linked to the primary trade route through Asia, the Silk Road, one of the oldest and most important land routes.

REVIEW What locations or regions were part of the European trade network? **Main Idea and Details**

▶ **This image from the thirteenth century shows a typical medieval shop filled with goods.**

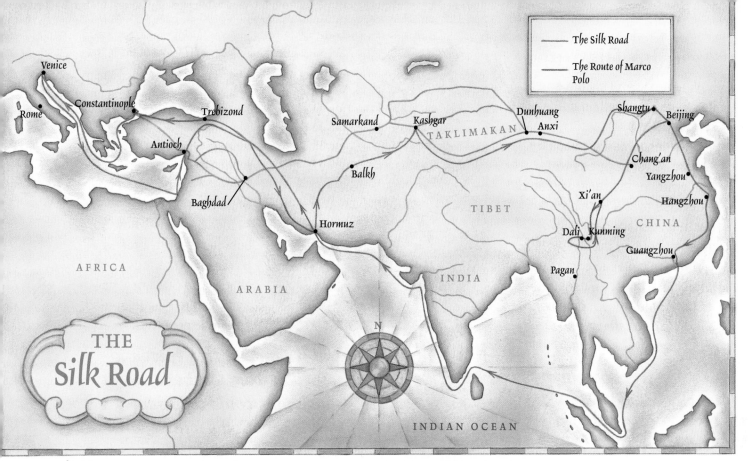

The map shows cities including Venice, Rome, Constantinople, Trebizond, Antioch, Baghdad, Samarkand, Kashgar, Balkh, Hormuz, Dunhuang, Anxi, Shangtu, Beijing, Chang'an, Yangzhou, Xi'an, Hangzhou, Dali, Kunming, Guangzhou, and Pagan. Regions labeled include AFRICA, ARABIA, TAKLIMAKAN, TIBET, INDIA, CHINA, and the INDIAN OCEAN.

Legend:
— The Silk Road
— The Route of Marco Polo

THE
Silk Road

▶ The name *Silk Road* is a nineteenth-century term coined by the German scholar Ferdinand von Richthofen. Marco Polo traveled the entire length of the Silk Road to cross Asia.

The Silk Road

We know much about the Silk Road from the travels of Marco Polo. His accounts of China's riches fascinated Europeans.

At about 4,000 miles in length, the Silk Road was not one single route across Central Asia. It was several different routes and branches, each passing through different settlements. However, all routes set out from the Chinese capital, Chang'an under the Han dynasty. They all reached Dunhuang on the edge of the Taklimakan Desert. At Dunhuang the road branched. The northern route, which led to Baghdad, is shown above on the map.

Caravans to China carried gold, ivory, and precious stones. Caravans from China brought silk, furs, ceramics, jade, bronze objects, lacquer, and iron. Ideas traveled both ways—Buddhism came to China via the Silk Road.

The Silk Road was physically difficult for travel. In addition, bandits made travel dangerous.

Caravans needed their own defense forces. In some places, forts and defensive walls were constructed along part of the route to protect the caravans.

In 1271 Marco Polo left Venice, Italy, for Shangtu. Under the Mongols, Polo remained in China as a guest for 17 years. In his writings, he describes how Genghis Khan unified the region:

> *"He then made himself master of cities and provinces . . . . and appointed governors to them."*

Once the numerous states in the region were united under the Mongol Empire, the Silk Road became important as a path for communication between different parts of the Empire. When the Silk Road came under the protection of the Mongols, it became safe for travel.

REVIEW What goods traveled along the Silk Road to and from China? **Main Idea and Details**

The Plague

When medieval culture was at its greatest strength, the **Plague** hit Europe.

The Plague was a **bubonic plague**, a very aggressive **epidemic**, or the rapid spread of a disease over a wide area. Bacteria, usually carried by rodents, caused the Plague.

A bubonic plague occurs when fleas infest rodents, usually rats, and then they move to humans. The fleas then transfer the

National Library of Australia

▶ Carved 75 years after the Plague, this woodcut illustrates the connection between trade and the spread of disease.

bacteria from the rat, through a bite, to the human. The rat and the human die, while the flea lives.

Today, we know how a bubonic plague spreads. However, in the fourteenth century, no one knew how and why the Plague spread. As one account says,

> *"And from what this epidemic came, all wise teachers and physicians could only say that it was God's will."*

Some historians suggest that the Plague began in Central Asia in the late 1320s and spread east to China. The Plague then spread west along the Silk Road, reaching the Black Sea by 1347.

The first European cases of the disease started in **Genoa**, Italy. An epidemic in a seaport town such as Genoa is especially dangerous. Ships from all directions came to and from Genoa. As a result, rats could spread the Plague from country to country in ships.

People were terrified that they would get the Plague. Some thought that they could get it by looking at someone who had the Plague. Here is an eyewitness account from Agnolo di Tura, of Siena:

> *". . . And they died by the hundreds, both day and night, and all were thrown in those ditches and covered with earth. And as soon as those ditches were filled, more were dug."*

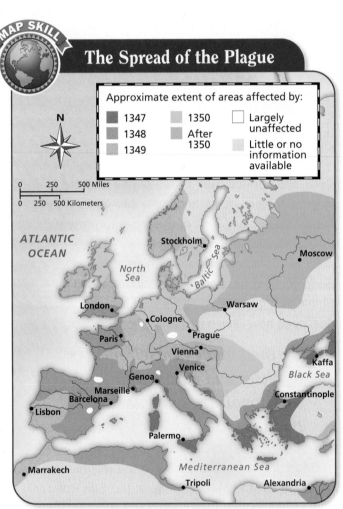

MAP SKILL

The Spread of the Plague

Approximate extent of areas affected by:

- 1347
- 1348
- 1349
- 1350
- After 1350
- Largely unaffected
- Little or no information available

N

0   250   500 Miles
0   250   500 Kilometers

ATLANTIC OCEAN
North Sea
Baltic Sea
Stockholm
Moscow
London
Cologne
Warsaw
Paris
Prague
Vienna
Venice
Kaffa
Black Sea
Genoa
Marseille
Barcelona
Constantinople
Lisbon
Palermo
Marrakech
Mediterranean Sea
Tripoli
Alexandria

▶ Scholars do not know for certain why some small pockets in Europe were not affected by the Plague.

MAP SKILL Use a Map Key *What areas were largely unaffected by the Plague?*

Effects of the Plague

- 25–33% Population loss in Europe
- Businesses go bankrupt
- Deaths cause labor shortages
- Trade declines and towns disappear
- Construction and building projects stop
- Food supply decreases and people starve

CHART SKILL Interpret a Chart *How did the Plague affect the growth of towns?*

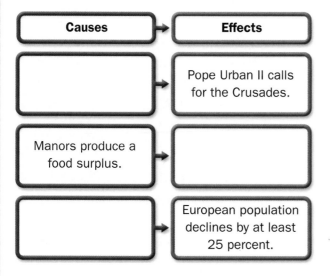

▶ Fleas drank the blood of rats that carried the bacteria that caused the Plague. Then the bacteria multiplied in the fleas. Finally, the fleas would bite humans, transfering the bacteria through their saliva.

An attack of bubonic plague does not last long, but the disease has a very high death rate. The Plague killed about one-fourth to one-third of Europe's population from 1347 to 1352. Despite the negative effects of the Plague (see chart at the left), fewer people meant that serfs became more valuable to lords. Serfs enjoyed a higher standard of living and more independence.

REVIEW What economic effects did the Plague have on Europe? **Cause and Effect**

Summarize the Lesson

- **1000** Trade began to grow in Europe.
- **1095** Pope Urban II called for the Crusades.
- **1271** Marco Polo traveled to China along the Silk Road.
- **about 1347** The Plague reached Europe.

LESSON 4   REVIEW

Check Facts and Main Ideas

1. Cause and Effect On a separate piece of paper, fill in the missing cause or effect in the blanks below.

Causes		Effects
	→	Pope Urban II calls for the Crusades.
Manors produce a food surplus.	→	
	→	European population declines by at least 25 percent.

2. Who issued the call for the Crusades, and why?

3. In addition to goods, what else traveled along trade routes such as the Silk Road.

4. What caused the Plague?

5. Critical Thinking: *Detect Bias* Why might some historians say that the Plague began in Central Asia?

Link to ⚬⚬ Science

Make a Hypothesis The bacteria that caused the Plague was *yersinia pestis.* Look in an encyclopedia, science book, or on the Internet to determine how bacteria form. Write a hypothesis, or educated guess, explaining how bacteria divide and spread.

Map and Globe Skills

Use a Time Zone Map

What? A time zone map is a map that indicates the relative time for a location. Earth is divided into 24 standard time zones, 23 full zones and two half zones. Each of the full zones represents a time interval of one hour.

The International Date Line is an imaginary line halfway around the world from Greenwich, England. It roughly parallels the 180° longitude line. The world's nations have agreed that this line will be used to designate where new days begin on Earth.

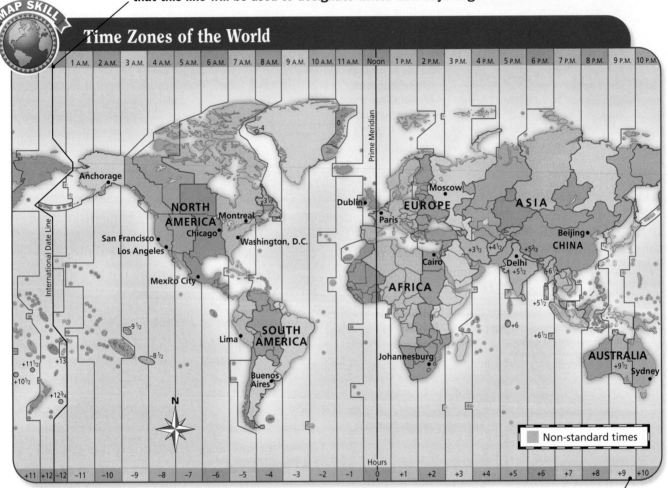

Time Zones of the World

1 A.M. 2 A.M. 3 A.M. 4 A.M. 5 A.M. 6 A.M. 7 A.M. 8 A.M. 9 A.M. 10 A.M. 11 A.M. Noon 1 P.M. 2 P.M. 3 P.M. 4 P.M. 5 P.M. 6 P.M. 7 P.M. 8 P.M. 9 P.M. 10 P.M.

International Date Line

Prime Meridian

Anchorage

NORTH AMERICA
Montreal
San Francisco
Los Angeles
Chicago
Washington, D.C.
Mexico City

-4
0
-3½
-9½
-8½

Dublin
Paris
EUROPE
Moscow
ASIA
Cairo
AFRICA
Beijing
CHINA
Delhi +5½
+3½ +4½ +5⅔
+6¼
+5½
+6
+6½

Lima
SOUTH AMERICA
Buenos Aires

Johannesburg

AUSTRALIA
+9½
Sydney

N

+11½ +13
+10½
+12¾

Hours

☐ Non-standard times

+11 +12 -12 -11 -10 -9 -8 -7 -6 -5 -4 -3 -2 -1 0 +1 +2 +3 +4 +5 +6 +7 +8 +9 +10

Positive and negative numbers show the difference between local time and Greenwich Mean Time (GMT).

Anchorage   Los Angeles   Chicago   Montreal   Buenos Aires

Why? In the late 1880s, international scientists created 24 time zones to standardize time keeping. They divided Earth into 24 time zones because since Earth rotates 360° every day (or 24 hours), they could establish each time zone 15° apart. To simplify, 360 divided by 15 equals 24. Sometimes, boundaries of the time zones had to be changed to keep with political boundaries such as countries.

How? The following steps will help you use a time zone map to find the local time for a specific location—for example Moscow, Russia.

1. Find Moscow on the time zone map.

2. Match the color with positive and negative numbers at the top of the map to the color used for Moscow's time zone.

3. Read the time given, 3:00 P.M.

Think and Apply

1. How did scientists create the time zones?

2. According to the time zone map, what is the time difference between Los Angeles, California, and Washington, D.C.?

3. If it is 6 P.M. in Washington, D.C., what is the local time in Los Angeles?

4. What is the time difference between Mexico City, Mexico, and Chicago, Illinois? Explain.

Internet Activity

For more information, go online to the Atlas at **www.sfsocialstudies.com.**

ublin

Paris

Moscow

Delhi

Beijing

Sydney

600   800

800
Charlemagne was crowned emperor by Pope Leo III.

c. 800
Vikings began to invade Charlemagne's empire.
Feudalism began to rise.

Chapter Summary

Sequence

On a separate piece of paper, put these events in their correct order.

- The Magna Carta is signed.
- Vikings launch invasions on Europe.
- Charlemagne becomes ruler.
- The First Crusade takes place.

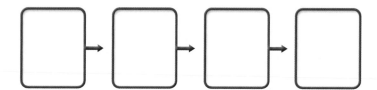

Vocabulary

Match each word with the correct definition or description.

1 monarch (p. 401)

2 feudalism (p. 401)

3 serf (p. 401)

4 knight (p. 401)

5 guild (p. 404)

6 chivalry (p. 401)

a. warrior trained to fight on horseback

b. person who lived and farmed on land owned by a lord

c. social, political, and economic system of the Middle Ages

d. group of people united by a common trade

e. supreme ruler

f. knight's code

People and Terms

Write a sentence explaining why each of the following people and terms is important in the study of the Middle Ages. You may use two or more in a single sentence.

1 Charlemagne (p. 397)

2 Magna Carta (p. 398)

3 three-field rotation (p. 403)

4 Crusades (p. 407)

5 Silk Road (p. 409)

6 North European Plain (p. 393)

7 Rhine River (p. 394)

8 Leo III (p. 399)

9 Domesday Book (p. 397)

10 Christine de Pisan (p. 405)

Timeline

1000

1200

1400

1086
The Domesday Book was created.

1215
The Magna Carta was signed.

1347
The Plague reached Europe.

1400
Feudalism began to decline.

Facts and Main Ideas

1. Who called for the First Crusade?

2. How were serfs and slaves alike and different?

3. **Time Line** About how long did the feudal system last?

4. **Main Idea** What are the four major land regions of Europe?

5. **Main Idea** How did the Magna Carta change the way England was ruled?

6. **Main Idea** How did people's lives change during feudalism?

7. **Main Idea** How were the Crusades, trade, and the Plague related?

8. **Critical Thinking:** *Evaluate Information* What do you think was the greatest advancement in culture people made during the Middle Ages? Why?

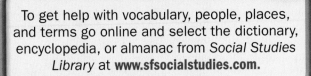

Internet Activity

To get help with vocabulary, people, places, and terms go online and select the dictionary, encyclopedia, or almanac from *Social Studies Library* at **www.sfsocialstudies.com.**

Write About History

1. **Write a journal entry** as a crusader who has reached Palestine (the Holy Land) during the First Crusade. What do you see? What do you hope to accomplish?

2. **Write a news bulletin** announcing the signing of the Magna Carta. Describe its contents and why it is newsworthy.

3. **Write a "help wanted" ad** inviting people to become merchants and traders along the Silk Road. Describe what qualifications are needed. Tell what kinds of people and things the merchant can expect to meet and see along the way.

Apply Skills

Use a Time Zone Map
Using the time zone map on page 412, answer the following questions.

1. What is the time difference, if any, between your state and Washington, D.C.?

2. How many time zones are in China?

3. If it is 9 A.M. in San Francisco, California, what time is it in Delhi, India?

The Round Table

Tales and legends are stories that are usually made up. Sometimes they try to explain something such as an historical event. This excerpt is from a medieval legend about King Arthur's Round Table. King Arthur appears in legends as early as A.D. 600 and as late as the 1300s. According to legend, Arthur was a Celtic ruler who fought against invaders from England. From this passage, what can you learn about the Middle Ages?

King Arthur filled his Round Table with the best knights in all the world. But for many years, one seat remained empty. No one could sit on it and live, which is why it was called the Siege Perilous, or seat of danger. Merlin prophesied that when a knight came to claim the Siege Perilous, the days of the Round Table would be drawing to a close.

One day a young knight clad in red armor appeared at court, without weapons. He bowed to King Arthur, walked straight to the Siege Perilous, and sat down. The knights gasped. But behind the young knight appeared in letters of gold, "Galahad, the High Prince."

"Welcome," said King Arthur. "Please tell us who you are."

"I am Sir Galahad, and my mother, Elaine, is the daughter of King Pelles, the Maimed King."

"I have heard of King Pelles, who lies crippled at the castle of Carbonek. But I did not know he had a grandson. And yet, Sir Galahad, I feel I know you. You look like Sir Lancelot as a young man."

"This is not surprising," said Lancelot, "for he is my son."

[from DK The Illustrated Book of Myths: Tales and Legends of the World, retold by Neil Philip]

Review

Main Ideas and Vocabulary

TEST PREP

Read the passage below and use it to answer the questions that follow.

The years from about 500 to 1500 are often called the Middle Ages. During that period, people from different parts of the world came into contact with one another, often for the first time. This contact and interaction included armed conflicts and the <u>bartering</u> of goods.

The Byzantine Empire maintained a capital at Constantinople, a city at the center of several trade routes. Christianity flourished in the Byzantine Empire until the 1000s, when the empire began to decline as it fought losing battles against the Muslims.

In the 600s, Islam, based on the teachings of Muhammad, rose in Arabia. Under Muhammad's successors, Muslim Arabs conquered northern Africa, bringing Islam with them. Muslim traders and sailors also spread Islam. African empires in eastern, western, and southern Africa developed along major trade routes.

Isolation helped Chinese society to be both stable and self-sufficient. In the 1200s, Mongol warriors, led by Kublai Khan, swept into China. The Khan established the Mongol Empire, marking the first time that China came under foreign rule.

Japanese culture was influenced by contact with China. For example, the Japanese borrowed the Chinese system of writing. Japan began to cast off Chinese influences during the late 700s and early 800s. The 1100s marked civil wars resulting in a form of military government led by a shogun.

In Europe feudalism and the manor system rose and declined. Royal power was limited under the Magna Carta. To take back the Holy Land, the Crusades were launched in 1095. Towns grew and trade thrived. But much of that changed when the plague hit Europe.

1 According to the passage, what two items helped influence the future of world regions?
  A feudalism and serfs
  B Islam and empires
  C conflicts and trade
  D language and time

2 In the passage, the word *bartering* means—
  A growing   **C** throwing away
  B trading   **D** making

3 According to the passage, what religion was carried by traders?
  A Christianity   **C** feudalism
  B Buddhism   **D** Islam

4 What is the main idea of the passage?
  A There were many wars between 500 and 1500.
  B Muslim traders conquered lands.
  C Trade and religion helped shape the future of many regions.
  D Japan borrowed ideas from China.

Test Talk

Use the map to help you find the answer.

People and Terms

Match each person or term to its definition.

1 Sumanguru (p. 375)

2 Genghis Khan (p. 352)

3 Shah Jahan (p. 349)

4 Ming dynasty (p. 353)

5 Solomonid dynasty (p. 382)

6 bubonic plague (p. 410)

a. an epidemic

b. defeated by Sundiata at Battle of Kirina

c. ruled Ethiopia for more than 700 years

d. ruthless Mongol warrior

e. overthrew the Mongols

f. built Taj Mahal for his wife

Apply Skills

Prepare a Time Zone Map

Make a time zone map. Show the time zones on a globe or map for several different cities around the world.

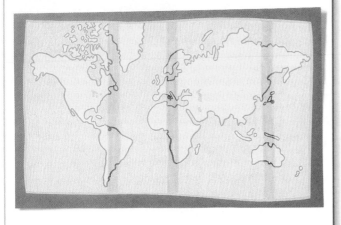

Write and Share

Present a Television News Magazine Segment
Prepare a 10-minute segment about the impact of trade in the Middle Ages. Work with your classmates to choose a news anchor, a reporter, and people to interview. Be sure to include the viewpoints of people such as rulers, traders, merchants, serfs, and religious leaders. Have the remaining classmates write questions for the reporter to ask. Present your news segment to another class in your school.

Read on Your Own

Look for books like these in the library.

UNIT 5 Project

A Day in the Life

Make a documentary about living in a medieval village.

1 **Form** groups to choose topics to research about life in a medieval village. Find information about the village's buildings and the activities of people living in the village.

2 **Write** a script about people living in a medieval village.

3 **Build** a model of your village. Include buildings and the surrounding landscape.

4 **Present** your documentary to the class.

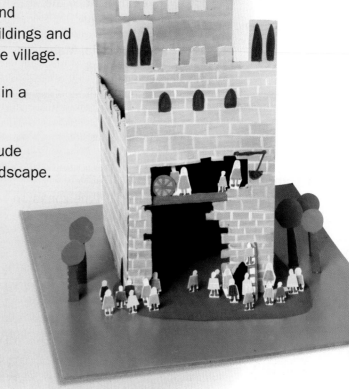

Internet Activity

Explore the Middle Ages on the Internet. Go to **www.sfsocialstudies.com/activities** and select your grade and unit.

Discovery, Expansion, and Revolutions

How do ideas make a nation?

UNIT 6

Begin with a Primary Source

1450   1500   1550   1600   1650

1455
Gutenberg Bible is printed.

1492
Columbus begins first voyage to the Americas.

1519
Magellan begins first voyage around the world.

1588
Spanish Armada is defeated by England.

1607
Jamestown is founded.

> *"Get gold, humanely if possible, but at all hazards—get gold."*
>
> —King Ferdinand of Spain, 1511

The power that European nations gained after 1500 was fueled by great advances in shipbuilding and navigation. This battle in the Gulf of Naples was painted by Pieter Brueghel.

1700   1750   1800   1850   1900

1760s
James Watt improves the steam engine.

1793
Reign of Terror begins in France.

1821
Mexico wins independence.

1871
German Empire is created.

1776 U.S. Declaration of Independence

Meet the People

Leonardo da Vinci

1452–1519
Birthplace: Vinci, near Florence, Italy
Artist, inventor
- Studied nature
- Made many inventions
- Painted the *Mona Lisa* and *The Last Supper,* among the world's most famous paintings

Vasco da Gama

c. 1469–1524
Birthplace: Sines, Portugal
Explorer
- Opened the first all-water trade route between Europe and Asia
- Led Portugal to become important trading and naval power in the Indian Ocean
- Named viceroy of India in 1524

Bartolomé de Las Casas

1474–1566
Birthplace: Seville, Spain
Historian, missionary
- Exposed the oppression of Native Americans by the Spanish
- Called for the abolition of Native American slavery
- Wrote *Historia de las Indias,* a history of the Indies

Martin Luther

1483–1546
Birthplace: Eisleben, Saxony (present-day Germany)
Religious reformer
- Leader of the Reformation
- Wrote a challenge to the Church, criticizing indulgences
- Publicly criticized the pope's claim to be the sole interpreter of the Bible

1400   1450   1500   1550   1600   1650

1452–1519 • Leonardo da Vinci

c. 1469–1524 • Vasco da Gama

1474–1566 • Bartolomé de Las Casas

1483–1546 • Martin Luther

1533–1603 • Elizabeth I

Elizabeth I

1533–1603

Birthplace: Greenwich, near London, England

English queen

- Reigned from 1558 until her death in 1603
- Under her reign, made Protestantism important in England
- Made England a great sea power and defeated the Spanish Armada

Marie-Olympe de Gouges

1748–1793

Birthplace: Montauban, France

Political activist, feminist

- Wrote *Declaration of the Rights of Woman and the Female Citizen,* calling for the equality of women
- Opposed the execution of Louis XVI
- Influenced feminists in other countries

Simón Bolívar

1783–1830

Birthplace: Caracas in present-day Venezuela

South American general, dictator, president

- Won independence for Bolivia, Colombia, Ecuador, Peru, and Venezuela from Spain
- President of Ecuador and Colombia
- Dictator of Peru
- Drew up constitution for Bolivia

Meiji

1852–1912

Birthplace: Kyoto, Japan

Japanese emperor

- Presided over the end of shogun rule of Japan
- Oversaw Japan's development into an industrial and military power
- Namesake of Meiji Era in Japan

1700   1750   1800   1850   1900   1950

1748–1793 • Marie-Olympe de Gouges

1783–1830 • Simón Bolívar

1852–1912 • Meiji

425

Discovery, Expansion, and Revolutions

Target Skill

Summarize

Summarizing information will help you pick out the main points of what you read. It will also help you make sense of the ideas you read or hear about.

You can use these four steps to write a summary.

- Read from start to finish.
- List the main points.
- Add important details to the list.
- Turn your list into a paragraph.

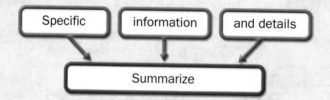

Specific → information → and details

↓

Summarize

Read the paragraph. Then read the **summary** that follows.

The Renaissance (rehn uh SAHNS) lasted from the 1400s to the 1600s. It began in Italy and spread to England, France, and other countries. During the Renaissance, scholars and artists studied the cultures of ancient Greece and Rome.

In summary, the Renaissance began in the 1400s. It spread from Italy to other European countries. During this time, people studied ancient Greek and Roman culture.

The Work of Bartolomé de Las Casas

Bartolomé de Las Casas (bahr toh loh MAY day lahs KAH sahs) lived from 1474 until 1566. He was one of the first Spanish missionaries to reach the island of Hispaniola, in the West Indies.

Las Casas was among the first Europeans to defend the rights of the native peoples. He worked hard to improve conditions for them. He wrote many essays and pamphlets, each detailing the thought processes that led him to oppose the Spanish treatment of these peoples.

One of his works was *In Defense of the Indians* (1552). In it Las Casas argues that every human being is free and rational by nature, and capable of unlimited growth.

Las Casas's views were contrary to those of philosophers such as Aristotle, who held that some people were slaves by nature and made to serve others.

Las Casas defended Native American resistance to Spanish conquest. He explained that the Spanish were coming to the Americas and acting as if they were kings in these new lands.

> *"Every king . . . can prohibit any person from entering his land, whether to engage in trade or to reside therein or for any other cause."*

Las Casas pointed out that Spanish explorers and generals acted as if they had a right to the gold. In support of his argument, he asked what the Spanish king would do if the French marched into Spain and took possession of the Spanish silver mines or the king's store of gold.

Las Casas continued to argue for the rights of the Native Americans until his death.

Use the reading strategy of summarize to answer these questions. Then write a summary of the selection.

1. What is the main idea of the selection?
2. What details will you place in your summary?

CHAPTER 15

New Beginnings

Lesson 1

1400s
Florence
People begin to look back at ancient Greek and Roman cultures.

1

Lesson 2

1492
West Indies
Adventurers, sailors, and explorers begin to find new trade routes.

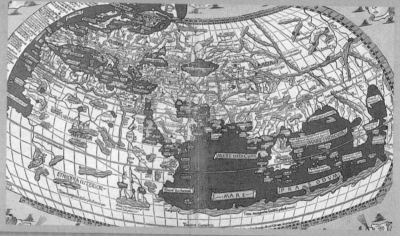

2

Lesson 3

1607
Jamestown
England establishes its first permanent colony in North America.

3

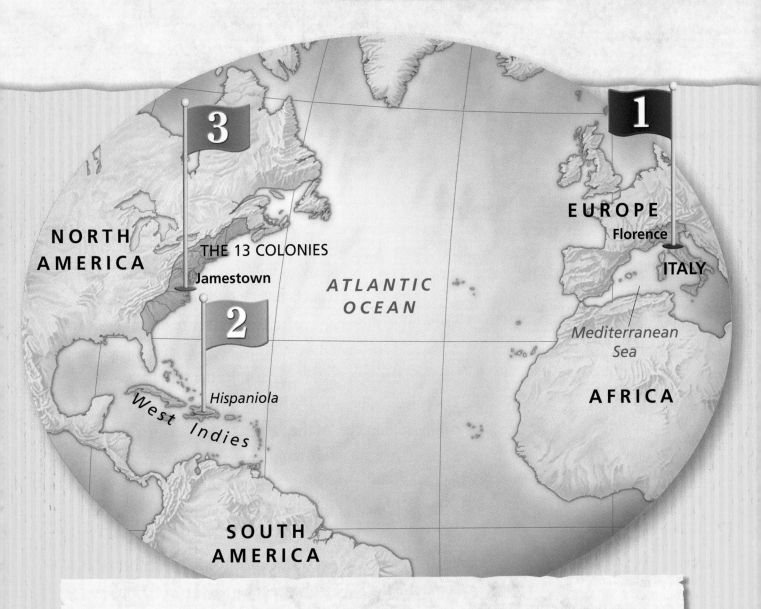

Why We Remember

In the 1400s, the effects of the Plague began to decrease. This is also when the Western world became interested in building a culture as grand as the cultures of ancient Rome and Greece. People took an interest in art, poetry, history, and moral philosophy. Adventurers sought new trade routes. Instead they found lands they did not know about. In their quest for riches, some people took advantage of native populations. All of these factors were a powerful influence on the world as we know it today.

ITALY
Milan · · Venice
· Florence

1400   1500

mid-1400s
Renaissance begins.

1455
Gutenberg introduces a Bible printed on a printing press.

1517
The Reformation begins.

The Renaissance

PREVIEW

Focus on the Main Idea
From the mid-1400s to the 1600s, Europeans had a renewed interest in art, literature, education, and the cultures of ancient Greece and Rome.

PLACES
Florence
Milan
Venice

PEOPLE
Petrarch
Raphael
Michelangelo
Leonardo da Vinci
Copernicus
Galileo
Johannes Gutenberg
Martin Luther

VOCABULARY
commerce
indulgence
excommunicate

TERMS
Renaissance
moveable type
Protestantism

EVENTS
Reformation
Council of Trent
Counter-Reformation

You Are There
It's a warm, sunny day in Florence, Italy, in the late 1500s. Yesterday, you watched the city celebrate the feast of Saint John, Florence's patron saint. The main event was a horse race through the city. Today, you're enjoying a stroll through the Boboli Gardens, behind the Pitti Palace. The palace belongs to the Medici, the most powerful family in Florence. At the far end of the gardens, on top of a hill, stands the newly built Forte Belvedere. You climb up to the battlements, and look out the openings to get a complete view of the city. You cannot miss the Duomo of Florence, a splendid cathedral. Next to it stands the Baptistery with its famous bronze doors. The cathedral's dome and the Baptistery's doors are just two examples of the stunning art of the time. From your perch on the Forte, you see that the city-state of Florence is a truly beautiful place.

Summarize As you read, summarize the events of the Renaissance to help you organize your learning.

The Awakening

In 1350 Italy consisted of many separate city-states. Three of the most important of these were **Florence,** **Milan,** and **Venice.** All of these city-states grew to importance through trade and commerce. **Commerce** is the buying and selling of a large quantity of goods. With great wealth, these city-states flourished economically, as well as intellectually.

Florence was the birthplace of the **Renaissance** (rehn uh SAHNS), the intellectual and economic movement that saw a revived interest in the art, social, scientific, and political ideas of ancient Greece and Rome. Some people believed that an understanding and appreciation of the cultures of ancient times could help people conduct their own lives. **Petrarch** (PEH trahrk), a poet and scholar, was a powerful influence on the early Renaissance. Petrarch encouraged people to seek out and study the philosophy and literature of the past. He also encouraged people to speak and write thoughtfully:

> **"The style is the man."**

▶ **Florence is known as the birthplace of the Renaissance. The large cathedral shown here is the Duomo of Florence.**

Petrarch meant that careless expression was a sign of careless thought.

As markets grew, merchants, bankers, and tradespeople became more prosperous. Prosperous people searched for ways to display their wealth. They wanted fine clothing and larger, more luxurious homes to display works of art. This cultural and economic rebirth began in Italy in the 1400s. By the 1600s it had spread to England, France, Germany, the Netherlands, and Spain.

REVIEW What did the Renaissance represent?
⟳ **Summarize**

MAP SKILL

Italian City-States, c. 1500

Other Italian states

SWISS CONFEDERATION

DUCHY OF SAVOY

FRANCE

DUCHY OF MILAN

REPUBLIC OF GENOA

REPUBLIC OF FLORENCE

PAPAL STATES

REPUBLIC OF VENICE

Adriatic Sea

HUNGARY

OTTOMAN EMPIRE

REPUBLIC OF GENOA

N

KINGDOM OF SARDINIA

Tyrrhenian Sea

KINGDOM OF NAPLES

KINGDOM OF SICILY

Mediterranean Sea

0   100   200 Miles
0 100 200 Kilometers

▶ **Several regions of fifteenth-century Italy were city-states.**

MAP SKILL Understand Borders *Which city-states bordered both the Adriatic Sea and the Tyrrhenian Sea?*

431

Art in the Renaissance

There were several reasons why the Renaissance began in Italy. Ancient ruins could be seen all over the Italian Peninsula. Trade made the Italian city-states wealthy. This wealth encouraged political leaders, businessmen, and the Catholic Church to hire artists to create beautiful works of art. There was a new respect for what humans were able to achieve.

Unlike medieval European artists, Renaissance painters and sculptors portrayed people and nature realistically. They were inspired by ancient Greek and Roman artists. They mastered the art of perspective, which creates the illusion that objects in paintings are closer or farther from the viewer. They learned to give depth to pictures as well as proportion to people, things, and buildings.

▶ **This painting of the Mother of Jesus was painted by Raphael.**

▶ **Michelangelo's statue of David was sculpted in marble and stands more than 13 feet tall.**

The Granger Collection

Among the most well-known Italian Renaissance artists were **Raphael,** **Michelangelo,** and **Leonardo da Vinci.** They were famous in their own time. Many people today still consider them to be geniuses. Raphael was noted for his lovely portraits of the Mother of Jesus. He was also noted for his mastery of perspective and architecture.

Michelangelo was not only a painter but also the finest sculptor of the Renaissance. He painted the Sistine Chapel in fresco and sculpted a series of works known as the *Pietà*. These statues portrayed the Mother of Jesus holding her son after he had been taken down from the cross. Michelangelo carefully chose his marble blocks by visiting the quarry where they were mined. There, he would wait until the sun rose, so that he could watch the sun shine through the marble. If there was a flaw in the marble, he could see it.

The greatest of the Renaissance artists may have been Leonardo da Vinci. He was a painter, sculptor, engineer, and scientist. His most famous paintings were the *Mona Lisa* and *The Last Supper*. He created statues of men and horses. As a scientist he investigated optics, or the study of light and vision, and dissected human bodies to study anatomy.

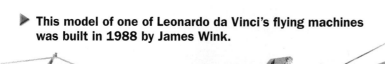

▶ **This model of one of Leonardo da Vinci's flying machines was built in 1988 by James Wink.**

Da Vinci is believed to be the first person to draw the human body accurately. He also experimented with mechanics, the study of forces on solids, liquids, and gases. He built models of aircraft (400 years before the first working airplane), a parachute, tanks, machine guns, and movable bridges. He kept notebooks on all his observations and experiments but he wrote them all backward so that these books can be read only by being held up to a mirror. He did not want people to read everything he wrote.

REVIEW What forms did Renaissance artists use to create their works of art? ↻ Summarize

---

An Asian Renaissance

At the same time the Renaissance was spreading throughout Europe, China and Japan were experiencing a cultural renaissance of their own. In China during the Ming dynasty there was a renewal of literature and the arts. Novels and dramas flourished. The Forbidden City, a beautiful palace, was built in Beijing. Theater thrived in Japan. Kabuki theater combined music, dancing, and elaborate costumes in performances that often lasted from morning to evening. Sometimes actors would stop the play so that they could talk to the audience. Sometimes the audience talked back. Other art forms grew prominent in Japan. Haiku poems, which have three lines and 17 syllables, became popular. The art of wood-block prints flourished. Multicolored wood-block art soon followed. This period made important contributions to urban Japanese culture.

▶ **Kabuki theater began in Japan in the 1500s. This actor is part of a present-day Kabuki performance.**

ASIA
MING DYNASTY
JAPAN
N

▶ **Matsuo Basho perfected Haiku poetry.**

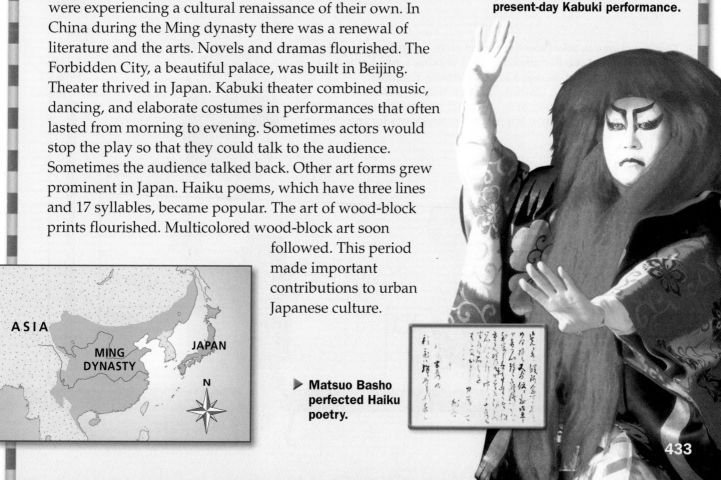

433

Revolution in Science

Renaissance thinkers believed that people should use reasoned thought and the scientific method to understand how the world works. Two of the most significant Renaissance scientists were **Copernicus** and **Galileo.** Both were astronomers and both taught that Earth moves around the sun.

Copernicus taught at the University of Cracow in Poland. His astronomical observations convinced Copernicus that Earth was not the center of the universe. He wrote out his ideas by 1510, but chose not to allow them to be published until 1540.

Galileo lived in Italy and taught at the University of Pisa. When he spoke out in favor of Copernicus's ideas, he was criticized by the Catholic Church. In 1609, only a year after the telescope was invented, Galileo built an improved telescope. He then did something revolutionary—he became the first person to point his telescope toward the sky. He used it to study the sky. However, Galileo's studies challenged the authority of the Catholic Church. He was put on trial and under house arrest for the

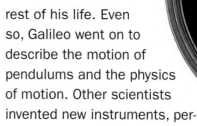

▶ Copernicus (left) and Galileo (below) helped to revolutionize our understanding of the universe.

rest of his life. Even so, Galileo went on to describe the motion of pendulums and the physics of motion. Other scientists invented new instruments, performed experiments, and made their ideas known.

REVIEW How did Copernicus and Galileo change people's ideas about the world?

↺ Summarize

▶ The inventions in this time line reveal some important contributions of the Renaissance. The printing press helped to spread ideas and increase literacy among European people. The others are instruments that helped either to measure more accurately or to see what humans could otherwise never see—two important requirements for the practice of science.

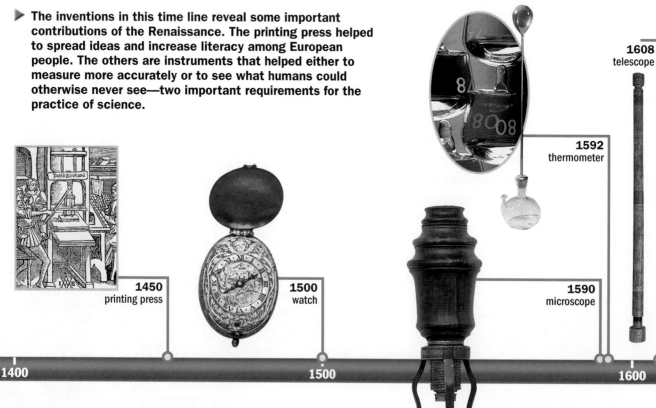

1450 printing press

1500 watch

1590 microscope

1592 thermometer

1608 telescope

1400

1500

1600

Renaissance Inventions

Probably the greatest advance in technology was **Johannes Gutenberg's** invention of a printing press that used **movable type,** or small reusable metal pieces for each letter and number. Gutenberg worked on his invention throughout the 1440s. In 1455 he introduced a Bible printed on his printing press.

Up until this time, books had to be copied by hand. Gutenberg's press produced books far more quickly than they could be produced by hand. As a result, books became affordable for the educated middle class. Readers wanted a variety of books, such as almanacs, travel books, romances, and poetry. As the demand for books grew, the book trade flourished throughout Europe. Other related industries, such as paper making and printing press building, also thrived. As a result, more people became literate and the economy strengthened.

In addition to the printing press, a variety of inventions was introduced during the Renaissance. Some have proven to be quite useful to society both then and now.

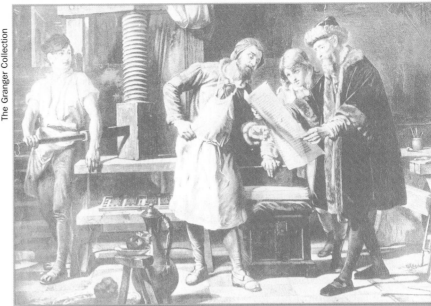

The Granger Collection

▶ **Johannes Gutenberg (on the far right) spent years perfecting his movable-type printing press. Here, he examines a page fresh off the press.**

Science & Society Picture Library

▶ **This is a modern reproduction of the Gutenberg printing press.**

As you already have read, Leonardo da Vinci experimented with mechanics, which is the study of forces on solids, liquids, and gases. Unfortunately, many of his inventions were too advanced for the existing technology of his time.

Other practical inventions included the watch, which was created in the early 1500s. A Dutchman invented a mainspring to power clocks. Until then, clocks had been driven by falling weights and had to remain stationary and upright for the weights to accurately operate. The mainspring allowed clocks to be portable and movable. In the late 1500s, a Dutch maker of eyeglasses discovered the principle of the compound microscope. In the 1670s, a single lens microscope was invented that could magnify an object up to 270 times its real size.

Another Dutch optician used the same principle to create an optical telescope in 1608. As you have read, Galileo soon improved on the original design of the telescope.

The air thermometer was invented in 1592. It worked by measuring a column of air in a glass tube. A person could use it to estimate temperature.

REVIEW How did Gutenberg's printing press change conditions in Europe? ↪ Summarize

The Need for Church Reform

Many Renaissance scholars in northern and western Europe turned their attention to the study of the Roman Catholic Church and its practices. The Church had become wealthy during the Middle Ages. With that wealth came corruption.

Among the practices these scholars objected to was the Church's willingness to accept money for **indulgences,** or pardons from punishment for sins. Originally, an indulgence could be gained only by performing works of charity. For example, a person could fast, give money to the poor, or make pilgrimages to holy places. However, by the beginning of the Renaissance, the Church allowed people to buy indulgences as a way to buy pardons for their sins. Indulgences were also granted to the crusaders before they set off for war.

One of the most vocal critics of this practice was **Martin Luther.** He believed that Christians should not be judged by the good works they

▶ **This wood engraving from the early 1500s depicts a church official selling indulgences.**

performed, but by their belief in God. In 1517 Luther wrote a challenge to the Church. He attacked the sale of indulgences. He stated that people should read and interpret the Bible themselves. The church dictated that only the pope, the leader of the Roman Catholic Church, or other church officials such as bishops and monks, could interpret the Bible on their own. Luther asked for a debate, or a public discussion.

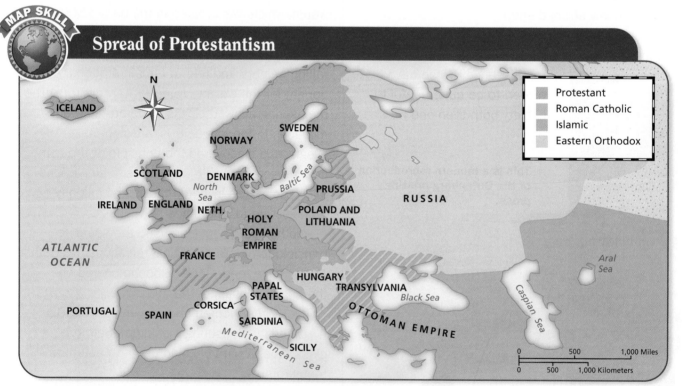

MAP SKILL

Spread of Protestantism

Protestant
Roman Catholic
Islamic
Eastern Orthodox

ICELAND

NORWAY

SWEDEN

SCOTLAND

DENMARK

North Sea

Baltic Sea

PRUSSIA

RUSSIA

IRELAND ENGLAND NETH.

POLAND AND LITHUANIA

HOLY ROMAN EMPIRE

ATLANTIC OCEAN

FRANCE

Aral Sea

HUNGARY

PAPAL STATES

TRANSYLVANIA

Black Sea

Caspian Sea

PORTUGAL SPAIN

CORSICA

SARDINIA

Mediterranean Sea

SICILY

OTTOMAN EMPIRE

0   500   1,000 Miles
0   500   1,000 Kilometers

▶ **By 1590 Protestantism had spread to many parts of Europe.**

MAP SKILL Use a Map Key *In which countries did Roman Catholic areas overlap with Protestant areas?*

Church officials reacted by **excommunicating,** or expelling, Luther from the Church. When he was asked if he would reconsider and take back his objections, Luther said,

> "... *my conscience is captive to the Word of God. I cannot and I will not recant [take back] anything ...*"

People who agreed with Luther and followed his teachings became known as Lutherans. Soon there were other groups of Christians, such as the followers of John Calvin, who no longer wished to be a part of the Roman Catholic Church.

These events were called the **Reformation** because these people wanted to reform, or change, Church beliefs and practices. This began a movement called **Protestantism,** since its supporters had protested against the Church.

The Catholic Church responded by calling the **Council of Trent** in 1545. These efforts were called the **Counter-Reformation** because they were against the Reformation. Roman Catholics

▶ **Martin Luther was the leader of the Protestant Reformation.**

still accepted that only the Church could explain the Bible. They also insisted that the pope was the highest authority in the Church. However, the council did begin some reforms, including a ban on the sale of indulgences.

As you read in Unit 4, Christianity split into an eastern church and a western church in 1054. Now the Reformation and the Counter-Reformation split western Christianity once again: into Catholics and Protestants.

REVIEW What were the Reformation and the Counter-Reformation? 🔄 **Summarize**

Summarize the Lesson

— **mid-1400s** The Renaissance began.
  └ **1455** Gutenberg published a printed version of the Bible.
— **1517** The Reformation began.

LESSON 1   REVIEW

Check Facts and Main Ideas

1. 🔄 **Summarize** On a separate piece of paper, write three short sentences that lead to the summary.

Events during the Renaissance brought great changes in the arts, science, literature, and ideas to Europe.

2. How did Petrarch influence the Renaissance?

3. What practices of the Roman Catholic Church led to the Reformation?

4. How does the Renaissance affect us today?

5. **Critical Thinking:** *Make Inferences* How did the Renaissance change people's thinking?

Link to ∞ **Writing**

Write an Essay Suppose you are Petrarch's assistant. Write an essay that describes and illustrates his quote: "The style is the man." Exchange your essay with a partner and ask him or her to evaluate it.

1492
Columbus's first expedition to the Americas

1519
Magellan begins
his journey around
the world.

1497
Vasco da Gama begins expedition to India.

Trade Routes and Conquests

PREVIEW

Focus on the Main Idea
European traders wanted additional trade routes, and rulers wanted to establish empires.

PLACES
Cape of Good Hope
West Indies

PEOPLE
Henry the Navigator
Bartolomeu Dias
Vasco da Gama
Ferdinand Magellan
Christopher Columbus
Isabella
Elizabeth I

VOCABULARY
circumnavigate
conquistador

TERMS
Treaty of Tordesillas
Columbian Exchange
Armada

You Are There
As Prince Henry's economic advisor, you've been asked to compare the cost of bringing gold to Portugal from Africa by sea to the cost of transporting it by land. Travel logs show that a single camel can travel about 3.5 miles per hour for about 10 hours a day—34 miles in one day. One camel can carry about 990 pounds of cargo. Most camel caravans have 1,000 camels.

Next, you discover that a ship travels about 2 miles per hour. However, the ship can move 24 hours a day. Most important is how much cargo a ship can carry—between 50 and 160 tons of cargo.

After you have made your calculations, you approach Prince Henry. You recommend that he spend whatever is necessary to establish and protect sea routes for trade with Africa.

Summarize As you read, summarize the information to help you better understand how Europeans started exploring and conquering other lands.

Portuguese Explorers

During the 1400s, Europeans developed an interest in gold and other riches from Africa. For years, travelers brought gold, silver, and ivory across land routes that connected Africa to the Mediterranean region. As you read in Unit 5, the land routes were costly, dangerous, and controlled by Muslim traders. As a Christian country, Portugal wanted to avoid land routes controlled by Muslims. Portugal took the lead in the expeditions to find new sea routes.

From 1419 until his death in 1460, Prince **Henry** of Portugal sent several expeditions to explore the west coast of Africa. He hoped to establish colonies there and break the Muslim control on trade routes. Henry's influence on voyages of exploration was so important that he came to be called Henry the Navigator.

In 1488 **Bartolomeu Dias** of Portugal sailed around the **Cape of Good Hope** at the southern tip of Africa. He would have continued on to India, but the ship's supplies were low. After consulting with his officers, Dias decided to turn back.

In 1497 **Vasco da Gama** sailed around the Cape of Good Hope to India. His voyage marked the first all-water

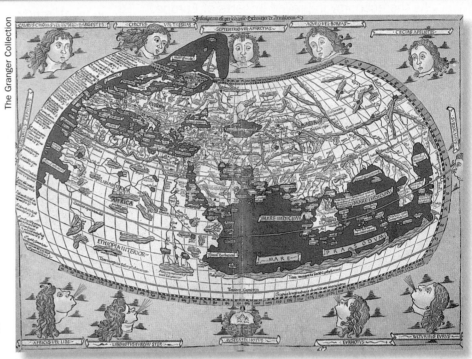

The Granger Collection

▶ **Thanks to the printing press, this world map, originally drawn by Ptolemy about A.D. 150, was widely available to navigators and sailors.**

trade route between Europe and Asia. Da Gama's second voyage to India, in 1502, established a Portuguese presence in India. Portugal soon became an important trading and naval power in the Indian Ocean.

Other nations soon took Portugal's lead. However, it was a Portuguese sea captain named **Ferdinand Magellan** who made one of the most important sea voyages of the age. Magellan thought it possible to reach the east by sailing around the southern tip of South America. In 1519 Magellan set out with five ships. Magellan did not live long enough to complete the voyage himself. He was killed while he and his crew visited an island in the Pacific Ocean.

In 1522, three years after Magellan had begun his voyage, a single ship—all that was left of the original five—arrived in Spain. It was the first ship to **circumnavigate,** or sail completely around, the world.

REVIEW Why did Catholic countries such as Portugal wish to find an ocean route to the African coasts? **Cause and Effect**

▶ **Galleons were sailing ships used mainly by the Spanish and Portuguese during the fifteenth and sixteenth centuries.**

East to West

As the economy improved in parts of Europe, the demand for goods from Asia—such as peppercorns, cloves, nutmeg, cinnamon, precious gems, and fine silk—increased. While the Portuguese worked to reach Asia by sailing around Africa, others thought sailing west would be easier. Among these was **Christopher Columbus,** an Italian sailor living in Portugal. In 1484 Columbus asked King John II of Portugal to sponsor a voyage to reach Asia by a western route. Because Portugal was committed to exploring the gold-producing coast of Africa, King John turned him down.

Columbus turned to Spain for funding. His first few requests were refused. Eventually, however, Queen **Isabella** agreed to fund Columbus's expedition. She wanted to spread Christianity and to compete with Portugal for wealth.

Columbus sailed from Spain on August 3, 1492. On October 12 he sighted land, an island in what is now called the **West Indies.** About two weeks later he sighted what he thought was Japan, also called Zipangu at that time.

> *"All my globes and world maps seem to indicate that the island of Japan is in this vicinity and I am sure that Cuba and Zipangu are one."*

By 1504 Columbus had completed three more expeditions.

REVIEW What benefits did Queen Isabella expect to get from Columbus's expedition? **Cause and Effect**

Map Adventure

You're an Explorer

It is 1497. Vasco da Gama has asked you to join his crew. You will be working on one of his four ships, sailing around the Cape of Good Hope. This voyage could open up trade routes to both India and China.

1. In July, you depart from Lisbon, Portugal. What direction do you sail to head toward the Cape of Good Hope?

2. You round the tip of Africa in November. How many months have you traveled?

3. You drop anchor off the coast of Mozambique. The people living there think that you are all Muslims. Why?

4. Your next major stop before India is Malindi. An Arab navigator joins your crew to show da Gama how to use the monsoon winds to reach Calicut. What ocean must you cross?

Conquering the Americas

As the Portuguese began exploring Africa, the Church expressed an interest in new territories. In 1452 Pope Nicholas V wrote an official letter that allowed explorers to make slaves of the native peoples of newly explored lands. Expeditions began to include missionaries, who tried to convert the native peoples to Christianity.

In 1494 the Church helped to draw up the **Treaty of Tordesillas.** This treaty divided the Americas between Spain and Portugal. This allowed the conquerors to claim great portions of the Americas for either Spain or Portugal.

The Spanish and Portuguese explorers believed that there was great wealth in the Americas. As you read in Unit 3, Hernando Cortes and Francisco Pizarro were **conquistadors,** or Spanish conquerors, who acquired wealth by conquering wealthy civilizations.

However, the conquerors soon discovered other riches: the foods grown by the Native Americans. These included maize (corn), tomatoes, potatoes, chocolate, and squash. Europeans introduced plants and animals to the Americas: wheat, sugar cane, cattle, pigs, and horses, among others. This exchange of goods between the Americas and Europe is known as the **Columbian Exchange.**

Diseases were also exchanged. Europeans brought over diseases such as smallpox, measles, and influenza. The Native Americans had never encountered these diseases before. Many died.

REVIEW What was the Treaty of Tordesillas?
↻ **Summarize**

MAP SKILL
European Voyages of Exploration

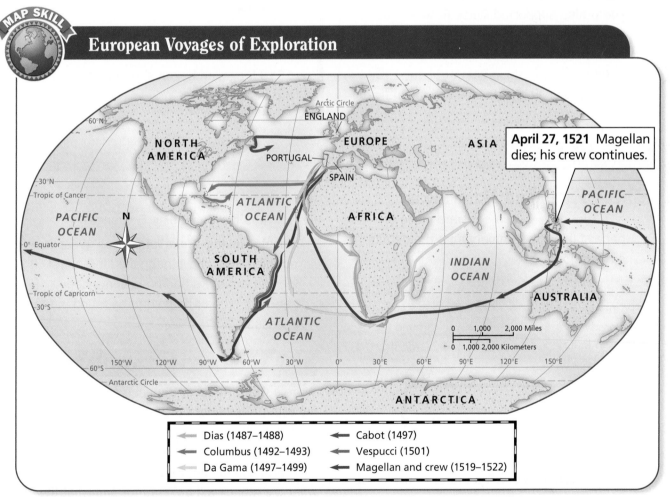

April 27, 1521 Magellan dies; his crew continues.

Legend:
- Dias (1487–1488)
- Columbus (1492–1493)
- Da Gama (1497–1499)
- Cabot (1497)
- Vespucci (1501)
- Magellan and crew (1519–1522)

▶ **From 1487 to 1522, a number of explorers completed voyages with different rates of success.**

MAP SKILL Use Latitude *Which explorer traveled to the farthest northern latitude? Which explorer traveled to the farthest southern latitude?*

The Spanish Armada

In 1496 King Henry VII of England funded the expedition of Italian explorer John Cabot to find a western route to Asia. When the expedition sailed the following year, Cabot explored the coast of North America. After Henry VII died, his son Henry VIII focused his attention on the religious changes taking place in Europe, not exploration. England became a Protestant nation under his rule. Under his daughter, Elizabeth I, England became a world sea power. Read more about Elizabeth I in the biography on page 443.

As queen of England, Elizabeth funded many expeditions after she came to power in 1558. Some of the English navigators, such as Sir Francis Drake, were pirates as well as explorers. These pirates attacked Spanish ships filled with gold and riches from their expeditions.

Elizabeth also supported Dutch Protestants who were fighting against Catholic Spain. In response in 1588, King Philip II of Spain sent the Armada (ar MAH dah), a fleet of about 130 warships, to attack England. The gold and intricate

▶ **The Spanish Armada clashes with English ships in this painting by Hendrik Cornelisz Vroom.**

designs on the Spanish ships were beautiful, but they made the ships heavy and slow. The plainer but swifter English ships had bigger and more powerful guns. Within a few days, the Armada was defeated.

REVIEW How did Queen Elizabeth make England a major sea power? **Main Idea and Details**

Summarize the Lesson

1488 Bartolomeu Dias reached the Cape of Good Hope.

1492 Christopher Columbus began his first expedition.

1519 Magellan began a journey around the world.

LESSON 2   REVIEW

Check Facts and Main Ideas

1. ⟳ **Summarize** On a separate piece of paper, fill in the summary from the details given below.

The Portuguese explored sea routes to India.	Columbus sailed west to reach Asia.	Magellan's crew sailed around the world.

↓ ↓ ↓

2. Why were Europeans interested in exploring Africa?

3. Where is the Cape of Good Hope?

4. What was the Columbian Exchange?

5. **Critical Thinking:** *Make Inferences* What do you think would have happened if the first Spanish explorers had been convinced there was little or no gold to be found in the Americas?

Link to ⊶ Writing

Write a Grant Request Suppose you are working with Christopher Columbus or Ferdinand Magellan. Your assignment is to prepare a grant request, asking investors for money to fund your expedition. Be sure you explain what the money will be used for and what the investor can expect in return.

Elizabeth I

1533–1603

Elizabeth I was the daughter of King Henry VIII of England. She received an excellent education. She studied French, Greek, Latin, and Italian. She wrote poetry.

When she was young, Elizabeth was caught in the religious power struggles between Catholics and Protestants. When her father died, Elizabeth's Protestant half-brother Edward VI became king. When a plot against Edward's life was discovered, Elizabeth was a suspect. Although she was only 15, she was brave and answered her accusers. Elizabeth was soon cleared of the charges.

After Edward died, Elizabeth's Catholic half-sister Mary became queen of England. When plans to overthrow Mary were discovered, Elizabeth, who was Protestant, was again accused. She was imprisoned in the Tower of London.

Elizabeth was released after two months, but Mary kept a close eye on her. After Mary's death, 25-year-old Elizabeth became queen. Elizabeth had learned to trust her instincts and make her own decisions. One important decision she made was not to get married. Marrying a member of the European nobility would force England to take sides in the rivalry between France and Spain. Elizabeth also enjoyed her independence:

BIOFACT

During Elizabeth's reign, many great writers lived in England. Perhaps the greatest of these was William Shakespeare, whose plays were performed in the Globe Theater, built in 1599.

> *"I would rather be a beggar and single than a queen and married."*

Elizabeth became one of England's most successful rulers. During her long reign England became one of Europe's major powers.

Learn from Biographies

How do you think Elizabeth's early experience made her a strong and independent ruler?

National Trust

For more information, go online to *Meet the People* at **www.sfsocialstudies.com.**

THE 13 COLONIES — Quebec
Jamestowh
Sandwich Islands
BRAZIL
NEW SOUTH WALES

PREVIEW

Focus on the Main Idea
As Europeans reached new lands, they spread their culture through settlement and colonization.

PLACES
Sandwich Islands
Brazil
Jamestown
New South Wales
Quebec

PEOPLE
James Cook
Jacques Cartier

VOCABULARY
colony
mercantilism

TERMS
encomienda
triangular trade

1500

1500s
The Spanish and Portuguese establish colonies in the Americas.

1600

1607
Jamestown becomes the first permanent English settlement in North America.

1608
The French establish their first settlement in North America at Quebec.

European Colonization

You Are There
You're one of the crew members on Captain James Cook's ship, the *Resolution*. Leaving your family in England in 1776 was hard. But being part of this expedition has been a life-changing experience. You've met many interesting people. However, you're all anxious to find what you're looking for—a northern passage that connects the Pacific Ocean to the Atlantic Ocean. After searching for months, you and your sister ship, the *Discovery*, head south.

You finally reach some islands. Captain Cook names them after a friend of his, the Earl of Sandwich. You search for weeks for a good harbor among these islands. When you finally set anchor, many people come to greet you.

▶ **This chief's ceremonial headdress is from the Cook Islands in the South Pacific Ocean.**

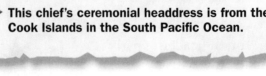

Summarize As you read, try to write a brief summary for each section to keep track of how Europeans colonized other lands.

Early Colonization

Where did **James Cook** land? The lands that Cook named the **Sandwich Islands** are in the Pacific Ocean. Today, we know them as the Hawaiian Islands.

Europeans began to look for faster passages to the east. On their expeditions and search for riches, they made contact with new peoples.

At first, Europeans were interested in finding new trade routes or new sources of trade goods. When Europeans arrived in a new land, they often wanted to use the resources there. Resources included more than just gold, silver, and ivory. Europeans also wanted to cultivate crops that they could export. They needed human labor to grow and harvest these crops.

The Europeans encouraged their fellow citizens to settle in the newly conquered lands. There the Europeans could manage the land. They could oversee the labor. These European settlements

National Maritime Museum

▶ **This portrait of James Cook was painted by Nathaniel Dance.**

were called **colonies** because they were physically separate from—but under the control of—another country.

The Europeans used an economic policy called **mercantilism** in their colonies. In this system, a country uses colonies to obtain raw materials to make into products. The colonies would also serve as new markets that could trade only with the ruling country. Under mercantilism, the function of a colony is to make the ruling country more wealthy and powerful.

REVIEW What advantages did ruling countries get from establishing colonies? Draw Conclusions

▶ **This cave painting of a European ship was created by Native Australians. It provides a glimpse of the impressions the people of Australia had during their early encounters with Europeans.**

Portugal and Spain

Portugal had begun exploring Africa in the early 1400s. The Portuguese had several motives. They wanted better access to the spice trade and they wanted to spread Christianity. However, when Portugal, along with Spain, looked to the Americas, they had an additional aim: colonization.

The Portuguese had landed in South America as early as 1500. However, they settled their first colony, **Brazil,** only when other European countries threatened to take it from them. Many Portuguese who did not own land in Portugal moved to Brazil to take a piece of land for themselves. There they set up sugar cane plantations and forced the Native Americans to work for them.

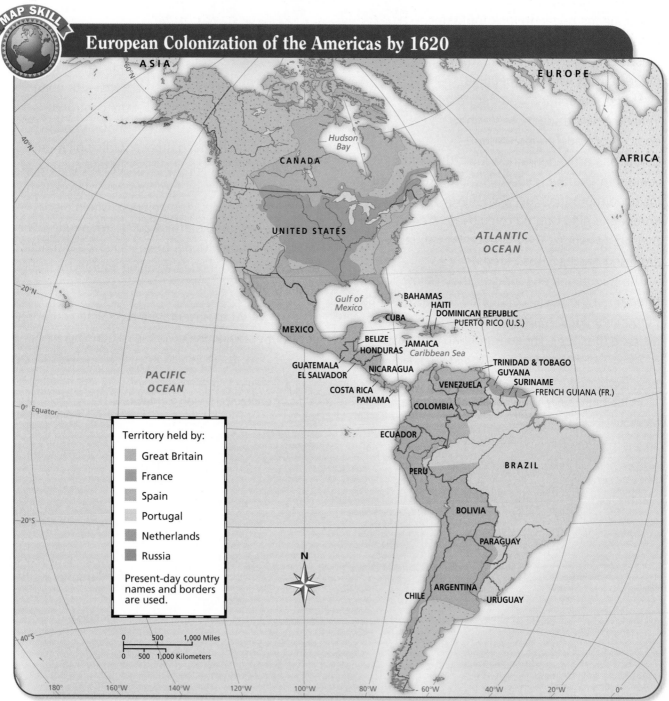

MAP SKILL

European Colonization of the Americas by 1620

Territory held by:
- Great Britain
- France
- Spain
- Portugal
- Netherlands
- Russia

Present-day country names and borders are used.

0   500   1,000 Miles
0 500 1,000 Kilometers

▶ **By 1620 many European nations had claimed territory in the Americas.**

MAP SKILL Understand the Equator *Which European nations held territories on the equator in the Americas?*

▶ This sixteenth-century picture shows a Portuguese soldier in the West African kingdom of Benin.

The Spanish formed a colony in the region where they had defeated the Aztecs. The Spanish colonists introduced the teachings of Christianity. They also forced the Native Americans to work. This system was known as the **encomienda.** The Spanish government allowed certain colonists the right to demand labor from the Native Americans of a particular area.

As you read in Lesson 2, Spanish conquests of lands in the Americas continued. By 1550 Spain controlled Mexico, Central America, part of South America, islands in the Caribbean, and part of the present-day southwestern United States.

REVIEW What was the cause of colonization?
Cause and Effect

English Colonies

Other European countries became interested in acquiring colonies. In England, there were several reasons why people began to think seriously about colonization. English merchants and other wealthy people saw colonies as a great source for new wealth. At the same time, some people in England were seeking religious and political freedom.

▶ These colonists are shown building Jamestown, England's first permanent colony in North America.

The first successful English colony in North America was established in **Jamestown** in 1607. It was planned by a group of investors who hoped it would bring them wealth. It paved the way for other settlements. England had established thirteen colonies in North America by 1732. By that time England had become part of Great Britain.

The British also set up the colony of **New South Wales** in Australia in 1788. Many of these colonists were convicts. At the time, Great Britain shipped criminals out of the country to relieve crowding in British prisons.

REVIEW Name two of the reasons the English wanted colonies in North America.
 Summarize

French Colonies

Explorations by **Jacques Cartier** in the 1530s led to France's claim to Canada. The French were disappointed when explorers were unable to find the kind of mineral riches the Spanish had found in Mexico and Peru. But Canada offered other kinds of riches to the French, especially furs such as beaver pelts. In 1608 France founded its first settlement in North America, **Quebec.** During the 1700s, the French settled in southern Canada and in what is today the U.S. state of Louisiana.

▶ Jacques Cartier explored Canada for France.

The Granger Collection

Clashes over land rights among the Native Americans, French, and British led to war in 1763 in North America. Great Britain defeated the French and the Native Americans seven years later, gaining all of Canada.

REVIEW Why did the French settle in North America? Summarize

The Slave Trade

Earlier in this lesson, you learned that the Portuguese and the Spanish had enslaved many Native Americans in their colonies. As time went by, the demand for additional workers increased. Many Native Americans were dying from over-work, cruel treatment, and exposure to European diseases. They often rebelled or escaped. Faced with this problem, European merchants began to transport slaves from Africa to work in America.

Europeans were familiar with the African cus-tom of making prisoners of people they captured in battle. These captives usually were treated fairly and might one day expect to gain their free-dom. Europeans began to purchase captives from the African leaders.

The English had also begun plantation agricul-ture in their colonies in the West Indies and on the North American mainland. Africans were first brought to Virginia in 1619. At first, many of these Africans were regarded as servants. They were bound for a period of years to the master who paid the ship captain for transporting them

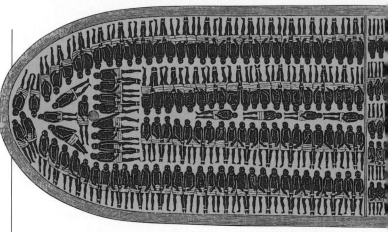

▶ This diagram shows how slaves were transported on the slave ships. This arrangement was meant to fit as many slaves as possible, with no concern for the comfort or safety of the slaves.

to America. However, by the 1640s, most Africans brought to the colonies were slaves, with no hope of freedom.

In 1672, England set up the Royal African Company. Colonial merchants also entered the business of transporting slaves to the colonies. These traders sold manufactured goods to leaders in West Africa in exchange for slaves.

MAP SKILL

Slavery and the Triangular Trade

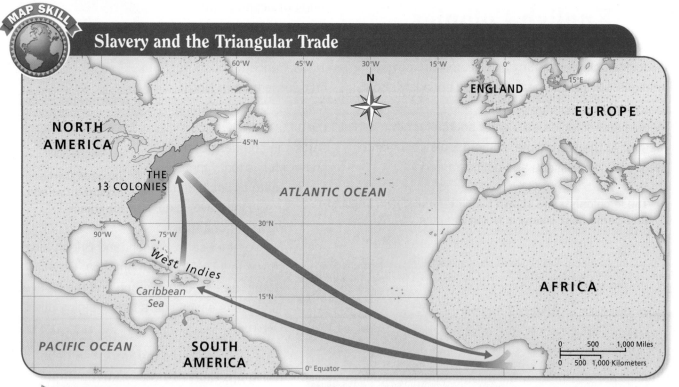

▶ Slaves were shipped to the Americas as part of the triangular trade.

MAP SKILL Trace Movement on Maps *In which direction did ships leaving the 13 colonies travel on the triangular trade?*

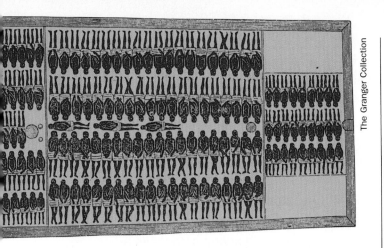

The slaves were transported to the West Indies. There, they were sold for sugar cane. The sugar cane was shipped to New England to be made into rum and other manufactured products. This trade arrangement came to be known as the **triangular trade.**

The most dehumanizing part of this trade may have been the Middle Passage. This was the journey of the slave ships across the Atlantic from Africa to America. The slaves were packed tightly into the holds of ships and chained together. They suffered through intense heat, painful illnesses, poor living conditions, and

rough seas. Many of the slaves would die during this grueling voyage, which lasted from four to six weeks.

To the European colonists, slaves were nothing but property. For the slaves, there was almost no hope of ever gaining freedom. Torn from their homelands and loved ones, most slaves ended up on plantations. There they worked very long hours in the fields six days a week. They lived in shacks under very harsh conditions. Each colony passed severe law codes that totally deprived African American slaves of any legal rights.

REVIEW What was the triangular trade and how did it work? **Summarize**

Summarize the Lesson

1500s The Portuguese and Spanish established colonies in the Americas.

1607 Jamestown became the first permanent English settlement in North America.

1608 The French established their first North American settlement at Quebec.

LESSON 3　　REVIEW

Check Facts and Main Ideas

1. **Summarize** On a separate piece of paper, fill in the missing details that lead to the summary.

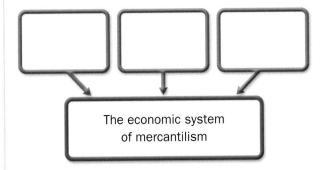

The economic system of mercantilism

2. What are colonies and how did they make European countries wealthy and powerful?

3. What was the encomienda?

4. What were some of the reasons for European colonization?

5. **Critical Thinking: *Solve Complex Problems*** How could Europeans have colonized other lands without forcing the native peoples to work for them?

Link to　　Writing

Write a Dialogue Write a dialogue between Native Americans and colonists who have just arrived from Europe. Write equal numbers of lines from the perspective of European colonists and of Native Americans.

449

Research and Writing Skills

Interpret Political Cartoons

What? You have probably turned to the editorial page in a newspaper. In editorials, news writers express opinions about current events. A political cartoon is a kind of editorial. It uses an image, often humorous, to make a point. Some political cartoons include some text. Others rely on pictures alone.

The cartoon on the left is an example of an early political cartoon. It shows Henry VIII, the king of England, seated upon his throne. The room is full of people. Some, but not all of them, appear to be upset. The cartoon is telling a story about an important moment in English history.

Why? According to a familiar saying, "a picture is worth a thousand words." This statement certainly rings true for political cartoons. As an image, a cartoon is able to communicate meaning on several levels. Its use of humor may soften a difficult or painful issue. Readers are often more open to a visual message than to straight text.

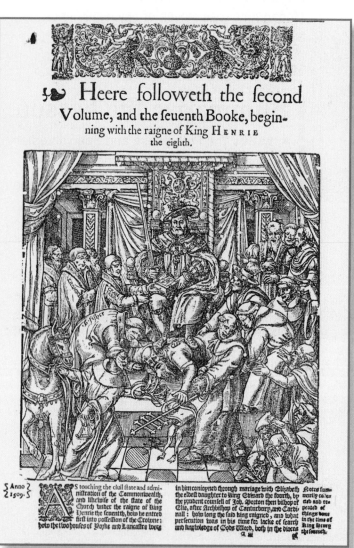

▶ **This cartoon deals with an important event during the rule of Henry VIII of England.**

WISDOM!

MikeKeefe 97 The Denver Post

> This modern political cartoon was created in 1997, at a time when many people were starting to use the Internet.

How? To understand a political cartoon, you must be able to identify the visual details. You must also interpret them correctly. What details do you notice in the cartoon of Henry VIII?

Notice that several of the people in this cartoon have their names written across their clothing. They were real people who were involved in this important event. This tradition—writing labels on people and objects to let readers know who they are or what they symbolize—is still used by many political cartoonists today. Henry VIII's name does not appear in the cartoon. The artist may have assumed (or hoped) that people would recognize the king. In political cartoons it is important to draw important people in a way that everyone can recognize them immediately.

Did you notice the figure lying down in front of the king? Notice that Henry is resting his feet on the man's back, hiding part of the man's name. This is Pope Clement VII of the Roman Catholic Church. Next to him is an English priest, who is trying to comfort the Pope. Alongside the king are two of his most important advisors.

In 1533 Henry VIII declared that he, not the Pope, was the head of the Church of England. This led England to break with Catholicism and become a Protestant nation.

Think and Apply

1. Look at the modern political cartoon at the top of this page. There are no famous people shown in this cartoon. It does not refer to a single event. However, it still deals with an important change in the world. In this cartoon, the changes are related to the growth of the computer industry and the Internet. What do you think the cartoonist is trying to tell us? Write your interpretation of this cartoon.

2. What are some other ways a cartoonist might show the same message in a political cartoon? You can sketch your cartoon idea or write a paragraph explaining what you would show.

3. Search for a political cartoon in a recent newspaper or magazine. Do you understand the point the cartoonist is trying to make? Write your interpretation of the cartoon. You may need to do some additional research to understand the cartoon's message.

CHAPTER 15 REVIEW

1450
1455
Gutenberg Bible was printed.
1492
Columbus began his westward voyages.

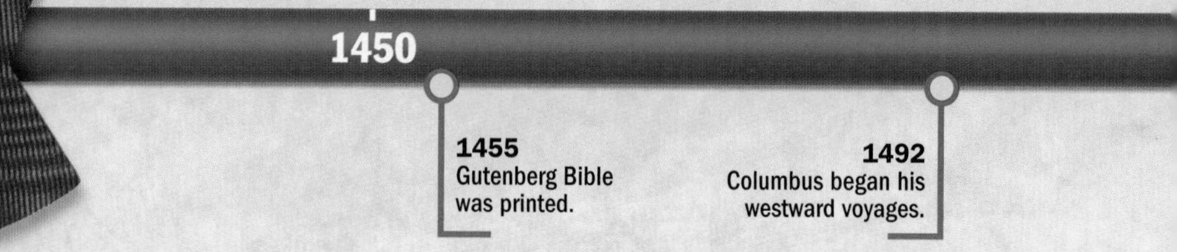

Chapter Summary

Summarize

Target Skill

On a separate piece of paper, write a summary that combines the ideas in this chapter.

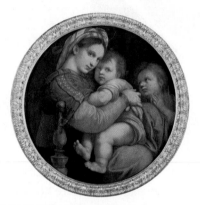

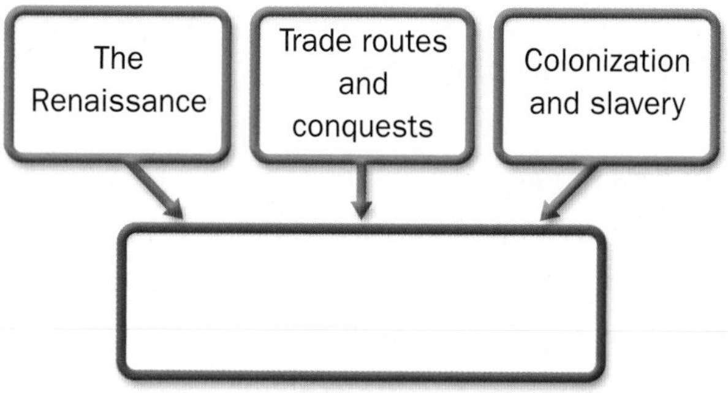

The Renaissance
Trade routes and conquests
Colonization and slavery

Vocabulary and Terms

Match each word with the correct definition or description.

1. **commerce** (p. 431)
2. **encomienda** (p. 447)
3. **conquistador** (p. 441)
4. **circumnavigate** (p. 439)
5. **mercantilism** (p. 445)

a. sail completely around the world

b. the buying and selling of goods

c. a system in which colonies are a source of raw materials

d. Spanish conquerors

e. a system that forced Native Americans to work for the Spanish

People and Events

Write a sentence explaining why each of the following people, terms, events is important. You may use two or more in a single sentence.

1. Reformation (p. 437)
2. Council of Trent (p. 437)
3. Isabella (p. 440)
4. Elizabeth I (p. 442)
5. Galileo (p. 434)
6. Armada (p. 442)
7. James Cook (p. 445)
8. Johannes Gutenberg (p. 435)
9. Leonardo da Vinci (p. 432)
10. Counter-Reformation (p. 437)

1500   1550   1600

1500s
Portuguese began
to colonize in
South America.

1517
Reformation began.

1588
Spanish Armada was defeated by England.

1607
Jamestown colony
was settled.

Facts and Main Ideas

1 Why was Prince Henry the Navigator looking for a new trade route?

2 What was the first permanent British colony in North America? When was it established?

3 What is slavery and how did the Europeans use it to create prosperous colonies?

4 **Time Line** Which three events occurred while the Portuguese were colonizing South America?

5 **Main Idea** What effect did Gutenberg's printing press have on European people?

6 **Main Idea** Name one reason why the English colonized North America.

7 **Main Idea** Explain how the triangular trade worked.

8 **Critical Thinking:** *Make Inferences* How were the searches for new trade routes related to colonization and slavery?

Apply Skills

Interpret Political Cartoons
Study the political cartoon below and then answer the questions.

1 Who is the person pictured in this cartoon?

2 Describe what the person in this cartoon is doing.

3 What is the cartoonist trying to say in this cartoon? Explain your answer.

Write About History

1 **Write a journal entry** as a sailor on Magellan's ship. What do you see? What is the purpose of your journey?

2 **Write a grant request** asking Queen Isabella to pay for a voyage to determine how to reach Asia by sailing west. Indicate what you think you will be able to bring the queen in return for her grant.

3 **Write a broadside poster** encouraging people to rethink their attitudes about slavery. Include reasons why slavery should be abolished, even if it is economically profitable.

Internet Activity

To get help with vocabulary, people, and terms, select dictionary, encyclopedia, or almanac from *Social Studies Library* at
www.sfsocialstudies.com.

CHAPTER 16
Ideas and Movements

Lesson 1

1773
Boston
New nations emerge in the Americas.

1

Lesson 2

1789
Paris
An angry mob storms the Bastille.

2

Lesson 3

After 1750
Great Britain
The Industrial Revolution begins in Great Britain.

3

Lesson 4

1876
Menlo Park
Thomas Edison's laboratory becomes a center of invention.

4

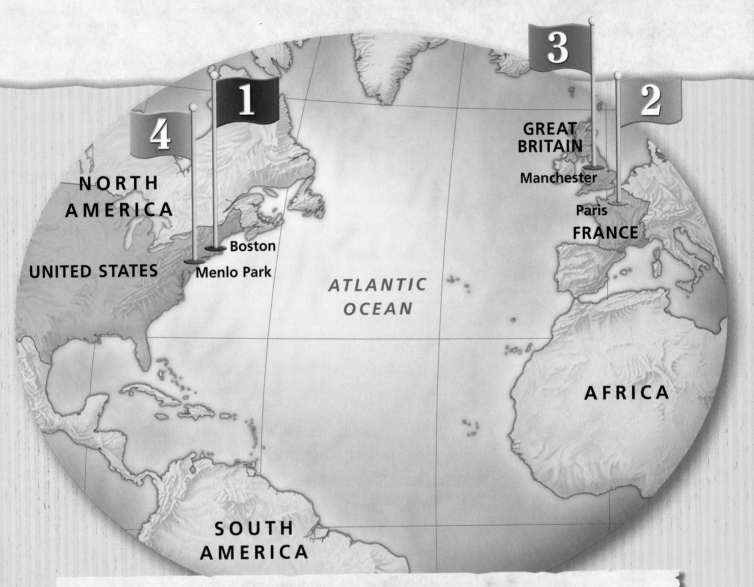

GREAT BRITAIN

Manchester

Paris

FRANCE

NORTH AMERICA

UNITED STATES

Boston

Menlo Park

ATLANTIC OCEAN

AFRICA

SOUTH AMERICA

Why We Remember

The way our government works, the kind of work we do, and the machines we use every day—all of these things have changed greatly in the last 200 years. Colonies in the Western Hemisphere became independent of their European masters. A revolution in France showed the world that kings could not be protected from new ideas about government. The Industrial Revolution and factory system transformed the way people make things. The Second Industrial Revolution brought us wave after wave of inventions that changed people's lives even further. Our way of life today is the result of a series of revolutions.

Boston
HAITI
Dolores

1750   1800   1850

1776
The 13 British colonies declare independence.

1821
Mexico wins independence.

1824
Simón Bolívar frees Peru from Spanish rule.

Revolutions in the Americas

PREVIEW

Focus on the Main Idea
New nations in the Americas broke free from European rule.

PLACES
Boston
Haiti
Dolores

PEOPLE
George Washington
Toussaint L'Ouverture
Miguel Hidalgo
José María Morelos
Agustín de Iturbide
Simón Bolívar
José de San Martín
Bernardo O'Higgins

VOCABULARY
legislature
massacre

TERMS
Declaration of Independence
United Provinces of Central America

EVENTS
Boston Massacre
Boston Tea Party
American Revolution
Battle of Saratoga

You Are There Your brother is out of breath. He just ran across town with the news. Your parents can barely believe it.

All last night, British troops were marching toward the town of Lexington. They were sure they would surprise the colonists.

The British arrived in Lexington just after daybreak. To their surprise, they found about 70 colonists waiting at the village green. Captain John Parker, the colonial leader, gave last-minute orders:

"Stand your ground. Don't fire unless fired upon. But if they want a war, let it begin here!"

A shot rang out and both sides began firing. As you listen to your brother's news, your family is a little afraid—but very excited. If we go to war now, you wonder, will we really be able to break free of British rule?

▶ **This soldier from the American Revolution wears the uniform of an infantryman in the Continental Army.**

Compare and Contrast As you read, look for the similarities and differences among the revolutions in the Americas.

The Roots of Conflict

For many years, the 13 British colonies in North America had largely governed themselves. Every colony had its own **legislature,** or lawmaking body. These legislatures made laws and set taxes.

This was about to change. Great Britain was deeply in debt. The British decided to tax the colonies. The colonists were furious. They believed that they should not be taxed without their approval. This was reflected in their rallying cry:

> *"No taxation without representation!"*

In 1770 an event occurred that weakened relations between the colonies and Great Britain. One winter night in **Boston,** Massachusetts, colonists began heckling British soldiers and throwing stones at them. Some soldiers fired into the crowd, killing several colonists. The incident became known as the **Boston Massacre.** A **massacre** is an event that causes the death of unresisting or helpless people.

New laws made the colonists angrier. In Boston colonists protested British rules that said that all tea had to be bought from only one company. On the night of December 16, 1773, about 60 colonists disguised as Native Americans boarded a tea ship in Boston Harbor. They threw the tea overboard, case by case. Colonists called this the **Boston Tea Party.** The act led the British government to close the port and to send troops to patrol the streets of Boston.

REVIEW What led the colonists to stage the Boston Tea Party? **Cause and Effect**

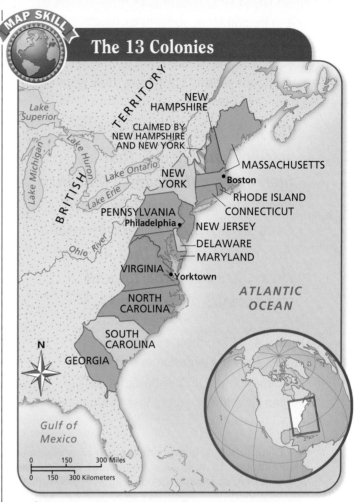

MAP SKILL

The 13 Colonies

▶ After 1770, the 13 British colonies in North America came into increasing conflict with Great Britain.

MAP SKILL Understanding Continents and Oceans *Which North American colony did not have a coastline on the Atlantic Ocean?*

▶ On the night of December 16, 1773, protesting colonists destroyed a shipload of tea from Great Britain.

The Granger Collection

457

The American Revolution

When Great Britain sent over more troops to force the colonists to obey Parliament's laws, the colonists decided to declare their independence. The result was the **Declaration of Independence.** The Americans clearly stated why they were splitting from Great Britain:

> *"We hold these truths to be self-evident [clear], that all men are created equal, that they are endowed [given] by their Creator with certain unalienable [absolute] rights; that among these, are life, liberty, and the pursuit of happiness."*

On July 4, 1776, the Declaration was approved. Now the Americans had to win their independence on the battlefield. The **American Revolution** would last five long years.

There was bitter fighting in every colony. One key victory came in 1777, when the Americans won the **Battle of Saratoga** in New York. Until that point, the Americans had been fighting alone. The victory at Saratoga convinced France that the Americans could win the war. As a result of the victory, France joined in an alliance with the Americans.

The war then shifted to the southern colonies, where the Americans won some important victories. Then, with the support of the French, General **George Washington** trapped a British force at Yorktown and forced it to surrender. In 1783 the British accepted the United States as an independent nation.

REVIEW Why did France decide to form an alliance with the Americans? 🔄 Summarize

▶ **The Declaration of Independence was written mostly by Thomas Jefferson.**

The Granger Collection

▶ **The Declaration of Independence, which announced the colonists' determination to split away from Great Britain, was approved on July 4, 1776, at Independence Hall in Philadelphia.**

The Granger Collection

Revolution in Haiti

In 1790 all of the lands south of the new United States were colonies of Europe. Spain ruled most of this territory. However, the first spark of revolt did not appear in a Spanish colony. It appeared in **Haiti,** then a colony of France. A few French planters controlled the island's great wealth. Most Haitians worked long hours on plantations as slaves.

In 1791 enslaved Africans revolted against French rule. **Toussaint L'Ouverture** (too SAINT loo ver TOOR) became the leader of the rebellion. L'Ouverture had escaped slavery and educated himself. Under his leadership, the slaves were able to drive French forces from the island. When French forces attempted to retake Haiti in 1802, L'Ouverture was captured and thrown into prison. Still, he did not give up the struggle. Before he died in prison he wrote:

> *"In overthrowing me, the French have only felled the tree of black liberty in [Haiti]. It will shoot up again for it is deeply rooted and its roots are many."*

The French failed to retake the island. In 1804 the Haitians declared their independence. Haiti became the first independent country in Latin America and the first republic led by a person of African descent.

REVIEW How was the revolution in Haiti different from the American Revolution? **Compare and Contrast**

▶ **Toussaint L'Ouverture (seated) became the leader of the Haitian Revolution.**

The Revolution Spreads

Meanwhile, much of Latin America remained under Spanish rule. On September 16, 1810, the struggle began to end colonial rule. A local priest in the village of **Dolores,** Mexico, called together villagers by ringing the church bell. Father **Miguel Hidalgo** (ee DAHL goh) asked them to revolt against the Spanish:

> *"My children, will you be free? Will you make the effort to recover from the hated Spaniards the lands stolen from your forefathers 300 years ago?"*

His words set off a struggle for freedom in Mexico. But the struggle did not end there. Father Hidalgo's words echoed throughout Latin America. They would become the rallying cry for Latin Americans who wanted independence. Many people under Spanish colonial rule longed for political and economic freedom.

Latin Americans were not allowed self-government. Officials appointed by the Spanish king made all of the important decisions. Latin American merchants could trade only with Spain. They could transport their goods only on Spanish ships. These strict rules held back Latin America's economic growth.

▶ **Father Miguel Hidalgo set off Mexico's struggle for freedom from Spain.**

National History Museum Mexico City/Dagli Orti/Art Archive

REVIEW Why did the people of Latin America struggle against Spanish rule? **Summarize**

Mexico, Central America, and South America

UNITED STATES

ATLANTIC OCEAN

Gulf of Mexico

BAHAMAS (1973)

MEXICO (1821)

CUBA (1902)

DOMINICAN REPUBLIC (1844)

JAMAICA (1962)

ST. KITTS AND NEVIS (1983)

ANTIGUA AND BARBUDA (1981)

GUATEMALA (1839)

BELIZE (1981)

HAITI (1804)

PUERTO RICO (U.S.)

DOMINICA (1978)

ST. LUCIA (1979)

HONDURAS (1838)

ST. VINCENT AND THE GRENADINES (1979)

Caribbean Sea

BARBADOS (1966)

EL SALVADOR (1841)

NICARAGUA (1838)

GRENADA (1974)

TRINIDAD AND TOBAGO (1962)

PANAMA (1903)

VENEZUELA (1830)

GUYANA (1966)

COSTA RICA (1838)

SURINAME (1975)

FRENCH GUIANA (FRANCE)

COLOMBIA (1819)

0° Equator

GALÁPAGOS ISLANDS (ECUADOR)

ECUADOR (1830)

PERU (1821)

BRAZIL (1822)

PACIFIC OCEAN

BOLIVIA (1825)

20°S

CHILE (1818)

PARAGUAY (1811)

N

URUGUAY (1828)

ARGENTINA (1816)

ATLANTIC OCEAN

Not yet independent

40°S

0   500   1,000 Miles
0   500   1,000 Kilometers

FALKLAND ISLANDS (GREAT BRITAIN)

120°W   100°W   80°W   60°W   40°W   20°W

▶ Beginning in the early 1800s, independence movements swept through Mexico, Central America, South America, and the Caribbean.

MAP SKILL Use a Historical Map *Which parts of Central America, South America, and the Caribbean still are not independent?*

▶ Mexico's struggle for independence from Spain is captured in this painting by Diego Rivera.

Independence for Mexico and Central America

Father Hidalgo's army began marching toward Mexico City. Father Hidalgo was captured by the Spanish and executed in 1811. But other leaders kept up the fight.

José María Morelos (moh RAY lohs) was a farm worker who had studied to become a priest. By 1813 his army controlled a large part of southern Mexico. However, Morelos frightened many Mexicans by announcing that he would seize land and give it to the peasants. Without support, Morelos was captured by the Spanish and executed in 1815.

A new revolution broke out in 1820. It was led by an army officer, **Agustín de Iturbide** (ah gus TEEN day ee toor BEE day), who had once supported the Spanish. In 1821 Iturbide fought off the Spanish and proclaimed independence for Mexico. Then he made himself emperor of Mexico. Opponents threw him out of office in 1823.

The people of Central America were inspired by Mexico's struggle for freedom. In 1821 they threw out the Spanish and joined Iturbide's short-lived empire of Mexico. But Central Americans did not want to be ruled by another country. So, in 1823, after Iturbide was removed from power, they joined together and formed the **United Provinces of Central America.** Later, the United Provinces split into the nations of Costa Rica, El Salvador, Guatemala, Honduras, and Nicaragua.

REVIEW What inspired the people of Central America to revolt against the Spanish? **Cause and Effect**

Literature and Social Studies

Latin American Liberator

Simón Bolívar is often called "the liberator" because he freed his people from Spanish rule. He did not seek power and greatness just for himself. In this passage from the biography *Simón Bolívar: Latin American Liberator* by Frank de Varona, do you think that Bolívar showed good judgment?

....

Simón Bolívar thought about the glory that would one day belong to the person who freed South America. But he also understood the danger of using this fame to seek personal power rather than freedom for all people. From then on, his ambition in life would be to achieve both liberty and glory.

461

Independence for South America

The struggle for South American independence took many years. In the northwestern part of South America, a brilliant young leader emerged. **Simón Bolívar** (see MOHN boh LEE vahr) dreamed of freeing South America from Spanish rule. Read more about Bolívar in the Biography on page 463. For 15 years, he led his troops through steamy rain forests and frigid mountains.

In the south, **José de San Martín** (hoh SAY day sahn mahr TEEN) forced out the Spanish. In Chile **Bernardo O'Higgins** organized an army. San Martín led his army through the rugged mountain passes of the Andes to join O'Higgins' army. Together, the two leaders defeated the Spanish. Chile became independent in 1818.

Peru had declared independence in 1821, but it lacked the strength to drive out all the Spanish forces. In 1824, high in the Andes, Bolívar's

▶ This painting shows José de San Martín and Bernardo O'Higgins crossing the Andes Mountains into Chile.

The Granger Collection

troops crushed a Spanish-led army. The struggle that had started with Father Hidalgo in Dolores was now complete. Almost all of Latin America was politically independent.

REVIEW Who were the leading figures of the South American revolutions and what did they accomplish? ⟳ Summarize

Summarize the Lesson

1776 The 13 British colonies declared independence.

1821 Mexico won independence.

1824 Simón Bolívar freed Peru from Spanish rule.

LESSON 1 **REVIEW**

Check Facts and Main Ideas

1. Compare and Contrast On a separate piece of paper, fill in the diagram to compare and contrast the revolutions in the Americas.

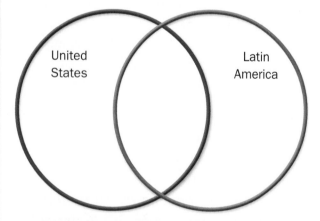

United States

Latin America

2. Why did the American colonists believe that they needed to break free of British rule?

3. Who was Father Miguel Hidalgo?

4. Name two restrictions that the Spanish government put on the people of Latin America.

5. Critical Thinking: *Evaluate Information* Why do you think the fight for South American independence took so many years?

Link to ⌗ **Geography**

Write a Description Study a relief map of South America. Write a report about the kind of landforms José de San Martín and his army should expect to find in Chile.

Simón Bolívar

1783–1830

Simón Bolívar was the son of wealthy Venezuelan landowners. Both his parents died when he was still a child. He was raised by an uncle and sent to study in Europe. Bolívar soon became interested in the ideas of liberty that had inspired the French Revolution of 1789. He was also greatly influenced by his teacher Simón Rodríguez. Bolívar credited Rodriguez with the revolutionary spirit that guided his life:

> *"You molded my heart for liberty, justice, greatness, and beauty."*

As a young adult, Bolívar pledged to devote his life to freeing South America from Spanish rule. He began by freeing the black slaves who worked on his land. He then turned toward freeing entire nations. In 1813 he led an army from Colombia (then known as New Granada) into Venezuela and defeated the Spanish. However, forces loyal to Spain soon regained control of Venezuela. Bolívar regrouped his army. In 1819 he led them across the Andes Mountains and into Colombia. His troops took the Spanish by surprise and defeated them.

BIOFACT

In 1828 Bolívar narrowly escaped assassination by diving out of a window minutes before his would-be murderers burst into his bedroom.

Bolívar played a key role in gaining independence for Colombia, Venezuela, Ecuador, Peru, and Upper Peru (present-day Bolivia). Bolívar wanted the newly independent nations to become a Federation of the Andes with himself as leader. However, his plan did not succeed. Revolts and disagreements brought an end to the federation. Even though Bolívar became very unpopular, today he is honored as the founding father of South American independence.

Learn from Biographies

Who and what influenced Simón Bolívar to fight for South American independence from Spain?

For more information, go online to *Meet the People* at **www.sfsocialstudies.com**.

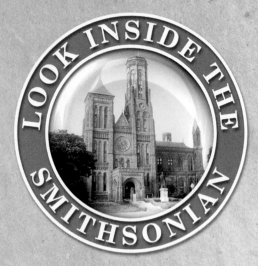

American Revolution

The American struggle for independence from Great Britain lasted five long years. The Americans had to endure many hardships—harsh winters and a lack of supplies—on the road to victory. Thanks to the leadership of George Washington and an alliance with France, the former colonies emerged from the war as a new nation: the United States.

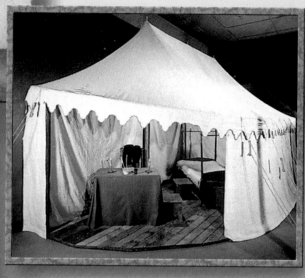

Washington's Field Tent
This field tent was used by George Washington during the American Revolution.

Washington Reviewing His Ragged Army at Valley Forge
From a Painting by William T. Trego

Washington Reviewing His Ragged Army at Valley Forge
William T. Trego's painting captures the hardships the Continental Army suffered during the winter of 1777. The image was used on a series of postage stamps issued as part of the United States Bicentennial in 1976.

Washington's Field Glass
George Washington used this field glass during the American Revolution. He may have used it to spy on enemy activity.

The Boston Massacre
This engraving by Paul Revere depicts the moment that British troops opened fire on a crowd of protesting colonists on March 5, 1770.

Washington Crossing the Delaware
From a Painting by Emanuel Leutze / Eastman Johnson

Washington Crossing the Delaware

This painting by Emanuel Leutze shows General George Washington and his troops as they crossed the Delaware River in December 1776, on their way to the Battle of Trenton. In 1976, as part of the United States Bicentennial, this image was released as a series of postage stamps.

American Grenadier Cap

Caps such as this one were worn by grenadiers, who were among the bravest and best-trained soldiers of the 1700s. This cap may have been worn by a grenadier fighting in the Battle of Trenton.

Officer's Regimental Coat
This coat was worn by Peter Gansevoort, a colonel with the Third New York Continental Regiment. Gansevoort would eventually become a general.

Artifacts are from the Smithsonian Institution.

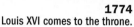

1750   1800

1774
Louis XVI comes to the throne.

1789
The Bastille falls; the *Declaration of the Rights of Man and of Citizen* is issued.

1793
Reign of Terror begins.

•Paris

FRANCE

PREVIEW

Focus on the Main Idea
The path of revolution turned violent in France.

PLACES
Paris

PEOPLE
Louis XVI
Marie Antoinette
Maximilien de Robespierre
Napoleon Bonaparte

VOCABULARY
monarchy

TERMS
Estates-General
estate
National Assembly
Bastille
Declaration of the Rights of Man and of Citizen
Reign of Terror
Napoleonic Code

EVENTS
French Revolution
Battle of Waterloo

The French Revolution

You Are There

1793: As you sit in a courtroom in Paris, you listen to the following dialogue:

JUDGE: Citizen, do you have anything to say before we pass sentence?

PRISONER: This trial is illegal. I am the king of France, and you are my subjects. You have no right to charge me with anything.

JUDGE: You have committed terrible crimes against the people of France. You have tried to destroy the Revolution. You have committed treason by conspiring with the enemies of France.

PRISONER: Rubbish! How can I commit treason against myself? I rule by the divine right of God and it is only to him that I have to answer.

JUDGE: Citizen, you have committed treason against the Revolution. You are sentenced to death.

▶ **This painting captures the determination of the Third Estate as they gathered to create a constitution for France.**

Summarize As you read, summarize the most important events of the French Revolution.

France in Trouble

France was one of the most powerful countries in Europe. Yet, by the middle of the 1700s, France's **monarchy,** or government in which a king, queen, or emperor has supreme power, was on the edge of collapse.

France's tax system was unfair. Peasants and the middle class paid heavy taxes while nobles paid almost nothing. The nobles, who made up about one percent of the population, owned nearly one-third of the land in France.

Louis XVI (LOO ee), who became king in 1774, was a weak ruler. Finding himself short of money, Louis decided to call a meeting of the Estates-General. The **Estates-General** was a group of advisers to the king.

The Estates-General represented the three **estates,** or classes, into which French society was officially divided. The First Estate was made up of church officials. The Second Estate was made up of nobles. The other 98 percent of the French people belonged to the Third Estate.

Each estate was represented in the Estates-General. Because the Third Estate represented most of the population, it demanded that each person at the meeting have one vote. When the king refused to grant this demand, members of the Third Estate formed into a group called the **National Assembly.** They then began to write a constitution for France. The **French Revolution** had begun.

REVIEW What were the three estates into which France was divided? Who belonged to each? **Main Idea and Details**

In this political cartoon, the Third Estate is shown carrying the nobles and priests on its back.

Louis XVI was the king of France at the beginning of the French Revolution.

New and Old Privileges

King Louis began gathering troops near the meeting. The people of Paris were outraged. On July 14, 1789, an angry mob attacked the Bastille (bah STEEL), a prison in Paris. The mob captured the prison and took the weapons stored there.

In its first days, the National Assembly took away all the privileges of the Church and nobles. Peasants no longer had to work without pay for nobles. Nobles and church leaders had to pay taxes. Many nobles had to sell their land at cheap prices to peasants.

In August 1789, the National Assembly adopted a *Declaration of the Rights of Man and of Citizen.* This document was inspired by the U.S. Declaration of Independence. The French declaration stated that all men are equal and have certain rights. These include freedom of speech, assembly, and religion, and the right to a fair trial.

Other rulers in Europe were frightened by the

▶ **Marie Antoinette**

French Revolution. Fearing that the revolution might spread, they sent armies into France. At first, the French armies were badly beaten. Panic swept the country. Mobs in Paris blamed Louis and the queen, Marie Antoinette (muh REE an twa NET), for the defeats.

REVIEW Why would other European rulers be frightened by the French Revolution?
Draw Conclusions

The Reign of Terror

Radical, or extreme, leaders soon took control of the revolution. In 1792 they took away all of the king's power and made France a republic.

The following year, the radicals put Louis on trial as a traitor. He was convicted by a single vote and put to death. Ten months later, Marie Antoinette was also executed.

A period of violence followed. It was known as the Reign of Terror. Thousands of citizens who were suspected of being against the revolution were put to death.

▶ **A mob stormed the Bastille in Paris on July 14, 1789.**

▶ **Maximilien de Robespierre**

A committee led by **Maximilien de Robespierre** (rohbz pee AIR) took over the government. Before long, the committee began executing anyone it suspected of being against the revolution.

Between 1793 and 1794, about 40,000 French people were executed. About half were beheaded by a new machine known as the guillotine (gee oh TEEN). Many leaders began to fear that they would be next to climb the steps to the guillotine. The final victims of the Reign of Terror were its leaders, including Robespierre.

Despite the violence of the Reign of Terror, the republic made many accomplishments. For example, slavery was ended in all of the French colonies. The republic also stripped away the privileges of the wealthy classes.

REVIEW Describe the Reign of Terror.
↻ Summarize

Napoleon

When the French Revolution began, **Napoleon Bonaparte** was a young officer in the army. Napoleon's rise to power was swift. He led the French army in victories against Great Britain and Austria and became a general at the age of 24. In 1799 Napoleon overthrew the republic. In 1804 he became emperor of France.

Napoleon strengthened the French government and restored order. He established a new system of laws for France called the **Napoleonic Code.** The Code is still the basis of French law today. The Code was based on the principles of Roman law. It preserved some of the important reforms made by the republic during the French Revolution. However, women lost some of the rights of citizenship that they had gained during the revolution.

▶ **This edition of the Napoleonic Code was published in 1804.**

REVIEW What was the Napoleonic Code and how did it affect the lives of women?
↻ Summarize

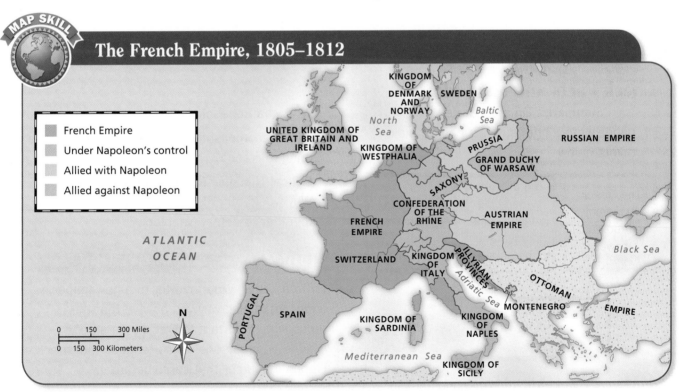

The French Empire, 1805–1812

MAP SKILL

French Empire
Under Napoleon's control
Allied with Napoleon
Allied against Napoleon

KINGDOM OF DENMARK AND NORWAY
SWEDEN
Baltic Sea
North Sea
UNITED KINGDOM OF GREAT BRITAIN AND IRELAND
KINGDOM OF WESTPHALIA
PRUSSIA
RUSSIAN EMPIRE
GRAND DUCHY OF WARSAW
SAXONY
CONFEDERATION OF THE RHINE
AUSTRIAN EMPIRE
ATLANTIC OCEAN
FRENCH EMPIRE
SWITZERLAND
KINGDOM OF ITALY
ILLYRIAN PROVINCES
Adriatic Sea
Black Sea
OTTOMAN
MONTENEGRO
EMPIRE
PORTUGAL
SPAIN
KINGDOM OF SARDINIA
KINGDOM OF NAPLES
Mediterranean Sea
KINGDOM OF SICILY

N

0   150   300 Miles
0   150   300 Kilometers

▶ **Napoleon made many conquests in Europe.**

MAP SKILL Use a Map Key *Which nations were allied with France? Which nations were allied against France?*

Napoleon's Conquests

Napoleon's goal was to establish his own empire. Napoleon made major conquests in Europe. His armies conquered Spain, much of present-day Germany, and Austria. However, the French Empire began to collapse in 1812, when Napoleon invaded Russia. Many French soldiers died in the invasion because they did not have the clothing or equipment needed during Russia's harsh winter.

Once again, the monarchs of Europe banded together. This time, they were successful. In 1813 the European allies defeated Napoleon. They exiled him, or forced him to leave. He was sent to an island in the Mediterranean Sea. However, he escaped to France in 1815.

Réunion des Musées Nationaux

▶ **Napoleon Bonaparte strikes a heroic pose in this painting by Jacques Louis David.**

Napoleon ruled France for 100 days. He was finally defeated by Britain and the European allies at the **Battle of Waterloo.** Napoleon was sent to the far-off island of St. Helena in the Atlantic Ocean, where he died in 1821.

REVIEW What were Napoleon's major conquests in Europe? ↻ **Summarize**

Summarize the Lesson

- **1774** Louis XVI came to the throne.
- **1789** Bastille fell; *Declaration of Rights of Man and of Citizenship* was issued.
- **1793** Reign of Terror

LESSON 2 ▸ REVIEW

Check Facts and Main Ideas

1. ↻ **Summarize** On a separate piece of paper, write a brief summary of the main points below.

| The French monarchy had too much power. | The Estates-General did not give equal representation to the estates. | France's tax system was unfair. |

↓ ↓ ↓

[ ]

2. How did Napoleon improve conditions in France?

3. Who was Robespierre?

4. What accomplishments did the republic bring to France?

5. **Critical Thinking:** *Recognize Point of View* Why would other European leaders band together to defeat Napoleon?

Link to ⬌ Writing

Write a Letter Write a letter to a newspaper editor explaining why you believe that the republic is important to France. Be sure to include comparisons of the republic with the French monarchy that came before it.

CITIZEN HEROES

BUILDING CITIZENSHIP
Caring
Respect
Responsibility
⭐ Fairness
Honesty
Courage

A Pioneer for Women's Rights

During the years of the French Revolution, Marie-Olympe de Gouges (oh LAMP duh GOOZH) asked that women be granted the same rights as men. Her demand was met with rejection and laughter from both men and women, but she continued to fight for what she believed in.

Musee de la Ville de Paris. Musee Carnavalet, Paris France

De Gouges was born in southwestern France in 1748. She began her career as a playwright. De Gouges's plays were considered extreme and often were not performed. The plays that were produced received harsh criticism.

De Gouges found other ways to spread her ideas about equality. She published pamphlets and articles. De Gouges's most famous work is the *Declaration of the Rights of Woman and the Female Citizen* (1791). This document was the first feminist manifesto, or public declaration. She began the *Declaration* with this challenge:

> *"Man are you capable of being just?*
> *It is a woman who asks you this question.*
> *Who has given you the authority to*
> *oppress my sex?"*

Bibliotheque Nationale de France

In the *Declaration,* de Gouges stated that women should have the same legal rights as men. She said that women should also receive an equal education. De Gouges was ahead of her time and was viewed as a threat. She was arrested, found guilty of treason, and sent to the guillotine.

De Gouges's work influenced women in other countries. A year after the *Declaration* was published, British writer Mary Wollstonecraft wrote a book about equal rights and education for women. These works helped to encourage the movement for women's rights.

Fairness in Action

Link to Current Events Research strategies the women's rights movement used to fight for equal rights. How do their experiences compare with de Gouges's experiences?

Research and Writing Skills

Compare Primary Sources

What? You have already learned that primary sources are snapshots of history. They come in many forms and translations.

You can use two primary sources from different time periods to compare and contrast how ideas were alike and different. Below are excerpts from the English Bill of Rights (1689) and the U.S. Constitution (1787).

XXVIII. WILLIAM the THIRD and MARY the SECOND, from 1688 to 1702.

BILL OF RIGHTS

The Granger Collection

"And for preventing all questions and divisions in this realm . . . in and upon which the unity, peace, tranquility and safety of this nation doth under God wholly consist and depend . . . the safety and welfare of this Protestant kingdom . . ."

tranquility: calmness, quiet
doth: does
posterity: later generations
ordain: pass into law

We the People of the United States, in Order to form a more perfect Union, establish Justice, insure domestic Tranquility, provide for the common defence, promote the general Welfare, and secure the Blessings of Liberty to ourselves and our Posterity, do ordain and establish this Constitution for the United States of America.

The Granger Collection

▶ **This scene depicts the signing of the U.S. Constitution.**

Why? By comparing primary sources, we can try to understand how one document might have influenced the writing of another.

The English wanted to limit the power of the monarchy. They used the main points of the Magna Carta (1215), which limited the king's power, to draw up the English Bill of Rights in 1689. This piece of legislation made England a **constitutional monarchy**, one in which the monarch's power is limited.

Beginning in the late 1600s, a philosophical movement called the **Enlightenment** began in Europe. This movement applied reason, or logical thinking, to understanding the laws of human nature. These ideas could then be used to improve society. Enlightenment writers such as John Locke inspired the American colonists to form ideas about self-government. The colonists then borrowed ideas from the Enlightenment, as well as the English Bill of Rights, to help in the writing of the Constitution.

How? In comparing primary sources, first you must use a dictionary to look up any words you do not know. You may be using a primary source that is in English but uses different words from those you are used to. For example, in the excerpt from the English Bill of Rights, you will see the word *doth*. We would say *does* instead of *doth*.

Then you must look for key words. In the selections that you read from both primary sources, make a list of key words, ideas, and subjects. Consider the writer or writers of the primary sources, as well as the audience.

Think and Apply

1. What are some common key words and ideas in both excerpts?

2. To whom are these documents addressed?

3. Summarize what you have learned by comparing these two primary sources.

473

1750   1800   1850   1900

1760s
James Watt improves the steam engine.

1807
Robert Fulton builds the first successful steamboat.

1829
The "Railroad Age" begins.

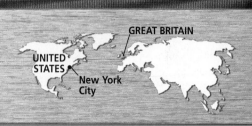

GREAT BRITAIN

UNITED STATES

New York City

The Industrial Revolution

PREVIEW

Focus on the Main Idea
The Industrial Revolution began in Great Britain and soon spread to other nations.

PLACES
Great Britain
Hudson River
New York City
Albany

PEOPLE
James Watt
George Stephenson
Robert Fulton
Charles Dickens

VOCABULARY
textile
factory
tenement

TERMS
domestic system
Industrial Revolution
steam engine
factory system

You Are There

Letter to the Editor
Manchester, England
February 15, 1831

Dear Editor:

I'm 15 years old and I work in a mill here in Manchester. I start work at five o'clock in the morning, six days a week. Many days I don't stop working until eight at night. I work the spinning machines, and I'm on my feet all day. My boss likes to hire children because he can pay us less than adults. Children also have smaller hands that can fit better inside the machines. A week ago, a girl lost her right hand in a machine, which started turning while her hand was in it.

I've worked here for seven years. My knees always hurt. Sometimes it hurts to breathe, too, because the factory is filled with cotton dust. I cough all of the time.

I expect I will work here all my life. That's if I don't get hurt. If I get hurt and can't work, I will starve because there's no one here to look out for me.

—Sophia

North Wind Picture Archives

Compare and Contrast As you read, think about the changes the Industrial Revolution made in the way goods were produced.

A New Way of Making Things

Between 1000 and 1750, humans or animals did nearly all of the work. There were some machines, but they were powered by hand, foot, or animal. Most goods were made at home. For example, workers would buy a raw material such as cotton from merchants, take it back to their cottages, and produce thread to make **textiles,** or cloth that is either woven or knitted. Making goods in the home is called the **domestic system.**

In Europe after 1750, new ideas arose about how to make and use machines to produce goods faster and on a larger scale. The change from human and animal power to machine power is known as the **Industrial Revolution.**

The invention of the **steam engine,** a machine that used the power of steam, kicked off the Industrial Revolution in **Great Britain.** The first useful steam engine was built early in the 1700s. During the 1760s, **James Watt** of Scotland improved the steam engine so that it could power large machines.

The next step was to lower costs by grouping machines together into one large place: a **factory.** Grouping machines in one place was known as the **factory system.**

REVIEW Summarize how the factory system was different from the domestic system.
Summarize

Great Britain and the Steam Engine

There were a number of reasons why Great Britain launched the Industrial Revolution. Great Britain had important natural resources, such as iron and coal. It also had many skilled workers, as well as people with money to invest in factories. It had a good transportation network, a system of roads and rivers to move goods to markets. Finally, it had colonies to supply raw materials and to buy goods.

By 1800 many new roads and canals had been built in Great Britain. Ten miles an hour was about as fast as anybody was able to travel in a horse-drawn coach or canal boat.

In 1825, **George Stephenson** attached a steam engine to wheels and put it on rails. The train engine could do the work of 40 teams of horses. In 1829 Stephenson's engine stunned people by reaching a top speed of 36 miles per hour. The "Railroad Age" had begun.

Steam power was also used to increase the speed of ships. The first successful steamboat was built by American **Robert Fulton.** In 1807 Fulton sailed a steamboat up the **Hudson River** from **New York City** to **Albany,** New York, at a speed of five miles an hour. By the 1840s, steamships were crossing the Atlantic Ocean.

REVIEW Why was Great Britain able to get an early lead in the Industrial Revolution? **Main Idea and Details**

▶ The moving parts of a steam engine are set in motion by introducing steam through the steam inlet.

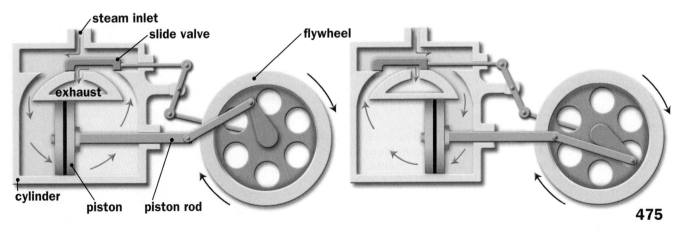

steam inlet
slide valve
flywheel
exhaust
cylinder
piston
piston rod

Terrible Conditions

Early factories were dark, dirty, and had poor air quality. Workers labored 12 to 15 hours a day, six days a week.

In the early days of the Industrial Revolution, most of the workers were women and children. They were paid much less than men. Children as young as five could be sent to work in textile mills. Even after the British government halted the use of children under nine in the textile industry in 1833, young children were still used in other industries.

Safety conditions were often poor. The machines had few, if any safety devices. Workers were often badly hurt. A worker who lost an arm or leg usually was fired without any payment.

One of the most dangerous jobs was that of the "scavenger." The youngest workers in the textile factories were usually employed as scavengers. They had to pick up the loose cotton from under the machinery by crawling under the running machines.

Coal was the cheap fuel that helped to drive the Industrial Revolution. Working conditions in the coal mines also were hard and dangerous. This is how one woman described her job in the mine:

> *"I have a belt round my waist and a chain passing between my legs, and I go on my hands and feet. The road is very steep, and we have to hold by a rope, and when there is no rope, by anything we can catch hold of."*

REVIEW Describe the working conditions in factories during the early Industrial Revolution.

⤵ Summarize

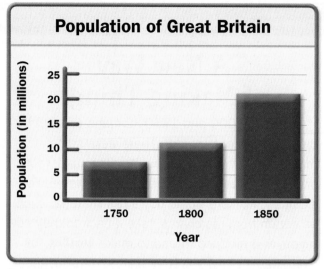

Population of Great Britain

▶ The Industrial Revolution helped the population of Great Britain to increase dramatically between 1750 to 1850.

GRAPH SKILL Use a Bar Graph *Did the population of Great Britain increase more between 1750 and 1800, or between 1800 and 1850?*

Growing Cities Have Many Problems

During the 1800s, Europe saw huge population growth. For example, in Great Britain the population went from a little more than 10 million in 1800 to more than 20 million in 1850.

As a result, Europe's cities grew rapidly. Before the Industrial Revolution, most people in Europe lived on farms or in small villages. After the Industrial Revolution began, more people started to move into towns and cities.

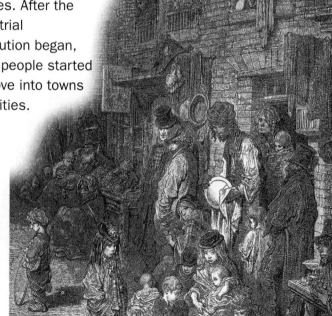

▶ The Industrial Revolution lured many people to cities such as London. Many lived in overcrowded slum apartments.

People moved into the cities because they were no longer able to earn their living on farms. As the use of machinery on farms increased, fewer farm workers were needed. At the same time, the growing number of factories in the cities provided many new jobs for workers.

In the cities, many workers lived in over-crowded slum apartments, called **tenements.** There were few public services for people in the tenements. For example, in the 1830s, the city of Birmingham, England, still used pigs to eat the garbage residents produced.

Writer **Charles Dickens** described a London slum:

> *"It was a town of machinery and tall chimneys, out of which serpents of smoke trailed. It had a black canal in it, and a river that ran purple with ill-smelling dye."*

Smoke filled the skies of industrial cities such as London.

REVIEW Why did so many people in Europe move to cities in the first half of the nineteenth century? **Cause and Effect**

Summarize the Lesson

- **1760s** James Watt improved the steam engine.
- **1807** Robert Fulton built the first successful steamboat.
- **1829** The "Railroad Age" began.

LESSON 3 REVIEW

Check Facts and Main Ideas

1. Compare and Contrast On a separate piece of paper, complete the diagram below.

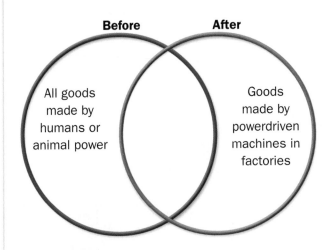

Before — All goods made by humans or animal power

After — Goods made by powerdriven machines in factories

2. What did James Watt's improvements to the steam engine accomplish?

3. What factors allowed Great Britain to get a head start in the Industrial Revolution?

4. Why did so many people move to cities between 1800 and 1850?

5. Critical Thinking: *Make Inferences* Why do you think the conditions were so bad in London factories and London slums?

Link to ⚭ Speech

Write a Speech Write a speech in which you try to draw attention to the terrible health problems caused by overcrowded slums and poor factory conditions in London.

Menlo Park
NEW JERSEY

1850   **1900**   **1950**

about 1850
U.S. industries start
using crude oil.

1877
Edison invents
the phonograph.

1913
Ford Motor Co. begins building
automobiles on an assembly line.

The Second Industrial Revolution

PREVIEW

Focus on the Main Idea
While business owners gained
more freedom from government
controls, workers struggled to
improve their working conditions.

PLACES
Menlo Park

PEOPLE
Thomas Edison
Karl Marx

VOCABULARY
corporation
reformer
strike

TERMS
Second Industrial Revolution
assembly line
capitalism
capitalist
market economy
traditional economy
laissez faire
labor union
socialism
command economy

You Are There

What will Thomas Edison dream up
next? All your life you've been hearing
about his wonderful inventions and
how some day they will improve people's lives. You haven't
actually met anyone who's used an electric light bulb in
their home. You've only heard stories about the kineto-
scope, an invention that seems to make photographs
move. However, you've just seen another of Edison's
inventions up close. It's a machine that holds a tube
wrapped in tin foil. When the machine is turned on, the
tube spins while a needle touches its surface.

All you can hear at first is a loud hissing and crackling.
As you listen closer, you hear something else. It's a softer,
more familiar sound. Somehow, that tube wrapped in tin
foil can store and then replay a human voice.

Main Idea and Details
As you read, keep track of the
machines you use today that
were first introduced during
the Second Industrial
Revolution.

1877
phonograph

1879
light bulb

1876
telephone

1875

New Sources of Power

The first Industrial Revolution had been based on the steam engine and coal. After the 1850s, the **Second Industrial Revolution** was powered by electricity, oil, and steel. New inventions began to change the way people lived and worked.

Thomas Edison and his assistants were responsible for many of the inventions that we are familiar with today: the electric light bulb, the phonograph (the ancestor of today's CD player), motion pictures, or movies, and others. Edison and others made important discoveries. Many of these inventions came out of Edison's laboratory in **Menlo Park,** New Jersey.

Steel bridges could cross wide rivers. Buildings with steel skeletons could rise higher and higher. Steel plows could break the heavy soil of the American Great Plains for planting.

In the 1850s industries in the United States started using crude oil. At first, crude oil was used for lighting and heating. Then came the development of the internal combustion engine. Oil could be made into gasoline to run these engines. This engine is used today in most cars, trucks, and buses.

Just as important was the power of electricity. Electricity supplied light and power to machines. It led to the development of new forms of communication, such as the telephone and telegraph. Later, inventors discovered how to use radio waves to send voices and music over long distances in virtually no time.

REVIEW How was the Second Industrial Revolution different from the first? **Compare and Contrast**

Corporations and Assembly Lines

At the beginning of the Industrial Revolution, a handful of people could build a factory and keep it going. However, by the early 1800s, large amounts of money were needed to open a factory. Railroad and steel-making companies had grown so large that it became very expensive to buy machines and pay workers.

A new type of business organization developed. It was called a corporation. **Corporations** provided a way to raise millions of dollars. They raised money by selling stock shares, or parts of the company, to the public. If the corporation made profits, those profits would be divided among the shareholders.

In time, business leaders tried to develop new ways to manufacture items. One such way was the **assembly line.** The assembly line was developed in the early 1900s by the U.S. automobile manufacturer Henry Ford. On the assembly line, the automobile traveled along a moving belt past a number of workers. Each worker added one part to the car, such as a door, until the car was complete. The assembly line made it possible to manufacture more items in a shorter period of time.

REVIEW What effect did the assembly line have on the manufacturing process? **Cause and Effect**

1890
movie camera

1885
automobile

1885

1895

Capitalism and Reformers

The economic system that arose during the Industrial Revolution was called capitalism. Under **capitalism**, private individuals own most factories and industries. These people run the businesses in order to make a profit. People who invested money were known as **capitalists.**

The capitalism that took hold in the industrialized nations was a market economy. In a **market economy,** the people make their own decisions about how to spend their money. To succeed in a market economy, capitalists have to know what people want. This influences the decisions that capitalists make about their businesses.

The market economy brought on by capitalism replaced a traditional economy. In a **traditional economy,** people work and spend their money in ways that do not change much from generation to generation.

One result of this change from a traditional to a market economy was that change occurred at a much quicker pace. Many questioned if all of these changes were better for people. Some people wanted the government to have some control over business.

Most capitalists believed that government controls were harmful to the growth of their businesses. The capitalists wanted to run their factories and businesses freely, without any government controls. These ideas about business were called *laissez faire* (LAY zay FAIR). *Laissez faire* is a French expression that means "leave it alone." Business owners believed that the system worked best when the government did not try to control it.

Many people were disturbed by the harsh conditions in the factory system. They rejected *laissez faire* ideas and wanted the government to correct many of the abuses. These people were known as **reformers,** because they wanted to keep capitalism but improve, or reform, it.

REVIEW Why did reformers reject *laissez faire* ideas? **Draw Conclusions**

Working Conditions

Pressure from reformers led governments in Europe and North America to pass laws that improved living and working conditions. For example, a British law limited the work day for children and women to ten hours. Other laws restricted the use of children and stopped the use of women, girls, and young boys in mines.

The workers themselves played a key role in improving conditions. They began to form labor unions to push their demands for better conditions. **Labor unions** represent all of the workers in a factory or an industry. They try to make the factory owner raise wages and improve working conditions. Unions use **strikes,** or the refusal to work, until their demands are granted.

In the 1700s, British workers had begun the first associations to help improve their working conditions. These were the first labor unions in Great Britain. As the unions grew more politically active, employers and the government grew hostile. In the early 1800s, many laws were passed to forbid labor unions. However, unions eventually became legal. By the late 1800s, workers' unions had become strong.

REVIEW How did people try to improve conditions for workers? **Summarize**

▶ **Union workers used strikes as a way of demanding better working conditions.**

North Wind Picture Archives

The Socialists

Reformers did not reject capitalism. They wanted to improve it. However, there were some people who blamed capitalism for many of society's problems. Some wanted to replace capitalism with an economic system called socialism. Under **socialism,** most industries, businesses, land, and natural resources are owned by the government, instead of individuals. Socialism was a form of **command economy,** in which the government or other central authority controls the flow of money.

Most socialists used peaceful means to promote their ideas. They formed political parties and struggled to win control of their nation's government in elections. However, some called for a revolution. One person who popularized socialist ideas and a revolt against the government was the German **Karl Marx.** He predicted a worldwide revolution that would bring about a society that had no separate economic classes.

During the 1800s and 1900s, many nations improved wages and working conditions. Workers in these nations gained many freedoms. They saw no need to overthrow the system.

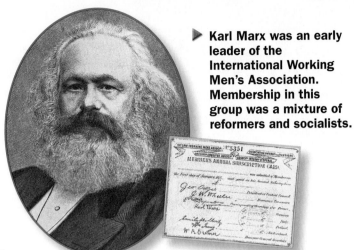

▶ Karl Marx was an early leader of the International Working Men's Association. Membership in this group was a mixture of reformers and socialists.

REVIEW How were Karl Marx's ideas different from those of many other socialists? Main Idea and Details

Summarize the Lesson

c. 1850 Industries in the United States started using crude oil.

1877 Edison invented the phonograph.

1913 Ford Motor Co. began building automobiles on an assembly line.

LESSON 4   REVIEW

Check Facts and Main Ideas

1. **Main Idea and Details** On a separate piece of paper, fill in the diagram to give examples of familiar machines that were invented during the Second Industrial Revolution.

> Many machines we use today were invented during the Second Industrial Revolution.

2. What is a corporation?

3. Why did reformers want to improve working conditions?

4. Who was Karl Marx?

5. **Critical Thinking:** *Make Generalizations* Do you believe that Thomas Edison's inventions improved people's lives? Explain your answer.

Link to ⚭ **Science**

Research on Your Own Thomas Edison spent years trying to develop electric lighting. Do some research to learn about the details of his experiments to design the light bulb.

1750   1775

1760s
James Watt improved
the steam engine.

1789
Bastille fell;
*Declaration
of Rights of
Man and of
Citizen* issued.

1793
Reign
of Terror began.

1776 13 British colonies declared independence.

Chapter Summary

Summarize

On a separate piece of paper, fill in the
missing summary from the details.

Many skilled workers	Large quantities of natural resources	A market for goods to be purchased

Vocabulary

Match each word with the correct definition or
description.

1 legislature
(p. 457)

2 monarchy
(p. 467)

3 textile
(p. 475)

4 factory
(p. 475)

5 strike (p. 480)

a. cloth that is either
woven or knitted

b. the refusal to work

c. a place where
machines are
grouped together

d. a government in
which a king,
queen, or emperor
has supreme
power

e. lawmaking body

People and Terms

Write a sentence identifying each of the following
people and terms and explain their significance.

1 George
Washington
(p. 458)

2 Simón Bolívar
(p. 462)

3 Bernardo
O'Higgins
(p. 462)

4 Declaration of
Independence
(p. 458)

5 Industrial
Revolution
(p. 475)

6 Thomas Edison
(p. 479)

7 Louis XVI
(p. 467)

8 capitalism
(p. 480)

9 socialism
(p. 481)

10 Napoleonic Code
(p. 469)

1821
Mexico won independence.

1876
Alexander Graham Bell invented the telephone.

1890
Edison invented a motion picture camera.

1913
Ford Motor Co. began building automobiles on an assembly line.

Facts and Main Ideas

1 Why did the British government tax the American colonists?

2 **Time Line** Which occurred first: the invention of the motion picture camera or the independence of Mexico?

3 **Main Idea** How did the policies of European nations lead to revolutions in the Americas?

4 **Main Idea** How did the French Revolution affect France and the rest of Europe?

5 **Main Idea** How did the Industrial Revolution affect people and economies?

6 **Main Idea** What was one important advantage to forming a corporation during the Second Industrial Revolution?

7 **Critical Thinking:** *Recognize Point of View* Do you think that the colonists in the Americas had the right to rebel against their government? Why or why not?

Write About History

1 **Write a journal entry** from the viewpoint of a French woman during the French Revolution. Should men and women get the same rights of citizenship?

2 **Write a "What If" story** describing what life might be like today if the Industrial Revolution had not occurred.

3 **Write an advertisement** urging colonists to join the movement to liberate Mexico. Make a poster using slogans, drawings, or other attention-grabbing techniques.

Apply Skills

Compare Primary Sources

Read the primary source below. Then answer the questions.

In 1819 the South American revolutionary leader Simón Bolívar spoke to other political leaders about the people and lands just liberated from the Spanish:

"We find that our quest for liberty is now even more difficult . . . for we, having been placed in a state lower than slavery, had been robbed not only of our freedom but also of the right to exercise an active domestic tyranny."

1 What important key word in this primary source is also used in one of the primary sources on page 472?

2 How is the meaning of that key word different in this primary source?

3 What was Simón Bolívar trying to tell his listeners?

Internet Activity

To get help with vocabulary, people, and terms, select dictionary, encyclopedia, or almanac from Social Studies Library at **www.sfsocialstudies.com**.

CHAPTER 17

Imperialism, Nationalism, and Unification

Lesson 1

**late 1800s
South Africa**
European countries divide up Africa into colonies.

1

Lesson 2

**1900
China**
China is forced to open its doors to all trading nations.

2

Lesson 3

**1867
Canada**
Canada becomes the first dominion of Great Britain.

3

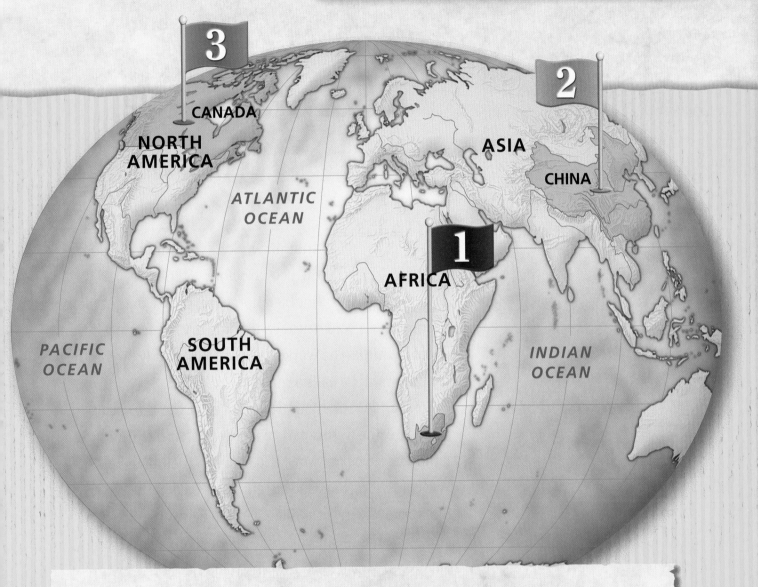

CANADA

NORTH
AMERICA

ATLANTIC
OCEAN

ASIA

CHINA

AFRICA

PACIFIC
OCEAN

SOUTH
AMERICA

INDIAN
OCEAN

Why We Remember

Today we live in a global culture. Most of us come into contact with people of many ethnic groups, nationalities, and religions. However, in the 1800s, interaction was more limited. For many people, such contact was only through the creation of colonies. The European powers wanted more resources. They were anxious to create empires. European powers began to search for lands they could colonize. The experiences of colonization brought diverse cultures face to face on a large scale. Colonization has had lasting effects on the world we live in today.

1850   1900

1857
Indian Mutiny

1869
Suez Canal opens.

1885
Congo Free State is set up.

GERMANY — Berlin
Suez Canal
EGYPT
INDIA — FRENCH INDOCHINA
CONGO FREE STATE
SOUTH AFRICA

PREVIEW

Focus on the Main Idea
By the 1800s, many European nations were building empires by conquering and colonizing other countries and territories.

PLACES
South Africa
India
Suez Canal
Indochina
Berlin
Congo Free State

PEOPLE
Cecil Rhodes
Victoria
Tilak
Leopold II

VOCABULARY
nationalism
imperialism
imperialist

EVENTS
Indian Mutiny
Berlin Conference

Expanding Empires

> **You Are There**
> Another work day begins. You watch as the people before you prepare for 12 hours of hot, hard, dirty work. At noon they receive a cold baked yam, some dry corn, and a little water to drink. The work master allows exactly 20 minutes for this snack he calls a meal.
>
> You barely remember the days before the European masters came to this part of the Congo. At one time your family raised corn, yams, and beans in their own fields. With older brothers and sisters you fished in the big river. Life was lively in your village. In the evenings, elders shared stories about village ancestors. You shared songs and jokes. Now it's sad to think these memories are growing dimmer and dimmer.

▶ Africans labored under harsh, often cruel conditions for the European conquerors.

Summarize As you read, try to summarize how European nations built world empires.

Nationalism and Imperialism

Why did the Europeans go into the Congo in Africa, conquer African peoples, and force them to work for their European masters? A powerful force called nationalism swept over Europe in the 1800s. **Nationalism** is a strong devotion to one's own country. For some people, nationalism meant wanting to unify or strengthen their country. For others, it meant believing that their country was better than all others.

Another idea that was often linked to nationalism was imperialism. In the 1800s, **imperialism** meant building up an empire by controlling or conquering lands in Africa, Asia, and elsewhere. The Europeans who promoted imperialism were called **imperialists.**

Imperialism made huge profits for the Europeans. European countries got raw materials such as cotton, rubber, oil, minerals, sugar, tea, and coffee from their colonies. In return, Europeans sold their own factory-made goods to the colonies—always at a nice profit.

▶ **Cecil Rhodes made a fortune in the diamond mines of South Africa.**

They believed that the conquered peoples were better off because of European influence. They believed they were spreading Christianity and European civilization to people they considered less advanced.

Many Europeans believed that they were better than the non-Europeans in their colonies. **Cecil Rhodes** was one such person. This British empire-builder developed diamond mines in **South Africa.** He became very rich. Rhodes said:

> *"I say that we are the first race in the world, and that the more of the world we inhabit [live in] the better it is for the human race."*

REVIEW Summarize the two powerful forces that swept over Europe in the 1800s.

🔄 Summarize

▶ **The Kimberley Mine in South Africa was founded after farmers started discovering diamonds on their land. This photo is from 1872, shortly after mining operations began.**

Empires in Asia and Africa

In the age of imperialism, Great Britain had the world's largest empire. British colonies were scattered all over the globe. During the reign of Queen Victoria, Great Britain's monarch, it was claimed that "the sun never sets on the British Empire." This meant that the British Empire had colonies all over the world. So even when the sun was setting in Great Britain, it was rising somewhere else in the empire.

India was a valuable colony to Great Britain. The British called India the "jewel in the crown." India held great riches. Great Britain had controlled parts of India since the 1600s. British rule there became known as the *Raj*. This word means "rule" or "reign" in Hindi, a language of India.

Many Indians were unhappy under the Raj. In 1857 Indian troops rebelled. The revolt, called the Indian Mutiny, was soon put down. In 1885 a group of Indians formed the Indian National Congress. In time, this organization would lead the way to that country's independence movement. A rebel Indian leader named Tilak expressed:

> ## "Freedom is my birthright and I will have it!"

▶ This illustration shows ships passing through the Suez Canal shortly after it was completed in 1869.

Great Britain extended its imperial activities into Egypt. The French had dug the Suez Canal across Egypt, beginning in 1859 and finishing ten years later. This waterway linked the Mediterranean Sea to the Indian Ocean. Because the canal shortened the sea route from England to India, the British wanted to control it. In an effort to fight French control of the canal, the British bought all of Egypt's ownership (44 percent) of the canal in 1875.

Other European nations also colonized in South and Southeast Asia. France took control of Indochina. This region includes present-day Vietnam, Cambodia, and Laos. The Netherlands controlled the islands that became Indonesia.

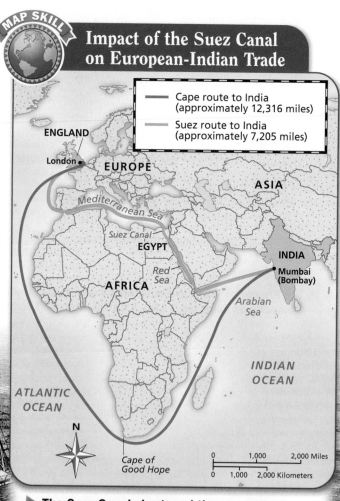

MAP SKILL

Impact of the Suez Canal on European-Indian Trade

— Cape route to India (approximately 12,316 miles)
— Suez route to India (approximately 7,205 miles)

ENGLAND
London
EUROPE
ASIA
Mediterranean Sea
Suez Canal
EGYPT
INDIA
Red Sea
Mumbai (Bombay)
AFRICA
Arabian Sea
ATLANTIC OCEAN
INDIAN OCEAN
N
Cape of Good Hope

0   1,000   2,000 Miles
0   1,000   2,000 Kilometers

▶ The Suez Canal shortened the sea route between England and India by more than 5,000 miles.

MAP SKILL Use Map Scale *If you could travel in a straight line, what would be the distance between London and Bombay, India?*

However, European imperialism reached its height in Africa. Spain and Portugal had long held lands there. Other European powers began to "scramble" for African lands. In 1884 the European powers decided to meet in Berlin, Germany, to partition, or divide up, Africa. They never invited any Africans to attend. At the Berlin Conference, France, Great Britain, Germany, Belgium, and Italy all claimed parts of African territory. Finally, only two African countries remained independent: Ethiopia and Liberia.

In Africa, European imperialism was at its harshest. Belgium's King Leopold II controlled the Congo region of Central Africa. In 1885 he

managed to have the Congo Free State set up with himself as ruler. Africans living in this area were forced to work for Leopold. Leopold was widely criticized for cruel treatment of the Africans. After 20 years of this cruelty, the Congo's population had fallen by about one-half.

European imperialism cast a long shadow over Africa's future. In Unit 8 you will read how, after years of struggle, the African nations gained their independence.

REVIEW Why did Great Britain want control of the Suez Canal? *Draw Conclusions*

Summarize the Lesson

1857 Indian troops, unhappy with British rule, revolted in the Indian Mutiny.

1869 Egypt's Suez Canal opened, making travel between Europe and India much faster.

1885 Belgium's King Leopold II set up the Congo Free State, which treated Africans brutally.

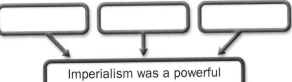
▶ **This woodcut offers a glimpse of life in an African village before contact with European conquerors.**

North Wind Picture Archives

LESSON 1 REVIEW

Check Facts and Main Ideas

1. ↻ **Summarize** On a separate piece of paper, fill in the details of the summary.

```
[   ]  →  [   ]  →  [   ]
            ↓   ↓   ↓
   Imperialism was a powerful
   force that led to European
   empires in the 1800s.
```

2. Why did some Europeans believe that imperialism would benefit people in colonies?

3. What evidence could you offer to show that King Leopold's rule in the Congo was harsh?

4. In what parts of the world did Europeans build their empires in the 1800s?

5. **Critical Thinking:** *Detect Bias* Do you think that Cecil Rhodes could back up his opinions with solid evidence? Why or why not?

Link to ⌘⌘ Writing

Write a Paragraph Explain whether or not you think that it was fair that no Africans were invited to the Berlin Conference. Explain how the outcome of the conference might have been different if they had attended.

Chart and Graph Skills

Interpret Circle Graphs

What? A circle graph shows the relationship between the parts and a whole. It can help you understand the relative proportions of the parts that make a whole. In a circle graph, an entire circle represents all, or 100 percent, of something. Half the circle represents 50 percent. A quarter circle represents 25 percent.

African Colonies and Protectorates (Area), 1914

The title of a circle graph tells you what quantity is illustrated. This graph illustrates the extent of colonization in Africa in 1914.

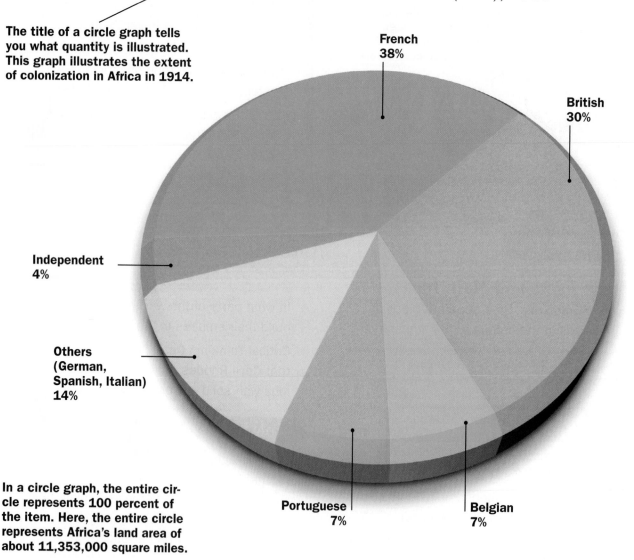

French
38%

British
30%

Independent
4%

Others
(German,
Spanish, Italian)
14%

Portuguese
7%

Belgian
7%

In a circle graph, the entire circle represents 100 percent of the item. Here, the entire circle represents Africa's land area of about 11,353,000 square miles.

In a circle graph, percents of the whole are shown by portions of the entire circle. Here, 38 percent is represented by a little more than one-third of the circle. From the graph you can read that 38 percent of Africa's land area was colonized by the French.

Why? A circle graph can make it easier to interpret data that describes parts of a whole. Smaller slices stand for smaller amounts. Larger slices stand for larger amounts.

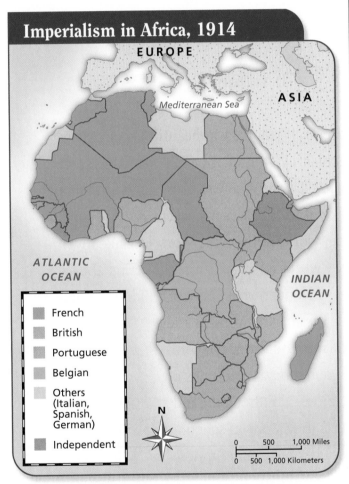

Imperialism in Africa, 1914

EUROPE

Mediterranean Sea

ASIA

ATLANTIC OCEAN

INDIAN OCEAN

N

0   500   1,000 Miles
0   500 1,000 Kilometers

Legend:
- French
- British
- Portuguese
- Belgian
- Others (Italian, Spanish, German)
- Independent

▶ **Use the colors indicated on the map and map key to match the countries with the circle graph on page 490.**

How? To use a circle graph to answer specific questions, compare the sizes of the graph portions. Often these portions are labeled with the percent of the whole they represent. For example, the graph on the previous page can be used to answer the questions "Which European country colonized the greatest portion of Africa?" and "Over how much land did it rule?"

First find the greatest portion on the graph. You can see that 38 percent is the greatest area represented.

Check the label to find out which country's holdings are represented. You can see that the French colonies covered about 38 percent of Africa in 1914.

Think and Apply

1. About what percent of Africa's land was ruled by the British?

2. Whose land holdings in Africa were greater, those of Great Britain or France? How do you know?

3. Explain how to use the graph to tell whether the following statement is true. "Together France and Great Britain controlled two-thirds of Africa's lands."

1800   1850   1900   1950

1839
First Opium War

1900
The Open Door Policy opens China's ports to all trading nations.

1904
Russia and Japan go to war over Manchuria.

MANCHURIA
Beijing
CHINA   JAPAN
Shanghai
Canton   Hong Kong
FORMOSA
(TAIWAN)
Macao

Imperialism in East Asia

PREVIEW

Focus on the Main Idea
China and Japan experienced Western imperialism in different ways.

PLACES
Hong Kong
Canton
Shanghai
Beijing
Macao
Formosa (Taiwan)
Manchuria

PEOPLE
Ci Xi
Matthew Perry
Meiji
Theodore Roosevelt

VOCABULARY
treaty port
compound
modernization

TERMS
Qing dynasty
Open Door Policy

EVENTS
Opium War

You Are There

May 30, 1888

Dear Diary,

The weather in Shanghai was beautiful again today. We had a picnic in Victoria Park. (It has a Chinese name, but I can't spell it.) The food was tasty. I had fun talking to Yvette in French. She says my accent is quite good! Yvette's father works in the treaty port, just like my poppa. But he works for France instead of England.

Sometimes I wonder what Chinese children are like. We never see them. Only workers and traders come into the European compound. I'd love to know what kinds of games the Chinese children play and which subjects they study in school. I bet Chinese children are not much different from Yvette and me.

Yours truly,
Claire

Cause and Effect As you read, keep in mind how actions of the European imperialists affected China and Japan.

The Middle Kingdom

Europeans colonized other parts of the world besides Africa. They were attracted to the riches of China. During the 1700s Britain had traded in China for tea, silk, and porcelain. However, Chinese officials strictly controlled this trade. They wanted as little contact with Europeans as possible.

Chinese culture was often isolated, or set apart, from other cultures. Their own word for China means "Middle Kingdom." The Chinese traditionally believed that their country was surrounded on all sides by inferior, "barbarian" peoples. The Chinese considered all foreigners who did not share Chinese customs, culture, and language to be barbarians.

As you read in Chapter 12, the Ming dynasty came to power in 1368. When that dynasty weakened, the **Qing** (CHIHNG) **dynasty** took power in 1644. Arts, learning, and trade flourished under the Qing. However, the Chinese would soon pay a price for trying to avoid contact with Europeans and European ideas.

In spite of its proud past, Chinese technology was not able to match the progress made by the Europeans. By the 1800s, China had fallen far behind Western nations. Chinese boats and weapons were inferior to modern European ships and guns. As time went on, the Qing dynasty became powerless to keep out the foreigners.

REVIEW Why were the Chinese opposed to foreigners? **Main Idea and Details**

▶ **This vase was created during the Qing dynasty. It features the crucifixion of Jesus, just one sign of the powerful hold Europeans had on China during this period.**

▶ **This view of Canton in about 1800 shows the increasing European presence in China. Note the European-style buildings.**

Western Imperialists in China

In the late 1700s, the British started bringing opium into China to trade for Chinese goods. Opium is a powerful and addictive drug. The Chinese government repeatedly told Great Britain to stop exporting opium. Great Britain refused. In 1839 China and Great Britain went to war over this issue. This war is known as the first **Opium War.** By 1842 Great Britain had defeated China. The British received **Hong Kong** in return. They then forced China to open five treaty ports. **Treaty ports** were port cities such as **Canton** and **Shanghai,** where Europeans had special trading rights. Europeans ran their own **compounds,** or enclosed areas with buildings in them. The Chinese police were not even allowed to arrest Europeans.

Soon, Great Britain wanted more treaty ports. In the late 1850s, the British, now joined by the French, fought against China in the second Opium War. They occupied China's capital, **Beijing** (bay JEENG), and forced China to open more treaty ports. By this time, Russia, Germany, and other countries wanted a piece of China. Even Portugal took the port of **Macao** (muh KOW).

Meanwhile, resentment had been growing in China. The Chinese government appeared unable to stop the European imperialists. A huge rebellion broke out in 1850. The Qing dynasty finally put down the revolt in 1864, but only after millions of Chinese had died.

A final blow for China came in 1894 when it went to war with Japan. Japanese forces easily defeated Chinese troops by 1895.

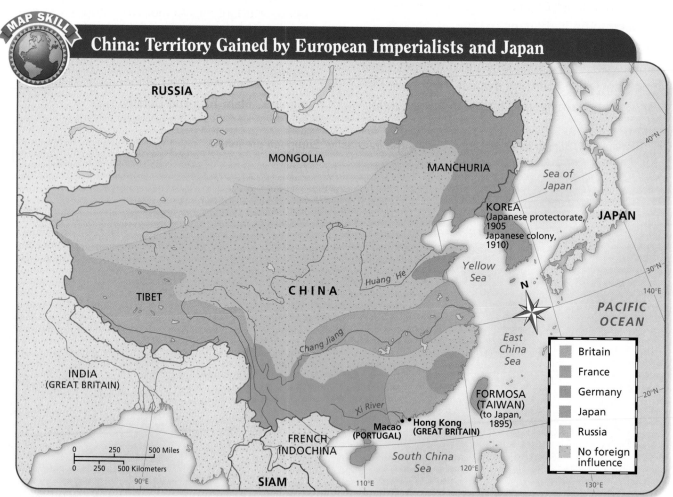

MAP SKILL

China: Territory Gained by European Imperialists and Japan

RUSSIA

MONGOLIA

MANCHURIA

Sea of Japan

KOREA
(Japanese protectorate, 1905
Japanese colony, 1910)

JAPAN

TIBET

CHINA

Huang He

Yellow Sea

N

40°N

30°N

140°E

PACIFIC OCEAN

INDIA
(GREAT BRITAIN)

Chang Jiang

East China Sea

Britain
France
Germany
Japan
Russia
No foreign influence

Xi River

Macao
(PORTUGAL)

Hong Kong
(GREAT BRITAIN)

FORMOSA
(TAIWAN)
(to Japan, 1895)

20°N

FRENCH INDOCHINA

South China Sea

120°E

0   250   500 Miles
0   250   500 Kilometers

90°E

SIAM

110°E

130°E

▶ Japan became an imperialist nation and gained territories from several countries.

MAP SKILL Use Latitude and Longitude *Which imperialist nation gained the territory located at 40° north, 120° east?*

► Empress Ci Xi was one of the most powerful women in China's history.

The Qing empress **Ci Xi** (tsee SHYEE), who kept out foreigners and prevented progress in China, expressed China's anger:

> *"The foreigners are the curse of China . . . . For forty years I have lain on brushwood and eaten bitterness because of them."*

In 1898 another revolt broke out in China. A powerful group known as "the Boxers" wanted to destroy all foreign influences. But again, the Europeans gained the upper hand. In 1900 they sent another army into Beijing and defeated the Boxers. The United States, which also was interested in China, set up an **Open Door Policy** in 1900. According to this policy, every country had equal opportunity to trade with China. With this policy, foreigners remained in control of China.

The days of European control of China were numbered. In Unit 7 you will read how the twentieth century brought dramatic changes to China.

REVIEW What were the effects of European imperialism on China? **Cause and Effect**

► The Chinese were powerless to prevent the British from bringing opium into China.

Japan and the West

In 1853 U.S. naval official **Matthew Perry** sailed warships into a Japanese harbor. He demanded that the Japanese authorities accept a letter from the U.S. president, demanding that Japan open treaty ports. In 1854 Japan opened its ports to trade.

As you read in Unit 5, Japan's shoguns had kept their country closed off from the outside world for two centuries. But some Japanese had begun to worry. They wondered if Japan would end up like China, a victim of Western imperialism.

In 1868, the last shogun handed over his power to a forward-looking emperor. This new leader, **Meiji** (MAY jee), and his advisors started Japan on a path of rapid modernization. **Modernization** is the process of bringing ways and standards into the present day. In this case, Japan wanted to improve technology to catch up with the West.

The Japanese now began to study Western science and industry. They built up and modernized their armed forces.

As Japan became more powerful, Western imperialists began to treat it differently from China. They ended their treaty port policies in Japan. Some governments even began to treat Japanese diplomats equally with Europeans.

► The first railway line in Japan began service in 1872. This painting details one of the train stations along the route.

As you have read, Japan defeated China in a war in 1895. As a result, Japan gained the island of **Formosa** (Taiwan). Japan also won influence in Korea, which it took over in 1910.

REVIEW Put the following events in correct order and give a date for each: Japan went to war with China; Japan took over Korea; The last shogun handed power over to Meiji; Matthew Perry arrived in Japan. **Sequence**

495

A New World Power

Meanwhile, Japan and Russia competed for control of **Manchuria,** the northeastern region of China. In 1904 they went to war. To the shock of the Western imperialists, Japan defeated Russia quickly. Japan was then considered a great world power, much like those in Europe. In 1905 Japan and Russia agreed to a peace treaty offered by U.S. President **Theodore Roosevelt.** Roosevelt later won a Nobel Peace Prize for helping to end this war.

Japan had proven that Asians could hold their own against the Western powers. In Unit 7 you will read how Japan and the United States clashed in a war.

REVIEW What event caused Japan to be considered a world power? **Main Idea and Details**

▶ **Japanese troops await an attack from the Russians in Manchuria in 1905.**

Summarize the Lesson

1839 The first Opium War began after Chinese officials demanded that Great Britain stop bringing opium into China.

1900 The Open Door Policy opened China's ports to all trading nations.

1904 Russia and Japan went to war over control of Manchuria.

LESSON 2 — REVIEW

Check Facts and Main Ideas

1. Cause and Effect On a separate piece of paper, fill in the missing cause or effect.

Great Britain fights China in the first Opium War.	→
	→ Japan opens its ports to the United States.
The Boxers rebel in China.	→

2. What traditional Chinese belief explains the name "Middle Kingdom" for China?

3. How did Japan change after Meiji came to power in 1868?

4. Before the 1800s, what contact did China and Japan have with Western countries?

5. Critical Thinking: *Make Inferences* Do you think the Qing dynasty provided the leadership needed to modernize China in the 1800s? Explain your answer.

Link to 🔗 Art

Analyze Visual Art Look at the Japanese painting in the right-hand column on page 495. What can you learn from this painting about Western influence in Japan?

Meiji
1852–1912

Emperor Meiji was the first Japanese ruler in more than two centuries who did not view Western nations and ideas with suspicion. The young emperor studied traditional Japanese subjects. However, he also studied German and European politics. These all greatly influenced his thought and rule.

In 1868 he was crowned emperor and changed his name from Mutsuhito to Meiji, which means "enlightened rule." He then took the "Charter Oath of Five Principles." The Charter Oath said that the Japanese would no longer live in the past:

"Evil customs of the past shall be discontinued, and new customs shall be based on the just laws of nature."

The government, economy, and military were modeled after those in the West. Meiji wore Western-style clothes and ate Western food. When Japan's first railway opened, Meiji appeared before the public to mark the occasion. Meiji also took an active role in the government.

BIOFACT

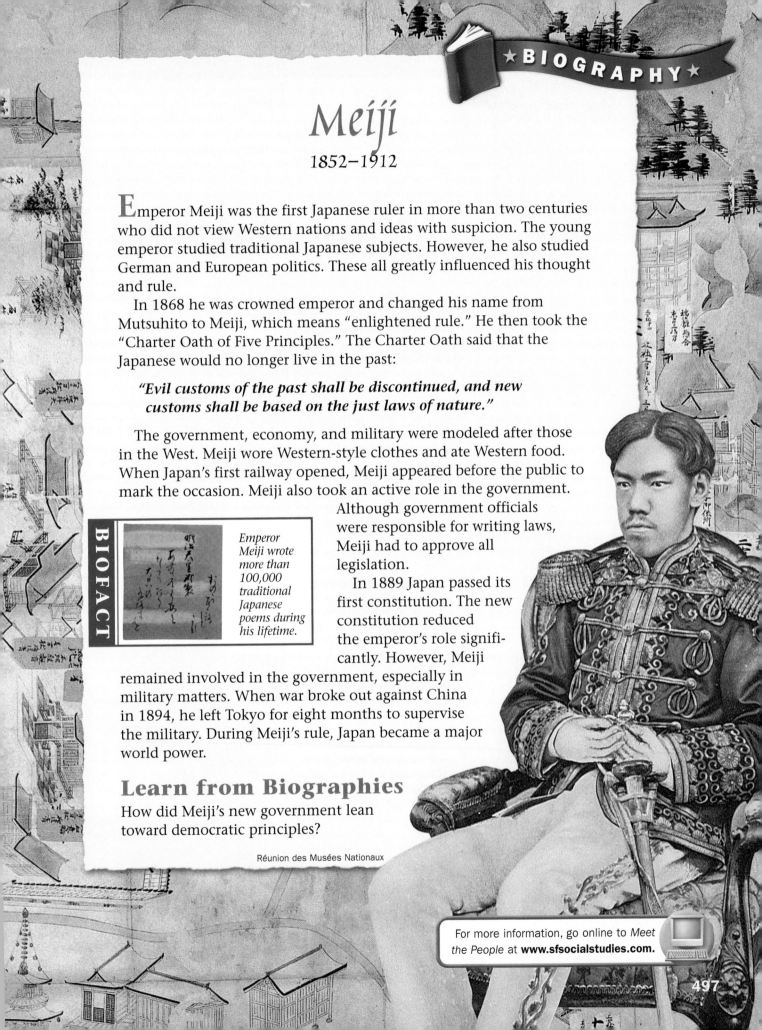

Emperor Meiji wrote more than 100,000 traditional Japanese poems during his lifetime.

Although government officials were responsible for writing laws, Meiji had to approve all legislation.

In 1889 Japan passed its first constitution. The new constitution reduced the emperor's role significantly. However, Meiji remained involved in the government, especially in military matters. When war broke out against China in 1894, he left Tokyo for eight months to supervise the military. During Meiji's rule, Japan became a major world power.

Learn from Biographies

How did Meiji's new government lean toward democratic principles?

Réunion des Musées Nationaux

For more information, go online to *Meet the People* at **www.sfsocialstudies.com.**

1850   1900

1861
Italy becomes a
unified nation.

1871
German Empire is created.

1867
Canada becomes a dominion.

New Nations

PREVIEW

Focus on the Main Idea
Nationalism led to new nations in
Europe and the British colonies.

PLACES
Germany
Italy
Prussia
Venice
Rome
Canada
Australia
New Zealand

PEOPLE
Giuseppe Mazzini
Otto von Bismarck
Wilhelm II
Camillo di Cavour
Victor Emmanuel II
Giuseppe Garibaldi
Sir John MacDonald
Sir Edmund Barton
William Hobson

VOCABULARY
dominion
parliament

You Are There
Over dessert and coffee your father and
Uncle Karl have a loud and bitter argument. Your father says that Italy has
been divided up like a pie for too long. Italians should have
their own nation. Uncle Karl protests that Italy is better off
under the strong, protective arm of Austria. They go back
and forth arguing until their faces turn bright red.
Everyone at the table shifts and squirms. Mother and Aunt
Cecilia try to change the subject. Later you begin to think
about what has been said. Doesn't it make sense for
Italians to have their own country? Why should Austria—
or any other country—rule Italy? You wonder if someone
will come forward to lead Italy in becoming
a unified nation.

▶ **Parts of present-day
Germany and present-day
Italy were controlled by
Austria-Hungary, whose flag
is pictured here.**

Sequence As you read, keep
the events that led to new
nations in their correct
chronological order.

Nationalism and Unification

In Lesson 1, you read how European nationalism contributed to imperialism. Nationalism also encouraged some countries to unify and build new nations. Two such nations were **Germany** and **Italy.**

For hundreds of years, there had been no German or Italian nation. France and Austria controlled parts of Germany. Austria also controlled northern Italy. A king ruled over the "Kingdom of the Two Sicilies" in southern Italy. The pope, or head of the Roman Catholic Church, ruled territories in central Italy.

In the 1800s, an Italian patriot named **Giuseppe Mazzini** (joo SEH peh mat ZEE nee) said:

▶ **Giuseppe Mazzini was an influential Italian patriot.**

> *"A nation is the universality [sum total] of citizens speaking the same language."*

The people of Italy wanted their own nation. Likewise, the people of Germany wanted a nation of their own.

Germans and Italians looked to Greece as an example. For nearly 500 years, the Ottoman Empire had ruled Greece. The Ottomans had a different language, customs, history, and religion than Greece had. In the 1820s, the people of Greece had fought a war of independence. Finally, in 1830, Greece became an independent nation. By the mid-1800s, the Germans and Italians were ready to fight for their own nations too.

REVIEW Describe the states of Germany and Italy before the 1850s. ↻ Summarize

MAP SKILL **Italy and Germany, 1850**

— German states
— Italian states

0   150   300 Miles
0   150   300 Kilometers

SWEDEN

North Sea

DENMARK

Baltic Sea

HOLSTEIN
OLDENBURG

MECKLENBURG-SCHWERIN

NETHERLANDS

HANOVER

P R U S S I A

RUSSIAN EMPIRE

BELGIUM

HESSE

SAXONY

THURINGIAN STATES

LUX.
LICHTENBURG
BADEN

BAVARIA

WÜRTTEMBURG

AUSTRIAN EMPIRE

FRANCE

SWITZ.

LOMBARDY & VENETIA

PARMA

MODENA

TUSCANY

PAPAL STATES

Adriatic Sea

OTTOMAN EMPIRE

KINGDOM OF SARDINIA

Corsica (FRANCE)

Tyrrhenian Sea

Sardinia

N

KINGDOM OF THE TWO SICILIES

Ionian Sea

Mediterranean Sea

Sicily

▶ **In 1850, Italy and Germany were made up of many states and territories, some of which were under the control of Austria-Hungary.**

MAP SKILL Use an Inset Map *What continent lies just to the south of the island of Sicily?*

A German Nation

Prussia was the largest and most powerful German state. Otto von Bismarck was its clever prime minister, or head of government. He led Prussia in three wars to unify Germany. Bismarck said he wanted to "put Germany in the saddle" in Europe.

Prussia first defeated its neighbor Denmark in 1864. Then it turned on Austria in 1866 and won a quick victory. Finally, Prussia fought France in 1870–1871. Again, Prussia won a quick victory. With all of these interfering neighbors out of the way, the Prussians declared Germany a united empire. Prussia's king became the kaiser (KEYE zuhr), or emperor, of unified Germany.

Germany grew rapidly into a powerful country. But its government, located in Prussia, was not democratic. Prussia was also the center of support for the military and warfare. A new kaiser, Wilhelm II, later explained:

> "We have . . . fought for our place in the sun and have won it. It will be my business to see that we retain this place in the sun unchallenged."

Wilhelm II meant that Germany had fought to become a great world power. France, Great Britain, and other European countries began to fear Germany's power and ambition. In Chapter 18, you will read how these fears helped draw Europe into war in 1914.

REVIEW Why were France and the other European powers fearful of a united Germany? **Cause and Effect**

Then and Now

German Reunification

In this lesson you have learned how German states united into one Germany in 1871. In 1990 Germany was reunited once again. How did this happen? After World War II, the United States and the Soviet Union set up separate "Germanys"—a democratic one in the west and a communist one in the east. Germany remained divided until the late 1980s. Changes in the Soviet Union allowed Germans to reach out across their borders. Today, Germany is again one country.

▶ The Brandenburg Gate (below) was completed in the 1790s to represent peace but became part of the Berlin Wall which separated East and West Germany from 1961 to 1989.

▶ The Berlin Wall was a grim reminder of a Germany divided in half. Finally, it was broken through in November 1989.

A United Italy

Meanwhile, a movement for unification was building in Italy. One leader of this movement, Giuseppe Mazzini, wanted Italians to overthrow their rulers and form a united, democratic Italy.

Another supporter of a united Italy was **Camillo di Cavour** (kuh VOOR), prime minister of the Kingdom of Sardinia. Cavour wanted to unify Italy under Sardinia's king, **Victor Emmanuel II.**

In 1859 Cavour formed an alliance with France to attack Austria, which controlled northern Italy. These allies soon drove the Austrians out of most

▶ **Garibaldi (seated beneath the tree) is surrounded by his patriotic troops, the Redshirts.**

of northern Italy. Most states in northern and central Italy then agreed to join with Sardinia under Victor Emmanuel II.

Another leader in the fight to unify Italy was **Giuseppe Garibaldi** (GAIR uh BALL dee). He gathered a small army known as the "Redshirts." To these brave patriots, Garibaldi said:

> *"I can offer you neither honors nor wages; I offer you hunger, thirst, forced marches, battles and death. Anyone who loves his country, follow me."*

Garibaldi's Redshirts freed Sicily, Naples, and other parts of southern Italy. In 1860 southern Italy united with most of the rest of the country under Victor Emmanuel II. In early 1861 the kingdom of Italy was formally announced. It would continue to grow for another nine years.

In 1866 Austria was involved in the war against Prussia that you read about. That gave Italy the opportunity to take over **Venice** and other nearby lands ruled by Austria. Finally, Italy took over **Rome** in 1870 and made that city the Italian capital.

REVIEW Summarize the main events leading to a united Italy in 1861. ⟳ Summarize

MAP SKILL
Italy and Germany, 1871

SWEDEN
DENMARK
Baltic Sea
North Sea
NETHERLANDS
UNITED KINGDOM
GERMAN EMPIRE
RUSSIAN EMPIRE
BELGIUM
LUXEMBOURG
FRANCE
SWITZERLAND
AUSTRO-HUNGARIAN EMPIRE
Adriatic Sea
OTTOMAN EMPIRE
Corsica (FRANCE)
KINGDOM OF ITALY
SPAIN
N
Tyrrhenian Sea
Sardinia
Ionian Sea
Sicily
Mediterranean Sea

0 150 300 Miles
0 150 300 Kilometers

▶ **By 1871 Italy and Germany were unified nations.**

MAP SKILL Observe Change Through Maps
Using this map and the map on page 499, explain what changes occurred in Italy and Germany between 1850 and 1871.

British Dominions

By the mid-1800s, the British were being pressured by some of their colonies for self-rule. Canada, Australia, and New Zealand had been settled by the British and other Europeans. Great Britain began preparing these colonies to become dominions. A dominion is a self-governing nation that still has ties with the ruling empire, in this case, the British Empire.

Each dominion set up a form of government like that of Great Britain. In this system, an elected legislature, or parliament, enacts laws and selects national leaders from its own members. Each dominion also had a governor-general, who represented the British king or queen but had little real power.

In 1867 the British Parliament made Canada the first dominion. Canada included four provinces: Quebec, Ontario, New Brunswick, and Nova Scotia. Canada set up its capital at Ottawa. Sir John MacDonald became Canada's first prime minister. In time, other provinces joined. Today, Canada has ten provinces and three territories.

British colonization of Australia began when colonists and convicts started to settle in New South Wales in 1788. This was the part of Australia that Captain James Cook had claimed for Great Britain. Soon many other people came to Australia and started other British colonies.

▶ Canada, Australia, and New Zealand all made the transition from British colonies to dominions.

MAP SKILL

Canada, New Zealand, and Australia

ARCTIC OCEAN

ASIA

CANADA

NORTH AMERICA

GREAT BRITAIN

EUROPE

ATLANTIC OCEAN

AFRICA

PACIFIC OCEAN

Equator 0°

SOUTH AMERICA

AUSTRALIA

NEW ZEALAND

N

0   1,500   3,000 Miles
0   1,500   3,000 Kilometers

60°

30°N

Equator 0°

30°S

0°

120°E   150°E   180°   150°W   120°W   90°W   60°W   30°W

▶ Between 1867 and 1907, the British colonies of Canada, Australia, and New Zealand became dominions.

MAP SKILL Understand the Equator *Which British dominions lie south of the equator?*

Many of the Aborigines, the original people to inhabit Australia, were pushed off their land by colonists. The lands the Aborigines were forced onto were often harsh and dry. It has been estimated that in the first half-century of colonial rule, the Aboriginal population of Australia dropped by one-half.

By the late 1800s, many Australians believed that their colonies should be united into a single nation. **Sir Edmund Barton** led the efforts to draw up a constitution for Australia. With British approval, Australia became a British dominion in 1901. Barton served as Australia's first prime minister.

New Zealand had originally been settled by Polynesian people called the Maori. British missionaries started to arrive in New Zealand in 1814, soon followed by other British colonists.

The alarmed Maori rebelled but were put down by British colonial forces. In 1840 British naval officer **William Hobson** signed a treaty with Maori chiefs. The treaty made New Zealand a British colony.

▶ **This Australian Aborigine is playing the didgeridoo, a traditional musical instrument of the Aborigines.**

In 1907 New Zealand became another British dominion. The new nation grew prosperous and attracted immigrants. However, strained relations continued between the Europeans and the Maori.

REVIEW Why do you think Canada, Australia, and New Zealand adopted a parliamentary form of government like Great Britain's? **Draw Conclusions**

Summarize the Lesson

1861 Italy became a united nation under King Victor Emmanuel II of Sardinia.

1867 Canada became the first British dominion.

1871 Germany became a united nation and declared itself an empire.

LESSON 3   REVIEW

Check Facts and Main Ideas

1. Sequence On a separate piece of paper, put the events in their correct time order.

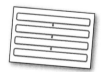

- Australia became a dominion.
- Canada became a dominion.
- Garibaldi freed southern Italy.
- Germany became an empire.
- Greece became independent.

2. How did the example of Greece give hope to nationalistic Germans and Italians?

3. What did the German Empire inherit from the powerful German state of Prussia?

4. How did nationalism lead to the formation of a unified Germany and Italy?

5. Critical Thinking: *Evaluate Information* Do you think that the British dominions were truly independent? Explain your answer.

Link to ⚭ Writing

Write a letter from Giuseppe Mazzini to Camillo di Cavour explaining why a united Italy should be democratic.

503

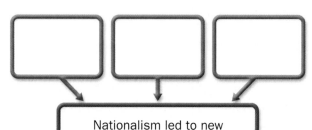

1840   1850

1839
First Opium War began.

1854
Japan opened to trade.

1857 Indian Mutiny

Chapter Summary

Target Skill

Summarize

On a separate piece of paper, break down the summary into three short sentences.

Nationalism led to new nations.

Vocabulary and Terms

Match the correct definition to the words below.

1 treaty port (p. 494)

2 dominion (p. 502)

3 nationalism (p. 487)

4 parliament (p. 502)

5 imperialism (p. 487)

a. an elected legislature

b. to build an empire by controlling or conquering lands

c. a self-governing nation that still has ties with a ruling empire

d. port city where Europeans had special rights

e. a devotion to one's own country

People and Events

Write a sentence explaining why each of the following people or events was important in the age of imperialism, nationalism, and unification. You may use two or more in a single sentence.

1 Otto von Bismarck (p. 500)

2 Indian Mutiny (p. 488)

3 Victoria (p. 488)

4 Camillo di Cavour (p. 501)

5 Opium War (p. 494)

6 Ci Xi (p. 495)

7 William Hobson (p. 503)

8 Berlin Conference (p. 489)

9 Theodore Roosevelt (p. 496)

10 Sir John MacDonald (p. 502)

1860	1870	1880	1890	1890

1861
Italy became a unified nation.

1871 German Empire was created.

1869 Suez Canal opened.

1867 Canada became a dominion.

1885
Congo Free State was set up.

1898 Boxer Rebellion began.

1904
War between Japan and Russia began.

Facts and Main Ideas

1 What did the British call "the jewel in the crown"? Why?

2 Which African countries remained independent after the Berlin Conference?

3 Explain why Great Britain and China fought the first Opium War.

4 **Time Line** How many years separated Italy's unification and the Boxer Rebellion?

5 **Main Idea** Why did the European imperialists want colonies?

6 **Main Idea** According to Giuseppe Mazzini, what defined a nation?

7 **Main Idea** How did Japan avoid becoming a target of Western imperialists?

8 **Critical Thinking: *Detect Bias*** Do you think that King Leopold II shared Cecil Rhodes's opinion that the white race was better than other races? Explain your answer.

Write About History

1 **Write a meeting notice** for an upcoming meeting of the Indian National Congress. Use persuasive writing to encourage fellow Indians to attend.

2 **Write a letter** from Beijing, China, to the United States about your feelings as a foreigner during the Boxer Rebellion.

3 **Write a diplomatic note** to the British Parliament asking that the Maori be given the right to their land in New Zealand.

Apply Skills

Interpret Circle Graphs

Students voted for the world history topics they enjoyed the most so far this school year. They then put the results into a circle graph.

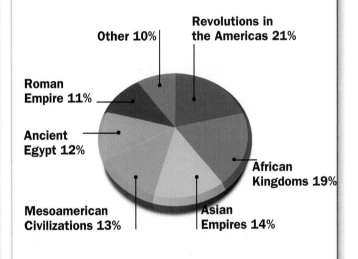

Other 10%

Revolutions in the Americas 21%

Roman Empire 11%

Ancient Egypt 12%

Mesoamerican Civilizations 13%

Asian Empires 14%

African Kingdoms 19%

1 Which topic was the students' favorite?

2 Which three topics took place on the continent of Africa?

3 Which topic was more popular, the Roman Empire or African kingdoms?

Internet Activity

To get help with vocabulary, people, and terms, select dictionary, encyclopedia, or almanac from *Social Studies Library* at **www.sfsocialstudies.com**.

End with a Song

Así es mi tierra

This song was written by Ignacío Fernández Esperón describing the beauty of Mexico. In English the title of this song means, "this is my land." Mexicans sometimes sing this song, which honors an important battle in Mexican history. After reading the translation, do you think that Esperón had a strong sense of nationalism when he wrote these words?

Words and Music by Ignacío Fernandez Esperón

A-sí es mi tie - rra, mo-re - ni - ta y lu - mi - no - sa; A - sí es mi
This is my coun-try, It's a land that's bright with beau-ty; This is my

tie - rra, tie-ne el al - ma he-cha de a - mor. A - sí es mi
coun - try, It's a land that's made to love. This is my

tie - rra, a-bun - da n-te y ge - ne - ro - sa; ¡Ay, tie - rra
coun - try, It has giv-en so much to me; Oh, my dear

2nd time to next stanza

mí - a co-mo es gra - to tu ca - lor!
coun - try, Wel-come are your gifts of love.

This is my land, both sun-bronzed and bright,
This is my land, with a soul made for love.
This is my land, abundant and generous,
Oh, my land, how pleasant is your warmth!
Your dawnings are so full of joy,
And your serenades are well-suited for love.
This is my land, flower of sadness,
Oh, my land, how pleasant is your warmth!

Sus al-bo-ra-das tan lle-ni-tas, de a-le-grí-a. Sus se-re-
When morn-ing light comes, Peo-ple greet the day with glad-ness. In hap-py

na-tas tan pro-pi-ci_as al a-mor. A-sí_es mi
sing-ing we hear mel-o-dies of love. This is my

tie-rra, flor de la me-lan-co-lí-a. ¡Ay, tie-rra
coun-try, Leav-ing fills me with such sad-ness; Oh, my dear

mí-a co-mo_es gra-to tu ca-lor!
coun-try, Wel-come are your gifts of love.

Main Ideas and Vocabulary

TEST PREP

Read the passage below and use it to answer the questions that follow.

During the Renaissance, Europeans developed a renewed interest in classical Greek and Roman culture. This inspired great changes in art, science, thought, and religion. Countries sought more profitable ways to bring goods to Europe. Adventurers explored the Americas, lands previously unknown to Europeans. The quest for wealth and power led Spain and Portugal to conquer the new lands. They mistreated the Native Americans. With Great Britain, they engaged in trading goods for slaves brought from Africa.

In the late 1700s people began to revolt against European rule in parts of the Americas. At about the same time, people in France rose up against their leaders, igniting the French Revolution.

Political revolutions were soon followed by the Industrial Revolution. Technological advances such as the steam engine and machines for producing textiles powered the Industrial Revolution. Economies changed from mostly rural and agricultural to mostly urban and industrial. New economic systems came into being, including capitalism and socialism.

European powers sought to <u>colonize</u> more lands, especially in Africa. But the European desires were the same as with the Americas—gain riches and work to rule and convert the people.

In the 1800s, some conflicts even led to the formation of new unified countries, such as Germany and Italy.

1 According to the passage, how did the industrial revolution affect European economies?
  A They changed from wealthy to poor.
  B They changed from agricultural and urban to industrial and rural.
  C They changed from agricultural and rural to industrial and urban.
  D They changed to colonial.

2 In the passage, the word *colonize* means—
  A take over a territory far from the country that governs it
  B bring Christianity to natives
  C start a revolution
  D begin a war

3 According to the passage, what items contributed to the Industrial Revolution?
  A trade
  B colonization of Africa
  C capitalism
  D steam engine and machines for making textiles

4 What is the main idea of the passage?
  A There have been a variety of changes since the 1700s.
  B Political revolutions produce industrial revolutions.
  C Ancient Greek and Roman culture inspired changes in religion and art.
  D African colonies prospered under European rule.

People and Terms

Write a complete sentence defining each term or explaining the importance of each person listed.

1 encomienda (p. 447)

2 Reign of Terror (p. 468)

3 capitalism (p. 480)

4 Open Door Policy (p. 495)

5 Karl Marx (p. 481)

6 Suez Canal (p. 488)

7 Marie-Olympe de Gouges (p. 471)

8 mercantilism (p. 445)

9 Elizabeth I (p. 442)

10 Armada (p. 442)

Write and Share

Present a Round Table Discussion Choose classmates to represent the points of view of the British government, British traders, and African natives. Form a round table discussion with a host. Write questions to ask the guests appearing on the show. Allow time for the guests to write the answers to the questions before the discussion starts. Invite another class to sit in on your discussion.

Read on Your Own

Look for books like these in the library.

Apply Skills

Create a Political Cartoon Draw a cartoon that shows your point of view about an important event. The cartoon can be about an event at your school, in the news, or in your own life. You can label different parts of your drawing to help people understand its meaning.

UNIT 6 Project

Arts and Letters

Create an infomercial about an important invention.

1 **Form** a group and choose an invention studied in this unit.

2 **Research** the invention. Write about the inventor and tell why he or she made the invention and when it was invented. Describe how the invention has helped people.

3 **Make** a poster or backdrop to advertise your invention.

4 **Present** your infomercial to your class. You may want to dress in the clothing of the time and add sound effects.

Internet Activity

Explore inventions on the Internet. Go to **www.sfsocialstudies.com/activities** and select your grade and unit.

A World in Opposition

*Why was much of the twentieth century
a time of war and change?*

1910

1920

1930

1940

1914–1918
The Great War
(World War I)

1929
Stock Market
Crash

1939–1945
World War II

> *"Never in the field of human conflict has so much been owed by so many to so few."*
>
> —said by Winston Churchill during the Battle of Britain, August 20, 1940

US 310

US 533

This photo of D-Day in 1944 shows all the forces of modern warfare—land, sea, and air—coming together for one big battle.

1950   **1960**   **1970**   **1980**

1945
United Nations
is founded.

Atomic
Age begins.

1950–1953
Korean War

1954–1975
Vietnam War

513

Meet the People

Woodrow Wilson

1856–1924

Birthplace: Staunton, Virginia

Lawyer, university professor, politician

- Governor of New Jersey, 1911–1913
- 28th President of the United States, 1913–1921
- Awarded Nobel Peace Prize in 1920 for helping to set up the League of Nations

Vladimir Lenin

1870–1924

Birthplace: Simbirsk, Russia

Revolutionary, writer

- Founded Russian Communist Party
- Led Bolshevik (Communist) Revolution in Russia, 1917
- Communist leader of Russia, 1917–1924

Winston Churchill

1874–1965

Birthplace: Oxfordshire, England

Politician, writer, artist

- In charge of the British Navy during the Great War (World War I)
- British Prime Minister 1940–1945, 1951–1955
- Led Great Britain to victory in World War II

Joseph Stalin

1879–1953

Birthplace: Gori, Georgia (part of the Russian Empire)

Revolutionary, dictator

- Dictator of Soviet Union, 1929–1953
- Imprisoned and executed millions of Soviet citizens
- Led Soviet Union to victory in World War II

1850	1860	1870	1880	1890	1900	1910	1920

1856 • Woodrow Wilson   1924

1870 • Vladimir Lenin   1924

1874 • Winston Churchill

1879 • Joseph Stalin

1884 • Eleanor Roosevelt

1889 • Adolf Hitler

1893 • Vera Brittain

1893 • Mao Zedong

Eleanor Roosevelt

1884–1962

Birthplace: New York, NY

Activist, writer, humanitarian

- First Lady of United States, 1933–1945
- United States delegate to United Nations, 1945, 1949–1951, 1961
- Helped draft the *United Nations Universal Declaration of Human Rights*, 1948

Adolf Hitler

1889–1945

Birthplace: Braunau, Austria

Dictator

- Dictator of Germany, 1933–1945
- Rearmed Germany in the 1930s and started World War II in 1939
- Killed millions of Jews and others in the Holocaust

Vera Brittain

1893–1970

Birthplace: Newcastle-under-Lyme, England

Writer, activist

- Volunteered as a nurse in the Great War
- Wrote *Testament of Youth* about her experiences in the war
- Supported women's rights, opposed war

Mao Zedong

1893–1976

Birthplace: Shao-shan, Hunan province, China

Soldier, revolutionary, writer

- Led Communist Party during the Long March and afterward
- Established People's Republic of China in 1949 and was its leader until his death
- Started the Cultural Revolution in 1966

1930   1940   1950   1960   1970   1980   1990   2000

1965

1953

1962

1945

1970

1976

515

UNIT 7

A World in Opposition

Cause and Effect

Cause	Effect
Cause A **cause** is why something happens.	**Effect** An **effect** is what happens.

- Sometimes writers use clue words and phrases such as *because*, *so*, *since*, *thus*, and *as a result* to signal cause and effect.

- A cause may have more than one effect. An effect may have more than one cause.

Read the following paragraph. **Cause** and **effect** have been highlighted.

In Chapter 17, you read about expanding empires and imperialism in the late 1800s. Nations wanted land, raw materials, and large numbers of people to buy their products. The effect was that these nations decided that they needed empires. Huge areas of Africa and Asia became colonies of Western countries. As a result, the people of those areas lost their independence.

Imperialism and War

As European countries grew strong and wealthy in the 1800s, they began to look for lands to colonize. This desire to have overseas colonies led to tension among the European powers.

For example, war almost broke out in 1911 over Morocco, a country in North Africa. When Germany tried to seize a port city there, Great Britain and France joined forces to stop it.

Italy and Germany were both new countries that had formed from smaller territories in the 1860s and 1870s. These nations tried to catch up with countries such as Great Britain and France in the race for colonies. Imperialism in Europe was at its height. German leaders believed that they needed a powerful navy to take and keep colonies. They then challenged Great Britain as a naval power. The British ship *Dreadnought,* shown above, was built as a warning to the German Navy.

Russia, France, and Great Britain all wanted land that was controlled by the Ottoman Empire (present-day Turkey). When European imperialism erupted into war in 1914, the Ottoman Empire opposed these countries.

Use the reading strategy of cause and effect to answer these questions.

1 What major cause of tension among European countries does this passage identify?

2 What caused Great Britain to consider Germany a threat to peace?

3 What caused the Ottoman Empire (Turkey) to decide to fight against Russia, France, and Great Britain when war broke out?

CHAPTER 18

The World at War

Lesson 1

1914
Sarajevo
An assassination helps
push nations
into war.

1

Lesson 2

1916
Verdun
War rages in Europe.

2

Lesson 3

1919
Paris
A peace conference
ends the Great War.

3

Why We Remember

Europeans are a variety of peoples living in countries on the same continent. They have their own cultures, languages, and customs. This has led to conflicts and civil wars. However, until 1914, most of these involved only a few countries. Some groups of people felt they were superior to others. Many had strong nationalist feelings about their country. This strained political relations between nations. These tensions eventually led to a world war. The effects of that war would continue to shape world events for the rest of the twentieth century.

1880   1900   1920

1882
Triple Alliance formed.

1907
Triple Entente formed.

1914
Great War begins.

AUSTRIA-HUNGARY
Sarajevo • SERBIA
BOSNIA AND HERZEGOVINA

PREVIEW

Focus on the Main Idea
Competition among nations pushed Europe toward war.

PLACES
Serbia
Bosnia and Herzegovina
Sarajevo

PEOPLE
Wilhelm II
Francis Ferdinand
Nicholas II

VOCABULARY
mobilization
neutral

TERMS
Triple Alliance
Triple Entente

Headed Toward War

You Are There

For weeks you have been looking forward to the national celebration of Queen Victoria's Diamond Jubilee. It's the sixtieth anniversary of her reign in Great Britain. The special day in June 1897 arrives. You and many thousands of others line the streets for this grand parade. Colorfully dressed soldiers from all parts of the British Empire—East Indians, Africans, Australians, New Zealanders, Canadians, and others—march in step. At the high point of the parade, the queen herself passes in a magnificent coach. Everyone smiles and enjoys the celebration. How could anyone guess that war was to come within the next two decades?

▶ Queen Victoria's Jubilees were often commemorated on stamps, plates, and mugs.

Cause and Effect As you read, look for causes of tension among European nations and its effect on Europe and the world.

520

Competition Among Nations

Queen Victoria's Diamond Jubilee was, in part, a celebration of the size and strength of Great Britain's empire. In Chapter 17, you read that nationalism and imperialism became strong forces in Europe in the late 1800s. They caused intense competition among the nations of Europe and produced dangerous disagreements.

A group of European nations challenged each other in a number of ways. These nations competed for colonies that were rich in natural resources. They used these resources to expand their growing industries. They tried to build up bigger navies and armies than their neighbors. In the early 1900s, the European Powers included Great Britain, France, Germany, Austria-Hungary, and Russia. Some thought that Italy belonged to this group too. As these nations competed, serious trouble developed.

France and Germany had problems left over from a war they fought in 1870–1871. After the war, Germany had taken over two French provinces. France wanted them back.

Since the early 1800s, the British Navy had ruled the seas. But by the 1890s, Germany's ruler, **Wilhelm II,** insisted on building a big, modern navy to compete with Great Britain. This caused tensions between Great Britain and Germany.

▶ **The British *Dreadnought* was completed in 1905.**

▶ **Kaiser Wilhelm II of Germany**

Austria-Hungary contained many different ethnic groups, such as Poles, Czechs, and Slovaks. These ethnic groups wanted to have countries of their own. Their nationalism made the rulers of Austria-Hungary afraid. In 1908 Austria-Hungary claimed two provinces in **Serbia,** its neighbor to the south: **Bosnia** (BAHZ nee uh) and **Herzegovina** (hairt suh goh VEE nuh). This made the Serbians angry and caused friction between the two countries.

By the early 1900s, imperialism was causing tension among the Great Powers. Europeans wanted more resources and felt they had a right to take over lands in Africa, Asia, and other places. However, little land was left to colonize. Nations scrambled for what was left. In 1911 Great Britain and France almost went to war with Germany over a port in Morocco. Europe was near a boiling point.

REVIEW What was the cause of friction between Great Britain and Germany?
↻ **Cause and Effect**

521

Alliances Lead to War

In the years leading up to what became known as the Great War, the European Powers joined together in two opposing alliances. The countries agreed to protect each other in case of attack.

In 1882 Germany, Austria-Hungary, and Italy formed an alliance known as the **Triple Alliance.** Ties between Germany and Austria-Hungary were especially strong. The ruling class of Austria spoke German, and the two countries shared a long border.

In 1907, Russia, France, and Great Britain formed the **Triple Entente** (ahn TAHNT). In French, *entente* means "understanding." Each country understood that an attack on one meant an attack on all. On the map below, identify the countries in both alliances.

Though alliances made countries feel safe, they actually helped push Europe toward war. Countries promised to help their allies if trouble arose. Many began to mobilize for war.

Mobilization is the preparations nations make before sending their armies into battle. These preparations include getting troops, supplies, and weapons ready. Once mobilization started, it was almost impossible to stop it.

In the summer of 1914, members of the Triple Alliance and the Triple Entente became locked in a quarrel that soon led to an all-out war. On June 28, 1914, Archduke **Francis Ferdinand** of Austria-Hungary, next in line for his nation's throne, was assassinated in **Sarajevo** (sair uh YAY voh), the capital of Bosnia. Because a Serbian nationalist was responsible for the crime, the leaders of Austria-Hungary wanted to punish Serbia. Czar (zar) **Nicholas II,** the ruler of Russia, believed that his country should protect Serbia. Many people in Serbia and Russia belonged to the same religion: Orthodox Christianity. Nicholas II responded to Austria-Hungary's threats by mobilizing his army.

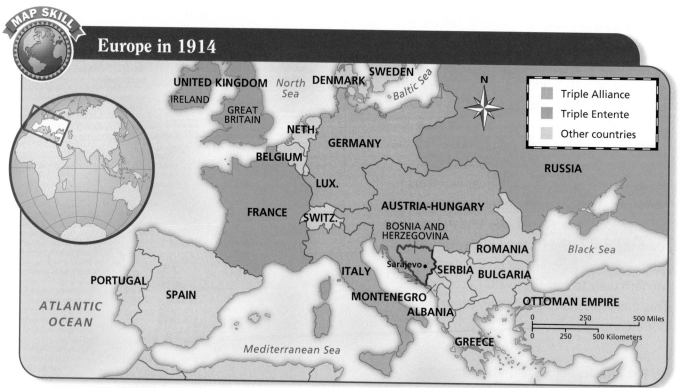

MAP SKILL

Europe in 1914

UNITED KINGDOM
IRELAND
North Sea
GREAT BRITAIN
DENMARK
SWEDEN
Baltic Sea
N
NETH.
GERMANY
BELGIUM
LUX.
FRANCE
SWITZ.
AUSTRIA-HUNGARY
BOSNIA AND HERZEGOVINA
RUSSIA
PORTUGAL
SPAIN
ITALY
Sarajevo •
SERBIA
BULGARIA
ROMANIA
Black Sea
MONTENEGRO
ALBANIA
OTTOMAN EMPIRE
GREECE
Mediterranean Sea
ATLANTIC OCEAN

Triple Alliance
Triple Entente
Other countries

0   250   500 Miles
0   250   500 Kilometers

▶ In 1914 Europe was divided into two main alliances. Notice that the Triple Entente surrounded the Triple Alliance.

MAP SKILL Use a Historical Map *What countries belonged to the Triple Alliance? What countries belonged to the Triple Entente?*

These events started a chain reaction that was soon felt throughout Europe. Germany declared war on Russia and Russia's ally, France. Then Germany invaded Belgium, Great Britain's ally and a neutral country, or one that does not take sides. Because Great Britain had a defensive treaty with Belgium, it declared war on Germany.

In August 1914, on the eve of the Great War, British foreign secretary Sir Edward Grey said,

> *"The lamps are going out all over Europe; we shall not see them lit again in our lifetime."*

The Great War—a war that affected many nations and peoples—had begun.

REVIEW What caused Great Britain to declare war on Germany in 1914? ↺ **Cause and Effect**

▶ **This photo of Archduke Francis Ferdinand and his wife, Sophie, was taken just minutes before their death.**

Summarize the Lesson

— **1882** Germany, Austria-Hungary, and Italy formed the Triple Alliance.

— **1907** Great Britain, France, and Russia formed the Triple Entente.

└ **1914** Archduke Francis Ferdinand was assassinated, triggering the Great War in Europe.

LESSON 1   REVIEW

Check Facts and Main Ideas

1. ↺ **Cause and Effect** On a separate piece of paper, fill in the chart below by listing one cause or effect.

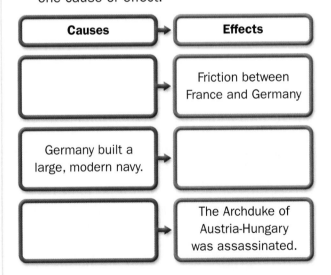

Causes	→	Effects
	→	Friction between France and Germany
Germany built a large, modern navy.	→	
	→	The Archduke of Austria-Hungary was assassinated.

2. What strong forces caused friction between the countries of Europe in the years leading up to 1914?

3. What was a cause of friction between France and Germany?

4. How did imperialism increase competition among nations in Europe?

5. **Critical Thinking:** *Make Inferences* Suppose the nations of Europe had not formed alliances in the years before 1914. Do you think a world war would have broken out? Explain.

Link to ⟡⟡ **Reading**

Make Connections Czar Nicholas II was the last ruler of the old Russian Empire. *Czar* means *caesar.* Go back and read through your textbook. Where have you seen the word "caesar" before? What does this tell us about past civilizations?

Chart and Graph Skills

Compare Parallel Time Lines

What? A time line is a type of chart that allows you to show events in a period of time. Events are shown in the order in which they occurred.

Parallel describes lines that are the same distance apart at every point. You can compare parallel time lines to show interesting time relationships. Look at the following parallel time lines. The first time line shows important events in the Great War. The second shows events that Adele, a student in Milwaukee, Wisconsin, recorded in her diary during the war years.

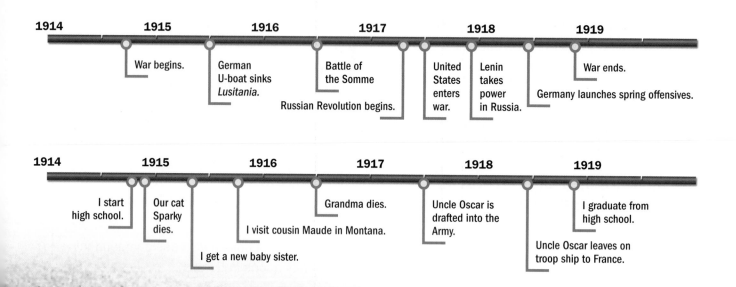

| 1914 | 1915 | 1916 | 1917 | 1918 | 1919 |

War begins.

German U-boat sinks *Lusitania*.

Battle of the Somme

Russian Revolution begins.

United States enters war.

Lenin takes power in Russia.

War ends.

Germany launches spring offensives.

| 1914 | 1915 | 1916 | 1917 | 1918 | 1919 |

I start high school.

Our cat Sparky dies.

I get a new baby sister.

I visit cousin Maude in Montana.

Grandma dies.

Uncle Oscar is drafted into the Army.

Uncle Oscar leaves on troop ship to France.

I graduate from high school.

524

Why? Parallel time lines help you compare events in different places or compare public events with personal events. In fact, as long as the time periods covered are the same, you can compare events from almost any place.

How? The parallel time lines on the previous page help you compare the public events of the Great War with the personal events in Adele's life.

One thing to be careful about when using a time line is reading dates correctly. Each blue tick mark on the time line stands for the beginning of a year (January 1). Everything to the *right*—until the next date's blue mark—is for that year. Look at the time line for Adele's diary. Find the *1915* label and blue mark. You can see on the time line that Adele's cat Sparky died toward the end of 1914. Adele's new baby sister was born sometime in early 1915.

Now look at the year 1914 on both time lines. You can see that the Great War began in Europe that year. During that same year, Adele started high school.

Think and Apply

1 What events happened in 1916? Which event do you think was most important to Adele? Why?

2 Which events in 1917 probably brought the war home to Adele?

3 Uncle Oscar fought for less than a year in the Great War. How do the parallel time lines give you this information?

1915

1920

1915
Italy joins
the Allies.

1916
Battles of
Verdun and
the Somme

1917
Russian
Revolution

1918
The Great War ends.

The Great War

May 15, 1915
a battlefield in France

Dear Anne,

I surely miss being home with you, Mother, and Father in Great Britain. You can't imagine what it's like to live in a trench. It's really just a deep ditch. Dirt and mud are all around—not to mention mice, rats, and bugs! But worst of all is the sound of German shells screaming overhead day and night. It's usually safe down here, six or eight feet below the ground. But many times we have to climb out of the trench and march into enemy lines. It's scary, but I know that fighting in this war is my duty to our country.

Your loving brother,

Ralph

▶ **A British soldier eats his dinner in a trench during the Great War.**

 Cause and Effect As you read, think about the effects of some of the most important battles of the Great War.

The War Begins

At the beginning of the war in August 1914, Germany had a plan to defeat France in six weeks. It sent an army through Belgium and into France. This army was supposed to encircle Paris, the French capital, and then attack the British and French armies.

The generals soon discovered that planning a war on maps is not the same as soldiers trudging through enemy territory. As one British soldier wrote home:

"People out here seem to think that the war is going to be quite short, why, I don't know; personally I see nothing to prevent it [from] going on forever."

In fact, the war continued for four long years. The German army came to a standstill opposite the French and British armies in France. This front, or line of battle, became known as the Western Front. Though huge battles raged, the armies hardly moved at all.

Meanwhile, Russia tried to push into Germany from the east. Russia also was fighting against Austria-Hungary, Germany's ally. The line of battle between Russia and Austria-Hungary became known as the Eastern Front. In August 1914, Germany won a great victory over Russia on Germany's eastern edge.

In November 1914 the Ottoman Empire entered the war on the side of Germany and Austria-Hungary. In 1915 Italy joined on the side of Great Britain, France, and Russia. The old Triple Entente, which you read about in Lesson 1, added Italy and became known as the Allied Powers. The old Triple Alliance—Germany and Austria-Hungary but minus Italy—was now known as the Central Powers. The Ottoman Empire and the border between Italy and Austria-Hungary soon became the sites of many battles.

REVIEW By 1915, what were the two main fronts in the Great War? **Summarize**

▶ Many soldiers, such as these British soldiers, were forced to live in protective trenches during the Great War.

The Granger Collection

527

A New Kind of War

The Great War proved deadlier than any earlier war. Thousands of soldiers were killed daily in battle. One reason for these terrible **casualties,** or wounded and killed soldiers, was a group of deadly new weapons.

For the first time, the machine gun was widely used in a major war. It allowed soldiers to shoot many times without reloading.

Still another new weapon was the tank, an armored vehicle mounted with guns. Tanks moved on tracks instead of wheels. This helped them to roll over land that soldiers could not travel easily on by foot.

One of the most horrifying new weapons was poison gas, which injured or killed many soldiers. Soldiers started wearing gas masks so that they would not breathe the deadly poison gas.

The Great War was the first war in which airplanes were used. In airplanes army pilots could see what was going on in enemy territory.

They could also drop bombs and fire guns from the airplanes.

Another reason for the war's high number of casualties was trench warfare. In **trench warfare,** armies dug deep trenches, or ditches, to shelter their troops. They strung barbed wire in front of the trenches to keep out the enemy.

When attacking, soldiers had to crawl out of the trench and move toward enemy soliders, who were waiting in their own trenches. Machine-gun fire sprayed the advancing troops. Shells from the enemy's big guns exploded all around them. The strip of land between the trenches of opposing armies became known as "No-Man's Land" for a good reason. It was no place for anybody!

One British soldier described watching fellow soldiers leading the way into battle:

> *"We were able to see our comrades [friends] move forward in an attempt to cross No-Man's Land, only to be mown down like meadow grass. I felt sick at the sight . . . and remember weeping."*

▶ **This gas mask was used during the Great War.**

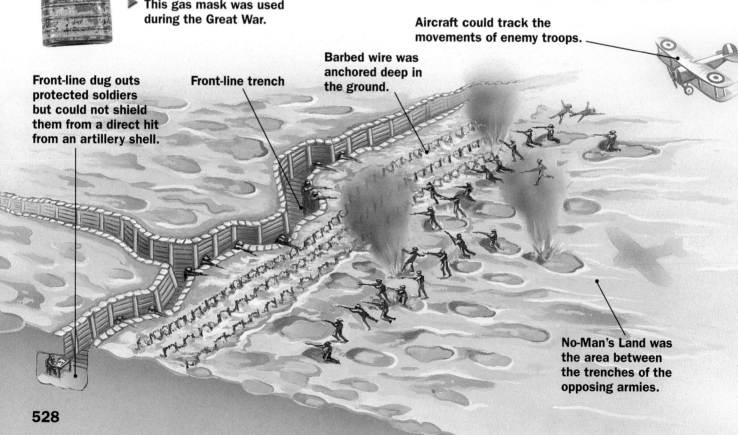

Aircraft could track the movements of enemy troops.

Barbed wire was anchored deep in the ground.

Front-line dug outs protected soldiers but could not shield them from a direct hit from an artillery shell.

Front-line trench

No-Man's Land was the area between the trenches of the opposing armies.

The Battles of Verdun and the Somme

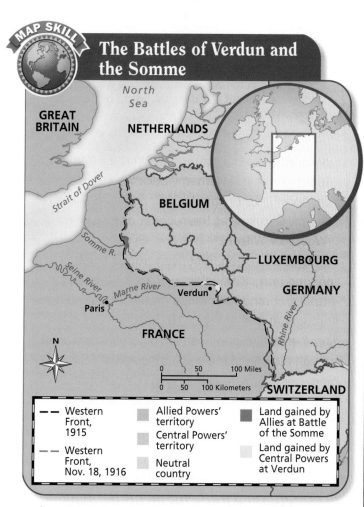

Map key:
- – – Western Front, 1915
- – – Western Front, Nov. 18, 1916
- ▪ Allied Powers' territory
- ▪ Central Powers' territory
- ▪ Neutral country
- ▪ Land gained by Allies at Battle of the Somme
- ▪ Land gained by Central Powers at Verdun

▶ **Neither side was able to make much progress at the Battles of Verdun and the Somme.**

MAP SKILL Use a Map Key *How did the Western Front change from 1915 to November 1916?*

Some of the war's fiercest battles were fought in these terrible conditions on the Western Front. Two of the worst took place in 1916. One was at **Verdun** (vair DUHN) in eastern France, and the other was at the **Somme** (SUHM) River.

Germany launched an attack on Verdun in February 1916. The French fought back, and the battle went on for the rest of the year. In the end, there were more than 500,000 French and German casualties. However, for all those months of death and suffering, Germany gained very little.

Meanwhile, the British Army led a powerful attack on the Germans at the Somme River. On July 1, 1916, the Allies stormed the German trenches. More British soldiers were killed that one day than on any other day in British history—

▶ **British nurses help a wounded soldier onto a stretcher.**

20,000. It was also the bloodiest day of the Great War. When the battle finally ended, the Allies had gained very little.

REVIEW Name at least one cause of the high number of casualties in the Great War. ⟳ Cause and Effect

Women's War Work

Although the soldiers fighting in the war were all men, women served in military roles too. Some 57,000 served in the British Women's Auxiliary Army Corps.

British women performed supportive tasks, including teaching soldiers how to use gas masks, driving ambulances, working in factories, and growing crops to feed everyone. Women also served as nurses. Sometimes this brought them close to the front lines. Like the men, these women often put their own lives in danger.

Germany had a special women's service in major cities. These women sewed uniforms for soldiers and sheets for hospital beds. German women also cooked and performed nursing duties.

REVIEW Name three of the tasks performed by British women during the Great War. **Main Idea and Details**

America Enters

When war broke out in 1914, the United States adopted a policy of neutrality. Many people did not want to get involved in the war. Some were even against sending food and supplies to help Great Britain. If the United States was going to enter the war, there needed to be a good reason for it.

Germany's leaders decided to take a big gamble. They would try to drive Great Britain out of the war by destroying British shipping. The British depended on trade for food and supplies. The Germans gambled that the British could be forced into defeat if German submarines sank their ships, cutting off Great Britain's food supply.

Germany's submarines were powerful weapons. But in the end, they brought a dangerous new enemy into the war on the side of the Allies—the United States.

In May 1915 a German submarine sank the *Lusitania*, a British ship. The *Lusitania* was carrying passengers, supplies, and probably weapons from the United States to Great Britain. Nearly 1,200 people died, including 128 Americans. The sinking of the *Lusitania* and several American commercial, or trade, ships by Germany pushed U.S. public opinion toward war.

In early 1917 many Americans also wanted to join the war after the British found a secret German telegram to the government of Mexico. In it Germany promised that it would restore to Mexico land that the United States had taken from it in 1846, if Mexico joined the war on the side of the Central Powers. When Great Britain

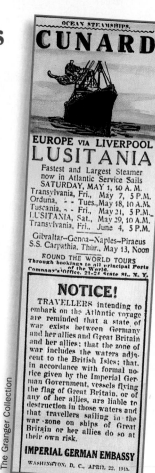

The Granger Collection

▶ **This advertisement from the *New York Herald* announces the sailing of the *Lusitania*. The "notice" in the advertisement is a warning to travelers about the dangers posed by German submarines.**

showed this telegram to the United States, feelings against Germany became stronger. On April 6, 1917, the U.S. Congress declared war on Germany at the request of President Woodrow Wilson.

As 1918 began, American troops began pouring into battlefields in France. German attacks crushed the Allies on the Western Front throughout the spring of 1918. However, by summer, two million fresh American soldiers were turning the tide of the war for the Allies. Still, many soldiers were being killed or wounded. Fanny Louise Cunningham, an American nurse on the Western Front, wrote:

> *"It broke your heart to see these fine young men carried off on stretchers with missing limbs, blinded, burned with gas and, in some cases shell-shocked. Many were only boys."*

By the fall of 1918, the Central Powers were exhausted. They gave up, one by one. First the Ottoman Empire surrendered, then Austria-Hungary. Germany held on until early November. Germany agreed to an **armistice,** or cease-fire, on November 11, 1918. After four long years, the fighting was finally over.

REVIEW What caused the United States to enter the war? What was the effect of this entry?
↻ **Cause and Effect**

The Russian Revolution

By 1917 people everywhere had grown tired of the war. In no other country were feelings running as strongly against the war as in Russia.

On the Eastern Front, the Russian Army had suffered terrible casualties, just as the French and British had on the Western Front. However, conditions in Russia were much worse. The Russian economy had collapsed. Military supplies were low. Food and fuel were limited.

The **Russian Revolution** broke out in March 1917. People demanded relief from their suffering. Russian soldiers joined the protesters. Russia's ruler, Czar Nicholas II, was forced to give up his throne. Russia's new rulers kept Russia in the war, but conditions did not improve. Russia was in a state of chaos, or disorder.

The Bolsheviks (BOHL shuh viks), or communists, led by **Vladimir Lenin** (LEH nuhn), promised peace, bread, and land to all Russians. They followed a form of socialism called **communism,** an economic and social system in which all resources are owned by a government led by a dictator. Aided by workers' and soldiers' councils called **Soviets,** the communists took over the government on November 7, 1917.

The Germans forced Russia to sign a treaty, giving up much land in the west. Lenin got peace,

▶ **Soldiers celebrate the Bolshevik Revolution.**

but at a high price.

Meanwhile, a bloody civil war broke out between the communists and the non-communists in Russia. The United States, Great Britain, Japan, and other nations sent troops and supplies to help the non-communists. The civil war in Russia raged on until 1920, when the communists triumphed. In 1922 Russia's communist leaders formed the **Soviet Union.**

REVIEW In Russia's civil war, which side had greater support among other nations? Explain your answer. **Draw Conclusions**

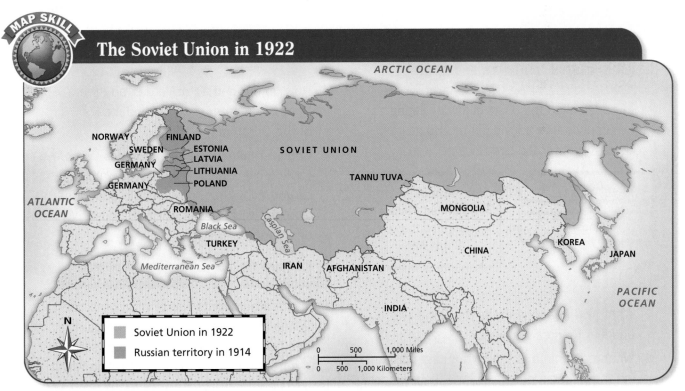

MAP SKILL

The Soviet Union in 1922

ARCTIC OCEAN

NORWAY
FINLAND
SWEDEN
ESTONIA
GERMANY
LATVIA
LITHUANIA
GERMANY
POLAND
SOVIET UNION
TANNU TUVA

ATLANTIC OCEAN

ROMANIA
MONGOLIA
Black Sea
Caspian Sea
TURKEY
CHINA
KOREA
Mediterranean Sea
JAPAN
IRAN
AFGHANISTAN
PACIFIC OCEAN
INDIA

N

Soviet Union in 1922
Russian territory in 1914

0   500   1,000 Miles
0   500   1,000 Kilometers

▶ **The borders of the Soviet Union were different from those of Russia.**

MAP SKILL Measure Distance *What was the distance between the eastern and western edges of the Soviet Union in 1922?*

Another Victory

The end of the Great War was a cause for celebration for the victorious nations. Soldiers went back to their families. Most women went back to taking care of their husbands and children. Returning soldiers wanted their jobs back from women who had filled in during the war.

However, between 1917 and 1920, women did gain an important victory of their own—the right to vote in national elections. After years of struggle by women, the Soviet Union, Canada, Germany, Great Britain, the United States, and others granted women the right to vote.

REVIEW How did women's lives change after the end of the Great War? **Main Idea and Details**

▶ **Members of the Women's Royal Air Force celebrate the armistice signing in 1918.**

Summarize the Lesson

- **1916** The Battle of Verdun and the Battle of the Somme raged on the Western Front.
- **1917** Lenin and the communists came to power in the Russian Revolution.
- **1918** The fighting ended when Germany signed an armistice on November 11.

Hulton-Deutsch Collection/Corbis

LESSON 2   REVIEW

Check Facts and Main Ideas

1. ↻ **Cause and Effect** On a separate piece of paper, fill in the chart below by listing two causes that convinced the United States to enter the Great War.

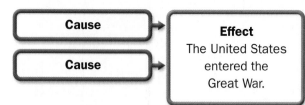

Cause	→	Effect
Cause	→	The United States entered the Great War.

2. What new weapons made the Great War deadlier than earlier wars?

3. What did Lenin and the communists promise the Russian people to gain their support in the Russian Revolution?

4. How do the battles of Verdun and the Somme summarize the experience of the Great War?

5. **Critical Thinking: *Make Inferences*** Given the terrible casualties in the Great War battles, do you think that some people questioned whether winning was worth the cost? Why or why not?

Link to ⬩⬥⬩ Science

Study Weather Fronts The term *front* is used for a line that separates enemy armies. It comes from meteorology, or weather science. Find a front on a weather map. Explain why it is like a front in war.

532

Vera Brittain

1893–1970

As a young girl growing up in Great Britain, Vera Brittain knew she wanted to be a writer. By the time she was 11, she had written and illustrated five "novels." Brittain loved to learn. She was determined to go to college, although it was uncommon for young women to attend college in the early 1900s. In 1914 she won a scholarship to a women's college at Oxford University in England. She started classes a few weeks after the Great War began. In 1915 Brittain left college to serve as a volunteer nurse in the war.

As a nurse, Brittain faced difficult experiences. She cared for wounded soldiers in freezing cold weather and poorly supplied field hospitals. Both her brother and one of her friends were killed in the war. The Great War turned Vera Brittain into a lifelong pacifist, or someone who opposes war. She once said:

> *"I hold war to be a crime against humanity, whoever fights it and against whomever it is fought."*

After the war, she graduated from Oxford and began a career as a writer. Brittain hoped to use "the power of ideas to change the shape of the world and even help to eliminate its evils." Brittain wrote more than 25 books and many essays. A number of her writings speak out against war. She also spent much of her time promoting rights and freedoms for women. Her best-known book is her autobiography, *Testament of Youth* (1933), which describes the horrors of war. The book quickly became a best seller.

BIOFACT

Brittain's Testament of Youth *was made into a movie in 1979.*

Learn from Biographies

Do you think Brittain's attitude toward war was different before the war? Explain your answer.

For more information, go online to *Meet the People* at **www.sfsocialstudies.com**.

1918

1919

1918
Germany signs armistice, ending the Great War.

1918
President Woodrow Wilson arrives in France.

1919
The Allies and Germany sign the Treaty of Versailles.

•Paris
FRANCE

After the War

PREVIEW

Focus on the Main Idea
The Allies tried to make a peace treaty that would solve all of Europe's problems.

PLACES
Paris
Rhineland

PEOPLE
Georges Clemenceau

VOCABULARY
holocaust
reparations
inflation

TERMS
Fourteen Points
Treaty of Versailles
League of Nations

You Are There Your teacher calls your attention to current events, though it's hard for you to concentrate. Spring has come to your hometown. Soon, school will be out.

The delegates at the Paris peace conference are trying to make a fair peace after the Great War, which just ended last fall. A newspaper article says that President Wilson has become an important leader at the peace conference. People in Europe seem to look up to Wilson as an example of democratic leadership.

As an American, you feel proud . . . but you wonder if someday you'll be helping in the war effort, like your older brother and sister have just done.

▶ **This painting by Sir William Orpen shows the delegates signing the peace treaty to end the Great War.**

Art Archive/Imperial War Museum/Art Archive

Cause and Effect As you read, take note of the changes the Great War caused in the map of Europe and in people's lives.

Results of the War

The Great War caused more suffering than any previous war in history. No one knows exactly how many people died. Government statistics indicate that more than eight million soldiers were killed. This number is about the same as the population of a large city. Millions of civilians, or non-soldiers, died too.

During the war, Ottoman officials forced Armenians, a minority group, from their homes. This terrible event became known as the Armenian Holocaust. Though no one knew it at the time, this holocaust, or mass killing, would be only the first of several in the twentieth century.

The Great War caused great property destruction as well. Areas near the Western Front, in France and Belgium, were especially hard-hit. People were homeless, and businesses were destroyed. Nations had run up huge debts to fight

▶ Between one-half million and one million Armenians were killed in the Armenian Holocaust in 1915–1916. These children are boarding a train to an orphanage.

the war. It has been estimated that the war cost more than $300 billion.

The Great War changed the map of Europe. Compare the two maps below. Empires disappeared, including the German Empire ruled by Kaiser Wilhelm II, the Russian Empire ruled by Czar Nicholas II, the Ottoman Empire, and the Empire of Austria-Hungary.

REVIEW Give three details to support the main idea that the Great War changed conditions in Europe. **Main Idea and Details**

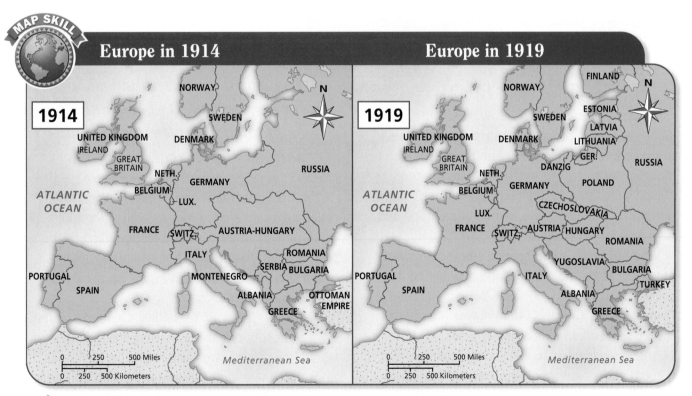

MAP SKILL

Europe in 1914

1914

NORWAY
SWEDEN
UNITED KINGDOM
IRELAND
DENMARK
GREAT BRITAIN
NETH.
BELGIUM
GERMANY
RUSSIA
ATLANTIC OCEAN
LUX.
FRANCE
SWITZ.
AUSTRIA-HUNGARY
ITALY
ROMANIA
SERBIA
BULGARIA
PORTUGAL
MONTENEGRO
SPAIN
ALBANIA
OTTOMAN EMPIRE
GREECE
Mediterranean Sea

0   250   500 Miles
0   250   500 Kilometers

Europe in 1919

1919

FINLAND
NORWAY
ESTONIA
SWEDEN
LATVIA
UNITED KINGDOM
IRELAND
DENMARK
LITHUANIA
GREAT BRITAIN
GER.
NETH.
DANZIG
RUSSIA
GERMANY
POLAND
ATLANTIC OCEAN
BELGIUM
LUX.
CZECHOSLOVAKIA
FRANCE
SWITZ.
AUSTRIA
HUNGARY
ROMANIA
YUGOSLAVIA
PORTUGAL
ITALY
BULGARIA
SPAIN
TURKEY
ALBANIA
GREECE
Mediterranean Sea

0   250   500 Miles
0   250   500 Kilometers

▶ The map of Europe changed significantly at the end of the Great War.

MAP SKILL Observe Change Through Maps *From which three old countries did the new nation of Poland receive land?*

FACT FILE

Casualties and Debt of the Great War

Country	Total Mobilized Forces	Wounded	Total Casualties	Cost in Dollars (rounded)
Russia (Soviet Union)	12,000,000	4,950,000	9,150,000	$22.3 billion
British Empire	8,904,467	2,090,212	3,190,235	$39.1 billion
France	8,410,000	4,266,000	6,160,800	$24.3 billion
Italy	5,615,000	947,000	2,197,000	$12.4 billion
United States	4,355,000	204,002	323,018	$22.6 billion
Japan	800,000	907	1,210	$40 million
Serbia	707,343	133,148	331,106	$400 million
Germany	11,000,000	4,216,058	7,142,558	$37.8 billion
Austria-Hungary	7,800,000	3,620,000	7,020,000	$20.6 billion
Ottoman Empire	2,850,000	400,000	975,000	$1.4 billion

▶ Red Cross workers, pictured here, cared for the wounded on both sides during the Great War.

Making Peace

On December 13, 1918, U.S. President Woodrow Wilson arrived in France. He came early to prepare for the peace conference that was to meet in Paris in January 1919. Many felt that Wilson's blueprint for peace, the Fourteen Points, would bring about a more democratic Europe and help prevent future wars.

When the peace conference opened, the leaders of Great Britain, France, and Italy joined the United States. From the start, Wilson and the French leader, Georges Clemenceau (KLEHM uhn soh), disagreed on almost every point. Clemenceau wanted to weaken Germany so that it could never again threaten France. This point of view collided with Wilson's ideas for a fair peace and cooperation between nations.

Earlier, President Wilson had said:

"The world must be made safe for democracy. Its peace must be planted upon the tested foundations of political liberty."

The final document, the Treaty of Versailles (vair SIGH), was a compromise containing ideas of both the French leader and Wilson. Wilson's fourteenth point, to create a "general association of nations" to help prevent future wars, became the League of Nations.

Under the Treaty of Versailles, Germany would have to accept blame for starting the war. It would have to remove forts and other defenses from the Rhineland, its western region bordering France. Finally, Germany would have to pay huge reparations, or payment for war losses, to the Allies.

▶ (seated left to right) Vittorio Orlando (Italy), David Lloyd George (Great Britain), Georges Clemenceau (France), and Woodrow Wilson (United States) at the peace conference in Paris

By 1927 the German economy had recovered slightly. However, the German people never forgot their suffering.

REVIEW What was the cause of Germany's inflation in the early 1920s? **Cause and Effect**

On June 28, 1919, the Allies signed the Treaty of Versailles with Germany. Germany's war-torn economy could not stand up to the strain of huge reparation payments. By the early 1920s, Germany was experiencing skyrocketing inflation, or the rapid increase in prices. Money became almost worthless. People had to bring along piles of it just to buy groceries. They also burned money because it was cheaper than buying coal to burn for heat.

Summarize the Lesson

- **December 1918** President Wilson arrived in France with ideas for establishing a fair peace.
- **January 1919** The peace conference began in Paris.
- **June 1919** Germany and the Allies signed the Treaty of Versailles.

LESSON 3   REVIEW

Check Facts and Main Ideas

1. **Cause and Effect** On a separate piece of paper, fill in the chart below by listing two effects in the blank boxes.

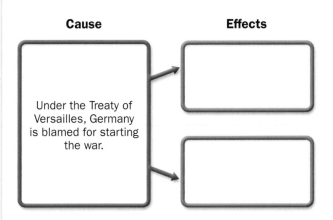

Cause | Effects

Under the Treaty of Versailles, Germany is blamed for starting the war.

2. What part of Europe was most affected by boundary changes after the Great War?

3. In what ways did the Treaty of Versailles punish Germany?

4. What was the major stumbling block in establishing the kind of fair and just peace that President Wilson wanted?

5. **Critical Thinking:** *Solve Complex Problems* What impact did paying reparations to the Allies have on Germany's economy?

Link to ⎯ **Reading**

Interpret a Poem Flanders is located in Belgium. Canadian John M. McCrae wrote "In Flanders Fields." The poem's first two lines read:
In Flanders fields the poppies blow
Between the crosses, row on row.
What tells you that this poem deals with the high number of casualties in the Great War?

537

1880   1890

1882
Triple Alliance
formed.

Chapter Summary

 Cause and Effect

On a separate piece of paper, fill in the chart by listing two causes and their effects of the Great War.

Causes	→	Effects

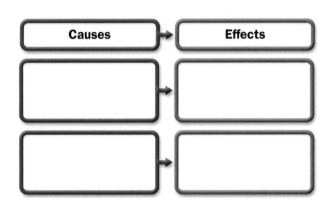

Vocabulary

Match each word with the correct definition or description.

1 neutral (p. 523)

2 mobilization (p. 522)

3 armistice (p. 530)

4 holocaust (p. 535)

5 reparations (p. 536)

6 inflation (p. 537)

7 casualties (p. 528)

a. cease-fire

b. mass killing

c. preparations for war

d. sums of money paid for war losses

e. not taking sides

f. wounded and killed soldiers

g. rapid increase in prices

People and Terms

Write a sentence explaining why each of the following people or terms was important in the events of the Great War. You may use two or more in a single sentence.

1 Wilhelm II (p. 521)

2 Francis Ferdinand (p. 522)

3 Triple Alliance (p. 522)

4 Central Powers (p. 527)

5 Woodrow Wilson (p. 530)

6 Vladimir Lenin (p. 531)

7 Allied Powers (p. 527)

8 Vera Brittain (p. 533)

9 Fourteen Points (p. 536)

10 League of Nations (p. 536)

1900	1910	1920

1897
The Diamond
Jubilee of
Queen Victoria

1907
Triple Entente formed.

1914 Great War began.

1918 Great War ended.

1917
Russian Revolution

1919 Treaty of Versailles

Facts and Main Ideas

1 How did alliances help start the Great War?

2 What type of warfare became common in battles during the Great War? Describe.

3 How were Woodrow Wilson's goals for peace different from those of the other Allied leaders?

4 **Time Line** About how many years after the start of the Great War did the Russian Revolution occur?

5 **Main Idea** How did some European nations challenge each other in the years before the Great War?

6 **Main Idea** Why did the United States enter the war in 1917?

7 **Main Idea** What did Allied leaders hope to do when they wrote the Treaty of Versailles?

8 **Critical Thinking:** *Recognize Point of View* From what you have read, do you think that Germany and Great Britain wanted to go to war? Explain.

Apply Skills

Compare Parallel Time Lines

Study the parallel time lines. Then answer the questions.

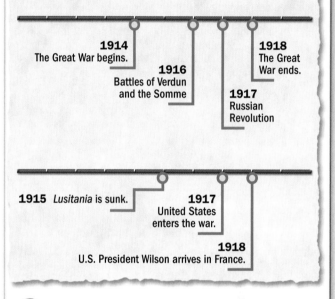

1914
The Great War begins.

1916
Battles of Verdun and the Somme

1918
The Great War ends.

1917
Russian Revolution

1915 *Lusitania* is sunk.

1917
United States enters the war.

1918
U.S. President Wilson arrives in France.

1 What was happening in Russia when the United States entered the war?

2 Was the Battle of Verdun before or after the sinking of the Lusitania?

3 How many years passed between the beginning of the Great War and the beginning of the U.S. involvement in the war?

Write About History

1 **Write a want ad** looking for someone to serve as note-taker at the meetings of the Paris peace conference.

2 **Write a letter** to a soldier fighting on the Western Front.

3 **Write a short poem** to honor soldiers who fought bravely in the Great War.

Internet Activity

To get help with vocabulary, people, and terms, select dictionary, encyclopedia, or almanac from *Social Studies Library* at **www.sfsocialstudies.com**.

539

CHAPTER 19

From Peace to War

Lesson 1

**The 1930s
Germany**
The stage is set for
another world war.

1

Lesson 2

**1939–1945
London**
World War II rages.

2

Lesson 3

**1945
New York City**
The world makes a
new beginning.

3

Why We Remember

Today many people of the world either enjoy or desire the benefits of freedom. However, in the 1920s and 1930s, many countries made the decision to abandon democracy. Hard times from economic depression convinced many people that a strong ruler—a dictator—was needed. Adolf Hitler, Benito Mussolini, Joseph Stalin, and military dictators in Japan rose to power. Their plans for national glory brought on the most destructive war the world has ever seen: World War II. Millions fought and died. We are all the children of their sacrifice.

1920   1930   1940

1922
Fascists take
control of Italy.

1929
Stock market crash/Great
Depression begins.

1933
Hitler becomes
dictator of Germany.

1931
Japan takes Manchuria.

PREVIEW

Focus on the Main Idea
Hard times set the stage for
another world war.

PLACES
Germany
Japan
China
Soviet Union

PEOPLE
Benito Mussolini
Adolf Hitler
Neville Chamberlain
Hirohito
Joseph Stalin

VOCABULARY
depression
fascism
Nazis
propaganda
aggression
annex
appeasement
collective

TERMS
Five-Year Plan

EVENTS
Great Depression
Spanish Civil War

Good to Bad Times

 On your walk home from school, you think about how nice it is that the war is over. The weekend is finally here. Father is taking you and your sister to a baseball game. You've never seen Babe Ruth play. In fact, you've never seen any of the New York Yankees play. You count the hours until Saturday's game. When you reach your driveway, Mother and Father greet you with smiling faces. Before you sits a beautiful, shiny black automobile with a red ribbon around it.

"Look what Father bought us!" Mother cries.

WOW! A brand new car. You can't believe how great things are. You don't want these good times to end.

▶ This advertisement for a luxury car dates from about 1927.

Cause and Effect As you read, think about conditions that may have caused the rise of dictators in Europe.

The 1920s

After the war, the economies of many European countries were weak. **Germany** was paying reparations. Europe had to be rebuilt. However, the United States became the strongest economic power in the world. Most Americans were living the good life. Some writers called this time the "Roaring Twenties."

Good times in the United States lasted less than a decade. During the Great War, the U.S. government had encouraged farmers to buy more land to increase production. Farmers took out loans to buy land. They promised to pay back the loans after the war. But after the war, Europeans went back to growing their own crops. When they stopped buying U.S. agricultural products, prices went down. Farmers did not make enough money to pay back their loans.

After the Great War, Americans also wanted to buy goods that were not available during the war. Factories switched from making weapons to making automobiles and radios. Like farmers, other Americans bought these goods on credit. Consumers soon ran out of credit and could not buy any more goods. When factories produced

▶ *Life* magazine captures the good times of the 1920s.

more goods than Americans were able to buy, prices fell and people lost their jobs.

In the late 1920s, people also borrowed money to buy stocks, or shares of companies, on credit. People investing their money in the stock market began to lose confidence in the economy. In October 1929, large numbers of investors began to sell their stock. Prices fell rapidly. When brokers demanded that investors pay back their loans, most could not repay them. Both the brokers and investors lost money. Hundreds of banks and businesses closed.

The prosperity that had begun in the early 1920s was swept away by the **Great Depression,** a worldwide business slump. A **depression** is a period of economic decline. During depressions, businesses close, people lose their jobs, and prices fall. Every country was hit hard, not just the United States. People around the world were out of work, food, and hope.

REVIEW How was borrowing money on credit one cause of the Great Depression? 🔄 **Cause and Effect**

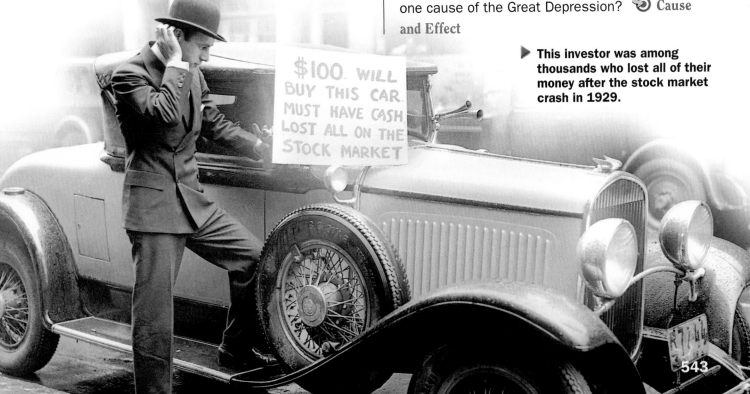

▶ This investor was among thousands who lost all of their money after the stock market crash in 1929.

New Dictators in Europe

Italian soldiers returned from the Great War to a country in poor condition. Workers went on strike. Factories stopped producing goods. Thousands of returning soldiers faced unemployment.

A new political movement called **fascism** (FASH ism) grew out of this troubled situation. Fascism is a form of government that stresses the nation above individuals. In a fascist country, the leader is usually a dictator who has total control over the government and industry.

The head of the Italian fascists, **Benito Mussolini** (MOO soh LEE nee), promised to make things better. When the fascists marched on Rome in

▶ **Benito Mussolini and Adolf Hitler became dictators in the 1920s and 1930s.**

October 1922, Mussolini took over the government as dictator.

Germany was still paying reparations when the Great Depression hit. As a result, by 1932, six million Germans were unemployed. Thousands joined Germany's fascist party, the National Socialists, or **Nazis.** Their leader, **Adolf Hitler,** promised to end hard times by restoring German military power. Hitler's ideas and plans were well known in Germany in part because of his book, *Mein Kampf* ("My Struggle").

Then and Now

Prices of Goods in the United States

How much money would you have needed to buy a sled or a doll in the 1930s? Why are prices today higher than they were back then? When governments print more money, that makes more money available. However, printing more money can actually decrease the value of the money. This causes inflation. Inflation causes an increase in prices. Look at the chart below to compare prices of goods taken from 1932 and 2001 advertisements.

	1932	2001
adult winter coat	$28.00	$99
table tennis	$23.50	$150
doll	$1.95	$19
table lamp	$1.00	$19

sled that steers
1932	$3.95
2001	$39.00

adult sweater
1932	$1.00
2001	$30.00

In January 1933 Hitler gained the top position in Germany's democratic government. Within two months, the Nazis took away most democratic freedoms. Hitler then became dictator of Germany.

Nazis were masters of **propaganda,** or the planned spread of certain beliefs. Propaganda was in the form of posters, pamphlets, or speeches. Nazis used propaganda to preach that the Jews were responsible for all of Germany's problems. They also said that the Germans were superior to all other ethnic groups.

Such Nazi ideas became widely known outside of Germany by 1938. Kristallnacht (krihs TAHL nahkt), a night of nationwide violence against Jews, showed the world how the Nazis treated Jews.

REVIEW What conditions in Germany and Italy led to the rise of dictators? **Cause and Effect**

Steps Toward War

Europe's new dictators quickly adopted a policy of **aggression,** which meant launching attacks on other countries. Both Hitler and Mussolini wanted to create empires. Beginning in the mid-1930s, they invaded lands that their armies could conquer easily. The leaders of Europe's strongest democracies, Great Britain and France, feared another war, so they did little to stop the aggressive acts.

Soon after taking power, Hitler began rebuilding Germany's armed forces, an action that violated the Treaty of Versailles. He had two goals: to regain territory in the east to bring together all German-speaking people and to take revenge for Germany's humiliating defeat in the Great War. The Treaty of Versailles had made the Rhineland, Germany's western region, off-limits to German troops. In 1936 Hitler ignored the treaty and sent troops into the Rhineland. Neither France nor Great Britain responded. Hitler's next move was to add Austria,

his homeland, to Germany. In March 1938, German troops marched into Austria and **annexed,** or attached, it to Germany. Both of these actions broke the Treaty of Versailles, but neither France nor Great Britain responded.

In September 1938 Hitler demanded that Czechoslovakia give up its German-speaking territories. He wanted to make them part of a greater Germany. To avoid war, British Prime Minister **Neville Chamberlain** suggested a conference. The result of the conference was an agreement: Germany was allowed to occupy the territory if Hitler promised to make no more claims in Europe. The agreement grew out of a policy called **appeasement,** or meeting the demands of an aggressor in order to preserve peace. In March 1939, however, Hitler broke the agreement. He seized the rest of Czechoslovakia.

Like Hitler, Mussolini had a plan of his own to take land for Italy. In 1935 he invaded Ethiopia in northeastern Africa. The League of Nations failed to stop this act of aggression. Then Italian and German troops went to Spain to join with fascist rebels against the government in the **Spanish Civil War.** This war ended with a fascist victory in 1939. Some historians later described this war as a "dress rehearsal" for what became World War II.

REVIEW Why did France and Great Britain ignore Hitler's breaking of the Treaty of Versailles? **Cause and Effect**

▶ **In 1938 Prime Minister Neville Chamberlain waves an agreement reached with Hitler, declaring "peace with honor."**

Japan Seizes an Empire

By 1930 military leaders began influencing **Japan.** As in Europe, nationalism began to rise. Japan's government encouraged nationalism through the worship of Emperor **Hirohito** (hir oh HEE toh). War and heroism were glorified.

As an island nation with few natural resources, Japan was dependent on the United States and other countries for raw materials. Japan's military leaders believed they could get the raw materials they needed by seizing Manchuria, a region in northeastern **China** with rich coal and iron deposits. The Chinese government was not strong enough to fight back. In 1931 Japan easily overran Manchuria.

▶ Hirohito became emperor of Japan in 1926.

Japan launched a full-scale war against China in 1937. The map below shows areas of China that Japan invaded. Millions died in the fighting. In Nanjing, then China's capital, the Japanese killed hundreds of thousands of the city's residents.

By late 1938, Japan's military leaders held most of eastern China and were planning to bring all of eastern and southeastern Asia under their control.

REVIEW What was the cause of Japan's invasion of Manchuria? ↻ **Cause and Effect**

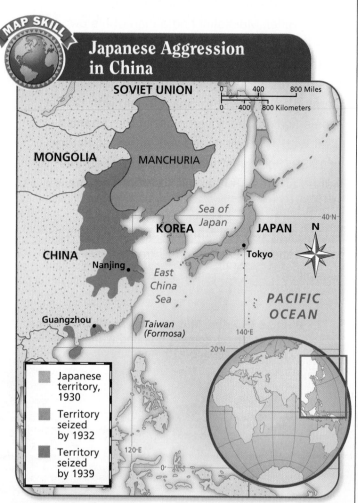

MAP SKILL

Japanese Aggression in China

SOVIET UNION

0   400   800 Miles
0   400   800 Kilometers

MONGOLIA

MANCHURIA

Sea of Japan

KOREA

JAPAN

N

40°N

CHINA

Nanjing

Tokyo

East China Sea

PACIFIC OCEAN

Guangzhou

Taiwan (Formosa)

140°E

20°N

■ Japanese territory, 1930

■ Territory seized by 1932

■ Territory seized by 1939

120°E

0°

▶ Japan took control of much of China in the 1930s.

MAP SKILL Use a Map Key *What parts of China did Japan invade?*

A Soviet Dictator

In 1922 the communists in Russia formed the Union of Soviet Socialist Republics, or the **Soviet Union.** The birth of this first communist nation had been long and violent. More than ten million Russians died during the civil war, which lasted from 1918 to 1920. Millions of Russians were left without food.

The Soviet leader, Lenin, tried to improve the failing economy. He allowed small peasant farmers and business people to operate without government control. This plan, called the New Economic Policy, helped the economy of the Soviet Union recover.

Lenin died in 1924, leaving the nation without a leader. Top Soviet officials became rivals in a struggle for power. By the late 1920s, the secretary general of the Communist Party, **Joseph Stalin,** had defeated all his opponents. He was now a dictator.

In 1928 Stalin rejected Lenin's New Economic Policy. That same year he launched the first of his **Five-Year Plans.** His plan had two goals. One was to turn farms into government collectives to increase crop production. **Collectives** are farms that are grouped together and run as a unit.

The second goal was to make the Soviet Union into an industrial giant. Stalin gave his reasons:

"We are 50 or 100 years behind the advanced countries. We must make good this lag in 10 years . . . or we will be crushed."

The peasants rebelled when Stalin tried to collectivize their land. Many of the wealthier peasants were sent to prison camps or killed. Farm production fell sharply, causing people to starve. Some historians believe five to seven million Soviet people died during this period.

Stalin's industrial drive was more successful. By the mid-1930s, the Soviet Union was second to the United States in industrial production. Still, many Soviet people did not like Stalin. In response, Stalin launched a program called the Great Terror. Millions of people were shot or sent to labor camps.

REVIEW How did Stalin plan to catch up to the economies of advanced countries? **Main Idea and Details**

▶ **These Russian refugees were taken away by train during a famine in 1922.**

Summarize the Lesson

- **1922** Fascists, led by Benito Mussolini, took control of Italy.
- **1931** Japan seized Manchuria from China.
- **1933** Adolf Hitler came to power in Germany.

LESSON 1 REVIEW

Check Facts and Main Ideas

1. **Cause and Effect** On a separate piece of paper, fill in the chart below by listing one important effect or cause.

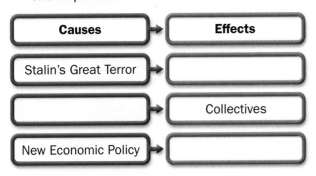

Causes	➜	Effects
Stalin's Great Terror	➜	
	➜	Collectives
New Economic Policy	➜	

2. Explain how inflation and the Great Depression affected world economies.

3. Define fascism and name two fascist countries from this lesson.

4. How did hard times lead to the rise of dictators in Italy and Germany?

5. **Critical Thinking:** *Make Inferences* Why do you think that Hitler repeatedly violated the Treaty of Versailles? Explain your answer.

Link to ⚭ Reading

Research Current Events Using newspapers, news magazines, and the Internet, research conflicts in the world today. Choose one conflict and prepare a report about it for your class.

1935   1940   1945

1939
World War II begins in Europe.

1941
Japan attacks U.S. ships
at Pearl Harbor.

1945
Nazi Germany surrenders.

1945
Japan surrenders.

World War II

PREVIEW

Focus on the Main Idea
World War II caused millions
of deaths and great destruction.

PLACES
Poland
London
Pearl Harbor
Stalingrad
Normandy
Berlin
Midway Island
Tokyo
Hiroshima
Nagasaki

PEOPLE
Winston Churchill
Franklin Roosevelt
Oveta Culp Hobby
Dwight Eisenhower
Douglas MacArthur
Harry Truman

TERMS
Axis Powers
Allies
Big Three
Women's Army Corps
D-Day
kamikaze

EVENTS
Battle of Britain

You Are There
At first, it seems like a holiday. You're going down into the "tube"—the London subway—at night with Mum and Dad and the neighbors. Mrs. Fenway, that nice older lady from downstairs, compares the bombing of London to a big slumber party. You bring your pajamas, pillows, and blankets and stay up very late. Mum says that Londoners always make the best of a bad situation.

In November 1940 London is in pretty bad shape. The Battle of Britain is in full swing, and every night German bombs are falling. Oh! There's one now. First you hear the rumble of planes overhead, then the scream of falling bombs, then the crash and roar of the explosions. You know that your family and friends will be safe here below tonight . . . but will you find your home still standing tomorrow morning?

► **Londoners seeking shelter and safety sleep in the subway at night during air raids.**

Cause and Effect As you read, look for the effects the actions of the Axis Powers had on the rest of the world.

Hitler's Aggression to 1939

Legend:
- Germany in 1935
- German territory occupied by troops against treaty, 1936
- Foreign territory under German control, March 1939

ESTONIA
LATVIA
LITHUANIA
SWEDEN
DENMARK
North Sea
Baltic Sea
EAST PRUSSIA
Elbe River
NETHERLANDS
GERMANY
Oder River
Vistula River
POLAND
BELGIUM
Rhine River
RHINELAND
LUX.
Danube River
CZECHOSLOVAKIA
FRANCE
AUSTRIA
SWITZERLAND
YUGO.
ITALY
Adriatic Sea

0   100   200 Miles
0   100   200 Kilometers

▶ Germany violated the Treaty of Versailles when it occupied the Rhineland in 1936.

MAP SKILL Use a Locator Map *Germany is part of what continent?*

World War II Begins

In August 1939, Stalin and Hitler signed an agreement. The two dictators promised not to attack each other. They also secretly agreed to attack and divide up **Poland.**

Hitler then set out on his plan to conquer Europe. On September 1 waves of German bombers, tanks, and troops crossed over into neighboring Poland. Within a few days, Great Britain and France declared war on Germany. Soon after, the Soviet Army invaded Poland from the east. World War II had begun.

Poland's collapse was followed by a period of calm. Then, in April 1940, Germany was on the move again, conquering the northern European countries of Denmark and Norway.

Meanwhile, **Winston Churchill** became prime minister of Great Britain in May. Churchill was the strong leader Great Britain needed. He knew that Hitler could not be trusted.

The Germans then marched into the Netherlands and Belgium. Next, Germany invaded France. Italy joined Germany by declaring war on France and Great Britain in June. Within a couple of weeks, France surrendered to Germany, leaving Great Britain to fight on alone.

The German Air Force soon launched an attack on Great Britain. In the **Battle of Britain,** day after day, British pilots defended England against German bombers. The Germans staged air raids on **London** and other cities. However, they could not destroy Britain's Royal Air Force or the will of the British people. Churchill was determined that Great Britain would fight on:

> *"We shall defend our island, whatever the cost may be. We shall fight on the beaches, we shall fight on the landing grounds, we shall fight in the fields and in the streets . . . we shall never surrender."*

Churchill's words of encouragement worked. The British fought on, and Hitler gave up on Great Britain.

Hitler's next move broke his agreement with Stalin. On June 22, 1941, the Germans attacked their ally, the Soviet Union. Expecting a quick victory, the Germans marched into Russia. The Soviet Union joined the side of Great Britain. The Germans held on until 1943. Then they retreated, or went back, to Germany.

REVIEW Why do you think Hitler gave up on his attacks against Great Britain? **Draw Conclusions**

The United States Enters the War

At the beginning of the war, the United States was at peace. However, U.S. President **Franklin Roosevelt** argued that all free countries would be endangered if the **Axis Powers**—Germany, Italy, and Japan—won the war. In order to aid the **Allies** —Great Britain, the Soviet Union, and China— Roosevelt asked for changes in laws that kept the United States neutral. Congress agreed. They then let the Allies buy war supplies.

With Great Britain fighting for its survival, the United States was the only country that could stop Japan from conquering Asia. The United States stopped exporting goods to Japan. As a result, the Japanese government decided to attack the United States.

On December 7, 1941, Japanese planes attacked the U.S. ships and airplanes anchored at **Pearl Harbor** in Hawaii. The surprise attack killed more than 2,300 people and destroyed or damaged 21 ships and 300 airplanes. President Roosevelt described the attack to Congress as follows:

> *"Yesterday, December 7, 1941— a date which will live in infamy [public disgrace]—the United States of America was suddenly and deliberately attacked by naval and air forces of the Empire of Japan."*

The United States immediately declared war on Japan. Germany and Italy then declared war on the United States.

▶ **Three damaged battleships during the Japanese attack on Pearl Harbor.**

▶ **A Japanese family about to be sent to a prison camp in California.**

The attack on Pearl Harbor made many Americans angry toward all of the Japanese, including Japanese Americans. In 1942 Roosevelt responded to this growing pressure and ordered all people of Japanese descent, or relation, to leave their homes on the West Coast. They were then sent to prison camps in various U.S. states. Nearly 50 years later, in 1988, Congress voted to grant $20,000 to each of the surviving Japanese Americans who had been sent to these camps.

REVIEW Why did the United States go to war in 1941?
◌ **Cause and Effect**

► Women contributed to the war effort, just as they had in World War I.

LIFE

JULY 19, 1943 10 CENTS
YEARLY SUBSCRIPTION $4.50

Wings Across America

Women in the War

During World War II women again helped in the war effort. As in World War I, women were not allowed to fight in combat. However, they had many more opportunities in war work that brought them closer to the front lines. Great Britain, the Soviet Union, and the United States all set up military organizations for women. Millions of women also went to work in defense plants, or factories that produced war weapons.

One U.S. organization that contributed to the war effort was the Women's Air Force Service Pilots (WASPs). Women pilots towed targets for training. They also moved aircraft around the country and abroad from factories to bases near enemy territory.

By the end of the war, the Soviet Union let women fight because of shortages in manpower. Great Britain also faced huge losses. For the first time in history, some British women were drafted, or called up for military service. However, British women were still not allowed to fight in combat. Germany did not allow women to help out much in the war. Many served as nurses or in the army in non-combat roles.

REVIEW How did women's roles in the war effort change over time? Compare and Contrast

The Tide Turns

By 1942 the United States and the Soviet Union had joined the Allies. The major Allied leaders—Franklin Roosevelt, Joseph Stalin, and Winston Churchill—were known as the Big Three. Roosevelt and Churchill agreed to concentrate on defeating Germany before Japan.

Stalin wanted a second fighting front, in Western Europe. Roosevelt and Churchill decided that the new front would be in Italy. However, the Allies first needed to drive the Axis Powers out of northern Africa. There the British were already fighting to hold on to Egypt and the Suez Canal.

In November 1942 the British stopped the Axis advance into Egypt at El Alamein. The battle was a turning point in the war. By May 1943 northern Africa was a clear base from which the Allies could invade Italy.

The Allies landed on the island of Sicily off the tip of Italy. In September 1943 they crossed over to the mainland and began a long, hard struggle up the Italian Peninsula. Though Italy had surrendered, Hitler and Mussolini still had control of central and northern Italy.

On the Eastern Front, intense Soviet fighting and the harsh winter of 1942 kept the Germans out of Moscow and Leningrad. In the spring, German forces moved south in an attempt to take Soviet oil fields. They met the Soviet Army at Stalingrad in late August. The battle raged for five months before the last German troops finally surrendered in February 1943. This battle was another key turning point in the war.

REVIEW What was the effect of the Battle of Stalingrad on Germany's invasion of the Soviet Union? Cause and Effect

► British officers lead troops of the British Empire from their desert camp in Egypt in 1940.

Hulton-Deutsch Collection/Corbis

Victory in Europe

After being attacked by Japan in late 1941, the United States began preparing for war. Millions of men entered the armed forces. Women served too. The commander of the Women's Army Corps, Oveta Culp Hobby, declared that every woman who served released a man for combat. Beatrice Hood Stroup, who served under Hobby, described her feelings about the war:

"It wasn't just my brother's country, or my husband's country, it was my country as well. And so this war wasn't just their war, it was my war, and I needed to serve in it."

National Archives

▶ Posters recruited women to work in factories to produce airplanes.

France. However, the Germans lacked the strength to keep it going.

While the Western Allies were freeing France from the Nazis, the Soviets were advancing from the east. By the spring of 1944, the Soviet troops had driven the Germans from the Soviet Union and then crossed into Eastern Europe. By April 1945, the Soviets held nearly all of Eastern Europe.

The United States astonished the world with its wartime production, including 86,000 tanks and 297,000 airplanes.

U.S. military production was put to the test on June 6, 1944. On this day, also known as D-Day, U.S. General Dwight Eisenhower led the Allied forces in history's largest invasion by sea. More than 4,700 ships carried over 150,000 soldiers from southern Great Britain to Normandy on the northern coast of France. By late June, one million Allied troops had landed.

On August 25, U.S. and French forces drove the last Germans out of Paris. In December the German Army launched a final attack on the border between Belgium and

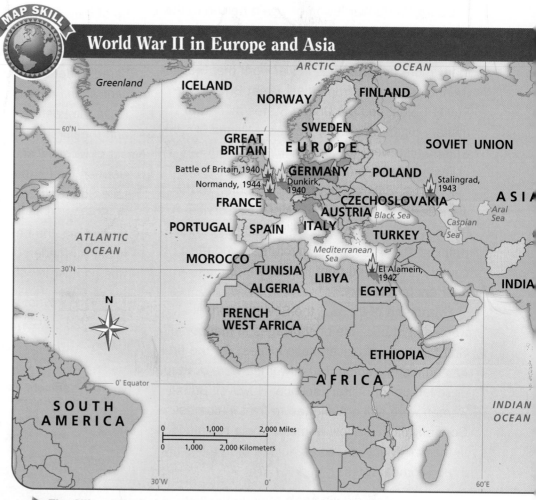

MAP SKILL

World War II in Europe and Asia

The Allies defeated Germany and Italy in Europe and Japan in Asia.

The Soviets then surrounded Germany's capital, **Berlin.** The Allies had marched from the west, and stood just outside of Berlin. Nazi Germany was finished. It surrendered to the Allies on May 7, 1945.

REVIEW How did U.S. war production help the Allies? ↻ **Cause and Effect**

Toward Victory Over Japan

The attack on Pearl Harbor gave Japan an important opportunity. While the United States was mobilizing for war, Japan expanded its empire in Asia. Within six months, Japan had conquered 100 million people. Japan easily took Hong Kong, Singapore, Thailand, and islands south of China. Japan already held large areas of China and Indochina, as well as all of Korea.

Only the islands of the Philippines, under U.S. General **Douglas MacArthur,** put up much resistance. MacArthur had to retreat from the Philippines in March 1942. By early May, the Philippines had surrendered. MacArthur promised, "I shall return."

Two sea battles cut off the Japanese advance in the Pacific. In May 1942, the Battle of the Coral Sea was fought entirely in the air between airplanes launched from aircraft carriers. Neither side won. However, it stopped the Japanese advance. In June the U.S. surprised and defeated the Japanese at **Midway Island,** west of Hawaii. The Battle of Midway was the first Allied victory in the Pacific.

REVIEW Why was the attack on Pearl Harbor an opportunity for the Japanese? **Main Idea and Details**

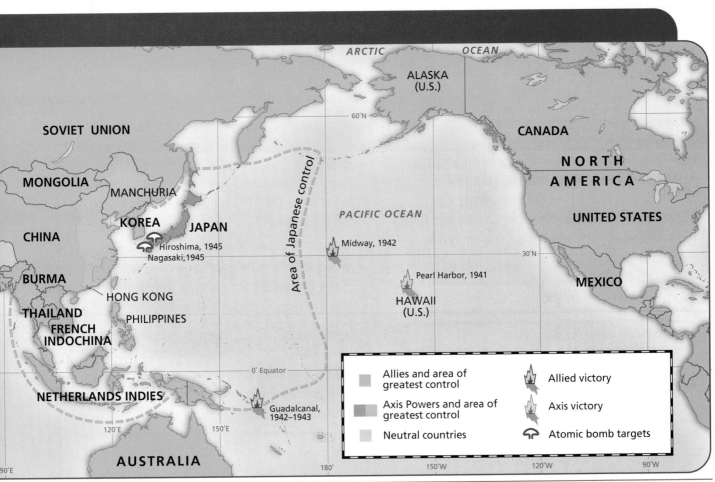

MAP SKILL Use Latitude and Longitude *What was the farthest eastern point of Japanese control?*

553

Dropping the Atomic Bomb

In August 1942 the United States began a military campaign in the Pacific. The U.S. defeat of Japan at Guadalcanal in February 1943 was a major victory.

General MacArthur returned to the Philippines in October 1944. Nearly 300 ships were involved in a battle that crushed the Japanese. However, Japan fought back with a dreadful new weapon— the **kamikaze** (kah mih KAH zee). These were pilots who flew airplanes directly into enemy warships. They faced certain death. In 1945 kamikazes sank at least 30 ships.

In March 1945, U.S. planes dropped firebombs on the Japanese city of **Tokyo.** One-fourth of the city's buildings were destroyed in this attack.

Meanwhile, President Roosevelt died in April 1945. The new U.S. President, **Harry Truman,** learned of a top-secret government program called the Manhattan Project. The scientists working on the project were developing an

atomic bomb. After testing a bomb in July, the United States warned Japan to surrender or be destroyed. Japan ignored the warning.

On August 6, 1945, the United States dropped an atomic bomb on the city of **Hiroshima** (hir uh SHEE muh). The bomb caused massive destruction and thousands of deaths. Still, Japan did not surrender. On August 9, the United States dropped a second atomic bomb, on the city of **Nagasaki** (nah guh SAH kee). Finally, the Japanese emperor urged his government to end the war. Japan surrendered on September 2, 1945. At last World War II was over.

REVIEW What finally caused Japan to surrender? Cause and Effect

Summarize the Lesson

- **1941** The United States entered World War II after Japan attacked Pearl Harbor.
- **1945** Germany surrendered to the Allies.
- **1945** Japan surrendered to the Allies.

LESSON 2   REVIEW

Check Facts and Main Ideas

1. Cause and Effect On a separate piece of paper, fill in the chart below with one effect of Hitler's attacks on the countries shown.

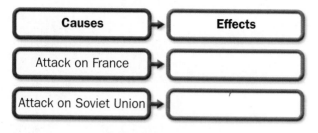

2. What made Hitler give up on invading Great Britain?

3. What was significant about D-Day?

4. What effect did dropping the atomic bomb have on Japan?

5. **Critical Thinking:** *Evaluate Information* What do you think might have happened if the United States had not entered the war in Europe? Explain your answer.

Link to ⬥⬥ Art

Design a Poster Create a poster to help inspire courage and hope in the people of London during the Battle of Britain.

554

Winston Churchill

1874–1965

Winston Churchill was born to an American mother and British father. He struggled in school as a child but later became one of the great leaders during World War II.

Throughout the 1920s, Winston Churchill was a member of Parliament in the British government. In the 1930s, he warned Great Britain of the growing threat of Nazism. When appeasement failed and Neville Chamberlain resigned as prime minister, Churchill accepted the position. He made it clear that Great Britain's goal was to defeat fascism. One of his most effective tools in rallying the British people was his gift of language. His first speech as prime minister was powerful and inspiring:

> *"You ask, what is our aim? I can answer in one word: victory, victory at all costs, victory in spite of all terror, victory however long and hard the road may be; for without victory there is no survival."*

During the war, Churchill woke at 8:00 A.M. every day. He spent hours reviewing the progress of the war. He then sent memos to military and government officials. After a one-hour nap, Churchill would work through the afternoon. He often spent the evening meeting with advisers until long after midnight.

During his long career, Churchill made mistakes and enemies. Few, however, would question his ability to use words to inspire others. As U.S. President John F. Kennedy once noted, Churchill "mobilized the English language and sent it into battle."

BIOFACT

Churchill was an amateur painter. He painted many landscapes using watercolors.

Chartwell Manor, Kent, UK/Bridgeman Art Library

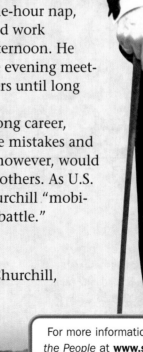

Learn from Biographies

From what you have read about Winston Churchill, how would you describe his personality?

For more information, go online to *Meet the People* at **www.sfsocialstudies.com**.

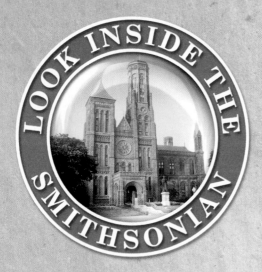

LOOK INSIDE THE SMITHSONIAN

A World at War

We can learn about World War I and World War II through artifacts such as objects people used or uniforms soldiers wore. By studying these artifacts, we gain a better understanding of what a soldier's or civilian's life was like during the world wars.

Hand-Me-Downs
Because the army was short on uniforms in World War II, some soldiers had to wear uniforms like this one that were left over from World War I.

Victory Gardens
During World War II, people were encouraged to grow their own gardens.

Kind of a Mess
American soldiers used this type of mess kit in World War II. Most of the food that soldiers ate came in cans.

Military Decorations
Some American soldiers were awarded medals such as the Silver Star, Italian Cross, and Purple Heart in World War II.

Limited Supplies
The United States issued the War Ration Book during World War II to reduce the usage of goods such as meat, butter, and petroleum.

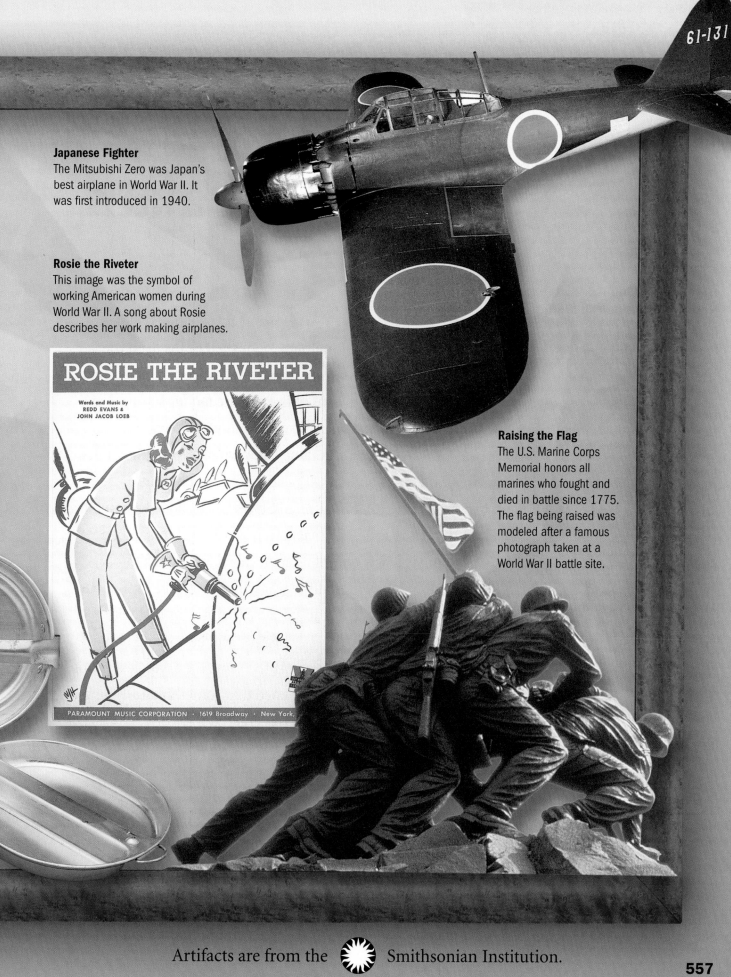

Japanese Fighter
The Mitsubishi Zero was Japan's best airplane in World War II. It was first introduced in 1940.

Rosie the Riveter
This image was the symbol of working American women during World War II. A song about Rosie describes her work making airplanes.

ROSIE THE RIVETER

Words and Music by
REDD EVANS &
JOHN JACOB LOEB

PARAMOUNT MUSIC CORPORATION · 1619 Broadway · New York,

Raising the Flag
The U.S. Marine Corps Memorial honors all marines who fought and died in battle since 1775. The flag being raised was modeled after a famous photograph taken at a World War II battle site.

Artifacts are from the Smithsonian Institution.

1945   1950

1945
Founding of the
United Nations

1948
Marshall Plan

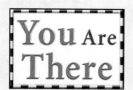

UN
Headquarters.

New York
City

The Aftermath

PREVIEW

Focus on the Main Idea
The Allies formed the United
Nations and helped shattered
nations rebuild.

PLACES
New York City

PEOPLE
Eleanor Roosevelt
George Marshall
Anne Frank

VOCABULARY
refugee
concentration camp
charter

TERMS
United Nations
Marshall Plan

You Are There
You're sitting at the kitchen table, helping Mom shell beans from the garden. It's so hot that you shift your chair to get directly in front of the electric fan for some relief. It's August, and a heat wave has hit your town.

You are enjoying a radio show when a voice interrupts with a news bulletin: "President Truman has just announced that the United States has exploded a bomb of tremendous destructive power over Hiroshima, Japan. The bomb is a new type of weapon called an atomic bomb."

Mom tells you that the war will probably be over soon. You're glad to hear this because that means that your brother will be coming home. At the same time, you feel frightened that something terrifying has entered the world.

The Granger Collection

▶ **Radios such as this one provided
people with news and entertainment.**

Cause and Effect As you read, identify effects of
the Allied victory in World War II on the postwar world.

Target Skill

The Most Terrible War

World War II was the first war in which an atomic bomb was used. It also brought more death and destruction than any other war. Cities such as Berlin and Tokyo had been bombed to ruins. About 40 to 50 million people were killed worldwide. Millions had been forced to flee their homes. Now Europe, China, and other areas were overflowing with **refugees,** or people who left their homeland for a safer place.

The Japanese cities of Hiroshima and Nagasaki had been hit by the first atomic bomb attacks in history. More than 100,000 were killed immediately. Thousands of survivors suffered burns and thousands more soon developed illnesses such as cancer.

However, nothing so horrified the world as the discovery of Nazi **concentration camps,** or places that held imprisoned people of a particular ethnic group or with particular political or religious beliefs. Nazi Germany put millions of people—mostly Jews—to death in such camps. The Nazi leaders had carried out their plan, which they called the "Final Solution," to get rid of Europe's Jews. They imprisoned millions in concentration camps, where people were forced to work.

No one will ever know exactly how many Jews were murdered in what came to be known as the Holocaust. Most historians believe that at least 6 million Jews died.

As Allied troops entered Nazi territory, they saw unbelievable suffering in the

▶ **World War II produced millions of refugees.**

Nazi camps. American reporter Meyer Levin described the survivors he saw:

> *"They were like none we have ever seen. Skeletal with feverish, sunken eyes, shaven skulls."*

REVIEW What were three terrible effects of World War II? 🔁 **Cause and Effect**

▶ **These young people in a concentration camp await liberation by Russian soldiers in September 1945.**

559

New Beginnings

Out of the war's destruction the Allies hoped to fashion a new and better world. U.S. President Franklin D. Roosevelt, among others, believed that an international peacekeeping organization was needed. Roosevelt died on April 12, 1945, just before the **United Nations,** or UN, formed.

Others carried on the work. On April 25, 1945, the first United Nations conference met and drew up a **charter,** or constitution. The United Nations became effective on October 24, 1945. In 1951 the UN moved to permanent headquarters in **New York City.**

In Chapter 18 you read that the Allies, after the Great War, had set up the League of Nations. Learning from the League's failures, the World War II Allies tried to make the UN stronger.

U.S. President Harry Truman named **Eleanor Roosevelt** to serve as a delegate to the UN when it met in early 1946. Mrs. Roosevelt was the wife of the late President Roosevelt. She also was a writer and experienced public speaker.

▶ **Eleanor Roosevelt fought for human rights.**

At the UN, Eleanor Roosevelt's most important work was as chairperson of the committee that wrote the *Universal Declaration of Human Rights.* This document set standards for human rights. The declaration has been a guideline for nations and rulers since the UN adopted it in 1948.

In Germany and Japan, the Allies brought war criminals to justice. They arrested the most important leaders and put them on trial. However, the chief war criminal, Adolf Hitler, escaped Allied justice. He had killed himself on April 30, 1945.

The economies of European countries failed to recover after the war. Europe needed to rebuild. It needed financial help. President Truman and his secretary of state, **George Marshall,** believed that the United States should help these countries. They persuaded Congress to pass the **Marshall Plan,** which went into effect in April 1948.

The United States sent $13 billion in aid to Europe. The Marshall Plan was a tremendous success. Within a few years, the economies of Western Europe were prospering. However, the countries of Eastern Europe were now under Soviet control. Soviet leader Joseph Stalin forced Eastern European countries to turn down America's offer of help. He did not want them to rely on the United States.

▶ **Ben Shahn's 1945 painting *Liberation* shows children playing in the rubble left by World War II.**

Estate of Ben Shahn/Licensed by VAGA, New York, NY/Museum of Modern Art

As the world made a new beginning, no one had expressed hope for humanity as much as Anne Frank. Anne was a Jewish girl who had lived in the Netherlands, a country in Europe. She went into hiding with her family. Anne kept a diary and wrote about her life in hiding. In 1944 she and her family were discovered and sent to concentration camps. In her diary she wrote:

> *"In spite of everything I still believe that people are really good at heart."*

Summarize the Lesson

- **1945** The United Nations charter was approved in April, and the United Nations opened in October.
- **1948** The United States began its aid program for Europe, the Marshall Plan.
- **1948** The United Nations adopted the Universal Declaration of Human Rights.

▶ **Anne Frank's diary has been translated into more than 60 languages.**

The Granger Collection

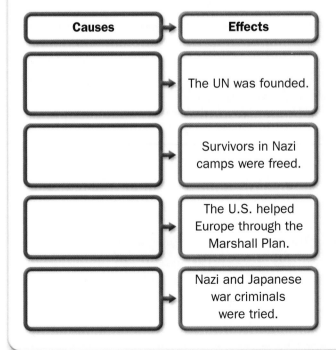

LESSON 3   REVIEW

Check Facts and Main Ideas

1. ↺ **Cause and Effect** On a separate piece of paper, fill in the chart below by listing the cause of each of the effects listed.

Causes	→	Effects
	→	The UN was founded.
	→	Survivors in Nazi camps were freed.
	→	The U.S. helped Europe through the Marshall Plan.
	→	Nazi and Japanese war criminals were tried.

2. What ill effects did survivors of the atomic bombings in Nagasaki and Hiroshima suffer?

3. Who was Anne Frank?

4. How did the United Nations give hope to the world?

5. **Critical Thinking:** *Evaluate Information* Why do you think Stalin did not want the Eastern European countries to take advantage of the Marshall Plan?

Link to ⬥ Writing

Write a Proposal You have been asked to write a proposal to give to your country's delegate to the United Nations. Use a topic from this lesson as the subject of your proposal. Suggest a solution to a problem or a way of preventing future problems.

561

Interpret Bar Graphs

What? A bar graph is a graph that shows different amounts by rectangles of different lengths. The three bar graphs shown here give information about World War II. The bars on each graph represent countries that were involved in the war. The numbers have been rounded off. For many of these countries, such as the Soviet Union, more exact numbers are not available for the first graph, *Military Casualties for World War II.*

Military Casualties for World War II

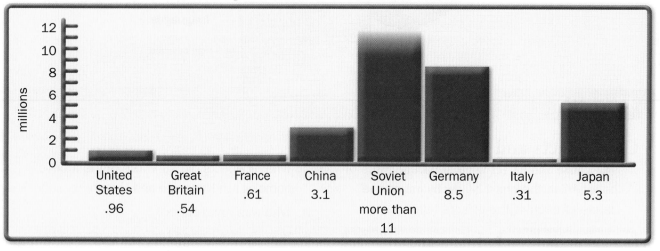

| United States .96 | Great Britain .54 | France .61 | China 3.1 | Soviet Union more than 11 | Germany 8.5 | Italy .31 | Japan 5.3 |

National Income of War Powers, 1937

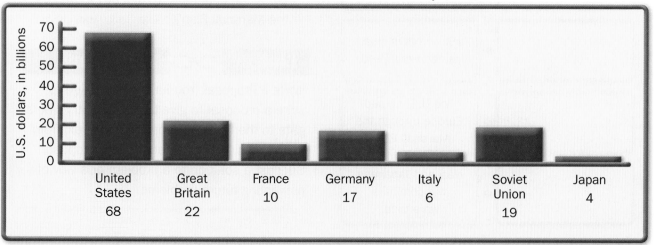

| United States 68 | Great Britain 22 | France 10 | Germany 17 | Italy 6 | Soviet Union 19 | Japan 4 |

Percentage of National Income Spent on Defense, 1937

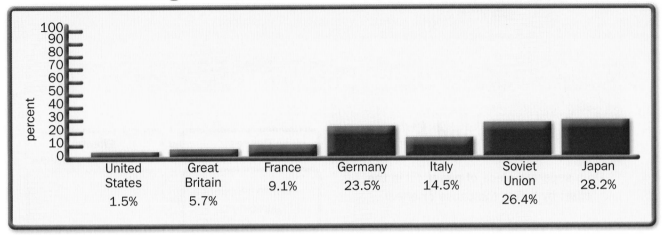

	percent
United States	1.5%
Great Britain	5.7%
France	9.1%
Germany	23.5%
Italy	14.5%
Soviet Union	26.4%
Japan	28.2%

Why? Graphing helps us understand relationships between amounts or numbers easily. Bars are simple visual objects. They are very easy for your eyes to scan to gather information.

How? Every bar graph has two axes, or labeled sides. (The word *axes* is the plural form of *axis*.) Usually, one axis only has labels. The base of the bars sits on this axis. The other axis usually has both a scale and a label. In mathematics the horizontal (side-to-side) axis is called the x-axis. The vertical (up-and-down) axis is called the y-axis.

Look at the graph *Military Casualties for World War II*. What do you see along the x-axis? Along the y-axis? In this graph, the bottoms of the bars sit on the x-axis. Names of countries label this axis. One name goes with each bar. The y-axis has a scale with numbers. Its label tells us the number of military casualties—soldiers killed or wounded in the war.

Now read the number of casualties for a particular country. Look at the x-axis. Find the bar for the United States. Scan upward to find the top of this bar. Then scan left to the y-axis. Note where on the axis your eye falls. You can see that the United States bar stops a little lower than one million on the scale. So its value must be a little

more than 900,000. Without a table of figures, you would not know the exact figure. But you could make a good guess based on the height of the bar.

Now study the other two graphs. One shows the national income of the World War II powers in 1937 (just before the war). The other shows the percentage of the national income being spent on defense during that same year.

Think and Apply

1. Which group of countries had more military casualties in World War II, the Allies or the Axis Powers?

2. Which group of countries had a higher total national income in 1937, the Allies or the Axis Powers?

3. Compare the bar graphs for *National Income of War Powers, 1937* and *Percentage of National Income Spent on Defense, 1937*. According to your comparison, which countries were mobilizing for war?

563

1920

1922
Fascists took control
of Italy.

Chapter Summary

Cause and Effect

Target Skill

On a separate piece of paper, fill in the
chart by listing the cause or effect.

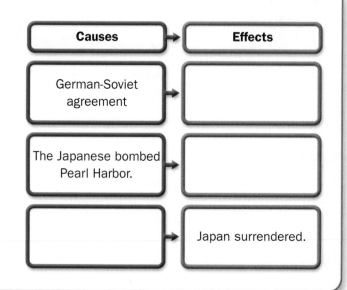

Causes	→	Effects
German-Soviet agreement	→	
The Japanese bombed Pearl Harbor.	→	
	→	Japan surrendered.

Vocabulary

Match each word with the correct definition or
description.

1 fascism
(p. 544)

2 propaganda
(p. 545)

3 Nazi
(p. 544)

4 annex
(p. 545)

5 charter
(p. 560)

a. a constitution

b. planned spread
of beliefs

c. attach or take
a territory

d. form of govern-
ment that
stresses nation
above individuals

e. Germany's fascist
party

People and Terms

Write a sentence explaining why each of the following people or terms was important in the
events of the 1930s and World War II. You may
use two or more in a single sentence.

1 Benito Mussolini
(p. 544)

2 Adolf Hitler
(p. 544)

3 Hirohito
(p. 546)

4 Axis Powers
(p. 550)

5 Winston Churchill
(p. 549)

6 Great Depression
(p. 543)

7 Allies (p. 550)

8 Dwight
Eisenhower
(p. 552)

9 D-Day (p. 552)

10 Eleanor
Roosevelt
(p. 560)

1930				1940					1950

1933
Hitler became
dictator of Germany.

1939
World War II began
in Europe.

1945
Nazi Germany surrendered.
Japan surrendered.
United Nations founded

1948
Marshall Plan
began.

1931
Japan seized Manchuria.

1941
Japan attacked U.S. at Pearl Harbor.

Facts and Main Ideas

1 What conditions helped dictators come to power in Italy and Germany after World War I?

2 What were the two goals of Stalin's first Five-Year Plan?

3 Why did the military leaders of Japan decide to bomb Pearl Harbor?

4 **Time Line** How long did World War II last in Europe?

5 **Main Idea** How did the rise of dictators help cause World War II?

6 **Main Idea** What event caused the United States to enter World War II?

7 **Main Idea** What did the Allies do to help the world recover after World War II?

8 **Critical Thinking:** *Evaluate Information* How accurate do you think the information about the Jews was in German propaganda?

Apply Skills

Interpret Bar Graphs

Use the skills you learned on pages 562–563 to answer the following questions. You will need to refer to the three bar graphs on those pages.

1 Based on the information shown, what country in 1937 may not have been worried about going to war?

2 What countries in 1937 may have been preparing to go to war?

3 What country shown on the bar graph had the lowest national income in 1937?

4 What country shown on the bar graph spent the highest percentage of its national income on defense in 1937?

Write About History

1 **Write a paragraph** from someone in the United States in 1940. Explain why you do—or do not—think the United States should get involved in the war in Europe between Nazi Germany and Great Britain.

2 **Write a radio script** for a radio broadcast at the time of the surrender of France in June 1940. Consider what the mood might have been at that time.

3 **Write a verdict** as a judge at a trial of a Nazi war criminal after World War II. Write a judgment at the end of the trial. Explain why you think the war criminal should be punished.

Internet Activity

To get help with vocabulary, people, and terms, select dictionary, encyclopedia, or almanac from *Social Studies Library* at **www.sfsocial studies.com**.

CHAPTER 20

The Cold War

Lesson 1

1948
Berlin
Tensions increase between the United States and the Soviet Union.

1

Lesson 2

1949
Beijing
China becomes a communist nation.

2

Lesson 3

1960s–1970s
Hanoi
The Cold War leads to fighting in Korea and Vietnam.

3

Why We Remember

After World War II, people longed for peace. In the past, countries went to war because of imperialism or nationalism. Now competition between communism and democracy took center stage. Communist countries believed that their system of state ownership of properties and businesses was fairer than one of private ownership. However, to enforce their ideas, communists had to destroy democratic freedoms. In this atmosphere, tensions between the Soviet Union and the United States led to a new kind of war—a "cold war."

1945   1955   1965

1948–1949
Berlin airlift

1949
North Atlantic Treaty Organization (NATO) forms.

Soviet Union makes an atomic bomb.

1962
Cuban missile crisis

Berlin •
WEST GERMANY   EAST GERMANY

The Soviets Advance

PREVIEW

Focus on the Main Idea
After 1945 the Soviet Union and the Allies broke off relations.

PLACES
Berlin
West Germany
East Germany
Cuba

PEOPLE
Nikita Khrushchev
John F. Kennedy

VOCABULARY
nuclear
containment

TERMS
Cold War
Truman Doctrine
North Atlantic Treaty Organization (NATO)
Warsaw Pact

EVENTS
Berlin airlift

You Are There While you listen to the radio, your parents and some of your neighbors are at the dining room table. They are debating about the speech that Winston Churchill gave at nearby Westminster College the other night. They keep using a phrase you have never heard before: "the Iron Curtain." Finally, you turn down the radio so you can listen more closely.

You're a little confused. Wasn't the Soviet Union one of our allies in the war? In his speech, Churchill warned that the Soviet Union is going to cut Eastern Europe off from the rest of the world. It will be behind an iron curtain. The adults are debating whether the Soviets would actually do something like that.

You begin to wonder: Does this mean we will be going back to war?

▶ **U.S. President Harry Truman introduces Winston Churchill at Westminster College in 1946.**

Cause and Effect As you read, consider the effects of the actions by the Soviet Union and Western countries after World War II.

New Superpowers

In the final weeks of World War II, Soviet troops met the Allied troops at Berlin, Germany. They had fought as Allies in a long war against Nazi Germany. Now their relationship was about to change.

With the Axis powers in ruins, the Soviet Union and the United States were now much stronger than any other countries. They had become "superpowers." However, the new superpowers soon found it hard to agree on anything.

During World War II, the "Big Three"—Great Britain's Churchill, U.S. President Roosevelt, and Soviet leader Stalin—had made plans for postwar Europe. They agreed to allow the nations of Eastern Europe to establish their own governments.

However, as the war drew to a close, Soviet troops marched into Eastern Europe. Stalin and the Soviet army forced communist governments on Poland, Czechoslovakia, Hungary, and other nations in the region. In this way, the Soviet Union gained political control of these countries. By 1948 all of Eastern Europe was communist.

Churchill said that the new communist rulers were putting up a wall between their countries and the West. This "wall" stopped trade and travel. In a speech Churchill made at Westminster College in Fulton, Missouri, he said:

Courtesy of FDR Library, Hyde Park, NY

▶ In 1945 the "Big Three" met to discuss plans for postwar Europe. Seated from left to right: Joseph Stalin, Franklin Roosevelt, and Winston Churchill.

"From Stettin in the Baltic to Trieste in the Adriatic an iron curtain has descended across the Continent."

Churchill's "iron curtain" became almost as familiar a term as "cold war." **Cold War** was the term used to describe the tension between the Soviet Union and the United States after World War II. The destructive power of **nuclear,** or atomic, weapons backed this "cold" war of words and threats.

REVIEW Why do you think the United States mistrusted the Soviet Union? Explain your answer. **Draw Conclusions**

▶ **The Iron Curtain was an imaginary wall that stretched from the Baltic Sea to the Adriatic Sea.**

IRELAND

UNITED KINGDOM

North Sea

DENMARK

Baltic Sea

NETHERLANDS

EAST GERMANY

ATLANTIC OCEAN

BELGIUM

POLAND

USSR

LUXEMBOURG

WEST GERMANY

FRANCE

SWITZERLAND

CZECHOSLOVAKIA

HUNGARY

ITALY

AUSTRIA

ROMANIA

PORTUGAL

YUGOSLAVIA

SPAIN

Adriatic Sea

Black Sea

BULGARIA

ALBANIA

A Divided Europe

At the close of World War II, the Allies agreed to divide Germany into zones of occupation. The Soviet Union, France, Great Britain, and the United States would each control a zone. Germany's capital, Berlin, would then be divided up in the same way.

As relations between the Soviet Union and the other Allies turned sour, these arrangements began to cause problems. Berlin was located inside the Soviet zone of occupation.

In June 1948 Stalin decided to push the French, British, and Americans out of Berlin. He stopped traffic coming into their sections of the city. People living in those zones now faced the threat of starvation.

U.S. President Harry S. Truman responded quickly with the Berlin airlift. An airlift is the transport of supplies by airplanes. For nearly a year, the people in the U.S., British, and French zones of Berlin survived on these supplies. In the end, Stalin had to give up. Only three years after the defeat of the Nazis, Berlin became a symbol of freedom to the world.

Truman worked to prevent Soviet communism from spreading into any other countries. This became known as a policy of containment. When Greece and Turkey faced Soviet pressure in 1947, Truman committed the United States to help these nations. This promise became known as the Truman Doctrine. In his address to Congress, Truman declared:

> *"The free peoples of the world look to us for support in maintaining their freedoms."*

The next year, Truman offered economic aid to any country, both in the East and the West, to encourage countries to resist communism.

In April 1949 the United States and its Western Allies set up the North Atlantic Treaty Organization (NATO). Members of this organization made a promise to each other. They promised that if one member were threatened by Soviet aggression, the others would come to its aid. In response, the Soviets set up the Warsaw Pact. This alliance was similar to NATO, but it was designed for the communist countries of Eastern Europe.

► The official NATO flag was approved in October 1953.

In May 1949, the Western Allies combined their zones of occupation to form the country of West Germany. The Soviets created East Germany from their zone. Now more than ever, an iron curtain divided Europe.

REVIEW What was the cause of the Berlin airlift? What was its effect? 🔄 **Cause and Effect**

► Berliners cheer as an American plane with supplies flies above them during the Berlin airlift.

The Nuclear Arms Race

In Chapter 19 you read how the United States dropped atomic bombs on two Japanese cities in 1945. Joseph Stalin realized that the Soviet Union would have to develop such weapons if it expected to keep up with the United States.

In 1949 the Soviet Union tested its first atomic bomb. This proved to the world that it was now a nuclear power too.

In the early 1950s, the United States tested a far more powerful weapon, the hydrogen bomb, or "H-bomb." Within a few years, the Soviet Union also had its own H-bombs. The Soviets and Americans, locked in their Cold War, now could threaten each other with complete destruction. Each side was determined to use the threat of nuclear war to make the other side back down.

People in both countries were afraid. Children grew up practicing drills in school for what to do in the event of a nuclear attack. Called "duck and cover," this drill resembled the procedure for a tornado drill. One student, looking back on this period, later reported:

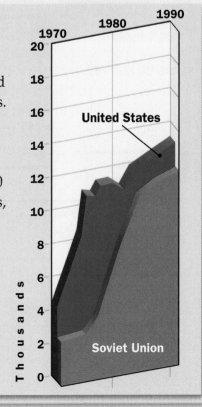

> "I was afraid because my parents and other adults seemed very worried. I remember our neighbors wondering if they should build a bomb shelter."

REVIEW Why did Stalin think the Soviet Union needed to develop its own nuclear weapons?
Draw Conclusions

FACT FILE

The Nuclear Arms Race, 1945–1990

After the United States used atomic bombs in World War II, it was only a matter of time until other countries developed nuclear weapons. The time line shows when other nations had "the bomb."

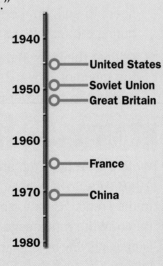

1940	
	— United States
1950	— Soviet Union
	— Great Britain
1960	
	— France
1970	— China
1980	

The nuclear race was mostly between the Soviet Union and the United States. By the 1980s, these two countries each had more than 10,000 nuclear weapons, as the graph at right shows.

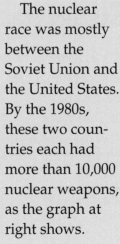

United States

Soviet Union

Thousands: 0 2 4 6 8 10 12 14 16 18 20
1970   1980   1990

The Cuban Missile Crisis

Sharp disagreements between the superpowers continued. The fear of nuclear attack was behind every action made by either side. When the new Soviet leader, Nikita Khrushchev, declared in 1956, "We will bury you," people in the United States felt more uneasy than ever.

In 1961 people were leaving East Germany in huge numbers to reach West Germany. Khrushchev responded. He had a wall built through the middle of Berlin. It became known as the Berlin Wall and stood for more than 25 years.

In October 1962, the world came dangerously close to nuclear war. U.S. spy planes took photos that showed that the Soviet Union was building missile bases in Cuba, a communist country. If the bases were completed, Soviet nuclear missiles would be only 90 miles from the southern tip of Florida. To keep missiles out of Cuba, President John F. Kennedy responded with a naval blockade, the use of force to prevent ships from reaching ports. For several days, the world trembled with fear. Finally, Khrushchev backed down.

► Soviet leader Nikita Khrushchev speaks at a United Nations conference.

REVIEW Did people leave East Germany before or after the Berlin Wall was built? Sequence

Summarize the Lesson

1948–1949 The United States and its Allies launched the Berlin airlift.

1949 The Soviet Union successfully tested its first atomic bomb.

1962 The United States and the Soviet Union came close to starting a nuclear war over Soviet missiles in Cuba.

LESSON 1 REVIEW

Check Facts and Main Ideas

1. ⟳ **Cause and Effect** On a separate piece of paper, fill in the chart below by listing three causes of the Cold War.

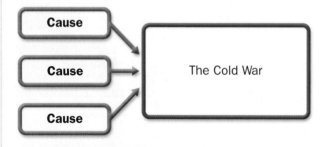

Cause → The Cold War

Cause →

Cause →

2. What was the purpose of the Berlin airlift?

3. What was the central issue of the Cuban missile crisis?

4. Why did Churchill's term, "the iron curtain," seem to sum up the situation in Europe during the Cold War so well?

5. **Critical Thinking:** *Make Inferences* How was the founding of NATO an effect of Stalin's attempt to take over Berlin? Explain.

Link to ○—⊂○ **Writing**

Write a Message You are a U.S. diplomat in 1948. The Soviets have just cut off all traffic to the French, British, and American zones of Berlin. Write a message to Joseph Stalin explaining why he should reconsider this action.

CITIZEN HEROES

BUILDING CITIZENSHIP

Caring
Respect
Responsibility
Fairness
★ Honesty
Courage

Reaching the Roof of the World

Tenzing Norgay's dream came true one cold day in 1953. He and Edmund Hillary became the first people to reach the top of Mt. Everest, the world's tallest mountain. However, Tenzing never thought that some people would turn his feat into a political issue.

Norgay was born in 1914 in Nepal, a country in southern Asia. His village was in the shadow of the Himalayas. As a boy he dreamed of climbing Mt. Everest. His people, the Sherpas, called it the "goddess mother of the world." He recalled:

> *"The pull of Everest was stronger for me than any force on Earth."*

Early on May 29, 1953, Norgay and his partner, New Zealander Edmund Hillary, set out from their camp. They were about 1,000 feet from the top of the mountain. They took turns leading the way. Both of them carefully planted their ice axes into the brittle ice as they inched upward. At 11:30 A.M. they reached the top—the roof of the world!

Norgay and Hillary were hailed as heroes. However, because Norgay was Asian and Hillary was of European descent, some people wanted to claim the achievement for the East or the West. They demanded to know who had reached the summit first.

Norgay gave the situation careful thought. Even though Norgay knew some people would be disappointed, he told the truth. In his autobiography *Tiger of the Snows* (1955), Norgay revealed that Hillary reached the top first. Norgay reached the summit moments later.

Honesty in Action

Link to Current Events Research the story of a person today who has demonstrated honesty. What risks did this person take in being honest in that particular situation?

Edmund Hillary/Royal Geographical Society Picture Library

573

Solve Complex Problems

What? A complex problem is one that needs to be considered carefully. If you make a bad decision in trying to solve a complex problem, the problem may only get worse. In October 1962, U.S. spy planes provided President John F. Kennedy with evidence that the Soviet Union was building missile bases in Cuba. From only 90 miles south of Florida, the Soviets or the Cubans would be able to launch nuclear missiles at any U.S. city.

President Kennedy had to make difficult decisions about how to get rid of the missiles—without setting off a nuclear war. Members of his Cabinet, military leaders, and others were called upon to advise him. Once decisions were made, Kennedy had to communicate them to the Soviet leader, Nikita Khrushchev, in Moscow.

▶ **U.S. President Kennedy (right) and Soviet Leader Khrushchev (above) had to deal with the threat of a nuclear war.**

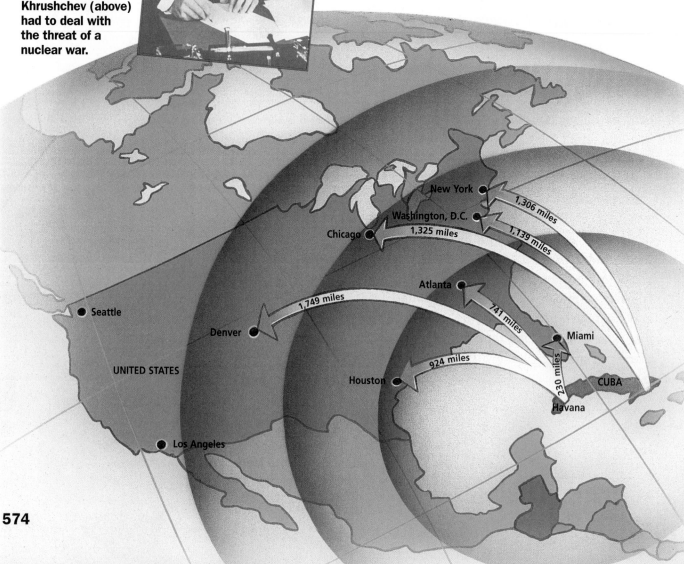

PROB NUCLEAR STORAGE BUNKER

BATCH PLANTS

PRE-FAB CONSTRUCTION MATERIALS

LAUNCH PAD

CONTROL BUILDING

PROTECTED VEHICLE POSITION

LAUNCH PAD

Defense Department Photo/AP/Wide World Photos

▶ **U.S. spy planes took aerial photos such as this one of the missile bases being built by the Soviets in Cuba. Labels (added later) indicate the different parts of the missile base.**

Why? It is always important to make decisions carefully. But when the stakes are high, finding effective ways to solve difficult problems is especially critical. President Kennedy had to deal with the Cuban missile crisis. He knew that the world's fate might rest in his hands. A poor decision might have led to nuclear war.

How? President Kennedy made a good decision right at the start. He carefully discussed all options, or possible actions, with a group of trusted advisers. By drawing on the experience of experts, he could feel confident of being well informed.

Next, President Kennedy refused to be rushed into making a decision. Some of his advisers wanted the United States to bomb the missile sites at once. However, the president realized that he had time to think. He knew the Soviets could not get the missile sites ready right away. He did not want to rush into any action.

Finally, Kennedy chose a plan of action. The plan satisfied the need to stop work on the missile sites without risking war with the Soviet Union. He placed a blockade on all Soviet ships coming to Cuba. This means that the U.S. Navy would prevent Soviet ships from reaching Cuba. The blockade would keep more Soviet missiles out of Cuba. It should also buy time for the two sides to work out a settlement.

Like President Kennedy, you might use the following strategy to solve complex problems:

· Carefully consider all your options. Seek advice from experts, or people whose judgment you respect.

· Do not allow yourself to be rushed into a decision. Give yourself time to think things through.

· Consider the consequence of each option. Try to find a solution that satisfies all requirements or most of them.

Think and Apply

1 What do you think might have happened in 1962 if President Kennedy had rushed into bombing the Cuban missile sites?

2 Why do you think that it is important for a leader to be willing to ask people for advice and to listen? Explain your answer.

3 Think of a situation in which you had to make a difficult decision. Did you use any parts of the strategy discussed here? Explain.

575

Beijing

CHINA

1910   **1930**   **1950**   **1970**

1911
China becomes a republic.

1949
Communists come to power.

1966
Cultural Revolution begins.

1976
Mao dies and the Cultural Revolution ends.

PREVIEW

Focus on the Main Idea
In a century of revolution, communists took control of China.

PLACES
Taiwan
People's Republic of China
Beijing
Taipei

PEOPLE
Sun Yat-sen
Chiang Kai-shek
Mao Zedong
Richard Nixon
Jiang Qing
Nien Cheng

VOCABULARY
proletarian

TERMS
Nationalist Party

EVENTS
Cultural Revolution

Communism in China

You Are There
Today, coming home from school, you notice that the street near your apartment building in Shanghai (shang HY), China, is blocked. You hear what sounds like a noisy parade. You try to remember what day it is. Oh, yes, it's August 23, 1966. You're sure it's not a special holiday.

By looking more closely at the paraders, you notice something. They all seem young—about the age of your teenage sister. They're all wearing red armbands. Many are shouting and waving a little red book. Some are carrying big poles that hold up huge banners. You try to make out some of the writing.

You turn to a girl next to you and ask, "What's going on?" "Don't you know?" she responds. "These are the Red Guards, marching in the Cultural Revolution."

▶ Copies of the "little red book": *Quotations from Chairman Mao Zedong*

 Cause and Effect As you read, try to identify causes and effects of the communist takeover of China in 1949.

A Struggle for Control of China

As you have just read, a revolution began in China in 1966. It was not the first revolution China went through in the twentieth century. In 1911 a revolution removed China's emperor and China became a country without a king or emperor—a republic. One of the leaders of that revolution was **Sun Yat-sen** (SUN YAHT SEN).

Sun Yat-sen started the Guomindang (GWOAH meen dang), or the **Nationalist Party.** When he died in 1925, **Chiang Kai-shek** (jee AHNG ky SHEK), became the Guomindang leader.

Meanwhile, the Communist Party of China was formed in 1921. In a few years, **Mao Zedong** (MOW ZUH DUNG) became the leader of the communists.

In the 1930s, the Nationalist Party ruled most of China. It wanted to get rid of the communists and nearly succeeded. However, a group of communists escaped to far northwest China. Their long, difficult journey during 1934 and 1935 became known as "The Long March." A man who later became an important government official described the Long March:

"For us, the darkest time . . . was . . . when we crossed the great grasslands near Tibet. . . . We not only had nothing to eat, we had nothing to drink."

During World War II, the Nationalist Party and the communists had to put aside their differences to fight Japan. But afterward they fought in a civil war. In 1949 the communists won and took over China. The nationalists then fled to **Taiwan** (ty WAHN), an island off China's coast.

REVIEW What were the effects of the civil war in China? 🔄 **Cause and Effect**

Yan'an

Huang Ho River

CHINA

Chang Jiang River

Zunyi

Ruijin

N

TAIWAN

—— Main Route of Red Army
⌐⌐⌐ Great Wall

Map Adventure

You're an American Journalist

The Chinese communists are making a 6,000-mile journey to escape from the nationalists. You're assigned to cover their story. The march begins in southeastern China in October 1934. About a year later, they set up a new base at Yan'an.

1. In January 1935, the communists hold a meeting at Zunyi. Locate Zunyi on the map.

2. What major river do the communists need to cross after turning their direction northward?

3. Along what human-made structure do the communists travel for many miles?

The People's Republic of China

When the communists took over China in 1949, they set up the **People's Republic of China** and made **Beijing** (bay JEENG) their capital. The Nationalist Party, led by Chiang, set up a government on Taiwan with its capital at **Taipei** (tie PAY).

The Communists began transforming China into a communist country. They also formed an alliance with the Soviet Union. In the next lesson, you will read how China supported its communist neighbor, North Korea, in the Korean War.

Mao and the Communists unified the country and improved the standard of living, especially for the poor. However, these improvements came at a cost. Mao's government took away democratic freedoms, including freedom of speech and religion. It invaded China's neighbor to the southwest, Tibet, forcing its leader to flee.

Mao's attempt to modernize China, "The Great Leap Forward," turned out to be a costly step backwards for China's economy. Like the Soviet Union in the 1930s, China tried to turn its farms into collectives. But the collectives were badly planned and badly run. The result was famine. A more serious attempt to change China was the **Cultural Revolution,** which you will read about in the next section.

> On his visit to China in 1972, U.S. President Richard Nixon shakes hands with China's leader, Mao Zedong.

Taiwan remained a problem for the People's Republic. After the communist takeover of mainland China, Taiwan took China's place in the United Nations, an organization that promoted peace. As it prospered, Taiwan maintained its independence. But the People's Republic claimed that Taiwan belonged to China.

In 1971 the United Nations dismissed Taiwan and invited the People's Republic of China to take its seat. In 1972, U.S. President **Richard Nixon** went to China and met with Mao. He hoped to improve relations between the United States and China. During this period, China had little to do with the Soviet Union. The two countries had broken off their friendship by 1960. They had been fighting over the border between the two countries and disagreed on the aims of communism.

REVIEW What were two achievements of Mao's communist government in China? What were two failures? **Summarize**

> The People's Republic of China adopted this as their national flag in 1949.

578

The Cultural Revolution

In 1966 Mao Zedong decided to start a new phase of revolution. He called this phase the "Great Proletarian Cultural Revolution." The word **proletarian** means "of the working class." The movement soon became known simply as the Cultural Revolution.

Mao's stated aim was to clear China of all "counter-revolutionary" elements. By this he meant all remaining privileges that interfered with his vision of an equal society without classes. Mao's closest ally in launching the Cultural Revolution was his wife, **Jiang Qing** (JANG CHEENG). For more than a decade, Jiang was to be one of the most powerful people in China.

Mao encouraged young people to take up his revolutionary cause. Millions of students joined the "Red Guards." They left their studies and marched in the streets. They teased and attacked many older people, as well as people in authority. Teachers and party officials came under attack, as did anyone who seemed to have a high standard of living. However, anyone opposed to the actions of the Red Guard could be seen as a counter-revolutionary element.

Soon, millions of people found their lives turned upside down. Attacks on older people and the well-educated became violent. Many people died.

Nien Cheng was a fairly wealthy resident of Shanghai in 1966. Because of her wealth, Nien Cheng was seen by the Red Guard as a privileged, counter-revolutionary element. She became a target of the Cultural Revolution. She later wrote about her experiences, describing the Red Guards in 1966:

> *"Red Guards were stopping buses, distributing leaflets, lecturing the passengers, and punishing those whose clothes they disapproved of. . . . On the sidewalks, the Red Guards led the people to shout slogans. Each group of Red Guards was accompanied by drums and gongs and . . . Mao's portrait."*

Nien Cheng was put in prison without any formal charge. She remained there for more than six years.

REVIEW What was the Cultural Revolution?
Main Idea and Details

▶ **In 1971, during the Cultural Revolution, China marked the 22-year anniversary of the Communist Revolution. This rally was held at the Gate of Heavenly Peace in Beijing.**

The Last Years

The Cultural Revolution continued for a decade. Schools were closed and students were sent to the countryside to do farm work. The army, backed by Mao, took control of China.

When Mao died in 1976, the Cultural Revolution came to an end. Jiang Qing held on to power until 1978, but she was

▶ **Jiang Qing was a cultural leader and spokeswoman.**

then put on trial and imprisoned. Leaders with different ideas for China then took power. Some of these leaders had been targets of the Cultural Revolution themselves.

REVIEW What was the effect of the Cultural Revolution on China? ↻ **Cause and Effect**

Summarize the Lesson

- **1911** China became a republic when the emperor was overthrown.
- **1949** Mao Zedong and the communists came to power after winning the civil war.
- **1966** The Cultural Revolution began.
- **1976** Mao Zedong died, and the Cultural Revolution came to an end.

LESSON 2 ▸ REVIEW

Check Facts and Main Ideas

1. ↻ **Cause and Effect** On a separate piece of paper, fill in the chart below by listing causes and effects.

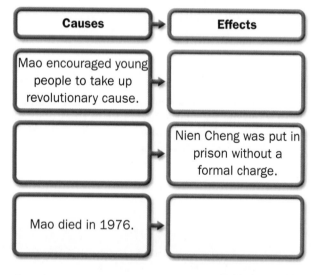

Causes	→	Effects
Mao encouraged young people to take up revolutionary cause.	→	
	→	Nien Cheng was put in prison without a formal charge.
Mao died in 1976.	→	

2. What political parties fought for control of China during the civil war of the late 1940s?

3. Who was Jiang Qing and what was her role in China's history?

4. What details can you provide to support the statement "The twentieth century was an era of revolution in China"?

5. **Critical Thinking:** *Detect Bias* Do you think you could believe everything the communist leaders in Beijing said about the government of Taiwan? Could you believe everything Taiwan's leaders said about the People's Republic of China? Explain your answer.

Link to ∞ Mathematics

Learn with Fractions Find the population of the United States and that of the People's Republic of China in a current almanac. To make the numbers easier to work with, round each figure to the nearest hundred million. Make a fraction like the model below:

$$\frac{\text{population of the United States}}{\text{population of China}}$$

Reduce the fraction to its lowest terms.

Mao Zedong
1893–1976

Mao was born a peasant. At the age of five, he was sent to work in rice fields. Two years later, he was allowed to go to school. Mao loved to read. He especially liked traditional Chinese novels about heroes who rebelled against their unfair rulers. Mao was a good student. However, his strict father made him quit school when he was 13 to return to farming.

In 1913 Mao attended a teacher's training school. There he became politically active. He joined in protests against the government.

BIOFACT

During the Cultural Revolution, people wore badges showing a picture of Mao. Some badges even glowed in the dark!

When the Russian Revolution broke out, Mao adopted Marxism. In 1921 he became the founder of the Chinese Communist Party. Mao believed that communism would take power away from landowners and other privileged people. He claimed that communism would help poor rural peasants. In 1927 Mao showed his confidence in the peasants in China:

"[S]everal hundred million peasants will rise like a mighty storm, like a hurricane, a force so swift and violent that no power, however great, will be able to hold it back."

All the peasants needed was a leader. Mao became that leader. After the 1949 revolution, he also became the leader of China.

Learn from Biographies

What events in Mao's life first reveal his political beliefs as an adult?

For more information, go online to *Meet the People* at **www.sfsocialstudies.com**.

1950 1960 1970

1953
The Korean War ends.

1950
The Korean War begins.

1965
The United States sends troops to Vietnam.

1975
North Vietnam takes over South Vietnam.

The Cold War Heats Up

PREVIEW

Focus on the Main Idea
The Cold War became a "hot" war in Korea and Vietnam.

PLACES
North Korea
South Korea
Indochina
North Vietnam
South Vietnam
Cambodia
Laos
Hanoi

PEOPLE
Ho Chi Minh
John F. Kennedy
Lyndon Johnson
Robert MacNamara

VOCABULARY
guerrilla
détente

TERMS
Viet Cong
domino effect
Vietnamization

EVENTS
Tet Offensive

▶ These "dog tags" belonged to a U.S. soldier during the Vietnam War.

You Are There

December 3, 1950

Dear Aunt Rosa,

I'm sorry I missed this year's Thanksgiving dinner. I hope the feast was delicious.

We got here just in time for the hottest summer Korea has had in years. The rains are supposed to help cool things off, but it was also a very dry summer.

We were supposed to get six weeks of training when we got here. But instead, they sent us into the field almost immediately.

Over Thanksgiving we were involved in some heavy fighting. We had a lot of casualties. Even worse was the rumor I heard that we were not just fighting the North Koreans, but the Chinese too.

They used to tell us we'd be out of here by Christmas. I'm starting to doubt it.

Say hi to Uncle Julio and the kids.

Your nephew,

Juan

Cause and Effect
As you read, look for effects of the wars in Korea and Vietnam on the United States.

The Korean War

In the previous lesson, you read that China became a communist nation under the leadership of Mao Zedong in 1949. Soon Asia, like Europe, became a battleground in the Cold War.

Since the end of World War II, Korea, a country to the southeast of China, had been a divided nation. The communists had taken control of the north. They were allied with the Soviet Union. Non-communists ruled in the south.

On June 25, 1950, North Korea launched an invasion of South Korea. President Harry S. Truman immediately requested action from the United Nations. In response, the United Nations agreed to support a military operation to help stop the invasion. However, the United States provided most of the equipment and troops.

President Truman appointed World War II hero Douglas MacArthur as the UN commander in Korea. MacArthur's troops made a brilliant landing on the west coast of South Korea. MacArthur's troops drove the North Korean army almost to the Chinese border.

China feared attack. They sent an army into North Korea against the UN troops. Soon the UN troops were forced to retreat.

General MacArthur and President Truman disagreed about how to fight the war. Truman and his advisers wanted to fight a limited war, not a total, all-out war. But MacArthur wanted to extend the war into China to win complete victory. In April 1951, Truman replaced MacArthur with another general.

In 1953 North Korea agreed to an armistice. The fighting stopped, but North and South Korea never officially signed a treaty to end the war.

REVIEW What event prompted U.S. and UN troops to fight a war in Korea?
🔄 Cause and Effect

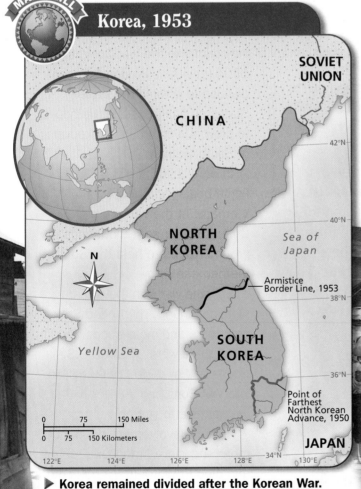

MAP SKILL Korea, 1953

Korea remained divided after the Korean War.

MAP SKILL Use Latitude and Longitude
What was the latitude line that divided Korea?

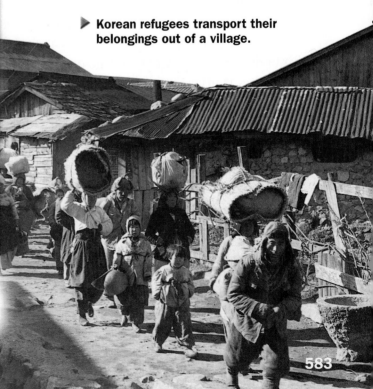

▶ **Korean refugees transport their belongings out of a village.**

583

The Vietnam War

The Korean War forced U.S. leaders to focus on the spread of communism in Asia. The war also showed that China was willing to fight for its communist neighbors.

A country just south of China—Vietnam—seemed to have much in common with Korea. Before 1954 Vietnam had been part of Indochina, a French colony. In 1954 the French lost this colony in a war against the Vietnamese people. A peace conference split Vietnam into two countries: a communist North Vietnam and a non-communist South Vietnam.

Unlike Korea, North Vietnam had a group of communist guerrillas, or hit-and-run fighters. The guerrillas were called the Viet Cong and they lived and fought mostly in South Vietnam. The Viet Cong and the North Vietnamese leader, Ho Chi Minh (HOH CHEE MIN), were determined to bring communist rule to the south.

The Granger Collection

▶ **An American soldier helps an elderly Vietnamese woman during the Vietnam War.**

U.S. President Dwight D. Eisenhower promised to help South Vietnam fight against communism. The president sent military advisers to build up South Vietnam's army and air force. In the early 1960s, President John F. Kennedy continued this policy and increased the number of advisers.

Meanwhile, South Vietnam's government was losing control of the country to the Viet Cong. In 1964 President Lyndon Johnson decided to commit the United States on a larger scale. He hoped to prevent a communist takeover of South Vietnam.

In early 1965 the U.S. Air Force began bombing North Vietnam. At the same time, the United States sent thousands of ground troops to help the South Vietnamese army.

Still, the war with the communists continued. The United States sent more and more troops. By 1966 there were 270,000 U.S. troops and by 1967, half a million. The Viet Cong and the North Vietnamese fought on.

As U.S. involvement deepened, more and more Americans fought and died in Vietnam. Opposition to the war began to surface in the United States.

Literature and Social Studies

The Clay Marble

Minfong Ho wrote about the terrible suffering of Cambodian children in the 1970s in *The Clay Marble*. Cambodia is a country in Southeast Asia. It is next to Vietnam. Fighting in the Vietnam War stretched into Cambodia. In this passage, a little girl wonders where her mother is after they have been forced to separate.

....

If only I could climb up this tree to the moon, I thought, drowsily, and curl up against its smooth curve, how comfortable I'd be tonight. Or I could hang on to it as it swept across the night sky, and search down far below for my mother.

President Johnson explained that the United States had to fight in Vietnam because of the **domino effect.** When dominoes are lined up and one domino falls, it knocks over the next domino, which knocks over the domino next to it. This continues until all the dominoes have fallen. President Johnson believed that if one country in Southeast Asia fell to communism, soon all of the countries in that region would fall.

By 1967 protests against U.S. involvement in the Vietnam War heated up all over the United States. In October a demonstration against the war brought 50,000 protesters to Washington, D.C. Antiwar protest activity became widespread on college campuses.

Television brought the Vietnam War into people's living rooms. Many Americans opposed the U.S. bombing of North Vietnam. President

► **This early protest against the Vietnam War took place in November 1965.**

Johnson hoped the bombing would convince North Vietnam to talk about peace.

REVIEW What was the domino effect, and why was it used to explain U.S. involvement in Vietnam? **Main Idea and Details**

HERE AND THERE

War in Algeria

At the same time that the United States was getting involved with Vietnam, France was losing its hold on Algeria. Like Vietnam, Algeria had been a French colony since the 1880s. Algerians formed an armed group to resist the French in 1954. This group carried out attacks on French colonists. The French responded by sending more troops. By 1959 the French president stated that Algerians should be given the right to decide their own future. Peace talks began in 1961. Algeria won its independence in 1962.

► **This ballot was used by Algerians to vote whether or not Algeria should become an independent nation.**

► **These Algerian troops fought for independence from the French.**

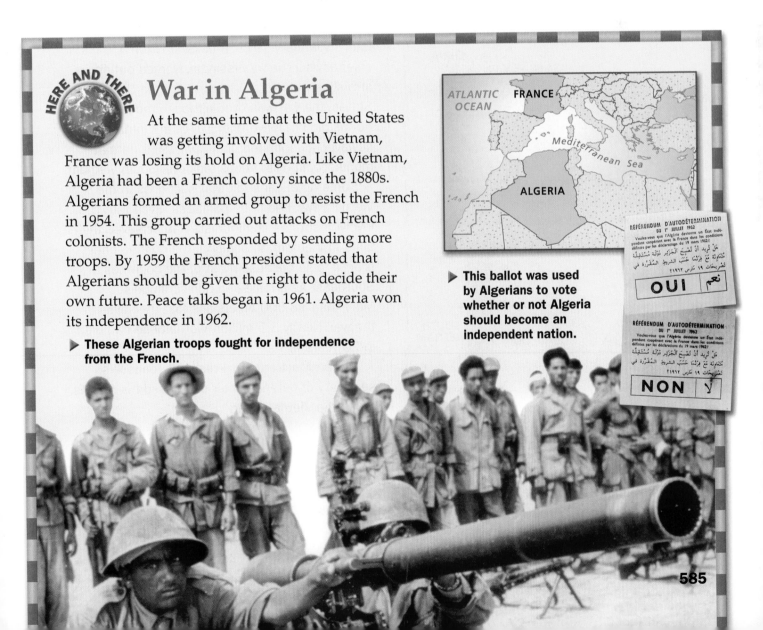

585

The War's Final Chapter

In 1968 the Viet Cong and North Vietnamese launched the **Tet Offensive.** This series of battles across South Vietnam showed that the North Vietnamese were a stronger opponent than the Americans had realized. His popularity damaged, President Johnson decided not to run for reelection. Richard Nixon became president in 1969. He had a plan to reduce the U.S. role in the Vietnam War. His plan was called **Vietnamization,** which turned over most of the ground fighting to the South Vietnamese Army. The number of American troops in the war dropped after 1969. The United States and North Vietnam were now conducting peace talks.

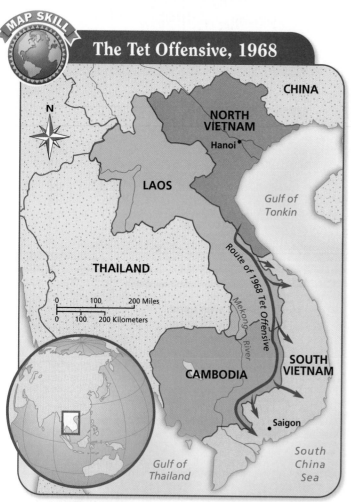

The Tet Offensive, 1968

▶ The Tet Offensive was a turning point in the Vietnam War.

MAP SKILL Trace Movement on Maps
In which direction did the North Vietnamese move during the Tet Offensive?

However, the United States continued to bomb North Vietnam heavily. The United States also extended the fighting into **Cambodia,** South Vietnam's neighbor.

The protests in the United States continued. In May 1970, a demonstration at Kent State University in Ohio turned tragic. National Guard troops sent there to stop the protests fired on students and killed four of them. That May, college campuses exploded in protest.

By 1972 the number of American ground troops fell to about 70,000. However, the United States continued to bomb North Vietnam, Cambodia, and **Laos** from the air. In December 1972 the United States launched the Christmas bombing of **Hanoi** and other cities in Vietnam. Many parts of Hanoi, including the airport, were destroyed.

The bombings in December would be the last major U.S. military action in Vietnam. One month later, in January 1973, President Nixon and his chief adviser, Henry Kissinger, worked out an armistice with North Vietnam. For the United States, the war was over, although the last U.S. troops did not leave until 1975. In Vietnam, however, it continued until April 1975. In that month, communist troops took over South Vietnam.

Some Americans felt that sacrifices in the Vietnam War had been pointless. Even with U.S. involvement, the communists had achieved their aims in Vietnam. In addition, the domino effect proved false because most of the countries in Southeast Asia remained non-communist. More than 58,000 Americans lost their lives in the war. Nearly 3.5 million Vietnamese had died in 20 years of war.

Robert MacNamara, President Johnson's secretary of defense, later expressed his regrets about the Vietnam War:

> *"We . . . acted according to what we thought were the principles . . . of this nation. We were wrong. We were terribly wrong."*

As U.S. involvement in the Vietnam War wound down, foreign relations were changing with other communist nations. Nixon and Kissinger started a period of **détente,** (day TAHNT) or the relaxation of tensions, with the Soviet Union and China. However, while relations improved, the nuclear arms race—and the Cold War—continued.

Express Newspapers/The Granger Collection

REVIEW Do you think that the United States should or should not have become involved in the Vietnam War? Explain your answer.
Draw Conclusions

Summarize the Lesson

- **1950** The Korean War began when North Korea invaded South Korea.
- **1953** An armistice ended the fighting in Korea.
- **1965** The United States sent troops to help South Vietnam fight against the communists.
- **1975** North Vietnam took over South Vietnam.

▶ **A U.S. government official greets former prisoners-of-war shortly after their release in February 1973.**

LESSON 3 REVIEW

Check Facts and Main Ideas

1. ↻ **Cause and Effect** On a separate piece of paper, fill in the chart below by listing a cause or effect.

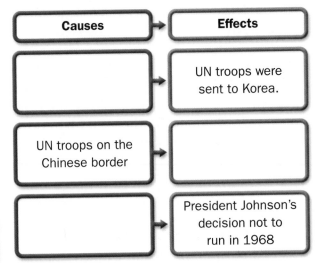

Causes	→	Effects
	→	UN troops were sent to Korea.
UN troops on the Chinese border	→	
	→	President Johnson's decision not to run in 1968

2. How did President Eisenhower help the government of South Vietnam fight against the Communists?

3. How did U.S. involvement in the war change under President Nixon?

4. How were the wars in Korea and Vietnam different from other disagreements with communist countries during the Cold War?

5. **Critical Thinking:** *Make Inferences* What events in other parts of the world would have convinced people that the domino effect would occur if Vietnam became a communist country?

Link to ⊶ Writing

Write a Letter to the Editor Suppose the year is 1967. Your city's newspaper has just printed an editorial supporting President Johnson's policy in the Vietnam War. Decide whether you support or oppose the war. Write a letter to the editor explaining your opinion for or against the war.

The Public Speaks Out

U.S. involvement in the Vietnam War divided the nation. It split the nation like no other issue since the Civil War, some 100 years earlier.

By 1967 public opinion was split over the war in Vietnam. Though many Americans still supported the war, protests against the war were increasing. Some demonstrations were peaceful. However, clashes between people of opposing views could be intense. As a result, the demonstrations sometimes grew violent. Many supporters of the war believed that some demonstrators were provoking the police and pro-war demonstrators on purpose.

On October 15, 1969, the largest antiwar protest in U.S. history took place. Millions of Americans skipped work or school to attend marches, demonstrations, religious services, and rallies. In Boston more than 100,000 people listened to speeches against the war. This protest was called the "Moratorium [strike] to End the War in Vietnam." Its goal was to send a strong message to President Richard Nixon. The protest suggested that a large number of ordinary American citizens wanted U.S. troops out of Vietnam.

However, for many Americans, supporting the war was a way of showing support for their country and for the American soldiers already in Vietnam.

"Then came the buildup in Vietnam and I watched the [poverty] program broken . . . and I knew that America would never invest the necessary funds or energies in . . . its poor . . . So I was increasingly compelled to see the war as an enemy of the poor and to attack it as such."

Martin Luther King, Jr., *civil rights activist, 1967*

> "China looms [appears] so high just beyond the frontiers that if South Vietnam went, it would . . . give the impression that the wave of the future in Southeast Asia was China and the Communists."
>
> **John F. Kennedy**, *U.S. President, 1963*

> "This war has already stretched the generation gap so wide that it threatens to pull the country apart."
>
> **Frank Church**, *U.S. senator, 1970*

> ". . . North Vietnam is carrying out . . . aggression against the South . . . The people of South Vietnam have chosen to resist this threat. At their request, the United States has taken its place beside them in their defensive struggle."
>
> **Aggression from the North,**
> *State Department White Paper on Vietnam, 1965*

Issues and You

Some Americans were against the idea of U.S. involvement in the Persian Gulf War of 1990–1991. Do some research to find out about the issues at stake and the reasons some Americans were against the use of force against Iraq. Write an essay to compare and contrast protests against the Gulf War with those against the Vietnam War.

1950   1955

1949
NATO formed.

1950–1953
Korean War

1948–1949
Berlin airlift

Chapter Summary

Target Skill

Cause and Effect

On a separate piece of paper, fill in three effects of communist aggression during the Cold War.

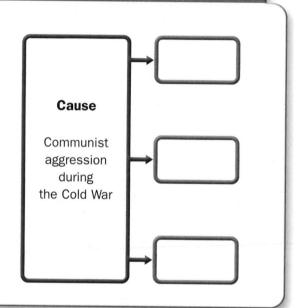

Cause

Communist aggression during the Cold War

Vocabulary

Match each word with the correct definition or description.

1 **containment** (p. 570)

2 **nuclear** (p. 569)

3 **détente** (p. 587)

4 **proletarian** (p. 579)

5 **guerrillas** (p. 584)

a. loosely organized fighters

b. relaxation of tensions

c. preventing the spread of communism

d. atomic

e. of the working class

People and Terms

Write a sentence explaining why each of the following people or terms was important in the events of the Cold War. You may use two or more in a single sentence.

1 John F. Kennedy (p. 572)

2 Cold War (p. 569)

3 NATO (p. 570)

4 Nikita Khrushchev (p. 572)

5 Chiang Kai-shek (p. 577)

6 Mao Zedong (p. 577)

7 People's Republic of China (p. 578)

8 Ho Chi Minh (p. 584)

9 Viet Cong (p. 584)

10 Vietnamization (p. 586)

1962
Cuban missile crisis

1965
United States sent troops to Vietnam.

1966
Cultural Revolution began in China.

1975
Last U.S. troops left Vietnam. North Vietnam took over South Vietnam.

1976
Mao Zedong died. Cultural Revolution ended.

Facts and Main Ideas

1. What happened to the World War II alliance of the Soviet Union, Great Britain, and the United States?

2. Name two political changes in the world between 1945 and 1950.

3. What U.S. president expanded military support for South Vietnam?

4. **Time Line** How long were U.S. troops in Vietnam?

5. **Main Idea** What were the two main sides in the Cold War?

6. **Main Idea** What were the two groups that fought for power during the civil war in China in the late 1940s?

7. **Main Idea** What were two "hot wars" during the Cold War?

8. **Critical Thinking:** *Make Inferences* Why do you think the Soviets were so eager to drive the Allies out of Berlin?

Apply Skills

Solve Complex Problems

Consider the following situation. Think how you might use the strategies presented on pages 574–575 of this chapter to find a solution. Then answer the questions.

You have just lost your backpack at school. You notice that one of your classmates has a backpack identical to the one you lost. When you ask him about the backpack, he says it was a gift from a relative.

1. Should you tell your teacher about the backpack? Why or why not?

2. What might be some consequences of confronting your classmate?

3. Can you think of some creative solutions other than (1) telling your teacher, or (2) confronting your classmate?

Write About History

1. **Write a journal entry** as someone who lives in the American zone of Berlin during the Berlin airlift. Write an entry describing the frequent arrival of airplanes bringing in supplies. Describe your feelings.

2. **Write a television news report** informing U.S. citizens about the Cuban missile crisis right after the crisis has ended.

3. **Write a paragraph** describing relations between South Korea and North Korea in the years since the end of the Korean War. You will need to research this topic before you write your paragraph.

Internet Activity

To get help with vocabulary, people, and terms, select dictionary, encyclopedia, or almanac from *Social Studies Library* at **www.sfsocialstudies.com.**

Over There

Broadway songwriter George M. Cohan (1878–1942) wrote "Over There" on April 7, 1917. This was the day after the United States entered the Great War. The song became the most popular song of the war. It later earned Cohan a special Congressional Medal. The song's opening notes imitate both a bugle and the bird call of a whippoorwill. To listeners the word "whippoorwill" suggested "Beat Kaiser Will"—that is, Kaiser Wilhelm II of Germany.

Words and Music by George M. Cohan

Review

Test Talk

Narrow the answer choices. Rule out answers you know are wrong.

Main Ideas and Vocabulary

TEST PREP

Read the passage below and use it to answer the questions that follow.

The twentieth century was a time of warfare. Imperialism, nationalism, and other forms of competition pushed European nations toward war. When the archduke of Austria-Hungary was assassinated in 1914, countries started mobilizing for war.

People expected the war to end quickly, but it did not. People called it the "Great War." <u>Casualties</u> were enormous. After the war, the Allies tried to make a peace that would prevent future wars. But they treated Germany harshly. Germany was told it would have to pay for the Allied war losses.

A new form of government appeared in Russia during the Great War. It was a communist government. In a communist system, everything is owned by the state. Under Lenin and Stalin, Russia became the Soviet Union.

Hard times from the Great Depression led to the rise of dictators in Germany and Italy. Military leaders took control of Japan. These three Axis Powers committed acts of <u>aggression</u>. These acts set the stage for World War II.

The Allies, led by the United States, Great Britain, and the Soviet Union, defeated the Axis Powers. After the war, they set up the United Nations to deal with future disagreements between countries.

The Soviet dictator, Stalin, wanted to spread communism worldwide. Mao Zedong led another communist country, China, after 1949.

Now the world experienced another kind of war. It was a cold war between communist and non-communist countries. This was mostly words and threats. However, "hot" wars flared in Korea and Vietnam during the Cold War.

1 According to the passage, what new kind of government played a major part in the politics of the twentieth century?
  A republic   **C** communist
  B royal   **D** council

2 In the passage the word *casualties* means—
  A easygoing manners
  B kindnesses
  C false remarks
  D killed or wounded soldiers

3 In the passage the word *aggression* means—
  A forceful taking   **C** generosity
  B concealment   **D** going backward

4 What is the main idea of this passage?
  A The Great War was brutal.
  B The United States has become very powerful.
  C The twentieth century was a time of warfare.
  D Russia had a revolution.

People and Terms

Match each person or term to its definition.

1. Triple Entente (p. 522)
2. Nicholas II (p. 522)
3. Georges Clemenceau (p. 536)
4. Central Powers (p. 527)
5. Oveta Culp Hobby (p. 552)
6. Nationalist Party (p. 577)

a. French leader during the Great War

b. group that removed the emperor and founded republic in China

c. ruler of Russia until 1917

d. head of the Women's Army Corps

e. alliance of Germany and Austria

f. alliance of Great Britain, France, and Russia

Apply Skills

Make Parallel Time Lines Create a poster displaying parallel time lines. Use events from your own life on one time line. Use public events on the other time line. Public events might include national events such as elections, weather events, or sports events.

You can use the tick marks on the time line to represent years, months, or weeks.

Write and Share

Honor Wartime Sacrifices The United States honors the people who make sacrifices during wartime. Many communities also have monuments and ceremonies to honor soldiers and civilian workers who contributed in times of war. Research ways in which your own community or state honors veterans. Write a paper on the subject and present it to your class. After presenting your paper, your class can break into small groups. Each group can then propose its own idea for a memorial or celebration in honor of veterans.

Read on Your Own

Look for books like these in your library.

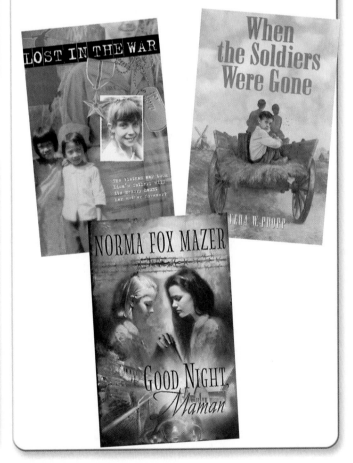

UNIT 7 Project

We Interrupt This Program

Participate in a "live" news conference from the past.

1 **Form** a group to present a special report about a historic event in this unit.

2 **Present** the event as breaking news. Focus on the event's significance in world history.

3 **Assign** jobs, including news anchors, government officials, reporters, and citizens.

4 **Write** a press release or a brief summary of the event and its significance.

5 **Create** a banner and bring in materials that help describe the event. You may choose to create a scenic background.

Internet Activity

Discover historic world events. Go to **www.sfsocialstudies.com/activities** and select your grade and unit.

New Nations and a New Century

How can you be a national citizen
and a global citizen?

Begin with a Primary Source

1950

1960

1970

1957
The European Economic
Community is created.

about 1960
Many sub-Saharan African
countries begin to gain
independence.

1967
The Six-Day War occurs
in the Middle East.

1973
The first global
oil crisis

Diana Ong's 2000 piece, *The Beat Goes On*, suggests the world's human diversity.

1980   1990   2000

1975
First personal computer

1989
Protest at Tiananmen Square

1991
Fall of the Soviet Union

1999 The euro is issued.

September 11, 2001
Terrorists attack the United States.

Meet the People

Mohandas Gandhi

1869–1948
Birthplace: Porbandar, India
Lawyer, writer, political and spiritual leader
- Leader of independence movement in India
- Promoted nonviolent resistance
- Assassinated in 1948 by religious extremist
- Influenced other world leaders, including Martin Luther King, Jr.

Rachel Carson

1907–1964
Birthplace: Springdale, Pennsylvania
Biologist, writer
- Worked for U.S. Fish and Wildlife Service
- Wrote *Silent Spring* (1962), which led to restrictions on pesticides
- Writings inspired creation of modern environmental movement

Mother Teresa of Calcutta

1910–1997
Birthplace: Skopje, Macedonia
Nun, missionary
- Roman Catholic nun, nurse, and teacher
- Founded the Missionaries of Charity in Calcutta, India, where she worked with the poor for more than 40 years
- Awarded the Nobel Peace Prize in 1979

Menachem Begin

1913–1992
Birthplace: Brest-Litovsk, Russia (present-day Belarus)
Military officer, political leader
- Served in Israeli parliament, 1949–1983
- Prime minister of Israel, 1977–1983
- Negotiated peace treaty between Israel and Egypt
- Shared 1978 Nobel Peace Price with Anwar el-Sadat

1860   1870   1880   1890   1900   1910   1920   1930

1869 • Mohandas Gandhi

1907 • Rachel Carson

1910 • Mother Teresa of Calcutta

1913 • Menachem Begin

1918 • Anwar el-Sadat

1922 • Julius Nyerere

Anwar el-Sadat

1918–1981

Birthplace: Mit Abu al-Kum, Egypt

Military officer, political leader

- President of Egypt, 1970–1981
- Negotiated peace treaty between Egypt and Israel
- Shared 1978 Nobel Peace Price with Menachem Begin
- Assassinated in 1981 by religious extremists

Julius Nyerere

1922–1999

Birthplace: Butiama, Tanganyika (present-day Tanzania)

Teacher, writer, political leader

- Led independence movement in Tanganyika
- Helped unite Tanganyika and Zanzibar to form Tanzania in 1964
- President of Tanzania, 1964–1984

Aung San Suu Kyi

1945–

Birthplace: Yangon (Rangoon), Myanmar (Burma)

Writer, human rights activist

- Leader of opposition to military dictatorship in Myanmar (Burma)
- Won 1991 Nobel Peace Prize for efforts to restore democracy in her country
- Awarded Presidential Medal of Freedom

Rigoberta Menchu

1959–

Birthplace: Chimel, Guatemala

Agricultural laborer, human rights activist

- Continued her father's fight for peace
- Activist for Indian rights in Guatemala
- Won 1992 Nobel Peace Prize for her efforts to achieve social justice for Guatemalan Indians

1940   1950   1960   1970   1980   1990   2000

1948

1964

1997

1992

1981

1999

1945 • Aung San Suu Kyi

1959 • Rigoberta Menchu

601

Reading Social Studies

New Nations

Draw Conclusions

A good reader puts together facts he or she reads and then creates a new idea, or a conclusion. Sometimes you may have more than one conclusion.

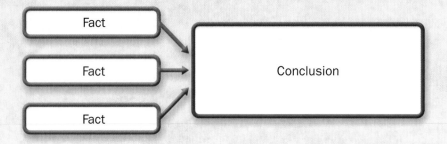

- Try to make a logical conclusion from the clues you have read.

- Use your own knowledge and experience to help you draw conclusions.

- Check to make sure that your conclusions make sense and are supported by the facts.

In this paragraph, the facts are highlighted in blue. The conclusion is in **boldface** type.

Jomo Kenyatta (JOH moh ken YAHT uh), the first leader of independent Kenya, studied in Great Britain. India's independence leader, Mohandas Gandhi (moh HAHN dahs GAHN dee), also studied law in Great Britain. Kwame Nkrumah (KWAH mee en KROO muh), the independence leader of Ghana, studied at American and British universities. **Many African and Asian independence leaders studied at universities in Western countries.**

Effects of Imperialism

European imperialism ended in most African and Asian nations more than 40 years ago. But people there are still experiencing the effects of imperialism. Sometimes these effects can be seen in the countries themselves.

You have read about some of the harsh rule of Europeans in Africa. Many colonial powers set up new economic and political systems. Some European countries did less to help their colonies prepare for independence than European countries did. Imperialist countries, such as Great Britain, took much of the wealth out of their colonies.

Nations in Africa and Asia have struggled to overcome the effects of these actions by European countries. Today, poverty and unstable governments in Africa can be partially traced back to imperialism.

On the other hand, Africans and Asians have gained some benefits from their former colonizers. Europeans helped many of their colonies set up universities. Two of these universities are located in Lagos, Nigeria, and Nairobi, Kenya. India has more than 8,000 universities and colleges.

Europeans also shared technology with Africans and Asians. You can see evidence of this in the skyscrapers of many African and Asian cities.

In India and other places, knowing the English language has been helpful. India is a huge land with many languages. The government encourages people to speak English as a second language. Knowledge of English has helped many Indians become successful in "hi-tech" industries such as computer software.

Use the reading strategy of drawing conclusions to respond to these items.

1 Explain why the following statement is or is *not* a good conclusion: "Imperialism affected the colonizing countries as much as their colonies."

2 Explain why the following statement is or is *not* a good conclusion: "The effects of European imperialism on Africa and Asia have been both harmful and beneficial."

3 List four facts that support the conclusion of this passage.

New Nations

Lesson 1

c. 1960
Africa
Many colonies in sub-Saharan Africa begin to gain independence from European powers.

1

Lesson 2

1967
West Bank
The Arab-Israeli conflict erupts into war.

2

Lesson 3

1989
Berlin
The gates to the Berlin Wall open, and communism crumbles.

3

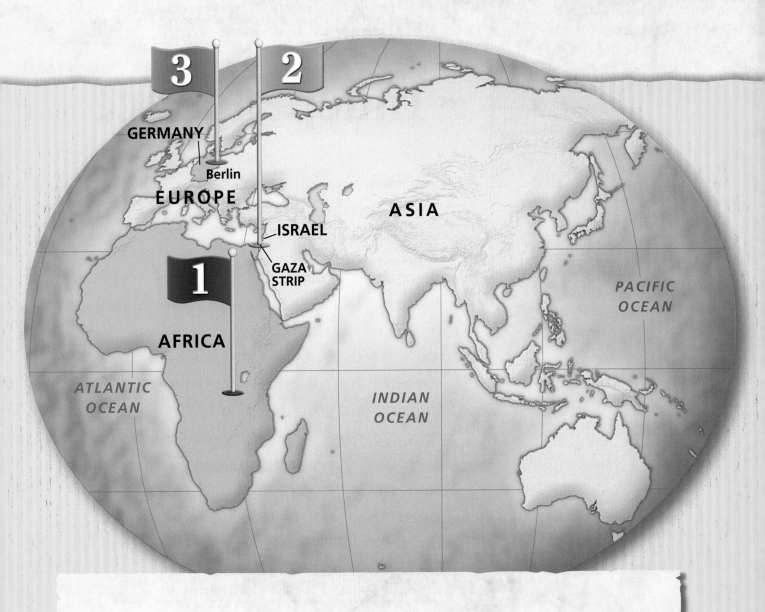

Why We Remember

You may have seen an old globe that your parents or grandparents used when they were in school. You would probably see names and borders that looked strange. In fact, since you were born, some nations have formed and others have vanished. From the world wars to the present, nations and governments changed from time to time. To understand where these nations came from, how they disappeared, or how they affect our lives today, we study history and other branches of social studies.

1940   2000

1947
India and
Pakistan gain
independence.

about 1960
Many sub-Saharan African nations
begin to gain independence from
European countries.

1997
China takes
control of
Hong Kong.

Independence

You Are There

Never has there been such an exciting
night. The skies above Nairobi explode
with fireworks. Crowds clap and roar
with each burst of color.

It's Kenya's independence day—December 12, 1963.
A gentle breeze brushes across your face. Near the Equator
in the highlands, Nairobi's weather is rather mild.

For longer than almost anyone can remember, the
British have been ruling the country. Your father and
mother worked for the Europeans, as did your grandparents and great-grandparents. Now Kenya will be truly free.
Tomorrow morning your schoolmaster will raise a new
flag. You will no longer sing "God Save the Queen."

Oh! Here comes the finale. The fireworks spell out
uhuru. In Swahili, this means "freedom!"

Draw Conclusions As you read, try to put facts
together to understand how former colonies became
independent nations.

▶ Hong Kong

▶ India

▶ Ghana

▶ Kenya

▶ South Africa

Decolonization

How did countries in sub-Saharan Africa such as Kenya gain independence? In Chapter 17, you read how European imperialists set up colonies in Africa, Asia, and elsewhere. After World War II, Africans began organizing into political groups to demand independence and fight for decolonization. Decolonization is the process of removing colonial rule, or control by another country.

Kwame Nkrumah (KWAH may neh KROO muh) was an independence leader in Ghana in western Africa. He and other Africans believed that freedom belonged to all people:

> *"Freedom is not something that one people can bestow on [give to] another as a gift. They claim it as their own and none can keep it from them."*

The path to freedom was different from country to country. As you read in Unit 7, colonies such as Algeria fought bitter wars of independence. By the 1950s, attitudes in Europe were changing. Great Britain had the most colonies in Africa. Now it was time to let them go.

Guinea and Ghana launched independence movements in 1950. But after 1960, decolonization and independence swept through sub-Saharan Africa. Kenya won its independence under the leadership of Jomo Kenyatta (JOH moh ken YAHT uh) in 1963. See the map on page 608 for independence dates of other African countries. By the mid-1970s, most of Africa was free of European imperialism.

REVIEW Why was it important when Guinea and Ghana launched independence movements in 1950? ⟳ Draw Conclusions

▶ Tanzania

▶ Zimbabwe

Challenges

In the early 1960s, many nations in sub-Saharan Africa were winning their independence from European countries. Some experienced decolonization very quickly. However, setting up strong governments proved difficult and challenging.

New African countries looked to their leaders for help. Julius Nyerere (nyuh RAIR ay) guided present-day Tanzania (tan zuh NEE uh) to independence from Great Britain beginning in 1961. Read more about Nyerere in the biography on page 613.

As you read in Unit 6, people living in the Belgian Congo had struggled under harsh colonial rule. Belgium gave little aid and training to the Congo army and government.

After the Congo won independence, the wealthy province of Katanga broke away from the Congo. The Congo then asked the United Nations (UN) for help. As a result, a UN army later forced Katanga to return to the Congo.

In 1965 Mobutu Sese Seko took control of the Congo in a coup d'état (KOO day TAH), or overthrow of the government. But the people of the Congo still were not free, as Mobutu ruled as a dictator for more than 30 years.

Some African nations had strong, capable leaders after decolonization, but others did not. Conflicts continued among some groups in sub-Saharan African nations. You will read more about some of these conflicts in Chapter 22.

REVIEW How did Mobutu disappoint hopes for a free Congo? ⟳ Draw Conclusions

▶ Jomo Kenyatta became Kenya's first president after independence was achieved.

Southern Africa

In the 1700s, many Europeans had started to settle in southern Africa. The British colony of Southern Rhodesia attracted many settlers.

In the 1960s, white Southern Rhodesians asked Great Britain for independence. Whites made up only 5 percent of the population but held the most farmland and controlled the government. Great Britain refused to recognize independence until Southern Rhodesia had a black majority in the government. In 1962 a constitution denied civil rights to blacks. By this time, many blacks had already joined groups to fight against the white government. In 1965 Southern Rhodesia's new white prime minister, Ian Smith declared independence.

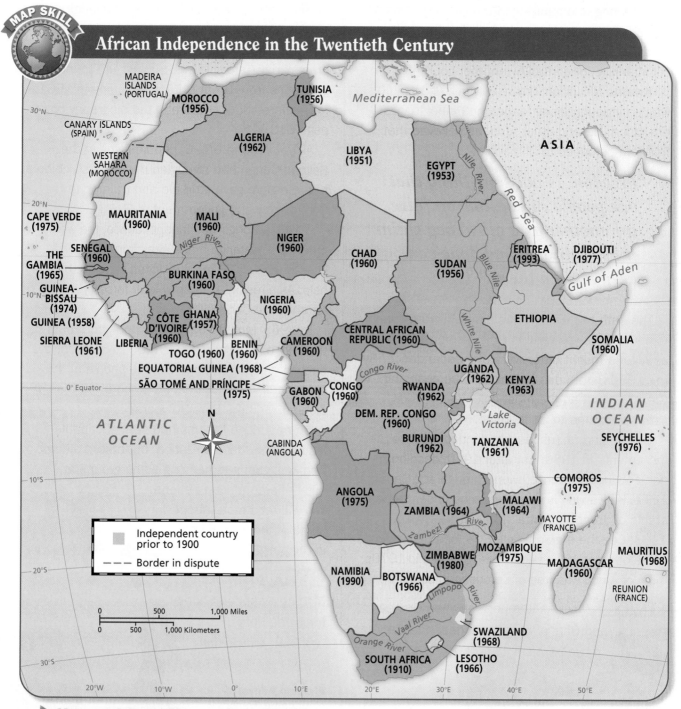

African Independence in the Twentieth Century

MADEIRA ISLANDS (PORTUGAL)
MOROCCO (1956)
TUNISIA (1956)
Mediterranean Sea
CANARY ISLANDS (SPAIN)
30°N
ALGERIA (1962)
LIBYA (1951)
EGYPT (1953)
ASIA
WESTERN SAHARA (MOROCCO)
Nile River
Red Sea
20°N
CAPE VERDE (1975)
MAURITANIA (1960)
MALI (1960)
NIGER (1960)
CHAD (1960)
SUDAN (1956)
ERITREA (1993)
DJIBOUTI (1977)
SENEGAL (1960)
Niger River
Blue Nile
Gulf of Aden
THE GAMBIA (1965)
10°N
GUINEA-BISSAU (1974)
BURKINA FASO (1960)
NIGERIA (1960)
GUINEA (1958)
CÔTE D'IVOIRE (1960)
GHANA (1957)
SIERRA LEONE (1961)
LIBERIA
TOGO (1960)
BENIN (1960)
CAMEROON (1960)
CENTRAL AFRICAN REPUBLIC (1960)
White Nile
ETHIOPIA
SOMALIA (1960)
EQUATORIAL GUINEA (1968)
SÃO TOMÉ AND PRÍNCIPE (1975)
0° Equator
GABON (1960)
CONGO (1960)
Congo River
UGANDA (1962)
RWANDA (1962)
KENYA (1963)
DEM. REP. CONGO (1960)
Lake Victoria
INDIAN OCEAN
ATLANTIC OCEAN
N
CABINDA (ANGOLA)
BURUNDI (1962)
TANZANIA (1961)
SEYCHELLES (1976)
10°S
COMOROS (1975)
ANGOLA (1975)
ZAMBIA (1964)
MALAWI (1964)
MAYOTTE (FRANCE)
Zambezi River
Independent country prior to 1900
Border in dispute
ZIMBABWE (1980)
MOZAMBIQUE (1975)
MADAGASCAR (1960)
MAURITIUS (1968)
NAMIBIA (1990)
BOTSWANA (1966)
Limpopo River
REUNION (FRANCE)
20°S
0 500 1,000 Miles
0 500 1,000 Kilometers
Vaal River
SWAZILAND (1968)
Orange River
30°S
SOUTH AFRICA (1910)
LESOTHO (1966)
20°W 10°W 0° 10°E 20°E 30°E 40°E 50°E

► Many sub-Saharan African nations gained independence in the twentieth century.

MAP SKILL Observe Change Through Maps *Compare the 1914 colonization map on page 491 with this map. What differences do you observe?*

Whites and blacks reached a settlement with the help of the British in 1979. National elections brought a black majority to power and a new prime minister, **Robert Mugabe** (moo GAH bay), to lead the country in 1980. Southern Rhodesia's name was then changed to **Zimbabwe** (zihm BAH bway).

South Africa has also had a long history of conflict between whites and blacks. Dutch settlers called Boers (later called Afrikaners) first came to the region in the 1600s. British settlers followed. These whites settled among the black Africans who were already living there, and they gave few rights to blacks. Blacks could not vote and only some owned land.

South Africa became independent in 1910. In 1948 an Afrikaner political party came to power. The government passed laws to **segregate,** or separate, whites from blacks and Asians. Blacks were forced to live apart from whites and go to separate schools. This system of laws was called **apartheid** (uh PART hayt), which means "apartness" in the language of the Afrikaners.

Political groups that had formed years before increased their protests against apartheid. One group, the African National Congress (ANC), was led by **Nelson Mandela.** In 1960 the South African government banned these groups and later imprisoned Mandela. Many young people became active in the protest against apartheid. In 1976 government forces killed 25 black children at a protest in the town of Soweto.

After the incident in Soweto, few nations wanted to continue trade relations with South Africa because of apartheid. In the 1980s, many countries placed **sanctions**, or penalties, on South Africa. For example, the United States and many European countries refused to buy South African goods. They hoped that sanctions would make the South African government do away with apartheid.

REVIEW Why did many countries place sanctions on South Africa? ↻ Draw Conclusions

A New Era

In 1990 South Africa's president, F.W. de Klerk, realized that the international boycott caused by sanctions was hurting South Africa. He also feared that apartheid would lead to civil war. As a result, he released Nelson Mandela from prison after 27 years. The two men held talks and made plans to end apartheid.

In 1994 all South Africans gained full voting rights, and Nelson Mandela was elected president. South Africa adopted a constitution that reflected many of Mandela's own ideas:

> *"I have fought against white domination and . . . against black domination. I have cherished the ideal of a democratic and free society in which all persons live together in harmony and with equal opportunities."*

Mandela helped reshape South Africa into a democracy. He served as president until 1999.

REVIEW Why was Mandela's election as president of South Africa important? ↻ Draw Conclusions

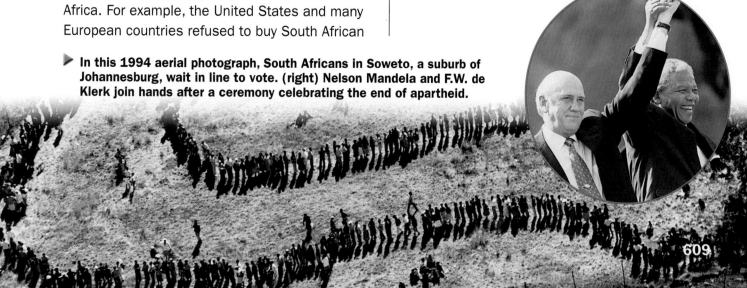

▶ **In this 1994 aerial photograph, South Africans in Soweto, a suburb of Johannesburg, wait in line to vote. (right) Nelson Mandela and F.W. de Klerk join hands after a ceremony celebrating the end of apartheid.**

609

East and Southeast Asia

Nations in East and Southeast Asia and the Pacific gained independence from European countries too. As in Africa, these nations gained independence in different ways.

In the 1930s, Japan took control of former European colonies. However, when the Allies defeated Japan in 1945, European countries tried to take back their former colonies in Asia.

In Chapter 20, you read about the long and bitter war in Vietnam. This war started as a struggle between the communists and France after World War II. France was forced to give up its control of Indochina (Vietnam) in 1954.

The British controlled Myanmar (Burma), Malaya, Singapore, and other lands in Southeast Asia. These countries became independent in the two decades following World War II. However, Malaya and some other states later joined to form the new nation of Malaysia.

The Netherlands had long controlled the rich island country of Indonesia. Indonesia fought for and won its independence in 1945. For independence dates of other countries in South and Southeast Asia, see the map below.

In Chapter 17, you read how Western imperialists took control of parts of China during the nineteenth century. In the twentieth century, the People's Republic of China was determined to end all foreign control of Chinese territory. **Hong Kong** had been held by the British for more than 150 years. In 1997 Great Britain turned over Hong Kong to China. Portugal gave its colony of Macao back to China in 1999. Both Hong Kong and Macao became special administrative regions of China. European imperialism disappeared from this region.

▶ **At a ceremony just before the transfer of Hong Kong to China, Chinese President Jiang Zemin welcomes Prince Charles of Great Britain.**

REVIEW How did the end of European imperialism change South and Southeast Asia? Draw Conclusions

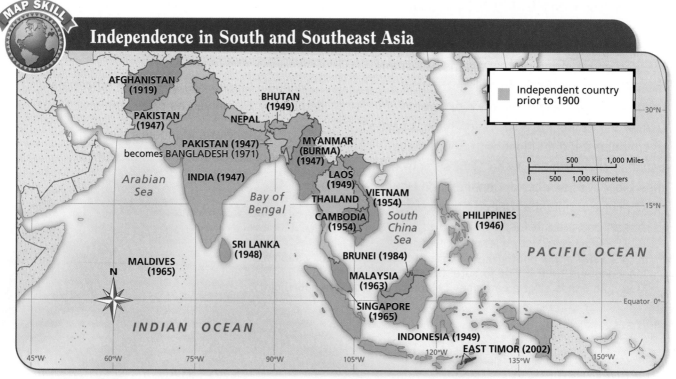

Independence in South and Southeast Asia

Independent country prior to 1900

AFGHANISTAN (1919)

PAKISTAN (1947)

NEPAL

BHUTAN (1949)

PAKISTAN (1947) becomes BANGLADESH (1971)

MYANMAR (BURMA) (1947)

INDIA (1947)

LAOS (1949)

Arabian Sea

Bay of Bengal

THAILAND

VIETNAM (1954)

CAMBODIA (1954)

South China Sea

PHILIPPINES (1946)

PACIFIC OCEAN

SRI LANKA (1948)

MALDIVES (1965)

BRUNEI (1984)

MALAYSIA (1963)

SINGAPORE (1965)

INDONESIA (1949)

EAST TIMOR (2002)

INDIAN OCEAN

0   500   1,000 Miles
0   500   1,000 Kilometers

N

45°W   60°W   75°W   90°W   105°W   120°W   135°W   150°W

30°N   15°N   Equator 0°

▶ **Which South and Southeast Asian nations were independent before 1900?**

MAP SKILL Use a Map Key *Which country became independent in the twenty-first century?*

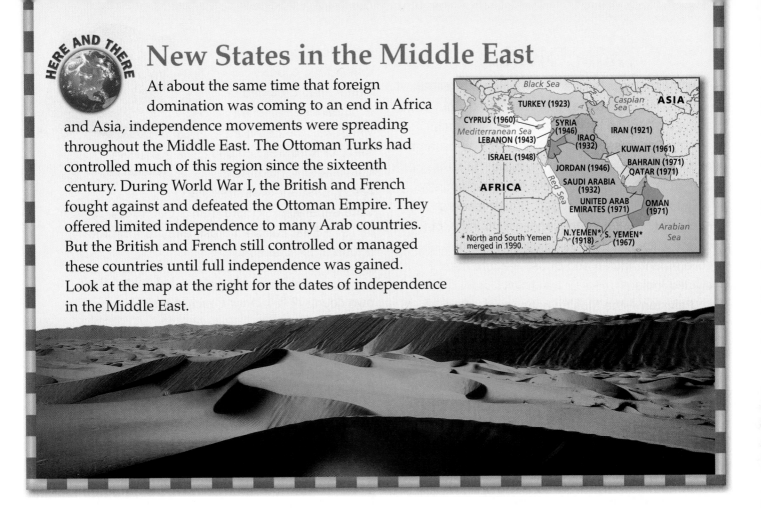

New States in the Middle East

HERE AND THERE

At about the same time that foreign domination was coming to an end in Africa and Asia, independence movements were spreading throughout the Middle East. The Ottoman Turks had controlled much of this region since the sixteenth century. During World War I, the British and French fought against and defeated the Ottoman Empire. They offered limited independence to many Arab countries. But the British and French still controlled or managed these countries until full independence was gained. Look at the map at the right for the dates of independence in the Middle East.

Map labels:
- TURKEY (1923)
- CYPRUS (1960)
- SYRIA (1946)
- LEBANON (1943)
- IRAQ (1932)
- IRAN (1921)
- KUWAIT (1961)
- ISRAEL (1948)
- BAHRAIN (1971)
- QATAR (1971)
- JORDAN (1946)
- SAUDI ARABIA (1932)
- UNITED ARAB EMIRATES (1971)
- OMAN (1971)
- N.YEMEN* (1918)
- S. YEMEN* (1967)
- ASIA
- AFRICA
- Black Sea
- Caspian Sea
- Mediterranean Sea
- Red Sea
- Arabian Sea

*North and South Yemen merged in 1990.

The Indian Subcontinent

In Unit 6, you read that India was a colony of Great Britain. The Indian National Congress, or "the Congress," opposed British rule. At first, the Congress attracted people of all religions. However, some Muslim members believed that Hindus were dominating the Congress. In 1906 many Muslims broke away and formed the All-India Muslim League.

About 1920 **Mohandas Gandhi** became the leader of India's independence movement. Gandhi knew that Great Britain could rule only as long as Indians cooperated. He urged people to stop buying British goods such as cloth and paying taxes on goods such as salt. Gandhi, whom the people called "Mahatma," or "great soul," wrote:

> *"In my humble opinion, noncooperation with evil is as much a duty as cooperation with good."*

Gandhi's methods of peaceful protest for freedom and democracy became known as nonviolent civil disobedience. **Civil disobedience** is the refusal to obey or cooperate with unjust laws. Gandhi's movement attracted millions of followers in India. In the 1960s, Martin Luther King, Jr., used similar methods to help gain equality for black Americans in the Civil Rights Movement in the United States.

REVIEW Why is nonviolent civil disobedience used to take action? ↻ **Draw Conclusions**

▶ Here, Gandhi is making cotton thread to weave his own clothes.

India Divides

Another Congress leader was Muhammed Ali Jinnah. He argued that the Congress did not pay enough attention to Muslim concerns. Jinnah left the Congress in the early 1930s and became head of the All-India Muslim League. He later demanded that Muslims have their own country.

Before World War II ended, British leaders had agreed to grant independence to India, but only if India's leaders could agree on a form of government. Indian and British leaders then divided India.

Pakistan —the Muslim nation that Jinnah had wanted—was created in August 1947. India became independent on the same day. However, dividing the country caused chaos and violence to break out. As a result, millions of Hindus left Pakistan for India, and millions of Muslims left India for Pakistan.

In 1948 Gandhi was shot and killed by a Hindu extremist. Jawaharlal Nehru (juh wah hur LAHL NAY roo), who had worked closely with Gandhi, then led India to become the democratic country Gandhi had dreamed of.

Jinnah led Pakistan, which was created from parts of northwestern and northeastern India. As a result, East and West Pakistan were separated by more than 1,000 miles. In 1971 East Pakistan broke away to form the nation of Bangladesh.

▶ Pakistan's national flag

REVIEW Why did Muslims in India want their own country? 🔄 Draw Conclusions

Summarize the Lesson

- **1947** India and Pakistan became independent when India was divided.
- **about 1960** Many sub-Saharan African colonies began to gain their independence from the European powers.
- **1997** Hong Kong became a special administrative region of China.

LESSON 1 REVIEW

Check Facts and Main Ideas

1. 🔄 **Draw Conclusions** On a separate piece of paper, fill in the missing facts.

```
[                    ]
        ↓
[ Hong Kong and Macao    ]   →   [ Independence
  became special              from European
  administrative regions       Powers was
  of China in the 1990s. ]     achieved in
                               different ways
[                    ]   →     and at different
                               times in sub-
                               Saharan Africa
                               and Asia. ]
```

2. How did black South Africans and Western countries react to apartheid?

3. Why did Gandhi believe that nonviolent civil disobedience was the way to gain independence for India?

4. Name four new nations that have formed in Asia and sub-Saharan Africa since World War II.

5. **Critical Thinking: *Fact or Opinion*** Find one fact and one opinion on page 607.

Link to 🔗 Geography

Use a Map Look at the map on page 610. How is the Indian subcontinent separated from the rest of Asia?

Julius Nyerere

1922–1999

Julius Nyerere was born in Tanganyika (present-day Tanzania), which at the time was ruled by the British. Nyerere attended Tanganyika's only high school, where he soon became a top student.

Nyerere eventually won an academic scholarship to study history and economics at the University of Edinburgh in Scotland. He became the first Tanganyikan ever to study in Great Britain. While in Scotland, he began to plan his future:

"Tanganyika's politics must be the politics of independence."

Nyerere became one of the leaders of the independence movement in sub-Saharan Africa. In 1955 he gave a powerful speech before the United Nations on the subject of independence. In 1961 Tanganyika achieved independence, and Nyerere became prime minister. When Tanganyika and Zanzibar formed the country of Tanzania in 1964, Nyerere was elected president.

Nyerere's vision for Tanzania was based on ideas of equality. Some of these ideas were rooted in socialism. Under his principle of *ujamaa,* or "familyhood," the government took control of industries and tried to improve harvests by forcing small farms to combine together. However, Nyerere's economic plans failed.

When Nyerere came to power, most Tanzanians could not read or write, and no national language existed. Tanzania was one of the world's poorest countries. Poverty and violence constantly threatened civil war. In 1985, after serving as president for four five-year terms, Nyerere resigned. By the end of his presidency, about 90 percent of Tanzanians could read and write. Nyerere's promotion of the Swahili language resulted in it becoming the country's national language. His free education policy has enabled more Tanzanians to read and write than the people of most other African nations.

BIOFACT

Nyerere translated two Shakespeare plays, Julius Caesar *and* The Merchant of Venice, *into Swahili.*

Julius Caezar
Mfasili JULIUS K. NYERERE
Oxford University Press

Learn from Biographies

What contributions did Nyerere make to help his country?

For more information, go online to *Meet the People* at **www.sfsocialstudies.com.**

LESSON 2

1940   2000

1948
The state of
Israel is created.

1967
Six-Day War between Israel and Arab states

1978
The Camp David Accords are
signed by Israel and Egypt.

The Middle East

PREVIEW

Focus on the Main Idea
The end of European control
and the creation of Israel
changed the Middle East.

PLACES
Palestine
Jerusalem
Israel
Egypt
West Bank
Golan Heights
Sinai Peninsula
Gaza Strip

PEOPLE
David Ben-Gurion
Gamal Abdel Nasser
Anwar el-Sadat
Menachem Begin

VOCABULARY
Zionism

TERMS
Arab nationalism
Palestinian Liberation
  Organization
Camp David Accords
Oslo Accords

EVENTS
Six-Day War

▶ **The Western Wall, sacred to
Jews, forms part of a larger wall
surrounding the Dome of the
Rock, which is sacred to
Muslims.**

614

You Are There
You turn on the television in your family room and find a documentary film on conflicts in the Middle East. You learn that this region stretches from the Mediterranean Sea to the western borders of Afghanistan and Pakistan. The program explains that this region was once part of the Ottoman Empire from the 1500s until the end of World War I. At that time, Great Britain and France took control of most of the Middle East.

You learn that the Babylonians forced many Jews out of Judah in about 600 B.C. in to what is called the Diaspora. Over time, some Jews returned to Judah.

In the first century A.D., the Romans forced all of the Jews out of Judah, a land they called Palestine. Centuries later many Jews began to call for a Jewish state in Palestine. During World War I, they persuaded the British government to support a Jewish state there.

Much of this is beginning to sound familiar to you, as you've heard it on the news.

Draw Conclusions As you read, identify the main facts of the Arab-Israeli conflict so that you can make logical conclusions.

A Growing Palestine

The movement to build a Jewish state in **Palestine** became known as **Zionism** (ZI uh niz um). Zionism comes from the word *Zion*, which became a synonym for **Jerusalem.** Zionism expressed hopes of the Jewish people for a homeland. Since the late 1800s, Zionism has come to mean the establishment of a Jewish state in Palestine. The British supported the establishment of a "national home for Jewish people" in Palestine.

Although there had been growing tensions between the Arabs and the small community of Jews living in Palestine before World War I, they had generally lived in peace. In the 1930s, anti-Semitism, or discrimination against Jews, in Europe caused more Jews to leave for Palestine and the United States.

However, persecution by Nazi Germany and the Holocaust led to the largest migration of Jews to Palestine. This large migration of Jews to Palestine soon led to growing tensions between Arabs and Jews.

After World War I, Great Britain and France took control of a large part of the Middle East. Great Britain had been governing Palestine. However, after World War II, Great Britain asked the United Nations (UN) to help with the growing conflict between Arabs and Jews. As a result, the UN proposed dividing Palestine into two states, creating one Arab state and one Jewish state.

REVIEW What was the cause of increasing Jewish migration to Palestine in the 1930s? **Cause and Effect**

▶ **David Ben-Gurion became the first prime minister of Israel in 1948.**

State of Israel

On May 14, 1948, the last British troops left Palestine. Jewish leader **David Ben-Gurion** declared the Jewish part of Palestine as the state of **Israel.**

Jews in Palestine celebrated, but Arab states opposed the division of Palestine and refused to recognize Israel. War then broke out between Arabs and Jews. The neighboring Arab countries of Syria, **Egypt,** and Jordan joined the Palestinian Arabs—now called Palestinians—in the fight against Israel.

Israel reached an armistice with its Arab neighbors by 1949. As a result, Israel gained a large portion of the land the UN had put aside for an Arab state. During the war, hundreds of thousands of Palestinians had fled Palestine and settled in refugee camps in Israel. Most settled in neighboring Arab states. More battles were to come between Israel and the Palestinians, as well as Arab states, in what became known as the Arab-Israeli conflict.

REVIEW How was the reaction different among Arabs and Jews to the declaration of the state of Israel? **Compare and Contrast**

Arab States

In the 1930s and 1940s, many Arab states gained their independence—Iraq and Jordan from Great Britain, and Syria and Lebanon from France. By the 1950s, most states in the Middle East had decolonized.

In Unit 6, you read that Great Britain had some control in keeping the Suez Canal open for British ships. In 1952 a coup d'etat ended the monarchy in Egypt. Two years later, **Gamal Abdel Nasser** became the prime minister and was determined to drive the British completely out of his country. He sent his forces to block the canal. In 1956 France, Great Britain, and Israel invaded Egypt, starting a war over the Suez Canal.

▶ **Gamal Abdel Nasser became president of Egypt in 1956.**

Nasser's actions gained wide support in the Arab world. No Arab leader in the Middle East had ever before stood up to Western nations. His goal of greater Arab unity, or **Arab nationalism,** became a powerful force throughout the Middle East.

REVIEW How did Nasser gain support from other Arab leaders in the Middle East? **Main Idea and Details**

Continuing Conflict

Israel and its Arab neighbors continued to fight wars in 1967 and 1973. The 1967 war, or the **Six-Day War,** ended with Israel in control of Palestine. Israel seized the **West Bank,** a large piece of land between Israel and Jordan, from Jordan. From Syria, Israel took the **Golan Heights** and from Egypt the **Sinai Peninsula** and the **Gaza Strip.**

The Gaza Strip and West Bank were home to more than 1 million Palestinians. Many Palestinians

recognized the **Palestinian Liberation Organization** (PLO) as representative of all Palestinians. Led by Yasir Arafat the PLO worked to create a Palestinian state. Some Arab leaders supported Palestinian attacks on Israel, but over time came to think that the best strategy was to make peace with Israel.

In the 1973 war, Arab states attacked Israel to try to regain land they had lost in 1967. This war caused an international oil crisis because Arab states placed an embargo on oil exports to Western countries, such as the United States, that supported Israel.

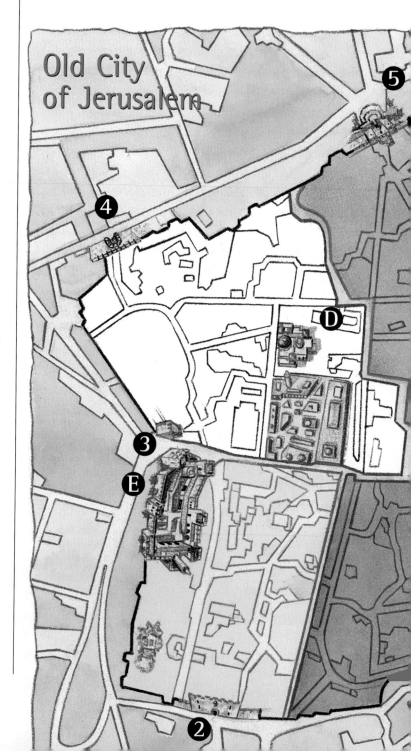

Old City of Jerusalem

In 1982 Israel invaded Lebanon following a series of Palestinian raids. Arafat and some of his followers fled to Tunisia in North Africa. In 1987 Palestinians in the Occupied Territories carried out an uprising—riots, demonstrations, and violence. Many Arab leaders wanted to stop the uprising. King Hussein of Jordan gave up his country's claims to the West Bank and East Jerusalem.

REVIEW How did the 1973 war between Israel and Arab states affect Western countries? Cause and Effect

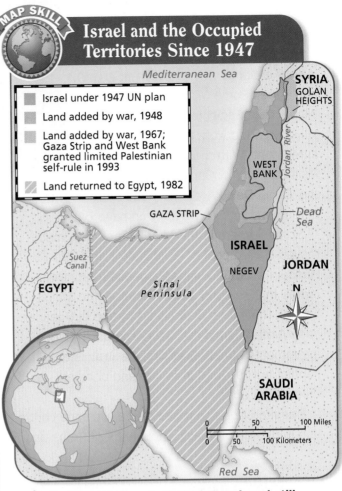

MAP SKILL
Israel and the Occupied Territories Since 1947

	Israel under 1947 UN plan
	Land added by war, 1948
	Land added by war, 1967; Gaza Strip and West Bank granted limited Palestinian self-rule in 1993
	Land returned to Egypt, 1982

▶ By the early twenty-first century Israel still occupied land taken in the Six-Day War.

MAP SKILL Human-Environment Interaction
What political boundary is formed by the Jordan River?

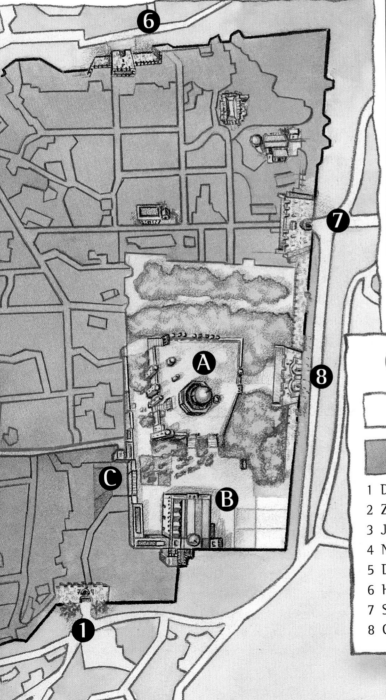

Old City of Jerusalem Map Key

☐ Christian	☐ Jewish
☐ Muslim	☐ Armenian (Eastern Orthodox)

1 Dung Gate
2 Zion Gate
3 Jaffa Gate
4 New Gate
5 Damascus Gate
6 Herod's Gate
7 St. Stephen's Gate
8 Golden Gate

A Dome of the Rock/Haram esh-Sharif
B El-Aqsa Mosque
C Western Wall of the Second Temple
D Church of the Holy Sepulchre
E The Citadel or Tower of David

Toward Peace

In 1978 Egypt's president **Anwar el-Sadat** (AHN wahr el-suh DAHT) and Israeli Prime Minister **Menachem Begin** (muh NAH chuhm BAY gihn) began to work toward a peace agreement. With the help of U.S. President Jimmy Carter, they signed the **Camp David Accords.** Read more about this agreement in the biography on page 619.

Some leaders in the Middle East have made moves toward peace. For example, in 1994 King Hussein of Jordan signed a peace treaty with Israel. In 1993 and 1995, Israeli Prime Minister Yitzhak Rabin (YIHT zak rah BEEN) and PLO leader Yasir Arafat signed the **Oslo Accords.** These agreements aimed at ending the Arab-Israeli conflict but resulted in failure and another Palestinian uprising in 2000.

Despite efforts to make peace, violence continues in the Middle East. Thousands of Arabs and

▶ **U.S. President Jimmy Carter joins hands with Anwar Sadat and Menachem Begin after the signing of the Camp David Accords.**

Israelis, as well as many of their leaders, have lost their lives in the Arab-Israeli conflict.

REVIEW How have efforts for peace on both sides affected the Arab-Israeli situation?

Summarize the Lesson

1948 The state of Israel, a homeland for Jews, was created.

1967 Israel and its Arab neighbors fought in the Six-Day War.

1978 Israel and the Egyptians signed the Camp David Accords.

LESSON 2 REVIEW

Check Facts and Main Ideas

1. ⟲ **Draw Conclusions** Copy the diagram below on a separate piece of paper. Then write a conclusion about how the state of Israel was created using the given clues.

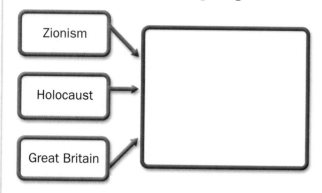

Zionism →

Holocaust →

Great Britain →

2. How did Arab nationalism affect the Middle East?

3. What was the result of the UN plan to divide Palestine into Jewish and Arab states?

4. How did Arab hopes for independence and Jewish hopes for a homeland in Palestine cause tension?

5. **Critical Thinking: *Evaluate Information*** In the Oslo Accords, Israel agreed to give land back to the Palestinians. The Palestinians then agreed to recognize Israel. Do you think this is a fair trade? Explain.

Link to 🔗 Mathematics

Compare Areas The area of the state of Israel is 8,130 square miles. The area of the state of Texas is 266,874 square miles. About how many states of Israel would fit inside Texas?

Menachem Begin
1913–1992

Anwar el-Sadat
1918–1981

On November 19, 1977, Egypt's president, Anwar el-Sadat, made history. He arrived in Israel to meet with Israel's prime minister Menachem Begin and address the Israeli Parliament. Sadat was the first Arab leader to visit Israel since its founding in 1948.

Begin welcomed Sadat warmly even though the nations were not at peace. Sadat was in Israel to take steps toward peace. As he told the Israeli Parliament:

> *"Let's fight no more wars; let's solve the very real differences between Arabs and Jews at a table, not on the battlefield."*

BIOFACT

Begin and Sadat were awarded the 1978 Nobel Prize for Peace for their efforts toward solving the Arab-Israeli conflict.

In September 1978, Begin and Sadat hammered out a peace agreement at Camp David, Maryland, with U.S. President Jimmy Carter. Sadat and Begin soon signed two agreements, known as the Camp David Accords. Israel agreed to withdraw its troops that had occupied Egypt's Sinai Peninsula since 1967. In return, Egypt agreed to establish peace with Israel. The two leaders also set up a process for a transition to self-rule for the Palestinian Arabs living in the Israeli-occupied West Bank and Gaza Strip. As Begin explained,

> *"We believe that if we achieve peace . . . we shall be able to assist one another . . . and a new era will be opened in the Middle East."*

The accords were hailed as a great achievement by most non-Arab states. However, many Arab states felt that Sadat was not backing the Arab cause. They did not want peace with Israel. In 1981 Sadat was assassinated by Muslim extremists.

Begin was also criticized for his role in the accords. A number of his supporters abandoned his political party after the accords were signed. In 1983 Begin resigned as prime minister following Israel's invasion of Lebanon.

Learn from Biographies

Why do you think Begin welcomed Sadat in 1977 even though Israel and Egypt were at war?

For more information, go online to *Meet the People* at **www.sfsocialstudies.com**.

• Berlin

1980	1990	2000

1985
Mikhail Gorbachev becomes the Communist Party leader of the Soviet Union.

1991
The Soviet Union falls.

1989
The gates of the Berlin Wall open.

Eastern Europe

PREVIEW

Focus on the Main Idea
Calls for greater freedom brought an end to communism in Eastern Europe.

PLACES
Berlin Wall
Czech Republic
Slovak Republic
Slovenia
Croatia
Bosnia and Herzegovina
Macedonia

PEOPLE
Lech Walesa
Mikhail Gorbachev
Boris Yeltsin

VOCABULARY
dissident
perestroika
glasnost

TERMS
Solidarity
Kremlin
Commonwealth of
Independent States

You Are There

It's a crisp autumn night in November 1989. A huge party is taking place right here in the heart of Berlin, Germany. The gates of the Berlin Wall are open!

East German guards let cars, bicycles, and people through as fast as they can cross the checkpoints. These same soldiers used to forbid anyone from crossing the border. But everyone seems happy tonight. Some are singing; others are laughing. A few even chip away at the tall concrete wall with hammers or drills. Fireworks go off; the crowd applauds.

You hold your grandmother's hand tightly. Tears well up in her eyes. "I remember when this wall went up," she says. "I never thought I'd see it come down." Even though it's well past your bedtime, you have been allowed to stay up late. You are excited to be part of history being made.

Draw Conclusions As you read, identify facts about how communism ended in Eastern Europe.

▶ **On November 10, 1989, on top of the Berlin Wall, Berliners celebrate the opening of the border between East and West Germany.**

Changes in Eastern Europe

In November 1989, the gates of the Berlin Wall were opened, allowing people to move freely into West Germany. East Germany's communist government soon fell. In 1990 East and West Germany were reunited into one country. By 1991 the destruction of the Berlin Wall was complete. All of these events that ended communist rule in Eastern Europe became known as the "Revolution of 1989."

In Chapter 18, you read how Russia became a communist country in 1917. After World War II, the Soviet Union forced communist governments on countries in Eastern Europe. Soviet leaders used force to keep these countries united under communism.

Beginning in the 1950s, some of these countries began to rebel against their communist governments. In 1953 people in East Germany protested against their communist government. In 1956 Hungary rebelled. In 1968 the people of Czechoslovakia (che kuh sloh VAH kee uh) demanded freedom. The Soviet Army quickly crushed these movements.

However, in the early 1980s, workers in Poland forced their government to accept a labor union that was free of communist control. The labor union was called Solidarity. An electronics technician named Lech Walesa (LEHK vah LEHN sah) led Solidarity. Before this time, labor unions in communist countries had been run by the government, rather than by workers.

By 1987 Soviet leader Mikhail Gorbachev (mee kah EEL GAWR buh chawf)

▶ **In Gdansk, Poland, Solidarity leader Lech Walesa speaks to shipyard workers.**

began calling for more freedoms. His call for freedom started a chain reaction throughout Eastern Europe. As a result, Poland held free elections in 1989. In 1990 the Poles elected Lech Walesa as president.

Hungary and Czechoslovakia also broke free of communist rule in 1989. A writer named Vaclav Havel (VAH tslahv HAH vehl) became president of Czechoslovakia. He had been a leading dissident, or protester against the government. Later, Czechoslovakia split into two countries, the Czech Republic and the Slovak Republic (Slovakia). (See the map on page R16.)

The end of communism also led to the breakup of Yugoslavia (yoo goh SLAH vee uh), another country in Eastern Europe. It also helped to form the newly independent nations of Slovenia, Croatia, Bosnia and Herzegovina, and Macedonia. In the next chapter, you will read about wars that were caused by the creation of these "breakaway" nations.

REVIEW Why did Eastern Europe change so rapidly after Gorbachev allowed greater freedom?
⟳ Draw Conclusions

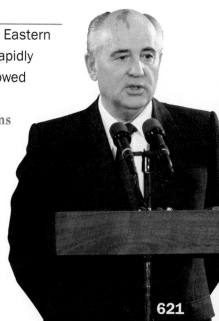

▶ **During the 1980s, Soviet leader Mikhail Gorbachev became a driving force for political and economic change.**

Communism Crumbles

During the Cold War, the Soviet Union and the United States spent huge sums of money on weapons. As a result, the Soviet Union had little money left over for other parts of the economy. For most people, the communist promise of a "worker's paradise" remained just an unfulfilled promise. Many lost faith in the communist system.

In 1985 Mikhail Gorbachev became the Communist Party leader. During his term, he introduced **perestroika,** or "restructuring," to reform the Soviet economy. Gorbachev also introduced **glasnost,** or "openness," to allow people some freedom of speech. He hoped that these policies would improve the economy, offer political freedom, and democratize the Soviet system.

Glasnost soon made people want greater self-government. In 1990 one of the 15 Soviet republics, Lithuania, declared independence. Other republics then began declaring their independence.

Some Soviet officials were unhappy with these changes. In August 1991, they attempted a coup d'état to overthrow Gorbachev. **Boris Yeltsin** (YELT suhn), president of the Russian Republic, successfully led demonstrations to stop the coup.

These events helped strengthen Yeltsin's popularity, and he gained more power than Gorbachev. In December 1991, Yeltsin and other leaders of the republics declared the end of the Soviet Union. Yeltsin then made the **Kremlin,** an old Moscow fort that had been the seat of Soviet government, the center for his government. Rejecting communism, Yeltsin began to change the Russian economy.

MAP SKILL

A New Eastern Europe

▶ The map of Eastern Europe changed after the fall of communism.

MAP SKILL Use a Map Key *Which former republics of the Soviet Union did not become members of the Commonwealth of Independent States?*

▶ **After the failed Soviet coup attempt, crowds celebrate outside the Kremlin, the center of the Soviet goverment in Red Square.**

The breakup of the Soviet Union in 1991 created 15 new nations. Look at the map on page 622 and locate these nations. Many of the nations joined a loose association called the **Commonwealth of Independent States.**

Mikhail Gorbachev resigned as president of the Soviet Union on December 25, 1991. Describing that day, he wrote:

> *"The promise I gave to the people . . . was kept: I gave them freedom."*

REVIEW What was the effect of *glasnost*?
Cause and Effect

Summarize the Lesson

1985 Mikhail Gorbachev became the Communist Party leader of the Soviet Union.

1989 Communist governments fell in Eastern Europe, and the gates of the Berlin Wall opened.

1991 The Soviet Union came to an end.

LESSON 3 REVIEW

Check Facts and Main Ideas

1. ↩ **Draw Conclusions** Copy the diagram below on a separate sheet of paper. Then fill in the conclusion based on the given facts.

> The communist system failed in Eastern Europe, and many people lost faith in communism. →

> Workers wanted labor unions free of communist control. →

> Eastern Europeans protested against their governments. →

2. What events does "the Revolution of 1989" describe?

3. Why did Gorbachev start the policy of *perestroika*? the policy of *glasnost*?

4. What changes did the end of communism bring to Eastern Europe?

5. **Critical Thinking: *Make Generalizations*** How did the Soviet response to protests in Eastern Europe in the 1950s and 1960s compare to those of Gorbachev in the 1980s?

Link to ⚭ **Writing**

Write an Editorial Suppose you are a member of Solidarity in Poland in 1980. Write an editorial explaining why your labor union should be controlled by workers, rather than by the communist government.

Thinking Skills

Determine Accuracy of Information

What? When you are reading a book, magazine, periodical, or newspaper, how do you know if the source is accurate? You face this issue when you are doing general reading or gathering information for a report. Determining the credibility of a source is an important skill. *Credibility* means "believability." If a source is not credible, then you should not take the information you are reading as fact.

Information is updated from time to time. Updated sources are more likely to be accurate. If you are using a source that is ten or more years old, you may want to double-check the information. This is especially important when you are using statistics or numbers. If you needed to find the population of a country for a research report, the most accurate statistic is from the most recent census. A census is an official national count of the people of a country or state. It is taken by about 90 percent of all countries in the world every ten years. Look at the information below from the U.S. Census Bureau. The population and growth rate of Russia by decade are given for the years 1960–2000.

The information in this table is provided by the U.S. Census Bureau. This bureau is a U.S. government office. A department within the U.S. Census Bureau gathers international population statistics.

Population and Growth Rate of Russia, 1960–2000

Year	Population	Growth Rate
1960	119,632,000	1.6
1970	130,245,000	0.9
1980	139,045,000	0.7
1990	148,082,000	0.6
2000	146,001,000	−0.1

source: U.S. Census Bureau

What conclusion can you draw from this table? The population growth rate, or the rate of population increase, drops after 1970 from 0.9 to 0.7. The rate decreases even more after 1990. From what you have read about the events in the Soviet Union between 1989–1991, make an inference. Does this information seem accurate? For example, people began to leave Russia when communism became weaker in the Soviet Union in the late 1980s. After 1991 Russians who wanted to get out of the former Soviet Union were free to leave.

Why? Almost anyone can write an article or a book. Sometimes writers have biases or prejudices that affect how they write about a topic. If you do not check the accuracy of a source, you may be reading or using incorrect information.

For example, under communist rule, the Soviet Union had tight rules on releasing information. There was no freedom of the press. The Soviet government often released false information, misleading its people and other nations.

However, in the mid-1980s, Gorbachev's policy of *glasnost* gave more freedom of the press. As Tankred Golenpolsky of the Soviet State Publishing Committee said in 1988, "It's more exciting right now to read than to live." Even more information became available to the public and the world after 1991.

How? Knowing about the author will help you determine whether the source is credible. Knowing how current the source is, or what the publication date is, helps you determine the accuracy of information.

Knowing the history of the former Soviet Union will help you determine the credibility of the selection below. If you did not know that the Soviet Union had strict rules on releasing information before 1986, you might think that the selection is inaccurate.

Think and Apply

Read the selection from *The New Russians* by Hedrick Smith, who won the Pulitzer Prize for International Reporting. Then answer the questions.

> *"Suddenly criticizing the Soviet past, the Soviet present, even the Soviet leadership, was not only tolerated [accepted], it was encouraged—in the press, books, theater, films, and on television . . . . Other books hidden away by Soviet authors came off the shelves . . . . Glasnost brought them out into the daylight."*

1 What information helps you determine whether or not the information from Hedrick Smith's book is accurate or not?

2 What other research might you need to do before you decide whether or not Smith's book has provided accurate information?

1940

1947
India and Pakistan gained independence.

1948
State of Israel was created.

1960

about 1960
Many colonies in sub-Saharan Africa began to gain independence.

Chapter Summary

Target Skill

Draw Conclusions

On a separate piece of paper, fill in a conclusion that the facts support.

Many colonies in sub-Saharan Africa became new nations after World War II.

Most colonies in South and Southeast Asia became new nations after World War II.

New countries and states formed in the middle East after the world wars.

The Soviet Union broke up into 15 new states in the 1990s.

Vocabulary

Match each word with the correct definition or description.

1 decolonization (p. 607)

2 coup d'état (p. 607)

3 apartheid (p. 609)

4 segregate (p. 609)

5 dissident (p. 621)

6 civil disobedience (p. 611)

a. protester against a harsh government

b. government policy of racial separation

c. to keep people of different races separate

d. overthrow of government by a small group

e. ending of colonial rule

f. refusal to obey unjust laws

People and Terms

Write a sentence explaining why each of the following people or terms was important in decolonization or the creation of new nations. You may use two or more in a single sentence.

1 Julius Nyerere (p. 607)

2 Robert Mugabe (p. 609)

3 Nelson Mandela (p. 609)

4 Mohandas Gandhi (p. 611)

5 Arab nationalism (p. 616)

6 Zionism (p. 615)

7 Kwame Nkrumah (p. 607)

8 Solidarity (p. 621)

9 Lech Walesa (p. 621)

10 Mikhail Gorbachev (p. 621)

1980	2000

1967 The Six-Day War

1978 The Camp David Accords were signed.

1989 The gates to the Berlin Wall opened.

1991 The Soviet Union fell.

1994 Nelson Mandela was elected president of South Africa.

1997 China took control of Hong Kong.

Facts and Main Ideas

1 What were two challenges of independence in Africa?

2 What is nonviolent civil disobedience and how did Gandhi use it to help India gain independence?

3 Name five nations that have formed in Europe since 1989.

4 **Time Line** How many years passed between the opening of the gates to the Berlin Wall and the end of the Soviet Union?

5 **Main Idea** How did Africa, South Asia, and Southeast Asia change after World War II?

6 **Main Idea** Name two important changes in the Middle East after World War II.

7 **Main Idea** How do the structures of the Soviet Union and the Commonwealth of Independent States differ?

8 **Critical Thinking:** *Make Inferences* Do you think that Mikhail Gorbachev believed in communism? Explain your answer.

Write About History

1 **Write a poem** expressing joy on the independence day of a country.

2 **Write a letter** home telling about events in Palestine in 1948 from a journalist's point of view.

3 **Write an editorial** about the fall of the Soviet Union.

Apply Skills

Determine Accuracy of Information

Your teacher may ask you to use additional reading materials with your textbook. As you read, you may find different explanations and statistics about an event. How will you decide which source is more accurate?

Read the passages below about the Palestinian population after the 1967 Arab-Israeli war. The first one is taken from your textbook.

"The Gaza Strip and West Bank were home to more than 1 million Palestinians."

"1.3 million Palestinians flee when Israel captures Gaza and West Bank during the Six-Day War."
United Nations Relief and Works Agency (UNRWA)

"Israel . . . acquire[d] the problem of administering more than a million Arabs in Gaza and the West Bank." Encyclopaedia Britannica

1 What information do these three sources provide?

2 Do you think that one source is more accurate than the others? If yes, explain why.

3 How would you check the accuracy of these sources?

Internet Activity

To get help with vocabulary, people, and terms, select dictionary, encyclopedia, or almanac from *Social Studies Library* at **www.sfsocialstudies.com.**

CHAPTER 22

Cooperation, Conflict, and Challenges

Lesson 1

1991
Maastricht
A treaty is signed in the Netherlands establishing what later became the European Union.

1

Lesson 2

1998
Kosovo
Civil war rages in the Balkans.

2

Lesson 3

2001
The United States
Americans unite and stand up with countries around the world against terrorism.

3

Locating Time and Place

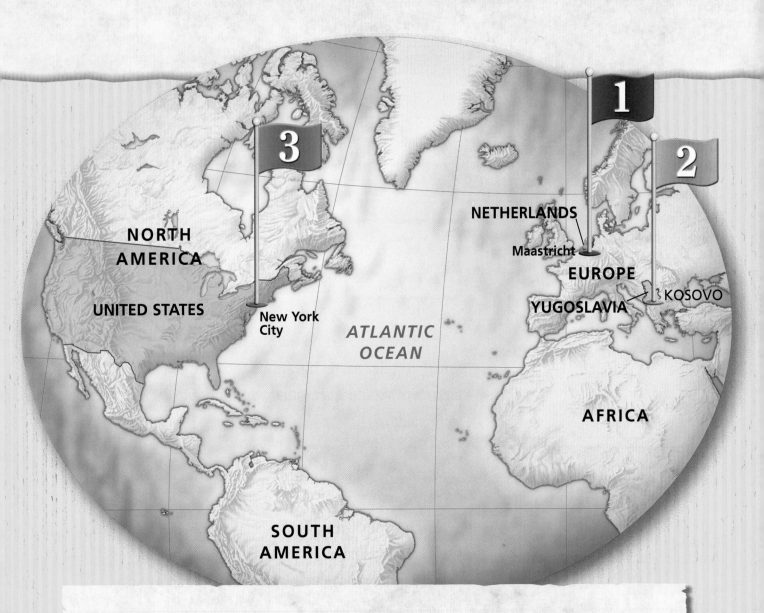

NETHERLANDS

Maastricht

NORTH
AMERICA

UNITED STATES

New York
City

ATLANTIC
OCEAN

EUROPE

YUGOSLAVIA

KOSOVO

AFRICA

SOUTH
AMERICA

Why We Remember

From your own experience, you know that working and playing together—rather than fighting—makes life richer. After many terrible wars in the twentieth century, many people began to cooperate to try to make the world better. They worked together in organizations such as the United Nations to promote peace. Nations opened up trade to share prosperity around the world. At the beginning of a new century, we enjoy the results of this cooperation. However, we still have conflicts. Thus, our new century is a time of cooperation, conflicts, and challenges.

NETHERLANDS

Maastricht •

1950   **1985**   **2000**

1957
The European
Economic Community
(EEC) is created.

1991
Mercosur is
organized.

1994
NAFTA
goes into
effect.

1999
The euro
is issued.

Economic Cooperation

PREVIEW

Focus on the Main Idea
World and regional economies
have become closely bound
together.

PLACES
Maastricht

PEOPLE
Bill Clinton

VOCABULARY
gross domestic product (GDP)
trading bloc
euro
trade agreement

TERMS
European Union (EU)
Association of Southeast Asian
  Nations (ASEAN)
Mercosur
North American Free Trade
  Agreement (NAFTA)
World Trade Organization (WTO)

You Are There
You're helping Dad fold laundry. You
pick up a shirt and look at the label.
"Made in Turkey. Where is Turkey?"
you ask.

Dad sends you to find the atlas. You look up Turkey and
find that it lies partly in Europe and partly in Asia. You
pick up other objects around your house to see where they
were made.

"How about this picture frame?" asks Dad. "Made in
Taiwan." The atlas shows that Taiwan is an island off
China's coast.

Now it's your turn. "My baseball cap? Made in the U.S.A.
I know where that is."

Dad's face lights up. He grabs the pen in his pocket.
"Fabriqué au Canada."

You're stumped. Then Dad
chuckles and says, "That's
French for 'Made in Canada'."

▶ **Every day goods from around the
world are produced and sold to
consumers.**

Cause and Effect As you read, consider how economic
cooperation among nations affects the global community.

Economies Without Borders

We live in a global economy. That is why you have objects that were made in many other countries.

Living in a global economy also means that what happens in one country soon affects others. Trade barriers, or things such as tariffs, quotas, or embargos, often hinder trade. As a result, many countries remove trade barriers by carrying on free trade with countries around the world. This means that they trade without tariffs. Removing tariffs can encourage trade.

In our global economy, the products we buy come from all over the world. For example, today automobile makers sell their cars worldwide. When your grandparents started driving, however, most cars sold in the United States were American-made.

The global economy has made some people and nations very wealthy. But it has also caused problems for some workers, communities, and economies. Industries have had to shut down because of increased competition. They could no longer compete in the global economy. Increased competition often leads to lower prices for consumers. But lower prices can sometimes cause lower profits for industries. In the United States, automobile manufacturing is such an industry. We have far fewer jobs in this industry today than we did 50 years ago.

Even in a global economy there are still sharp differences in wealth among countries. Wealthy nations include the United States, several European nations, and Japan. These nations are called developed nations. Their industries and economies are well-developed.

The global economy also includes developing nations whose industries and economies are in the process of developing. They do not have the

▶ **New cars parked at a port in Seattle, Washington, will soon make their way to other ports around the globe.**

great wealth that the developed nations have. Many developing nations are in Africa and Asia. Look at the pie graph below which compares gross domestic product of world regions. **Gross domestic product** (GDP) is the value of all final goods and services produced in a country in a year. It is a measure of a nation's wealth.

REVIEW What are some of the positive and negative effects of the global economy on nations? *Cause and Effect*

Gross Domestic Product

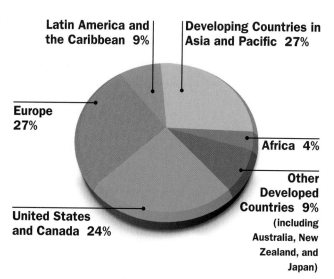

Latin America and the Caribbean 9%

Developing Countries in Asia and Pacific 27%

Europe 27%

Africa 4%

Other Developed Countries 9% (including Australia, New Zealand, and Japan)

United States and Canada 24%

▶ **The standard of living of countries and regions can be compared using GDP as an indicator.**

GRAPH SKILL Use a Circle Graph *Which countries or regions have the highest GDP?*

Trade and Cooperation

After World War II, many people believed that free trade between nations would lead to peace and prosperity. As a result, nations signed treaties to open up trade. They reduced or ended the use of tariffs with their trading partners.

Many nations joined regional trading blocs. A trading bloc is a group of countries that agree to trade under favorable conditions. Nations in a trading bloc reduce taxes on goods traded by countries within the trading bloc.

The trading bloc with the most nations is the European Union (EU). The origin of the EU began during the Cold War. In 1957 the European Economic Community was created to establish a common market. A common market is an economic union formed to increase trade and encourage cooperation among its members.

In 1991, 12 Western European leaders signed a treaty in Maastricht in the Netherlands. Within two years, the treaty had been approved by all members and the organization was renamed the European Community. The European Community later became part of the EU. Three more countries joined, bringing the total to 15. Since the fall of communism in the Soviet Union, many nations in Eastern Europe have been applying for membership in the EU. In 1999 the EU issued its own money, the euro. By having its own currency, EU members using the euro do not have to use exchange rates. As a result, EU nations began to export more manufactured goods than any other single nation in the world.

Western Europe was not the only place where a trading bloc formed. In 1967 five Southeast Asian countries formed the Association of Southeast Asian Nations (ASEAN). Like the EU, this organization aimed to reduce tariffs. It also wanted to promote economic cooperation.

REVIEW What are the benefits of belonging to a trading bloc? Main Idea and Details

▶ **The EU put the euro (pictured here) into circulation in 2002. International trade requires a system for exchanging currency between nations.**

MAP SKILL

Trading Blocs

▶ **The European Union and ASEAN are important trading blocs.**

MAP SKILL Compare Maps *What do the countries in these two maps have in common?*

American Trading Blocs

Trading blocs also developed in North and South America. In 1991 Argentina, Brazil, Paraguay, and Uruguay organized **Mercosur,** the "Southern Common Market." Before Mercosur, these nations had mostly traded with Europe and the United States. Mercosur has expanded and strengthened trade among these South American nations.

The United States, Canada, and Mexico became partners in a free trade zone called the **North American Free Trade Agreement (NAFTA),** which went into effect in 1994. The partnership had its roots in the 1989 trade agreement between the United States and Canada. A **trade agreement** outlines rules about the exchange of goods between countries.

The U.S.–Canada trade agreement was then extended to Mexico. After the leaders of the three countries signed the agreement in 1992, U.S. President **Bill Clinton** persuaded Congress to ratify, or approve, the full agreement in 1993. Over time, NAFTA must remove tariffs on most goods produced and sold in North America. This agreement has greatly expanded trade between the United States and Mexico.

In addition to specific regions of the world forming trading blocs, trading nations also set up several world organizations to promote free trade. The **World Trade Organization (WTO)** was created in 1995 to help nations settle trade disputes. The WTO makes sure that member nations follow their trade agreements.

REVIEW Why do you think President Clinton persuaded Congress to include Mexico in NAFTA? 🔄 **Draw Conclusions**

Summarize the Lesson

- **1957** The European Economic Community (EEC) was created.
- **1991** Mercosur was organized.
- **1994** NAFTA, the trading bloc including Canada, the United States, and Mexico, became fully operational.

LESSON 1   REVIEW

Check Facts and Main Ideas

1. **Cause and Effect** On a separate piece of paper, copy the diagram below. Write in the missing cause and effect.

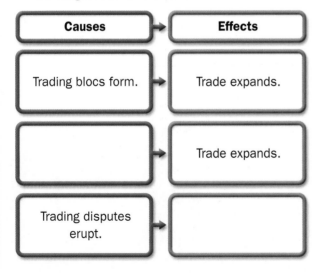

Causes	→	Effects
Trading blocs form.	→	Trade expands.
	→	Trade expands.
Trading disputes erupt.	→	

2. Define *gross domestic product.*

3. Name four trading blocs and list their members.

4. Explain the role of the World Trade Organization.

5. **Critical Thinking:** *Make Inferences* What might economic conditions be like in countries that belong to no trading blocs? Explain your answer.

Link to 🔗 Geography

Use a Map Look at a globe or a map of the world. How do you think physical geography affects how trading blocs form? What patterns can you identify?

Chart and Graph Skills

Interpret Cartograms

What? A cartogram is a special kind of graph based on a map. It stretches and bends the map outlines to represent data, or information.

The cartogram below represents the population of the world by country. It distorts the "real" map to give particular information about these nations.

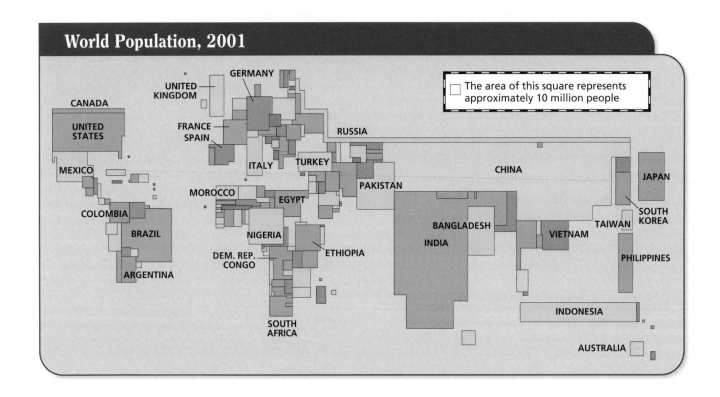

World Population, 2001

The area of this square represents approximately 10 million people

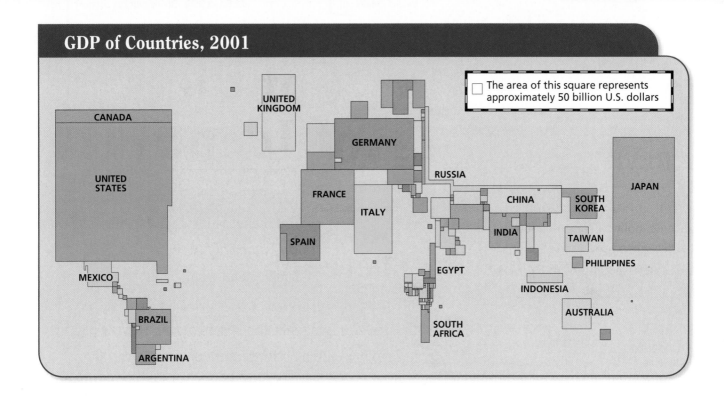

GDP of Countries, 2001

The area of this square represents approximately 50 billion U.S. dollars

CANADA

UNITED STATES

UNITED KINGDOM

GERMANY

RUSSIA

FRANCE

ITALY

SPAIN

CHINA

SOUTH KOREA

JAPAN

INDIA

TAIWAN

PHILIPPINES

MEXICO

EGYPT

INDONESIA

AUSTRALIA

BRAZIL

SOUTH AFRICA

ARGENTINA

Why? Graphs help us understand information at a quick glance. For this reason, they often make a big impact.

How? To use and understand a cartogram, you must know what the "real" map looks like. Look at the map of the world in the atlas in the back of your textbook. Now look at the cartogram on page 634. Did you notice that the cartogram makes some countries look much larger or much smaller?

Now look at the cartogram above. This cartogram represents gross domestic product (GDP) by country. Compare this cartogram with the cartogram on page 634. How have the shapes and sizes of some countries changed? To check the information on the cartograms, look in an almanac. You should be able to verify that the countries that look the largest on the cartogram have the highest GDP in the world. You should also be able to verify that the largest countries on the cartogram have the greatest population in the world. Check to see that the information in the almanac matches the information on the cartograms. You should be able to confirm your conclusions.

Think and Apply

1 Which countries have the largest population?

2 Which countries have the highest GDP?

3 What other data could you use to make a cartogram of the world?

YUGOSLAVIA
SERBIA
KOSOVO
MONTENEGRO

1950   **1970**   **1990**

late 1960s
Violence in Northern
Ireland breaks out.

1989 Protest at Tiananmen Square

1991–1992 Breakup of Yugoslavia

1993–1994 Massacres in Rwanda and Burundi lead to civil war.

1999
War breaks out in Kosovo.

Conflicts of Identity

PREVIEW

Focus on the Main Idea
Ethnic, political, and religious differences have led to violent conflicts around the world.

PLACES
Yugoslavia
Slovenia
Croatia
Serbia
Montenegro
Bosnia and Herzegovina
Kosovo
Rwanda
Burundi
Northern Ireland
Afghanistan
Myanmar
Chiapas
Tiananmen Square
Beijing

PEOPLE
Slobodan Milosevic
Mairead Corrigan Maguire
Mary Robinson
Aung San Suu Kyi
Rigoberta Menchú

VOCABULARY
ethnicity
multiethnic nation
ethnic cleansing
repressive

You Are There You pick up Marybeth Lorbiecki's book, *My Palace of Leaves in Sarajevo.* You've been wondering how the war that broke out in 1991 in Yugoslavia affected the lives of children. You hope that the letters of this 10-year-old girl will help give you a better picture of what it was like. You begin to read her book.

We use candles at night. No TV . . . .
Run to cellar many times. Bombs, and more bombs.
  Sit hours and hours . . . .
It is difficult to read. Noise is louder than
  thunder, it shakes me inside.
Father and Drini and I make pretend
  plays and stories, songs and dances.
  It is good almost as TV.

▶ **This Bosnian girl was among thousands of children affected by the 1991 war.**

Draw Conclusions As you read, identify religious, political, and ethnic conflicts to draw conclusions about conflicts of identity.

Identity and Ethnicity

The war that broke out in Marybeth's country was over identity or ethnicity. When people have the same **ethnicity** that means that they speak the same language, have the same customs, and share other cultural aspects. Many times people will go to war for economic and political reasons. Sometimes ethnic and religious differences are also factors in war.

A nation with many different ethnic groups is called a **multiethnic nation.** The former country of **Yugoslavia,** in the Balkans in southeastern Europe, is one example of a multiethnic nation. When the communists lost power in Yugoslavia, the country began to break apart.

Like the Soviet Union, Yugoslavia was a union of republics. In 1991 two of the six republics, **Slovenia** (sloh VEE nee uh) and **Croatia** (krow AY shuh), declared independence. **Serbia,** the largest republic in Yugoslavia, and **Montenegro** then fought a bitter war with Croatia. These civil wars were mainly fought over ethnicity. With help from the UN, most fighting in Croatia ended in 1998.

REVIEW How do differences in ethnicity cause conflicts? Cause and Effect

Kosovo

When the republic of **Bosnia and Herzegovina** declared independence in 1992, war broke out. The president of Serbia, **Slobodan Milosevic** (SLAW baw duhn mee LOH shehv ihtch), encouraged Serbs to carry out a policy of ethnic cleansing. **Ethnic cleansing** means to drive out or kill people who do not share the same identity. Thousands of refugees were forced out of Bosnia. Many countries tried to help end the war. They firmly believed that ethnic cleansing was wrong and violated human rights. With the help of other countries, a 1995 agreement—called the Dayton Accords—ended the war in Bosnia.

But wars continued to rage in this region. A district of Serbia, called **Kosovo,** became the next trouble spot. Most of the 2 million people there were Muslim Albanians called Kosovars. Kosovars wanted freedom and independence. In 1999 Milosevic sent in a mostly Serbian army. Soldiers burned and looted property and killed thousands of innocent people. They drove about 1 million Kosovars out of Kosovo.

In the end, NATO stepped in to help. NATO fighter jets bombed Belgrade, the capital of Serbia. They forced Milosevic to withdraw his army and provided help for refugees.

REVIEW Why did other countries get involved in the Kosovo conflict? Draw Conclusions

MAP SKILL

The Balkans

▶ The Balkans have been a hot spot for conflicts of identity or ethnicity.

MAP SKILL Use a Locator Map *In what region of Europe are the Balkans located?*

637

Central Africa

In the 1990s, the neighboring central African countries of **Rwanda** and **Burundi** exploded into civil war. The majority of the people in these two countries belong mainly to the Tutsi (TOO tze) and Hutu (HOO too) ethnic groups. Both are Bantu-speaking cultures and practice the same religion. However, they are distinct ethnic groups in that the Tutsi and Hutu have their own traditions. This difference has caused much tension and violence.

The army in Burundi, controlled by the Tutsi, killed thousands of Hutu citizens in 1993. The next year, the Hutu in control of Rwanda tried to wipe out the entire Tutsi population there. No one knows an exact number, but as many as 1 million Tutsi died.

Then the Tutsi took control in Rwanda and drove out the Hutu. More than 1 million Hutu refugees fled, mostly to the neighboring Democratic Republic of the Congo (DRC; Zaire). DRC rebel forces soon attacked the refugee camps and drove the Hutu back to Rwanda.

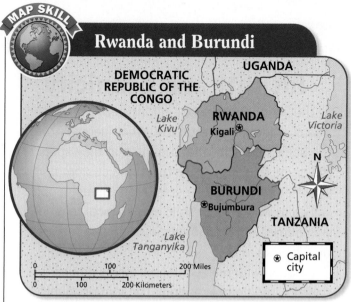

Rwanda and Burundi

▶ Civil war also has erupted inside and outside of Rwanda and Burundi over issues of identity.

MAP SKILL Understand Borders and Capitals
Which countries border Rwanda and Burundi?

The problems the Hutu and Tutsi survivors and returning refugees have faced are enormous. Villages and cities were badly damaged. People could not find jobs, shelter, or food.

REVIEW What caused the fighting between the Hutu and Tutsi in Burundi and Rwanda? Cause and Effect

Literature and Social Studies

What the World Needs

This poem was written by Elzbieta Jaworska when she was a teenager in Poland. Do you agree with what she thinks the world needs?

A little more kindness, a little less need,
A little more giving, a little less greed,
A little more gladness, a little less care,
A little more faith, a little more prayer,
A little more "we" and a little less "I,"
A little more laughter and a little less sigh,
A little more sunshine and brightening the view,
And a lot more friends, exactly like you.

▶ The group Doctors Without Borders sends volunteer doctors and other aid to refugees around the world. This German doctor helps a woman care for her child after major flooding hit Mozambique in 2000.

Northern Ireland

Disagreements between ethnic groups are not the only conflicts in the world. Fighting has focused on religious differences between Protestants and Catholics in Northern Ireland.

Ireland used to be all one country. But Great Britain, which held power in Ireland for hundreds of years, divided Ireland in 1920. Northern Ireland remained part of the United Kingdom. The rest of Ireland became an independent republic.

Most Irish are Catholics. However, in the six counties of Northern Ireland, Protestants are the majority and control much of the economy and government.

By the 1960s, the Protestant majority controlled Northern Ireland's parliament. As a result, the Catholic minority began a movement for civil rights. British troops were sent in and violence grew.

The conflict in Northern Ireland has caused the death of more than 3,000 people. Peace activists such as Mairead Corrigan Maguire are calling for the fighting to stop. She, like so many others, has lost family members to Catholic-Protestant violence. In 1976 she was awarded the Nobel Peace Prize. Maguire believes that people in the twenty-first century need to form new ideas of identity:

> *"It is fine to celebrate our diversity and our roots, but somehow we must . . . understand the most important identity that we have . . . the human family."*

REVIEW What conclusion can you draw about the effects of hostility in Northern Ireland? Draw Conclusions

MAP SKILL

United Kingdom

10°W   0°
60°N

0   100   200 Miles
0   100   200 Kilometers

NORTHERN IRELAND   SCOTLAND

N

UNITED KINGDOM

IRELAND

WALES   ENGLAND   NETHERLANDS

50°N   BELGIUM   GERMANY

ATLANTIC OCEAN   FRANCE

▶ Northern Ireland is one of four divisions of the United Kingdom.

MAP SKILL Use a Map *What are the other three divisions of the United Kingdom?*

The Struggle of Women

One struggle in the world involves about half of the population. This is the struggle of women for equality and freedom. In many countries, women have equality with men. In some, they have opportunities for good education and jobs too. But in other countries, the status of women is very low.

In 1996 a religious political party, called the Taliban, came to power in Afghanistan. The Taliban drove women out of the workforce and girls out of schools. Women doctors were not allowed to practice medicine. Some female patients were not able to get medical care.

Policies like those of the Taliban caused a reaction in the global community. Mary Robinson of Ireland became the United Nations High Commissioner for Human Rights in 1997. She has encouraged nations to ratify the Convention on the Elimination of Discrimination Against Women. This document has been called the "human rights charter for women."

REVIEW Why does the United Nations support equal rights for women? Draw Conclusions

▶ Mary Robinson served as president of Ireland before heading the UN Commission for Human Rights.

Struggles for Change

Many people have fought for human rights and freedom in the world. Even though greater democracy has come to nations such as Taiwan, South Korea, Chile, and others, people still struggle for freedom. Today, some nations have repressive governments. A **repressive** government is one that denies citizens basic human rights. Freedom of speech is one example of a human right. Another is freedom from arrest without just cause or reason.

Aung San Suu Kyi is just one of many people who have fought for human rights and political freedom. She has led the struggle against the repressive government led by military rulers in **Myanmar** (Burma), which has one of the world's worst records on human rights. An army officer named Ne Win took over the government there in a coup d'état in 1962. His ruling group has refused to give up power, even after losing national elections. It has also imprisoned many opponents like Aung San Suu Kyi. Read more about her in the biography on page 642.

People have also fought for political changes in the Americas. In 1994 people living in **Chiapas** (chee AH pahs), Mexico's poorest state, rebelled against the government. They were angry about the living conditions there. Many farm workers and laborers had lost their land to wealthy farmers and landowners. They also wanted more of a voice in the government.

Some economic and political changes have been made in Chiapas. However, many farm workers continue to seek greater rights and better living conditions.

In Guatemala **Rigoberta Menchú** led a group of workers in a strike against plantation owners. Her work earned her world wide recognition. Read more about Rigoberta Menchú on page 643.

REVIEW What rights did Aung San Suu Kyi and peasants in Chiapas fight for? Compare and Contrast

Limited Freedom

The People's Republic of China is another nation that has been criticized for its human rights record. The ruling Communist Party there has begun to allow the Chinese people some economic freedom. For example, they can start their own businesses. But the government still denies people human rights, such as freedom of speech. The Chinese Communist Party does not want to give up its hold on power.

▶ On May 25, 1989, students seeking more freedom, protested at Tiananmen Square in Beijing.

▶ A sign by a tree blocking a road welcomes people to the rebel state of Chiapas.

BIEN VENIDOS AL MUNICIPIO ZAPATISTA EMILIANO ZAPATA
ESTADO REBELDE DE CHIAPAS
CABEBERA MUNICIPAL COMUNIDAD CHACTOJ

640

In the spring of 1989, students gathered for a mass protest in **Tiananmen** (tyahn ahn mehn) **Square** in **Beijing**, China. They demanded more freedom. Chinese leaders sent the army into Tiananmen Square to crush the protests. Hundreds were killed. Many students were arrested and imprisoned. One student leader remembered it sadly:

> *"On a day in June that should have belonged to a season of fresh flowers, my people, my countrymen, my classmates . . . fell."*

Even though the mass protest was put down by the Communist government, their fight was seen by millions of people on television. This event showed people around the world how in some places others must fight for rights that are often taken for granted elsewhere.

REVIEW What do the governments of China and Myanmar have in common? Compare and Contrast

Summarize the Lesson

late 1960s Violence broke out in Northern Ireland.

1989 Protest at Tiananmen Square

1993–1994 Civil war broke out between Tutsi and Hutu peoples in Rwanda and Burundi.

1999 War in Kosovo left millions of refugees.

LESSON 2   REVIEW

Check Facts and Main Ideas

1. 🔄 **Draw Conclusions** On a separate piece of paper, copy the diagram below. Write a conclusion based on the given facts.

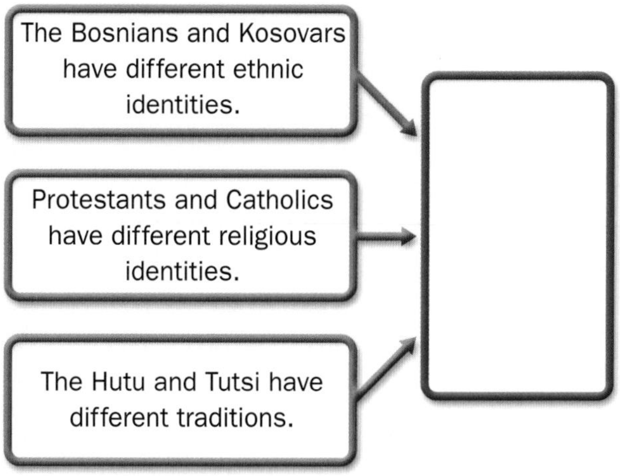

   ```
   The Bosnians and Kosovars
   have different ethnic
   identities.

   Protestants and Catholics
   have different religious
   identities.

   The Hutu and Tutsi have
   different traditions.
   ```

2. What caused thousands of refugees to flee Bosnia and Herzegovina in the 1990s?

3. How are the situations in central Africa and Northern Ireland alike and different?

4. Name three places in the world where people have been struggling for freedom or human rights.

5. **Critical Thinking: *Detect Bias*** Do you think countries that do not give equal status to men and women are showing a bias? Why or why not?

Link to 🔗 Reading

Vocabulary in Context Read the following statement. Then in your own words, write a definition for the underlined word. Use the surrounding words to help you.

> *In a society where the rights . . . of women are <u>constrained</u>, no man can be truly free. He may have power, but he will not have freedom.*
> —*Mary Robinson*

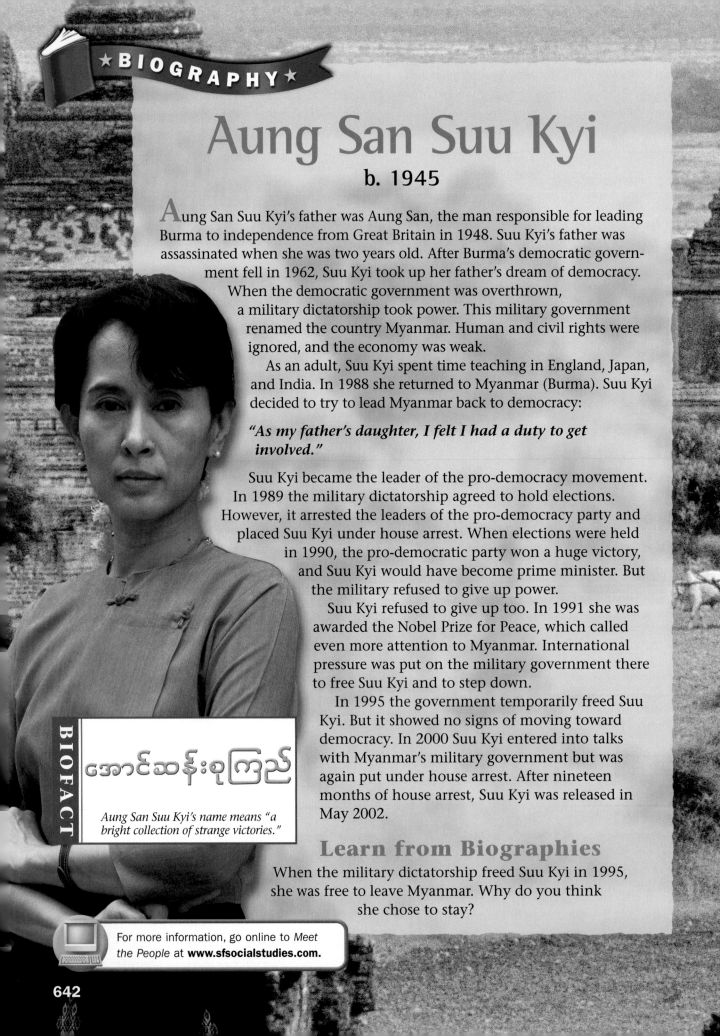

Aung San Suu Kyi

b. 1945

Aung San Suu Kyi's father was Aung San, the man responsible for leading Burma to independence from Great Britain in 1948. Suu Kyi's father was assassinated when she was two years old. After Burma's democratic government fell in 1962, Suu Kyi took up her father's dream of democracy. When the democratic government was overthrown, a military dictatorship took power. This military government renamed the country Myanmar. Human and civil rights were ignored, and the economy was weak.

As an adult, Suu Kyi spent time teaching in England, Japan, and India. In 1988 she returned to Myanmar (Burma). Suu Kyi decided to try to lead Myanmar back to democracy:

"As my father's daughter, I felt I had a duty to get involved."

Suu Kyi became the leader of the pro-democracy movement. In 1989 the military dictatorship agreed to hold elections. However, it arrested the leaders of the pro-democracy party and placed Suu Kyi under house arrest. When elections were held in 1990, the pro-democratic party won a huge victory, and Suu Kyi would have become prime minister. But the military refused to give up power.

Suu Kyi refused to give up too. In 1991 she was awarded the Nobel Prize for Peace, which called even more attention to Myanmar. International pressure was put on the military government there to free Suu Kyi and to step down.

In 1995 the government temporarily freed Suu Kyi. But it showed no signs of moving toward democracy. In 2000 Suu Kyi entered into talks with Myanmar's military government but was again put under house arrest. After nineteen months of house arrest, Suu Kyi was released in May 2002.

BIOFACT

အောင်ဆန်းစုကြည်

Aung San Suu Kyi's name means "a bright collection of strange victories."

Learn from Biographies

When the military dictatorship freed Suu Kyi in 1995, she was free to leave Myanmar. Why do you think she chose to stay?

For more information, go online to *Meet the People* at **www.sfsocialstudies.com**.

CITIZEN HEROES

BUILDING CITIZENSHIP

Caring
Respect
Responsibility
Fairness
Honesty
★ Courage

The Struggle for Peace

Rigoberta Menchú knows poverty and heartbreak first-hand. As a Mayan Indian, she was born in 1959 into poverty. Growing up in a small Guatemalan village, Menchú watched poor farmers being forced off their small plots of land by rich landowners.

For years Guatemalan soldiers had been killing thousands of poor farmers. But Guatemala's military governments had done nothing to stop this.

In the 1970s, many of Guatemala's poor farmers joined together to stand up for their rights. Rigoberta Menchú's father led one of these organizations but was killed by government forces in 1980. Despite the danger involved, Menchú took over as leader of her father's organization. She led sugar and cotton workers in a massive strike against plantation owners. The government tried to arrest Menchú, but she fled the country. While out of the country, Menchú spoke about poverty and lack of human rights in Guatemala.

For her efforts, Menchú was awarded the 1992 Nobel Prize for Peace. Upon receiving the award she stated:

"I consider this prize not as an award to me personally, but . . . in the struggle for peace, for human rights, and for the rights of indigenous [native] people . . . ."

Guatemala no longer has a military government, but the military remains strong. Poor farmers and political activists still fear kidnappings and death. Using the $1.2 million she received with the Nobel Peace Prize, Menchú has set up a human rights foundation and continues to work for peace.

Courage in Action

Link to Current Events What kind of risk did Menchú take in her fight for peace in Guatemala? Research a person or a group of people who have taken risks to make peace.

1970	1980	1990	2000

1988
Bomb on airliner explodes over Lockerbie, Scotland.

1995
Truck bomb destroys a federal building in Oklahoma City.

2001
Terrorist attacks occur in New York City and near Washington, D.C.

Political Conflicts and Challenges

PREVIEW

Focus on the Main Idea
People around the world continue to stand up against terrorism and work toward peace.

PLACES
Barbary States
Lockerbie
Oklahoma City
New York City
Washington, D.C.

PEOPLE
Thomas Jefferson
George W. Bush
Elie Wiesel

VOCABULARY
terrorism

You Are There

September 11, 2001: You've been watching and listening to news reports with your parents all day long. You're stunned by the horrible images on TV.

You're sad but feel safe at home with your family. The TV station shows some live video footage of emergency rescue workers.

"Look!" you cry out. "It's Uncle Nat! He's carrying a woman to the ambulance."

A news reporter turns to your uncle and says, "You're a hero."

"I'm just doing my job," he replies.

You're so proud of Uncle Nat. Now you know a real hero!

You wonder if heroes are ever frightened or worried. Do you have to be a rescue worker or soldier to be heroic? You wonder what it takes to be a hero.

▶ In the United States, there are more than 150,000 emergency medical technicians and paramedics who wear badges such as this one.

Draw Conclusions As you read, put facts together to understand how and why many people have been standing up against terrorism and working toward peace.

International Struggles

Throughout world history, many people have performed heroic acts in the face of danger. Many heroes have been part of the fight and struggle against international terrorism. **Terrorism** is the use of violence and fear to achieve political goals. Terrorism can take the form of assassinations, bombings, hijackings, kidnappings, or chemical and germ warfare. It is often used against civilians, or ordinary citizens.

Terrorism has been a part of world history for centuries. In the twentieth century, international terrorist attacks increased as groups used terror-ism to carry out their political agendas. For example, in June 1914, a member of the Black Hand Serbian terrorist organization assassinated Austrian Archduke Franz Ferdinand. This event started a chain reaction throughout Europe, which eventually led to World War I. Beginning in the late 1950s, a group fighting for Algerian independence from France carried out terrorist attacks against French colonists.

Look at the map below to locate major international terrorist attacks since 1978.

REVIEW What is terrorism and how is it used?
Main Idea and Details

Major International Terrorist Attacks, 1978–2001

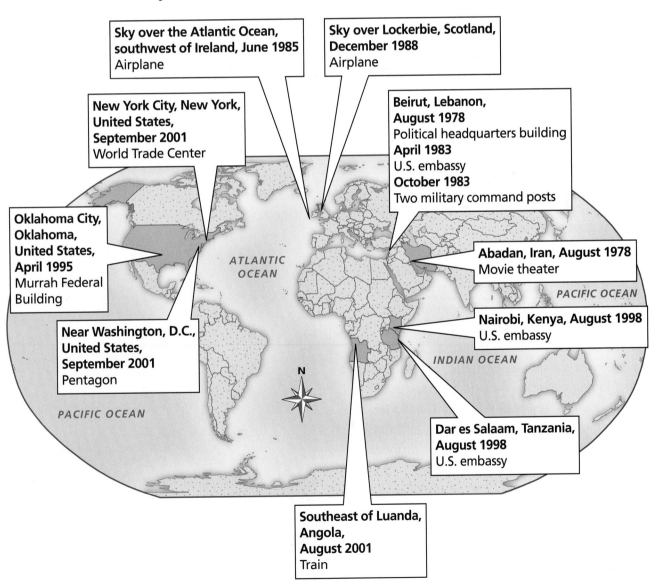

Sky over the Atlantic Ocean, southwest of Ireland, June 1985
Airplane

Sky over Lockerbie, Scotland, December 1988
Airplane

New York City, New York, United States, September 2001
World Trade Center

Beirut, Lebanon, August 1978
Political headquarters building
April 1983
U.S. embassy
October 1983
Two military command posts

Oklahoma City, Oklahoma, United States, April 1995
Murrah Federal Building

Abadan, Iran, August 1978
Movie theater

Near Washington, D.C., United States, September 2001
Pentagon

Nairobi, Kenya, August 1998
U.S. embassy

Dar es Salaam, Tanzania, August 1998
U.S. embassy

Southeast of Luanda, Angola, August 2001
Train

ATLANTIC OCEAN
PACIFIC OCEAN
INDIAN OCEAN
PACIFIC OCEAN

Terrorism Against Americans

Terrorist attacks on Americans and on American property and interests are not new. In the late eighteenth century, pirates of the Barbary States on the coast of North Africa began attacking U.S. and European commercial ships in the Mediterranean Sea. They held the crews for ransom, or in exchange for money.

When Thomas Jefferson became President in 1801, he wanted to end piracy overseas to protect American rights. In a letter, Jefferson wrote about the determination of the United States to stand up against piracy:

> *"If we wish our commerce to be free and uninsulted, we must let [other] nations see that we have an energy which at present they disbelieve."*

After diplomatic negotiations failed, Jefferson sent a naval squadron to stop piracy in the Mediterranean. As a result, the Barbary States signed a treaty ending the attacks on U.S. commercial ships.

But by the twentieth century, terrorists began to target civilians, as well as military forces. For example, in April 1983, a car bomb exploded at the U.S. embassy in Lebanon. In December 1988, a terrorist bomb destroyed an American airplane over Lockerbie, Scotland. In April 1995, a truck bomb exploded outside the Murrah Federal Building in Oklahoma City, Oklahoma. In 1998 bombs planted by international terrorists exploded outside two U.S. embassies in Tanzania and Kenya.

The United States had been responding to and taking a stand against terrorism for many years. But our country faced a new challenge on September 11, 2001.

▶ **In this painting, the U.S. Navy is shown capturing an Algerian ship in the war with the Barbary States.**

On that morning, international terrorists crashed two hijacked airplanes into the 110-story twin towers of the World Trade Center in New York City. Thousands of people working in the twin towers were killed, and both buildings were completely destroyed. On the same day, international terrorists crashed a third hijacked airplane into the Pentagon, the headquarters for the Department of Defense, in Arlington, Virginia, a suburb of Washington, D.C.

It is believed that passengers on a fourth hijacked airplane performed heroic acts to prevent the destruction of other possible targets. However, the plane crashed in a field in Shanksville, Pennsylvania. About 3,000 people from some 40 nations were killed in the September 11 terrorist attacks.

▶ **The twin towers of the World Trade Center were international symbols of economic power. They were also important landmarks in the New York City skyline.**

The American people responded to these terrorist attacks with courage and heroism. Thousands of rescue workers, firefighters, police officers, emergency workers, and volunteers rushed to the scenes of the attacks. They risked their lives to save the lives of others.

Adults and children around the country also responded. Some people donated blood. Others donated money to funds and organizations that had been set up for victims and their families. In support of the United States, people hung American flags on houses, businesses, and government buildings around the nation and in countries around the world.

The U.S. government and military also responded immediately. President George W. Bush addressed the nation with these words:

> *"Terrorist attacks can shake the foundations of our biggest buildings, but they cannot touch the foundation of America. These acts shatter steel, but they cannot dent the steel of American resolve [determination]."*

In the weeks following the attacks, Congress passed tougher antiterrorism laws. Air travel had declined greatly, so funding was made available

▶ After the terrorist attacks of September 11, 2001, U.S. airports and airlines increased security measures.

to the airline industry to help with economic recovery. Airports, skyscrapers, train and bus stations, and other public buildings increased security.

The terrorist attacks on the United States on September 11, 2001, provoked, or caused, a unified response by the United States. By October 7, the United States, aided by other nations, had gathered evidence that the Taliban government in Afghanistan was protecting the terrorist group responsible for the attacks. On that day, the United States, with its ally Great Britain, began bombing Taliban military targets in Afghanistan.

By December Taliban rule over Afghanistan had been replaced. Efforts to establish a new government had also begun.

REVIEW How did Americans respond to the terrorist attacks on September 11, 2001?
Summarize

Terrorist Attacks Against Civilians

Date	Location	Target	Attacker
1988	Lockerbie, Scotland	Civilians	International terrorists
1995	Oklahoma City	Civilians	Domestic terrorist
1998	Tanzania and Kenya	Civilians	International terrorists
2001	New York City and near Washington, D.C.	Civilians	International terrorists

▶ Terrorist attacks against Americans have taken different forms.

CHART SKILL Use a Chart *How are these terrorist attacks alike and different?*

Working Together

The United States was not the only nation to respond to the terrorist attacks on September 11. Countries all over the world have responded and supported the fight against terrorism. As **Elie Wiesel,** a Holocaust concentration camp survivor and winner of the Nobel Prize for Peace said:

" . . . it is incumbent upon [required of] us to choose between escape and solidarity, shame and honor. The terrorists have chosen shame. We choose honor."

FACT FILE

The World Unites

After the terrorist attacks on September 11, Americans and many people around the world vowed to unite in the fight against terrorism. With President George W. Bush, New York City Mayor Rudolph Giuliani, and New York Governor George Pataki, rescue workers, firefighters, police officers, volunteers, and political and religious leaders worldwide also responded. They began working together to help support victims, families of victims, and businesses destroyed and damaged as a result of the attacks.

► **During a peace vigil in Northern Ireland, people hold up cut-out doves of peace.**

Acts of terrorism are often caused by differences—in religion, ethnicity, or political beliefs—among peoples. People around the world have tried to work together to promote peace.

For example, disagreements between Protestants and Catholics led to acts of terrorism in Northern Ireland. Mairead Corrigan Maguire founded the Community of the Peace People to help unite Protestants and Catholics.

Disputes between Arabs and Jews in the Middle East have also led to acts of terrorism. In response, some Arabs and Jews have worked together to promote peace and understanding of differences. In the summer of 2001, Chicago Symphony Orchestra conductor Daniel Barenboim led a concert program performed by young Palestinians and Jewish musicians to show that people of different identities can work together.

REVIEW How have people and countries around the world responded to acts of terrorism? *Main Idea and Details*

Summarize the Lesson

1988 Bomb on airplane exploded over Lockerbie, Scotland.

1995 Truck bomb destroyed a federal building in Oklahoma City.

2001 Terrorist attacks hit New York City and near Washington, D.C.

LESSON 3   REVIEW

Check Facts and Main Ideas

1. ⤺ **Draw Conclusions** On a separate piece of paper, copy the diagram below. Fill in the missing facts that support the conclusion.

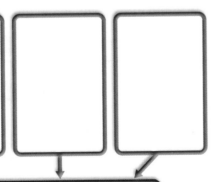

President Jefferson sent a naval squadron to stop piracy in the Mediterranean

People throughout history have stood up against terrorism.

2. What is terrorism and when is it used?

3. How has the United States responded to acts of terrorism?

4. How have people around the world responded to acts of terrorism?

5. Critical Thinking: *Solve Complex Problems* What can governments around the world do to stand up to terrorists and terrorism?

Link to ∞ Writing

Make of list Write down several objectives for working toward peace. Consider new ways that people can help promote peace together.

1950   1960

1957
The European Economic Community
was created.

1962
Military takeover
in Burma

Chapter Summary

Draw Conclusions

On a separate piece of paper, fill in three facts that support the given conclusion.

The world has seen examples of cooperation, conflicts, and challenges.

Vocabulary

Match each word with the correct definition or description.

1 trading bloc (p. 632)

2 ethnicity (p. 637)

3 gross domestic product (p. 631)

4 repressive (p. 640)

5 euro (p. 632)

a. denying citizens basic civil rights

b. common culture, religion, and customs of a group

c. currency of the EU

d. a measure of a nation's wealth

e. a group of countries that agrees to trade under favorable conditions

People and Terms

Write a sentence explaining why each of the following people or terms was important in world events since World War II. You may use two or more in a single sentence.

1 European Union (p. 632)

2 Mercosur (p. 633)

3 Bill Clinton (p. 633)

4 George W. Bush (p. 647)

5 Aung San Suu Kyi (p. 640)

6 Rigoberta Menchú (p. 640)

7 Mary Robinson (p. 639)

8 Slobodan Milosevic (p. 637)

9 Mairead Corrigan Maguire (p. 639)

10 ASEAN (p. 632)

late 1960s
Violence broke out in
Northern Ireland.

1989 Tiananmen Square massacre

1991–1992
Breakup of Yugoslavia

1994
NAFTA began.

1996
Taliban takeover in Afghanistan

1999
War in
Kosovo

1967 ASEAN was formed.

2001 Terrorist attacks hit New York City and near Washington, D.C.

Facts and Main Ideas

1 What is a trading bloc?

2 How did Chinese communist leaders react to students protesting in Tiananmen Square in 1989?

3 Which republics pulled out of Yugoslavia? Which republic used force against them?

4 **Time Line** How many years were there between the breakup of Yugoslavia and the war in Kosovo?

5 **Main Idea** How has economic cooperation brought about the global economy?

6 **Main Idea** Why do differences of identity sometimes lead to conflict?

7 **Main Idea** How has the world responded to acts of terrorism?

8 **Critical Thinking:** *Fact or Opinion* Acts of terrorism against Americans have been committed for centuries.

Write About History

1 **Write an advertisement** for a new product your company is trying to market in a foreign nation.

2 **Write an eyewitness account** of the events in Tiananmen Square in June 1989. Identify your point of view—student, soldier, bystander, or reporter.

3 **Write a preamble,** or introduction, to a new constitution for a nation that has decided to guarantee full equality for women.

Apply Skills

Interpret Cartograms

Turn to the atlas in the back of your textbook. Look at a map of South America. Then look at the cartogram below representing population and answer the following question.

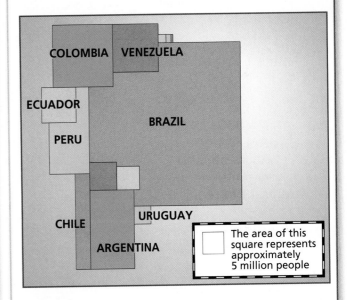

COLOMBIA VENEZUELA

ECUADOR

PERU

BRAZIL

CHILE URUGUAY

ARGENTINA

The area of this square represents approximately 5 million people

1 How does the map of South America on page R9 compare to the cartogram?

Internet Activity

To get help with vocabulary, people, and terms, select dictionary, encyclopedia, or almanac from *Social Studies Library* at www.sfsocialstudies.com.

Living in the 21st Century

Lesson 1

2000s
Calcutta
Population is growing and changing, especially in megacities.

1

Lesson 2

2000s
Antarctica
People cause environmental damage and work to repair it.

2

Lesson 3

2000s
Iguaçu Falls
We seek new energy sources and ways to produce and conserve energy.

3

Lesson 4

2000s
Space
New technology changes people's lives.

4

Locating Time and Place

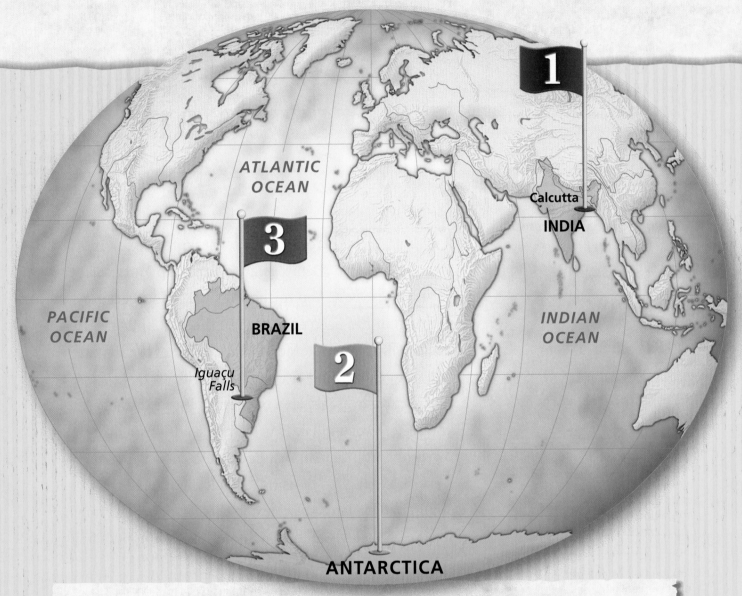

ATLANTIC OCEAN

PACIFIC OCEAN

INDIAN OCEAN

1

Calcutta

INDIA

3

BRAZIL

Iguaçu Falls

2

ANTARCTICA

Why We Remember

As you live your daily life, you are part of history being made. You make choices and solve problems that affect other people and places. For example, you buy products made in a particular country. By doing this, you contribute to the wealth of that country. Decisions you make about how to use electricity affect energy supplies and the environment. You use technology, which is constantly being improved. Some day in the future you may look at a social studies textbook. As you thumb through the pages, you may think: "I was there! I was part of history."

1850　　　1900　　　1950　　　2000

about 1900
One out of 10 people live in cities.

about 1960
More people began moving from developing to developed countries.

2000
About half of the world's population lives in cities.

Population Growth and Change

PREVIEW

Focus on the Main Idea
Population growth and movement present challenges in today's world.

PLACES
Mexico City
Calcutta
Madagascar

PEOPLE
Mother Teresa

VOCABULARY
millennium
megacity
demographer
immigration
zero population growth

▶ Mexico City is one of the most populated cities in the world.

You Are There
Your family settles into the car at Benito Juárez Airport in Mexico City. You're coming here to live because your father has been appointed to the U.S. Embassy. He keeps telling you that Mexico City is one of the largest and most interesting cities in the world.

The car moves fast on a busy road. In the distance, you see crowded hillsides with thousands of small dwellings. You've read that people are coming to the city too fast to get good housing. See all the haze? That's smog. Dad explains that Mexico City sits in a bowl much like Los Angeles, California. Sometimes the polluted air settles over the city.

You reach the downtown area and pass by wide boulevards and parks bright with flowers. Everywhere you see people—shopping, hurrying, and buying snacks from street vendors. It's not hard to believe that Mexico City has nearly 20 million residents. You begin to look forward to the exciting year ahead.

Draw Conclusions As you read, put facts together to identify how the population is growing and changing in many parts of the world.

Population Growth

By the late twentieth century, Mexico City was the most populated city in the world. It was less populated a century ago. However, population growth is not unique to Mexico City. It is happening all over the world.

Earth is home to billions of people. A millennium is one thousand years. At the beginning of the second millennium, the world population stood at about 6 billion people. When your grandparents were in school, the world had about half that many people. The graph below shows how rapidly population has grown.

Many of the world's people are moving to urban, or city, areas. Cities usually offer more job opportunities than rural, or country, areas. But many cities are growing so fast that they cannot provide housing for the people who live in them. Urban areas cannot always provide basic necessities such as clean water and good housing.

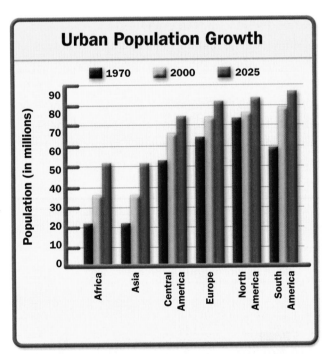

Urban population growth has increased greatly in many regions of the world since 1970.

GRAPH SKILL Use a Bar Graph *Which region is projected to have the largest urban population by 2025?*

▶ **Mother Teresa talks to children at an orphanage in Calcutta, India.**

By 2000 there were more than 20 megacities in the world. A megacity is a city region with 10 million or more people. Tokyo, New York City, and São Paulo are all megacities.

Calcutta, India, is also a megacity, but it is one of the world's poorest cities. According to some estimates, 600,000 people are homeless in Calcutta. They live on the city streets.

You may have heard of Mother Teresa. She was a Roman Catholic nun who wanted to help the poorest people in Calcutta. She lived and worked in Calcutta's slums for more than 40 years.

Mother Teresa helped set up soup kitchens, hospitals, and shelters for homeless people. She provided hospices, or places for dying people to be sheltered and cared for.

Like others of the late twentieth century, Mother Teresa believed in people. She said:

> *"Do not wait for leaders; do it alone, person to person."*

In 1979 Mother Teresa received the Nobel Peace Prize. She is known to the world as one who made a difference in the lives of thousands of people.

REVIEW How did Mother Teresa help the people of India? ⟳ **Draw Conclusions**

655

Population Movement

You have already learned that people throughout the world are moving to urban areas. The migration of people from rural to urban areas increased during the Industrial Revolution in the late 1800s. By 1900 only about 1 out of 10 people in the world lived in cities. More people moved from the countryside to cities in the first half of the twentieth century for economic opportunities.

By the 1960s, people began moving from developing countries to more developed countries. Today, most of these people on the move continue to seek a better life. Populations in developing countries are rising so fast that many governments can no longer provide good housing and clean water. They also do not have enough jobs for all of the people. Unemployment is high in many developing countries.

The population is growing much faster in many developing nations than in most developed nations. For example, in **Madagascar,** off the coast of East Africa, the population is increasing at more than 3 percent a year. By contrast, the population growth rate in the United States is about 0.9 percent, which means that its population doubles in size in about 77 years. At a 3 percent growth rate, a country's population doubles in less than 25 years. Population is also growing rapidly in developing nations such as

▶ People crowd a market in Guatemala, a country whose population has nearly doubled since 1975.

Guatemala, Ethiopia, and the Philippines.

On the other hand, population is growing little or not at all in countries such as Sweden, Italy, and Japan. These are all developed nations.

REVIEW How are high population growth rates affecting developing countries? **Cause and Effect**

Immigration

Population changes are important to study because they affect how people live and work. Scientists who study population trends are called **demographers** (di MAH gruh furz).

Many demographers believe that the status of women affects the rate of population growth. In developed countries, women often have good opportunities for education. Educated women tend to have children later, and fewer of them. In developing countries, women sometimes have fewer job and educational opportunities.

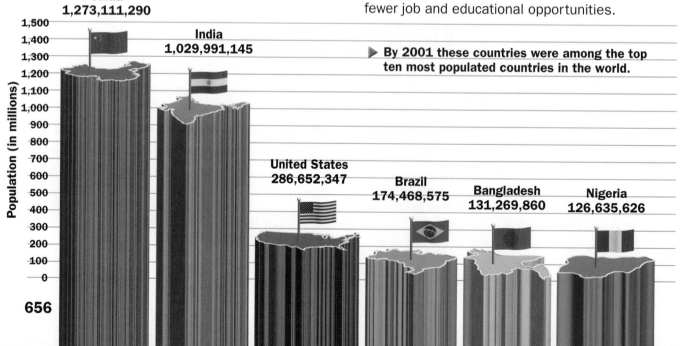

China
1,273,111,290

India
1,029,991,145

▶ By 2001 these countries were among the top ten most populated countries in the world.

United States
286,652,347

Brazil
174,468,575

Bangladesh
131,269,860

Nigeria
126,635,626

Population (in millions)

1,500
1,400
1,300
1,200
1,100
1,000
900
800
700
600
500
400
300
200
100
0

Immigration from developing countries is changing the population and cultures of many developed countries. **Immigration** is the process of people moving to a new country to stay permanently or for a long time. For example, France has received many immigrants from former French colonies in North Africa. Now one of France's national foods is *couscous,* a hot-cereal dish from Arab countries. Some demographers believe that more people in France now attend mosques than churches. This is because most immigrants from North Africa are Muslims.

REVIEW How has immigration changed countries? Main Idea and Details

A Population Explosion?

Not long ago, demographers spoke of a "population explosion." They compared population to something wildly out of control—like the explosion of a bomb. Some of these scientists painted very grim pictures of the world's future.

Today, many demographers see evidence of slowing population growth. In some developed countries, **zero population growth** has been reached. This means that just enough babies are being born to balance population loss.

Some demographers even think that by later in the twenty-first century, the world's population might begin to shrink. In the meantime, growing population remains a challenge in many cities and developing countries.

REVIEW In your own words, explain the idea of zero population growth. Summarize

Summarize the Lesson

c. 1900 One out of 10 people lived in cities.

c. 1960 More people began moving from developing to developed countries.

2000 About half of the population lived in urban areas.

LESSON 1   REVIEW

Check Facts and Main Ideas

1. Draw Conclusions On a separate piece of paper, copy the diagram below. Write a conclusion based on the facts in the diagram.

| More people have migrated to developed countries. |
| More people have migrated to urban areas. |
| More people have migrated to places with more opportunities. |

2. Why are people moving to cities?

3. In which parts of the world is the population growing the fastest?

4. Name one challenge that population movement presents.

5. **Critical Thinking: *Make Generalizations*** How does immigration affect populations in developed and developing countries?

Link to 🔗 Mathematics

Draw a Line Graph Suppose the population of a megacity was 4 million in 1960, 6 million in 1980, and 12 million in 2000. Sketch a line graph to show the growth of this megacity, or describe how the line would look.

Map and Globe Skills

Compare Distribution Maps

What? Distribution maps are maps that show where something, such as people or natural resources, is distributed, or spread, across the area shown on the map. The world population distribution map below shows where people are distributed around the world.

Distribution maps often use dots to show population density, or where people live. Look at the population distribution map below.

Why? Distribution maps are useful because they are very flexible. You can make distribution maps to show how *anything* is distributed. Do you want to know where certain animals live? Look at a wildlife distribution map. How about where certain kinds of industries are located? Use an economic distribution map.

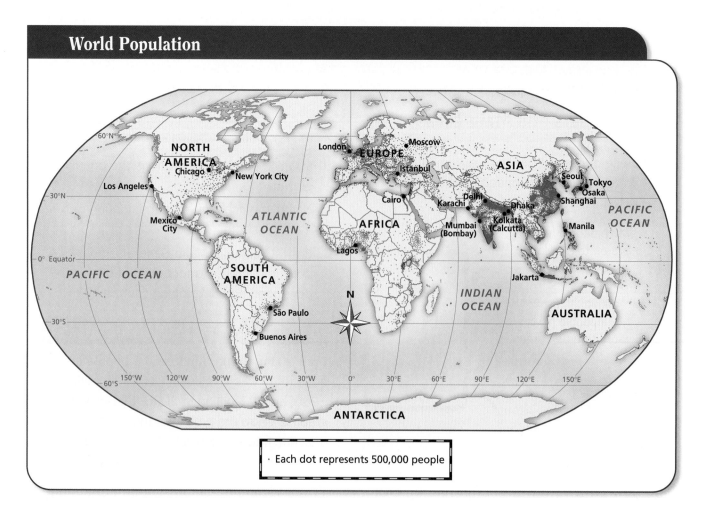

World Population

Each dot represents 500,000 people

Major Oil and Gas Fields

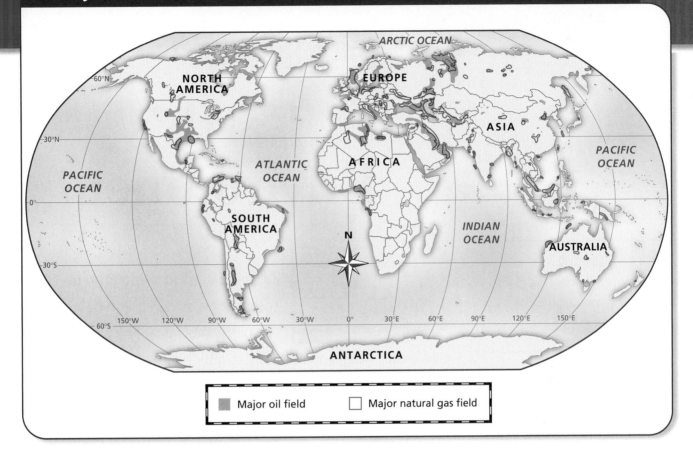

Major oil field   Major natural gas field

Meteorologists, or people who study Earth's atmosphere and weather patterns, use distribution maps to see where rain has fallen. Environmentalists use distribution maps to determine where pollution is found. Businesses use them to show where their offices are located.

How? You can learn a lot by comparing different types of distribution maps that show the same area. For example, by comparing a world population distribution map to a distribution map showing where oil and gas fields are located, you can learn if there are large populations living near important energy resources. You can also learn where important resources are located.

To compare distribution maps, follow these steps.

1. Read the title of the maps to learn what each map shows.
2. Study the map keys on both maps to learn what the symbols and colors on the map mean.

3. Note what is alike and different in the distribution of things on both maps.

Use the World Population map on page 658 and the Major Oil and Gas Fields map on this page to answer the following questions.

1 In what regions of the world is population density the greatest?

2 On which continents are the major oil and gas fields located?

For more information, go online to the Atlas at **www.sfsocialstudies.com.**

1960　　1970　　1980　　1990　　2000

1962
Silent Spring
is published.

1970
The Environmental Protection
Agency is established.

1997
The Kyoto Protocol
is written.

PREVIEW

Focus on the Main Idea
People are working together to repair damage to Earth's environment.

PLACES
Antarctica

PEOPLE
Rachel Carson

VOCABULARY
global warming
carbon dioxide
greenhouse effect
pesticide
environmentalist
endangered species
deforestation
desertification
pollution

TERMS
Environmental Protection
Agency

▶ People in developed countries generate the most garbage. In response, more people have started recycling programs to reduce waste.

Earth's Environment

You Are There Camping in the back country of Yosemite National Park in California is one of the best vacations you've ever had. Today, you're hiking to a high lookout with a wide view of the whole valley. It's hard work keeping up with Mom and Dad. But they say this view is really worth the effort.

As you round the last corner, your eyes follow the path out onto the ledge of the lookout. You take a deep breath . . . and then you see it. Just in front of the guardrail is a huge plastic garbage bag. Through a rip, it is spilling out cans, spoiled food, pop bottles, and other junk.

"Tourist trash," says Mom. "Some people have no respect for our planet." Though the view of the valley is awesome, you can't really enjoy it. You're bothered by the way that some people have treated this beautiful place.

Cause and Effect As you read, consider how humans affect Earth's environment and what they are trying to do to take care of it.

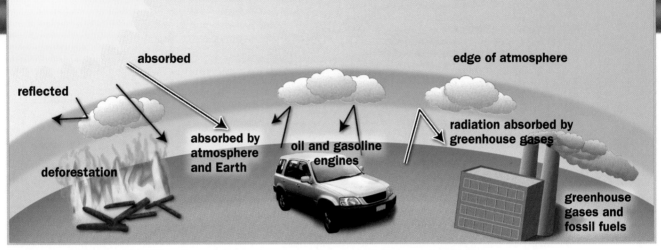

The greenhouse effect is often compared to how air warms inside a greenhouse.

DIAGRAM SKILL Use a Diagram *What conclusion can you draw from the diagram about the greenhouse effect?*

The Environment

Global warming is a gradual increase in the average temperature of Earth's surface. Many scientists agree that Earth's temperature is rising, but they do not agree on why it is rising or what the causes and effects might be.

Human activities such as burning gasoline in cars produce a gas called carbon dioxide. **Carbon dioxide** and other gases trap heat that is radiated from the earth. Radiation from the earth then warms the atmosphere. This process is called the **greenhouse effect.**

Some scientists estimate that carbon dioxide in the atmosphere has increased by about 25 percent since the mid-1800s. Burning fuels such as coal and oil in factories, houses, and cars has caused most of this increase.

In the 1960s, many people became more aware of how human activity was affecting our natural environment. They believed that some economic development was harmful to nature.

In 1962 a scientist named **Rachel Carson** wrote *Silent Spring.* This book described how **pesticides,** or chemicals that are used to kill pests such as insects, were killing off birds and other animals. Carson explained how mornings were becoming silent:

> *"Early mornings are strangely silent where once they were filled with the beauty of bird song."*

Silent Spring convinced some people to become environmentalists. An **environmentalist** is a person who favors taking measures to protect Earth's natural environment. People began pressing for laws to protect the environment.

In 1970 the U.S. Congress set up the **Environmental Protection Agency.** This agency serves as a watchdog for the environment. Later, Congress passed laws to protect **endangered species,** or animals and plants that could die out. In Europe, "green" political parties formed. Through political action, they worked to pass environmental laws.

REVIEW How did some people respond to *Silent Spring*? Cause and Effect

▶ Rachel Carson holding *Silent Spring,* her book that sparked environmentalism

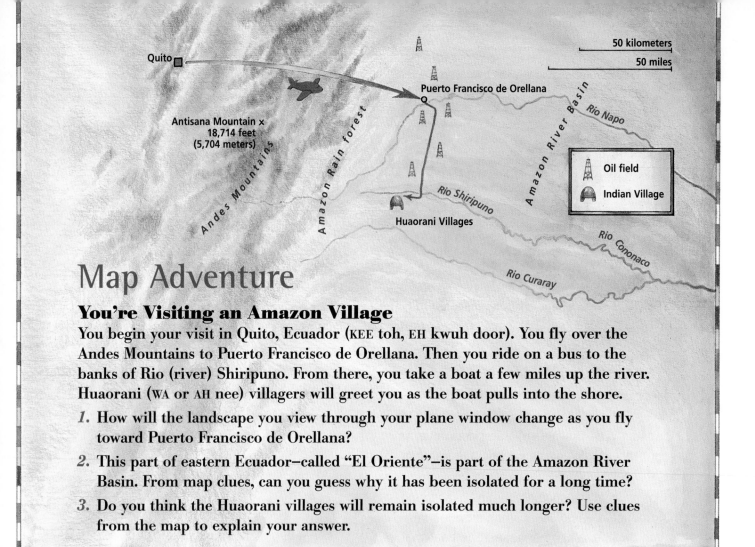

Map Adventure

You're Visiting an Amazon Village

You begin your visit in Quito, Ecuador (KEE toh, EH kwuh door). You fly over the Andes Mountains to Puerto Francisco de Orellana. Then you ride on a bus to the banks of Rio (river) Shiripuno. From there, you take a boat a few miles up the river. Huaorani (WA or AH nee) villagers will greet you as the boat pulls into the shore.

1. How will the landscape you view through your plane window change as you fly toward Puerto Francisco de Orellana?

2. This part of eastern Ecuador—called "El Oriente"—is part of the Amazon River Basin. From map clues, can you guess why it has been isolated for a long time?

3. Do you think the Huaorani villages will remain isolated much longer? Use clues from the map to explain your answer.

Problems and Solutions

Some environmentalists believe that global warming will continue unless people take steps to slow or stop it. In 1997 officials from more than 160 countries met in Kyoto, Japan, to draw up a treaty on global warming called the Kyoto Protocol. The treaty urged nations to agree to reduce the production of greenhouse gases such as carbon dioxide over time.

But most nations have not adopted the treaty because they believe it will disrupt their economies. The treaty must be ratified by at least 55 countries. For more developed countries, the treaty offers emission credits in return for pollution control efforts.

Another problem in the world is feeding rapidly growing populations. Farmers have cut down forests to grow crops. This process is called **deforestation.** The deforestation of rain forests in South America, Africa, and Southeast Asia has added to global warming. Deforestation has removed the trees, which absorb carbon dioxide gases. As a solution to deforestation, people have planted trees.

Global warming is not the only example of climate change caused by human activity. Throughout history, fertile land has been lost through a process called **desertification.** In this process, farmers plow fields, and animals overgraze the land. Topsoil becomes loose, dries up, and blows away. Desertification has been devastating in parts of Africa.

The effect of humans on the environment has also reached the poles of the earth. For example, **Antarctica,** the fifth largest continent on Earth, was the last continent to be explored. It is also the highest, driest, and coldest continent. Only scientists live there. However, tourism in Antarctica has grown in the past several decades. Some 15,000 tourists visit there each year. Rusted cans and plastic wrappers are just some of the ways people have polluted parts of

Antartica. **Pollution** is the process of making the environment dirty. A visible form of pollution is waste such as garbage. As a solution to pollution, people recycle aluminum, paper, and glass.

REVIEW What agricultural practices have harmed the land? Summarize

Summarize the Lesson

1970 The U.S. Congress set up the Environmental Protection Agency.

1997 The Kyoto Protocol was written.

▶ **Trash left by tourists in Antarctica harms the environment and wildlife.**

LESSON 2 REVIEW

Check Facts and Main Ideas

1. Cause and Effect On a separate piece of paper, copy the diagram below. Fill in the effects.

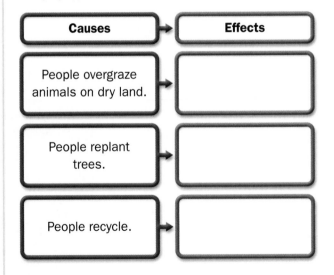

Causes	→	Effects
People overgraze animals on dry land.	→	
People replant trees.	→	
People recycle.	→	

2. What is an environmentalist?

3. What has happened to the amount of carbon dioxide in Earth's atmosphere?

4. How have people helped to solve environmental problems in the last 50 years?

5. Critical Thinking: *Evaluate Information* Do you think that humans have done more good or harm to Earth? Why or why not?

Link to ⚭ Science

Research and Report Carbon dioxide is not the only greenhouse gas, although it is the most plentiful. Use an encyclopedia or Internet resource to identify another greenhouse gas. Explain how it is produced.

1970	1980	1990	2000

1973
First global
oil crisis

1986
Chernobyl
nuclear accident

2001
George W. Bush begins campaign
to help make the United States
self-sufficient.

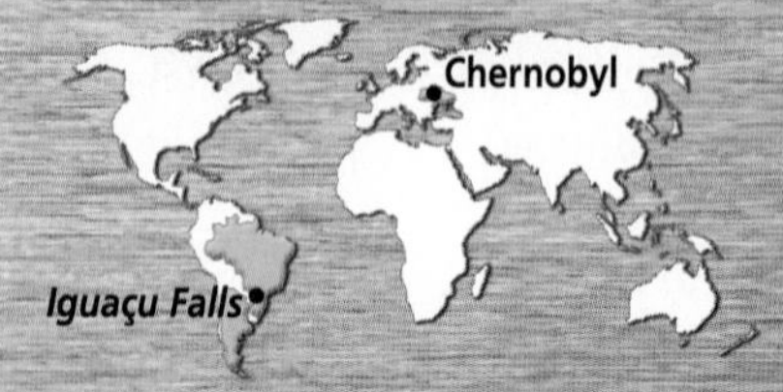

Chernobyl

Iguaçu Falls

Energy

PREVIEW

Focus on the Main Idea
As energy sources become less plentiful, we look for new ways to produce and conserve energy.

PLACES
Chernobyl
Iguaçu Falls
Niagara Falls

PEOPLE
George W. Bush

VOCABULARY
conservation
fossil fuel
nonrenewable resource
renewable resource
hydroelectric energy
geothermal energy

TERMS
Organization of Petroleum
 Exporting Countries (OPEC)

▶ **An offshore drilling rig in the Gulf of Mexico**

You Are There
Mom is a petroleum engineer. When your friends find out what she does, they picture her wearing an oil-spattered outfit and carrying a clipboard.

Actually, Mom does most of her work in an office watching a computer screen. Today, she has let you visit her at work!

Mom brings up the 3-D imaging software she uses to look at rocks far underground. You see bands of stuff in different colors. It looks like a layered cake. Mom hands you 3-D goggles and says, "Put these on." Wow! Now you feel like you are *inside* the rock layers.

"There!" says Mom. "Look at that pool of liquid. That might be oil."

She tells you that it's important for us to keep looking for more sources of oil so we don't have to rely on oil from other countries. However, she also explains that we should reduce our use of fuels and find alternative sources of energy too.

Draw Conclusions As you read, identify how energy is produced and where new energy sources might be located.

Using Energy

Energy keeps our world going. We depend on natural resources to keep producing the energy we need. As world population has grown rapidly, demand for energy has skyrocketed. A growing population, new industries, and new technologies demand more energy.

Keeping up with this demand for energy is one of the biggest challenges we face in the twenty-first century. We need to find new energy sources and new ways to produce energy. We also need to learn how to stop wasting energy. Conservation, or limiting our use of energy, is one solution to this energy crisis.

Do you ever wonder when you plug in your computer or television where the electricity comes from? It is generated in a power plant, which uses power lines to get electricity to your home. Most power plants burn fuel to produce steam from water. The pressure of the steam then drives a generator.

We burn a lot of coal, petroleum (oil), and natural gas to run generators in power plants. We use these fuels in other ways too. In a huge chemical plant called a refinery, gasoline is extracted, or taken out, from petroleum. As you know, gasoline makes most of our cars run.

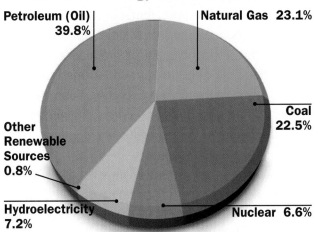

Sources of Energy as Percent of Total

Petroleum (Oil) 39.8%
Natural Gas 23.1%
Coal 22.5%
Nuclear 6.6%
Hydroelectricity 7.2%
Other Renewable Sources 0.8%

GRAPH SKILL Use a Circle Graph *Which source of energy is used more than others?*

Coal, petroleum, and natural gas make up more than 80 percent of world energy sources. They are fossil fuels, which formed long ago, deep in the earth from rotting plants and animals. Part of the trouble with fossil fuels is that they take so long to form. Fossil fuels are nonrenewable resources because they can not be easily replaced. Look at the time line below to see when some scientists believe that fossil fuels will run out.

REVIEW What are some causes of the rapidly increasing demand for energy? Cause and Effect

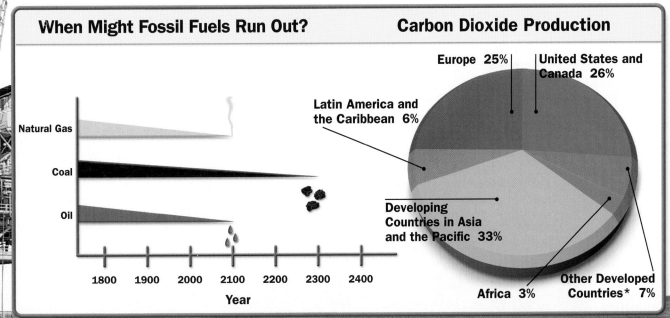

When Might Fossil Fuels Run Out?

Natural Gas
Coal
Oil

Year: 1800 1900 2000 2100 2200 2300 2400

Carbon Dioxide Production

Europe 25%
United States and Canada 26%
Latin America and the Caribbean 6%
Developing Countries in Asia and the Pacific 33%
Africa 3%
Other Developed Countries* 7%

*including Australia, New Zealand, and Japan

Meeting Energy Needs

Because most developed countries have relied on fossil fuels for energy, they have faced many challenges. For example, much of the world's oil reserves are located in the Middle East. In 1973 many of the world's biggest oil producers cut their production of petroleum and formed the Organization of Petroleum Exporting Countries (OPEC). They also raised oil prices. This caused a global oil crisis. People waited in long lines to fill their cars with gasoline.

Because the United States imports a great deal of the oil it uses, it has relied on OPEC. To avoid a future energy supply crisis, U.S. President George W. Bush began a campaign in 2001 toward self-sufficiency.

Another problem with fossil fuels is that they give off carbon dioxide when they burn. You read in Lesson 2 how this gas is collecting in Earth's atmosphere, trapping warmth. Fossil fuels are thought by some to be the main cause of global warming.

One nonrenewable resource that does not give off carbon dioxide is nuclear energy. A nuclear power plant uses steam pressure to drive a generator. But instead of burning a fossil fuel, it uses nuclear fuel. In nuclear fuel, heat is produced by splitting atoms. Though nonrenewable, nuclear fuel could last for thousands of years.

Nuclear power seems to be a good alternative energy source. However, sometimes things can go wrong in a nuclear power plant. In 1986 the Chernobyl (chair NOH buhl) nuclear power plant in the Soviet Union (now Ukraine) had a terrible accident. Gases and steam blew off the top of the concrete building. Radioactive gases escaped into the atmosphere. About 30 people died. However, some scientists think an additional 40,000 cancer deaths will occur over time because of the population's exposure to nuclear radiation.

Another problem with nuclear power is the waste it produces. This material, which remains radioactive for thousands of years, must be buried deep underground.

REVIEW What are the advantages and disadvantages of using nuclear power as an alternative energy source? **Main Idea and Details**

Alternative Energy

Some people think that we should use more renewable resources such as solar energy, water, and wind because they cannot be used up easily like nonrenewable resources can. Some power plants are using giant windmills to drive generators. Others use water power from rapidly flowing rivers or dams. This type of energy is called hydroelectric energy. Waterfalls are a great source of hydroelectricity. Iguaçu Falls on the border between Argentina and Brazil is a major source of hydroelectricity in South America. Niagara Falls in Canada provides a portion of the province of Ontario's energy needs.

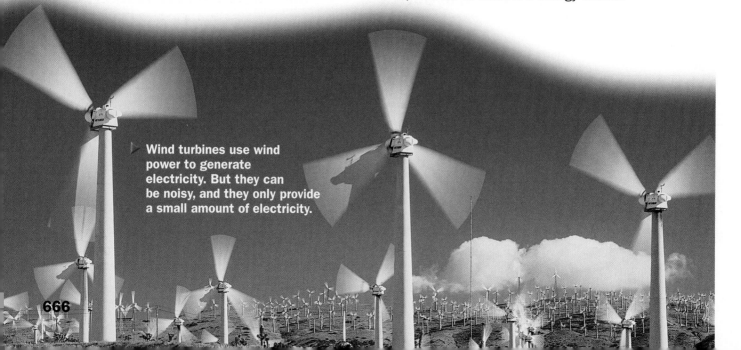

Wind turbines use wind power to generate electricity. But they can be noisy, and they only provide a small amount of electricity.

Another alternative, or other, energy source is **geothermal energy.** This is energy from super-hot water underground. Many power plants could tap into this source. But alternative energy sources can only make a minor contribution to our energy needs. Some are available in only certain parts of the world.

Scientists are trying to create entirely new ways of producing energy. One area of research is nuclear fusion. *Fusion* means "joining together." In nuclear fusion, atoms are combined instead of split apart. This process releases energy and does not produce dangerous waste products.

To tackle our energy challenges, we can also look at making changes to the fuel-guzzling machines we use. For example, we can try to make automobiles and trucks more energy efficient. Engineers in automobile companies are developing hybrid cars. These cars are smaller and lighter than traditional cars. They have much smaller gasoline engines.

▶ **Iguaçu Falls consists of some 275 waterfalls.**

REVIEW What conclusion can you make about the alternative energy sources we use?
⟳ **Draw Conclusions**

Summarize the Lesson

1973 The first global oil crisis occurred.

1986 The Chernobyl nuclear accident polluted vast areas of eastern Europe.

2001 George W. Bush began an energy campaign to help make the United States self-sufficient.

LESSON 3   REVIEW

Check Facts and Main Ideas

1. ⟳ **Draw Conclusions** On a separate piece of paper, copy the diagram below. Write a conclusion based on the given facts.

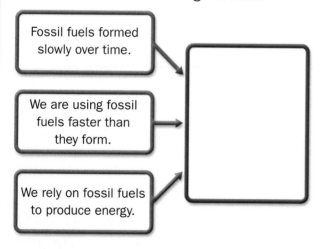

Fossil fuels formed slowly over time.

We are using fossil fuels faster than they form.

We rely on fossil fuels to produce energy.

2. What are fossil fuels and which one will probably run out first?

3. List a benefit and a disadvantage of nuclear energy.

4. Identify alternative energy sources we use today.

5. **Critical Thinking: *Solve Complex Problems*** Make a list of the qualities a good energy source has.

Link to ⬡⬡ Science

Electricity from Lightning In this lesson, you have read about generating electricity in power plants. Explain whether or not you believe lightning could be used to produce electricity. Explain your conclusion.

1950   **1975**   **2000**

1957
First
satellite

1975
First personal
computer

1995
U.S. *Atlantis* docks
with Russia's *Mir*.

2000
Human Genome Project identifies thousands of human genes.

NORTH AMERICA   EUROPE   ASIA
AFRICA
SOUTH AMERICA   AUSTRALIA

Technology

PREVIEW

Focus on the Main Idea
Technology gives us many benefits, but it cannot solve every human problem.

PEOPLE
Yuri Gagarin
Neil Armstrong
Edwin Aldrin
Charles DeLisi
David A. Smith
Flossie Wong-Staal

VOCABULARY
space station
satellite

TERMS
National Aeronautics and Space
   Administration (NASA)
Human Genome Project

You Are There

Snug in your spacesuit, you step off of the space shuttle and onto a space station. You close your eyes. You've dreamed of this day. You remember reading about the U.S. space shuttle *Atlantis* docking with the Russian space station *Mir* (meer) in 1995. Russian and American crews then began working together to do important experiments and repair satellites on the space station. Soon, astronauts came from many other nations to work on *Mir*.

You're thrilled that you were chosen to work on the International Space Station. You know that you will work and sleep here for many days and do important work. You wonder if the inside of the space station is like a railroad car because other astronauts have described it that way. You open your eyes and take another step. Now it's your turn to make history.

Draw Conclusions
As you read, put facts together to understand how we solve problems with technology.

▶ In 1965 Edward H. White II became the first American to leave his spacecraft and "walk" in space.

New Technology

Just like the space station *Mir*, technology can develop quickly. A **space station** is a large **satellite,** or human-made object sent into space, that serves as a scientific base. It can also be used as a refueling station for spacecraft or a launching pad for other satellites.

Technology has helped us learn more about our universe and change and improve our lives. However, there are problems that come with advancing technology.

Technology includes using knowledge, resources, and tools to accomplish or improve something. In prehistory, technology was very basic. It included advancements in toolmaking from stone to copper. Today, when we make more powerful computers to process more information faster, that is technology.

In fact, for the past 50 years, computers have played a part in most of our technology. Fast-developing technology has helped space travel skyrocket. The former Soviet Union put the first satellite into orbit in 1957. It was called *Sputnik I.* Today, telephones, cable television, and other communications depend on satellites.

Technology helped astronaut **Yuri Gagarin** of the Soviet Union to become the first human in space in April 1961. The U.S. government space agency, the **National Aeronautics and Space Administration (NASA),** sent the first humans, **Neil Armstrong** and **Edwin Aldrin,** to walk on the moon in July 1969. All of this was made possible with technology.

REVIEW What are two important new technologies of the twentieth century?
Summarize

Computers

Then and Now

One of the first modern computers was developed by American John Atanasoff. It was completed in 1946 and called an Electronic Numerical Integrator and Computer, or ENIAC. Weighing some 30 tons and filling the space of a small room, ENIAC could only complete one task at a time.

Personal computers (PCs) that fit on your desktop were developed in 1975. PCs could be used at home or work by one person and were much faster than ENIAC. By the mid-1990s, a computer could be held in someone's hand! With a hand-held computer, you can browse the Internet and download information while you are away from your PC.

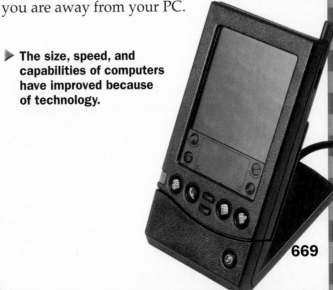

▶ The size, speed, and capabilities of computers have improved because of technology.

New Possibilities

Another new form of technology that developed in the late twentieth century was the mapping of genes. Genes are the basic blueprint for life. Scientists have learned how to substitute genes from one cell to another. They can even mix genes from different species, or life forms.

The **Human Genome Project** is an international effort to find all of the more than 30,000 human genes. It was launched in 1990, five years after **Charles DeLisi** and **David A. Smith** led the first conference to investigate the possibility of such a project. By 2000 researchers were able to map out thousands of human genes. By understanding genes, researchers can try to explain how genetic diseases develop and find a cure for such diseases.

Technology has helped researchers and scientists identify human genes. However, there are social and legal issues involved. The information that we learn about genes could be used for other purposes. Even though the cause of disease is the main goal of discovering genes, it may not be the only one.

REVIEW How can technology help researchers learn about human genes? ⟳ Draw Conclusions

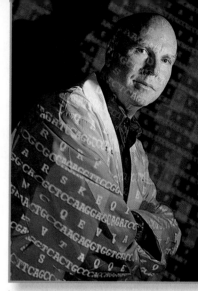

▶ **J. Craig Venter, a leading genomic scientist, stands in front of a projection from the human genetic code.**

DORLING KINDERSLEY EYEWITNESS BOOK

Telecommunication

Communication is the sharing of information, ideas, and thoughts. It has been a vital part of human life since prehistory. Over time, methods of communication have improved. Today, we can even rely on telecommunication— messages that can be transmitted by radio, telephones, and satellites—to communicate with people around the world.

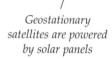

Geostationary satellites are powered by solar panels

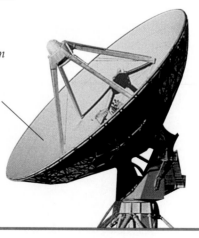

Ground station receives signals from the satellites

Satellite Systems

About 200 communication satellites are in orbit around the Earth. The satellites receive signals from transmitter dishes, amplify them, and then relay them back to a ground station. In this way, the signals are transmitted to other continents, enabling instant worldwide telecommunication.

670

Limits

Many scientists today are doing research on a disease called Acquired Immunodeficiency Syndrome, or AIDS. AIDS is a deadly disease that attacks people's immune systems. Scientists are using technology to help find a cure.

Flossie Wong-Staal has helped lead the way in AIDS research. In the early 1980s, she joined the group in the United States that identified human immunodeficiency virus, or HIV, the AIDS virus. Researchers in France made the same discovery at the same time.

AIDS illustrates both the power and limits of technology. Anti-AIDS drugs can now keep infected people healthy for years. But these drugs are very expensive. Only some people can afford them. People in developing countries cannot usually afford to buy anti-AIDS drugs.

In 2001 UN Secretary-General Kofi Annan urged nations to contribute money to help fight AIDS in Africa. Southern Africa has the largest number of people infected with HIV in the world.

The AIDS crisis in Africa demonstrates that technology cannot solve every problem. Still, technology has been part of our human history from the beginning. It continues to impact how we live.

REVIEW What is the main goal of the technologies discussed in this section?
🔄 Draw Conclusions

Summarize the Lesson

— **1957** The Soviet Union launched the world's first artificial satellite, *Sputnik I.*

— **1975** The first personal computer became available to the public.

— **2000** The Human Genome Project identified thousands of genes.

LESSON 4   REVIEW

Check Facts and Main Ideas

1. 🔄 **Draw Conclusions** On a separate piece of paper, copy the diagram below. Write a conclusion based on the given facts.

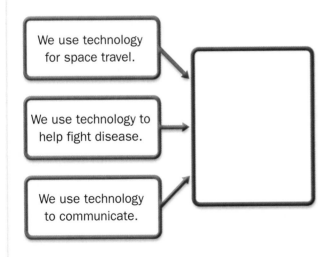

We use technology for space travel.

We use technology to help fight disease.

We use technology to communicate.

2. Explain how we have used technology in space.

3. What is the Human Genome Project?

4. Give an example of a problem that technology might solve and an example of a problem that it cannot solve.

5. **Critical Thinking:** *Evaluate Information* Of the technologies discussed in this lesson, which do you think is most important? Explain your answer.

Link to ◦—◦ Technology

Be an Inventor What could you invent that would improve an aspect of human life? Would your invention help solve a problem in your community or school? Describe your invention and then draw a sketch or make a model to present to the class.

1950   1960

1957
First successful satellite

about 1960
More people began moving from developing to developed countries.

1962
Silent Spring was published.

Chapter Summary

Target Skill

Draw Conclusions

On a separate piece of paper, copy the diagram below. Write a conclusion based on the given facts in the diagram.

Fossil fuels are nonrenewable resources.

The world's population is increasing.

Technology can improve our lives.

Vocabulary

Match each word with the correct definition or description.

1 demographer (p. 656)

2 environmentalist (p. 661)

3 global warming (p. 661)

4 fossil fuel (p. 665)

5 satellite (p. 669)

a. coal, petroleum, natural gas

b. a person who supports taking measures to protect environment

c. a gradual increase in Earth's average temperature

d. a scientist who studies population trends

e. an object that is sent into space and orbits Earth

People and Terms

Write a sentence explaining why each of the following people or terms was important in events since World War II. You may use two or more in a single sentence.

1 Mother Teresa (p. 655)

2 Rachel Carson (p. 661)

3 Environmental Protection Agency (p. 661)

4 NASA (p. 669)

5 Yuri Gagarin (p. 669)

6 Neil Armstrong and Edwin Aldrin (p. 669)

7 George W. Bush (p. 666)

8 OPEC (p. 666)

9 Human Genome Project (p. 670)

10 Flossie Wong-Staal (p. 671)

1970	1980	1990	2000

1970
The EPA
was set up.

1975
First personal
computer

1973 First global oil crisis

1986
Chernobyl nuclear
accident

1990
Human
Genome
Project was
launched.

1997
The Kyoto Protocol
was written.

2000
More than half of the
world's population
lived in cities.

Facts and Main Ideas

1 In what parts of the world is population growing the fastest?

2 How has technology changed since prehistory?

3 **Time Line** How many years were there between the publication of *Silent Spring* and the nuclear accident at Chernobyl?

4 **Main Idea** How is the world's population different today than it was about 50 years ago?

5 **Main Idea** How are we trying to solve environmental problems?

6 **Main Idea** How are we trying to solve energy problems?

7 **Main Idea** Can technology solve every human problem? Explain your answer.

8 **Critical Thinking:** *Evaluate Information* Do you think it is important to use technology to find a cure for a genetic disease? Why or why not?

Apply Skills

Compare Distribution Maps
Look at the map below. Then answer the questions.

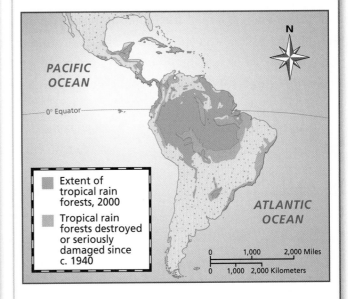

Legend:
- Extent of tropical rain forests, 2000
- Tropical rain forests destroyed or seriously damaged since c. 1940

PACIFIC OCEAN

0° Equator

ATLANTIC OCEAN

N

0   1,000   2,000 Miles
0 1,000 2,000 Kilometers

1 Look at the map on page 658. What is population density where tropical rain forests are located?

2 What can you conclude from the maps above and on page 658 about rain forests and population density in this region?

Write About History

1 **Write an energy-saving plan** for your family.

2 **Write a short biography** of one of the following people: Rachel Carson, Mother Teresa of Calcutta, or George W. Bush. Use encyclopedias or the Internet to do your research.

3 **Write three personal guidelines** for using environmental resources.

Internet Activity

To get help with vocabulary, people, and terms, select dictionary, encyclopedia, or almanac from *Social Studies Library* at **www.sfsocialstudies.com.**

End with a Poem

The Garden We Planted Together

by Anuruddha Bose

This poem was written by an 11-year-old boy from India in honor of the fiftieth anniversary of the United Nations. As you have learned, the United Nations was created in 1945 as a world peacekeeping organization. After reading Anuruddha's poem, consider why he chose this subject. What do you think the garden symbolizes?

From all over the world
together they came,
to make a garden
with shovels and spades.

Disagreement crept in—
which flowers to grow?
So they sat in a circle
And agreed row by row.

They wrote down their rules
in a big, mighty book
and promised to keep them
by hook and by crook.

With the book to guide them,
they grew beautiful flowers,
each of them equal,
none higher, none lower.

When some flowers grow weak
or ready to die,
the children get together,
new solutions to try.

They share water and seeds,
all must have enough,
the book just demands it
when the going gets tough.

The garden remains a symbol
to all, its flowers are fifty years
old this fall. The book is known
as a charter of peace—its rules
are still valid, so read if you please.

Unit Review

Main Ideas and Vocabulary

TEST PREP

Read the passage below and use it to answer the questions that follow.

When World War II ended in 1945, European countries still held many colonies. Most colonies were in Africa and Asia. Soon they began demanding independence.

Mohandas Gandhi used new methods of nonviolent <u>civil disobedience</u> to gain independence for India in 1947.

By the 1960s, many nations in sub-Saharan Africa were becoming independent too. However, black Africans in South Africa had to struggle to gain full civil rights.

The state of Israel was created in 1948, which led to the Arab-Israeli Conflict. Later, the fall of communism in Eastern Europe led to the creation of more new nations.

The world faced many new ideas and challenges in the late twentieth century and early twenty-first century. Cooperation led to free trade and the global economy. Nations drew together and formed <u>trading blocs</u> to help promote regional trade.

Along with cooperation, though, conflicts broke out. Many conflicts were based on differences of identity. Ethnic conflict tore apart Yugoslavia and Rwanda. International terrorism posed new challenges.

Scientists developed new areas of research. Industry used the research to create new products. Computers soon changed the way people lived and worked.

Humans blasted into space. Astronauts walked on the moon and set up space stations. Scientists began to research human genes and find cures for diseases.

1 According to the passage, what forces led to creation of so many new nations after 1945?
A communist takeovers
B hatred, greed
C the end of imperialism, the fall of communism
D inflation, unemployment

2 In the passage the term *civil disobedience* means—
A going to prison
B opposing someone by any means necessary
C setting up an new nation
D opposing someone or something by not cooperating

3 In the passage the term *trading blocs* means—
A open-air markets
B groups of countries trading to their advantage
C efforts to stop trade
D tariffs

4 What is the main idea of the passage?
A The world is full of conflict.
B We live in a time of new nations, ideas, and challenges.
C Mohandas K. Gandhi was a great person.
D Science is changing our world.

Use the diagram to help you find the answer.

Vocabulary

Match vocabulary word to its definition.

1. millennium (p. 655)
2. deforestation (p. 662)
3. *glasnost* (p. 622)
4. renewable resource (p. 666)
5. *perestroika* (p. 622)
6. immigration (p. 657)

a. restructuring

b. one thousand years

c. clearing of trees

d. openness

e. natural resource that can be replaced

f. process of people moving to a new place to live

Write and Share

Present Radio Interviews Choose someone to be the moderator of a radio talk show. The moderator will interview people that students have read about in the unit. Let other students volunteer for these guest parts. Have remaining classmates write questions that the moderator will ask the guests. Give guests time to write their answers before showtime.

Read on Your Own

Look for books like these in your library.

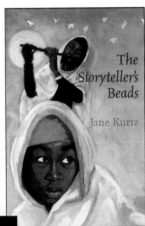

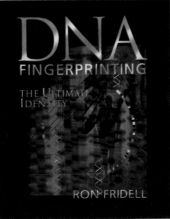

Apply Skills

Prepare a Cartogram using a topic from this unit. For example, compare how much garbage is produced by a country or how much energy is produced by a country or countries. Use encyclopedias, books, and the Internet to gather your statistics. Use colored paper or markers to make the cartogram.

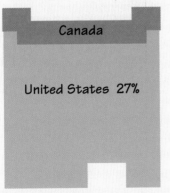

Energy Consumption

Canada

United States 27%

Discovery CHANNEL SCHOOL

UNIT 8 Project

Making Contact

Design a Web page about the history of communication.

1 **Form** groups and choose a communication method or invention that helped people communicate. Write about the development of the communication method or invention you chose.

2 **Use** pictures wherever possible. You may choose to include a timeline.

3 **Draw** your Web page. Include text, pictures, and other graphics that represent your method or invention. If possible, create your Web page on the computer.

4 **Present** your Web page to the class.

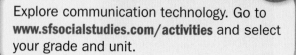
Internet Activity

Explore communication technology. Go to **www.sfsocialstudies.com/activities** and select your grade and unit.

Reference Guide

Table of Contents

Atlas

Satellite Photograph of the Continents	R2
The World: Political	R4
The World: Physical	R6
The Americas: Political	R8
The Americas: Physical	R9
Asia and the Pacific Islands: Political	R10
Asia and the Pacific Islands: Physical	R12
Africa: Political	R14
Africa: Physical	R15
Europe: Political	R16
Europe: Physical	R17
Australia and New Zealand: Political and Physical	R18
Arctic/Antarctica	R19

Geography Terms	**R20**
Countries of the World	**R22**
World History Time Line	**R29**
Gazetteer	**R41**
Biographical Dictionary	**R50**
Glossary	**R58**

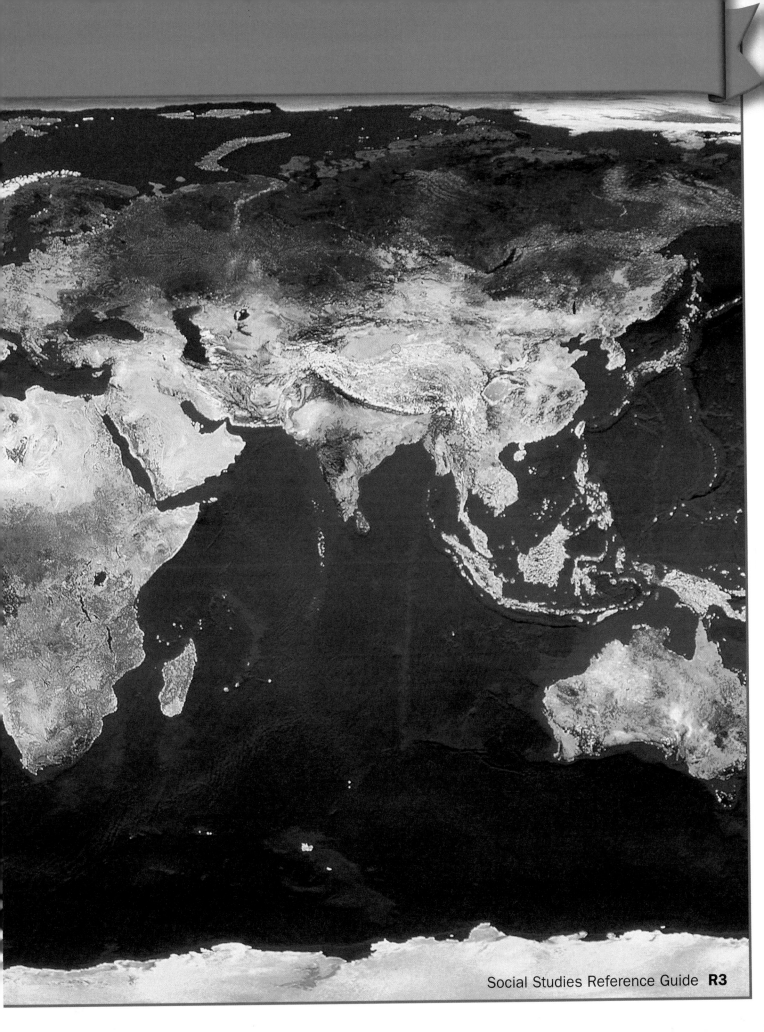

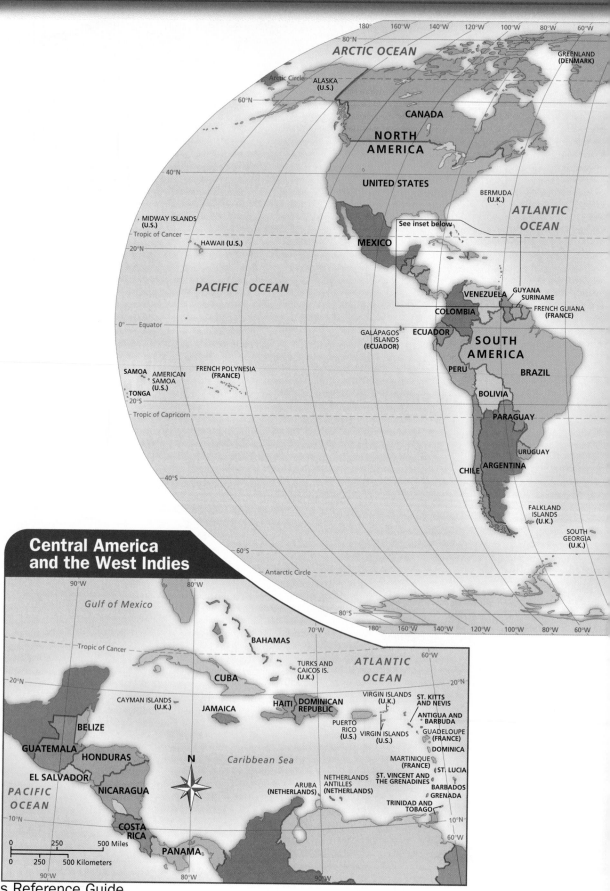

Central America and the West Indies

ARCTIC OCEAN

Arctic Circle

SPITSBERGEN (NORWAY)   SVALBARD (NORWAY)

ICELAND   See inset below

RUSSIA   ASIA   60°N

EUROPE

KAZAKHSTAN   MONGOLIA   40°N

AZORES IS. (PORTUGAL)

GEORGIA   UZBEKISTAN   KYRGYZSTAN   NORTH KOREA   JAPAN
ARMENIA   TURKMENISTAN   TAJIKISTAN   SOUTH KOREA
TURKEY
TUNISIA   LEBANON   SYRIA   AZERBAIJAN   AFGHANISTAN   CHINA   PACIFIC OCEAN

MOROCCO   ISRAEL   JORDAN   IRAN
NARY IS. (SPAIN)   KUWAIT   BAHRAIN   PAKISTAN   NEPAL   BHUTAN   Tropic of Cancer
WESTERN   ALGERIA   LIBYA   EGYPT   QATAR   INDIA   MYANMAR   TAIWAN   WAKE ISLAND (U.S.)   20°N
SAHARA (MOROCCO)   SAUDI   UNITED   (BURMA)
ARABIA   ARAB   BANGLADESH   LAOS   NORTHERN   MARSHALL ISLANDS
MAURITANIA   MALI   NIGER   CHAD   SUDAN   ERITREA   YEMEN   OMAN   EMIRATES   THAILAND   VIETNAM   MARIANA IS. (U.S.)
APE VERDE   BURKINA   DJIBOUTI   GUAM (U.S.)
SENEGAL   FASO   BENIN   AFRICA   SRI   CAMBODIA   PHILIPPINES   PALAU   FEDERATED STATES OF MICRONESIA
GUINEA   GHANA   NIGERIA   CENTRAL   ETHIOPIA   LANKA   BRUNEI   KIRIBATI
SIERRA   AFRICAN REP.   MALAYSIA
LEONE   CAMEROON   SOMALIA   MALDIVES   SINGAPORE   Equator   0°
LIBERIA   UGANDA   KENYA   NAURU
CÔTE D'IVOIRE   TOGO   INDONESIA   PAPUA
SÃO TOMÉ AND PRÍNCIPE   GABON   RWANDA   NEW   SOLOMON
GUINEA-   EQUATORIAL   REP.   DEM. REP.   BURUNDI   GUINEA   ISLANDS
BISSAU   GUINEA   CONGO   CONGO   TANZANIA   SEYCHELLES   TUVALU
AMBIA   INDIAN   VANUATU   FIJI
ATLANTIC   ANGOLA   MALAWI   COMOROS   OCEAN   20°S
OCEAN   ZAMBIA   MOZAMBIQUE   NEW
NAMIBIA   ZIMBABWE   MADAGASCAR   MAURITIUS   CALEDONIA (FRANCE)
BOTSWANA   RÉUNION (FR.)
AUSTRALIA
SOUTH   SWAZILAND
AFRICA   LESOTHO

N

0   1,000   2,000 Miles
0   1,000   2,000 Kilometers
Scale accurate at Equator

KERGUELEN
ISLANDS
(FRANCE)

NEW
ZEALAND   40°S

60°S

Antarctic Circle

ANTARCTICA   80°S

0°W   20°W   0°   20°E   40°E   60°E   80°E   100°E   120°E   140°E   160°E   180°

N

FINLAND

NORWAY   SWEDEN   ESTONIA

North   RUSSIA
IRELAND   UNITED   Sea   DENMARK   LATVIA
KINGDOM   Baltic Sea   LITHUANIA
RUSSIA   BELARUS
NETHERLANDS
ATLANTIC   BELGIUM   GERMANY   POLAND
OCEAN   LUXEMBOURG   CZECH   UKRAINE
REPUBLIC
FRANCE   LIECHTENSTEIN   SLOVAKIA   MOLDOVA
SWITZERLAND   AUSTRIA   HUNGARY   ROMANIA
SLOVENIA
PORTUGAL   MONACO   CROATIA   YUGOSLAVIA   Black Sea
ANDORRA   SAN   BOSNIA AND
SPAIN   CORSICA   MARINO   HERZEGOVINA   BULGARIA
(FR.)   ITALY   MACEDONIA
BALEARIC IS.   SARDINIA   ALBANIA
(SP.)   (IT.)
GIBRALTAR (U.K.)   Mediterranean   GREECE
Sea   SICILY
(IT.)   CRETE
MALTA   (GR.)

0   250   500 Miles
0   250   500 Kilometers

Atlas
The World: Physical

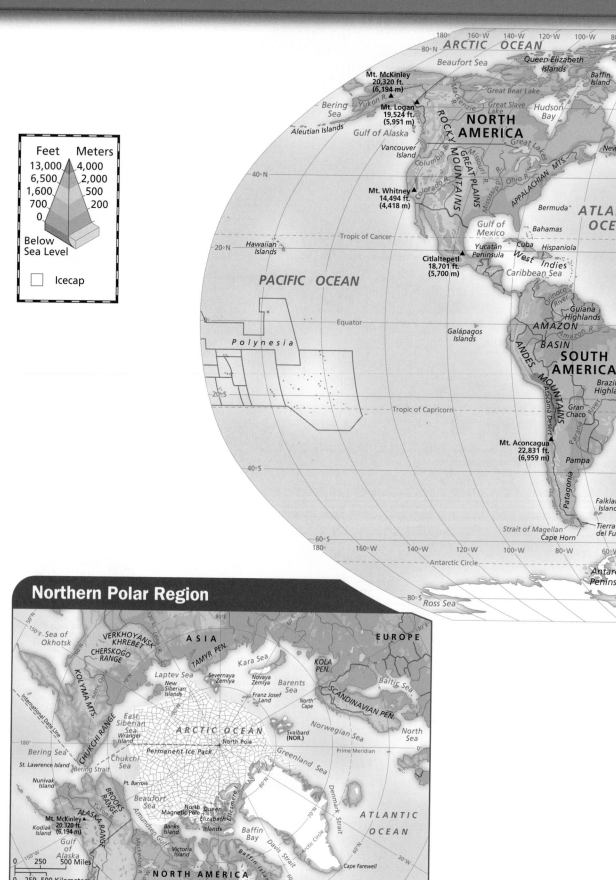

Feet | Meters
13,000 | 4,000
6,500 | 2,000
1,600 | 500
700 | 200
0 | 0
Below Sea Level

Icecap

ARCTIC OCEAN

Beaufort Sea

Queen Elizabeth Islands

Baffin Island

Greenla

Mt. McKinley
20,320 ft.
(6,194 m)

Mt. Logan
19,524 ft.
(5,951 m)

Bering Sea

Aleutian Islands

Gulf of Alaska

Vancouver Island

Mackenzie

Great Bear Lake

Great Slave Lake

Hudson Bay

NORTH AMERICA

ROCKY MOUNTAINS

GREAT PLAINS

Missouri R.

Ohio R.

Mississippi R.

APPALACHIAN MTS.

Great Lakes

Newfoundland

Azore

40°N

Mt. Whitney
14,494 ft.
(4,418 m)

Columbia R.

Colorado R.

Bermuda

ATLANTIC OCEAN

Tropic of Cancer

Citlaltepetl
18,701 ft.
(5,700 m)

Yucatán Peninsula

Gulf of Mexico

Bahamas

Cuba

Hispaniola

West Indies

Caribbean Sea

Cape Verd
Islan

20°N

Hawaiian Islands

PACIFIC OCEAN

Galápagos Islands

Orinoco River

Guiana Highlands

AMAZON BASIN

Amazon R.

SOUTH AMERICA

Brazilian Highlands

Equator

Polynesia

ANDES MOUNTAINS

Atacama Desert

Gran Chaco

Paraná River

20°S

Tropic of Capricorn

Mt. Aconcagua
22,831 ft.
(6,959 m)

Pampa

Patagonia

Falkland Islands

40°S

Strait of Magellan

Tierra del Fuego

Cape Horn

180°

160°W

140°W

120°W

100°W

80°W

60°W

40°

Antarctic Circle

60°S

80°S

Ross Sea

Antarctic Peninsula

Weddel Sea

Northern Polar Region

50°N

Sea of Okhotsk

VERKHOYANSK KHREBET

CHERSKOGO RANGE

KOLYMA MTS.

ASIA

TAMYR PEN.

90°E

Laptev Sea

Severnaya Zemlya

Kara Sea

Novaya Zemlya

Franz Josef Land

Barents Sea

KOLA PEN.

EUROPE

30°E

Baltic Sea

SCANDINAVIAN PEN.

New Siberian Islands

North Cape

International Date Line

CHUKCHI RANGE

East Siberian Sea

Wrangel Island

180°

ARCTIC OCEAN

North Pole

Svalbard (NOR.)

Norwegian Sea

North Sea

Prime Meridian

0°

Bering Sea

St. Lawrence Island

Bering Strait

Chukchi Sea

Permanent Ice Pack

Greenland Sea

Nunivak Island

BROOKS RANGE

Pt. Barrow

Beaufort Sea

Magnetic Pole

North Pole

Queen Elizabeth Islands

Ellesmere I.

ATLANTIC OCEAN

Denmark Strait

70°N

Mt. McKinley
20,320 ft.
(6,194 m)

ALASKA RANGE

Kodiak Island

Gulf of Alaska

Banks Island

Victoria Island

Baffin Bay

Davis Strait

Baffin Island

Arctic Circle

60°N

30°W

0   250   500 Miles

0   250   500 Kilometers

150°W

Mackenzie R.

NORTH AMERICA

90°W

Cape Farewell

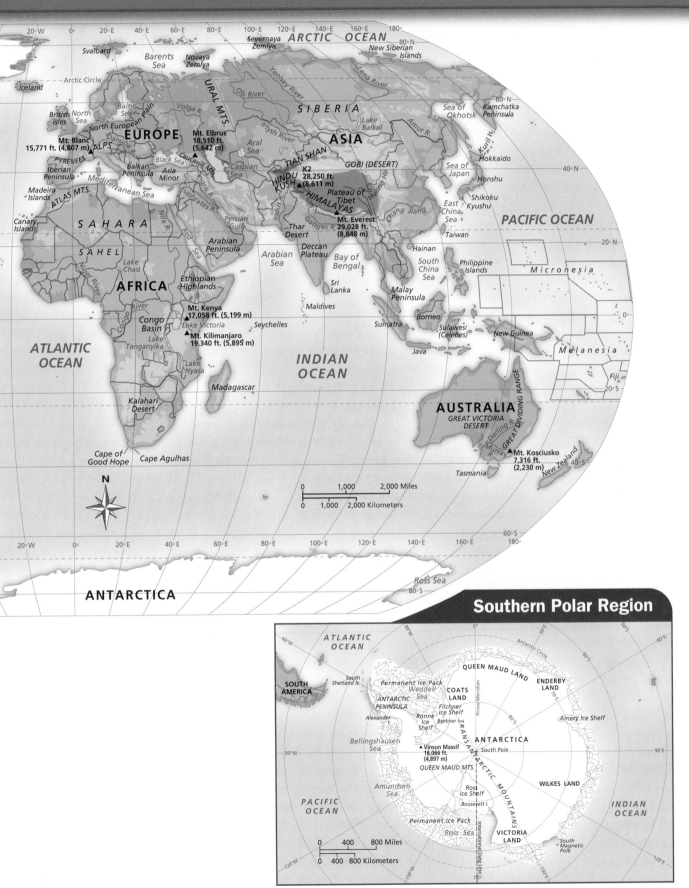

20° W · 0° · 20° E · 40° E · 60° E · 80° E · 100° E · 120° E · 140° E · 160° E · 180°

ARCTIC OCEAN

80° N

Severnaya Zemlya
New Siberian Islands

Svalbard
Barents Sea
Novaya Zemlya

Iceland
Arctic Circle

60° N

British Isles
North Sea
Baltic Sea
North European Plain
Volga R.
URAL MTS.
Ob River
Yenisey River
Lena River
S I B E R I A
Sea of Okhotsk
Kamchatka Peninsula

EUROPE
Mt. Blanc 15,771 ft. (4,807 m)
ALPS
PYRENEES
Iberian Peninsula
Balkan Peninsula
Black Sea
Asia Minor
Danube R.
Caucasus Mts.
Mt. Elbrus 18,510 ft. (5,642 m)
Aral Sea
Caspian Sea
A S I A
TIAN SHAN
Irtysh River
Lake Baikal
Amur R.
Kuril Is.
Hokkaido
Sea of Japan
40° N
Honshu

ATLAS MTS.
Mediterranean Sea
Tigris R.
Euphrates R.
HINDU KUSH
K2 28,250 ft. (8,611 m)
GOBI (DESERT)
Huang He
Plateau of Tibet
HIMALAYAS
Shikoku
Kyushu
East China Sea
Chang Jiang

Madeira Islands
S A H A R A
Nile R.
Red Sea
Persian Gulf
Arabian Peninsula
Indus R.
Thar Desert
Ganges R.
Mt. Everest 29,028 ft. (8,848 m)
Taiwan
PACIFIC OCEAN
20° N

Canary Islands
S A H E L
Lake Chad
Niger River
Arabian Sea
Deccan Plateau
Bay of Bengal
Hainan
South China Sea
Philippine Islands
M i c r o n e s i a

AFRICA
Ethiopian Highlands
Sri Lanka
Malay Peninsula

0°
Congo River
Mt. Kenya 17,058 ft. (5,199 m)
Lake Victoria
Seychelles
Maldives
Sumatra
Borneo
Sulawesi (Celebes)
New Guinea
0°

ATLANTIC OCEAN
Congo Basin
Lake Tanganyika
Mt. Kilimanjaro 19,340 ft. (5,895 m)
INDIAN OCEAN
Java
M e l a n e s i a
Fiji
20° S

Lake Nyasa
Madagascar
AUSTRALIA
GREAT VICTORIA DESERT
GREAT DIVIDING RANGE

Kalahari Desert
Darling R.
Murray R.
Mt. Kosciusko 7,316 ft. (2,230 m)
New Zealand
40° S

Cape of Good Hope
Cape Agulhas
Tasmania

N

0 · 1,000 · 2,000 Miles
0 · 1,000 · 2,000 Kilometers

60° S

ANTARCTICA
Ross Sea
80° S

20° W · 0° · 20° E · 40° E · 60° E · 80° E · 100° E · 120° E · 140° E · 160° E · 180°

Southern Polar Region

ATLANTIC OCEAN
60° W
30° W
0°
30° E
60° E
Antarctic Circle

SOUTH AMERICA
South Shetland Is.
Permanent Ice Pack
Weddell Sea
COATS LAND
QUEEN MAUD LAND
ENDERBY LAND

ANTARCTIC PENINSULA
Filchner Ice Shelf
Prime Meridian
70° S

Alexander I.
Ronne Ice Shelf
Berkner I.
Amery Ice Shelf

90° W
Bellingshausen Sea
Vinson Massif 16,066 ft. (4,897 m)
QUEEN MAUD MTS.
ANTARCTICA
South Pole
80° S
90° E

Amundsen Sea
WILKES LAND

PACIFIC OCEAN
Ross Ice Shelf
Roosevelt I.
INDIAN OCEAN

Permanent Ice Pack
Ross Sea
VICTORIA LAND
South Magnetic Pole

0 · 400 · 800 Miles
0 · 400 · 800 Kilometers

120° W
150° W
180°
150° E
120° E

ASIA

ARCTIC OCEAN

EUROPE

Bering Strait

Beaufort Sea

Baffin Bay

GREENLAND (DENMARK)

Arctic Circle

ALASKA (U.S.)

Yukon R.

Juneau

Labrador Sea

Hudson Bay

CANADA

Lake Winnipeg

NORTH AMERICA

Great Lakes

Québec

St. Lawrence

Vancouver

Seattle

Ottawa

Toronto

New York

Washington, D.C.

ATLANTIC OCEAN

San Francisco

UNITED STATES

Mississippi

Los Angeles

Rio Grande

Gulf of Mexico

Nassau

BAHAMAS

DOMINICAN REPUBLIC

Tropic of Cancer

MEXICO

Havana

CUBA

PUERTO RICO (U.S.)

VIRGIN IS. (U.S.)
ST. KITTS & NEVIS
ANTIGUA & BARBUDA

Guadalajara

Kingston

HAITI

San Juan

GUADELOUPE (FR.)

Mexico City

BELIZE

JAMAICA

Port-au-Prince

Santo Domingo

DOMINICA
MARTINIQUE (FR.)

GUATEMALA

Belmopan

ST. LUCIA

HONDURAS

Caribbean Sea

ST. VINCENT AND THE GRENADINES

BARBADOS

Guatemala

Tegucigalpa

GRENADA

San Salvador

NICARAGUA

TRINIDAD & TOBAGO

EL SALVADOR

Managua

Caracas

GUYANA

PACIFIC OCEAN

San José

Panama

VENEZUELA

Georgetown

Paramaribo

Cayenne

COSTA RICA

PANAMA

Bogotá

FRENCH GUIANA (FR.)

COLOMBIA

SURINAME

Quito

ECUADOR

SOUTH AMERICA

Amazon R.

Galápagos Islands (EC.)

BRAZIL

São Francisco R.

N

PERU

Cuzco

Lima

Brasília

Lake Titicaca

La Paz

BOLIVIA

Sucre

Rio de Janeiro

Tropic of Capricorn

PARAGUAY

São Paulo

Asunción

National border

National capital

Other City

ARGENTINA

URUGUAY

Santiago

Buenos Aires

Concepción

La Plata

Montevideo

CHILE

0   500   1,000 Miles

0   500   1,000 Kilometers

Tierra del Fuego

Falkland Islands (U.K.)

ATLANTIC OCEAN

160°E   180°   160°W   140°W   120°W   100°W   80°W   60°W   40°W   20°W   0°   20°E

60°N   80°N   40°N   20°N   0°   20°S   40°S

20°N   0°   20°S   40°S

ASIA

EUROPE

ARCTIC
OCEAN

160°E

80°N

60°N

80°N

60°N

20°E

Bering
Strait

Beaufort
Sea

Baffin
Bay

180°

Yukon R.

Arctic Circle

0°

Mackenzie R.

Labrador
Sea

40°N

160°W

Hudson
Bay

CANADIAN SHIELD

ROCKY MOUNTAINS

GREAT PLAINS

Lake
Winnipeg

Great
Lakes

St. Lawrence R.

ATLANTIC
OCEAN

20°N

CASCADES

Missouri R.

SIERRA NEVADA

Great
Salt L.

Ohio R.

APPALACHIAN MTS.

NORTH
AMERICA

Colorado R.

Mississippi R.

Tropic of Cancer

BAJA
CALIFORNIA

SIERRA MADRE
OCCIDENTAL

SIERRA MADRE
ORIENTAL

Rio Grande

Gulf of
Mexico

Cuba

Hispaniola

20°N

20°N

YUCATAN
PENINSULA

Jamaica

WEST INDIES

PACIFIC
OCEAN

Caribbean Sea

ISTHMUS OF
PANAMA

Orinoco R.

0°

0°

AMAZON
BASIN

Amazon R.

SOUTH
AMERICA

São Francisco R.

N

ANDES
MOUNTAINS

Lake
Titicaca

BRAZILIAN
HIGHLANDS

Feet	Meters
13,000	4,000
6,500	2,000
1,600	500
700	200
0	0

Below
Sea Level

Icecap

20°S

ATACAMA
DESERT

Paraguay R.

Paraná R.

Paraná R.

20°S

Tropic of Capricorn

PAMPAS

PATAGONIA

ATLANTIC
OCEAN

40°S

40°S

0   500   1,000 Miles

0   500   1,000 Kilometers

Tierra del Fuego

160°W

140°W

120°W

100°W

80°W

60°W

40°W

20°W

0°

Atlas
Asia and the Pacific Islands: Political

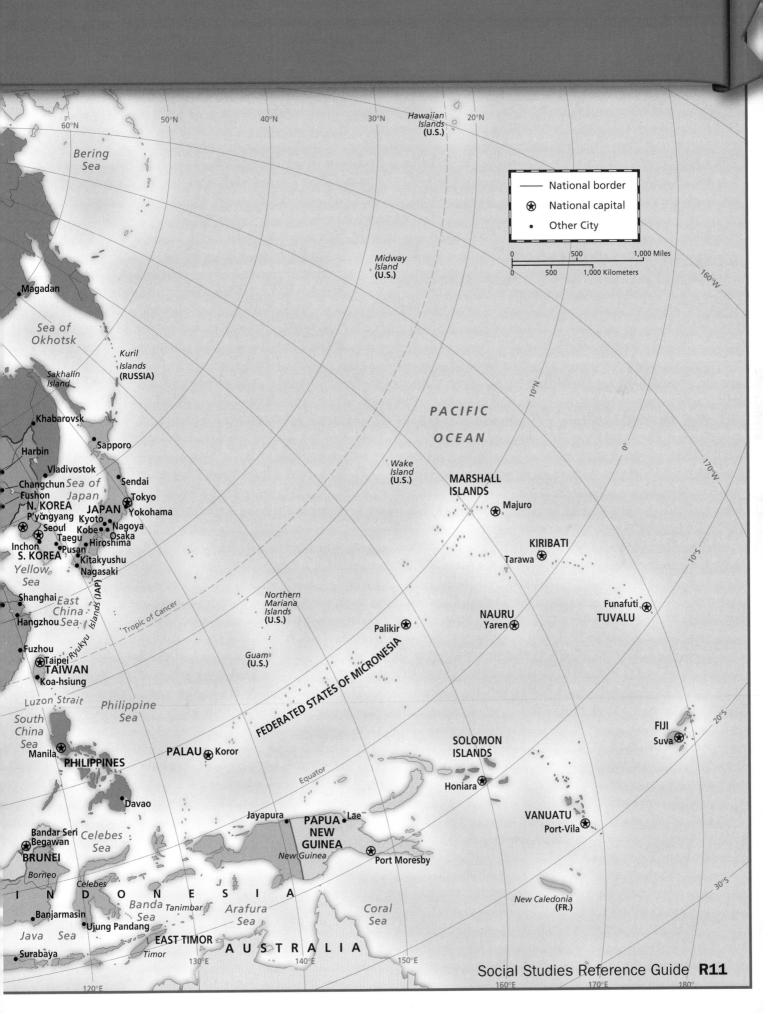

Bering
Sea

60°N   50°N   40°N   30°N   20°N

Hawaiian
Islands
(U.S.)

Magadan

Sea of
Okhotsk

Kuril
Islands
(RUSSIA)

Midway
Island
(U.S.)

Sakhalin
Island

Khabarovsk

Harbin
Vladivostok
Changchun   Sendai
Fushon   Sea of
N. KOREA   Japan   Tokyo
P'yŏngyang   Yokohama
Seoul   Kyoto Nagoya
Taegu   Kobe   Osaka
Inchon   Pusan Hiroshima
S. KOREA Kitakyushu
Nagasaki

Sapporo

JAPAN

Wake
Island
(U.S.)

MARSHALL
ISLANDS

Majuro

10°N

PACIFIC

OCEAN

National border
National capital
Other City

0   500   1,000 Miles
0   500   1,000 Kilometers

160°W

170°W

0°

KIRIBATI

Tarawa

Yellow
Sea

Shanghai   East
China
Hangzhou   Sea

Fuzhou
Taipei
TAIWAN
Koa-hsiung

Ryukyu Islands (JAP)

Tropic of Cancer

Northern
Mariana
Islands
(U.S.)

Palikir

FEDERATED STATES OF MICRONESIA

Guam
(U.S.)

NAURU
Yaren

Funafuti
TUVALU

10°S

Luzon Strait
South
China
Sea

Philippine
Sea

Manila

PHILIPPINES

PALAU   Koror

Equator

SOLOMON
ISLANDS

Honiara

FIJI
Suva

20°S

Davao

Bandar Seri   Celebes
Begawan   Sea
BRUNEI

Borneo   Celebes

Jayapura   PAPUA   Lae
NEW
GUINEA
New Guinea
Port Moresby

VANUATU
Port-Vila

New Caledonia
(FR.)

30°S

I N D O N E S I A

Banjarmasin
Ujung Pandang
Java   Sea

Banda
Tanimbar Sea

EAST TIMOR

Arafura
Sea

Coral
Sea

Surabaya

Timor

A U S T R A L I A

120°E   130°E   140°E   150°E   160°E   170°E   180°

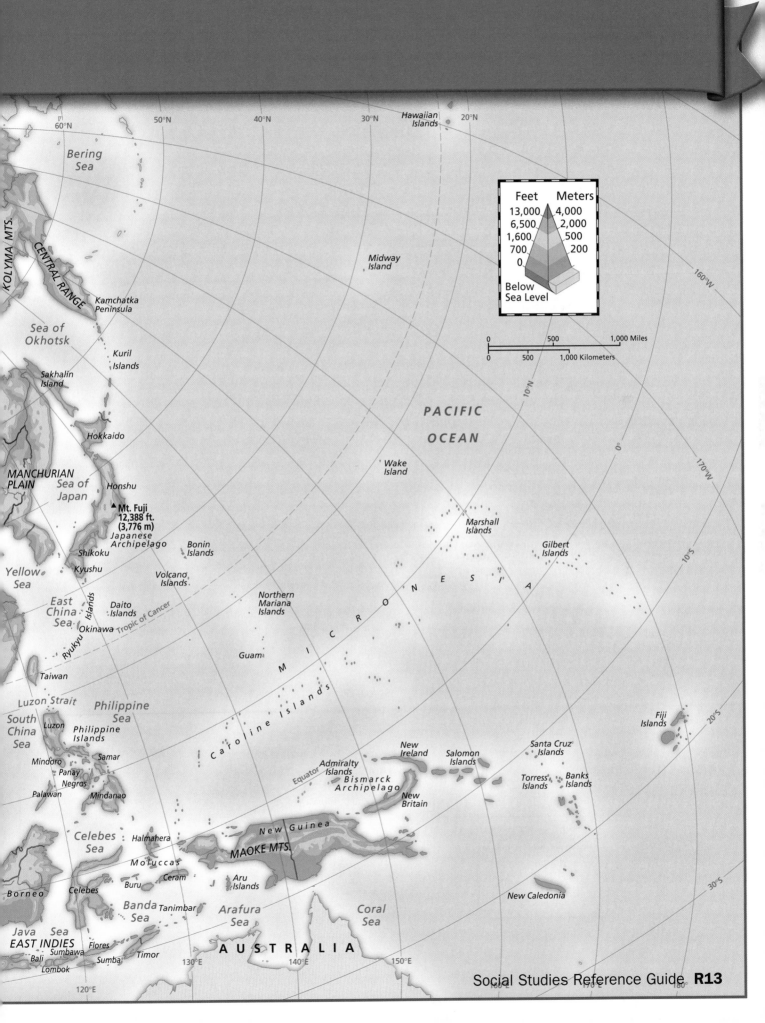

KOLYMA MTS.

*Bering
Sea*

CENTRAL RANGE

*Kamchatka
Peninsula*

*Sea of
Okhotsk*

*Kuril
Islands*

*Sakhalin
Island*

Hokkaido

MANCHURIAN
PLAIN

*Sea of
Japan*

Honshu

▲ Mt. Fuji
12,388 ft.
(3,776 m)
*Japanese
Archipelago*

Shikoku

Kyushu

*Yellow
Sea*

*East
China
Sea*

*Daito
Islands*

Okinawa Tropic of Cancer

Ryukyu Islands

Taiwan

Luzon Strait

*South
China
Sea*

*Philippine
Sea*

Luzon

*Philippine
Islands*

Mindoro

Samar

Panay

Negros

Palawan

Mindanao

*Celebes
Sea*

Halmahera

Moluccas

Ceram

Buru

Borneo

Celebes

*Banda
Sea*

Tanimbar

Java Sea

EAST INDIES

Flores

Bali

Sumbawa

Sumba

Lombok

Timor

*Arafura
Sea*

*Coral
Sea*

A U S T R A L I A

*Bonin
Islands*

*Volcano
Islands*

*Northern
Mariana
Islands*

Guam

M I C R O N E S I A

Caroline Islands

*Admiralty
Islands*

*Bismarck
Archipelago*

New Guinea

MAOKE MTS.

*Aru
Islands*

*Midway
Island*

*Wake
Island*

*Marshall
Islands*

*Gilbert
Islands*

PACIFIC

OCEAN

*New
Ireland*

*New
Britain*

*Salomon
Islands*

Equator

*Santa Cruz
Islands*

*Torress
Islands*

*Banks
Islands*

New Caledonia

*Fiji
Islands*

*Hawaiian
Islands*

60°N
50°N
40°N
30°N
20°N
160°W
170°W
10°N
0°
10°S
20°S
30°S
120°E
130°E
140°E
150°E

Feet	Meters
13,000	4,000
6,500	2,000
1,600	500
700	200
0	

Below
Sea Level

0   500   1,000 Miles
0   500   1,000 Kilometers

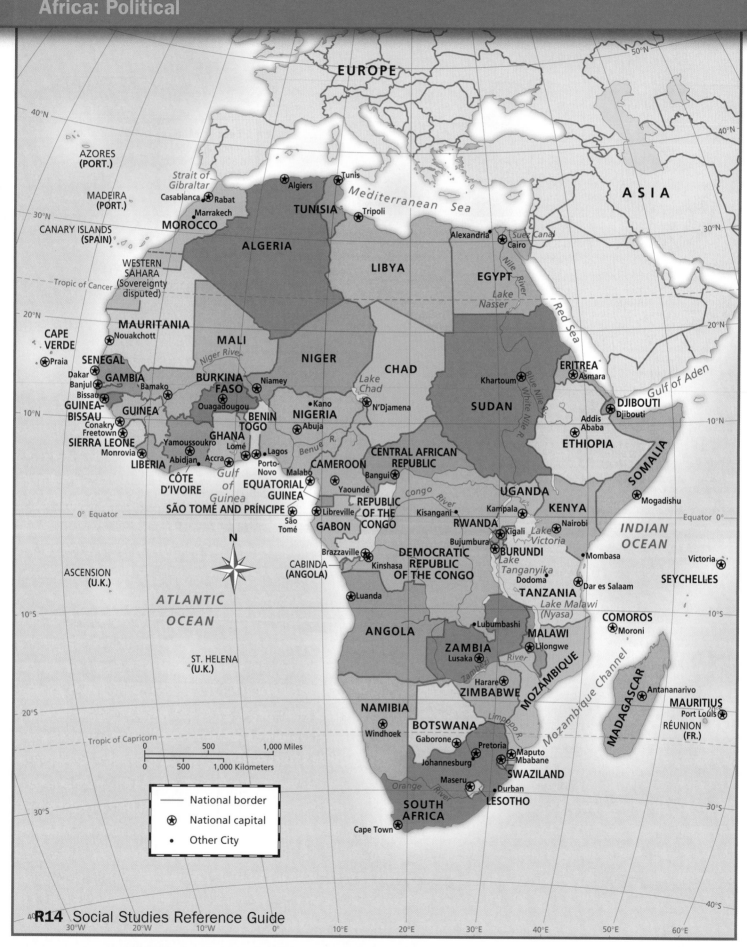

EUROPE

ASIA

Strait of Gibraltar

Mediterranean Sea

Azores (PORT.)

MADEIRA (PORT.)

Casablanca • Rabat
• Marrakech
MOROCCO

Algiers
TUNISIA
Tunis
Tripoli

CANARY ISLANDS (SPAIN)

WESTERN SAHARA (Sovereignty disputed)

ALGERIA

LIBYA

Alexandria
Suez Canal
Cairo

EGYPT

Nile River

Lake Nasser

Tropic of Cancer

20°N

MAURITANIA
Nouakchott

MALI

NIGER

CHAD

Khartoum

SUDAN

Blue Nile R.
White Nile R.

ERITREA
Asmara

Red Sea

Gulf of Aden

CAPE VERDE
• Praia

SENEGAL
Dakar
Banjul
GAMBIA
Bissau
GUINEA-BISSAU
Conakry
Freetown
SIERRA LEONE
Monrovia

Bamako

BURKINA FASO
Ouagadougou

Niamey

Niger River

• Kano
NIGERIA
Abuja

N'Djamena

Addis Ababa

DJIBOUTI
Djibouti

ETHIOPIA

SOMALIA

GUINEA

BENIN
TOGO

GHANA
Yamoussoukro
Lomé
Accra
Abidjan
LIBERIA
CÔTE D'IVOIRE

Porto-Novo
Lagos

Benue R.

CENTRAL AFRICAN REPUBLIC

Gulf of Guinea

CAMEROON
Malabo
Yaoundé
EQUATORIAL GUINEA
SÃO TOMÉ AND PRÍNCIPE
São Tomé

Bangui

Congo River

UGANDA
Kampala

KENYA

Mogadishu

0° Equator

GABON
Libreville

REPUBLIC OF THE CONGO

Kisangani

RWANDA
Kigali
Bujumbura
BURUNDI

Lake Victoria

Nairobi

INDIAN OCEAN

Equator 0°

ASCENSION (U.K.)

ATLANTIC OCEAN

Brazzaville
CABINDA (ANGOLA)

Kinshasa

DEMOCRATIC REPUBLIC OF THE CONGO

Lake Tanganyika
Dodoma

Mombasa

Victoria

SEYCHELLES

ST. HELENA (U.K.)

Luanda

TANZANIA

Dar es Salaam

10°S

Lubumbashi

ANGOLA

ZAMBIA
Lusaka

Lake Malawi (Nyasa)

MALAWI
Lilongwe

COMOROS
Moroni

10°S

River

Zambezi River

MOZAMBIQUE

MADAGASCAR
Antananarivo

MAURITIUS
Port Louis

RÉUNION (FR.)

Tropic of Capricorn

NAMIBIA
Windhoek

Harare
ZIMBABWE

Limpopo R.

Mozambique Channel

BOTSWANA
Gaborone

Pretoria
Johannesburg

Maputo
Mbabane
SWAZILAND

Orange River

Maseru
LESOTHO

Durban

500   1,000 Miles

0   500   1,000 Kilometers

SOUTH AFRICA

Cape Town

N

National border
National capital
Other City

30°W   20°W   10°W   0°   10°E   20°E   30°E   40°E   50°E   60°E

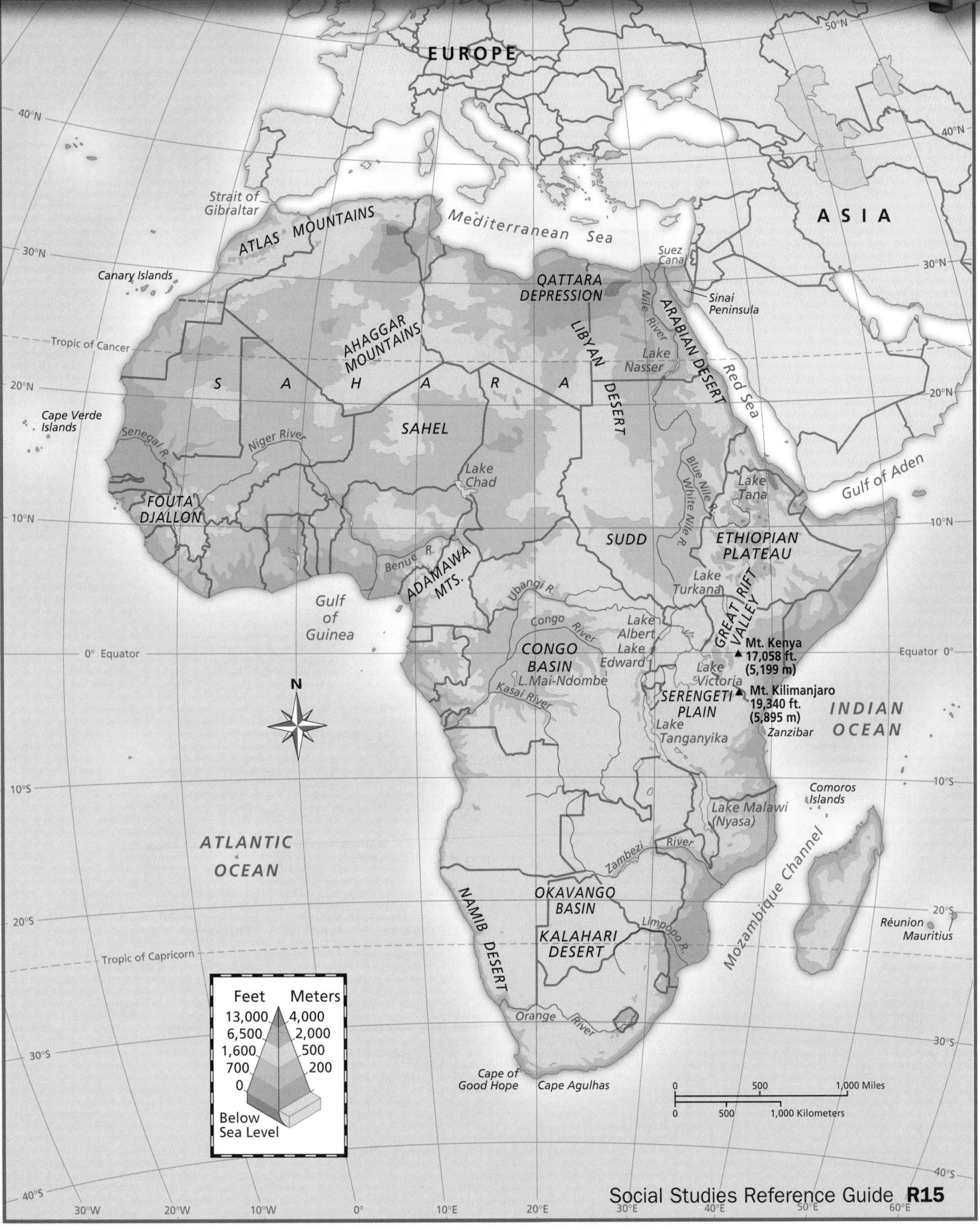

EUROPE
ASIA
Strait of Gibraltar
ATLAS MOUNTAINS
Mediterranean Sea
Suez Canal
Sinai Peninsula
Canary Islands
QATTARA DEPRESSION
AHAGGAR MOUNTAINS
LIBYAN DESERT
ARABIAN DESERT
Nile River
Lake Nasser
Red Sea
Tropic of Cancer
S A H A R A
Cape Verde Islands
SAHEL
Senegal R.
Niger River
Lake Chad
Blue Nile R.
White Nile R.
Lake Tana
Gulf of Aden
FOUTA DJALLON
SUDD
ETHIOPIAN PLATEAU
Benue R.
ADAMAWA MTS.
Lake Turkana
GREAT RIFT VALLEY
Ubangi R.
Gulf of Guinea
Congo River
Lake Albert
Lake Edward
Mt. Kenya 17,058 ft. (5,199 m)
0° Equator
Equator 0°
CONGO BASIN
L.Mai-Ndombe
Kasai River
Lake Victoria
Mt. Kilimanjaro 19,340 ft. (5,895 m)
SERENGETI PLAIN
Lake Tanganyika
Zanzibar
INDIAN OCEAN
N
Comoros Islands
Lake Malawi (Nyasa)
ATLANTIC OCEAN
Zambezi River
Mozambique Channel
NAMIB DESERT
OKAVANGO BASIN
KALAHARI DESERT
Limpopo R.
Réunion
Mauritius
Tropic of Capricorn
Orange River
Cape of Good Hope
Cape Agulhas
Feet
Meters
13,000
4,000
6,500
2,000
1,600
500
700
200
0
Below Sea Level
0
500
1,000 Miles
0
500
1,000 Kilometers
50°N
40°N
30°N
20°N
10°N
10°S
20°S
30°S
40°S
30°W
20°W
10°W
0°
10°E
20°E
30°E
40°E
50°E
60°E

Feet · Meters
13,000 · 4,000
6,500 · 2,000
1,600 · 500
700 · 200
0
Below Sea Level
☐ Icecap

ARCTIC OCEAN

Arctic Circle

KOLA PENINSULA

LAPLAND

Lake Onega

Lake Ladoga

Gulf of Bothnia

Norwegian Sea

Faeroe Is. (DEN.)

Glittertind 8,110 ft. (2,472 m) ▲

KJØLEN MTS.

SCANDINAVIAN PENINSULA

Shetland Is. (U.K.)

Prime Meridian

Lake Vänern

ATLANTIC OCEAN

Ben Nevis ▲ 4,406 ft. (1,343 m)

North Sea

JUTLAND PENINSULA

Baltic Sea

NORTHERN EUROPEAN PLAIN

Dnieper R.

British Isles

Vistula R.

Thames R.

RUHR VALLEY

Elbe River

Oder River

English Channel

Seine River

Rhine R.

Danube River

Dniester River

CARPATHIAN MTS.

Loire River

Bay of Biscay

Mt. Blanc 15,771 ft. (4,807 m) ▲

Matterhorn 14,692 ft. (4,478 m) ▲

A L P S

Po River

TRANSYLVANIAN ALPS

Black Sea

MASSIF CENTRAL

Rhône River

DINARIC ALPS

Danube River

BALKAN MTS.

Garonne R.

PYRENEES

A P E N N I N E S

Adriatic Sea

BALKAN PENINSULA

Bosporus

Douro R.

Ebro R.

Corsica

ITALIAN PENINSULA

MESETA

Tagus River

Sardinia

Tyrrhenian Sea

PINDUS MTS

Dardanelles Aegean Sea

ASIA

IBERIAN PENINSULA

Balearic Is.

Ionian Sea

PELOPONNESE

M e d i t e r r a n e a n

Strait of Gibraltar

Gibraltar (U.K.)

Sicily

S e a

Crete

AFRICA

0 · 250 · 500 Miles
0 · 250 · 500 Kilometers

N

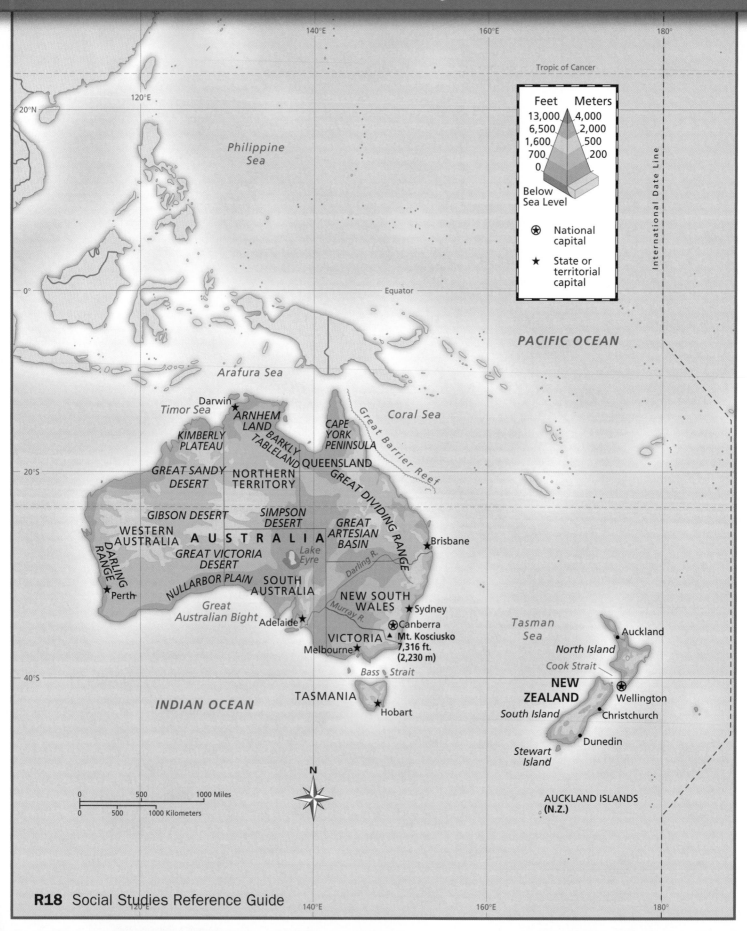

Tropic of Cancer

20°N

120°E

140°E

160°E

180°E

International Date Line

Philippine Sea

Feet | Meters
13,000 | 4,000
6,500 | 2,000
1,600 | 500
700 | 200
0 |
Below Sea Level

⊛ National capital

★ State or territorial capital

0°

Equator

PACIFIC OCEAN

Arafura Sea

Coral Sea

Darwin

Timor Sea

ARNHEM LAND

CAPE YORK PENINSULA

Great Barrier Reef

KIMBERLY PLATEAU

BARKLY TABLELAND

GREAT SANDY DESERT

NORTHERN TERRITORY

QUEENSLAND

20°S

GIBSON DESERT

SIMPSON DESERT

GREAT DIVIDING RANGE

WESTERN AUSTRALIA

A U S T R A L I A

GREAT ARTESIAN BASIN

DARLING RANGE

GREAT VICTORIA DESERT

Lake Eyre

Brisbane ★

NULLARBOR PLAIN

SOUTH AUSTRALIA

Darling R.

Perth ★

Great Australian Bight

Murray R.

NEW SOUTH WALES

Sydney ★

Tasman Sea

Auckland

Adelaide ★

⊛ Canberra

VICTORIA

▲ Mt. Kosciusko 7,316 ft. (2,230 m)

North Island

Cook Strait

Melbourne ★

NEW ZEALAND

Wellington ⊛

40°S

Bass Strait

INDIAN OCEAN

TASMANIA

South Island

Christchurch

Hobart ★

Dunedin

Stewart Island

N

AUCKLAND ISLANDS (N.Z.)

0   500   1000 Miles
0   500   1000 Kilometers

120°E

140°E

160°E

180°E

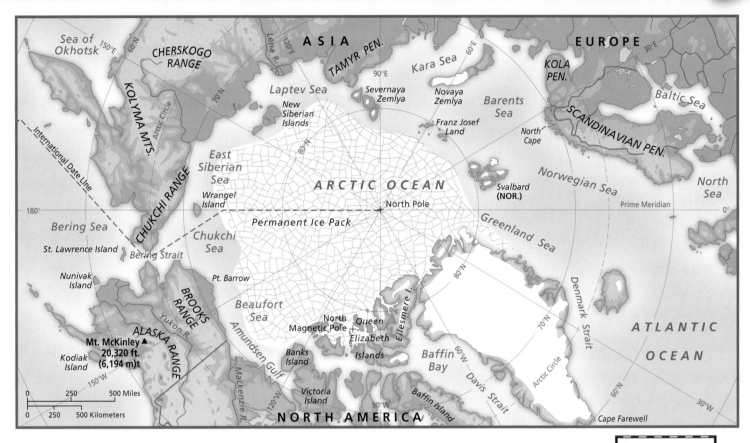

Sea of Okhotsk
150°E
60°N
CHERSKOGO RANGE
KOLYMA MTS.
Arctic Circle
ASIA
TAMYR PEN.
Lena R.
120°E
Kara Sea
90°E
60°E
EUROPE
30°E
KOLA PEN.
Baltic Sea
SCANDINAVIAN PEN.
Laptev Sea
Severnaya Zemlya
Novaya Zemlya
Barents Sea
North Cape
Norwegian Sea
North Sea
New Siberian Islands
70°N
80°W
Franz Josef Land
Svalbard (NOR.)
International Date Line
East Siberian Sea
ARCTIC OCEAN
North Pole
Prime Meridian
0°
180°
Wrangel Island
Permanent Ice Pack
Greenland Sea
80°N
Denmark Strait
70°N
ATLANTIC OCEAN
Bering Sea
CHUKCHI RANGE
Chukchi Sea
St. Lawrence Island
Bering Strait
Pt. Barrow
Beaufort Sea
Ellesmere I.
Nunivak Island
BROOKS RANGE
North Magnetic Pole
Queen Elizabeth Islands
60°W
Baffin Bay
Arctic Circle
60°N
Mt. McKinley ▲ 20,320 ft. (6,194 m)†
ALASKA RANGE
Yukon R.
Amundsen Gulf
Banks Island
30°W
Kodiak Island
150°W
Victoria Island
120°W
Mackenzie R.
Davis Strait
Baffin Island
Cape Farewell
NORTH AMERICA

0   250   500 Miles
0   250   500 Kilometers

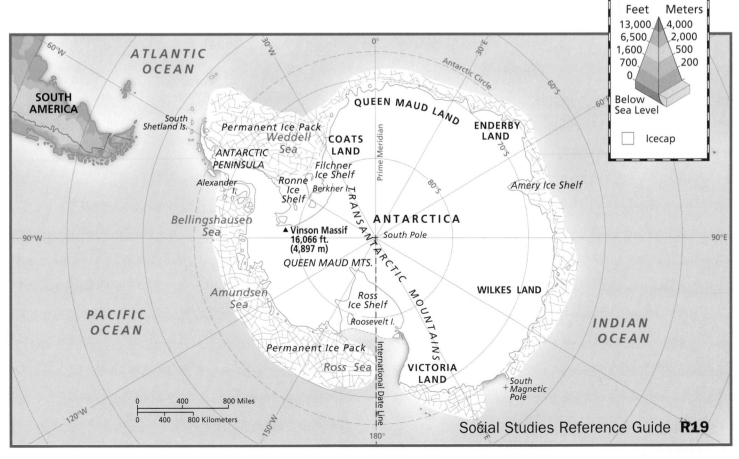

60°W
ATLANTIC OCEAN
30°W
0°
Antarctic Circle
30°E
SOUTH AMERICA
South Shetland Is.
Permanent Ice Pack
Weddell Sea
QUEEN MAUD LAND
ENDERBY LAND
60°S
ANTARCTIC PENINSULA
COATS LAND
Prime Meridian
70°S
Alexander I.
Filchner Ice Shelf
Ronne Ice Shelf
Berkner I.
Amery Ice Shelf
Bellingshausen Sea
TRANSANTARCTIC MOUNTAINS
ANTARCTICA
80°S
90°W
▲ Vinson Massif 16,066 ft. (4,897 m)
South Pole
90°E
QUEEN MAUD MTS.
Amundsen Sea
WILKES LAND
PACIFIC OCEAN
Ross Ice Shelf
INDIAN OCEAN
Roosevelt I.
Permanent Ice Pack
120°W
International Date Line
VICTORIA LAND
South Magnetic Pole
Ross Sea
150°W
150°E
180°

Feet   Meters
13,000   4,000
6,500   2,000
1,600   500
700   200
0
Below Sea Level
☐ Icecap

0   400   800 Miles
0   400   800 Kilometers

Geography Terms

archipelago group or chain of islands

basin bowl-shaped area of land surrounded by higher land

bay narrower part of an ocean or lake that cuts into land

canal narrow waterway dug across land mainly for ship travel

cataract steep, large waterfall

coast land at the edge of a large body of water such as an ocean

coastal plain area of flat land along an ocean or sea

delta triangle-shaped area of land at the mouth of a river

desert very dry, barren land without trees

dune hill of sand formed by wind

glacier giant sheet of ice that moves very slowly across land

gulf large body of water with land around part of it

island land with water all around it

isthmus narrow strip of land connecting two larger land areas

lake large body of water with land all or nearly all around it

mountain a very high hill

mountain range long row of mountains

mouth place where a river empties into another body of water

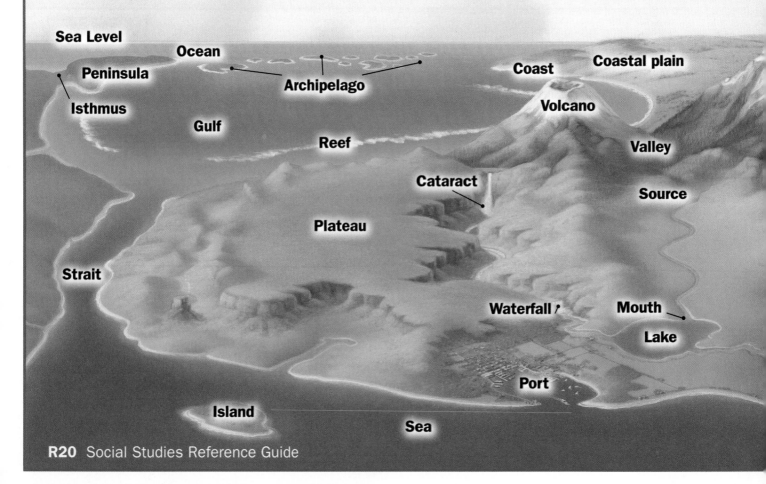

oasis fertile spot in a desert, with water and green vegetation

ocean any of the four largest bodies of water on Earth

peak pointed top of a mountain

peninsula land with water on three sides

plain very large area of flat land

plateau high, wide area of flat land, with steep sides

port place, usually in a harbor, where ships safely load and unload goods and people

reef off-shore ridge, often of limestone, along a coastline, at or near the surface of a sea or ocean

riverbank land at a river's edge

sea large body of water somewhat smaller than an ocean

sea level an ocean's surface, compared to which land can be measured either above or below

source place where a river begins

steppe wide, treeless plain

strait narrow channel of water joining two larger bodies of water

tributary stream or river that runs into a larger river

valley low land between mountains or hills

volcano mountain with an opening at the top formed by violent bursts of steam and hot rock

waterfall steep falling of water from a higher to a lower place

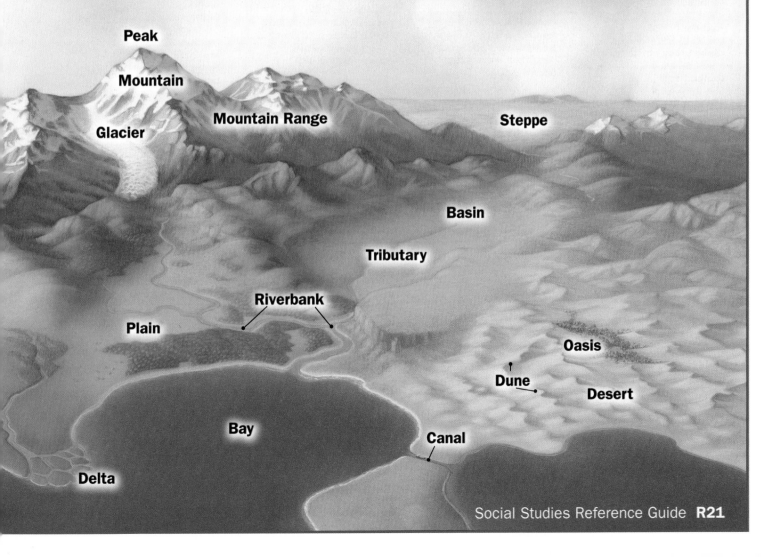

Countries of the World

Afghanistan
Capital: Kabul
Population: 26,813,057
Area: 250,010 sq mi;
    647,500 sq km
Leading Exports: fruits and nuts, handwoven carpets, and wool
Location: Asia

Albania
Capital: Tirana
Population: 3,490,435
Area: 11,101 sq mi; 28,750 sq km
Leading Exports: metals and metallic ores, textiles
Location: Europe

Algeria
Capital: Algiers
Population: 31,193,917
Area: 919,626 sq mi;
    2,381,740 sq km
Leading Exports: petroleum and natural gas
Location: Africa

Andorra
Capital: Andorra la Vella
Population: 67,627
Area: 181 sq mi; 468 sq km
Leading Exports: tobacco products and furniture
Location: Europe

Angola
Capital: Luanda
Population: 10,366,031
Area: 481,370 sq mi;
    1,246,700 sq km
Leading Exports: oil, petroleum products, and diamonds
Location: Africa

Anguilla
Capital: The Valley
Population: 12,132
Area: 35 sq mi; 91 sq km
Leading Exports: lobster and salt
Location: North America (Caribbean Sea)

Antigua and Barbuda
Capital: Saint John's
Population: 66,970
Area: 170 sq mi; 442 sq km
Leading Exports: petroleum products and manufactured goods
Location: North America (Caribbean Sea)

Argentina
Capital: Buenos Aires
Population: 37,384,816
Area: 1,068,339 sq mi;
    2,766,890 sq km
Leading Exports: wheat, corn, oilseed, and manufactured goods
Location: South America

Armenia
Capital: Yerevan
Population: 3,336,100
Area: 11,506 sq mi; 29,800 sq km
Leading Exports: diamonds, scrap metal, and copper
Location: Asia

Australia
Capital: Canberra
Population: 19,357,594
Area: 2,968,010 sq mi;
    7,686,850 sq km
Leading Exports: coal, gold, wheat, wool, and iron ore
Location: Australia

Austria
Capital: Vienna
Population: 8,150,835
Area: 32,376 sq mi; 83,858 sq km
Leading Exports: machinery and equipment, iron, and steel
Location: Europe

Azerbaijan
Capital: Baku
Population: 7,771,092
Area: 33,438 sq mi; 86,600 sq km
Leading Exports: oil, gas, machinery, and cotton
Location: Asia

The Bahamas
Capital: Nassau
Population: 297,852
Area: 5,382 sq mi; 13,940 sq km
Leading Exports: pharmaceuticals, rum, and seafood
Location: North America (Caribbean Sea)

Bahrain
Capital: Manama
Population: 645,361
Area: 239 sq mi; 620 sq km
Leading Exports: petroleum and petroleum products
Location: Asia

Bangladesh
Capital: Dhaka
Population: 131,269,860
Area: 55,600 sq mi; 144,000 sq km
Leading Exports: garments, jute and jute goods, and leather
Location: Asia

Barbados
Capital: Bridgetown
Population: 275,330
Area: 166 sq mi; 430 sq km
Leading Exports: sugar, molasses, rum, and clothing
Location: North America (Caribbean Sea)

Belarus
Capital: Minsk
Population: 10,350,194
Area: 79,926 sq mi; 207,600 sq km
Leading Exports: machinery and equipment, chemicals
Location: Europe

Belgium
Capital: Brussels
Population: 10,258,762
Area: 11,780 sq mi; 30,510 sq km
Leading Exports: iron, steel, machinery, and chemicals
Location: Europe

Belize
Capital: Belmopan
Population: 256,052
Area: 8,865 sq mi; 22,960 sq km
Leading Exports: sugar, citrus fruits, bananas, and clothing
Location: North America

Benin
Capital: Porto-Novo
Population: 6,590,782
Area: 43,484 sq mi; 112,620 sq km
Leading Exports: cotton, oil, and palm products
Location: Africa

Bermuda
Capital: Hamilton
Population: 63,503
Area: 23 sq mi; 59 sq km
Leading Exports: re-export of pharmaceuticals
Location: North America (Atlantic Ocean)

Bhutan
Capital: Thimphu
Population: 2,049,412
Area: 18,147 sq mi; 47,000 sq km
Leading Exports: cardamom, gypsum, timber, and handicrafts
Location: Asia

Bolivia
Capital: La Paz and Sucre
Population: 8,300,463
Area: 424,179 sq mi;
    1,098,580 sq km
Leading Exports: metals, natural gas, soybeans, gold, and wood
Location: South America

Bosnia and Herzegovina

Capital: Sarajevo
Population: 3,922,205
Area: 19,782 sq mi; 51,233 sq km
Leading Exports: none
Location: Europe

Botswana

Capital: Gaborone
Population: 1,586,119
Area: 231,812 sq mi;
    600,370 sq km
Leading Exports: diamonds, copper, and nickel
Location: Africa

Brazil

Capital: Brasilia
Population: 174,486,575
Area: 3,286,600 sq mi;
    8,511,965 sq km
Leading Exports: iron ore, soybeans, citrus, and coffee
Location: South America

Brunei

Capital: Bandar Seri Begawan
Population: 336,376
Area: 2,228 sq mi; 5,770 sq km
Leading Exports: oil and natural gas
Location: Asia

Bulgaria

Capital: Sofia
Population: 7,707,495
Area: 42,824 sq mi; 110,910 sq km
Leading Exports: machinery and agricultural products
Location: Europe

Burkina Faso

Capital: Ouagadougou
Population: 12,272,289
Area: 105,873 sq mi;
    274,200 sq km
Leading Exports: cotton, gold, and animal products
Location: Africa

Burundi
Capital: Bujumbura
Population: 6,223,897
Area: 10,746 sq mi; 27,830 sq km
Leading Exports: coffee, tea, and cotton
Location: Africa

Cambodia
Capital: Phnom Penh
Population: 12,491,501
Area: 69,902 sq mi; 181,040 sq km
Leading Exports: timber, rubber, and rice
Location: Asia

Cameroon
Capital: Yaounde
Population: 15,803,200
Area: 183,574 sq mi; 475,440 sq km
Leading Exports: petroleum products, coffee, and cotton
Location: Africa

Canada
Capital: Ottawa
Population: 31,592,805
Area: 3,851,940 sq mi; 9,976,140 sq km
Leading Exports: wood pulp, timber, petroleum, and machinery
Location: North America

Cape Verde
Capital: Praia
Population: 405,163
Area: 1,556 sq mi; 4,030 sq km
Leading Exports: fish, bananas, and hides
Location: Africa (Atlantic Ocean)

Central African Republic
Capital: Bangui
Population: 3,576,884
Area: 240,542 sq mi; 622,980 sq km
Leading Exports: diamonds, timber, cotton, coffee, and tobacco
Location: Africa

Chad
Capital: N'Djamena
Population: 8,707,078
Area: 495,772 sq mi; 1,284,000 sq km
Leading Exports: cotton, cattle, textiles, and fish
Location: Africa

Chile
Capital: Santiago
Population: 15,328,467
Area: 292,269 sq mi; 756,950 sq km
Leading Exports: copper, fish, and chemicals
Location: South America

China
Capital: Beijing
Population: 1,273,111,290
Area: 3,705,533 sq mi; 9,596,960 sq km
Leading Exports: textiles, garments, and machinery
Location: Asia

Colombia
Capital: Bogota
Population: 40,349,388
Area: 439,751 sq mi; 1,138,910 sq km
Leading Exports: petroleum, coffee, coal, and bananas
Location: South America

Comoros
Capital: Moroni
Population: 596,202
Area: 838 sq mi; 2,170 sq km
Leading Exports: vanilla, cloves, and perfume oil
Location: Africa (Indian Ocean)

Congo, Democratic Republic of the
Capital: Kinshasa
Population: 53,624,718
Area: 905,599 sq mi; 2,345,410 sq km
Leading Exports: copper, coffee, diamonds, cobalt, and oil
Location: Africa

Congo, Republic of the
Capital: Brazzaville
Population: 2,894,336
Area: 132,051 sq mi; 342,000 sq km
Leading Exports: oil, lumber, sugar, and cocoa
Location: Africa

Costa Rica
Capital: San José
Population: 3,773,057
Area: 19,730 sq mi; 51,100 sq km
Leading Exports: coffee, bananas, textiles, and sugar
Location: North America

Côte d'Ivoire
Capital: Yamoussoukro
Population: 16,393,221
Area: 124,507 sq mi; 322,460 sq km
Leading Exports: cocoa, coffee, wood, and petroleum
Location: Africa

Croatia
Capital: Zagreb
Population: 4,334,142
Area: 21,830 sq mi; 56,538 sq km
Leading Exports: textiles and transportation equipment
Location: Europe

Cuba
Capital: Havana
Population: 11,184,023
Area: 42,805 sq mi; 110,860 sq km
Leading Exports: sugar, tobacco, and nickel
Location: North America (Caribbean Sea)

Cyprus
Capital: Nicosia
Population: 762,887
Area: 3,572 sq mi; 9,250 sq km
Leading Exports: citrus, potatoes, grapes, wine, and clothing
Location: Europe (Mediterranean Sea)

Czech Republic
Capital: Prague
Population: 10,264,212
Area: 30,388 sq mi; 78,703 sq km
Leading Exports: machinery and manufactured goods
Location: Europe

Denmark
Capital: Copenhagen
Population: 5,352,815
Area: 16,630 sq mi; 43,094 sq km
Leading Exports: meat products, dairy products, and furniture
Location: Europe

Djibouti
Capital: Djibouti
Population: 460,700
Area: 8,495 sq mi; 22,000 sq km
Leading Exports: hides and coffee
Location: Africa

Dominica
Capital: Roseau
Population: 70,786
Area: 290 sq mi; 750 sq km
Leading Exports: bananas, soap, bay oil, vegetables, and citrus
Location: Caribbean Sea

Dominican Republic
Capital: Santo Domingo
Population: 8,581,477
Area: 18,815 sq mi; 48,730 sq km
Leading Exports: iron, nickel, sugar, gold, coffee, and cocoa
Location: North America (Caribbean Sea)

Ecuador
Capital: Quito
Population: 13,183,978
Area: 109,487 sq mi; 283,560 sq km
Leading Exports: petroleum, bananas, shrimp, cocoa
Location: South America

Egypt
Capital: Cairo
Population: 69,536,644
Area: 386,675 sq mi; 1,001,450 sq km
Leading Exports: oil and petroleum products, cotton, and textiles
Location: Africa

El Salvador
Capital: San Salvador
Population: 6,237,662
Area: 8,124 sq mi; 21,040 sq km
Leading Exports: coffee, sugar cane, and shrimp
Location: North America

Equatorial Guinea
Capital: Malabo
Population: 486,060
Area: 10,831 sq mi; 28,050 sq km
Leading Exports: coffee, oil, and cocoa
Location: Africa

Eritrea
Capital: Asmara
Population: 4,298,269
Area: 46,844 sq mi; 121,320 sq km
Leading Exports: livestock, sorghum, and textiles
Location: Africa

Estonia
Capital: Tallinn
Population: 1,431,471
Area: 17,414 sq mi; 45,226 sq km
Leading Exports: textiles, food products, and machinery and equipment
Location: Europe

Ethiopia
Capital: Addis Ababa
Population: 65,891,874
Area: 435,201 sq mi; 1,127,127 sq km
Leading Exports: coffee, leather products, and gold
Location: Africa

Countries of the World

Fiji
Capital: Suva
Population: 844,330
Area: 7,054 sq mi; 18,270 sq km
Leading Exports: sugar, gold, processed fish, and lumber
Location: Oceania

Finland
Capital: Helsinki
Population: 5,175,783
Area: 130,132 sq mi; 337,030 sq km
Leading Exports: paper and pulp, machinery, and chemicals
Location: Europe

France
Capital: Paris
Population: 59,551,227
Area: 211,217 sq mi; 547,030 sq km
Leading Exports: machinery and transportation equipment
Location: Europe

Gabon
Capital: Libreville
Population: 1,221,175
Area: 103,351 sq mi; 267,670 sq km
Leading Exports: oil, timber, manganese, and uranium
Location: Africa

The Gambia
Capital: Banjul
Population: 1,411,205
Area: 4,363 sq mi; 11,300 sq km
Leading Exports: peanuts, peanut products, and fish
Location: Africa

Georgia
Capital: T'bilisi
Population: 4,989,285
Area: 26,912 sq mi; 69,700 sq km
Leading Exports: citrus, tea, and wine
Location: Asia

Germany
Capital: Berlin
Population: 83,029,536
Area: 137,808 sq mi; 356,910 sq km
Leading Exports: vehicles, machines, machine tools, and chemicals
Location: Europe

Ghana
Capital: Accra
Population: 19,894,014
Area: 92,104 sq mi; 238,540 sq km
Leading Exports: cocoa, gold, timber, and bauxite
Location: Africa

Greece
Capital: Athens
Population: 10,623,835
Area: 50,944 sq mi; 131,940 sq km
Leading Exports: manufactured goods, foodstuffs, and wine
Location: Europe

Grenada
Capital: Saint George's
Population: 89,227
Area: 131 sq mi; 340 sq km
Leading Exports: bananas, cocoa, nutmeg, fruits, and vegetables
Location: North America (Caribbean Sea)

Guatemala
Capital: Guatemala City
Population: 12,974,361
Area: 42,044 sq mi; 108,890 sq km
Leading Exports: coffee, sugar, bananas, and cardamom
Location: North America

Guinea
Capital: Conakry
Population: 7,613,870
Area: 94,930 sq mi; 245,860 sq km
Leading Exports: bauxite, alumina, diamonds, gold, and coffee
Location: Africa

Guinea Bissau
Capital: Bissau
Population: 1,315,822
Area: 13,946 sq mi; 36,210 sq km
Leading Exports: cashews, peanuts, shrimp, fish, and palm kernels
Location: Africa

Guyana
Capital: Georgetown
Population: 697,181
Area: 83,033 sq mi; 214,970 sq km
Leading Exports: sugar, gold, bauxite, rice, and shrimp
Location: South America

Haiti
Capital: Port-au-Prince
Population: 6,964,549
Area: 10,700 sq mi; 27,712 sq km
Leading Exports: light manufactured products, coffee, and mangoes
Location: Caribbean Sea

Holy See (Vatican City)
Capital: Vatican City
Population: 890
Area: 0.17 sq mi; 0.44 sq km
Leading Exports: none
Location: Europe

Honduras
Capital: Tegucigalpa
Population: 6,406,052
Area: 43,280 sq mi; 112,090 sq km
Leading Exports: bananas, coffee, shrimp, and zinc
Location: North America

Hungary
Capital: Budapest
Population: 10,106,017
Area: 35,920 sq mi; 93,030 sq km
Leading Exports: machinery, equipment, and manufactured goods
Location: Europe

Iceland
Capital: Reykjavík
Population: 277,906
Area: 39,770 sq mi; 103,000 sq km
Leading Exports: fish and fish products
Location: Europe

India
Capital: New Delhi
Population: 1,029,991,145
Area: 1,269,389 sq mi; 3,287,590 sq km
Leading Exports: clothing, chemicals, gems, and jewelry
Location: Asia

Indonesia
Capital: Jakarta
Population: 228,437,870
Area: 636,000 sq mi; 1,919,440 sq km
Leading Exports: oil and gas, textiles, rubber, and plywood
Location: Asia

Iran
Capital: Tehran
Population: 66,128,965
Area: 634,562 sq mi; 1,643,452 sq km
Leading Exports: petroleum, carpets, and fruit and nuts
Location: Asia

Iraq
Capital: Baghdad
Population: 23,331,985
Area: 168,760 sq mi; 437,072 sq km
Leading Exports: oil
Location: Asia

Ireland
Capital: Dublin
Population: 3,840,838
Area: 27,136 sq mi; 70,280 sq km
Leading Exports: machinery, chemicals, and electronics
Location: Europe

Israel
Capital: Jerusalem
Population: 5,938,093
Area: 8,019 sq mi; 20,770 sq km
Leading Exports: machinery, electronics, and cut diamonds
Location: Asia

Italy
Capital: Rome
Population: 57,679,825
Area: 116,310 sq mi; 301,230 sq km
Leading Exports: metals, motor vehicles, textiles, and clothing
Location: Europe

Jamaica
Capital: Kingston
Population: 2,665,636
Area: 4,243 sq mi; 10,990 sq km
Leading Exports: bauxite, sugar, bananas, and rum
Location: Caribbean Sea

Japan
Capital: Tokyo
Population: 126,771,662
Area: 145,888 sq mi; 377,835 sq km
Leading Exports: machinery, motor vehicles, and electronics
Location: Asia

Jordan
Capital: Amman
Population: 5,153,378
Area: 35,637 sq mi; 92,300 sq km
Leading Exports: phosphates, fertilizers, and potash
Location: Asia

Kazakhstan
Capital: Astana
Population: 16,731,303
Area: 1,049,191 sq mi; 2,717,300 sq km
Leading Exports: oil, ferrous and nonferrous metals
Location: Asia

Kenya
Capital: Nairobi
Population: 30,765,916
Area: 224,970 sq mi;
582,650 sq km
Leading Exports: tea, coffee,
petroleum products, and cement
Location: Africa

Kiribati
Capital: Tarawa
Population: 91,149
Area: 277 sq mi; 717 sq km
Leading Exports: copra and fish
products
Location: Oceania

Korea, North
Capital: P'yongyang
Population: 21,968,228
Area: 46,542 sq mi; 120,540 sq km
Leading Exports: minerals and
metallurgical products
Location: Asia

Korea, South
Capital: Seoul
Population: 47,904,370
Area: 38,025 sq mi; 98,480 sq km
Leading Exports: electronics,
electrical equipment, and motor
vehicles
Location: Asia

Kuwait
Capital: Kuwait
Population: 2,041,961
Area: 6,881 sq mi; 17,820 sq km
Leading Exports: oil
Location: Asia

Kyrgyzstan
Capital: Bishkek
Population: 4,753,003
Area: 76,644 sq mi; 198,500 sq km
Leading Exports: wool, meat, cotton,
metal, and shoes
Location: Asia

Laos
Capital: Vientiane
Population: 5,497,459
Area: 91,432 sq mi; 236,800 sq km
Leading Exports: wood products,
coffee, and tin
Location: Asia

Latvia
Capital: Riga
Population: 2,385,231
Area: 24,750 sq mi; 64,100 sq km
Leading Exports: timber and ferrous
metals
Location: Europe

Lebanon
Capital: Beirut
Population: 3,627,774
Area: 4,016 sq mi; 10,400 sq km
Leading Exports: agricultural
products, chemicals, and textiles
Location: Asia

Lesotho
Capital: Maseru
Population: 2,177,062
Area: 11,719 sq mi; 30,350 sq km
Leading Exports: wool, mohair,
wheat, cattle, and peas
Location: Africa

Liberia
Capital: Monrovia
Population: 3,225,837
Area: 43,002 sq mi; 111,370 sq km
Leading Exports: iron ore, rubber,
coffee, and diamonds
Location: Africa

Libya
Capital: Tripoli
Population: 5,240,599
Area: 679,385 sq mi;
1,759,540 sq km
Leading Exports: oil, refined
petroleum products, and food
products
Location: Africa

Liechtenstein
Capital: Vaduz
Population: 32,204
Area: 62 sq mi; 160 sq km
Leading Exports: specialty machinery
and dental products
Location: Europe

Lithuania
Capital: Vilnius
Population: 3,610,535
Area: 25,175 sq mi; 65,200 sq km
Leading Exports: machinery, mineral
products, and foodstuffs
Location: Europe

Luxembourg
Capital: Luxembourg
Population: 442,972
Area: 998 sq mi; 2,586 sq km
Leading Exports: finished steel
products and chemicals
Location: Europe

Macedonia
Capital: Skopje
Population: 2,046,209
Area: 9,781 sq mi; 25,333 sq km
Leading Exports: manufactured
goods
Location: Europe

Madagascar
Capital: Antananarivo
Population: 15,982,563
Area: 226,665 sq mi;
587,040 sq km
Leading Exports: coffee, vanilla,
cloves, shellfish, and sugar
Location: Africa

Malawi
Capital: Lilongwe
Population: 10,548,250
Area: 45,747 sq mi; 118,480 sq km
Leading Exports: tobacco, tea, and
sugar
Location: Africa

Malaysia
Capital: Kuala Lumpur
Population: 22,229,040
Area: 127,322 sq mi;
329,750 sq km
Leading Exports: electronic
equipment, petroleum, rubber,
and palm oil
Location: Asia

Maldives
Capital: Male
Population: 301,475
Area: 116 sq mi; 300 sq km
Leading Exports: fish and clothing
Location: Asia (Indian Ocean)

Mali
Capital: Bamako
Population: 11,008,518
Area: 478,783 sq mi;
1,240,000 sq km
Leading Exports: cotton, livestock,
gold, peanuts, and fish
Location: Africa

Malta
Capital: Valletta
Population: 394,583
Area: 122 sq mi; 316 sq km
Leading Exports: machinery and
transportation equipment
Location: Europe (Mediterranean
Sea)

Marshall Islands
Capital: Majuro
Population: 70,822
Area: 70 sq mi; 181 sq km
Leading Exports: coconut oil, fish,
trochus shells
Location: Oceania

Mauritania
Capital: Nouakchott
Population: 2,667,859
Area: 397,969 sq mi;
1,030,700 sq km
Leading Exports: iron ore, fish, fish
products, and livestock
Location: Africa

Mauritius
Capital: Port Louis
Population: 1,189,825
Area: 718 sq mi; 1,860 sq km
Leading Exports: textiles, sugar, and
clothing
Location: Africa (Indian Ocean)

Mexico
Capital: Mexico City
Population:
101,879,171
Area: 761,632 sq mi;
1,972,550 sq km
Leading Exports: oil, petroleum
products, coffee, and silver
Location: North America

Micronesia,
Federated States of
Capital: Palikir
Population: 134,597
Area: 271 sq mi; 702 sq km
Leading Exports: fish, bananas, and
black pepper
Location: Oceania

Moldova
Capital: Chisinau
Population: 4,430,654
Area: 13,012 sq mi; 33,700 sq km
Leading Exports: foodstuffs, wine,
tobacco, fur, and leather
Location: Europe

Monaco
Capital: Monaco
Population: 31,693
Area: 0.77 sq mi; 2 sq km
Leading Exports: none
Location: Europe

Mongolia
Capital: Ulaanbaatar
Population: 2,654,999
Area: 604,270 sq mi;
1,565,000 sq km
Leading Exports: copper, livestock,
animal products, and cashmere
Location: Asia

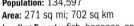

Countries of the World

Morocco
Capital: Rabat
Population:
30,645,305
Area: 172,420 sq mi;
446,550 sq km
Leading Exports: food, beverages, and phosphates
Location: Africa

Mozambique
Capital: Maputo
Population:
19,371,057
Area: 309,506 sq mi;
801,590 sq km
Leading Exports: shrimp, cashews, cotton, and sugar
Location: Africa

Myanmar (Burma)
Capital: Yangon (Rangoon)
Population: 41,994,678
Area: 261,979 sq mi;
678,500 sq km
Leading Exports: textiles, clothing, teak, rice, and hardwood
Location: Asia

Namibia
Capital: Windhoek
Population: 1,797,677
Area: 318,707 sq mi;
825,418 sq km
Leading Exports: diamonds, copper, gold, zinc, and lead
Location: Africa

Nauru
Capital: no official capital
Population: 11,845
Area: 8 sq mi; 21 sq km
Leading Exports: phosphates
Location: Oceania

Nepal
Capital: Katmandu
Population: 25,284,463
Area: 54,365 sq mi; 140,800 sq km
Leading Exports: carpets, clothing, rice, wheat, and leather goods
Location: Asia

Netherlands
Capital: Amsterdam
Population:
15,981,472
Area: 16,033 sq mi; 41,523 sq km
Leading Exports: machinery and equipment, flowers, and chemicals
Location: Europe

New Zealand
Capital: Wellington
Population: 3,864,129
Area: 103,741 sq mi;
268,680 sq km
Leading Exports: wool, beef, fish, and foodstuffs
Location: Oceania

Nicaragua
Capital: Managua
Population: 4,812,569
Area: 50,000 sq mi; 129,494 sq km
Leading Exports: coffee, cotton, rice, sugar, seafood, and gold
Location: Central America

Niger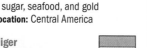
Capital: Niamey
Population: 10,355,156
Area: 489,208 sq mi;
1,267,000 sq km
Leading Exports: uranium ore and animal products
Location: Africa

Nigeria
Capital: Abuja
Population: 126,635,626
Area: 356,682 sq mi;
923,770 sq km
Leading Exports: oil, cocoa, timber, and rubber
Location: Africa

Norway
Capital: Oslo
Population: 4,503,440
Area: 125,186 sq mi;
324,220 sq km
Leading Exports: pulp and paper products, petroleum products, and natural gas
Location: Europe

Oman
Capital: Muscat
Population: 2,622,198
Area: 82,034 sq mi; 212,460 sq km
Leading Exports: petroleum and food
Location: Asia

Pakistan
Capital: Islamabad
Population:
144,616,639
Area: 310,414 sq mi;
803,940 sq km
Leading Exports: cotton, textiles, clothing, and rice
Location: Asia

Palau
Capital: Koror
Population: 18,766
Area: 177 sq mi; 458 sq km
Leading Exports: trochus, tuna, copra, and handicrafts
Location: Oceania

Panama
Capital: Panama City
Population: 2,845,647
Area: 30,194 sq mi; 78,200 sq km
Leading Exports: bananas, shrimp, sugar, coffee, and clothing
Location: North America

Papua New Guinea
Capital: Port Moresby
Population: 5,049,055
Area: 178,266 sq mi;
461,690 sq km
Leading Exports: gold, copper ore, oil, and wood products
Location: Oceania

Paraguay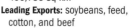
Capital: Asuncion
Population: 5,734,139
Area: 157,052 sq mi;
406,750 sq km
Leading Exports: soybeans, feed, cotton, and beef
Location: South America

Peru
Capital: Lima
Population:
27,483,864
Area: 496,243 sq mi;
1,285,220 sq km
Leading Exports: copper, zinc, and fish products
Location: South America

Philippines
Capital: Manila
Population: 82,841,518
Area: 115,834 sq mi;
300,000 sq km
Leading Exports: electronics, textiles, and food products
Location: Asia

Poland
Capital: Warsaw
Population:
38,633,912
Area: 120,731 sq mi;
312,680 sq km
Leading Exports: machinery, transportation equipment, manufactured goods, and coal
Location: Europe

Portugal
Capital: Lisbon
Population: 10,066,253
Area: 35,553 sq mi; 92,080 sq km
Leading Exports: clothing, machinery, cork, and paper
Location: Europe

Qatar
Capital: Doha
Population: 769,152
Area: 4,416 sq mi; 11,437 sq km
Leading Exports: petroleum products
Location: Asia

Romania
Capital: Bucharest
Population: 22,364,022
Area: 91,702 sq mi; 237,500 sq km
Leading Exports: metals, metal products, and mineral products
Location: Europe

Russia
Capital: Moscow
Population:
145,470,197
Area: 6,592,734 sq mi;
17,075,200 sq km
Leading Exports: petroleum, petroleum products, wood products, and metals
Location: Europe and Asia

Rwanda
Capital: Kigali
Population: 7,312,756
Area: 10,170 sq mi; 26,340 sq km
Leading Exports: coffee, tea, hides, and tin ore
Location: Africa

Saint Kitts and Nevis
Capital: Basseterre
Population: 38,819
Area: 104 sq mi; 261 sq km
Leading Exports: machinery, food, electronics, and beverages
Location: North America (Caribbean Sea)

Saint Lucia
Capital: Castries
Population: 156,260
Area: 239 sq mi; 620 sq km
Leading Exports: bananas, clothing, cocoa, and vegetables
Location: North America (Caribbean Sea)

Saint Vincent and the Grenadines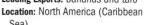
Capital: Kingstown
Population: 115,461
Area: 150 sq mi; 389 sq km
Leading Exports: bananas and taro
Location: North America (Caribbean Sea)

Samoa
Capital: Apia
Population: 179,466
Area: 1,104 sq mi; 2,860 sq km
Leading Exports: coconut products and fish
Location: Oceania

San Marino
Capital: San Marino
Population: 26,937
Area: 23 sq mi; 60 sq km
Leading Exports: stone, lime, wood, and chestnuts
Location: Europe

São Tomé and Príncipe
Capital: Sao Tome
Population: 165,034
Area: 386 sq mi; 1,001 km
Leading Exports: cocoa, coffee, and palm oil
Location: Africa

Saudi Arabia
Capital: Riyadh
Population: 22,757,092
Area: 757,011 sq mi; 1,960,582 sq km
Leading Exports: petroleum and petroleum products
Location: Asia

Senegal
Capital: Dakar
Population: 10,284,929
Area: 75,752 sq mi; 196,190 sq km
Leading Exports: fish, peanuts, and phosphates
Location: Africa

Seychelles
Capital: Victoria
Population: 79,326
Area: 176 sq mi; 455 sq km
Leading Exports: fish, cinnamon bark, and copra
Location: Africa (Indian Ocean)

Sierra Leone
Capital: Freetown
Population: 5,426,618
Area: 27,700 sq mi; 71,740 sq km
Leading Exports: diamonds, coffee, and cocoa
Location: Africa

Singapore
Capital: Singapore
Population: 4,300,419
Area: 250 sq mi; 647 sq km
Leading Exports: electronics and refined petroleum products
Location: Asia

Slovakia
Capital: Bratislava
Population: 5,414,937
Area: 18,860 sq mi; 48,845 sq km
Leading Exports: machinery and transportation equipment
Location: Europe

Slovenia
Capital: Ljubljana
Population: 1,930,132
Area: 7,837 sq mi; 20,296 sq km
Leading Exports: metals and transportation equipment
Location: Europe

Solomon Islands
Capital: Honiara
Population: 480,442
Area: 10,985 sq mi; 28,450 sq km
Leading Exports: fish, timber, and cocoa
Location: Oceania

Somalia
Capital: Mogadishu
Population: 7,253,137
Area: 246,210 sq mi; 637,660 sq km
Leading Exports: bananas, animals, fish, and hides
Location: Africa

South Africa
Capital: Pretoria (administrative), Cape Town (legislative), Bloemfontein (judicial)
Population: 43,586,097
Area: 471,027 sq mi; 1,219,912 sq km
Leading Exports: gold, minerals, metals, and diamonds
Location: Africa

Spain
Capital: Madrid
Population: 40,037,995
Area: 194,892 sq mi; 504,750 sq km
Leading Exports: motor vehicles. textiles, olives and olive oil, and manufactured goods
Location: Europe

Sri Lanka
Capital: Colombo
Population: 19,408,635
Area: 25,333 sq mi; 65,610 sq km
Leading Exports: textiles, garments, tea, and diamonds
Location: Asia (Indian Ocean)

Sudan
Capital: Khartoum
Population: 35,080,373
Area: 967,532 sq mi; 2,505,810 sq km
Leading Exports: gum arabic, cotton, and peanuts
Location: Africa

Suriname
Capital: Paramaribo
Population: 433,998
Area: 63,041 sq mi; 163,270 sq km
Leading Exports: aluminum, shrimp, and fish
Location: South America

Swaziland
Capital: Mbabane (administrative) Lobamba (royal and legislative)
Population: 1,104,343
Area: 6,641 sq mi; 17,360 sq km
Leading Exports: beverage concentrates, sugar, and fruit
Location: Africa

Sweden
Capital: Stockholm
Population: 8,873,052
Area: 173,738 sq mi; 449,964 sq km
Leading Exports: machinery, motor vehicles, and paper products
Location: Europe

Switzerland
Capital: Bern
Population: 7,283,274
Area: 15,943 sq mi; 41,290 sq km
Leading Exports: machinery, machine equipment, and food products
Location: Europe

Syria
Capital: Damascus
Population: 16,728,808
Area: 71,501 sq mi; 185,180 sq km
Leading Exports: petroleum, textiles, cotton, and fruit
Location: Asia

Taiwan
Capital: Taipei
Population: 22,370,461
Area: 13,892 sq mi; 35,980 sq km
Leading Exports: electrical machinery, electronics, and textiles
Location: Asia

Tajikistan
Capital: Dushanbe
Population: 6,578,681
Area: 55,253 sq mi; 143,100 sq km
Leading Exports: cotton, aluminum, fruit, and vegetable oil
Location: Asia

Tanzania
Capital: Dodoma
Population: 36,232,074
Area: 364,914 sq mi; 945,090 sq km
Leading Exports: coffee, cotton, tobacco, tea, and cloves
Location: Africa

Thailand
Capital: Bangkok
Population: 61,797,751
Area: 198,463 sq mi; 511,770 sq km
Leading Exports: machinery, rice, rubber, and garments
Location: Asia

Togo
Capital: Lome
Population: 5,153,088
Area: 21,927 sq mi; 56,790 sq km
Leading Exports: phosphates, cotton, cocoa, and coffee
Location: Africa

Tonga
Capital: Nuku'alofa
Population: 104,227
Area: 289 sq mi; 748 sq km
Leading Exports: squash, fish, and vanilla
Location: Oceania

Trinidad and Tobago
Capital: Port-of-Spain
Population: 1,169,682
Area: 1,981 sq mi; 5,130 sq km
Leading Exports: petroleum and petroleum products
Location: North America (Caribbean Sea)

Tunisia
Capital: Tunis
Population: 9,705,102
Area: 63,172 sq mi; 163,610 sq km
Leading Exports: phosphates, chemicals, and agricultural products
Location: Africa

Countries of the World

Turkey
Capital: Ankara
Population: 66,493,970
Area: 301,394 sq mi;
780,580 sq km
Leading Exports: manufactured products, cotton, textiles, and foodstuffs
Location: Europe and Asia

Turkmenistan
Capital: Ashgabat
Population: 4,603,244
Area: 188,463 sq mi;
488,100 sq km
Leading Exports: natural gas, cotton, and oil
Location: Asia

Tuvalu
Capital: Funafuti
Population: 10,838
Area: 10 sq mi; 26 sq km
Leading Exports: copra
Location: Oceania

Uganda
Capital: Kampala
Population: 23,985,712
Area: 91,139 sq mi; 236,040 sq km
Leading Exports: coffee, cotton, and tea
Location: Africa

Ukraine
Capital: Kiev
Population: 48,760,474
Area: 233,098 sq mi;
603,700 sq km
Leading Exports: fuel and petroleum products, chemicals, and metals
Location: Europe

United Arab Emirates
Capital: Abu Dhabi
Population: 2,407,460
Area: 32,000 sq mi; 82,877 sq km
Leading Exports: oil, natural gas, and dried fish
Location: Asia

United Kingdom
Capital: London
Population: 59,647,790
Area: 94,529 sq mi; 244,820 sq km
Leading Exports: manufactured goods, machinery, fuels, and chemicals
Location: Europe

United States
Capital: Washington, D.C.
Population: 278,058,881
Area: 3,717,939 sq mi;
9,629,091 sq km
Leading Exports: capital goods, automobiles, and consumer goods
Location: North America

Uruguay
Capital: Montevideo
Population: 3,360,105
Area: 68,041 sq mi; 176,220 sq km
Leading Exports: wool, meat, rice, and leather products
Location: South America

Uzbekistan
Capital: Tashkent
Population:
25,155,064
Area: 172,748 sq mi;
447,400 sq km
Leading Exports: cotton, gold, natural gas, and minerals
Location: Asia

Vanuatu
Capital: Port-Vila
Population: 192,910
Area: 4,710 sq mi; 12,200 sq km
Leading Exports: copra, beef, cocoa, timber, and coffee
Location: Oceania

Venezuela
Capital: Caracas
Population: 23,916,810
Area: 352,156 sq mi;
912,050 sq km
Leading Exports: petroleum, bauxite, aluminum, and steel
Location: South America

Vietnam
Capital: Hanoi
Population: 79,939,014
Area: 127,248 sq mi;
329,560 sq km
Leading Exports: textiles, rice, crude oil, coffee, rubber, and sea products
Location: Asia

Yemen
Capital: Sanaa
Population: 18,078,035
Area: 203,857 sq mi;
527,970 sq km
Leading Exports: oil, cotton, coffee, fish, hides, and fruit
Location: Asia

Yugoslavia (Serbia and Montenegro)
Capital: Belgrade
Population: 11,101,833
Area: 39,436 sq mi; 102,350 sq km
Leading Exports: manufactured goods, food, and raw materials
Location: Europe

Zambia
Capital: Lusaka
Population: 9,770,199
Area: 290,594 sq mi;
752,610 sq km
Leading Exports: copper, zinc, cobalt, and lead
Location: Africa

Zimbabwe
Capital: Harare
Population: 11,365,366
Area: 150,809 sq mi;
390,580 sq km
Leading Exports: agricultural and mineral products and clothing
Location: Africa

World History Time Line
Prehistory

3.5 million | 35,000 B.C. | 30,000 | 25,000 | 20,000 | 15,000 | 10,000 | 5000 | 1000 B.C.

AFRICA

3.5 million years ago
The first humans probably appeared

5500–3500 B.C.
Cave walls painted in Tassili

3000 B.C. or earlier
Farmers in Nile River Valley developed irrigation systems

5000 B.C.
Crops first cultivated in Egypt

THE AMERICAS

9500 or more B.C.
Humans probably crossed the Bering land bridge from Asia into North America

9000 B.C.
Clovis culture established in the Americas

7000 B.C.
"Cave of the Hands" painted

4000 B.C. or earlier
Corn first cultivated in Mexico

ASIA AND PACIFIC

10,000 B.C.
Herding of goats began in Persia (present day = Iran)

8000 B.C.
New Stone Age began in Southwest Asia as agriculture developed

5000 B.C. or earlier
Farmers in Mesopotamia developed irrigation systems

7000 B.C. or earlier
Wheat and barley first cultivated in Southwest Asia

6000 B.C. or earlier
Rice first cultivated in China

EUROPE

30,000 B.C.
Stone-Age people made cave paintings at Chauvet (France)

15,000 B.C.
Cave paintings made at Lascaux (France)

13,000 B.C.
Cave paintings made at Altamira (Spain)

World History Time Line

3500 B.C.   **3250 B.C.**   **3000 B.C.**   **2750 B.C.**   **2500 B.C.**   **2250 B.C.**   **2000 B.C.**

AFRICA

3200 B.C.
Civilization arose in Nubia

3150 B.C.
King Menes united Lower and Upper Egypt

2575 B.C.
Egyptians invaded Nubia

2600 B.C.
Great Pyramid begun at Giza in Egypt

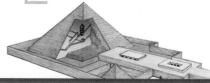

THE AMERICAS

3000 B.C.
Inuit settled in northern Canada

2500 B.C.
Period of drought ended across North America; people returned to the Great Plains and hunted buffalo

ASIA AND PACIFIC

3500 B.C.
People settled in the Indus River Valley

3500 B.C.
City-states of Mesopotamia arose

3200 B.C.
Writing invented in Sumer

2500 B.C.
Height of Harappa and Mohenjo-Daro civilizations

2334 B.C.
Sargon of Akkad united Mesopotamia into world's first empire

2000 B.C.
Xia legendary period began in China

2100 B.C.
City-state of Ur gained control of Mesopotamia

1800 B.C.
Abraham's cover (agreement) with God marked the beginning of Judaism

EUROPE

3000 B.C.
Minoan culture arose on Crete

1750 B.C.	1500 B.C.	1250 B.C.	1000 B.C.	750 B.C.	500 B.C.	250 B.C.	A.D. 1

AFRICA

1570 B.C.
New Kingdom
began in Egypt

814 B.C.
Traditional date of
founding of Carthage by
seafaring Phoenicians

600 B.C.
Nubian city-state of Meroë
arose as a great trade center

100 B.C.
Bantu
people
began
spreading
across
Africa

146 B.C.
Rome destroyed
Carthage at the end of
the Third Punic War

750 B.C.
Nubian kings began
a century of rule
as pharaohs of Egypt

THE AMERICAS

1200 B.C.
Olmec civilization arose in Mexico

900 B.C.
Chavín culture
appeared in
ancient Peru

300 B.C.
Decline of Olmec
civilization

200 B.C.
Chavín culture
disappeared from
ancient Peru

700 B.C.
Adena culture
appeared in
Ohio Valley

100 B.C.
Hopewell culture arose in east-
central North America

ASIA AND PACIFIC

1760 B.C.
Shang
dynasty
began rule in
China; writing
used on
oracle bones

1400 B.C.
Phoenicians
developed alphabet

1500 B.C.
Aryans migrated
into India

1000 B.C.
King David
united the
Hebrews

563 B.C.
Siddhartha
Gautama,
the Buddha,
born in India

350 B.C.
Mencius
began to
spread
the
teachings
of
Confucius

214 B.C.
Shi
Huangdi
connected
existing
walls
to form
the Great
Wall

206 B.C.
During the Han
dynasty, civil
service exams were
set up in China

1027 B.C.
Zhou dynasty
founded in China

551 B.C.
Confucius born
in Lu Province,
China

before 1750 B.C.
Hammurabi ruled Babylonia,
developed first extensive law code

500 B.C.
Lydians minted the region's first coins

EUROPE

1600 B.C.
Latins settled along
Italy's Tiber River

Minoan culture
reached its height

1400 B.C.
Mycenae arose
on Greek
mainland

900 B.C.
Greek city-state of
Sparta began
conquering its neighbors

500s B.C.
Democracy
appeared in some
Greek city-states;
Rome set up
a republic

27 B.C.
Augustus became
first Roman emperor

753 B.C.
According to legend, Rome founded

336 B.C.
Alexander the Great became
king of Macedonia on the
death of Philip II

1250 B.C.
Troy and
Mycenae
fought in the
Trojan War

Social Studies Reference Guide **R31**

World History Time Line
A.D. 1–600

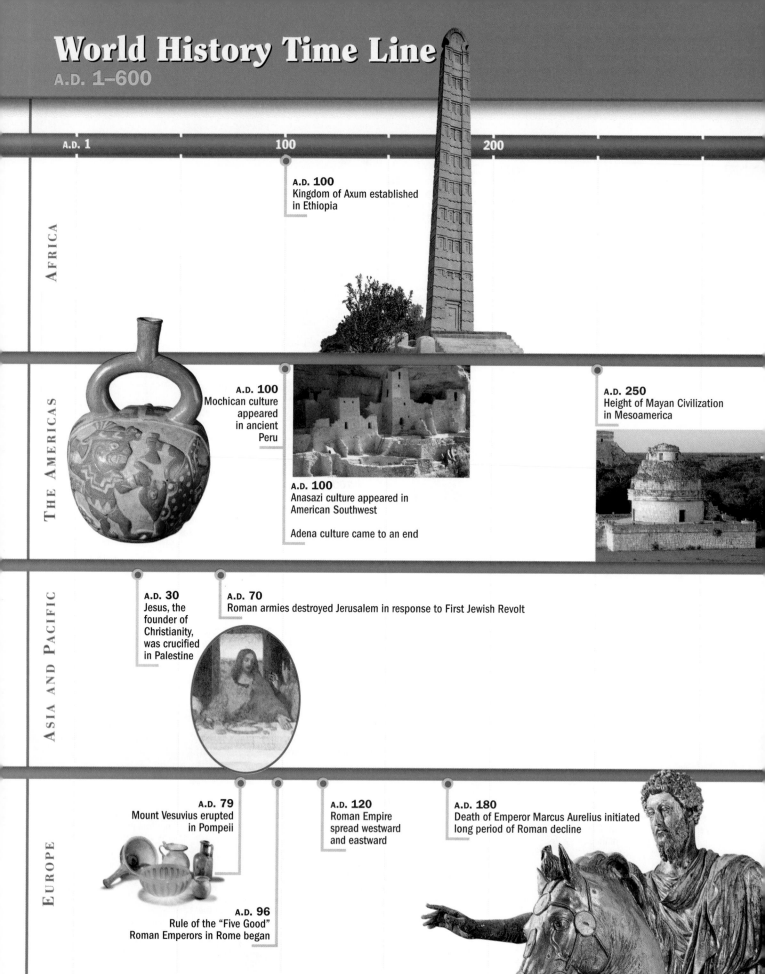

AFRICA

A.D. **100**
Kingdom of Axum established in Ethiopia

THE AMERICAS

A.D. **100**
Mochican culture appeared in ancient Peru

A.D. **100**
Anasazi culture appeared in American Southwest

Adena culture came to an end

A.D. **250**
Height of Mayan Civilization in Mesoamerica

ASIA AND PACIFIC

A.D. **30**
Jesus, the founder of Christianity, was crucified in Palestine

A.D. **70**
Roman armies destroyed Jerusalem in response to First Jewish Revolt

EUROPE

A.D. **79**
Mount Vesuvius erupted in Pompeii

A.D. **96**
Rule of the "Five Good" Roman Emperors in Rome began

A.D. **120**
Roman Empire spread westward and eastward

A.D. **180**
Death of Emperor Marcus Aurelius initiated long period of Roman decline

300   400   500   600

A.D. 330
King Ezana of Axum converted to Christianity

A.D. 350
Axum invaded former Kush capital of Meroë

A.D. 429
The Germanic Vandals invaded North Africa and began a century of raiding

AFRICA

A.D. 300
Hohokam culture appeared in American Southwest

A.D. 500
Hopewell culture came to an end

THE AMERICAS

A.D. 570
Muhammad, founder of Islam, was born in Arabia

A.D. 320
A golden age began under the Gupta dynasty in India

A.D. 589
Sui dynasty unified China

ASIA AND PACIFIC

A.D. 380
Christianity became the official religion of the Roman Empire

A.D. 476
Last Roman emperor in the West overthrown; Constantinople became center of Roman (Byzantine) power

A.D. 527
Justinian began rule of Byzantine Empire

A.D. 537
The largest church in Constantinople, the Hagia Sophia, was completed

A.D. 330
Constantinople became the new capital of the Roman Empire

EUROPE

A.D. 313
Christianity gained recognition as a Roman religion

World History Time Line
600 to 1200

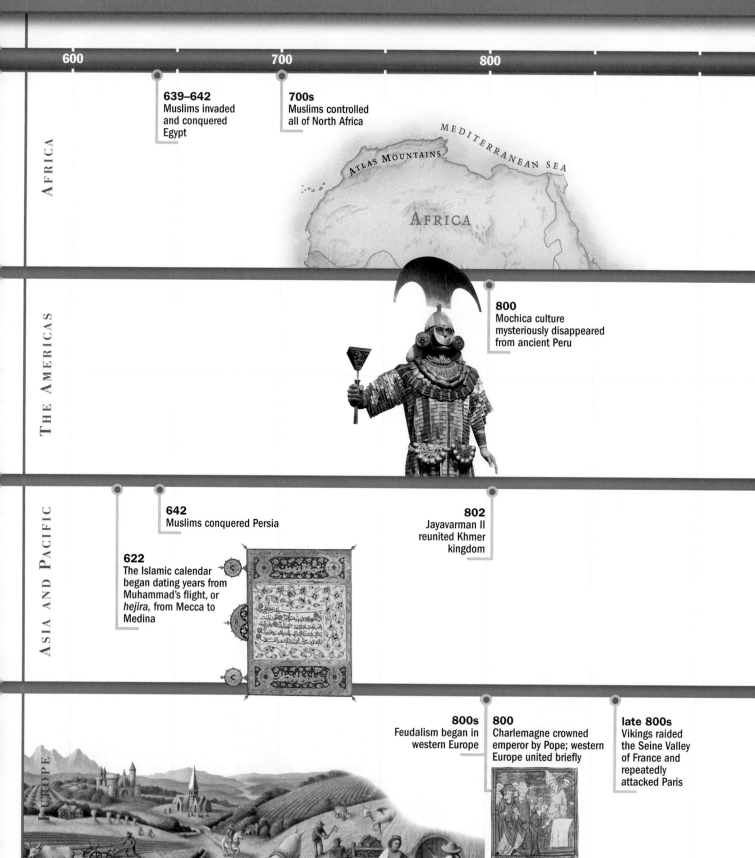

600

700

800

AFRICA

639–642
Muslims invaded and conquered Egypt

700s
Muslims controlled all of North Africa

ATLAS MOUNTAINS

MEDITERRANEAN SEA

AFRICA

THE AMERICAS

800
Mochica culture mysteriously disappeared from ancient Peru

ASIA AND PACIFIC

642
Muslims conquered Persia

622
The Islamic calendar began dating years from Muhammad's flight, or *hejira*, from Mecca to Medina

802
Jayavarman II reunited Khmer kingdom

EUROPE

800s
Feudalism began in western Europe

800
Charlemagne crowned emperor by Pope; western Europe united briefly

late 800s
Vikings raided the Seine Valley of France and repeatedly attacked Paris

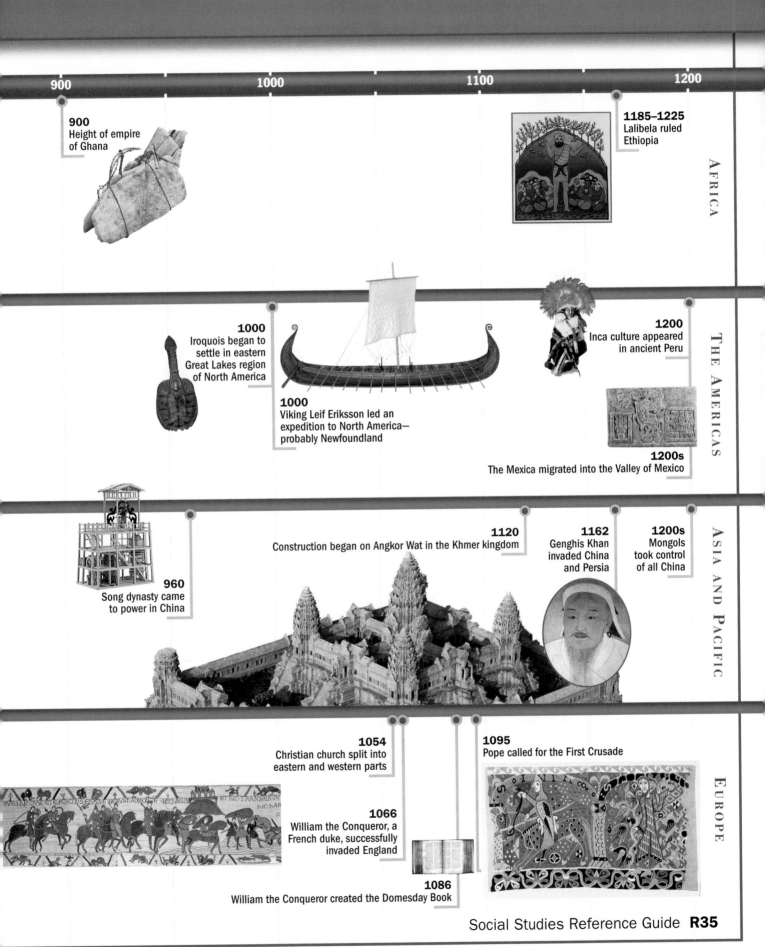

900 · **1000** · **1100** · **1200**

AFRICA

900
Height of empire of Ghana

1185–1225
Lalibela ruled Ethiopia

THE AMERICAS

1000
Iroquois began to settle in eastern Great Lakes region of North America

1000
Viking Leif Eriksson led an expedition to North America—probably Newfoundland

1200
Inca culture appeared in ancient Peru

1200s
The Mexica migrated into the Valley of Mexico

ASIA AND PACIFIC

1120
Construction began on Angkor Wat in the Khmer kingdom

1162
Genghis Khan invaded China and Persia

1200s
Mongols took control of all China

960
Song dynasty came to power in China

EUROPE

1054
Christian church split into eastern and western parts

1095
Pope called for the First Crusade

1066
William the Conqueror, a French duke, successfully invaded England

1086
William the Conqueror created the Domesday Book

Social Studies Reference Guide **R35**

World History Time Line
1200 to 1800

1200	1300	1400

AFRICA

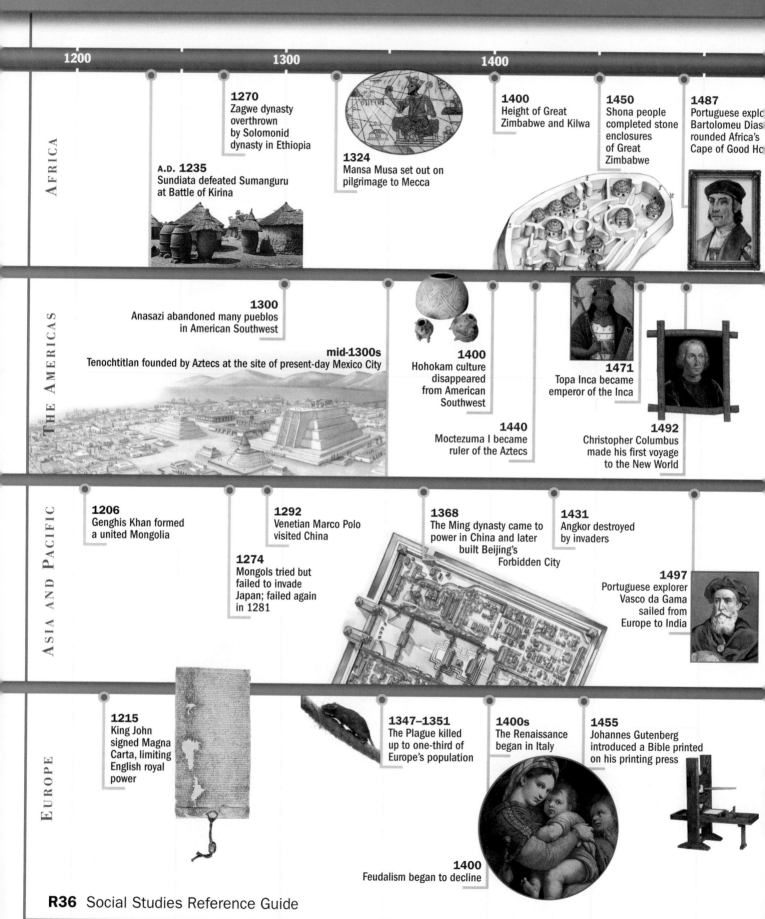

1270
Zagwe dynasty overthrown by Solomonid dynasty in Ethiopia

A.D. 1235
Sundiata defeated Sumanguru at Battle of Kirina

1324
Mansa Musa set out on pilgrimage to Mecca

1400
Height of Great Zimbabwe and Kilwa

1450
Shona people completed stone enclosures of Great Zimbabwe

1487
Portuguese explo[rer] Bartolomeu Dias rounded Africa's Cape of Good Ho[pe]

THE AMERICAS

1300
Anasazi abandoned many pueblos in American Southwest

mid-1300s
Tenochtitlan founded by Aztecs at the site of present-day Mexico City

1400
Hohokam culture disappeared from American Southwest

1440
Moctezuma I became ruler of the Aztecs

1471
Topa Inca became emperor of the Inca

1492
Christopher Columbus made his first voyage to the New World

ASIA AND PACIFIC

1206
Genghis Khan formed a united Mongolia

1274
Mongols tried but failed to invade Japan; failed again in 1281

1292
Venetian Marco Polo visited China

1368
The Ming dynasty came to power in China and later built Beijing's Forbidden City

1431
Angkor destroyed by invaders

1497
Portuguese explorer Vasco da Gama sailed from Europe to India

EUROPE

1215
King John signed Magna Carta, limiting English royal power

1347–1351
The Plague killed up to one-third of Europe's population

1400s
The Renaissance began in Italy

1455
Johannes Gutenberg introduced a Bible printed on his printing press

1400
Feudalism began to decline

1500	1600	1700	1800

AFRICA

early 1500s
Portuguese invasions in eastern and southern Africa; start of Atlantic slave trade

1591
Empire of Songhai weakened

1500
The kingdom of Benin became a powerful trading empire

1799
The Rosetta stone was decoded by Jean Champollion

THE AMERICAS

1521
Spaniard Hernando Cortes conquered the Aztec Empire

1532
Spaniard Francisco Pizarro conquered Inca Empire

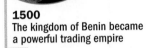

1570
Iroquois League formed in eastern North America

1607
First permanent English settlement in America at Jamestown, Virginia

1763
Great Britain gained Canada after defeating France in war

1776
The original 13 British colonies in America declared independence

1789
The United States of America began with George Washington as president

ASIA AND PACIFIC

1526
The Mogul Empire began in India

1603
Shoguns of Tokugawa dynasty began rule in Japan

1630
Construction began on Taj Mahal in India

1788
British colony of New South Wales established in Australia

EUROPE

1517
The Protestant Reformation began in Germany

1588
England defeated the Spanish Armada

1769
James Watt improved the steam engine

1558
Elizabeth I became queen of England

1789
The French Revolution began

1545
The Council of Trent began its work of reforming the Catholic Church

1799
Napoleon Bonaparte took control of the French government

Social Studies Reference Guide **R37**

World History Time Line
1800 to 1950

1800 1810 1820 1830 1840 1850 1860 1870

AFRICA

1869
Suez Canal completed across part of Egypt

THE AMERICAS

1807
Robert Fulton invented the steamboat in the United States

1818
Chile gained independence from Spain

1821
Mexico gained independence from Spain

1861–1865
U.S. Civil War ended in emancipation of slaves and outlawing of slavery

1867
Canada became a British dominion

ASIA AND PACIFIC

1853-1854
U.S. Commodore Matthew Perry opened Japan to trade with the West

1868
The Meiji emperor came to power in Japan, ending the rule of shoguns

1839
First Opium War started between China and Great Britain

1840
William Hobson signed Treaty of Waitangi with the Maori

EUROPE

1804
Napoleon I became emperor of France

1820s
The first railroad was used in Great Britain

1815
Napoleon I defeated at the Battle of Waterloo and exiled

1871
German Empire proclaimed after French defeat in Franco-Prussian War

1870
Italian unification made complete by capture of Rome from the papacy

1880   **1890**   **1900**   **1910**   **1920**   **1930**   **1940**   **1950**

1885
Congo Free State set up in Africa under King Leopold of Belgium

1911
Crisis in Morocco almost pushed Great Britain and France into war with Germany

1912
African National Congress founded in South Africa as "South African Native National Congress"; renamed 1923

1942–1943
North Africa became a major theater (location of battles) of World War II

1948
South Africa's National Party came to power and began instituting *apartheid*

1889
Thomas Edison invented the motion picture camera

1910
Revolution broke out in Mexico, beginning a long period of reform

1913
Ford began building automobiles on an assembly line

1929
The Great Depression began

1917
United States joined Great Britain and France in The Great War

1878
Alexander Graham Bell invented the telephone

1941
Japan attacked Pearl Harbor, United States entered World War II

1945
United Nations founded in San Francisco; later moved to New York City

1948 The United States launched the Marshall Plan to aid war-torn Europe

---

1885
The Indian National Congress formed

1898
Boxer Rebellion broke out in China

1900
Open Door Policy opened Chinese ports to all trading nations

1905
Japan defeated Russia in the a war to control Manchuria

1937
Japan launched a full-scale war against China

1945
Hiroshima and Nagasaki bombed; the Atomic Age began

1948
Jewish state of Israel proclaimed; first Arab-Israeli war broke out

1949
Communists, led by Mao Zedong, won control of mainland China in civil war

---

1882
Germany, Austria-Hungary, and Italy formed the Triple Alliance

1901
Queen Victoria died in Great Britain, closing the end of the Victorian Age

1914–1918
World War I raged in Europe and elsewhere

1922
Russia's communist leaders formed the Soviet Union

1939–1945
World War II

1949
The United States and its European allies formed NATO

1933
The Nazis under Adolf Hitler took power in Germany

1917
The Russian Revolution broke out, leading to Bolshevik (communist) rule

Social Studies Reference Guide **R39**

World History Time Line

1950	1960	1970	1980	1990	2000	2010

AFRICA

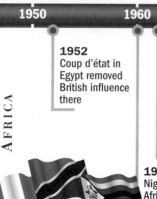

1952
Coup d'état in Egypt removed British influence there

1964
Tanganyika and Zanzibar united to become Tanzania

1962
Algeria gained independence from France after a long, bloody war

1960
Nigeria, Congo, and many other sub-Saharan African nations gained independence

1980
Robert Mugabe led blacks to power in Zimbabwe, formerly Rhodesia

1998
U.S. embassies bombed in Tanzania and Kenya

1994
Nelson Mandela led black majority to power in South Africa

1993-1994
Ethnic war in Rwanda and Burundi led to hundreds of thousands of deaths

THE AMERICAS

1967
U.S. protest movement against the war in Vietnam intensified

1969
The United States put the first astronauts on the moon

1975
The first personal computers

1991
Mercosur, the "Southern Common Market," organized

1994
North American Free Trade Agreement (NAFTA) extended to Mexico

1973
United States signed treaty with North Vietnam

2001
Terrorists attacked New York City and the Pentagon

1999
Canada created the territory of Nunavut for its Inuit people

ASIA AND PACIFIC

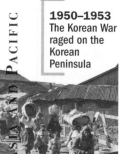

1950–1953
The Korean War raged on the Korean Peninsula

1965
Massive U.S. military buildup began in Vietnam

1967
Six-Day War between Israel and Arab States

1971
New nation of Bangladesh created

1978
Egypt and Israel signed the Camp David Accords

1975
Communists took control of all Vietnam

1989
Chinese student protest crushed by army in Beijing's Tiananmen Square

1997
Great Britain turned control of Hong Kong over to the People's Republic of China

1993
Israel and the PLO signed the Oslo Accords

EUROPE

1957
The Soviet Union launched Sputnik I, the world's first artificial satellite

late 1960s
Violence broke out between Catholics and Protestants in Northern Ireland

1957
The Common Market (later European Union) created

1980
Polish workers founded Solidarity, a trade union free of communist control

1989–1991
Communist governments fell in Eastern Europe; the Berlin Wall opens; East and West Germany reunited

1991
After a failed coup attempt by the communists, the Soviet Union collapsed

2002
European Union put the euro into circulation

1999
NATO countries bombed Serbia to stop ethnic cleansing in Kosovo

Gazetteer

This Gazetteer is a geographic dictionary that will help you locate and pronounce places in this book. Latitude and longitude are given for cities. The page numbers tell you where each place appears on a map (m) or in the text (t).

Aegean Sea (i jē′ən sē) the sea that separates Greece from Asia Minor (m. 247, t. 247)

Afghanistan (af gan′ə stan) a country in Southwest Asia (t. 639)

Agra (ä′grə) a city in India; capital of the Mogul Empire and home of the Taj Mahal; 27°N, 78°E (m. 348, t. 347)

Akkad (ak′ad) a city-state in northern Mesopotamia, the ruler of which conquered all the city-states of Mesopotamia and formed the world's first empire (m. 40, t.41)

Albany (ȯl′bə nē) the capital of New York; 42°N, 73°W (t. 475)

Alexandria (al′ig zan′drē ə) an Egyptian seaport city on the Mediterranean, a center of trade and learning in the Hellenistic Age; 31°N, 30°E (m. 267, t. 269)

Altamira (əl tə mē′rə) a site in Spain where prehistoric paintings appear on the ceiling of a cave (t. 28)

Altiplano (äl tə plä′nō) a region of plateaus and plains in the Andes (m. 187, t. 187)

Amazon Rain Forest (am′ə zon rān fôr′ist) the largest rain forest on Earth (m. 187, t. 187)

Amazon River (am′ə zon riv′ər) the world's second longest river, located in the northern half of South America (m. 187, t. 187)

Andes Mountains (an′dēz moun′tənz) the world's longest mountain chain, located in western South America (m. 187, t. 187)

Angkor (ang′kôr) the first royal city of the Khmer Kingdom (m. 356, t. 357)

Angkor Wat (ang′kôr wät) a temple featuring magnificent towers; built in the 1100s by the Khmer people in present-day Cambodia (m. 357, t. 357)

Antarctica (ant′ärk′tə kə) the fifth largest continent on Earth; also the highest, driest, and coldest continent (t. 663)

Anyang (an yäng′) a town in eastern China known for its artifacts of bone (m. 109, t. 107)

Appalachian Mountains (ap′ə lā′chən moun′tənz) a range in eastern North America (m. 210, t. 209)

Arabian Peninsula (ə rā′bē ən pə nin′sə lə) peninsula in Southwest Asia, bounded by the Red Sea, the Persian Gulf, and the Arabian Sea (m. 334, t. 335)

Asia Minor (ā′zhə mī′nər) the western edge of Asia (m. 247, t. 247)

Assyria (ə sir′ē ə) region at the foot of the Zagros Mountains in the Upper Tigris River Valley (t. 52)

Athens (ath′ənz) a city-state that was the best example of ancient Greek democracy; the capital of modern Greece; 38°N, 23°E (m. 247, t. 255)

Atlas Mountains (at′ləs moun′tənz) a mountain range that separates the Sahara from the Mediterranean (m. 371, t. 371)

Australia (ȯ strā′ lyə) an island continent southeast of Asia; became a dominion of Britain (m. 502, t. 502)

Axum (aks′əm) a kingdom in East Africa that began as a trading settlement (m. 380, t. 381)

Babylon (bab′ə lon) a city-state in Mesopotamia (m. 49, t. 49)

Babylonia (bab′ə lō′nē ə) an empire that included all of Mesopotamia as well as some neighboring city-states (m. 49, t. 49)

Balkan Peninsula (bȯl′kən pə nin′sə lə) a stretch of land that extends southward into the eastern part of the Mediterranean Sea (m. 247, t. 247)

Pronunciation Key

a in hat	ō in open	sh in she
â in care	ȯ in all	th in thin
ā in age	ô in order	ᴛʜ in then
ä in far	oi in oil	zh in measure
e in let	ou in out	ə = a in about
ē in equal	u in cup	ə = e in taken
ėr in term	u̇ in put	ə = i in pencil
i in it	ü in rule	ə = o in lemon
ī in ice	ch in child	ə = u in circus
o in hot	ng in long	

Gazetteer

Beijing (bā′jing′) the capital of China; 40°N, 116°E (m. 101, t. 101)

Benin (be nēn′) a West African kingdom that became an empire by 1500 (m. 380, t. 384)

Beringia (bə rin′jē ə) a prehistoric "land bridge" that once connected Asia and North America (m. 15, t. 14)

Berlin (bər lin′) the capital of Germany and site of the Berlin Conference in 1884; 52°N, 13°E (t. 489)

Berlin Wall (bər lin′ wawl) a wall built in 1961 to divide the German city of Berlin into a communist eastern and a non-communist western half; the wall was finally torn down in 1989 (t. 621)

Black Sea (blak sē) a large sea bordered by Turkey, Bulgaria, Romania, Ukraine, Russia, and Georgia (m. 323, t. 324)

Bodh Gaya (bōd gä′yä) the town in northern India where Siddhartha was enlightened and became Buddha (m. 140, t. 142)

Bosnia and Herzegovina (boz′nē ə and hėr′tsə gə vē′nə) a Balkan country, once part of Yugoslavia (m. 522, t. 521)

Boston (bô′stən) the capital of Massachusetts and site of colonial protests against the British; 42°N, 71°W (t. 457)

Brazil (brə zil′) a country in South America; originally a Portuguese colony (m. 446, t. 446)

Burundi (bù rün′dē) a central African nation affected by civil war in the 1990s (t. 638)

Byzantine Empire (biz′n tēn′ em′pīr) an empire of lands that formed the eastern part of the Roman Empire with its center at the city of Constantinople (t. 323)

Byzantium (bi zan′tē əm) an old Greek city, renamed Constantinople, that became the center of the Byzantine Empire; present-day Istanbul (t. 301)

Cahokia (ka hō′kē ə) the largest temple mound site in North America (m. 220, t. 221)

Calcutta (kal kut′ə) a megacity in India; 22°N, 88°E (t. 655)

Cambodia (kam bō′ dē ə) a country in Southeast Asia; part of the Khmer civilization (m. 357, t. 357)

Canaan (kā′nən) Eastern Mediterranean land in which Abraham resettled around 1800 B.C. (t. 55)

Canada (kan′ə də) a large nation in the north part of North America (t. 223)

Canadian Shield (kə nā′dē ən shēld) a vast plateau region north of the Interior Plains in North America (m. 210, t. 209)

Canton (kan ton′) a former British treaty port in China; now called Guangzhou (m. 492, t. 494)

Cape of Good Hope (kāp ov gùd hōp) the southern tip of Africa (m. 440, t. 439)

Carthage (kär′thij) an important Phoenician trading post in North Africa (m. 58, t. 58)

Cave of the Hands (kāv ov ᴛʜə handz) a cave in Patagonia, a land in southern South America, where people painted on the walls thousands of years ago (t. 27)

Central Plateau (sen′trəl pla tō′) a high, flat area in the center of the Plateau of Mexico (t. 163)

Central Uplands (sen′trəl up′ləndz) low mountains and high plateaus in the central region of Europe (t. 393)

Chang'an (shəng′än) a capital city in Central Asia on the Silk Road (m. 409, t. 409)

Chauvet (shō vä′) a site in southern France with 32,000-year-old cave paintings and artifacts (m. 26, t. 29)

Chavín (chä vēn′) an ancient city in southern South America; home to the Chavín people (m. 190, t. 191)

Chernobyl (chėr nō′bəl) site in Ukraine of a nuclear power plant accident in 1986 (t. 666)

Chiapas (chē ä′päs) Mexico's poorest state (t. 640)

Chichén Itzá (chē chen′ ēt zä′) an ancient Mayan city located on the Yucatan Peninsula (m. 168, t. 171)

China (chī′nə) a large country in East Asia (m. 350, t. 351)

Clovis (klō′vis) city in New Mexico near where archaeologists found many early human-made objects (m. 15, t. 12)

Coastal Range (kō′stl rānj) a small mountain range in North America, between the Great Basin and the Pacific Ocean (t. 209)

Colosseum (kol′ə sē′əm) a famous Roman arena (m. 288, t. 291)

Congo Free State (kong′gō frē stāt) a Belgian colony in Africa under King Leopold II (t. 489)

Constantinople (kon stan tə nō′pəl) the capital of the Byzantine Empire (m. 322, t. 324)

Crete (krēt) an island in the eastern Mediterranean Sea; the center of Minoan civilization (m. 247, t. 250)

Croatia (krō ā′shə) a Balkan nation, once part of Yugoslavia (t. 621)

Cuba (kyü′bə) Caribbean nation in which the Soviet Union attempted to build missile bases in 1962 (t. 572)

Cuzco (küz′kō) the capital of the Inca empire (m. 198, t. 197)

Czechoslovakia (chək ə slō vä′kē ə) a central European country invaded by Germany in 1939 (t. 545)

Czech Republic (chək ri pub′lik) a nation formed after Czechoslovakia split into two countries in 1993 (t. 621)

 **D**

Danube River (dan′yüb riv′ər) Europe's second longest river (m. 393, t. 394)

Deccan Plateau (dek′ən pla′tō) a dry, high region south of the Indo-Ganges Plain (m. 124, t. 126)

Deir el-Medina (dīr əl mə dē′nə) a village built for workers at the Valley of the Kings in Egypt (t. 88)

Dolores (dō lôr′əs) a village in which the end of colonial rule in Mexico began (t. 459)

Dunhuang (dun hwang′) a Chinese city on the edge of the Taklimakan Desert (m. 406, t. 409)

 **E**

Eastern Ghats (ē′stərn gȯts) rolling mountains east of the Deccan Plateau in southern India (t. 126)

East Germany (ēst jėr′mə nē) a former country created by the Soviet Union after World War II (m. 569, t. 570)

Edo (ē′dō) the Japanese shogun capital, renamed Tokyo; 35°N, 140°E (m. 362, t. 361)

Egypt (ē′jipt) an ancient kingdom and present-day country in northeastern Africa (m. 79, t. 79)

England (ing′glənd) the southernmost and largest part of the island of Great Britain (m. 396, t. 397)

Ethiopia (ē′thē ō′pē ə) a country in East Africa (m. 383, t. 382)

Europe (yu̇r′əp) a continent to the north of Africa, connected to Asia in western Russia (m. 393, t. 393)

 **F**

Fertile Crescent (fėr′tl kres′nt) a curved region with rich soil in the Middle East where one of the first civilizations developed (m. 35, t. 35)

Florence (flôr′əns) an important Italian city-state that became the birthplace of the Renaissance; 44°N, 11°E (t. 431)

Forbidden City, The (fər bid′n sit′ē, ᴛʜə) the palace of the Chinese emperor in Beijing (t. 351)

Formosa (fôr mō′sə) an island colonized by China and later renamed Taiwan (m. 494, t. 495)

 **G**

Ganges River (gan′jēz riv′ər) an important river in India; Hindus believe it represents purity (m. 136, t. 138)

Ganges River Valley (gan′jēz riv′ər val′ē) the land surrounding the Ganges River (m. 124, t. 131)

Gao (gou) a city east of Timbuktu and capital of the Songhai Empire (m. 377, t. 378)

Gaza Strip (gä′zə strip) an area of eastern Mediterranean land seized by Israel in the Six-Day War (m. 617, t. 616)

Genoa (jen′ō ə) a seaport town in Italy (m. 410, t. 410)

Germany (jėr′mə nē) a nation in central Europe (m. 499, t. 499)

Ghana (gä′nə) an ancient kingdom in West Africa (m. 377, t. 375)

Giza (gē′zə) a city in Egypt where the Great Pyramid is located; 30°N, 31°E (m. 84, t. 87)

Golan Heights (gō′län hīts) an area of southwestern Asia seized by Israel in the Six-Day War (m. 617, t. 616)

Pronunciation Key

a in hat	ō in open	sh in she
â in care	ȯ in all	th in thin
ā in age	ô in order	ᴛʜ in then
ä in far	oi in oil	zh in measure
e in let	ou in out	ə = a in about
ē in equal	u in cup	ə = e in taken
ėr in term	u̇ in put	ə = i in pencil
i in it	ü in rule	ə = o in lemon
ī in ice	ch in child	ə = u in circus
o in hot	ng in long	

Gazetteer

Great Basin (grāt bā′sn) an area of basins and ranges west of the Rocky Mountains (m. 210, t. 209)

Great Britain (grāt brit′n) the largest island of Europe; made up of England, Scotland, and Wales (t. 475)

Great European Plain (grāt yùr′ə pē′ən plān) a vast expanse of land in Europe; includes southeastern England (t. 393)

Great Lakes, The (grāt lāks, ᴛнə) a chain of five freshwater lakes in North America (t. 224)

Great Plains (grāt plānz) a large, grassy region in the western Interior Plains of North America (m. 210, t. 209)

Great Rift Valley (grāt rift val′ē) a valley in East Africa (m. 371, t. 372)

Great Serpent Mound (grāt sėr′pənt mound) a large, snake-shaped mound created by the Adena people (m. 220, t. 219)

Great Zimbabwe (grāt zim bä′bwä) a city in southeastern Africa that reached its height in about 1400; features large stone enclosures (m. 383, t. 384)

Guangxi Zhungzu (gwäng shē zəng jü) a region in southern China that has one of the best climates for farming (m. 101, t. 102)

Guiana Highlands (gē ä′nə hī′ləndz) a land of vast tropical forests in northern South America (m. 187, t. 188)

Gulf of Mexico (gulf ov mek′sə kō) a part of the Atlantic Ocean east of Mexico (m. 163, t. 164)

Gulf Stream (gulf strēm) a powerful ocean current that brings warm water from the Gulf of Mexico to Europe (t. 394)

★ **H** ★

Hagia Sophia (hä yē′ə sō fē′ə) a great domed cathedral in Constantinople (present-day Istanbul, Turkey) (t. 326)

Haiti (hā′tē) a former French colony in the Caribbean Sea and the first republic led by a person of African descent (m. 460, t. 459)

Hanoi (hä noi′) the former capital of North Vietnam and capital of present-day Vietnam 21°N, 106°E (m. 586, t. 586)

Harappa (hə rä′pə) the site of one of the earliest civilizations in South Asia (m. 122, t. 126)

Himalayas (him′ə lā′əz) a mountain range in southern Asia; includes the highest point on Earth (m. 101, t. 103)

Hippodrome (hip′ə drōm) a huge building in Constantinople and the site of chariot races (t. 324)

Hiroshima (hir′ō shē′mə) Japanese city that was the site of the first atomic bomb dropped in a war, on August 6, 1945; 34°N, 132°E (m. 553, t. 554)

Hong Kong (hong′ kong′) a British colony in China, received after the first Opium War and returned to China in 1997; 22°N, 114°E (m. 494, t. 494)

Huang River (hwäng riv′ər) a river that cuts through the North China Plain (m. 101, t. 102)

Huang River Valley (hwäng riv′ər val′ē) the area surrounding the Huang River (m. 101, t. 102)

Hudson River (hud′sən riv′ər) a river that runs through the state of New York (t. 475)

★ **I** ★

Iguaçu Falls (e′gwä sü fälz) a waterfall on the border between Argentina and Brazil; a major source of hydroelectricity in South America (t. 666)

India (in′dē ə) a large country on the Indian subcontinent (t. 346)

Indian Ocean (in′dē ən ō′shən) an ocean south of Asia, west of Australia, and east of Africa (m. 124, t. 124)

Indochina (in′dō chī′nə) a peninsula in Southeast Asia that includes Vietnam, Cambodia, and Laos (t. 488)

Indo-Ganges Plain (in′dō gan′jēz plān) a region in India through which the Ganges and Brahmaputra Rivers flow (m. 124, t. 125)

Indus River Valley (in′dəs riv′ər val′ē) the land surrounding the Indus River in Pakistan (t. 125)

Interior Plains (in tir′ē ər plānz) large plains between the Rocky Mountains and Appalachian Mountains in North America (m. 210, t. 209)

Ionian Sea (ī ō′nē un sē) the sea that separates western Greece from southeastern Italy (m. 247, t. 248)

Israel (iz′rē əl) Jewish kingdom founded by David around 1000 B.C.; a country in southwestern Asia (m. 54, t. 57)

Italian Peninsula (i tal′yən pə nin′sə lə) an arm of land surrounded by the Mediterranean, Tyrrhenian, and Adriatic seas; location of the country of Italy (m. 277, t. 277)

Italy (it′l ē) a country in southern Europe, on a peninsula in the Mediterranean Sea (m. 501, t. 499)

Jamestown (jāmz′ toun′) the first permanent English colony in North America (t. 447)

Japan (jə pan′) a nation that consists of four large islands and many smaller islands in the western Pacific Ocean, east of the Asian mainland (m. 360, t. 361)

Jenne-jenno (je nā′ je nō′) an ancient city in West Africa, located southeast of Timbuktu on the Niger River; the oldest known city in sub-Saharan Africa (m. 377, t. 377)

Jerusalem (jə rü′sə ləm) the capital of the kingdom of Israel; 32°N, 35°E (m. 57, t. 57)

Judah (jü′də) the southern region of Israel that became its own kingdom after the death of Solomon (m. 57, t. 57)

Kenya (ken′ yə) an eastern African nation that won its independence in 1963 (t. 607)

Kilwa (kil′wä) a southern African city involved in the gold and ivory trade (m. 383, t. 383)

Kish (kish) an early city-state in Mesopotamia (t. 38)

Kosovo (kō′sə vō) an area in Serbia and site of a violent conflict in 1999 (m. 637, t. 637)

Koumbi (küm′bē) the capital of the kingdom of Ghana (t. 375)

Kush (kush) a Nubian kingdom freed from Egypt in 1650 B.C. (m. 93, t. 94)

Kyoto (kyō′tō) a major city in Japan; 35°N, 136°E (m. 362, t. 362)

Lagash (lə′gash) an early city-state in Mesopotamia (t. 38)

Lake Texcoco (lāk tā skō′kō) the lake on which the Mexica settled (t. 176)

Lake Titicaca (lāk tit′ə kä′kə) a lake in the Altiplano in South America (m. 187, t. 188)

Laos (lä′ōs) a country in Southeast Asia; once part of the Khmer civilization (m. 357, t. 357)

Lascaux (ləs kou′) a site in southern France with cave art from about 17,000 years ago (t. 28)

London (lun′dən) the capital of Great Britain; 51°N, 0° (t. 549)

Lower Egypt (lō′ər ē′jipt) the region of Egypt that surrounds the Nile Delta (m. 79, t. 79)

Lu Province (lü prä′vins) the birthplace of Confucius (m. 114, t. 115)

Maastricht (mäs′trikt) a town in the Netherlands that was the site of the signing of the treaty that created the European Union (m. 630, t. 632)

Macao (mə kou′) a former Portuguese treaty port in China (m. 494, t. 494)

Macedonia (mas′ə dō′nē ə) an ancient country in northern Greece; a nation formed after the breakup of Yugoslavia (m. 263, t. 264)

Machu Picchu (mäch′ü pēk chü) a city built by the Inca people on a mountaintop in the Andes Mountains in present-day Peru (m. 198, t. 197)

Madagascar (mad′ə gas′kər) an island off the coast of East Africa (t. 656)

Mali (mä′lē) an empire in West Africa (m. 377, t. 376)

Manchuria (man chùr′ē ə) the northeastern region of China, seized by Japan in 1931 (m. 494, t. 496)

Marathon (mar′ə thon) a plain northeast of Athens, Greece (t. 261)

Mecca (mek′ə) a city located along the shore of the Red Sea on the Arabian Peninsula; the birthplace of Muhammad; 21°N, 40°E (m. 332, t. 331)

Medina (mə dē′nə) a town on the Arabian Peninsula where Muhammad found people eager to hear his teachings on Islam (m. 332, t. 331)

Pronunciation Key

a in hat	ō in open	sh in she
â in care	o· in all	th in thin
ā in age	ô in order	ᴛʜ in then
ä in far	oi in oil	zh in measure
e in let	ou in out	ə = a in about
ē in equal	u in cup	ə = e in taken
èr in term	u· in put	ə = i in pencil
i in it	ü in rule	ə = o in lemon
ī in ice	ch in child	ə = u in circus
o in hot	ng in long	

Gazetteer

Mediterranean Sea (med′ə tə rā′nē ən sē) a large body of water bordered by Europe, Asia, and Africa (m. 247, t. 247)

Memphis (mem′fis) a city on the Nile in Egypt; 25°N, 31°E (m. 82, t. 80)

Menlo Park (mən′lō pärk) a town in New Jersey where Thomas Edison had his laboratory (t. 479)

Meroë (mər′ō ē′) a capital city of Nubia (m. 93, t. 93)

Mesoamerica (mes′ō ə mer′ə kə) a region that extends from southern North America to the central part of Central America (m. 163, t. 163)

Mesopotamia (mes′ə pə ta′me ə) an area of flat land between the Tigris and Euphrates Rivers where one of the first civilizations emerged (m. 35, t. 35)

Mexico City (mek′sə kō sit′ē) capital of Mexico and the most populated city in the world; 19°N, 99°W (t. 655)

Midway Island (mid′wā i′lənd) site, west of Hawaii, of an important battle in World War II (m. 553, t. 553)

Milan (mi lan′) an important city-state in Italy during the Renaissance; 45°N, 9°E (t. 431)

Mississippi River (mis′ə sip′ē riv′ər) located in North America, the main river of one of the largest river systems in the world (m. 210, t. 209)

Moche Valley (mō′chə val′ē) the home of the Mochica people (m. 190, t. 192)

Mohenjo-Daro (mō hen′jō där′ō) an ancient city in the Indus River Valley in Pakistan (m. 128, t. 129)

Mongolia (mong gō′lē ə) a country in northern Asia (m. 352, t. 352)

Monte Verde (mon′tə vər′dā) site in Chile near where archaeologists found artifacts dating to 12,500 years ago (m. 15, t. 16)

Mount Everest (mount ev′ər ist) the highest peak in the Himalayas and the tallest mountain on Earth (m. 124, t. 123)

Mount Kilimanjaro (mount kil′ə mən jär′ō) the highest mountain in Africa (m. 371, t. 372)

Mount Olympus (mount ō lim′pəs) a mountain in northern Greece thought by the ancient Greeks to be the home of their gods (m. 252, t. 254)

Myanmar (Burma) (mī än′mär) a country in South Asia with a repressive government (t. 640)

Mycenae (mī sē′nē) an early city-state of Greece (m. 247, t. 251)

Nagasaki (nä gə sä′kē) a port city in Japan and site of the second atomic bomb dropped in a war, on August 9, 1945; 33°N, 130°E (m. 553, t. 554)

Nanjing (nän′ jing′) the capital of China during the Japanese occupation (m. 546, t. 546)

Napata (nap′ət ə) the capital of the African kingdom of Kush (m. 93, t. 95)

Nazareth (naz′ər əth) a city in ancient Palestine and the home of Jesus (m. 294, t. 295)

New South Wales (nü south wālz) a British colony for convicts in Australia (t. 447)

New York City (nü yôrk sit′ē) the largest city in the United States; 40°N, 74°W (t. 475)

New Zealand (nü zē′lənd) a colony that became a dominion of Britain (m. 502, t. 502)

Niagara Falls (nī ag′rə fälz) waterfalls on the boundary between the United States and Canada; provides a portion of the energy needs of the Canadian province of Ontario (t. 666)

Nile River (nīl riv′ər) the longest river in the world, it flows from East Africa to Egypt (m. 82, t. 79)

Nile River Valley (nīl riv′ər val′ē) the area of land surrounding the Nile River (m. 79, t. 79)

Nineveh (nin′ə və) the capital of the Assyrian Empire and the site of a great library under King Ashurbanipal (m. 49, t. 52)

Nippur (nip ər′) an early city-state in Mesopotamia (t. 38)

Normandy (nôr′mən dē) a region in northern France and the site of the D-Day invasion on June 6, 1944 (m. 552, t. 552)

North China Plain (nôrth chī′nə plān) the region where human settlement and culture began in China (m. 101, t. 101)

Northern Ireland (nôr′тнərn īr′lənd) a part of the United Kingdom located in the northeastern part of the island of Ireland; the site of fighting between religious groups (m. 639, t. 639)

North European Plain (nôrth yür′ə pe′ən plān) the northern part of the Great European Plain (m. 393, t. 393)

North Korea (nôrth kô rē′ ə) the communist nation of a divided Korea on the Korean peninsula in eastern Asia (m. 583, t. 583)

North Vietnam (nôrth vē et näm′) the communist nation of Vietnam (m. 586, t. 584)

Northwest Mountains (nôrth′west′ moun′tən) a region in Europe that is poor for farming (m. 393, t. 393)

Nubia (nü′bē ə) a large African kingdom to the south of Egypt (m. 93, t. 93)

Nunavut (nü′nə vüt′) a province in northern Canada and the home of many of the Inuit people (m. 223, t. 223)

Oklahoma City (ō′klə hō′mə sit′ē) capital city of the U.S. state of Oklahoma; the sight of a terrorist attack in 1995; 35°N, 97°W (t. 646)

Olympia (ō lim′pē ə) an area of ancient Greece where the Olympic Games were first held (m. 247, t. 254)

Osaka (ō sä′kə) a major city in Japan; 34°N, 135°E (m. 362, t. 362)

Pakistan (pak′ə stan) a Muslim nation in southern Asia; created by the division of India in 1947 (m. 610, t. 612)

Palestine (pal′ə stīn) a Roman province on the eastern coast of the Mediterranean Sea (t. 295)

Pampas (pam′pəz) a vast grassland in the southern plains of South America (m. 187, t. 188)

Pantanal (pän tə näl′) the world's largest wetland, located in South America (m. 187, t. 187)

Paris (pār′is) the capital of France; 49°N, 2°E (m. 529, t. 468)

Pearl Harbor (pėrl här′bər) a port in Hawaii attacked by the Japanese on December 7, 1941 (m. 553, t. 550)

Peloponnesus (pel ə pə nē′səs) a part of the Greek peninsula (m. 247, m. 263)

People's Republic of China (pē′pəlz ri pub′lik uv chī′nə) the name given to China after the communist takeover in 1949 (t. 578)

Peru (pə rü′) a dry, rough country in western South America (m. 190, t. 191)

Philippines (fil′ə pēnz′) an island nation in the Pacific Ocean (m. 553, t. 553)

Phoenicia (fə nish′ə) an ancient country on the Mediterranean Sea, south of Asia Minor (t. 267)

Plateau of Mexico (pla tō′ ov mek′sə kō) a high, flat area in central Mexico (t. 163)

Poland (pō′lənd) a country east of Germany (m. 549, t. 549)

Prussia (prush′ə) the largest and most powerful German state before unification (m. 499, t. 500)

Quebec (kwi bek′) the first permanent French settlement in North America (t. 447)

Rhineland (rīn′land) the western region of Germany bordering France (t. 536)

Rhine River (rīn riv′ər) the main river of the busiest inland system of waterways in the western part of Europe (m. 393, t. 394)

Rocky Mountains (rok′ē moun′tənz) a mountain range that stretches through western Canada and the United States (m. 210, t. 209)

Rome (rōm) a city near the middle of the western coast of Italy; 42°N, 12°E (m. 277, t. 277)

Russia (rush′ə) a large country in Eastern Europe and north Asia (m. 522, t. 496)

Rwanda (rü än′də) a central African nation affected by civil war in the 1990s (t. 638)

Pronunciation Key

a in hat	ō in open	sh in she
â in care	ȯ in all	th in thin
ā in age	ô in order	ŦH in then
ä in far	oi in oil	zh in measure
e in let	ou in out	ə = a in about
ē in equal	u in cup	ə = e in taken
ėr in term	u̇ in put	ə = i in pencil
i in it	ü in rule	ə = o in lemon
ī in ice	ch in child	ə = u in circus
o in hot	ng in long	

Gazetteer

★ S ★

Sahara (sə har′ə) the largest desert in the world (m. 371, t. 371)

Sahiwal (sə ē′wəl) a town in east-central Pakistan; the center of the cotton industry (m. 126, t. 126)

Salamis (sal′ə məs) the site of a mighty sea battle between Greece and Persia (t. 261)

Sandwich Islands (sand′wich ī′ləndz) a group of islands in the Pacific Ocean; now known as the Hawaiian Islands (t. 445)

Sarajevo (sar′ə yä′vō) the capital of Bosnia and Herzegovina; 44°N, 18°E (m. 522, t. 522)

Sardinia (sär din′ē ə) an island near Italy (m. 499, t. 501)

Scandinavia (skan′də na′vē ə) a northwestern region of Europe; includes the nations of Denmark, Sweden, and Norway (m. 396, t. 397)

Sea of Marmara (sē uv mär′mər ə) a small sea that lies between Europe and Asia Minor (m. 322, t. 324)

Serbia (sėr′bē ə) a country in southeastern Europe (m. 522, t. 521)

Shanghai (shang hī) a former British treaty port in China; 31°N, 121°E (m. 492, t. 494)

Sierra Madre Occidental (sē er′ə mäd′drä ok′sə den′tl) a mountain range to the west of the Plateau of Mexico (m. 163, t. 163)

Sierra Madre Oriental (sē er′ə mäd′drä ôr′ē en′tl) a mountain range to the east of the Plateau of Mexico (m. 163, t. 163)

Sinai Peninsula (sī′nī pə nin′sə lə) an area of land seized by Israel in the Six-Day War (m. 617, t. 616)

Skara Brae (skä′rä brā) a Stone Age village in Northern Scotland discovered by archaeologists in the 1800s (t. 22)

Slovak Republic (slō′vak ri pub′lik) an Eastern European nation formed after Czechoslovakia split into two countries (t. 621)

Slovenia (slō vē′nē ə) a southeastern European nation formed after the breakup of Yugoslavia (t. 621)

Snaketown (snāk toun) the modern name of the Hohokam's largest village (m. 212, t. 213)

Sofala (sō fä′lä) a southern African city involved in the gold and ivory trade (m. 383, t. 383)

Somme, The (səm, ᴛнə) a river in eastern France (m. 529, t. 529)

Songhai (song gī′) an empire near the Niger River (m. 377, t. 378)

South Africa (south af′rə kə) an African nation that was ruled under a system of apartheid until the early 1990s (m. 608, t. 609)

South Korea (south kô rē′ə) the republic of a divided Korea on the Korean peninsula in eastern Asia (m. 583, t. 583)

South Vietnam (south vē et näm′) the former non-communist part of Vietnam in Southeast Asia (m. 586, t. 584)

Soviet Union (sō′vē et ÿu nyən) the former country formed by Russia's communist leaders in 1922 (m. 531, t. 531)

Soweto (sō wə′tō) a town in South Africa that was the site of the killing of black children in 1976 (t. 609)

Sparta (spär′tə) an ancient Greek city-state that was under strict military rule (m. 252, t. 255)

Stalingrad (stä′lin grad) a city in the Soviet Union and the site of fierce fighting in World War II; present-day Volgograd (m. 552, t. 551)

Suez Canal (sü ez′ kə nal′) a man-made waterway that connects the Mediterranean Sea with the Indian Ocean (m. 488, t. 488)

Sumer (sü′mər) a powerful city-state in southern Mesopotamia (m. 40, t. 41)

★ T ★

Taipei (tī pā′) the capital of Taiwan; 25°N, 121°E (t. 578)

Taiwan (tī wän′) an island nation that became Nationalist China (m. 577, t. 577)

Tanzania (tan′zə nē′ə) an African nation that gained independence in 1961 (m. 608, t. 607)

Tassili (tas ē′le) an area in the North African country of Algeria; the site of ancient cave paintings (m. 13, t. 13)

Tenochtitlan (tä nòch′tē tlan′) the capital city of the Aztecs (m. 175, t. 176)

Thebes (thēbz) a Greek city-state that defeated Sparta (m. 263, t. 264)

Tiananmen Square (tyän′än mən skwär) an area in Beijing where students gathered for a mass protest in 1989 (t. 641)

Tiber River (tī′bər riv′ər) a river in Italy (m. 277, t. 277)

Tibetan Plateau (ti bət′n pla tō′) a rocky region in the west of China (m. 101, t. 103)

Tikal (tē käl′) a city-state of the Maya that is now an important ruin (m. 170, t. 170)

Timbuktu (tim′buk tü′) a major trading city in Mali (m. 377, t. 377)

Tokyo (tō′kē ō) the capital city of Japan; 35°N, 139°E (t. 554)

Topper site (top′ər sīt) a place in South Carolina where archaelogists found artifacts that were up to 18,000 years old (m. 15, t. 16)

Troy (troi) a city on the western coast of Asia Minor; site of the legendary Trojan War (m. 252, t. 253)

Umma (ü′mə) an early city-state in Mesopotamia (t. 38)

Upper Egypt (up′ər ē′jipt) the region south of the Nile Delta (m. 79, t. 79)

Ur (ėr) an early city-state in Mesopotamia (m. 38, t. 38)

Ural Mountains (yür′əl moun′tənz) a mountain range that separates Eastern Europe from Asia (m. 393, t. 393)

Uruk (ėr′ük) a large Sumerian city-state in Mesopotamia (t. 41)

Valley of Mexico (val′ē ov mek′sə kō) an area of Mesoamerica (t. 176)

Venice (ven′is) an important city-state during the Renaissance; 45°N, 12°E (t. 431)

Verdun (vər dun′) a city in northeastern France; 49°N, 5°E (m. 529, t. 529)

Volga River (vol′gə riv′ər) the longest river in Europe (m. 393, t. 394)

Washington, D.C. (wäsh′ing tən) the capital city of the United States; located between Maryland and Virginia along the Potomac River 38°N, 77°W (t. 646)

West Bank (west bangk) an area of land seized by Israel in the Six-Day War (m. 617, t. 616)

Western Ghats (wə′stərn gôts) rolling mountains west of the Deccan Plateau in southern India (m. 124, t. 126)

West Germany (west jėr′mə nē) a former European country created by the Allies after World War II (m. 569, t. 570)

West Indies (west in′dēz) islands in the Caribbean (m. 438, t. 440)

Yucatán Peninsula (yü kə′tan′ pə nin′sə lə) an arm of land that sticks out into the Gulf of Mexico (m. 163, t. 164)

Yugoslavia (yü′gō slä′vē ə) a former country in southeastern Europe (m. 637, t. 637)

Zimbabwe (zim bä′bwā) a southern African nation, formerly known as Southern Rhodesia (m. 608, t. 609)

Pronunciation Key

a in hat	ō in open	sh in she
â in care	ȯ in all	th in thin
ā in age	ô in order	ᴛʜ in then
ä in far	oi in oil	zh in measure
e in let	ou in out	ə = a in about
ē in equal	u in cup	ə = e in taken
ėr in term	u̇ in put	ə = i in pencil
i in it	ü in rule	ə = o in lemon
ī in ice	ch in child	ə = u in circus
o in hot	ng in long	

Biographical Dictionary

This Biographical Dictionary tells you about the people in this book and how to pronounce their names. The page numbers tell you where the person first appears in the text.

A

Abraham c. 1800 B.C. A shepherd living in Ur who is considered by Jewish people to be the first Jew. p. 55

Akbar (ak′bär) 1542–1605 Grandson of Babur who became the greatest Mogul emperor. His reign from 1556 to 1605 brought most of the Indian subcontinent under Mogul rule. p. 348

Akhenaten (äk′ə′nät ən) Egyptian ruler who changed his name from Amenhotep IV and called for the worship of one god, Aton. p. 90

Aldrin, Edwin 1930– American astronaut who walked on the moon in 1969. p. 669

Alexander 356 B.C.–323 B.C. Known as "Alexander the Great," the king of Macedonia who conquered a vast empire in Europe, Asia, and Africa. p. 267

Alexius Comnenus (ä leks′ē us kōm nən′us) 1048–1118 Byzantine emperor who appealed to the pope for Christian knights to fight against the Turks. p. 407

al-Khwarizmi (al kwär′əz mē) c. 780–850 Muslim mathematician who developed algebra. p. 336

Amanirenas first century B.C. Queen of Kush who led military expeditions and built monuments. p. 95

Arafat, Yasir (är′ə fat, yä′sər) 1929– Leader of the PLO who signed a peace pact with Israel in 1993. p. 616

Archimedes (ar kə mē′dēz) c. 287 B.C.–212 B.C. Scientist of the Hellenistic Age who was the first person to explain how levers work. p. 270

Aristotle (ar′ə stot′l) 384 B.C.–322 B.C. Ancient Greek philosopher and student of Plato who wrote more than 170 books. p. 262

Armstrong, Neil 1930– American astronaut who became the first human to walk on the moon in July of 1969. p. 669

Ashoka c. 304 B.C.–237 B.C. Grandson of Chandragupta Maurya. Who used stone columns to mark the territory of his empire and make announcements. p. 133

Ashurbanipal (ash ür bän′ē päl) reign 668 B.C.–627 B.C. King of Assyria from 668 B.C. to 627 B.C. when it was at its largest and most powerful. p. 52

Augustus (ȯ gus′təs) 63 B.C.–A.D. 14 Ancient Roman emperor whose rule began a long period of prosperity and peace called the Pax Romana, or "the Roman Peace." for the Roman Empire. p. 289

B

Babur (bä′bər) 1483–1530 Muslim ruler who conquered parts of northern India and founded the Mogul Empire. p. 348

Ban Zhao (ban jou) c. 100 B.C. Chinese scholar and historian of the Han dynasty who continued the work of Sima Qian. p. 111

Barton, Sir Edmund 1849–1920 Australian leader who drew up his country's first constitution. p. 503

Begin, Menachem (bā′gin, mə nä′kəm) 1913–1992 Israeli prime minister who worked toward peace in the Middle East by signing a peace accord between Egypt and Israel in 1978. p. 619

Ben-Gurion, David 1886–1973 Israeli leader who declared the state of Israel in 1948. p. 615

Bismarck, Otto von 1815–1898 Prussian prime minister who unified Germany in the 1800s. p. 500

Bolívar, Simón (bō lē′vär, sē mōn′) 1783–1830 South American soldier and revolutionary leader who liberated northwestern South America from the Spanish. p. 462

Brittain, Vera 1893–1970 British writer who became a pacifist after serving as a nurse in World War I. p. 533

Bush, George W. 1946– Forty-third president of the United States who began a campaign toward energy self-sufficiency and against terrorism in 2001. p. 647

C

Caligula (kə lig′yə lə) 12–41 Cruel ancient Roman emperor who was assassinated by members of his bodyguard. p. 289

Carson, Rachel 1907–1964 American scientist who wrote *Silent Spring*, warning of the harmful effects of pesticides on the environment. p. 661

Cartier, Jacques (kär tyā′, zhäk) 1491–1557 French explorer who claimed Canada for France. p. 447

Cavour, Camillo di (dē kä vür′, kä mē′lō) 1810–1861 Prime minister of Sardinia who supported a unified Italy. p. 501

Chamberlain, Neville 1869–1940 British prime minister who pursued a policy of appeasement with Adolf Hitler before World War II. p. 545

Chandragupta Maurya (chən drə gup′tə mou′rē ə) 360 B.C.–298 B.C. Soldier who started the Mauryan Empire, the first Indian empire, and later became a monk. p. 135

Charlemagne (shär′lə mān) 742–814 King of the Franks who was later crowned emperor of the former Roman Empire in western Europe. p. 397

Chiang Kai-shek (chang′ kī′shek′) 1887–1975 Leader of the Nationalist Party in China who set up a nationalist government in Taiwan. p. 577

Churchill, Winston 1874–1965 Prime Minister of Great Britain in 1940 who led the country to victory in World War II. p. 549

Ci Xi (tsē shyē′) 1835–1908 Chinese empress who tried to keep out foreigners and prevented further progress in China. p. 495

Claudius (klȯ′dē əs) 10 B.C.–A.D. 54 Ancient Roman emperor after Caligula who tried to improve conditions in the Empire. p. 289

Clemenceau, Georges (kləm′ən sō, jôr′jə) 1841–1929 Leader of France who opposed U.S. President Woodrow Wilson's ideas for a fair peace and cooperation between nations after World War I. p. 536

Clinton, Bill 1946– Forty-second president of the United States who extended free trade throughout North America. p. 633

Columbus, Christopher c. 1451–1506 Italian sailor who sailed to the Americas from Spain in 1492. p. 440

Commodus (kum mō′dəs) 161–192 Ancient Roman emperor who succeeded his father, Marcus Aurelius, and began the decline of the Roman Empire. p. 299

Confucius (kən fyü′shəs) c. 551 B.C.–479 B.C. Chinese teacher of morals that came to embody the core of Confucianism. p. 115

Constantine (kon′stən tēn) c. 275–337 Christian emperor who made Christianity equal to all other religions in Rome and reunited the Roman Empire after Diocletian had divided it into two parts. p. 296

Cook, James 1728–1779 English sea captain who searched for a northern passage to the Pacific. p. 445

Copernicus (kə pėr′nə kəs) 1473–1543 Renaissance scientist who taught that Earth moves around the sun. p. 434

Cortés, Hernando (kôr tez′, hər nan′dō) 1485–1547 Spanish conquistador who defeated the Aztecs in 1521. p. 180

Cyrus II c. 585 B.C.–529 B.C. Persian king who established the Persian Empire. p. 132

da Gama, Vasco (də gä′mə, väs′kō) c. 1469–1524 Portuguese explorer who sailed around the Cape of Good Hope to India, establishing the first all-water route from Europe. p. 439

Darius I c. 550 B.C.–486 B.C. Persian king who expanded the Persian Empire to include India. p. 132

David 1030 B.C.–965 B.C. Second king of Israel who unified the kingdom of Israel. p. 57

da Vinci, Leonardo (də vin′chē, lē′ō när′dō) 1452–1519 Renaissance artist who painted the *Mona Lisa* and made contributions to science. p. 432

Deborah c. 1200 B.C. Female Hebrew judge who encouraged a military leader to gather the peoples of Israel to attack the Canaanites. p. 56

de Gouges, Marie-Olympe 1748–1793 French political activist and feminist who wrote the *Declaration of the Rights of Woman and the Female Citizen,* calling for the equality of women. p. 471

Deganawidah (deg än ä wē′də) c. 1550–1600 Native American leader who founded the Iroquois Confederacy. p. 225

de Klerk, F. W 1936– President of South Africa who ended the policy of apartheid. p. 609

Dias, Bartolomeu (dē′əs, bär tō′lō myü) c. 1450–1500 Portuguese explorer who sailed around the Cape of Good Hope in 1488. p. 439

Dickens, Charles 1812–1870 English writer who often wrote about the London slums. p. 477

Diocletian (dī ō klē′shən) c. 245–316 Ancient Roman emperor who restored order and strengthened the economy of the Roman Empire, dividing it into two parts. p. 300

Pronunciation Key

a in hat	ȯ in all	sh in she
ā in age	ō in open	th in thin
â in care	ô in order	ᴛʜ in then
ä in far	oi in oil	zh in measure
e in let	ou in out	ə = a in about
ē in equal	u in cup	ə = e in taken
ėr in term	u̇ in put	ə = i in pencil
i in it	ü in rule	ə = o in lemon
ī in ice	ch in child	ə = u in circus
o in hot	ng in long	

Biographical Dictionary

Edison, Thomas 1847–1931 American inventor who created many items such as the electric light bulb, the phonograph, and the motion picture. p. 479

Eisenhower, Dwight D. 1890–1969 U.S. general who led the Allied forces on D-Day, history's largest invasion by sea, during World War II. He later became the thirty-fourth president of the United States. p. 552

Elizabeth I 1533–1603 Queen of England who built up the English navy and promoted the arts. p. 442

Enheduanna (en hä′dü wän ä) c. 2330 B.C. Daughter of Sargon and was appointed the high priestess of Ur. p. 45

Euclid (yü′klid) c. 300 B.C. Greek mathematician who developed the system of plane geometry. p. 271

Eudocia (yü′dō shē′ə) c. 400–460 Wife of Eastern Roman Emperor Theodosius II who converted to Christianity and had much influence on her husband's reign. p. 305

Ezana (ā′zä nä) c. 330 King of Axum Ethiopia who converted to Christianity. p. 381

Ferdinand, Francis 1863–1914 Archduke of Austria-Hungary whose assassination was a factor that led to World War I. p. 522

Frank, Anne 1929–1945 Young Jewish girl who kept a diary of her experiences during the Holocaust in World War II. p. 561

Fulton, Robert 1765–1815 American inventor who built the first steamboat in 1807. p. 475

Gagarin, Yuri 1934–1968 Soviet cosmonaut who became the first human in space in 1961. p. 669

Galileo (gal′ə lē′ō) 1564–1642 Renaissance scientist who studied motion and who was imprisoned by the Church for his belief that Earth moves around the sun. p. 434

Gandhi, Mohandas (gän′dē, mō hän′dəs) 1869–1948 Indian political and religious leader who believed in nonviolent civil disobedience and led India to independence in 1947. p. 611

Gaozu (gou′zü′) 256 B.C.–195 B.C. First ruler of the Han dynasty who lifted the ban on books in China. p. 111

Garibaldi, Giuseppe (gar′ə bȯl′dē, jü zep′ä) 1807–1882 Italian patriot and soldier who led a small army called the "Redshirts" to unify southern Italy. p. 501

Genghis Khan (jəng′gis kän) c. 1162–1227 Mongolian leader who united the nomadic tribes of northern Asia to form a unified Mongolia. p. 352

Gilgamesh (gil′gä məsh) c. 2700 B.C. Sumerian king whose adventures were recorded in the *Epic of Gilgamesh*. p. 44

Gorbachev, Mikhail (gôr′bə chȯf, mē′kil′) 1931– Communist Party leader and last president of the Soviet Union who called for and allowed more freedom in Eastern Europe. p. 621

Gutenberg, Johannes (güt′n bėrg, yō′hän) c. 1390–1468 German craftsman who invented the movable-type printing press in the 1440s. p. 435

Hammurabi (ham′ü rä′bē) c. 1810 B.C.–1750 B.C. King of Babylon who came to rule all of Mesopotamia and established a written code of laws known as the Code of Hammurabi. p. 51

Hannibal (han′ə bəl) 247 B.C.–183 B.C. Carthaginian general who launched an invasion on the Romans from Spain by crossing the Alps. p. 285

Hatshepsut (hat shəp′süt) reigned c. 1498 B.C.–1483 B.C. Queen of ancient Egypt who proclaimed herself pharaoh and ruled during the New Kingdom. p. 91

Henry the Navigator 1394–1460 Portuguese prince who encouraged expeditions to explore the west coast of Africa. p. 439

Hidalgo, Miguel (ē däl′gō, mē gəl′) 1753–1811 Mexican priest who encouraged a revolt in Mexico. p. 459

Hillary, Edmund 1919–2001 New Zealand mountain climber who was the first person to reach the top of Mount Everest. p. 573

Hippocrates (hi pok′rə tēz) c. 460 B.C.–377 B.C. Ancient Greek doctor who is often called the "father of medicine." p. 270

Hirohito (hir′ō hē′tō) 1901–1989 Emperor of Japan during World War II who surrendered to the United States. p. 546

Hitler, Adolf 1889–1945 German dictator who led Nazi Germany against the Allies in World War II. p. 544

Hobby, Oveta Culp 1905–1995 American commander of the U.S. Women's Army Corps during World War II. p. 552

Hobson, William 1793–1842 British naval officer who signed a treaty making New Zealand a colony. p. 503

Ho Chi Minh (hō′ chē′ min′) 1890–1969 Communist leader of the Viet Cong in Vietnam who was determined to bring communist rule to South Vietnam. p. 584

Homer c. 900 B.C.–800 B.C. Ancient Greek poet who composed two poems, the *Iliad* and the *Odyssey*, about the Trojan War. p. 253

Hussein 1935–1999 King of Jordan who gave up his country's claim to the West Bank in order to foster peace with Israel. p. 618

Ibn Battuta (əb′ən ba tü′tä) c. 1304–1368 Great traveler and historian of the Islamic world. p. 336

Inca Viracocha (in kä′ vē rä kō′chä) c. 1435 Incan ruler who fled his empire in 1438 because he thought it would be defeated by the Chancas. p. 198

Isabella 1451–1504 Spanish queen who funded Columbus's expedition to America. p. 440

Iturbide, Agustín de (dä ē tür bē′dä, ȯ gus tēn′) 1783–1824 Spanish army officer who defeated Spain and proclaimed independence for Mexico. p. 461

Jayavarman II (jä yä vär′mən) c. 770–850 God-king of the Khmer who reunited the kingdom in 802. p. 357

Jefferson, Thomas 1743–1826 Third president of the United States who stood up to piracy against Americans off the Barbary coast. p. 646

Jesus c. 4 B.C.–A.D. 29 A young Jewish man who taught in Palestine and founded Christianity. p. 295

Jiang Qing (jyäng chēng) 1914–1991 Wife of Mao Zedong who led the Cultural Revolution in China in the 1960s and 1970s. p. 579

Jinnah, Muhammed Ali 1876–1948 Muslim nationalist and political leader who called for the formation of the separate Muslim state of Pakistan. p. 612

John 1167–1216 English king whose lords forced him to agree to the Magna Carta in 1215, which limited royal power. p. 398

Johnson, Lyndon B. 1908–1973 Thirty-sixth president of the United States who escalated the commitment of U.S. forces in Vietnam in an effort to prevent a communist takeover of South Vietnam. p. 584

Julius, Caesar (jü′lyəs sē′zər) 100 B.C.–44 B.C. Ancient Roman general whose murder led to the end of the Roman Republic. p. 286

Junius Brutus sixth century B.C. Ancient Roman leader who, with his supporters, forced the Etruscans out of Rome. p. 278

Justinian 483–565 Byzantine emperor who brought the Empire to its height under his rule and told his scholars to collect the laws of the ancient Romans and organize them into a code of laws. p. 327

Kashta reigned c. 777–750 B.C. King of Kush who conquered Upper Egypt. p. 94

Kennedy, John F. 1917–1963 Thirty-fifth president of the United States who prevented the Soviet Union from building missile bases in Cuba. p. 572

Kenyatta, Jomo (ken yä′tə, jō′mō) 1890–1978 African independence leader in Kenya who became that country's first prime minister and president. p. 607

Khrushchev, Nikita (krüsh′chȯf, ni kē′tə) 1894–1971 Leader of the Soviet Communist Party in the 1950s and 1960s who divided Berlin with a wall and tried to build missile bases in Cuba. p. 572

Khufu (kü′fü) c. 2600 B.C. Egyptian pharaoh for whom the Great Pyramid at Giza was built. p. 87

Kublai Khan (kü′blə kän) 1215–1294 Grandson of Genghis Khan and founder of the Mongol (Yuan) dynasty. p. 352

Lalibela (lä lē bə′lä) reigned 1185–1225 Zagwe king who built eleven Christian churches in Ethiopia. p. 382

Laozi (lou′dzē′) c. sixth century B.C. First great teacher of Daoism who taught before Confucius. p. 117

Pronunciation Key

a in hat	ȯ in all	sh in she
ā in age	ō in open	th in thin
â in care	ô in order	ᴛʜ in then
ä in far	oi in oil	zh in measure
e in let	ou in out	ə = a in about
ē in equal	u in cup	ə = e in taken
ėr in term	u̇ in put	ə = i in pencil
i in it	ü in rule	ə = o in lemon
ī in ice	ch in child	ə = u in circus
o in hot	ng in long	

Biographical Dictionary

Lenin, Vladimir 1870–1924 Communist leader who took over the government of Russia after the revolution and later formed the Soviet Union. p. 531

Leopold II 1835–1909 Belgian king who cruelly ruled the Congo region of Africa in the late 1800s. p. 489

Louis XVI 1754–1793 French king who was overthrown during the French Revolution. p. 467

Luther, Martin 1483–1546 German priest whose protest to the Roman Catholic Church in 1517, started the Reformation. p. 436

MacArthur, Douglas 1880–1964 U.S. general who commanded forces in the Pacific, including the Philippines, during World War II. p. 553

MacDonald, Sir John 1812–1872 Canadian who became the first prime minister of Canada. p. 502

Magellan, Ferdinand c. 1480–1521 Portuguese sailor who led a group of ships, one of which was the first to circumnavigate the world. p. 439

Maguire, Mairead Corrigan 1944– Northern Irish social worker who was awarded the Nobel Prize for Peace in 1976 for her work toward ending the violence in Northern Ireland. p. 639

Manco Capac c. 1200 Founder of the Inca dynasty who led the Inca to settle in Cazco. p. 197

Mandela, Nelson 1918– African National Congress leader who was the first black president of South Africa. p. 609

Manetho c. 300 B.C. Egyptian priest and advisor who began keeping records of the ancient Egyptian kings. p. 85

Mansa Musa (män′sä mü′sä) c. 1324 King of Mali who is best known for his pilgrimage to Mecca. p. 376

Mao Zedong (mou′ zǔ dǔng′) 1893–1976 Chinese communist leader and founder of the People's Republic of China. p. 577

Marco Polo (pō′lō) c. 1254–1324 Venetian merchant, world traveler, and writer who remained in China as a guest for 17 years. p. 409

Marcus Aurelius (mär′kus ȯ rē′lē əs) 121–180 Ancient Roman philosopher, general, and emperor who was perhaps the greatest of Rome's "Five Good Emperors." p. 293

Marie Antoinette (mə rē′ an′twə net′) 1755–1793 Wife of Louis XVI and Queen of France during the French Revolution. p. 468

Marshall, George 1880–1959 U.S. Secretary of State under President Harry S. Truman who believed the United States should help all countries recover after World War II. p. 560

Marx, Karl 1818–1883 German economist and philosopher who popularized socialist ideals and predicted that a revolution would erase economic classes. p. 481

Mazzini, Giuseppe (mat zē′nē, jü zep′ä) 1805–1872 Italian patriot who fought to create a unified nation. p. 499

McNamara, Robert 1916– U.S. Secretary of Defense under President Lyndon B. Johnson who supported the build-up of U.S. forces in Vietnam but later questioned U.S. involvement in the war. p. 586

Meiji (mā′jē) 1852–1912 Japanese emperor who started Japan on a path of rapid modernization and adoption of Western ways. p. 495

Menchú, Rigoberta (men′chyü, rē gō bər′tä) 1959– Guatemalan woman who was awarded the Nobel Prize for Peace in 1992 for her work toward civil rights for Guatemala's poor farmers. p. 640

Mencius (mən′shē əs) c. 371 B.C.–289 B.C. Disciple of Confucius who is regarded as second only to Confucius as the cofounder of Confucianism. p. 117

Menes (mē′nēz) c. 3150 B.C. Legendary ancient Egyptian king who is credited with uniting Lower and Upper Egypt. p. 85

Michelangelo 1475–1564 Renaissance painter and sculptor who sought realism in his art. p. 432

Milosevic, Slobodan (mē lō′shəv ətch, slȯ′bȯ dən) 1941– President of Serbia who encouraged Serb fighters to carry out a policy of ethnic cleansing. p. 637

Minos (mī′nəs) Legendary King of the Minoan civilization in Crete. p. 250

Moctezuma I (mok tə zü′mä) c. 1390–1469 Aztec ruler of the Aztec Empire who increased its size and wealth. p. 178

Moctezuma II (mok tə zü′mä) 1466–1520 Aztec emperor who was the last to reign the Aztec Empire before it fell to Spain. p. 180

Morelos, José María (mō rä′lōs, hō sä′ mä rē′ä) 1765–1815 Mexican farmer and priest who helped lead the fight for Mexican independence. p. 461

Moses c. 1400 B.C.–1200 B.C. Hebrew prophet and teacher who led the Hebrews out of slavery in Egypt and received the Ten Commandments from God. p. 55

Mother Teresa 1910–1997 Roman Catholic nun who helped the poorest people of Calcutta, India, for decades p. 655

Mugabe, Robert (mü gä′bā, rə′bərt) 1924– African nationalist who became the prime minister of Zimbabwe (formerly Rhodesia). p. 609

Muhammad (mu häm′əd) c. 570–632 Founder of Islam. p. 331

Mussolini, Benito (mü′sə lē′nē, bən ē′tō) 1883–1945 Italian dictator who led Italy in World War II against the Allies. p. 544

Napoleon Bonaparte (nə pō′lē ən bō′nə pärt) 1769–1821 French general and military genius who named himself emperor of France in 1804. p. 469

Nasser, Gamal Abdel 1918–1970 Modern Egyptian leader who drove the British out of Egypt in 1956. p. 616

Nebuchadnezzar II (nə bə kəd nəz′ər) c. 630 B.C.–562 B.C. Chaldean dynasty king of Babylon who took over much of the former Assyrian Empire and ordered massive building projects. p. 52

Nero (nir′ō) 37–68 Ancient Roman emperor upon whose death civil war broke out. p. 289

Nicholas II 1868–1918 Czar of Russia during World War I who became the last Russian emperor.. p. 522

Nixon, Richard 1913–1994 Thirty-seventh president of the United States who visited China in 1972 and, in 1974, became the only president to resign from office. p. 578

Nkrumah, Kwame (nə krü′mə, kwä′mä) 1909–1972 Ghanaian leader who headed the independence movement and later became Ghana's first prime minister. p. 607

Norgay, Tenzing (nôr′gā, tən′zing) 1914–1986 Sherpa who was one of the first people to reach the top of Mount Everest. p. 573

Nyerere, Julius (nyə rār′ā, jü′lyəs) 1922–1999 Tanganyikan leader who worked for the independence of Tanzania from Great Britain and later became that country's first president. p. 607

O'Higgins, Bernardo 1778–1842 South American army leader who helped gain Chile's independence in 1818. p. 462

Pachacuti (pä chä kü′tē) c. 1391–1473 Incan emperor and son of Inca Viracocha who defeated the Chancas and extended his empire. p. 203

Paul died c. A.D. 68 Disciple of Jesus who helped spread his teachings throughout the Roman Empire. p. 296

Pericles (per′ə klēz′) c. 490 B.C.–429 B.C. Ancient Athenian leader who strove to make Athens the center of art and literature and who was responsible for building the Parthenon. p. 255

Perry, Matthew 1794–1858 U.S. naval officer who sailed to Japan and opened the country to trade with the West in 1853. p. 495

Peter died c. A.D. 67 Disciple of Jesus who helped spread his teachings throughout the Roman Empire. p. 296

Petrarch, Francesco (pə′trärk, fran səs′kō) 1304–1374 Italian poet and scholar who often encouraged people to speak and write thoughtfully. p. 431

Pizarro, Francisco (pi zär′ō, fran sis′kō) c. 1478–1541 Spanish conquistador who defeated the Incas. p. 201

Plato (plā′tō) c. 428 B.C.–347 B.C. Ancient Greek philosopher and disciple of Socrates who was one of the most famous thinkers of ancient Greece. p. 262

Pythagoras (pə thag′ər əs) c. 580 B.C.–500 B.C. Ancient Greek philosopher and mathematician whose ideas led to the field of geometry. p. 271

Rabin, Yitzhak (rä bēn′, yət zäk′) 1922–1995 Israeli prime minister who worked toward peace in the Middle East by signing the Oslo Accords in 1993. p. 618

Raphael 1483–1520 Renaissance painter who is known for his Madonnas. p. 432

Regulus c. 250 B.C. Ancient Roman general who was defeated and captured in a war between Rome and Carthage. p. 283

Pronunciation Key

a in hat	ȯ in all	sh in she
ā in age	ō in open	th in thin
â in care	ô in order	ŦH in then
ä in far	oi in oil	zh in measure
e in let	ou in out	ə = a in about
ē in equal	u in cup	ə = e in taken
ėr in term	ů in put	ə = i in pencil
i in it	ü in rule	ə = o in lemon
ī in ice	ch in child	ə = u in circus
o in hot	ng in long	

Biographical Dictionary

Rhodes, Cecil (rōdz, sē′səl) 1853–1902 British imperialist who believed that Europeans were better than non-Europeans in the colonies. p. 487

Robespierre, Maximilien de (də rōbz′pyer, mäk′sē mē lyan′) 1758–1794 Radical leader who became a key figure in the French Revolution. p. 469

Robinson, Mary 1944– First female president of the Republic of Ireland who later became the United Nations High Commissioner for Human Rights in 1997. p. 639

Romulus Augustulus (rom′yə las ô gus′tə lus) c. 464–? Last emperor of the Western Roman Empire in A.D. 476 at age twelve and reigned for only eleven months. p. 304

Roosevelt, Eleanor 1884–1962 Wife of U.S. President Franklin D. Roosevelt who became a delegate to the United Nations, a writer, and a public speaker. p. 560

Roosevelt, Franklin D. 1882–1945 Thirty-second president of the United States and the longest serving president who led the country during most of World War II. p. 550

Roosevelt, Theodore 1858–1919 Twenty-sixth president of the United States who was responsible for peace between Japan and Russia in 1905. p. 496

el-Sadat, Anwar 1918–1981 Egyptian president who made peace with Israel in 1978. p. 619

San Martín, José de (dā sän mär tēn′, hō sā′) 1778–1850 Argentine soldier who helped defeat the Spanish in Chile. p. 462

Sargon c. 2400 B.C.–2300 B.C. Akkadian king who united all of the city-states of Mesopotamia under his rule, forming the world's first empire. p. 45

Scipio (skip′ē ō) c. 185 B.C.–129 B.C. Ancient Roman general who attacked Carthage and forced Hannibal to retreat from Rome. p. 285

Sese Seko, Mobutu (sə sā′ sā kō, mō bü′tü) 1930–1997 African president of Zaire (Democratic Republic of the Congo) who overthrew the government in 1965 and ruled as dictator until 1997. p. 607

Shah Jahan (shä jə hän′) 1592–1666 Grandson of Akbar and Mogul ruler from 1628 to 1658 who ordered the construction of the Taj Mahal. p. 349

Shi Huangdi (shē′ hwäng dē) c. 259 B.C.–210 B.C. King of Qin who created the first unified Chinese empire and became the first Chinese emperor. p. 110

Shikibu, Murasaki c. 978–1014 Japanese court lady who wrote *The Tale of Genji*, the world's first novel. p. 361

Shulgi c. 2100 B.C. King of the Sumerian dynasty of Ur who was also the son of Ur-Nammu. p. 46

Siddhartha Gautama (sid där′tə gô′tə mə) c. 563 B.C.–483 B.C. Ancient Indian religious leader who came to be known as the Buddha, or the "Enlightened One," and founded Buddhism. p. 141

Sima Qian (sü′mən chə′en) c. 100 B.C. Chinese astronomer who became the first Chinese historian after writing a complete history book on China. p. 111

Socrates (sok′rə tēz′) c. 470 B.C.–399 B.C. Ancient Greek philosopher who developed an approach to teaching based on asking questions. p. 262

Solomon c. 1000 B.C. Son of David and King of Israel. p. 57

Sonni Ali (sün′nē ä lē′) c. 1500 King of Songhai who increased trade and learning in the empire of Songhai. p. 378

Stalin, Joseph 1879–1953 Dictator of the Soviet Union who fought on the side of the Allies during World War II and led the Soviet Union against the United States in the Cold War. p. 546

Stephenson, George 1781–1848 British engineer who invented the locomotive. p. 475

Sumanguru (sü mən gü′rü) c. 1203 King of Ghana who defeated the Soninke king and controlled Koumbi. p. 375

Sundiata (sün′ dē ä′tä) 1210–1255 King of Mali who established a long-lived system of government and made Mali into one of the greatest trading kingdoms in Africa. p. 376

Sun Yat-sen (sün′ yät′sən′) 1866–1925 Chinese leader who led a revolutionary movement in China that began in 1911. p. 577

Suryavarman II (sər yä vär′mən) c. 1150 Khmer king who oversaw the construction of the magnificent towers of Angkor Wat. p. 357

Suu Kyi, Aung San (sü kyē, än sän) 1945– Myanmar opposition leader who was awarded the Nobel Prize for Peace in 1991 for leading a pro-democracy movement in Myanmar (Burma). p. 642

Tarquin (tär′kwin) c. 510 B.C. Etruscan leader and the last king of ancient Rome. p. 278

Theodora c. 500–548 Wife of Byzantine Emperor Justinian who was also his most trusted advisor. p. 327

Theodosius (thē ō dō′sē əs) 347–395 Ancient Roman emperor who made Christianity Rome's official religion in 380. p. 296

Thutmose III c. 1400s B.C. New Kingdom pharaoh who conquered Nubia and brought ancient Egypt to the height of its power. p. 94

Tilak 1856–1920 Indian rebel leader who helped guide India to independence. p. 488

Tokugawa Ieyasu (tō kü gä′wä ē yä′sü) 1543–1616 First shogun of the Tokugawa dynasty of Japan who also began a policy of isolation. p. 361

Topa Inca c. 1471 Inca ruler and son of Pachacuti who doubled the size of the empire. p. 198

Toussaint L'Ouverture (tü sän′ lü vər tür′) 1743–1803 Former slave who led a revolt against the French in Haiti. p. 459

Toyotomi Hideyoshi (toi yō tō′mē hĭ dä yō′shē) 1537–1598 Japanese general who united Japan after civil war in 1590. p. 361

Truman, Harry S. 1884–1972 Thirty-third president of the United States after Franklin Roosevelt died, Truman authorized the use of the atomic bomb on Japan. p. 554

Urban II c. 1035–1099 Pope who issued a plea to free the Holy Land Palestine from the Turks, launching the Crusades. p. 407

Ur-Nammu c. 2200 B.C.–2100 B.C. Sumerian king who founded the last and most successful dynasty of Ur. p. 46

Victor Emmanuel II 1820–1878 Sardinian king who began to rule a unified Italy in 1860. p. 501

Victoria 1819–1901 Queen of Great Britain who oversaw the expansion of the British Empire and claimed that "the sun never sets" on it. p. 488

Virgil (vėr′jəl) 70 B.C.–19 B.C. Ancient Roman poet who wrote the legend the *Aeneid*. p. 253

Walesa, Lech (və wen′sə, lək) 1943– Polish steel worker who led the Solidarity labor union and became president after communists lost control of the Polish government. p. 621

Washington, George 1732–1799 General of the United States in the Revolutionary War who later became the first president of the United States. p. 458

Watt, James 1736–1819 Scottish inventor who improved the steam engine, enabling it to power large machines. p. 475

Wilhelm II 1859–1941 German ruler who insisted on building a big, modern navy to compete with Great Britain. p. 521

William the Conqueror c. 1028–1087 Norman king who conquered England in 1066. p. 397

Wilson, Woodrow 1856–1924 Twenty-eighth president of the United States who, during World War I, negotiated peace based on the Fourteen Points and helped form the League of Nations. p. 530

Wu Di (wü dē) c. 87 B.C. Chinese emperor who increased authority during the Han dynasty. p. 111

Wu Hou (wü jou) 625–705 First Chinese empress who ruled during the Tang dynasty and unified the empire. p. 351

Yeltsin, Boris 1931– First president of the Russian Republic, which formed in 1991 after the breakup of the Soviet Union. p. 622

Zheng He c. 1371–1435 Chinese explorer who led seven voyages westward under the Ming dynasty. p. 355

Pronunciation Key

a in hat	ȯ in all	sh in she
ā in age	ō in open	th in thin
â in care	ô in order	ᴛн in then
ä in far	oi in oil	zh in measure
e in let	ou in out	ə = a in about
ē in equal	u in cup	ə = e in taken
ėr in term	u̇ in put	ə = i in pencil
i in it	ü in rule	ə = o in lemon
ī in ice	ch in child	ə = u in circus
o in hot	ng in long	

Glossary

The Glossary will help you understand the meanings and pronounce the vocabulary words in this book. The page number tells you where the word or term first appears.

 **A**

absolute power (ab′sə lüt pou′ər) the power to control every part of a society (p. 357)

adobe (ə dō′bē) a brick formed from mud and straw that is dried in the sun (p. 214)

aggression (ə gresh′ən) a policy of launching attacks on the territory of others (p. 545)

agora (ag′ər ə) an outdoor marketplace in ancient Greece (p. 249)

agriculture (ag′rə kul chər) the raising of plants or animals for human use (p. 21)

alliance (ə lī əns) an agreement made between two or more groups or nations (p. 177)

Allied Powers (al′īd pou′ərz) an alliance between Great Britain, France, Russia, and Italy in World War I (p. 527)

Allies (al′īz) an alliance between Great Britain, France, the Soviet Union, China, and the United States in World War II (p. 550)

alpaca (al pak′ə) a domesticated animal from the Andes Mountains (p. 187)

Analects (a nə leks′) a collection of sayings by Confucius (p. 116)

ancestor (an′ses tər) a relative who lived longer ago than a grandparent (p. 111)

annex (ə neks′) to attach or to add (p. 545)

anthropology (an′thrə pol′ə jē) the study of how people have developed and live in cultural groups (p. 27)

apartheid (ə pärt′hāt) a system of laws in South Africa, which kept blacks and whites separate (p. 609)

Apostle (ə pos′əl) one of twelve disciples chosen by Jesus to help him preach and spread the Word of God (p. 295)

appeasement (ə pēz′mənt) to preserve peace by meeting the demands of an aggressor (p. 545)

Appian Way (a′pē′ən wā) a famous ancient Roman road (p. 287)

aqueduct (ak′wə dukt) structures used to carry flowing water from a distance (p. 170)

Arab nationalism (ar′əb nash′ə nə liz′əm) Arab unity, which became a powerful force under Egyptian President Gamal Abdel Nasser (p. 616)

archaeologist (är′kē ol′ə jist) a scientist who uncovers evidence, or proof, from the past (p. 11)

archaeology (är′kē ol′ə jē) the study of past cultures through the things that remain such as buildings, tools, or pottery (p. 11)

archipelago (är′kə pel′ə gō) a close group of islands (p. 188)

arid (ar′id) dry (p. 210)

aristocracy (ar′ə stok′rə sē) a government controlled by a few wealthy people (p. 255)

aristocrat (ə ris′tə krat) a person who is a member of a high social class (p. 361)

Armada (är mä′də) a fleet of warships (p. 442)

armistice (är′mə stis) a cease-fire (p. 530)

artifact (är′tə fakt) an object made by people long ago (p. 11)

artisan (är′tə zən) a craftsperson such as a potter or weaver (p. 38)

Assembly (ə sem′blē) in ancient Greece, an Athenian governing body of all citizens older than eighteen (p. 255)

assembly line (ə sem′blē lin) a way to manufacture items in which each worker contributes one part along a moving belt or line to make a whole product (p. 479)

Association of Southeast Asian Nations, (ASEAN) a trading bloc of Southeast Asian nations (p. 632)

astrolabe (as′trə lāb) and instrument used by navigators to determine latitude (p. 337)

auction (ȯk′shən) to sell something to the highest bidder (p. 299)

Axis Powers (ak′sis pou′ərz) alliance between Germany, Italy, and Japan in World War II (p. 550)

 **B**

balsa (bȯl′sə) a small reed boat (p. 188)

Bantu (ban′tü) any of a number of languages with word similarities in Africa (p. 373)

barter (bär′tər) to exchange one kind of good or service for another (p. 59)

basin and range (bā′sn and rānj) a low area of land with a small mountain range (p. 209)

Bastille (ba stēl′) a former prison in Paris and site of the beginning of the French Revolution (p. 468)

Big Three (big thrē) the major Allied leaders—Franklin Roosevelt, Joseph Stalin, and Winston Churchill (p. 551)

biome (bī′ōm) a place that has a distinct climate, plants, and animals (p. 188)

Book of Documents (bùk ov dok′yə mənts) Zhou dynasty text that Confucius interpreted and revived (p. 115)

Brahman (brä′mən) believed by Hindus to be the universal truth being, which is the source of everything (p. 138)

brahmin (brä′mən) a priest who held the highest position in Aryan society (p. 131)

Bronze Age (bronz āj) a period of history when bronze was mainly used to make items such as tools and weapons (p. 108)

bubonic plague (byü bon′ik plāg) an epidemic spread to humans by fleas from rats (p. 410)

Buddha, the (bü′də) the "Enlightened One," what Siddhartha Gautama came to be known (p. 141)

Buddhism (bü′diz əm) the religion that is based on the teachings of the Buddha (p. 141)

burial mound (ber′ē əl mound) a small hill of dirt built over the grave of a person (p. 219)

Byzantine Empire (biz′n tēn′ em′pīr) an empire of lands formerly part of the Roman Empire with its center at the city of Constantinople (p. 301)

Byzantine Orthodox Church (biz′n tēn′ ôr′thə doks chèrch) the early Christian church in the Eastern Roman Empire of which the emperor was head (p. 302)

caesar (sē′zər) an ancient Roman emperor (p. 286)

caliph (kā′lif) a successor to Muhammad (p. 332)

capitalism (kap′ə tə liz′əm) an economic system in which private individuals own most businesses and resources (p. 480)

capitalist (kap′ə tə list) a person who follows capitalism and invests in factories and industries (p. 480)

caravan (kar′ə van) a group of people and animals traveling together (p. 331)

carbon dating (kär′bən dāt′ing) a method of estimating the age of something after it has died (p. 23)

carbon dioxide (kär′bən dī ok′sid) a gas produced by the burning of gasoline (p. 661)

caste (kast) in Hinduism, a lifelong social group into which one is born (p. 139)

casualty (kazh′ü əl tē) a wounded or killed soldier (p. 528)

catacomb (kat′ə kōm) an underground room used as a burial site (p. 295)

cataract (kat′ə rakt′) a waterfall (p. 80)

cathedral (kə thə′drəl) a large, important Christian church (p. 327)

causeway (kòz′wā′) raised bridges made of land (p. 176)

cenote (sā nō′tā) natural wells on the Yucatán Peninsula (p. 171)

Central Powers (sen′trəl pou′ərz) an alliance between Germany, Austria-Hungary, and the Ottoman Empire in World War I (p. 527)

charter (chär′tər) a constitution (p. 560)

chinampa (chən äm′pä) man-made island (p. 176)

chivalry (shiv′əl rē) a knight's code of behavior (p. 401)

Christianity (kris′chē an′ə tē) the monotheistic religion based on the life, teachings, and death of Jesus (p. 295)

circumnavigate (sèr′kəm nav′ə gāt) to travel around the world (p. 439)

city-state (sit′ē stāt) a city that is an individual unit, complete with its own form of government and traditions (p. 38)

civil disobedience (siv′əl dis′ə bē′dē əns) the refusal to obey or cooperate with unjust laws (p. 611)

civilization (siv′ə lə zā′shən) a group of people who have a complex and organized society within a culture (p. 35)

civil service (siv′əl sèr′vis) the practice of using skills and talents to work in the government (p. 111)

climate (klī′mit) the average weather conditions of a place over a long span of time (p. 23)

Pronunciation Key

a in hat	ō in open	sh in she
â in care	ò in all	th in thin
ā in age	ô in order	ᴛʜ in then
ä in far	oi in oil	zh in measure
e in let	ou in out	ə = a in about
ē in equal	u in cup	ə = e in taken
èr in term	ù in put	ə = i in pencil
i in it	ü in rule	ə = o in lemon
ī in ice	ch in child	ə = u in circus
o in hot	ng in long	

Glossary

Code of Hammurabi (kōd ov ham′ú rä′bē) a set of laws established by Hammurabi (p. 50)

codex (kō′deks) a folding-screen book containing information about predicting the future and religious rituals (p. 172)

Cold War (kōld wôr) the tension between the Soviet Union and the United States after World War II (p. 569)

collective (kə lek′tiv) farms that are grouped together and run by the government (p. 546)

colony (kol′ə nē) a settlement far from the country that governs it (p. 445)

Columbian Exchange (kə lum′bē ən eks chānj′) the transfer of goods and diseases from Europe to America and American items back to Europe (p. 441)

command economy (kə mand′ i kon′ə mē) an economy in which the government or other central authority controls the flow of money (p. 481)

commerce (kom′ərs) the buying and selling of a large quantity of goods (p. 431)

common market (kom′ən mär′kit) an economic union (p. 636)

communism (kom′yə niz′əm) a form of socialism in which all resources are owned by a government led by a dictator (p. 531)

compound (kom′pound) a set-aside area (p. 494)

concentration camp (kon′sən trā′shən kamp) a place that holds imprisoned people of a particular ethnic group or for their political or religious beliefs (p. 559)

concrete (kon′krēt′) a building material made from a mixture of crushed stone, sand, cement, and water (p. 287)

Confucianism (kən fyü′shə niz′əm) a way of thinking and living based on the teachings of Confucius (p. 116)

conquer (kong′kər) to defeat (p. 45)

conquest (kon′kwest) the defeat of another group (p. 52)

conquistador (kon kē′stə dôr) a Spanish conqueror (p. 441)

conservation (kən sər vā′shən) the use of resources carefully and wisely (p. 657)

consul (kon′səl) in ancient Rome, one of two officials who managed the government and the army (p. 283)

containment (kən tān′mənt) a policy of preventing Soviet communism from spreading into new countries or states (p. 570)

convent (kon′vent) a community of nuns (p. 401)

corporation (kôr′pə rā′shən) a business organization (p. 479)

Counter-Reformation (koun′tər-ref′ər mā′shən) response and reforms by the Roman Catholic Church to the Protestant Reformation (p. 437)

coup d'état (kü′dā tä′) the overthrow of a government (p. 607)

covenant (kuv′ə nənt) an agreement (p. 55)

Crusades (krü sādz′) major military expeditions by Christians to win back control of Palestine (Holy Land) and to protect the Byzantine Empire (p. 407)

culture (kul′chər) the way in which individuals and groups react with their environment, including their technology, customs, beliefs, and art (p. 27)

cuneiform (kyü nē′ə fôrm) a form of wedge-shaped writing used in ancient times (p. 43)

daimyo (dī myō) a powerful samurai who controlled many other samurai and governed large areas of farmland in Japan (p. 359)

Daoism (dou′izəm) the belief in finding the "way," or the dao, of the universe (p. 117)

D-Day (dē′dā′) June 6, 1944, the date that Allied forces landed in France in World War II in the largest invasion by sea in history (p. 552)

Declaration of Independence (dek lə rā′shən ov in di pen′dəns) the document written in 1776 that said the American colonies were free and independent states and no longer part of Great Britain (p. 458)

Declaration of the Rights of Man and of Citizen a document that established the rights of citizens under a French republic (p. 468)

decolonization (dē kol′ə nə zā′shən) the process of replacing colonial rule with self-rule (p. 607)

deforestation (dē fôr′ist ā′shən) the clearing of land, which causes loss of forests and less fertile land (p. 662)

Delian League (də lē′ən lēg) in ancient Greece, an alliance between Athens and other Greek city-states (p. 263)

delta (del′tə) a triangular-shaped area at the mouth of some rivers (p. 79)

democracy (di mok′rə sē) a government by the people (p. 255)

demographer (di mog′rə fər) a person who studies population trends (p. 656)

depression (di presh′ən) a period of sharp economic decline (p. 543)

descendant (di sen′dənt) a person born later into the same family (p. 55)

desertification (di zėrt′ə fə kā′shən) the drying up of land along a desert (p. 662)

détente (dā tänt′) a relaxation of tensions, especially between nations (p. 587)

deva-raja (dā′və-rä′jə) according to Hindu rites, a god-king (p. 357)

dharma (där′mə) in Hinduism, the order of the universe (p. 138)

dictator (dik′tā tər) a person who has total control over the people (p. 283)

disciple (də sī′pəl) one of a small group of people who followed Jesus (p. 295)

dissident (dis′ə dənt) a protester against a government (p. 621)

diverse (də vėrs′) different (p. 27)

Domesday Book (dümz′dā′ bůk) a book made in 1086 that helped King William keep track of all of the people and property in England (p. 397)

domestic system (də mes′tik sis′təm) a system in which goods were made in the home, rather than in factories (p. 475)

domesticate (də mes′tə kāt) to tame (p. 19)

dominion (də min′yən) a self-governing nation with strong ties to a ruling empire (p. 502)

domino effect (dom′ə nō ə fekt′) a theory that the fall of one item will lead to the fall of all adjoining items like dominoes that are lined up when one is toppled (p. 585)

double cropping (dub′əl krop′ping) a process in which two crops are grown on the same land in the same year (p. 102)

dynasty (di′nə stē) a ruling family (p. 45)

★ E ★

economy (i kon′ə mē) the way people use and manage resources (p. 89)

Eightfold Path (āt′fōld path) the Buddhist way of living that can help Buddhists find relief from their suffering (p. 143)

emperor (em′pər ər) the ruler of an empire (p. 289)

empire (em′pīr) a large territory consisting of many different places under the control of a single ruler (p. 45)

encomienda (en kō mē ən′də) a Spanish system that allowed colonists to demand labor from Native Americans (p. 447)

endangered species (en dān′jərd spē′shēz) an animal or plant that is in danger of dying out completely (p. 661)

enlightenment (en līt′n mənt) in Buddhism, a state of pure goodness, the goal of reincarnation (p. 142)

environmentalist (en vī′rən men′tl ist) a person who tries to solve environmental problems (p. 661)

Environmental Protection Agency a U.S. agency that watches the environment (p. 661)

epidemic (ep′ə dem′ik) a disease that spreads quickly (p. 410)

estate (e stāt′) a class or order in pre-Revolutionary French society (p. 467)

Estates-General (e stātz′jen′ər əl) in pre-Revolutionary France, a representative assembly that advised the king (p. 467)

etching (ech′ing) an imprinted drawing or design (p. 213)

ethnic cleansing (eth′nik klən′zing) to drive out or kill people who do not share the same ethnicity or identity (p. 637)

ethnicity (eth nis′ə tē) a group of people with the same language, customs, and culture (p. 637)

euro (yůr′ō) the money of the European Union (p. 632)

European Union, (EU) (yůr′ə pē′ən yü′nyən) a European trading bloc (p. 632)

excavation site (ek′skə vā′shən sīt) a site where archaeologists uncover artifacts (p. 20)

excommunicate (eks′kə myü′nə kāt) to expel from a church (p. 437)

Pronunciation Key

a in hat	ō in open	sh in she
â in care	ȯ in all	th in thin
ā in age	ô in order	ŦH in then
ä in far	oi in oil	zh in measure
e in let	ou in out	ə = a in about
ē in equal	u in cup	ə = e in taken
ėr in term	ů in put	ə = i in pencil
i in it	ü in rule	ə = o in lemon
ī in ice	ch in child	ə = u in circus
o in hot	ng in long	

Glossary

factory (fak′tər ē) a building that houses many machines (p. 475)

factory system (fak′tər ē sis′təm) the grouping of machines in one place (p. 475)

fascism (fash′iz′əm) a form of government that stresses the nation above individuals (p. 544)

fertile (fėr′tl) rich, as in soil (p. 35)

feudalism (fyü′dl iz′əm) a social, political, and economic system used in the Middle Ages (p. 401)

Five-Year Plan (fiv′yir plan) an economic plan first launched by Soviet Party leader Joseph Stalin in 1928 (p. 546)

fossil fuel (fos′əl fyü′əl) a fuel formed long ago deep in the earth from prehistoric plants and animals (p. 665)

Four Noble Truths (fôr nō′bəl trüᴛʜz) in Buddhism, beliefs about human suffering (p. 143)

Fourteen Points (fôr′tēn′points) U.S. President Woodrow Wilson's blueprint for peace in Europe after World War I (p. 536)

geography (jē og′rə fē) the study of the relationship between physical features, climate, and people (p. 27)

geothermal energy (jē ō thėr′məl en′ər jē) energy that is produced from super-hot, underground water (p. 667)

glacier (glā′shər) a huge ice sheet (p. 12)

gladiator (glad′ē ā tər) in ancient Rome, a professional fighter (p. 291)

glasnost (glaz′nost) "openess", a policy introduced by Mikhail Gorbachev in 1985 to allow the Soviet people some freedom of speech (p. 622)

global warming (glō′bəl wôr′ming) a gradual increase in the temperature of Earth's surface (p. 661)

Golden Age (gōl′dən āj) a period of time in ancient Athens when magnificent temples were built; artists created statues and monuments; and philosophers extended human knowledge (p. 262)

Gospels (gos′pəlz) in Christianity, the four books of the Bible known as the New Testament (p. 295)

Great Depression (grāt di presh′ən) a period of economic decline that began in 1929 and lasted until about 1939 (p. 543)

Great Wall (grāt wôl) a wall in China originally built for protection from northern invaders that over centuries was extended to more than 4,300 miles (p. 110)

Great Zimbabwe (grāt zim bä′bwā) a kingdom in Africa of some 11,000 people that reached its height about 1400 (p. 384)

greenhouse effect (grēn′hous ə′fekt′) the process by which carbon dioxide in Earth's atmosphere traps heat from the sun, raising the temperature of Earth's surface (p. 661)

griot (grēō′) a professional storyteller from Africa (p. 376)

gross domestic product, (GDP) (grōs də mes′tik prod′ekt) a measure of a country's wealth (p. 631)

guerrilla (gə ril′ə) a hit-and-run fighter (p. 584)

guild (gild) a group of craftspeople or merchants who are united by a common interest (p. 404)

hajj (haj) a pilgrimage to Mecca (p. 331)

Han dynasty (hän di′nə stē) a dynasty that lasted from 206 B.C. to A.D. 220 in China (p. 111)

harvest (här′vist) to gather (p. 20)

Hellenistic Age (hel′ə nis′tik āj) a period of time when ancient Greek and Asian cultures mixed (p. 268)

helot (hel′ət) a slave (p. 255)

hieroglyphics (hī′ər ə glif′iks) a form of writing based on pictures (p. 86)

Hinduism (hin′dü iz′əm) the main religion of India that is based on Aryan beliefs (p. 137)

hippodrome (hi′pə′drōm) an ancient Greek stadium used for horse and chariot racing (p. 324)

holocaust (hol′ə kôst) a mass killing (p. 535)

Human Genome Project (hyü′mən je′nōm proj′ekt) an international project launched in 1990, to locate all of the human genes (p. 670)

hydroelectric energy (hī′drō i lek′trik en′ər jē) electricity produced by using the energy of flowing water (p. 666)

Ice Age (īs āj) a period of time when glaciers covered great stretches of land (p. 12)

icon (ī′kon) a religious image (p. 328)

immigration (im′ə grā′shən) to leave a home country and go to another country to stay permanently (p. 657)

immortal (i môr′tl) to live forever (p. 254)

imperialism (im pir′ē ə liz′əm) a system of building an empire by conquering lands around the world (p. 487)

imperialist (im pir′ē ə list) a person who promotes imperialism (p. 487)

independent (in′di pen′dənt) free (p. 94)

indulgence (in dul′jəns) in the Roman Catholic Church, a pardon for sin (p. 436)

Industrial Revolution (in dus′trē əl rev′ə lü′shən) a period of time in society when human and animal power changed to machine power (p. 475)

inflation (in flā′shən) a rapid increase in prices (p. 537)

internal combustion engine (in tėr′nl kəm bus′chən en′jən) a machine that uses the power of a controlled burning of fuel (p. 479)

irrigation (ir ə gā′shən) a system of transporting water to crops (p. 36)

Islam (is′lam) the monotheistic religion revealed to and based on the teachings of Muhammad (p. 331)

jihad (ji häd′) in Islam, a military or peaceful "struggle" (p. 333)

Judaism (jü′dē iz′əm) the monotheistic religion founded by Abraham (p. 55)

Justinian Code (ju stin′ē ən kōd) laws of the ancient Romans collected by Byzantine scholars and organized into a code of laws for the Byzantine Empire under Emperor Justinian (p. 327)

kamikaze (kä′mi kä′zē) World War II Japanese pilots who flew into enemy warships to destroy them (p. 554)

knight (nīt) a feudal warrior trained and prepared to fight on horseback (p. 401)

labor union (lā′bər yü′nyən) a group of workers that gathers together to raise wages and improve working conditions (p. 480)

lady (lā′dē) a woman of nobility (p. 405)

laissez faire (les′ā fâr′) "leave it alone," a policy in which the government does not try to control something such as business operations (p. 480)

landform (land′fôrm′) a natural feature of Earth's surface such as a valley, plain, hill, or mountain (p. 27)

Late Stone Age (lāt stōn āj) the end of the New Stone Age (p. 27)

League of Nations (lēg ov nā′shənz) an organization of nations formed after World War I to promote cooperation and peace (p. 536)

legislature (lej′ə slā′chər) a group of elected people who make laws (p. 457)

levee (lev′ē) a dike used to control flooding (p. 102)

llama (lä′mə) a domesticated animal from the Andes Mountains (p. 187)

loess (lō′is) a yellowish brown soil that blows in from a desert (p. 101)

long house (lông′ hous′) a large, rectangular building used by the Iroquois that housed many families (p. 224)

Magna Carta (mag′nə kär′tə) an English charter (1215) that limited royal power (p. 398)

Mandate of Heaven (man′dāt ov hev′ən) in dynastic China, the divine right to govern for the good of all people (p. 116)

manor system (man′ər sis′təm) in the Middle Ages, a way to manage feudal lands (p. 402)

marathon (mar′ə thon) the longest race in the Olympics, a footrace of about 26 miles (p. 261)

market economy (mär′kit i kon′ə me) an economy in which the people make their own decisions about how to spend money (p. 480)

Marshall Plan (mär′shəl plan) a plan that offered U.S. financial help to Europe after World War II (p. 560)

massacre (mas′ə kər) the killing of many helpless people (p. 457)

Pronunciation Key		
a in hat	ō in open	sh in she
â in care	ȯ in all	th in thin
ā in age	ô in order	ᴛʜ in then
ä in far	oi in oil	zh in measure
e in let	ou in out	ə = a in about
ē in equal	u in cup	ə = e in taken
ėr in term	u̇ in put	ə = i in pencil
i in it	ü in rule	ə = o in lemon
ī in ice	ch in child	ə = u in circus
o in hot	ng in long	

Glossary

meditation (med′ə tā′shən) in Buddhism, a way of clearing the mind (p. 142)

megacity (meg′ə sit′ē) a city region with more than 10 million people (p. 655)

mercantilism (mėr′kən ti liz′əm) a system in which a country uses its colonies to obtain raw materials, makes products from the raw materials, and then sells the goods back to the colonists (p. 445)

mercenary (mėr′sə ner′ē) a hired soldier (p. 264)

Mercosur (mėr kō′sər) a trading bloc of South American countries (p. 633)

Messiah (mə′sī ə) in Judaism, a leader sent by God; in Christianity, the savior, Jesus, God in human form (p. 296)

Middle Ages (mid′l ājs) a period in European history that lasted from about 500 to about 1500 (p. 397)

middleman (mid′l man) a person who goes between buyers and sellers (p. 112)

migrate (mī′grāt) to move from one place to another (p. 12)

millennium (mə len′ē əm) a period of 1,000 years (p. 655)

Ming dynasty (ming dī′nəstē) a dynasty that lasted from 1368 to 1644 in China (p. 353)

Minoan (mi nō′ən) an early Greek civilization that developed on the island of Crete (p. 250)

missionary (mish′ə ner′ē) a person who teaches a religion to people with different beliefs (p. 401)

mobilization (mō′bə li zā′shən) the preparations nations make before sending their armies into battle (p. 522)

modernization (mod′ər ni zā′shən) the process of bringing ways and standards to those of the present (p. 495)

monarch (mon′ərk) a king or queen who is a supreme leader (p. 401)

monarchy (mon′ər kē) government in which a king, queen, or emperor has supreme power (p. 467)

monastery (mon′ə ster′ē) a community where monks live, study, and pray (p. 401)

Mongol (Yuan) dynasty (mong′gəl dī nə′stē) a dynasty that began with Kublai Khan's conquest of southern China and Burma in 1287 (p. 352)

monk (mungk) a man who devotes his life to religion and lives in a monastery (p. 401)

monotheism (mon′ə thē iz′əm) the worship of only one God (p. 55)

monsoon season (mon sün′) rainy season in monsoon climates in which winds blow from the southwest for six months (p. 125)

mosque (mosk) a Muslim place of worship (p. 332)

movable type (mü′və bəl tīp) small, reusable metal blocks used to print letters and numbers (p. 435)

multiethnic nation (mul′tē eth′nik nā′shən) a nation with different ethnic groups living together (p. 637)

mummy (mum′ē) a preserved dead body (p. 87)

Muslim (muz′ləm) a believer in Islam (p. 331)

myth (mith) a traditional story that may include gods and goddesses and often tries to explain events in nature (p. 253)

Napoleonic Code (nə pō′lē on′ik kōd) a system of French laws under Emperor Napoleon I (p. 469)

National Aeronautics and Space Administration, (NASA) the United States space agency (p. 669)

National Assembly (nash′ə nəl ə sem′blē) the revolutionary assembly made up of members of the third estate of France, which served as the French parliament (p. 467)

nationalism (nash′ə nə liz′əm) a strong devotion to one's country (p. 487)

Nationalist Party (nash′ə nə list pär′tē) the party started by Sun Yat-sen after China became a republic in 1911 (p. 577)

navigator (nav′ə gā′tər) a person skilled at guiding ships (p. 337)

Nazis (nä′tsēz) the National Socialists, Germany's former fascist party (p. 544)

neutral (nü′trəl) one that does not take sides (p. 523)

New Stone Age (nü stōn āj) the late period of the Stone Age when humans made great improvements in technology (p. 19)

New Testament (nü tes′tə mənt) the part of the Christian Bible that contains the Gospels (p. 295)

nobility (nō bil′ə tē) a high-ranking social class (p. 115)

nomad (nō′mad) a person who travels from place to place without a permanent home (p. 22)

nonrenewable resource (non ri nü′ə bl ri sôrs′) a resource that cannot be replaced (p. 665)

Normans (nôr′mənz) a group of invaders that settled in northern France (p. 397)

North American Free Trade Agreement, (NAFTA) an agreement that created a free-trade zone between the United States, Canada, and Mexico (p. 633)

North Atlantic Treaty Organization, (NATO) a military alliance set up by the United States and its Western Allies after World War II (p. 571)

nuclear (nü′klē ər) atomic (p. 569)

nun (nun) a woman who devotes her life to religion and lives in a convent (p. 401)

oba (ō′bə) a king of Benin (p. 384)

Old Stone Age (ōld stōn āj) the early, longer period of the Stone Age when little progress was made (p. 19)

Olympic Games (ō lim′pik gāmz) athletic contests held by the ancient Greeks about 3,500 years ago and revived in modern times (p. 254)

Open Door Policy (ō′pən dôr pol′ə sē) a policy set up in 1900 by the United States in which any country could trade with China (p. 495)

oracle bone (ôr′ə kəl bōn) a bone commonly used during the Shang dynasty in China to predict the future (p. 108)

oral tradition (ôr′əl trə dish′ən) the passing down of stories from person to person orally (p. 253)

papyrus (pə pī′rəs) a plant whose stems are used to make a kind of paper (p. 80)

parliament (pär′lə mənt) an elected legislature (p. 502)

patrician (pə trish′ən) a wealthy, powerful citizen of ancient Rome (p. 283)

patriotism (pā′trē ə tiz′əm) a sense of pride in one's country (p. 285)

Pax Romana (paks′ rō mä′nä) "Roman Peace," a time when ancient Rome was prosperous and peaceful (p. 289)

peninsula (pə nin′sə lə) land that is nearly surrounded by water (p. 164)

perestroika (per′ə stroi′ka) "restructuring"; a reform movement introduced by Mikhail Gorbachev to restructure the Soviet economy (p. 622)

persecute (per′sə kyüt) to punish (p. 296)

pesticide (pes′tə sīd) a chemical that is used to kill insects or other pests (p. 661)

pharaoh (fer′ō) in ancient Egypt, a god-king (p. 85)

philosopher (fə los′ə fər) a person who studies truth and knowledge (p. 262)

pictograph (pik′tə graf) a picture that represents a word (p. 107)

pilgrimage (pil′grə mij) a journey to a place of religious importance (p. 331)

pillage (pil′ij) to rob (p. 303)

pit house (pit′ hous) a dwelling used by the Hohokam and made from digging a hole in the ground and covering it with logs (p. 213).

plague (plāg) an epidemic of an often fatal disease (p. 263)

Plague, the (plāg) an attack of bubonic plague that killed about 25–30 percent of Europe's population from 1347 to 1352 (p. 410)

plain (plān) an area of flat land (p. 35)

plateau (pla tō′) an area of high, flat land (p. 36)

plebeian (pli bē′ən) a common citizen of ancient Rome (p. 283)

plunder (plun′dər) valuables taken in war (p. 251)

policy of isolation (pol′ə sē ov ī sə lā′shən) a policy whereby foreigners are forced out of a country and traveling abroad is outlawed (p. 363)

pollution (pə lü′shən) the process of making the environment dirty (p. 663)

polytheism (pol′ē thē′iz əm) the worship of many gods (p. 42)

pope (pōp) the leader of the Roman Catholic Church (p. 302)

prehistory (prē his′tər ē) the long period of time before people developed systems of writing and written language (p. 11)

proletarian (prō′lə târ′ē ən) of, or belonging to, the working class (p. 579)

propaganda (prop′ə gan′də) the planned spread of certain beliefs (p. 545)

Protestantism (prot′ə stən tiz′əm) the religion of Protestants, or Christians who led a movement against the beliefs and practices of the Roman Catholic Church (p. 437)

Pronunciation Key

a in hat	ō in open	sh in she
â in care	ȯ in all	th in thin
ā in age	ô in order	ŦH in then
ä in far	oi in oil	zh in measure
e in let	ou in out	ə = a in about
ē in equal	u in cup	ə = e in taken
ėr in term	u̇ in put	ə = i in pencil
i in it	ü in rule	ə = o in lemon
ī in ice	ch in child	ə = u in circus
o in hot	ng in long	

Glossary

pueblo (pweb′lō) a structure of adobe brick (p. 214)

pyramid (pir′ə mid) a large stone building to serve as a house for the dead (p. 87)

Qin dynasty (chin dī′nə stē) the Chinese dynasty founded by the first Chinese emperor, Shi Huangdi in 221 B.C. (p. 110)

quipu (kē′pü) a knotted rope used by the Incas to keep records (p. 199)

Quran (kô rän′) the holy book of Islam (p. 331)

Ramadan (räm′ə dän′) the ninth month of the Muslim calendar (p. 332)

reason (rē′zn) logical thinking (p. 262)

Reformation (ref′ər mā′shən) the religious movement in Europe that aimed at reforming the Roman Catholic Church but led to the establishment of Protestantism (p. 437)

reformer (ri fôr′mər) a person who tries to change or improve something (p. 480)

refugee (ref′yə jē′) a person who leaves his or her homeland for a safer place (p. 559)

region (rē′jən) an area on Earth with common physical features (p. 38)

Reign of Terror (ran ov ter′ər) a period of violence during the French Revolution when thousands of citizens were put to death (p. 468)

reincarnation (rē′in kär nā′shən) the Hindu belief that the spirit or soul goes from one life to the next (p. 138)

Renaissance (ren′ə säns′) the intellectual and economic movement that began in the mid-1400s and lasted until the 1600s that saw a revived interest in the art, social, scientific, and political thoughts of ancient Greece and Rome (p. 431)

renewable resource (ri nü′ə bəl ri sôrs′) a natural resource that can be replaced (p. 666)

reparations (rep′ə rā′shənz) a payment for war losses (p. 536)

representative (rep′ri zen′tə tiv) a person elected to represent the people (p. 283)

repressive (ri pres′iv) something that restrains (p. 640)

republic (ri pub′lik) a form of government in which citizens have the right to choose their leaders (p. 283)

Rig Veda (rig vā′də) one of the best-known books of the Vedas, containing more than 1,000 hymns (p. 137)

Roman Catholic Church (rō′mən kath′ə lik chėrch) the early Christian church in the Western Roman Empire of which the Pope was head (p. 302)

Rosetta Stone (rō zet′ə stōn) a stone on which a passage was written in three languages: Greek, Egyptian hieroglyphics, and a form of Egyptian cursive writing (p. 86)

Russian Revolution (rush′ən rev′ə lü′shen) the revolution that overthrew Russian Czar Nicholas I in 1917, later establishing the Bolshevik government under Vladimir Lenin (p. 531)

samurai (sam′ü rī′) a member of the Japanese warrior class (p. 361)

sanction (sangk′shən) a penalty placed against a country to force it to change its ways or policies (p. 609)

Sanskrit (san′skrit) the main language of the Aryans (p. 130)

satellite (sat′l it) an object that is sent into space and orbits Earth (p. 669)

savanna (sə van′ə) a short grassy plain (p. 371)

scribe (skrīb) a professional writer (p. 43)

scrub land (skrub land) an area of low-growing vegetation (p. 188)

segregate (seg rə gāt) to separate (p. 609)

Senate (sen′it) a governing body in which ancient Roman representatives served (p. 283)

serf (sėrf) a person who lived on and farmed feudal land (p. 401)

Shang dynasty (shang dī′nə stē) a dynasty that lasted from 1760 B.C. to 1500 B.C. in China (p. 108)

shogun (shō′gun) a high-ranking military commander in Japan (p. 362)

Silk Road (silk rōd) a trading route that connected Europe and lands of the former Roman Empire with China (pp. 112, 409)

silt (silt) a mixture of soil and small rocks (p. 79)

slavery (slā′vər ē) the practice of one person owning another person (p. 55)

snowhouse (snō hous) a house of snow blocks used by the Inuit (p. 223)

social division (sō′shəl də vizh′ən) a group that does a certain type of work (p. 22)

socialism (sō′shə liz′əm) an economic system in which the government owns businesses, land, and natural resources (p. 481)

society (sə sī′ə tē) an organized community with established rules and traditions (p. 42)

Socratic method (sō krat′ik meth′əd) an approach to teaching developed by the Greek philosopher, Socrates, which involves teaching people to think by asking questions (p. 262)

sod house (sod hous) a shelter made from blocks of earth (p. 223)

Solidarity (sol′ə dar′ə tē) a Polish labor union that resisted communist control (p. 621)

Song dynasty (sông dī′nə stē) a dynasty that lasted from 960 to 1279 in China (p. 351)

Soviet (sō′vē et) a Russian workers' council (p. 531)

space station (spās stā′shən) a large, orbiting scientific base used by humans in space (p. 669)

steam engine (stēm en′jən) a machine that uses the power of steam (p. 475)

Stone Age (stōn āj) the period of time when humans relied primarily on stone tools (p. 19)

strike (strīk) the refusal to work until demands are met (p. 480)

subcontinent (sub kon′tə nənt) a large area of land that is separated from other countries by water and land (p. 123)

subsistence farming (səb sis′təns fär′ming) the process of growing food mainly for self-consumption (p. 125)

sudra (sü′dru) a serf in Hindu society (p. 131)

Sui dynasty (swāy dī′nə stē) a dynasty that lasted from 581 to 618 in China (p. 351)

surplus (sėr′pləs) an extra supply (p. 21)

Swahili (swä hē′lē) a culture and language that combines African and Arabic cultures and languages (p. 383)

synagogue (sin′ə gòg) a Jewish place of worship (p. 257)

Taj Mahal (täj′ mə häl′) a magnificent tomb built by the Indian ruler Shah Jahan in memory of his wife (p. 346)

Tang dynasty (täng dī′nə stē) a dynasty that lasted from 618 to 907 in China (p. 351)

technology (tek nol′ə jē) the way in which humans produce the items they use (p. 19)

temple mound (tem′pəl mound) hill of dirt built for ceremonies (p. 221)

Ten Commandments (ten kə mand′mənts) a set of laws that provides guidance for the worship of God and rules for moral behavior (p. 55)

tenement (ten′ə mənt) an overcrowded slum apartment building (p. 477)

terrace (ter′is) a platform of earth (p. 101)

terrorism (ter′ə riz′əm) the use of violence and fear to achieve political goals (p. 645)

Tet Offensive (tet ə fen′siv) a series of battles launched by the Viet Cong and North Vietnamese across South Vietnam in 1968 (p. 586)

textile (tek′stīl) cloth that is either woven or knitted (p. 475)

theocracy (thē ok′rə sē) a system of government in which the rulers are believed to represent the will of the gods (p. 169)

three-field rotation system (thrē′ fēld′ rō tā′shən sis′təm) in the Middle Ages, a system whereby the planting of crops on manor lands alternates between three fields (p. 403)

Torah (tôr′ə) the first five books of the Hebrew Bible (p. 56)

trade agreement (trād äg rē′mənt) an agreement with rules about the exchange of goods between countries (p. 633)

trading bloc (trā′ding blok) a group of nations that agrees to trade under favorable conditions (p. 632)

Pronunciation Key

a in hat	ō in open	sh in she
â in care	ò in all	th in thin
ā in age	ô in order	ᴛʜ in then
ä in far	oi in oil	zh in measure
e in let	ou in out	ə = a in about
ē in equal	u in cup	ə = e in taken
ėr in term	ù in put	ə = i in pencil
i in it	ü in rule	ə = o in lemon
ī in ice	ch in child	ə = u in circus
o in hot	ng in long	

Glossary

treaty port (trē′tē pôrt) Asian port cities that were open to trade with Western countries (p. 494)

Treaty of Tordesillas (trē′tē ov tôr də sē′yä) the 1494 agreement that divided any newly discovered territories between Spain and Portugal (p. 441)

Treaty of Versailles (trē′tē ov vėr sī′) the document signed at the end of World War I between the Allies and Germany (p. 536)

trench warfare (trench wôr′fär′) the use of deep ditches to shelter troops in battle (p. 528)

triangular trade (trī ang′gyə lər trād) a trade arrangement in which manufactured goods were traded for slaves, slaves were sold for raw materials such as sugar cane, and raw materials were made into manufactured products for sale (p. 449)

tribune (trib′yün) in ancient Rome, men who were appointed to protect the rights of plebeians (p. 284)

tributary (trib′yə ter′ē) a small stream that flows into a larger stream or river (p. 209)

Triple Alliance (trip′əl e li′əns) an alliance formed in 1882 between Germany, Austria-Hungary, and Italy (p. 522)

Triple Entente (trip′əl än tänt′) an alliance formed in 1907 between Russia, France, and Great Britain (p. 522)

Truman Doctrine (trü′mən dok′trən) U.S. President Harry S. Truman's commitment of the U.S. military to help nations resisting communism (p. 570)

tundra (tun′drə) a cold, flat area where trees cannot grow (p. 210)

typhoon (tī fün′) a tropical storm with heavy winds and rough seas (p. 361)

ulama (ü′lä mə) an ancient Olmec ball game (p. 175)

unify (yü′nə fī) to unite, combine, or bring together (p. 85)

United Nations, (UN) (yü ni′tid nā′shənz) an international peacekeeping organization that was created in 1945 (p. 560)

vandal (van′dl) a person who destroys property (p. 303)

Vedas (vā′dəs) "Books of Knowledge" that contain much of the stories and songs of the Aryans (p. 130)

Viet Cong (vē et′ kȯng′) Vietnamese communist guerillas (p. 584)

Vietnamization (vē et nä′mə zā′shən) Richard Nixon's plan to reduce the role of the United States in the Vietnam War (p. 586)

Warsaw Pact (wôr′sȯ pakt) a military alliance of the communist countries of Eastern Europe signed after World War II (p. 570)

wattle (wät′l) a wall material made from branches and vines intertwined with logs (p. 219)

wetland (wet′land′) land that is covered with moist soil (p. 187)

wigwam (wig′wom) a dome-shaped hut made of branches covered with animal skins or woven mats (p. 220)

Women's Army Corps (wim′ənz är′mē kôr) a female division of the U.S. Army in World War II (p. 552)

World Trade Organization, (WTO) (wėrld trād ôr′gə nə zā′shən) an international body created to help nations settle trade disputes (p. 633)

zero population growth (zir′ō pop′yə lā′shən grōth) the balance between new babies born and people lost due to death (p. 657)

Zhou dynasty (jou di′nə stē) the largest of the Chinese dynasties, lasting from 770–221 B.C. (p. 108)

ziggurat (zig′ù rat) a huge, pyramid-shaped structure consisting of a series of stacked, rectangular platforms (p. 41)

Zionism (zī′ə niz′əm) a movement that began in the 1800s to set up a Jewish state in Palestine (p. 615)

Zoroastrianism (zôr′ō as′trē ə niz′əm) a religion founded by the Persian prophet Zoroaster based on the belief of one god as supreme and the enemy of evil (p. 132)

Index

This Index lists the pages on which topics appear in this book. Page numbers after an *m* refer to a map. Page numbers after a *p* refer to a photograph. Page numbers after a *c* refer to a chart, graph, or diagram.

Aborigines, 503
Abraham, 55, 332
absolute power, 357
Abu Bakr, 335
Acquired Immunodeficiency Syndrome (AIDS), 671
Acropolis, *m*H6, *m*258, *m*259
Adefa, 382
Adena culture, 219, 220, *m*220
adobe, 214
Adriatic Sea, *m*431
Aegean Sea, 247, 248, 250, *m*247, *p*248
Aeneas, 253
Aeneid, 253
Afghanistan, H11, 124, 639, 647, R22, *m*H11, *m*124, *m*610
Africa, 368–373, 439, 441, 449, 489, 551, 607, 608, 671, R14, R15, *m*608, *c*631, *c*655
See also East Africa, West Africa
African Americans, 611
African National Congress (ANC), 609
Afrikaner, 609
aggression, 545
agora, 249, *p*249
Agra, 348, *m*345
agriculture, 21
AIDS, 671
Akbar, 348, 349
Akhenaten (Amenhotep IV), 90
Akkad, 41, 42, 43
Alaric, 303
Albany, New York, 475
Aldrin, Edwin, 669
Alexander the Great, 266–269, *p*266–268
Alexandria, Egypt, 269, *m*245
Alexius Comnenus, 407
algebra, 336
Algeria, 585, *m*585

Algonquian, 224
Algonquin, 224
alliance, 177, 522
Allied Powers (Allies), 527, 529, 530, 536, 537, 550–553
All-India Muslim League, 611, 612
almanac, 364, 365, H18
alphabet, 58, 59, 248, *p*292
Alpine Mountain System, 393
Alps, 393
Altamira, 28, 29
alternative energy, 666
Altiplano, 187, 188, *p*187
Amanirenas, 95
Amazon rain forest, 187, 188, 228, *p*187
Amazon River, 188
American Indians. *See* Native Americans
American Revolution, 456–458, 464–465, *p*464–465
Americans, ancient, 7, 12, 14, 16, *m*15
American Southwest, 14, 212–215
Americas, the, 159, 441, R8, R9, *m*446
Amon-Ra, 81, 85, 91, *p*81, *p*85
Analects, 116
Anasazi culture, 214, 215, *m*214
Anatolia, 335
ancestor, 111
Andes Mountains, 187–189, 191, 197, *p*187, *m*198
Angkor, 357, 358, *m*345, *m*358
Angkor Wat, 356–358, *p*356, *m*357
Antarctica, 663, R19, *p*663
anthropology, 27
anti-Semitism, 615
Antoinette, Marie. *See* Marie Antoinette
Anu, 42
Anyang, 107–109, *m*99, *m*109
apartheid, 609
Aphrodite, *p*254

Apollo, *p*254
Apostles, 295, 296, *p*295
Appalachian Mountains, 209
appeasement, 545
Appian Way, 287
aqueduct, 170, 278, 279, 292, *p*279
Arabian Peninsula, 335, *m*321
Arabic language, 335, 383
Arab-Israeli conflict, 615–619
Arab nationalism, 616
Arafat, Yasir, 616
archaeologist, 11
archaeology, 11
Archimedes, 270, 271
Archimedes' screw, *p*271
archipelago, 188
Arctic, 223, R19
Ares, *p*254
Argos, *m*261
arid, 210
aristocracy, 255, 361
Aristotle, 264, 265, *p*262
Armada, 442
Armenian Holocaust, 535, *p*535
armistice, 530, 586
Armstrong, Neil, 669
Arthur, King, 416
artifact, 11, 12
artisan, 38
Aryans, 130, 137
Ashoka, 133, 141
Ashurbanipal, 52
Asia, 7, 12, 268, 344, 408, 409, 440, R12, R13, *m*345, *m*347, *m*391, *m*409, *c*631, *c*655
Asia Minor, 247, 407, *m*247
Así es mi tierra, 506, 507
Asimov, Isaac, 229, *p*229
Assembly, 255
assembly line, 479
Association of Southeast Asian Nations (ASEAN), 632, *m*632
Assyria, 52, 57, 95
astrolabe, 337, 338, *p*337
astronomy, 53, 337, 434

Atacama Desert, 188
Athena, 252, 253, *p*252, *p*254, *p*262
Athens, Greece, 253, 255, 260–264, H6, *m*245, *m*258, *m*261, *m*263
atlas, H18, R1–R21
Atlas Mountains, 371, *m*371
atomic bomb, 554, 559, 571
Augustus, 288, 289, *p*288
Aurangzeb, 349
Australia, 445, 447, 502, 503, R18, *m*502, *c*631
Austria-Hungary, 498, 499, 501, 521, 522, 527, *p*498, *m*501, *c*536
automobile industry, 479, 667
Axis Powers, 550, 551, 569
Axum, 381, 382
Aymara culture, *p*188
Aztec Empire, 174–181, *m*161, *m*175
Aztlán, 177

Babur, 348
Babylon, 49–53, *m*49
Babylonian Empire, 49–53, *m*49
Bahrain, *p*333, *m*611
Balkan Peninsula, 247, *m*247
Balkans, *m*637
balsa, 188
Bangladesh, 124–126, 612, *m*124, *p*125, *c*656
banking, 336
Bantu, 373, *m*373
Ban Zhao, 111
barbarian, 303
Barbary States, 646
bar graph, *c*562, *c*563
barley, 34, 188
barter, 59, 408
Barton, Sir Edmund, 503
basalt, 163
basin, 209
Bastille, 468, *p*468

Index

battle. *See* specific battles
Bayeux Tapestry, *p*397
Begin, Menachem, 618, 619, *p*618, *p*619
Beijing, China, 101, 104, 353, 494, 578, 641, *m*H9, *m*H13, *m*345
Belgian Congo, 607
Belize, *m*163
Ben-Gurion, David, 615, *p*615
Benin, 384, 385, *p*447
Beothuk, 404
Berber, 375
Beringia, 14, *m*15
Bering Strait, 14
Berlin airlift, 570, *p*570
Berlin Conference, 489
Berlin, Germany, 489, 553, 570
Berlin Wall, 500, 572, 621, *p*500, *p*621
Bhutan, 124, *m*124, *m*610
bias, 216, 217, 281
Big Three, 551, 569, *p*569
Bill of Rights (England), 472, 473
biome, 188
Bismarck, Otto von, 500
"black land," 80
Black Sea, 324
Blanc, Mount, *m*393
block printing, 354
Boat on the Lake, A, 148, 149
Bodh Gaya, 142, *m*121
Boer, 609
Bolívar, Simón, 461–463, *p*463
Bolivia, 188
Bolsheviks, 531
Bonaparte, Napoleon. *See* Napoleon Bonaparte
Book of Documents, 115
book trade, 435
Bosnia and Herzegovina, 521, 621, 637
Bosporus, 324, *p*324
Boston, Massachusetts, 457
Boston Massacre, 457
Boston Tea Party, 457
Boxer Rebellion, 495, R39
Brahma, 138, *p*137
Brahman, 138
Brahmaputra River, 125
brahmin, 131

branch-banking, 336
Brandenburg Gate, *p*500
Brazil, 446, *m*446, *c*656
Britain. *See* England, Great Britain
Britain, Battle of, 549
British Empire, 502
Brittain, Vera, 533, *p*533
Bronze Age, 108
bronze mirror, *p*110
bronze sculpture, 385, *p*385
bubonic plague, 410
Budapest, Hungary, *p*394
Buddha, the, 141–143, *p*141
Buddhism, 141–143, 361, 409, *m*142, *p*143
bull leaping, 246, 250, *p*246
burial mound, 219, 220, *p*219
Burundi, 638, *m*638
Bush, George W., 647, 666, *p*648
Byzantine Empire, 301, 304, 321–329, 407, *m*321, *m*327
Byzantine Orthodox Church, 302, 328, *m*327
Byzantium, 301, 324

Cabot, John, 442, *m*441
Caesar, Julius. *See* Julius Caesar
Cahokia, 221, *p*218
Cahokia Mounds State Historic Site, 221
Calcutta, India, 655
calendar, 24, 75, 81, 165, 172, 337
Caligula, 289
caliph, 332, 335
Calvin, John, 437
Cambodia, 356–358, 584, 586, *m*138, *m*357, *m*358, *m*610
Camp David Accords, 618, 619
Canaan, 55
Canada, 207, 447, 502, 633, *m*207, *m*210, *m*502, *c*631
Canadian Shield, 209
canal, 81, 213
Canton, 494, *p*493
Cape of Good Hope, 439, *m*178, *m*440
capital, 270

capitalism, 480, 481
capitalist, 480
capitularies, 399
Cappadocia, *p*302
caravan, 331, 334, 372, 409
caravel, *p*423
carbon dating, 23
carbon dioxide, 661, 666
Caribbean, *m*460
caribou, 223
Carpathian Mountains, 393
Carson, Rachel, 661, *p*661
Carter, Jimmy, 618, *p*618
Carthage, 58, 282, 285, *m*275
Catholic Church, 434
Cartier, Jacques, 447, *p*447
cartograms, *c*634, *c*635
Caso, Alfonso, 202
caste, 139
catacomb, 294, 295, *p*294
Catalan Atlas, *p*315
cataract, 80, 83, 93, *m*79, *m*82, *p*83
cathedral, 327, *p*401
Catholic Church, 434
Catholics, 639
causeway, 176
cave art, 13, 26–29, *p*3, *p*13, *p*28, *p*29, *c*25
Cave of the Hands, 3, 27
Cavour, Camillo di, 501
cenote, 171
Central Africa, 27, 638
Central America, 159, 163, 461, *m*163, *m*460, *c*655
Central Asia, 347, 409, 410, *m*347
Central Plateau, 163
Central Powers, 527, 530
Central Uplands, 393, *m*393
Chaco Culture National Historic Park, *p*214
Chamberlain, Neville, 545, *p*545
Champollion, Jean, 86
Chancas, 198, 203
Chandragupta Maurya, 133, 135
Chang'ian, 409, *m*409
Charlemagne, 397, 399, *p*399
charter, 560
"Charter Oath of Five Principles," 497
Chartres Cathedral, 401
Chauvet, 29
Chavín, 191, 193
chemistry, 336

Chernobyl power plant, 666
Chiang Kai-shek, 577, 578
Chiapas, Mexico, 640
Chichén Itzá, 171, *p*172
child labor, 476, 480
Chile, 16, 188, 462, *m*H14
China
  ancient civilization in, 99, 101, 107, *m*101
  climate of, 104, 105
  communism in, 576–581
  Confucianism and, 115, 116
  European imperialism and, 493, 494, *m*494
  geography of, 100–103
  Han dynasty in, 111
  hundred schools of thought and, 117
  inventions and, 112
  Japan and, 361, 546
  Korean War and, 583
  Pakistan and, 126
  plague and, 410
  population of, *m*H13, *c*656
  Qin dynasty and, 110, 113
  Renaissance and, 433
  Shang dynasty and, 108
  Silk Road and, 409, *m*409
  Zhou dynasties and, 108–110, *m*109
chinampa, 176
China, People's Republic of, 578–581, 610, 640, *p*578
Chinese language, 107
chivalry, 401
Christianity, 294–297, 302, 328, 381, 382, 401, 407, 437, 439–441, *m*296
church. *See* specific churches
Church, Frank, 589, *p*589
Churchill, Winston, 513, 549, 551, 555, *p*555, *p*569
circle graph, *c*490, *c*491
circumnavigation, 439
citizenship, 17, 88, 255, 290, 293, 339, 471, 573, 643, H4–H5
city, 476, 477
city-state, 38
civil disobedience, 611
civilization, 35
Civil Rights Movement, 611
civil service, 111
civil war, 201, 286, 289, 398, 531, 546, 638
Ci Xi, 495, *p*495

class system, 42
Claudius, 239, 289
Clay Marble, The, 584
Clemenceau, Georges, 536, p537
climate, 23
climate zone, 371
climograph, 104, 105
Clinton, Bill, 633
clock, 435
Clovis, New Mexico, 7, 12, 14, 16
coal, 665, c665
coal mining, 476
Coastal Lowlands, 209
Coastal Range, 209
Code of Hammurabi, 50, 51, p50
codex, 172, p172
coffin, 87, p87
coins, 59, p59, p264, p301
Cold War, 569, 571, 582, 587
collective, 546, 547, 578
Colombia, 463, m163
colony, 439, 444–449, 457–459, 485, 487–489, 493–496, 521, 585, m457
Colosseum, 291, p291
Columbian Exchange, 441
Columbus, Christopher, 178, 229, 440, m441, p229
columns, 270, p270
command economy, 481
commerce, 431
Commodus, 299, p299
common market, 632
Commonwealth of Independent States, 623
communism, 531, 546, 569, 576–581, 583–586, 621, 640, 641
compass rose, H11
compound, 494
computer, 387, 669
concentration camp, 559, 561
concrete, 287
Confucianism, 116, 117
Confucius, 115–117, p115
Congo, Democratic Republic of the, 638, mH12, m638
Congo Free State, 489
Congo River, 372
conquistador, 441
conservation, 665
Constantine, 296, 301, 319, 324, p296, p301

Constantinople, 301, 322, 324, 325, 329, 341, m275, p301, p325
constitutional monarchy, 473
Constitution of the United States, 472, p473
consul, 283
continent, R2, R3
Continental Army, p456
convent, 401
Convention on the Elimination of Discrimination Against Women, 639
Cook Islands, 444
Cook, James, 444, 445, p445
Copernicus, 434, p434
Coral Sea, Battle of the, 553
Corinth, m261
corn, p28
corporation, 479
Cortés, Hernando, 180, 181
cottage, 402
cotton, 126, p126
Council of Trent, 437
Counter-Reformation, 437
countries, R22–R28
coup d'état, 607, 622
covenant, 55
craft guild, 404
Crete, 250, 251, m245
Croatia, 621, 637
crown, 85, p85
Crusades, 407, 408, m407, p408
Cuban missile crisis, 572, 574, 575
Cultural Revolution, 578–580
culture, 6, 27, 28
cuneiform, 43, 59, p43
Cuzco, 197, 198, 200, 203
Cyrus II, 132, p132
Czechoslovakia, 545, 621
Czech Republic, 621

da Gama, Vasco, 439, 441
daimyo, 361, 362
Danube River, 394, p394
Daoism, 117
Darius I, 132

David, King, 57, p432
da Vinci, Leonardo, 432, 433, 435
Dayton Accords, 637
D-Day, 552, p513
Deborah, 56, 57, p57
Deccan Plateau, 126
decision making, H5
Declaration of Independence, 458, 468, p458
Declaration of the Rights of Man and of Citizen, 468
Declaration of the Rights of Woman and the Female Citizen, 471
decolonization, 607
deforestation, 394, 662, c661
Deganawidah, 225
de Gouges, Marie-Olympe, 471
Deir el-Medina, 88
de Klerk, F. W., 609, p609
Delian League, 263
DeLisi, Charles, 670
delta, 79, 83, m82
democracy, 245, 255
demographer, 656
Deng Xiaoping, c111
depression, 543
descendants, 55, 214
desert, 370, 371
desertification, 662
détente, 587
deva-raja, 357
developed nation, 631, 656
dharma, 138, 139
Diamond Jubilee, 520, p520
diamond mine, 487
Dias, Bartolomeu, 178, 439, m441
Diaz, Bernal, 155
Dickens, Charles, 477
dictator, 283, 541, 544, 546
dictionary, H18
Diocletian, 300
disciple, 295, p295
dissident, 621
distribution map, 658, 659, H13
diverse, culture, 27
divine kingship, 42
Doctors Without Borders, 638
dog tag, p284
Dolores, Mexico, 459

Dome of the Rock, p331
Domesday Book, 397
domestication, 19, 20, 22, 187
domestic system, 475
dominion, 502, 503
domino effect, 585, 586
double cropping, 102
Drake, Sir Francis, 442
Dreadnought, p521
dromos, p255
drought, 214
duck and cover, 571
Dunhuang, 409
Duomo of Florence, 430, p431
dynasty, 45

earthquake, 123, 319
Earth's circumference, 336
Earth's orbit, 172
East Africa, 12, 27, 369, 372, 381
East Asia, 492–496
East Timor, m610
Eastern Europe, 408, 560, 569, 620–623, m622
Eastern Front, 527, 531
Eastern Ghats, 126
Eastern Highlands, 188
Eastern Orthodox Church, 328, m327, m436
Eastern Roman Empire, 303, m303
Eastern Zhou, 109, m109
East Germany, 570, 572, 621
economy, 89, 480, 631–633
Edison, Thomas, 478, 479
Edo, Japan, 361, 362, m345, m362
education, 111, 284
Edward VI, 443
Egypt
　Alexander the Great and, 267
　Camp David Accords and, 618, 619
　civilization in, 77
　Fertile Crescent and, 35
　Hebrews and, 55
　hieroglyphics and, 86
　Kush and, 95
　Mansa Musa and, 376

Index

Nile River and, 75, 78, 80–83, 89, *m*82
Nubia and, 92–94, *m*93
pharaohs and, 89–91
social classes and, 89
Suez Canal and, 488, 616
surgical tools and, *p*17
technology and, 89
tomb construction and, 88
trade and, 89
unification of, 85
Eightfold Path, 143
Eisenhower, Dwight, 552, 584
electricity, 479, 665
Electronic Numerical Integrator and Computer (ENIAC), 669
elements, *p*116
Elizabeth I, 442, 443, *p*443
El Salvador, *m*163, *m*170
El Tajin, *p*169
emblem, *p*404
emperor, 288, 289, 296, 302
empire, 45, 66, 487–489
encomienda, 447
encyclopedia, 364, 365, H18
endangered species, 661
energy, 665–667
England, 397, 398, 447, 451, 472, 473, *m*391, *m*639
England, Church of, 451
Enheduanna, 45
Enki, 42
enlightenment, 142
Enlightenment, the, 473
Enlil, 42
environment, 661–663
Environmental Protection Agency, 661
Epic of Gilgamesh, 43, 44
epidemic, 410
equal-area map projection, 167
equator, 167
estate, 467
Estates-General, 467
etching, 213
Ethiopia, 382, 489, 545
ethnic cleansing, 637
ethnicity, 637
Etruscan, 278
Euclid, *p*270
Eudocia, 305, *p*305
Euphrates River, 35, *p*35
euro, 632, *p*632
Europe
Byzantine Empire and, *m*321
colonization and, 444–449

cultures and, 28
dictators and, 544
early peoples and, 12
geography of, 393, 394, *m*393
global economy and, 632
Great War and, 522, *m*522, 535
gross domestic product of, *c*631
imperialism and, 487–489, 492–496
Industrial Revolution and, 476
Middle Ages and, 391–411, *m*391
physical map, R17
political map, R16
population of, *c*655
Roman Empire and, 292
Truman Doctrine and, 570
World War II and, 549, 560
European Community, 632
European Powers, 521, 522
European Union (EU), 632, *m*632
Everest, Mount, 123, 573, *p*123, *m*347
excavation site, 20, 78
excommunication, 437
Ezana, 381

factory, 475–477, 479, 480
factory system, 475
fair, 408
fascism, 544
feminism, 471
Ferdinand, King, 423
Fertile Crescent, 34, 35, 52, *p*34, *p*35
feudalism, 401–402
Final Solution, 559
First Cataract, *p*83
First Estate, 467
First Temple, 54
fishing, 394, *p*126
Five Good Emperors, 289, 293
Five Pillars of Islam, 332, 333
Five-Year Plan, 546
flooding, 75, 81, 102, 125
Florence, Italy, 430, 431, *m*429

flying machine, *p*433
Forbidden City, 350, 351, 353
Ford, Henry, 479
Formosa, 495
fossil fuel, 665, 666, *c*661
Four Noble Truths, 143
Fourteen Points, 536
France
Algeria and, 585
American Revolution and, 458
China and, *m*494
colonization and, 447, *m*446
French Revolution and, 466–469
Great War and, 527, 529, 536, *c*536
Haiti and, 459
Napoleon and, 469–470, *m*469
Triple Entente and, 522
World War II and, 549, 552
Francis Ferdinand, 522, *p*523
Frank, Anne, 561
frankincense, 381
Franks, 399
freedom of speech, 640
free trade, 632
French Revolution, 466–469
Fulton, Robert, 475

Gagarin, Yuri, 669
Galahad, Sir, 416
Galileo, 434, *p*434
galleon, *p*439
Gandhi, Mohandas, 611, *p*611
Ganga Mai, 138
Ganges River, 125, 136, 138, *m*121, *p*136
Gao, 378
Gaozu, 111
"Garden We Planted Together, The," 674
Garibaldi, Giuseppe, 501
gasoline, 665
Gate of Heavenly Peace, p579
Gaza Strip, 616, *m*617
generalization, 217
genetics, 670
Genghis Khan, 352, 409
Genoa, Italy, 410

geography, 27, H8
geometry, 271
geothermal energy, 667
German tribes, 299, 303
Germany
division of, 570
Great War and, 523, 527, 529–531, 536, *c*536
imperialism and, 489, 517, 521, *m*494
nationalism and, 499, 500, *m*499, *m*501
Nazis and, 544, 545, 552
reunification of, 500, 621
Triple Alliance and, 522
World War II and, 549–551, 553, *m*549
Ghana, 375, 607, *m*377
Gila River, 213
Gilgamesh, 43, 44, *p*44
Giuliani, Rudolph, *p*648
Giza, 87, *m*77, *p*94
glacier, 12
gladiator, 291, 299, *p*291
glasnost, 622, 625
global economy, 631
Global Positioning Satellite, 195
global warming, 661, 662
Globe Theater, 443
gods
ancient Egypt and, 81
ancient Greece and, 243, 253, 254, *p*254
Aztecs and, 179
Hinduism and, 137, 138
Incas and, 203
Islam and, 331
Khmer kingdom and, 357
Maya and, 171, 172, *p*172
Nubians and, 93
Olmec and, 169
Roman Empire and, 296
Golan Heights, 616, *m*617
gold, 369, 375, 376, 384
Golden Age of Athens, 260–263
Goodyear, Albert, 7, 16
Gorbachev, Mikhail, 621, 622, *p*621
Gospels, 295
"Governor, The," *p*131
Great Basin, 209
Great Britain
American Revolution and, 457, 458
Arab-Israeli conflict and, 615

Berlin airlift and, 570
British Empire and, 488,
    493, 494, 517, 521,
    m494
colonization and, 447,
    m446
decolonization and,
    607–612
dominions of, 502, 503,
    m502
Great War and, 523, 527,
    529, 530, c536
Industrial Revolution and,
    475, 476, c476
Triple Entente and, 522
working conditions of, 480
World War II and,
    549–551, 555
Great Charter, 398
Great Depression, 543, 544
Great European Plain, 393
Great Lakes, 220, 224
Great Leap Forward, 578
Great Mosque, p331
Great Plains, 209
Great Plaza at Tikal, p171
Great Pyramid, 87
Great Rift Valley, 372, m371,
    p371, p372
Great Seal, p398
Great Serpent Mound, 219,
    p219
Great Stupa, p133
Great Temple, 114, 115, p115
Great Terror, 547
Great Wall of China, 110,
    353, p110–111
Great War (World War I),
    523–537, 556, m529, c524,
    c536
Great Zimbabwe, 384, m369,
    p384
Greece, ancient, 135, 243,
    246–259, 260–263, m245,
    m247, m258, m259
greenhouse effect, 661,
    c661
Greenwich Mean Time, m412
griot, 376, 379
**gross domestic product
    (GDP),** 631, c631
Guangxi Zhungzu, 102
Guatemala, 173, 643, m163,
    m170
guerrilla, 584
Guiana Highlands, 188
guild, 404

Guinea, 607
Gula, p42
Gulf of Mexico, 164, 169,
    394, m163, m170
Gulf Stream, 394
Gupta Empire, 133, 134, 348
Gutenberg, Johannes, 435

Hagia Sophia, 319, 326–328
haiku, 433
Haiti, 459
hajj, 331, 333, 336
Hammurabi, 49–51, p51
Han dynasty, 111, 112
**Hanging Gardens of
    Babylon,** 48, 53, p52
Hannibal, 285
Hanoi, 586
Harappa, Pakistan, 126, 129
harvest, 20
Hatshepsut, 90, 91, p91
Havel, Vaclav, 621
Hawaiian Islands, 445
H-bomb, 571
Hebrew Bible, 55, 56
Hebrews, 55
hejira, m332
Helen, 253
Hellenistic Age, 268–271
helot, 255
hemisphere, H8
Henry VII, 442
Henry VIII, 442, 443, 450,
    451, p450
Henry, Prince, 439
Hera, p254
Herculaneum, 280
Hermes, p254
Herodotus, 308
Heyerdahl, Thor, p27
Hiawatha, 225
Hidalgo, Miguel, 459, 461,
    p459
hidden agenda, 217
hieroglyphics, 86, 172, p86
highlands, 163
Hillary, Edmund, 573
Himalayas, 103, 123
Himeji Castle, p361
Hinduism, 136–139, 349, 611,
    612, m138
Hindu Kush mountains, 124,
    m124

Hippocrates, 270
Hippocratic Oath, 270
Hippodrome, 324
Hirohito, 546
Hiroshima, 554, 559
Hispaniola, m429
Hitler, Adolf, 544, 545, 549,
    551, 560, p544
Hobby, Oveta Culp, 552
Hobson, William, 503
Ho Chi Minh, 584
Hohokam culture, 213, 215,
    p213, m214
holocaust, 535, 559, 615
Holocaust, 559
Holy Land, 407
Holy Roman Empire, m407,
    m436
Holy Spirit, 297
Homer, 253
Honduras, m163, m170
Hong Kong, 104, 494, 610,
    mH13
Hopewell culture, 220, 221,
    m220
Huang River, 102, p102
Huang River Valley, 99, 102,
    107
Huaorani, 662
Hudson River, 475
Human Genome Project,
    670
human rights, 560, 637, 640
human sacrifice, 179
**hundred schools of
    thought,** 117
Hungary, p394
Huns, 134, 303, 348, m303
hunting and gathering, 10,
    11, 17, 27, 404
Hutu, 638
hybrid car, 667
hydroelectric energy, 666,
    c665
hydrogen bomb, 571
Hyksos, 89
Hymn of the Nile, 80

Ibn Battuta, 336, 337, 339,
    353, 383
Ice Age, 7, 12, 24, 27, m15
Iceman, 23
icon, 328, p328

identity, 637
Iguaçu Falls, 666
Iliad, 253
immigration, 656, 657
immortal, 254
imperialism, 487–489,
    492–496, 517, 603, m494,
    c490
Inca Empire, 196-203, m198
Inca Trail, 200, m200
Inca Viracocha, 198
In Defense of the Indians,
    427
independence movement,
    456–463, m460
India, 124–126, 132–134,
    136–139, 348, 439, 603,
    611, 612, m124, m130,
    c656
Indian Mutiny, 488
Indian National Congress,
    488, 611
Indian Ocean, 124, 383, 439,
    m124
Indochina, 488, 584, 610
Indochina Peninsula, 357,
    m357
Indo-Ganges Plain, 125
Indonesia, 610, m610
indulgence, 436, 437
Indus River, 125
Indus River Valley, 121, 125,
    129, 130, m121, m130
Industrial Revolution,
    474–477
inferences, 60
In Flanders Fields, 537
inflation, 537, 544
insects, domestication of,
    22
Interior Plains, 209
intermediate direction, H11
**internal combustion
    engine,** 479
International Date Line, 412
**International Working
    Men's Association,** p481
Internet, 386, 387, H17
Inti, 203
Intipunco Stairway, p200
Inuit, 223, 226–227, 232,
    p223, p233
Inundation, 75
invention, 112, 175, 270,
    434, 435, 478, 479
Ionian Sea, 248
Iran, 132, mH11, m611

Index

Iraq, 35, *m*611
Ireland, 639, *m*632, *m*639
iron, 250, 351
Iron Curtain, 569, *m*569
Iroquois, 224, 225
Iroquois Confederacy, 225
irrigation, 36, 81, 126, 203, 213, 214, 357, *p*336
Isabella, Queen, 440
Ishtar Gate, *p*53
Islam, 321, 330–339, 407, *m*332, *m*436
isolation, policy of, 363
Israel, 35, 56–57, 295, 615–617, *m*57, *m*617
Issus, 267, *m*267
Istanbul, 301, *p*301
Italian Peninsula, 277, 278, *m*277
Italy
    fascism and, 544
    Great War and, 527, *c*536
    imperialism and, 517
    nationalism and, 499, 501, *m*499, *m*501
    olive production and, *p*395
    Renaissance and, 430–437, *m*431
    Triple Alliance and, 522, *m*522
    World War II and, 550, 551
Iturbide, Agustín de, 461

Jackson, Andrew, 216, 217
jade, *p*162
Jael, 56
Jahan, Shah, 346, 349
Jamestown, 447, *m*429, *p*447
Japan, 360–363, 440, 494–497, 546, 550, 554, 559, *m*362, *m*494, *c*536, *c*631
Japanese American, 550
Jataka Tales, The, 141
Jayavarman II, 357
Jefferson, Thomas, 458, 646
Jenne-jenno, 377
Jerusalem, 54, 57, 305, 401
Jesus, 24, 295, 296, 332, 407, *p*295, *p*493
Jews, 54–57, 132, 545, 559, 561, 615
Jiang Qing, 579, 580, *p*580

jihad, 333
Jinnah, Muhammed Ali, 612
John, King, 398
John II, King, 440
Johnson, Lyndon, 584–586
Jordan, 35, 295, 618, *m*611
Judah, 57, 614, *m*57
Judaism, 54–57
Julius Caesar, 280, 281
Junius Brutus, 278
junk, *p*493
Justinian, 327–329, *p*329
Justinian Code, 327
jute, 20

K2 mountain, 124, *m*124, *m*347
Ka' ba, *p*331
kabuki, 433, *p*433
kaiser, 500
kamikaze, 361, 554
Kampfer, Engelbert, 363
Kampuchea, 358
karma, 138
karst hills, 102, *p*102
Kashta, 94
Katanga, 607
Kennedy, John F., 572, 574, 584, 589, *p*574, *p*589
Kent State University, 586
Kenya, 607, 646, *c*647
Kenyatta, Jomo, 607, *p*607
key word, 387
Khmer, 356–359
Khrushchev, Nikita, 572, 574, *p*574
Khufu, 87
Kilimanjaro, Mount, 372, *m*371, *p*372
Kilwa, 383
Kimberley Mine, *p*487
King, Martin Luther, Jr., 588, 611, *p*588
kingship, 42, 85, 382, 398, 401
Kirina, Battle of, 376, 379
Kish, 38
Kissinger, Henry, 586, 587
knight, 401–403, 416
Korea, 583, *m*583
Korean War, 583
Kosovars, 637
Kosovo, 637

Koumbi, 375
Kremlin, 622, *p*623
Krishna, 138
Kristallnacht, 545
Kublai Khan, 352, 353
Kung Fuzi, 115
Kush, 94, 95
Kyoto, Japan, 362, *m*362
Kyoto Protocol, 662

labor union, 480, 621
Lacandon Maya, 228
Lagash, 38
laissez faire, 480
Lakshmana, *p*131
Lalibela, 382
Lancelot, Sir, 416
land bridge, 14, *m*15
landform, 27
Laos, 357, 586, *m*357, *m*610
Laozi, 117
Las Casas, Bartolomé de, 427, *p*427
Lascaux, 28
Last Supper, The, *p*295
lateen sail, *p*338
Late Stone Age, 27, 29
Latin America, 459, 462, *c*631
Latin language, 292
Latins, 278
latitude, 194, 195, H9, *m*441
law code, 50, 60, 290, 321, 327, 335, 398, 399, 449, 469
League of Nations, 536, 560
Lebanon, 35, *m*611
legend, 416
legislature, 457
Lenin, Vladimir, 531, 546
Leopold II, 489
levee, 102, *p*102
lighthouse at Alexandria, *p*269
limestone, 102, 164, *p*102
line graph, 340, 341
Lockerbie, Scotland, 646, *c*647
loess, 101
London, England, 549, *p*477
long house, 224
longitude, 194, 195, H9
Long March, 577

lord, 398, 401, 403, 408
"lost wax" process, *p*385
Louis XVI, 467, 468, *p*467
L'Oúverture, Toussaint, 459, *p*459
Lower Egypt, 79, 85, *m*79, *m*82
Lower Nubia, *m*93
Luoyang, 109, *m*109
Lu Province, 115, *m*99
Lusitania, 530
Lutheran, 437
Luther, Martin, 436, 437, *p*437
Lydians, 58, 59

Maastricht treaty, 632
Macao, 494, 610
MacArthur, Douglas, 553, 554, 583
MacDonald, Sir John, 502
Macedonia, 264, 266–268, 621
machine gun, 528
Machu Picchu, 197, 200, 203
MacNamara, Robert, 586
Madagascar, 686
Magellan, Ferdinand, 439
Magna Carta, 398, 473
Maguire, Mairead Corrigan, 639
Mahabharata, 130, *p*131
Maha Bodhi, *p*140
Makurra, 381
Malaysia, 610, *m*610
Maldives Islands, 124, 127, *m*124, *m*610
Mali, 339, 376–379, *m*369, *m*377
mammoth, *p*24
Manchuria, 496, 546
Manco Capac, 197
Mandate of Heaven, 116
Mandela, Nelson, 609, *p*609
Manetho, 85
Manhattan Project, 554
manor house, 402
manor system, 402, 403
Mansa Musa, 374, 376, 377, *p*374
Mantinea, *m*261
Maori, 503
Mao Zedong, 577–581, *p*578, *p*581, *c*111

map making, 336
maps,
  Africa, R14–R15
  Arctic and Antarctica, R19
  Asia and the Pacific
    Islands, R10–R11,
    R12–R13
  Australia and New
    Zealand, R18
  Central America and the
    West Indies, R4
  distribution, 658–659
  features of, H11
  Europe, R5, R16–R17
  Hemispheres, H8
  latitude on, H9, 194–195
  longitude on, H9, 194–195
  North America, R8–R9
  Northern Polar Region, R6
  physical, H11, R6–R7, R9,
    R11, R15, R17, R18, R19
  political, R8, R10, R14,
    R16, R18
  population density, H13,
    658
  projections of, H10,
    166–167
  purpose of, 83, 337
  road, H14
  satellite, R2–R3
  scales of, H12, 82,
    258–259
  South America, R8–R9
  Southern Polar Region, R7
  time zone, H15, 412
  world, R4–R5, R6–R7
marathon, 261
Marathon, Battle of, 261
Marco Polo, 315, 409, *p315*
Marcus Aurelius, 289, 293,
  299, *p293*
Marie Antoinette, 468, *p468*
market economy, 480
Marshall, George, 560
Marshall Plan, 560
Marx, Karl, 481, *p481*
Masai, *p372*
massacre, 457
mastaba, 87
Master Kung, 115
mathematics, 53, 134, 172,
  270, 271, 336
Mauryan Empire, 133
Mayan civilization, 168,
  170–173, *m161*
Mazzini, Giuseppe, 499, 501,
  p499

meadowland, 403
Mecca, 330–333, 339, 376,
  m321
medicine, 262, 270, 337
Medieval world, 313, 350,
  390
Medina, 331
meditation, 142
Meditations, 293
Mediterranean climate,
  371, 395
Mediterranean Sea, 35, 247,
  248, 277, *m35, m247, m277*
megacity, 655
Megara, *m261*
Meiji, 495–497, *p497*
Mein Kampf, 544
Memphis, Egypt, 80, 83, 85,
  p94, m82
Menchú, Rigoberta, 640,
  643, *p643*
Mencius, 117
Menes, King, 85
Menlo Park, 479
mercantilism, 445
Mercator map projection,
  167, H10
mercenary, 176, 264, 299
merchant guild, 404
Mercosur, 633
Meroë, 93, 381, *m77, m93*
Meroitic language, 93, *p95*
Mesoamerica, 159, 162–165,
  175–181, 215, *m163*
Mesopotamia, 35, 37–42,
  45–47, 49–53, *m35, m38*
Messiah, 296
Mexica, 176
Mexico, 173, 202, 210, 459,
  461, 530, 633, 640, *m163,*
  m170, m175, m210, m460
Mexico City, 655
Michaelmas, 400, 401
Michelangelo, 432
microscope, 434–435, *p434*
Middle East, 611, 614–619
Middle Kingdom (China),
  493
Middle Kingdom (Egypt),
  85, 89
middleman, 112
Middle Passage, 449
Midway Island, 553
migration, 12, 14–16, 130,
  251, 347, 372, 615, 656,
  m15, m130
Milan, Italy, 431

millennium, 655
milling stone, *p28*
Milosevic, Slobodan, 637
Minfong Ho, 584
Ming dynasty, 351, 353, 355,
  433, 493, *c111*
Minoan civilization, 250,
  251
Minos, King, 250
mint plant, 20
missionary, 401, 441
Mississippian culture, 221,
  m220
Mississippi River, 209
Mitsubishi Zero, 557, *p557*
mobilization, 522
Mobutu Sese Seko, 607
Moche Valley, 192
Moctezuma I, 178
Moctezuma II, 180, 181, *p181*
modernization, 495
Mogul Empire, 348, 349,
  m348
Mohenjo-Daro, 129, *m121,*
  p129
Mohica, 192, 193
moldboard plow, *p403*
monarch, 402
monarchy, 467
monastery, 401
Mongol dynasty, 351, 352,
  361, 409, *m352*
Mongolia, 352
monk, 401
monotheism, 55
monsoon season, 125, 337,
  p122
Monte Albán, 202
Monte Verde, Chile, 16
**"Moratorium to End the
  War in Vietnam,"** 588
Morelos, José María, 461
Morocco, 378
mosaic, *p329*
Moses, 55, 56, 332
mosque, 332, 333, 376, 377,
  p376
Mother Civilization, 169
Mother of Jesus, *p432*
Mother Teresa, 655, *p655*
mound building, 218–221,
  m220
movable type, 435
muezzin, *p332*
Mugabe, Robert, 609
Muhammad, 331, 332, 335
multiethnic nation, 637

mummy, 87, *p87*
Murasaki Shikibu, 361
Muslim, 331, 349, 376, 378,
  441, 611–612
Mussolini, Benito, 544, 545,
  551, *p544*
Myanmar (Burma), 640, 642,
  m138, m610
Mycenae, 251
myrrh, 381
myth, 252–254, 275

Nagasaki, Japan, 362, 554,
  559
Nanjing, 546
Napata, 95
Napoleon Bonaparte, 469,
  470, *p470*
Napoleonic Code, 469, *p469*
Nasser, Gamal Abdel, 616,
  p616
**National Aeronautics and
  Space Administration
  (NASA),** 669
National Assembly, 467, 468
nationalism, 487, 499, 501,
  521, 546, 616
Nationalist Party (China),
  577
Native Americans, 211–221,
  427, 447, 448
natural gas, 665, *c665*
navigation, 337–338
navy, 521
Nazareth, 295, *m275*
Nazis, 544, 545, 552, 553, 559
Nebuchadnezzar, 52, 53, 57
Nefertiti, 90
Nehru, Jawaharlal, 612
Nepal, 124, *m124, m138,*
  m610
Nero, 289, *p289*
Netherlands, 488, 610, *m446*
neutral, 523, 529, 550
New Economic Policy, 546
Newfoundland, 404
New Kingdom of Egypt, 85,
  88, 89, 90
New Mexico, 7, 12, 14, 16
New South Wales, 447, 502
news periodical, 364, H19
New Stone Age, 18, 19, 22,
  23

Index

New Testament, 295, 407
New York City, 475, 560, 646, c647
New Zealand, 502, 503, R18, m502, c631
Niagara Falls, 666
Niani, 379
Nicaragua, m163
Nicholas II, 522, 531
Nien Cheng, 579
Nigeria, 250, c656
Niger River, 372, 376–378, m377
Nile River, 74, 75, 78, 79, 80, 81, 83, p75, p83, m77, m79, m82
Nile River Valley, 79, m77, m82
nilometer, 75, p75
Nineveh, 52
Ninhursag, 42
Nippur, 38
Nixon, Richard, 578, 586, 587, p578
Nkrumah, Kwame, 607
Noba, 381
nobility, 115, 361, 405, 443, 467, 468
Nok people, 250
nomad, 22, 103
No-Man's Land, 528, p528
nonrenewable resource, 665, 666
Norgay, Tenzing, 573
Normandy, 552
Norodom Sihanouk, 358
North America, 159, 207–211, 447, m166, m167, m207, c655
North American Free Trade Agreement (NAFTA), 633
North Atlantic Treaty Organization (NATO), 570, 637
North China Plain, 99, 101, m99
Northern Ireland, 639, 649, m639
North European Plain, 393, 394, m393
North Korea, 583
North Vietnam, 584–587
Northwest Mountains, 393, 395, m393
Nubia, 92–94, m93
Nubian Desert, m82
nuclear energy, 666, 667, c665

nuclear fusion, 667
nuclear weapons, 569, 571, 572, c571
nun, 401
Nunavut, 223, m223
Nyerere, Julius, 607, 613, p613

oba, 384, 385
obsidian, 163
Octavian, 288, p288
Odysseus, 253, p253
O'Higgins, Bernardo, 462, p462
Ohio, 219
oil, 479, 665, 666
Oklahoma City, 646, c647
Old Kingdom of Egypt, 85, 89
Old Stone Age, 18, 19, 25, c25
olive, p395
Olmec, 168–170, 175, m170
Olympic Games, 254, p254
Olympus, Mount, 254
Open Door Policy, 495
Opium War, 494
oracle bone, 108
oral tradition, 253, 379
Organization of Petroleum Exporting Countries (OPEC), 666
Orkney Islands, p18
Osaka, Japan, 362, m362
Oslo Accords, 618
Ottoman Empire, 301, 499, 517, 527, 611, c536

Pachacuti, 198, 203, p203
Pacific Islands, R10, R11
pacifism, 533
painting, 432
Paiute people, 14, p14
Pakistan, 124–126, 129, 612, H11, m124, m610, p126
Palestine, 295, 296, 407, 614, 615, 616
Palestinian Liberation Organization (PLO), 616
Pampas, 188

Pantanal, 187, p187
papermaking, 80, 112, p80
papyrus, 80, p80
parallel time lines, 24, 25, c24, 25, 524, 525
Paris, France, 468, 527, 552
Paris peace conference, 534, 536, p537
parliament, 502
Parsis, 132
Parthenon, 257, p262
Passover, 57
Patagonia, 188
Pataki, George, p648
patrician, 283–286
patriotism, 285
Paul, 296
Pax Romana, 289
Pearl Harbor, 550, p550
peasant, 402–403, 467, 468, c401
Peloponnesian War, 263, 264, m263
Peloponnesius, 250
penguins, p663
peninsula, 164
Pentagon, 646
Pepin III, 399
perestroika, 622
Pericles, 255, 257, 263, p257
Perry, Matthew, 495
persecution, 296
Persian Empire, 131, 132, 260, 261, 267, 268, m132, m263
Persian Gulf, 39
Persian Gulf War, 589
Persian Wars, 308
personal computer (PC), 669
perspective, 432
Peru, 185, 188, 191, 462
pesticide, 661
Peter, 296
Petrarch, 431
petroleum, 665, 666, c665
pharaoh, 85–91
Pheidippides, 261
Philippines, 553, 554, m610
Philip II of Macedon, 266, p266
Philip II of Spain, 442
philosopher, 262
Phoenicians, 58, 59
phonograph, 478, 479
physical map, H11
Piankhi, 94
pictograph, 107, p107

picture writing, 43, 86, 107
Pieta, 432
pilgrimage, 331, 333, 336, 339, 376
pillage, 303
Pillars of Islam, 332, 333
Piraeus, m261
pirate, 442, 646
Pisan, Christine de, p405
pit house, 213
Pizarro, Francisco, 201, p201
plague, 263
Plague, the, 410, 411, m410
plain, 35
Plain of Issus, 267, m267
plantation, 448, 449
plant life, 20
Plateau of Mexico, 163
plate tectonics, 123
Plato, 248, 262, 264, p262
plebeian, 283, 284
Pliny the Younger, 280
plunder, 251
poison gas, 528
Poland, 549, 621
policy of isolation, 363
political cartoon, 450, 451, p450, p467
political map, H11
pollution, 663
Polo, Marco. See Marco Polo
polytheism, 42, 81, 295, 331, p191
Pompeii, 280, 281, p281
pope, 302, 401, 436, 437, 451, 499
Popol Vuh, 171
population, 655–657, c634, c635, c655, c656, m658, m659
Portolan chart, p325
Portugal, 383–385, 439–441, 446, m446
Poseidon, p254
power plant, 665–667
prehistoric art, 28, 29. See also cave art
prehistory, 11
primary souce, H16, 3, 29, 37, 43, 50, 51, 52, 55, 61, 63, 71, 80, 85, 91, 111, 116, 135, 137, 142, 155, 181, 203, 228–229, 239, 248, 255, 257, 265, 270, 280 –281, 284, 285, 286, 289, 291, 293, 295, 305, 307, 315, 328,

329, 331, 335, 339, 352,
353, 358, 363, 379, 383,
399, 407, 409, 410, 423,
427, 437, 440, 443, 457,
458, 459, 463, 471,
472–473, 476, 477, 487,
488, 495, 497, 499, 500,
501, 513, 523, 527, 528,
530, 532, 547, 549, 550,
552, 553, 561, 569, 570,
571, 573, 577, 579, 581,
586, 588–589, 599, 607,
609, 611, 613, 619, 623,
625, 639, 641, 642, 643,
646, 647, 648, 655, 661
prime meridian, H9
printing press, 435, *p*435,
*c*434
problem solving, H5
proletarian, 579
propaganda, 545
prophet, *p*57
protest, 585, 586, 588
Protestantism, 436, 437,
442, 443, 639, *m*436
Prussia, 500, 501
Ptolemy, 336, *p*439
pueblo, 214
Pueblo Bonito, 214, *p*214
**Puerto Francisco de
Orellana,** 662, *m*662
Punic Wars, the, 285, *p*285
pyramid, 87, 89, 170, *p*87,
*p*169
Pythagoras, 271

Qin dynasty, 110
Qing dynasty, 493, 494
Quebec, 447
Quechua, *p*189
Quetzalcóatl, 179, 181, *p*179
quipu, 199, *p*199
***Quotations of Chairman
Mao Zedong,*** *p*576
Quran, 330, 331, 335, 346,
*p*330

Rabin, Yitzhak, 618
"Railroad Age," 475
rain forest, 228, 229, 371

Raj, 488
rajah, 130
Rama, *p*131
Ramadan, 332
Ramayana, 130
Ramses II, *p*90
range, 209
Raphael, 432, *p*303
ration book, 556, *p*556
reason, 262
Red Cross, *p*536
Red Guard, 579
Red Land, 78, 80
Redshirt, 501
reference book, 364, 365
Reformation, 437
reformer, 480, 481
refugee, 559, 637, 638
region, 38
Regulus, 282, 283, *p*282
Reign of Terror, 468, 469
reincarnation, 138
Remus, 276, 277
Renaissance, 430–437
renewable resource, 666
reparations, 536, 537
representative, 283
repressive government, 640
republic, 283
research report, 144, 145,
280, 281, 364, 365, 386,
387, H16, H22
Resurrection of Jesus, 296
Revolution of 1989, 621
Rhineland, 536, 545
Rhine River, 394
Rhodes, Cecil, 487, *p*487
Rhodesia, 608
Rig Veda, 137
Rihla, 339
ritual, 108
road building, 200, 287, *p*287
road map, H14
**Robespierre, Maximilien
de,** 469, *p*469
Robinson map projection,
167, H10
Robinson, Mary, 639
**Rock Churches of
Cappadocia,** *p*302
Rocky Mountains, 209, *m*207
Rodríguez, Simón, 463
Roman Catholic Church,
302, 436, 437, *m*327, *m*436
Roman Empire, 288–293,
294–296, 298–304, 323,
325, *m*275, *m*290, *m*300

Roman law, 290
Roman Republic, 282–287,
*m*286
Roman roads, 287, *p*287
Roman spirit, 283
Rome, 276–279, 401, 407,
*m*275, *m*277, *m*300
Romulus, 276, 277
Romulus Augustulus, 304
Roof of the World, 103
Roosevelt, Eleanor, 560,
*p*560
Roosevelt, Franklin, 550,
551, 554, 560, *p*569
Roosevelt, Theodore, 496
Rosetta Stone, 86, *p*86
Rosie the Riveter, 557, *p*557
Round Table, 416, *p*417
Runnymede, 398
rural area, 655
Russia, 470, 496, 522, 527,
530, 531, *m*446, *m*494,
*c*536
Russian Revolution, 530,
531
Rwanda, 638, *m*638

Sadat, Anwar el-, 618, 619,
*p*618, *p*619
Sahara, 371, 372, *m*369,
*m*371, *p*371
Sahiwal, Pakistan, 126
Saint George, Church of,
*p*382
Salamis, battle at, 261
salt, 375, *p*375
Samuelson, Joan Benoit,
*p*254
samurai, 361, 362
sanctions, 609
Sandwich Islands, 444, 445
San Martín, José de, 462,
*p*462
Sanskrit, 130
Santorini, *p*248
Sappho, 243
Sarajevo, 522
Saratoga, Battle of, 458
Sardinia, Kingdom of, 501
Sargon, 45, 47, *p*47
satellite, 669
savanna, 371, *p*371
Savior of the World, 382

scale, 83, H12
Scandinavia, 397
scavenger, 476
Scipio, 285
scribe, 43, 84, 86, 89, *p*84
scroll painting, *p*109
scrub land, 188
sculpture, 385, 432, *p*385,
*p*432
seal, 223
Sea of Marmara, 324
search engine, 386, 387, H17
secondary source, 280, 281,
H16
Second Estate, 467
**Second Industrial
Revolution,** 478–481
seeds, 20
segregation, 609
Seljuk Turks, 407
Senate, Roman, 283, *p*239
Seneca, 291
sequence of events, 6
Serbia, 521, 522, 637, *c*536
serf, 401–403, 408
Sermon on the Mount, 295
Shakespeare, William, 443
Shang dynasty, 108, *m*109
Shanghai, 494, *m*H13
Shanksville, Pennsylvania,
647
Shi Huangdi, 110, 111, 113,
*p*113, *c*110
Shiva, 138, *p*137
shogun, 362, 363, 495
Shub-ad (Puabi), Queen, *p*45
Shulgi, 46
Siberia, 7
Sicily, 277, *m*277
Siddhartha Gautama, 141
Siege of Antioch, *p*408
Siege Perilous, 416
Sierra Madre Occidental, 163
Sierra Madre Oriental, 163
Silent Spring, 661
silk, 108
Silk Road, 99, 112, 408–410,
*m*409
silt, 79, 102, 125
Sima Qian, 111
Sinai Peninsula, 616, *m*617
Sipan, Lord of, *p*192
Six-Day War, 616
Sixth Cataract, 83, *m*82, *m*93
Skara Brae, 18, 19, 22, *p*22
slavery, 55, 89, 255, 285,
441, 448, 449, 469, *m*448

Index

slave ship, *p*448
Slovak Republic, 621
Slovenia, 621, 637
Smith, David A., 670
Smith, Ian, 608
Snaketown, 213
snowhouse, 223
social division, 22
socialism, 481, 531, 613
society, 42
Socrates, 262, 265, *p*262, *p*265
Socratic method, 262, 265
sod house, 223
Sofala, 383
Solidarity, 621
Solomon, 54, 57
Solomonid dynasty, 382
Somme, Battle of the, 529, *m*529
Song dynasty, 351
Songhai, 378, *m*377
Soninke, 375
Sonni Ali, 378
South Africa, 487, 609, *m*H12
South America, 14, 159, 185–189, 446, 447, 462, *m*166, *m*167, *m*185, *m*460, *c*655
South Asia, 121–127, 132, 144, 145, *m*124
South Carolina, 7, 10, 16
Southern Africa, 608, 609
Southern Rhodesia, 608
South Korea, 583
South Vietnam, 584–587
Soviet, 531
Soviet Union
    Cold War and, 571, *c*571
    communism and, 622
    Cuban Missile Crisis and, 572, 574, 575
    Germany and, 621
    Iron Curtain and, 569, 670
    Russian Revolution and, 531, *m*531
    as a superpower, 569
    World War II and, 546, 547, 549, 552, 553, 560
Soweto, 609
space station, 669
spade money, *p*109
Spain
    Americas and, 441, 446, 447, 459, 461–463, *m*446
    Armada and, 442
    Aztec Empire and, 180, 181
    Inca Empire and, 201
    Las Casas and, 427

    olive production and, *p*395
    Rome and, *p*279
Spanish Civil War, 545
Sparta, Greece, 253, 255, 261, 263, *m*245, *m*261, *m*263
Sputnik I, 669
Sri Lanka, 124, 127, *m*124, *m*610, *p*127
Stalingrad, Battle of, 551
Stalin, Joseph, 546, 547, 549, 551, 560, 570, 571, *p*569
Standard of Ur, *p*38, *p*39
stars, 171
steamboat, 475
steam engine, 475, *c*475
stelae, *p*381
Stephenson, George, 475
step pyramid, 87
Stone Age, 17–20, 22, 28
storytelling, 232, 376, 379
strike, 480
subcontinent, 123
submarine, 530
subsistence farming, 125
Sudan, the, 93
sudra, 131
Suez Canal, 488, *p*488, *m*488
sugar beet, 20
Sui dynasty, 351
Sumanguru, 375, 376, 379
Sumer, 41–43, 46, 47, 60
Sundiata, 376, 379, *p*379
sunflower, *p*20
sun worship, 81, 90, 91, 179, 203
Sun Yat-sen, 577
superheroes, 107
surgical tools, 17, *p*17
surplus, 37, 38, 66, 403
survey, H21
Suryavarman II, 357
Suu Kyi, Aung San, 640, 642, *p*642
Swahili, 383, 613
sweet potato, *p*27
synagogue, 57, 295
Syria, 616

Taipei, Taiwan, 578
Taiwan, 495, 577, 578
Taj Mahal, 346, 347, 349
Tale of Genji, The, 361
Taliban, 639, 647

Tanganyika, 613
Tang dynasty, 351
tank, 528
Tanzania, 607, 613, 646, *m*H12, *c*647
tariff, 631
Tarquin, 278
taxes, 49, 95, 111, 199, 348, 362, 457, 467
technology, 19, 89, 130, 345, 603, 669–671
telescope, 434, 435, *p*434
temple mound, 221
Ten Commandments, 55, *p*55
tenement, 477
Ten Kings, Battle of the, 130
Tenochtitlan, 155, 176–178, 180, 181, *m*161, *p*177
terrace, 101
terrorism, 645–649
Testament of Youth, 533
Tet Offensive, 586, *m*586
tetrarchy, *p*300
Texcoco, Lake, 176, 177
textile, 475
Thailand, *m*138, *m*357, *m*610
Thebes, 83, 264, *m*82, *p*94
theocracy, 169, 171
Theodora, 327, 329, *p*329
Theodosius, 296
Theodosius II, 305
thermometer, 435, *p*434
Thesmophoria, 243
Third Estate, 467, *p*466, *p*467
Thrace, *m*247, *m*263
three-field rotation system, 403
Three Sisters, 27
threshing, *p*20
Thutmose III, 94, *p*94
Tiananmen Square, 641
Tiber River, 277, 278, *m*277
Tibetan Plateau, 103, *p*103
Tierra del Fuego, 188
Tigris River, 35, *p*35
Tikal, 170, 171, *p*160
Tilak, 488
Timbuktu, 377
time lines, 24, 25, *c*24, *c*25, *c*524, *c*525
time zone map, 412, 413, H15
Titicaca, Lake, 188, 197
toga, 284, *p*284, *p*288
Tokugawa dynasty, 361–363
Tokugawa Ieyasu, 361, 362, *p*362
Tokyo, Japan, 362, 554, *m*362

tomb building, 88, 113, 346, *p*188
tomb painting, *p*79, *p*85
tools, 11, 12, 16, 17, 19, 95, *p*17
Topa Inca, 198
Topper site, 7, 16
Torah, 56, 57, *p*56
Tordesillas, Treaty of, 441
Totonac, 169
Tower of Babel, 52
Toyotomi Hideyoshi, 361
trade
    Africa and, 369, 375, 378, 379, 381, 385, *m*383
    ancient China and, 99, 110, 112
    ancient Egypt and, 89, 94
    ancient Greece and, 248
    Byzantine Empire and, 324
    European colonization and, 445, 449
    in the global economy, 631–633
    Hopewell culture and, 220
    Islamic culture and, 335, 336, 338
    Italy and, 431
    Japan and, 362, 363
    Maya and, *p*172
    Medieval Europe and, 391, 408
    Mesopotamia and, 38, 39
    Olmec and, 169
    Phoenicians and, 58, 59, *m*58
    Plague and, 411
    Portugal and, 439
trade agreement, 633
trading bloc, 632, 633
traditional economy, 480
transportation network, 475
treaty. *See* specific treaties
treaty port, 494, 495
trench warfare, 528, *p*528
triangular trade, 449, *m*448
tribune, 284
tributary, 209
trigonometry, 336
trinity, 297
Triple Alliance, 522, *m*522
Triple Entente, 522, 527, *m*522
Trojan War, 252, 253
Troy, 253
Truman Doctrine, 570
Truman, Harry, 554, 560, 570, 583
truth, 138
tundra, 210

tunic, *p*284
Turkey, 301, 517, *m*611, *c*536
Tutankhamen, 90
Tutsi, 638
typhoon, 361

Uhl, Christopher, 229, *p*229
ulama, 175
Umma, 38
Union of Soviet Socialist Republics. *See* Soviet Union
United Kingdom, 639, *m*639
See also England, Great Britain
United Nations, 560, 583, 615, 639
United Provinces of Central America, 461
United States
China and, 578
climate and, 210, *m*210
Cold War and, 571, *c*571
Constitution and, 472, *p*473
Cuban Missile Crisis and, 572, 574, 575
Declaration of Independence and, 458, *p*458
in the global economy, 631, 633
Great War and, 530, *c*536
gross domestic product of, *c*631
Industrial Revolution and, 479
Japan and, 496
Korean War and, 583
Native American bias and, 216, 217
in the 1920s, 543
North America and, 207, *m*207
population of, *c*656
Russia and, 496
as a superpower, 569
and terrorism and, 646–648
Truman Doctrine and, 570
Vietnam War and, 584–588
World War II and, 550–554
Universal Declaration of Human Rights, 560
untouchable, 139
Upper Egypt, 79, 85, *m*79, *m*82
Upper Nubia, *m*93

Ur, 38, 45, 46
Ural Mountains, 393, *m*393
urban area, 655
Urban II, 407
Ur-Nammu, 46
Uruk, 38, 41
Urumchi, 105

Valley of Mexico, 176, 178
Valley of the Kings, 88
Vandal, 303
Vedas, 130, 137, *p*130, *p*137
vegetarian, 139
Venezuela, 463
Venice, Italy, 431, 501
Verdun, Battle of, 529, *m*529
Versailles, Treaty of, 536, 537, 545
Vesuvius, Mount, 280
Victor Emmanuel II, 501
Victoria, Queen, 488, *p*520
victory garden, 556
Viet Cong, 584, 586
Vietnam, 584–588, 610, *m*357, *m*610
Vietnamization, 586
Vietnam War, 584–588
Vikings, 397
Virgil, 253
Vishnu, 138, 358, *p*137, *p*358
Visigoths, 303, *m*303
volcano, 163
Volga River, 394
voting rights, 532, 609

Walesa, Lech, 621, *p*621
war crime, 560
war medals, 556, *p*556
Warsaw Pact, 570
Washington, D.C., 646, *c*647
Washington, George, 458
wasteland, 403
waterfall, 80, 187, 666
Waterloo, Battle of, 470
waterwheel, 394, *p*336
Watt, James, 475
wattle, 219
Web site, 386, 387
wedding, *p*139
West Africa, 369, 373–379, 448, *m*377

West Bank, 616, *m*617
West Indies, 440, 449
Western Civilization, 245
Western Europe, 408
Western Front, 527, 529, 530
Western Ghats, 126
Western Roman Empire, 303, 304, *m*303
Western Wall, *p*614
Western Zhou, 108, *m*109
West Germany, 570, 572, 621
West Indies, 440
wheel, 173, *p*46
Wiesel, Elie, 648
wigwam, 220, *p*220
Wilhelm II, 500, 521, *p*521
William of Tyre, *p*408
William the Conqueror, 397
Wilson, Woodrow, 530, 534, 536, *p*537
women
in ancient China, 108, 111, *p*109
in ancient Egypt, 89, 91
in ancient Greece, 243, 255, 256
and equal rights, 639
in the factory system, 476
in the French Revolution, 471
in the Great War, 529
in Hebrew society, 56, *p*57
in Kush, 95
in Mayan civilization, 173
in the Middle Ages, 405
population growth and, 656
in Roman Republic, 283, *p*284
in South Asia, *p*125
voting rights and, 532
in World War II, 551, *p*552
Women's Air Force Service Pilots (WASPs), 551
Women's Army Corps, 552
Women's Auxiliary Army Corps (British), 529
Women's Royal Air Force, *p*532
Wong-Staal, Flossie, 671
wood-block art, 433
world map, R4–R7
World Trade Center, 646, *p*646
World Trade Organization (WTO), 633
World War I. *See* Great War
World War II, 545, 548–555, 556–557, 559–561, 569,

*m*552, *p*556–*p*557, *c*563
World Wide Web, 387
writing systems, 43, 86, 107, 129, 171, *p*43, *p*86, *p*107
Wu Di, 111
Wu Hou, 351

Xia legendary period, 107

Yeltsin, Boris, 622
Yemen, *m*611
yin and yang, *p*117
Yorktown, Battle of, 458
Yucatán Peninsula, 164, *m*161
Yugoslavia, 637, *m*637

Zagros Mountains, 35, *m*35
Zagwe dynasty, 382
Zambezi River, 372
Zapotec, 202
zero, 172, 336
zero population growth, 657
Zeus, 252, 254, *p*254
Zheng He, 355
Zhou dynasty, 108, 109, 110, *m*109
Zhuang, 103
ziggurat, 41, 46, 52, *p*41
Zimbabwe, 609
Zionism, 615
Zipangu, 440
Zoroastrianism, 132

Credits

Text

"Battling Everest" by Michael Burgan. Reprinted by permission of NGS Image Collection.

From *The Cambridge Illustrated History of China* by Patricia Buckley Ebrey. © Cambridge University Press 1996. Reprinted with the permission of Cambridge University Press.

Song "A Boat on the Lake." Reprinted by permission of Pearson Education, Inc.

Excerpt from *Jataka Tales* edited by Nancy DeRoin. Copyright © 1975 by Nancy DeRoin. Reprinted by permission of Houghton Mifflin.

"The Garden We Planted Together" by Anuraddha Bose from *A World in Our Hands.* Copyright © 1995 by Peace Child Charitable Trust. Reprinted by permission of Tricycle Press.

"What the World Needs" by Elzbieta Jawarska from *A World in Our Hands.* Copyright © 1995 by Peace Child Charitable Trust. Reprinted by permission of Tricycle Press.

From *My Palace of Leaves in Sarajevo* by Marybeth Lorbiecki. Copyright © 1997 by Marybeth Lorbiecki. Reprinted by permission of the Selman Literary Agency.

From *Horizon History of Africa,* pg. 188. Copyright © 1971 by American Heritage Publishing Co., Inc., a subsidiary of McGraw-Hill, Inc. Reprinted by permission of AMERICAN HERITAGE, Inc.

Song "Over There" words and music by George M. Cohan. Reprinted by permission.

From #67 "Hymn of the Nile" from *A Comparative Study of the Literature of Egypt, Palestine and Mesopotamia,* edited by T. Eric Peet. Reprinted by permission.

Excerpt from "The Earth and the People" found in Magic Words Poems by Edward Field. Copyright © 1998 by Edward Field. Reprinted by permission.

Cover page from The Parade Magazine, October 28, 2001. Reprinted by permission.

Fair Use

Quotes from pgs. 61 & 71 from *Side-By-Side: A Photographic History of America Women in War* by Vickie Lewis. Copyright © 1999 by Vickie Lewis. New York: Stewart, Tabori & Chang, 1999.

From *Mesopotamia: The Mighty Kings.* New York: Time-Life Books, 1995.

From *The Code of Hammurabi,* translated by L.W. King. The Avalon Project at the Yale Law School, 1996. http://www.yale.edu/lawweb/avalon/hamframe.htm.

From *The Sea Traders* by Maitland Edey. New York: Time-Life Books, 1974.

From *The Epic of Gilgamesh,* translated by N.K. Sandars. London: Penguin, 1972.

From *Babylonians* by H.W.G. Saggs. Berkeley and Los Angeles, California: University of California Press, 2000.

From *The Sumerians: Their History, Culture and Character* by Samuel Noah Kramer, pages 238 and 341. Chicago & London: The University of Chicago Press, 1963.

From *S.C. dig challenges theory of First Americans* by Henry Eichel. http://www.cgcas.org/topper.htm [central gulf coast archaeology society]

From *Rio Pinturas Cave Paintings The Hands of Time* by Carlos Manuel Conto. http://www.argentime.com/eng/issues/009/02manos.htm.

From "Found Wonders in A Secret Cave" by Nancy Fritz as appeared in *Popular Science,* 6/1/95.

From *The First Cities* by Dora Jane Haroblin. New York: Time-Life Books, 1973.

From *The Life and Death of Adolph Hitler* by Adolph Payne, pg. 131. New York: Praeger Publishers, 1973.

From *A Time to Break the Silence* by Martin Luther King, Jr. http://stum.finda.com/instructor/swensson.king.html.

From *Life and Death in Shanghai* by Nien Cheng, pg. 64 & 65. New York: Grove Press, Inc.

From *Deaths of Man* by Edwin S. Shneidman, pg. 184. New York: Quandrangle/The New York Times Book Co. , 1973.

From *History of the Twentieth Century, Vol. 2* by Martin Gilbert, pg. 659. New York: Wm. Morrow and Company, Inc.

From *Why Lenin? Why Stalin?* by Theodore H. Von Laue, pg. 196. New York: J.B. Lippincott Company.

From *New York Times Great Lives of the Twentieth Century* edited by Galb, Rosenthal and Siegal, pg. 106. New York: Times Books, a division of Random House, Inc., 1988.

From *Twentieth Century Speeches* edited by Brian MacArthur, pg. 56. London: The Penguin Group, 1992.

From *British Novelists between the Wars* edited by George M. Johnson, pg. 50. Detroit, Washington, D.C., London: A Bruccoli Clark Layman Book, Gale Research.

Excerpt from *The Clay Marble* by Minfong Ho, pg. 73. New York: Farrar Straus Giroux. Published simultaneously in Canada: HarperCollins Canada, Ltd., 1991.

Excerpt from *The Vietnam Reader,* edited by Walter Capps, pg. 206. New York: Routledge, an imprint of Routledge, Champan and Hall, Inc., 1991.

From *The March of Folly* by Barbara Tuchman, pg. 304. New York: Ballantine Books, a division of Random House, Inc., 1985.

Frank Church quote from http://www.vietnamwarnet/quotations/quotations.htm.

From *The Wit and Wisdom of Winston Churchill,* edited by James C. Humes, pg. 142 & 119-120. New York: HarperPerennial, a division of HarperCollins Publishers, 1994.

Winston Churchill quote from *International Church Society Website,* http://www.winstonchurchill.org/bonmots.htm#owed.

From *Familiar Quotations* by John Bartlett, 15th and 125th anniversary edition, pg. 909. New York: Little, Brown and Company (Inc.), 1980.

From *Oxford Dictionary of Quotations,* pgs. 632 and 488, edited by Elizabeth Knowles. New York: Oxford University Press, 1999.

From *Historic World Leaders,* edited by Anne Commire, pg. 387. Michigan: Gale Research, Inc., 1994.

Quotation from *Premier Chou En-Lai,* pg. 90. New York: Thomas Y. Crowell Company.

Published simultaneously in Canada: Fitzhenry & Whiteside Limited.

From *The First World War* by Martin Gilbert, pg. 133. New York: Henry Holt and Company, 1994.

From *Horizon History of Africa,* pg. 73. Heritage Publishing Company, 1971.

From *The Power of Gold* by Peter L. Bernstein. New York, NY: John Wiley & Sons, Inc. 2000.

From *The Tanner Lectures on Human Values, Volume 18,* edited by Grethe B. Peterson. Salt Lake City, UT: University of Utah Press, 1997.

From *Women Prime Minister and Presidents* by Olga S. Opfell. Jefferson, NC: McFarland & Company, Inc., 1993.

From *Nobel Prize Winners Supplement 1987–1991,* edited by Paula McGuire. New York, NY: The H.W. Wilson Company, 1992.

From *Nobel Prize Winners, 1992–1996 Supplement,* edited by Clifford Thompson. New York, NY: The H.W. Wilson Company, 1997.

From *Crisis in Tiananmen: Reform and Reality in Modern China* by Ti Mu and Mark V. Thompson. San Francisco, CA: China Books & Periodicals, Inc. 1989.

From *Great Lives of the Twentieth Century,* edited by Arthur Gelm, A.M. Rosenthal and Marvin Siegel. New York, NY: Times Books, 1988.

From *Nelson Mandela's life of struggle* found on http://www.bbc.co.uk/leeds/news/042001/26/mandela_biog.shtml.

From *EUROPE: A History* by Norman Davies. New York, NY: Oxford University Press, 1996

From *Encyclopaedia Britannica, Volume 3.* Chicago, IL: The University of Chicago, 1990

From *Simón Bolíva: Latin American Liberator* by Frank de Varona. Brookfield, CT: The Millbrook Press, 1993.

From *The History of the Haitian Revolution and the Economic Adjustment to Emancipation: 1791–1804* by Sapna Mehta. Seminar Paper 1999.

From *The Dictionary of Biographical Quotations* edited by Richard Kenin and Justin Wintle. New York, NY: Alfred A. Knopf, 1978.

Quote by Christopher Columbus from *Early European Adventurers and the Opening of Japan* by Richard Pflederer found on http://www.mercatormag.com/103_pfled.html.

Quote by Martin Luther from *Luther at the Imperial Diet of Worms (1521)* found on http://www.luterh.de/e/worms.html.

From *A Global History, From Prehistory to the Present* by L.S. Stavrianos. Englewood Cliffs, NJ: Prentice Hall a division of Simon & Schuster, 1991.

From *Historic World Leaders (4) North & South America A-L,* edited by Anne Commire, Associate editor, Deborah Klezmer. Washington, DC: Gale Research Inc, 1994.

From *Historic World Leaders (2) Europe A-K,* edited by Anne Commire, associate editor, Deborah Klezmer. Washington, DC: Gale Research Inc, 1994.

From *Quotable Women of the Twentieth Century,* edited by Tracy Quinn. New York, NY: William Morrow & Company, Inc.,1999.

From *The New Russians* by Hedrick Smith. New York, NY: Random House, Inc. 1990.

Quote by Mikhail Sergeyevich Gorbachev from *Oxford Dictionary of Quotations.* New York, NY: Oxford University Press, 1999.

Quote by Mahatma Gandhi from *Oxford Dictionary of Quotations.* New York, NY: Oxford University Press, 1999.

Quote by Kwame Nkrumah from *Oxford Dictionary of Quotations.* New York, NY: Oxford University Press, 1999.

From *The Nobel Peace Prize for 1978* found on http://www.nobel.se/peace/laureates/1978/press.html.

From *Historic World Leaders, Volume 1, Africa, Middle East, Asia, Pacific* edited by Anne Commire. Washington, DC: Gale Research, 1994.

Quote by Bartolomé de Las Casa from *The Legacy of Bartolomé de Las Casas* by Benjamin Keane found on http://osu.orst.edu/dept/philosophy/ideas/papers/keen.html#11.

From *Simpson's Contemporary Quotations* compiled by James B. Simpson, 1988 found on http://www.bartleby.com/63/82/3082.html.

From *The Dragon Empress* by Marina Warner. New York, NY: The Macmillan Company, 1972.

From *The Clay Marble* by Minfong Ho. New York, NY: A Sunburst Book, Farrar, Straus, Giroux, 1991.

From *Lessons of the Rain Forest* edited by Suzanne Head and Robert Heinzman. San Francisco, CA: Sierra Club Books, 1990.

From *A Concise History of the World* by J.M. Roberts. New York, NY: Oxford University Press, 1995.

Excerpt from Pliny from *The Destruction of Pompeii, 79 AD* found on http://www.ibiscom.com/pompeii.htm.

From *The Horizon Book of Ancient Greece,* edited by William Harlan Hale. New York, NY: American Heritage Publishing Co., Inc., 1965.

From *A Short History of China* by Hilda Hookham. New York, NY: St. Martin's Press, 1970.

From *Theosophy World, November 1998* found on http://www.theosophy.net/tw-text/TW9811.txt.

From *A Traveller's History of India, 2e* by Sinharaja Tammita-Delgoda, edited by Denis Judd. Brooklyn, NY: Interlink Books, 1999.

From http://home.cfl.rr.com/crossland/Ancientcivilizations/Ancient_Egypt/ancient_egypt.html.

From "The Fabled Land Punt" from *Ancient Record of Egypt Historical Documents from the Earliest Times to the Persian Conquest, Vols., II, IV* by James Breasted. Chicago, IL: University of Chicago Press.

From *Historic World Leaders (5): North & South American M-Z,* edited by Anne Commire, associate editor, Deborah Klezmer. Washington DC: Gale Research Inc., 1994.

From *Isaac Asimov's Book of Science and Nature Quotations* by Isaac Asimov. 1988. Found on http://department.stthomas.edu/recycle/forest.htm.

From *What Life Was Like Amid Splendor and Intrigue, Byzantine Empire AD330-1453.* By the editors of Time-Life Books, Alexandria, VA.

From *World Book Encyclopedia "Muhammed" M, Volume 13.* Chicago, IL: World Book, Inc.

From *The Travel of Ibn Battuta: "Ibn Battuta in Mali"* found on http://www.humanitites.ualberta/ca/history111/weeksept29/sept29.tut2.html.

From *Rokugo-no-Watash;, The Rokugo Ferry Crossing* found on http://www.us-japan.org/edomatsu/Rokugo/story.html.

From http://www.visit-mekong/com/cambodia/thigstodo/

From *The Royal Kingdoms of Ghana, Mali, and Songhay* by Patricia & Fredrick McKissack. New York, NY: Henry Holt and Company, 1994.

From *African Empires...found on* http://barney.gonzaga/edu/-sbennet3/mead/lessonplans/africanempires.htm.

From *African Civilization Revisited* by Basil Davidson. African World Press, 1991.

From *World Book Encyclopedia, Volume F.* Chicago, IL: World Book, Inc.

From "Heart of Sky" *The Popul Vuh: The Mayan Book of the Dawn of Life,* translated by Dennis Tedlock.

Maps:

MapQuest.com, an America Online, Inc. company

Illustrations:

8, 11, 14 Yoshi Miyake; 16, 19, 24 Higgins Bond; H17, 24, 25, 31, 104, 105, 159, 171, 272, 340, 341, 343, 386, 412, 413, 475, 476, 490, 505, 524, 562, 563, 571, 590, 624, 631, 642, 647, 655, 656, 661, 665, R29 Jeff Grunewald; 32, 41 Randal Birkey; 34, 35, 38, 80, 187, 261, 323, 337, 371, 409, 440, 577 Susan J. Carlson; 37, 85, 94 Ralph Voltz; 43, 55, 292 Dan McGeehan; 44, 47, 51, 160, 176, 177, 219, 308, 309, 353, 368, 384, 616, 617 Robert Lawson; 45, 148, 149, 506, 507 Ilene Robinette; 52, 53, 72, 135, 181, 317, 329, 379 Chris Butler; 64, 148, 308 Eliza Holliday; 64, 65 Carmelo Blandino; 89, 401 Linda Pierce; 107, 116 Gladys Rosa-Mendoza; 157, 225, 592, 593 Tony Crnkovich; 166, 220, 268, 271, 287, 400 William Graham; 200, 662 Chet Jezierski; 206, 213, 351, 390, 402, 403, 416, 417 Tom Metcalf; 228, 229 Guy Porfirio; 232, 233, 588 Neal Armstrong; 453 Jeff Osier; 524 Joann Daley; 528, 569, 574 Andy Zito; 674, 675 Jordan Dalton

Photographs:

Every effort has been made to secure permission and provide appropriate credit for photographic material. The publisher deeply regrets any omission and pledges to correct errors called to their attention in subsequent editions.

Unless otherwise acknowledged, all photographs are the property of Scott Foresman, a division of Pearson Education.

Front Matter: III (TL) Hubert Stadler/Corbis; IV Werner Forman Archive/Art Resource, NY; V Felipe Davalos/NGS Image Collection; VI Scala/Art Resource, NY; VII (TR) Bibliothèque Nationale Paris/The Art Archive; VIII Robert Frerck/Odyssey Productions; IX Scala/Art Resource, NY; X U.S. Coast Guard; XI Diana Ong/SuperStock; H4 (TC) Robin Sachs/PhotoEdit, (TL) Michael Newman/PhotoEdit, (TR) Mary Kate Denny/PhotoEdit, (BL) Rudi Von Briel/PhotoEdit, (BR) © Comstock Inc., (BC) Fotopic/Camerique/H. Armstrong Roberts; H5 (L) Myrleen Ferguson Cate/PhotoEdit, (R) © 2003 Frank Siteman/Mira Media Image Resource Alliance; H6 SuperStock, (C) © Antonio M. Rosario/Getty Images/Image Bank, (R) © Patrick Ward/Corbis; H7 (L) Réunion des Musées Nationaux/Art Resource, NY, (R) © Yann Arthus-Bertrand/Corbis; H8 Earth Imaging/Stone; H16 Jeff Greenberg/Stock Boston; H20 © Richard Hutchings/PhotoEdit

Cover:

Roy Ooms/Masterfile Corporation

Karen Su/China Span

Unit 1:

1 Hubert Stadler/Corbis; 2, 3 Kenneth Garrett; 4 (CL) Scala/Art Resource, NY, (L) Archaeological Museum Aleppo/Dagli Orti/Art Archive, (CR) National Gallery Budapest/Dagli Orti/Art Archive, (R) Musée du Louvre Paris/Dagli Orti/Art Archive; 5 (CL), (CR) Corbis-Bettmann, (R) Chris Hellier/The Granger Collection, New York, (L) The Granger Collection, New York; 7 Kenneth Garrett/National Geographic; 8 (C) © Macduff Everton/Corbis (B) Archivo Iconografico, S.A./Corbis; 10 British Museum/© Dorling Kindersley; 12 American Museum of Natural History/© Dorling Kindersley; 13 Erich Lessing/Art Resource, NY; 17 Scala/Art Resource, NY; 18 © John Garrett/Corbis; 20 (T) Doranne Jacobson/International Images, (B) Eileen Tweedy/Art Archive; 21 Butser Ancient Farm/© Dorling Kindersley; 22 (T) Scott Camazine, (B) © Macduff Everton/Corbis; 23 (CL) Kenneth Garrett; 25 Galleria di Storia ed Arte Udine/Dagli Orti/Art Archive; 26 Reunion des Musées Nationaux/Art Resource, NY; 27 (B) Bettmann/Corbis, (T) Artville; 28 (B) Grant Heilman Photography, (C) Runk/Schoenberger/Grant Heilman Photography, (T) Archivo Iconografico, S.A./Corbis; 29 Kenneth Garrett; 30 Reunion des Musées Nationaux/Art Resource, NY; 32 (B) Scala/Art Resource, NY, (T) British Museum, (BC) Art Directors & TRIP Photo Library; 34 Burke/Triolo Productions/FoodPix; 36 Chris Stowers/Panos Pictures; 38, 39 British Museum; 40 National Museum Damascus Syria/Dagli Orti/Art Archive; 42 (TL), (TR) British Museum, (B) Erich Lessing/Art Resource, NY; 43 British Museum; 44 (L) Musée du Louvre Paris/Dagli Orti/Art Archive, (R) Eric Lessing/Art Resource, NY; 46 SEF/Art Resource, NY; 47 (R) Eric Lessing/PhotoEdit, (L) Topham Picturepoint/Image Works; 48 Topham Picturpoint/Image Works; 50 © Gianni Dagli Orti/Corbis; 51 British Museum; 52 The Metropolitan Museum of Art, Gift of John D. Rockefeller, Jr., 1932. (32.143.2) Photograph ©1981 The Metropolitan Museum of Art; 53 Art Directors & TRIP Photo Library; 54 Scala/Art Resource, NY; 56 (L) The Jewish Museum, NY/Art Resource, NY, (R) Jewish Museum/© Dorling Kindersley; 57 (T) © Chris Hellier/Corbis, (B) Andy Crawford/© Dorling Kindersley; 58 National Geographic; 59 American Numismatic Association; 60 (B) Siede Preis/PhotoDisc, (L) Courtesy of the Oriental Institute of the University of Chicago, (R) AFP/Corbis; 61 (T) Archaeological Museum Bagdad/Dagli Orti/Art Archive, (B) Siede Preis/PhotoDisc; 63 Topham Picturepoint/Image Works,

Unit 2:

69, 70, 71 Werner Foreman Archive/Art Resource, NY; 72 (CL) Araldo de Luca/Corbis, (L) Erich Lessing/Art Resource, NY, (R) Doranne Jacobson/International Images; 73 (R) Asian Art & Archaeology, Inc./Corbis, (CL) Giraudon/Art Resource, NY, (L) The British Library/Art Archive, (CR) British Museum; 75 (T) Robert Caputo/Stock Boston, (TR) © Dorling Kindersley; 76 (C) John Woodcock/© Dorling Kindersley, (B) © Roger Wood/Corbis, (T) Erich Lessing/Art Resource, NY; 78 Kenneth Garrett; 79 Erich Lessing/Art Resource, NY; 80 North Carolina Museum of Art/Corbis; 81 (TL) Art Directors & TRIP Photo Library, (TR) Dagli Orti/The Art Archive; 83 Robin White/FotoLex Associates; 84 Egyptian Museum Cairo/Dagli Orti (A)/Art Archive; 85 (B) Fitzwilliam Museum, University of Cambridge/Bridgeman Art Library International Ltd.; 86 (BR), (BC) British Museum/© Dorling Kindersley, (TL) Boltin Picture Library, (TR) Art Resource, NY; 87 (T) The Newark Museum/Art Resource, NY, (B) John Woodcock/© Dorling Kindersley; 88 (BR) Dagli Orti (A)/Art Archive, (B) B. Turner/Art Directors & TRIP Photo Library; 89 Erich Lessing/Art Resource, NY; 90 Stuart Westmorland/Danita Delimont; 91 (R) H. Rogers/Art Directors & TRIP Photo Library, (Bkgd) Wolfgang Kaehler, (L) Boltin Picture Library; 92 © Roger Wood/Corbis; 93 Museum of Fine Arts, Boston; 94 Egyptian Museum Cairo/Dagli Orti (A)/Art Archive; 95 British Museum; 96 Egyptian Museum Cairo/Dagli Orti (A)/Art Archive; 97 Kenneth Garrett; 98 (B) Archivo Iconografico, S.A./Corbis, (T) Catherine Platt/Panos Pictures, (C) Lowell Georgia/Photo Researchers, Inc.; 100 (B) WorldSat International/Photo Researchers, Inc., (B) Catherine Platt/Panos Pictures; 102 (T) © Lowell Georgia/Corbis, (B) Picture Press/Corbis; 103 (T) © Galen Rowell/Corbis; 104, 105 Wolfgang Kaehler; 106 Lowell Georgia/Photo Researchers, Inc.; 107 Genius of China Exhibition/The Art Archive; 108 Art Archive; 109 (T) Museum of Fine Arts, Boston, (B) British Museum; 110 (T) Asian Art & Archaeology, Inc/Corbis, (B) © Keren Su/Corbis; 111 Giraudon/Art Resource, NY; 112 Asian Art & Archaeology, Inc/Corbis; 113 (R) The British Library/Art Archive, (Bkgd) Mercury Press International, (L) Wolfgang Kaehler; 114 © Dorling Kindersley; 115 (B) Dennis Cox/ChinaStock, (T) Archivo Iconografico, S.A./Corbis; 116 (B) N. Ray/Art Directors & TRIP Photo Library, (TL), (TC), (TR), (TCR) PhotoDisc, (TCL) © Dorling Kindersley; 117 (T) Réunion des Musées Nationaux/Art Resource, NY; 118 WorldSat International/Photo Researchers, Inc.; 119 Asian Art & Archaeology, Inc/Corbis; 120 (B) Neil Cooper/Panos Pictures, (BC) Doranne Jacobson/International Images, (TC) Paolo Koch/Photo Researchers, Inc., (T) Panos Pictures; 122 (BL) Frank Schreider/Photo Researchers, Inc., (BR) R. Cracknell/Art Directors & TRIP Photo Library; 124 © Alan Oddie/PhotoEdit; 125 (T) E.R. Degginger/Color-Pic, Inc., (B) Panos Pictures; 126 (B) Mercury Press International, (T) Art Directors & TRIP Photo Library, (TL) Dinodia/Art Directors & TRIP Photo Library; 127 © Howard Davies/Corbis; 128 Borromeo/Art Resource, NY; 129 (T) National Museum Karachi/Dagli Orti (A)/Art Archive, (B) Paolo Koch/Photo Researchers, Inc.; 130 Milind A. Ketkar/Dinodia Picture Agency; 131 (T), (BL) Victoria and Albert Museum, London/Art Resource, NY, (BR) © Danny Lehman/Corbis; 132 © Chris Hellier/Corbis; 133 (T) Giraudon/Art Resource, NY, (B) Doranne Jacobson/International Images; 134 British Museum; 135 E.R. Degginger/Color-Pic, Inc.; 136 Doranne Jacobson/International Images; 137 (TC) Reunion des Musées Nationaux/Art Resource, NY, (BC) Boltin Picture Library, (B) Musée Guimet Paris/Dagli Orti (A)/Art Archive, (T) M. Amirtham/Dinodia Picture Agency; 139 © David H. Wells/Corbis; 140 Dinodia Picture Agency; 141 (B) Werner Forman Archive/Art Resource, NY, (T) Mary Evans Picture Library; 142 Doranne Jacobson/International Images; 143 Neil Cooper/Panos Pictures; 146 (T) Borromeo/Art Resource, NY, (B) © Alan Oddie/PhotoEdit

Unit 3:

153, 154, 155 Felipe Davalos/NGS Image Collection; 156 (CR) Archivo Iconografico, S.A./Corbis, (L) North Wind Picture Archives, (CL), (R) Pedro de Osma Museum Lima/Mireille Vautier/Art Archive; 157 (CL) Scala/Art Resource, NY, (L) Réunion des Musées Nationaux photo: Franck Raux/Art Resource, NY, (R) Instituto de Investigaciones Antropoligicas/Alfonso Caso Fund/Instituto de Investigaciones Antropoligicas; 159 (T) Robert Frerck/Odyssey Productions, (R) Werner Forman/Biblioteca Universitaria, Bologna, Italy/Art Resource, NY; 160 (T) © Charles & Josette Lenars/Corbis, (C) Robert Frerck/Odyssey Productions; 162 (BL) Museum of Mankind London/Eileen Tweedy/Art Archive, (B) Charles & Josette Lenars/Corbis; 164 (B) © Macduff Everton/Corbis, (R) Larry Dunmire/D. Donne Bryant Stock Photography; 165 International Images; 168 © Gianni Dagli Orti/Corbis; 169 Robert Frerck/Odyssey Productions; 170 Danny Lehman/Corbis; 171 Robert Frerck/Odyssey Productions; 172 (T) © Charles & Josette Lenars/Corbis, (B) INAH/© Dorling Kindersley; 174 D. Donne Bryant Stock Photography; 175 Werner Forman/Museum fuer Voelkerkunde, Hamburg, Germany/Art Resource, NY; 178 Ancient Art & Architecture Collection, Ltd./Bridgeman Art Library International Ltd.; 179 INAH/© Dorling Kindersley; 180 Biblioteca Nacional, Madrid, Spain/Bridgeman Art Library International Ltd.; 181 (L) Kunsthistorisches Museum, (R) North Wind Picture Archives; 182 © Danny Lehman/Corbis; 184 (T) Robert Frerck/Woodfin Camp & Associates, (B) Katsuyoshi Tanaka/Woodfin Camp & Associates, (BC) Bruning Museum Lambayeque Peru/Mireille Vautier/The Art Archive, (C) Album/J. Enrique Molina/Art Archive; 186 Robert Frerck/Odyssey Productions; 187 (BL) Robert Frerck/Woodfin Camp & Associates, (TR) © Michael & Patricia Fogden/Corbis, (TL) © Stephanie Maze/Corbis, (BR) © Craig Lovell/Corbis; 188 Robert Frerck/Odyssey Productions; 189 Doranne Jacobson/International Images; 190 J. Enrique Molina/Art Archive; 191 (B) Archaeological Museum Lima/Dagli Orti/Art Archive, (T) Werner Forman Archive/David Bernstein Fine Art, NY/Art Resource, NY; 192, 193 Robert Frerck/Odyssey Productions; 196, 197 Katsuyoshi Tanaka/Woodfin Camp & Associates; 197 (T) Bruning Museum Lambayeque Peru/Mireille Vautier/The Art Archive; 198 Jorge Ianiszewski/Art Resource, NY; 199 (T) Newberry Library, Chicago, (B) Loren McIntyre/Woodfin Camp & Associates; 200 Robert Frerck/Odyssey Productions; 201 Franck Raux/Réunion des Musées Nationaux/Art Resource, NY; 202 Alfonso Caso Fund/Instituto de Investigaciones Antropoligicas; 203 (T), (TR) Pedro de Osma Museum Lima/Mireille Vautier/Art Archive, (C) Tom Till Photography, Inc.; 204 (B) Robert Frerck/Odyssey Productions, (T) Jorge Ianiszewski/Art Resource, NY; 206 (T) Bob Clemenz Photography, (BC) © Richard A. Cooke/Corbis, (B) Werner Forman/American Museum of Natural History, New York, N.Y., U.S.A./Art Resource, NY; 208 (L) Bob Clemenz Photography, (R) R. Hamilton Smith, (C) © James Randklev/Getty Images/Stone; 209 (CL) Willard Clay Photography, (L) © Layne Kennedy/Corbis, (R) © Douglas Peebles/Corbis, (CR) © Danny Lehman/Corbis; 211 Doranne Jacobson/International Images; 212 © Richard A. Cooke/Corbis; 214 Bob & Suzanne Clemenz/Bob Clemenz Photography; 215 © Richard A. Cooke/Corbis; 216 (T) The Granger Collection, New York, (B) Smithsonian American Art Museum, Washington DC/Art Resource, NY; 218 Cahokia Mounds State Historic Site; 219 © Richard A. Cooke/Corbis; 221 © Michael Lewis/Corbis; 222 Werner Forman/American Museum of Natural History, New York/Art Resource, NY; 223 AP/Wide World; 225 (Bkgd) With permission of the Royal Ontario Museum © ROM/Royal Ontario Museum, (L) D. Robert & Lorri Franz/Corbis; 226, 227 Smithsonian Institution; 229 (T) Giraudon/Art Resource, NY, (C) Ben Asen, (B) image courtesy of Pennsylvania State University with permission from Christopher Uhl; 230 Doranne Jacobson/International Images

Unit 4:

237, 238, 239 Scala/Art Resource, NY; 240 (L) A.K.G., Berlin/SuperStock, (CL), (CR) Araldo de Luca/Corbis, (R) Réunion des Musées Nationaux/Art Resource, NY; 241 (L) Augustus of Primaporta, circa 20 BC/Corbis, (CL) Vanni Archive/Corbis, (CR) SuperStock, (R) Erich Lessing/Art Resource, NY; 243 (B) © Mimmo Jodice/Corbis, (T) © Araldo de Luca/Corbis, (TR) © Gianni Dagli Orti/Corbis; 244 (T) Nimatallah/Art Resource, NY, (TC) North Wind Picture Archives, (BC) Réunion des Musées Nationaux/Art Resource, NY, (B) Archivo Iconografico, S.A./Corbis; 246 © Wolfgang Kaehler/Corbis; 248 (B) SuperStock, (T) © Gail

Jang/Stone, (BL) Siede Preis/PhotoDisc, (C) Topham/Image Works; 545 Hulton/Archive Photos; 546 AP/Wide World; 547 Hulton/Archive; 548 Bettmann/Corbis; 550 (B) The Granger Collection, New York, (T) AP/Wide World; 551 (TR) Wings Across America, (TL) © 2001 Owen/Black Star, (B) Hulton-Deutsch Collection/Corbis; 552 National Archives; 555 (Bkgd), (R) Hulton/Archive Photos, (L) Chartwell Manor, Kent, UK/Bridgeman Art Library International Ltd.; 556, 557 The Smithsonian Institution; 558 The Granger Collection, New York; 559 (T) Fred Ramage/Keystone/Archive Photos, (B) AP/Wide World; 560 (T) Courtesy of FDR Library, Hyde Park, NY (B) James Thrall Soby Bequest. Photograph © 2001 The Museum of Modern Art, New York © Estate of Ben Shahn/Licensed by VAGA, New York, NY; 561 (T) AP/Wide World, (B) The Granger Collection, New York; 564 Wings Across America; 566 (C) Bettmann/Corbis, (B) AP/Wide World, (T) Courtesy of FDR Library, Hyde Park, NY; 568 Bettmann/Corbis; 569 Courtesy of FDR Library, Hyde Park, NY; 570 (B) Bettmann/Corbis, (T) Courtesy North Atlantic Treaty Organization; 571 (T) © 1999 Owen/Black Star, (B) Bettmann/Corbis; 572 © Magnum Photos; 573 Edmund Hillary/Royal Geographical Society, London; 574 (R) Cecil Stoughton/TimePix, (L) Time Magazine, © Time Inc./TimePix; 575 AP/Wide World; 576 © Macduff Everton/Corbis; 578 (T) © Magnum Photos, (B) © Dorling Kindersley; 579 Bettmann/Corbis; 580 Hulton/Archive Photos; 581 (R) AP/Wide World, (Bkgd) Harry Redl/Black Star, (L) David King; 582 © Steve Raymer/Corbis; 584 (B) AP/Wide World, (T) Hulton/Archive by Getty Images; 585 (B) AP/Wide World, (TC) Hulton/Archive Photos, (BC) © AFP, (T) Hulton-Deutsch Collection/Corbis; 587 Express Newspaper/Hulton/Archive/Getty Images; 589 (T) SuperStock, (C) Douglas Corry/PictureQuest, (B) Bettmann/Corbis; 590 Courtesy North Atlantic Treaty Organization; 592 © The Norman Rockwell Museum at Stockbridge/2002 Christie's Images, Inc.

Unit 8:

597, 598, 599 Diana Ong/SuperStock; 600 (L) Elliott & Fry/Hulton/Archive by Getty Images, (CL) Erich Hartmann/© Magnum Photos, (R) Hulton/Archive by Getty Images, (CR) Hulton-Deutsch Collection/Corbis; 601 (L), (CL), (CR) Hulton/Archive by Getty Images, (R) Eric Risberg/AP/Wide World; 603 (T) Raghu Rai/© Magnum Photos, (B) © Chris Hellier/Corbis; 604 (C) S. Kanno/Photri, Inc., (B) Thomas Kienzle/AP/Wide World, (T) Dream Maker Software; 606 Dream Maker Software; 607 Agence France Press/Archive Photos/Hulton/Archive by Getty Images; 609 (T) Reuters/Juda Ngwenya/Hulton/Archive/Getty Images, (B) Denis Farrell/AP/Wide World; 610 David Longstreath/AP/Wide World; 611 (T) Stuart Franklin/© Magnum Photos, (B) Vithalbhai Jhaveri/GandhiServe e.K; 613 (R) © AFP, (Bkgd) Wolfgang Kaehler, (L) Translated by Julius Nyerere/Oxford University Press; 614 S. Kanno/Photri, Inc.; 615 Horst Tappe/Hulton/Archive/Getty Images; 616 Charles Bonnay/TimePix; 618 Bob Daugherty/AP/Wide World; 619 (BR) Sahm Doherty/TimePix, (T) Corbis, (Bkgd) © Richard T. Nowitz/Corbis, (BL) Bettmann/Corbis; 620 Thomas Kienzle/AP/Wide World; 621 (T) Bettmann/Corbis, (B) © David & Peter Turnley/Corbis; 623 David & Peter Turnley/Corbis; 625 J. Lee/Tropix Photo Library; 628 (T) © Frank Wing/PhotoDisc, (B) Reuters/TimePix, (C) © David & Peter Turnley/Corbis; 630 C Squared Studios/PhotoDisc; 631 © Bruce Hands/Stone; 632 © Frank Wing/PhotoDisc; 634 © Chris Shinn/Stone; 636 © David & Peter Turnley/Corbis; 638 © Per-Anders Pettersson/Prestige/Getty Images News Services; 639 Paul McErlane/AP/Wide World; 640 (R) Reuters/Arthur Tsang/Hulton/Archive/Getty Images, (L) © AFP; 642 (L) © Alison Wright/Corbis, (Bkgd) Radhika Chalasani/Sipa Press; 643 Rolando Gonzalez/© AFP; 644 Marc Schauber; 646 (B) © Joseph Sohm/Visions of America/Corbis, (T) Hulton/Archive by Getty Images; 647

Julie Jacobson/AP/Wide World; 648 (T) Reuters/TimePix, (BL) AP/Wide World, (BC) Richard Drew/AP/Wide World, (BR) Antonio Cotrim/© AFP; 649 Peter Mcerlane/AP/Wide World; 650 © Frank Wing/PhotoDisc; 652 (T) Fotos & Photos/Index Stock Imagery, (TC) PhotoLink/PhotoDisc, (BC) Paul Schutzer/TimePix, (B) NASA; 654 SuperStock; 655 Santosh Basak/AP/Wide World; 656 Fotos & Photos/Index Stock Imagery; 660 Ecoscene/Corbis; 661 AP/Wide World; 663 PhotoLink/PhotoDisc; 664, 665 © Terry Vine/Getty Images/Stone; 666 © A & L Sinibaldi/Stone; 667 Paul Schutzer/TimePix; 668 NASA; 669 (L) AP/Wide World, (R) The Image Bank;

End Matter: R2 Earth Imaging/Stone; R22 (TL) Flag Research Center; R30 (TCR) Detail/Smithsonian American Art Museum, Washington DC/Art Resource, NY/(Detail); R32 (BR) © Arthur Tilley/Getty Images/FPG; R35 (TCL) American Museum of Natural History/© Dorling Kindersley, (TCC) National Maritime Museum/© Dorling Kindersley; R37 (TCR) The Granger Collection, New York; R38 (TCCR) The Granger Collection, New York; R39 (TCR) The Military Picture Library/Corbis, (TCC) Hulton-Deutsch Collection/Corbis, (TCL) Smithsonian Institution; R40 (BL) Hulton/Archive, (TCLB) TimePix, (TL) Flag Research Center; Endsheets: (C) D. Logan/H. Armstrong Roberts; (BC) Frans Lemmens; (TC), (TL), (TR), Corbis; (C) Garry Black/Masterfile Corporation; (BL) Anthony Johnson; (LC) PhotoDisc; INAH/© Dorling Kindersley; Jorge Ianiszewski/Art Resource, NY; Museum of Mankind London/Eileen Tweedy/Art Archive; © Canada Post Corporation, 1898. Reproduced with Permission/The Art Archive; © Dorling Kindersley; The Granger Collection, New York; Bob Clemenz Photography; (CC) Robert Frerck/Odyssey Productions; (BC) Christine Osborne Pictures; Gianni Dagli Orti/Corbis; The Studio Dog/PhotoDisc